Cadillac
CTS & CTS-V
Automotive
Repair Manual

by Jeff Killingsworth
and John H Haynes

Member of the Guild of Motoring Writers

Models covered:

Cadillac CTS and CTS-V

2003 through 2014

Does not include information specific to
All-Wheel Drive (AWD) models or turbocharged models

(21015 - 4U3)

ABCDE
FGHIJ
KLMNO
P

Haynes Publishing Group

Sparkford Nr Yeovil

Somerset BA22 7JJ England

Haynes North America, Inc

861 Lawrence Drive

Newbury Park

California 91320 USA

Acknowledgements

Wiring diagrams provided exclusively for Haynes North America, Inc by Valley Forge Technical Information Services.

A book in the Haynes Automotive Repair Manual Series

Printed in the U.S.A.

ISBN-13: 978-1-62092-240-8
ISBN-10: 1-62092-240-1

Library of Congress Control Number: 2016938862

Contents

Haynes mechanic and photographer with a 2010 Cadillac CTS

About this manual

Its purpose

The purpose of this manual is to help you get the best value from your vehicle. It can do so in several ways. It can help you decide what work must be done, even if you choose to have it done by a dealer service department or a repair shop; it provides information and procedures for routine maintenance and servicing; and it offers diagnostic and repair procedures to follow when trouble occurs.

We hope you use the manual to tackle the work yourself. For many simpler jobs, doing it yourself may be quicker than arranging an appointment to get the vehicle into a shop and making the trips to leave it and pick it up. More importantly, a lot of money can be saved by avoiding the expense the shop must pass on to you to cover its labor and overhead costs. An added benefit is the sense of satisfaction and accomplishment that you feel after doing the job yourself.

Using the manual

The manual is divided into Chapters. Each Chapter is divided into numbered Sections, which are headed in bold type between horizontal lines. Each Section consists of consecutively numbered paragraphs.

At the beginning of each numbered Section you will be referred to any illustrations which apply to the procedures in that Section. The reference numbers used in illustration captions pinpoint the pertinent Section and the Step within that Section. That is, illustration 3.2 means the illustration refers to Section 3 and Step (or paragraph) 2 within that Section.

Procedures, once described in the text, are not normally repeated. When it's necessary to refer to another Chapter, the reference will be given as Chapter and Section number. Cross references given without use of the word "Chapter" apply to Sections and/or paragraphs in the same Chapter. For example, "see Section 8" means in the same Chapter.

References to the left or right side of the vehicle assume you are sitting in the driver's seat, facing forward.

Even though we have prepared this manual with extreme care, neither the publisher nor the author can accept responsibility for any errors in, or omissions from, the information given.

NOTE

A **Note** provides information necessary to properly complete a procedure or information which will make the procedure easier to understand.

CAUTION

A **Caution** provides a special procedure or special steps which must be taken while completing the procedure where the Caution is found. Not heeding a Caution can result in damage to the assembly being worked on.

WARNING

A **Warning** provides a special procedure or special steps which must be taken while completing the procedure where the Warning is found. Not heeding a Warning can result in personal injury.

Introduction

This manual covers the Cadillac CTS coupe, sedan and sport wagon. Available with either 2.8L, 3.0L, 3.2L and 3.6L V6 engines or 5.7L, 6.0L and 6.2L V8 engines.

The engine drives the rear wheels through either a five- or six-speed manual or automatic transmission via a driveshaft and rear independent driveaxles.

Suspension is independent at all four wheels; coil spring/shock absorber assemblies are used at the front with parallel upper and lower control arms, and coil springs and telescopic shock absorbers are used at the rear, with upper and lower control arms and trailing arms. The rack-and-pinion steering unit is mounted on the suspension crossmember.

The brakes are disc at the front and rear, with power assist standard. An Anti-lock Brake System (ABS) is standard on all models.

Vehicle identification numbers

Modifications are a continuing and unpublicized process in vehicle manufacturing. Since spare parts manuals and lists are compiled on a numerical basis, the individual vehicle numbers are essential to correctly identify the component required.

Vehicle Identification Number (VIN)

This very important identification number is stamped on a plate attached to the dashboard inside the windshield on the driver's side of the vehicle (see illustration). The VIN also appears on the Vehicle Certificate of Title and Registration. It contains information such as where and when the vehicle was manufactured, the model year and the body style.

Manufacturer's Certification Regulation label

The Manufacturer's Certification Regulation label is attached to the driver's side door opening (see illustration). The label contains the name of the manufacturer, the month and year of production, the Gross Vehicle Weight Rating (GVWR), the Gross Axle Weight Rating (GAWR) and the certification statement.

VIN engine code

Counting from the left, the engine code letter designation is the 8th character. On all models covered by this manual the engine codes are:

T .... 2.8L V6 engine (2005 through 2009 models)
G .... 3.0L V6 engine (2010 models)

Y .... 3.0L V6 engine (2011 models)
5 .... 3.0L V6 engine (2012 and later models)
N .... 3.2L V6 engine (2003 and 2004 models)
7 .... 3.6L V6 engine (2004 through 2009 models)
V .... 3.6L V6 engine (2008 through 2010 models)
D .... 3.6L V6 engine (2011 models)
3 .... 3.6L V6 engine (2012 and later models)
P .... 5.7L V8 engine (2004 models)
S .... 5.7L V8 engine (2005 models)
U .... 6.0L V8 engine (2006 and 2007 models)
W .... 6.2L V8 engine (2009 and later models)
P .... 6.2L V8 engine (2010 and and later models)

VIN model year code

Counting from the left, the model year code letter designation is the 10th character. On all models covered by this manual the model year codes are:

3 2003
4 2004
5 2005
6 2006
7 2007
8 2008
9 2009
A 2010
B 2011
C 2012
D 2013
E 2014

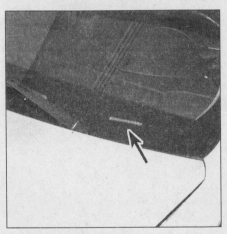

The Vehicle Identification Number (VIN) is visible through the driver's side of the windshield

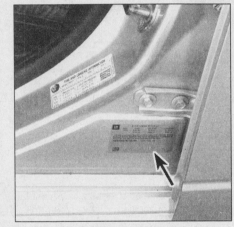

The Manufacturer's Certification Regulation label is located on the driver's door opening

Location of the engine identification number - V6 engine

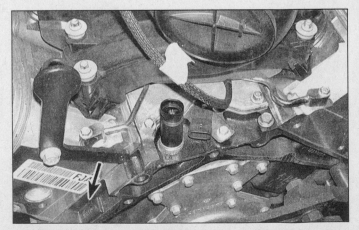

Typical location of the engine identification number - V8 engine

Engine number

On V6 models, the engine identification number is stamped into a machined pad on the lower left rear (driver's side) of the engine block **(see illustration)**.

On V8 models, the engine identification number is stamped into a machined pad on the left rear (driver's side) of the engine block, behind the cylinder head **(see illustration)**.

Transmission identification

The transmission identification is listed on a Manufacturer's RPO code list or on a sticker attached to the transmission. The codes are as follows:

Code	Transmission
M35	Getrag (76 mm), 5-speed manual transmission
MV1, MV7	Aisin AY6 (85 mm), 6-speed manual transmission
M12, MG9	Tremec (85 mm), 6-speed manual transmission
M82	5L40-E, 5-speed automatic transmission
MV3, M22	5L50-E, 5-speed automatic transmission
MYA	6L45, 6-speed automatic transmission
MYB	6L50, 6-speed automatic transmission
MYD	6L90, 6-speed automatic transmission

Recall information

Vehicle recalls are carried out by the manufacturer in the rare event of a possible safety-related defect. The vehicle's registered owner is contacted at the address on file at the Department of Motor Vehicles and given the details of the recall. Remedial work is carried out free of charge at a dealer service department.

If you are the new owner of a used vehicle which was subject to a recall and you want to be sure that the work has been carried out, it's best to contact a dealer service department and ask about your individual vehicle - you'll need to furnish them your Vehicle Identification Number (VIN).

The table below is based on information provided by the National Highway Traffic Safety Administration (NHTSA), the body which oversees vehicle recalls in the United States. The recall database is updated constantly. **Note:** *This a partial list containing only the General Motors Corporation dealer recalls. There are additional aftermarket recalls available.* For the latest information on vehicle recalls, check the NHTSA website at www.nhtsa.gov, www.safercar.gov, or call the NHTSA hotline at 1-888-327-4236.

Recall date	Recall campaign number	Model(s) affected	Concern
March 24, 2003	03V115000	2003 CTS	Some models have a condition in which the intermediate steering shaft bolt may be loose. An improperly tightened bolt could loosen, resulting in separation of the upper and lower steering shafts, causing a loss of vehicle control. If this happens while the vehicle is moving, a crash could result.
July 15, 2003	03V250000	2003 CTS	Some models fail to comply with the requirements of Federal Motor Vehicle Safety Standard No. 225, "child restraint anchorage system." The owner's manual does not explain the meaning of the location symbols for the child restraint lower universal anchorage system. This does not meet the requirements of the standard.
September 16, 2003	03V346000	2004 CTS	Some models fail to comply with the requirements of Federal Motor Vehicle Safety Standard No. 207, "seating systems." One or both front anchor tabs for the front bucket seats are not engaged in the floor pan reinforcement slots. A seat with only one tab engaged or neither engaged would not meet the static rearward loading test requirements of the standard. In some crash conditions, the seat could pivot rearward and its occupant or a rear seat occupant could be injured.

Recall date	Recall campaign number	Model(s) affected	Concern
June 03, 2004	04V273000	2004 CTS	On some models, the lower control arm ballstud nut/washer assemblies with washers were made of the wrong material. The washers may fracture and become loose or fall away from the vehicle, reducing clamp load. Separation of the control arm ballstud and steering knuckle, due to disengagement of the tapered attachment and retaining nut, is possible. If the control arm separates from the knuckle, the affected corner of the vehicle will drop and the control arm would be forced downward, contacting the wheel. The affected wheel could tilt outward and create a dragging action that would tend to slow the vehicle and create a tendency for the vehicle to turn in the direction of the affected wheel. In extreme situations, the affected wheel assembly could separate from the vehicle. Separation of the wheel assembly would also sever that wheel's hydraulic brake hose and result in diminished braking performance of the vehicle, which could result in a crash.
January 20, 2005	05V024000	2004 CTS	On some models, an interaction between the sensing and diagnostic module and vehicle's electrical system may cause the driver's frontal airbag and/or roof-mounted side impact airbag to deploy when the ignition key is turned to the "ON" position. A person positioned for driving may receive minor injuries, such as abrasions, from contact with a deploying airbag.
January 20, 2006	06V020000	2005, 2006 CTS	Some models equipped with V6 engines may have a condition where fuel is no longer supplied to the engine. This condition occurs without the illumination of the fuel level low indicator light or the warning chime. If the engine stops running, the operator will not be able to restart the vehicle which could increase the risk of a crash.
October 03, 2007	07V468000	2007 CTS	Some models fail to comply with the requirements of Federal Motor Vehicle Safety Standard No. 118, "power operated window, partition, and roof panel systems." Under the standard, the sunroof may only be closed when the ignition is on, or after the ignition is turned off, but before either of the front doors are opened. The affected vehicles may exhibit a condition where the sunroof can be closed after the ignition is turned off and the doors are opened. This standard specifies requirements for power operated window, partition, and roof panel systems to minimize the likelihood of death or injury from their accidental operation.
December 19, 2007	07V589000	2005, 2006, 2007 CTS	On some models, the rear axle pinion seal does not meet all of the specifications and may experience a fluid leak. A rear differential failure may cause loss of motive power and possibly loss of control, increasing the risk of a crash.

Recall date	Recall campaign number	Model(s) affected	Concern
November 05, 2008	08V582000	2009 CTS	Some models fail to conform to the requirements of Federal Motor Vehicle Safety Standard No. 208, "Occupant Crash Protection." Under certain conditions, a software condition within the passenger sensing system may disable the front passenger airbag when it should be enabled or enable it when it should be disabled. In a vehicle crash, if the front passenger airbag does not operate as designed, increased personal injury could occur.
March 15, 2010	10V105000	2004, 2005, 2006, 2007 CTS	Some models currently registered in or originally sold in Connecticut, Delaware, Illinois, Indiana, Iowa, Maine, Maryland, Massachusetts, Michigan, Minnesota, Missouri, New Hampshire, New Jersey, New York, Ohio, Pennsylvania, Rhode Island, Vermont, Washington D.C., West Virginia and Wisconsin have a condition in which the front brake hose fitting at the caliper may corrode due to snow or water, containing road salt or other contaminants entering and being retained in the routing sleeve. If the fitting corrodes significantly, the brake hose-tube interface may develop a leak. The brake hose-tube interface may rupture suddenly without prior warning and increase vehicle stopping distance may occur, increasing the risk of a crash.
June 04, 2010	10V240000	2008, 2009 CTS	On some models equipped with a heated washer fluid system (HWFS), a recall was implemented in 2008 to add a fuse to the control circuit harness to address the potential consequences of a printed circuit board (PCB) electrical short. However, there have been new reports of thermal incidents on HWFS modules after this improvement was installed. These incidents resulted from a new failure mode attributed to the device's thermal protection feature. The significance varies from minor distortion to considerable melting of the plastic around the HWFS fluid chamber. It is possible for the heated washer module to ignite and a fire may occur.
September 13, 2010	10V414000	2009, 2010 CTS and CTS-V	Some models fail to comply with the requirements of Federal Motor Vehicle Safety Standard No. 208, "Occupant Crash Protection." Dealers will replace the glove compartment assembly and, in some vehicles, modify the instrument panel structure. This service will be performed free of charge.
November 18, 2010	10V575000	2004 through 2011 Chevy Colorado/GMC Canyon	On some models the top tether anchor for the front center seat is not accessible and the owner's manual does not include instructions regarding how to use the top tether. Lack of access to the top tether anchor and a lack of instructions as to how to use it, may result in improper installation of a child restraint. Improper installation of a child restraint can result in a reduction in the restraint's performance in the event of a crash and an increased risk of injury or death to the child seated in the restraint.

Recall date	Recall campaign number	Model(s) affected	Concern
December 17, 2010	10V644000	2005, 2006, 2007 CTS	Some models have a condition in which repeated flexing of the passenger sensing system mat in the front passenger seat may cause the mat to kink, bend, or fold. This flexing can break the connections in the mat. If this occurs, the sensor may not detect the presence of a front seat passenger and will disable the airbag. Non-deployment of the front passenger airbag in the event of a crash necessitating that airbag's deployment may reduce protection of the passenger and increase the risk or severity of injury to them.
January 6, 2011	11V007000	2011 Chevy Colorado/ GMC Canyon	On some models the rear axle cross pins were not properly heat treated and could fracture and become displaced within the rear axle. Should the pin shift out of position, it could create an interference condition and cause the rear axle to lock. The driver may not be able to maintain directional control of the vehicle and a crash could occur without warning.
February 11, 2011	11V089000	2009, 2010 CTS	Some models have a condition in which a wax coating on the rear suspension toe link jam nuts may allow the nut(s) to loosen. If a nut sufficiently loosens, the toe link could separate and the rear wheel would be able to turn inboard or outboard. Owners may hear a metallic clanking noise coming from the rear of the vehicle that may warn of a loosening nut. The driver may experience sudden changes with vehicle handling and may not be able to control the vehicle, increasing the risk of a crash.
May 6, 2011	11V276000	2011 Chevy Colorado/ GMC Canyon	On some models the windshield wiper motor crank arm nut may not be tightened to specification. When the wipers are operated with a build-up of snow or ice, or if the wipers are operated on a dry windshield, the nut could loosen. If there is sufficient loosening of the nut, the wipers could become inoperative. Driver visibility could be reduced increasing the risk of a crash.
June 28, 2011	11V337000	2011 Chevy Colorado/ GMC Canyon	Some models equipped with a 2.9 or 3.7 liter engine and a four-speed automatic transmission may have been built with an automatic transmission adjustment clip that may not retain the shift cable in the correct position. if the shift cable is not in the correct position, the PRNDL shift lever may not accurately reflect the position of the transmission gear. The driver could move the shifter to "Park" and remove the ignition key, but the transmission gear may not be in "Park." The driver may not be able to restart the vehicle, and the vehicle could roll away as the driver or other occupants exit the vehicle or have exited, resulting in the possibility of the vehicle striking them or someone around the vehicle, or could result in a crash without warning.

Recall date	Recall campaign number	Model(s) affected	Concern
November 02, 2011	11V536000	2012 CTS	Some models may have a condition in which the power vacuum brake boost pushrod retention nut may not be torqued to the proper specification. If the nut is not torqued to the proper specification, the nut could loosen and allow the pushrod to separate from the brake pedal. This could result in a loss of ability to brake and a vehicle crash.
November 17, 2011	11V552000	2012 Chevy Colorado/ GMC Canyon	Some models may have been produced with driver safety belt buckle electrical connector terminals that do not fit snugly with the connector pins, causing the connection to be intermittent. The loose connections may cause the driver to not receive a visual or audible warning that the driver seat belt is not fastened, thereby increasing the risk of personal injury in the event of a crash.
December 19, 2012	12V594000	2010 through 2012 Chevy Colorado/GMC Canyon	On some models the hood may be missing the secondary hood latch. If the primary hood latch is not engaged, the hood could open unexpectedly. During vehicle operation, this could obstruct the view of the driver and increase the risk of a crash.
May 15, 2014	14V253000	2014 CTS manufactured between June 10, 2013 to February 26, 2014	On some models, if the wiper system is left on after the key is removed and the windshield becomes covered with ice and snow (causing the wipers' movement to be restricted) and the vehicle's battery goes dead and needs a jump start, the wiper module may fail and the wipers become inoperative. This could cause restricted visibility, increasing the risk of a crash.
June 19, 2014	14V338000	2014 CTS manufactured between June 10, 2013 to March 20, 2014	Some models may have a defective transmission shift cable that may disconnect from either the bracket on the transmission shift lever or the bracket on the transmission. This could cause the vehicle to roll away when the occupants are exiting the vehicle
July 2, 2014	14V394000	2003 through 2014 CTS manufactured between August 16, 2001 through April 28, 2014	On some models, the weight of the key ring, road conditions or some other jarring event may cause the ignition switch to move out of the RUN position, turning off the engine. With the ignition key out of the RUN position, the vehicle's airbag system may not deploy if the vehicle is involved in a crash, increasing the risk of an injury.
July 23, 2014	14V446000	2014 CTS	Some models may have an incomplete weld on the seat hook bracket assembly. The front seats on the may not stay secured in place during a collision, causing occupants to become injured during a crash.
October 01, 2014	14V614000	2013, 2014 CTS	module that is contaminated, which could cause it to fail. The vehicle could stall and the driver may experience a loss of handling, increasing the risk of a crash.

Buying parts

Replacement parts are available from many sources, which generally fall into one of two categories - authorized dealer parts departments and independent retail auto parts stores. Our advice concerning these parts is as follows:

Retail auto parts stores: Good auto parts stores will stock frequently needed components which wear out relatively fast, such as clutch components, exhaust systems, brake parts, tune-up parts, etc. These stores often supply new or reconditioned parts on an exchange basis, which can save a considerable amount of money. Discount auto parts stores are often very good places to buy materials and parts needed for general vehicle maintenance such as oil, grease, filters, spark plugs, belts, touch-up paint, bulbs, etc. They also usually sell tools and general accessories, have convenient hours, charge lower prices and can often be found not far from home.

Authorized dealer parts department: This is the best source for parts which are unique to the vehicle and not generally available elsewhere (such as major engine parts, transmission parts, trim pieces, etc.).

Warranty information: If the vehicle is still covered under warranty, be sure that any replacement parts purchased - regardless of the source - do not invalidate the warranty!

To be sure of obtaining the correct parts, have engine and chassis numbers available and, if possible, take the old parts along for positive identification.

Maintenance techniques, tools and working facilities

Maintenance techniques

There are a number of techniques involved in maintenance and repair that will be referred to throughout this manual. Application of these techniques will enable the home mechanic to be more efficient, better organized and capable of performing the various tasks properly, which will ensure that the repair job is thorough and complete.

Fasteners

Fasteners are nuts, bolts, studs and screws used to hold two or more parts together. There are a few things to keep in mind when working with fasteners. Almost all of them use a locking device of some type, either a lockwasher, locknut, locking tab or thread adhesive. All threaded fasteners should be clean and straight, with undamaged threads and undamaged corners on the hex head where the wrench fits. Develop the habit of replacing all damaged nuts and bolts with new ones. Special locknuts with nylon or fiber inserts can only be used once. If they are removed, they lose their locking ability and must be replaced with new ones.

Rusted nuts and bolts should be treated with a penetrating fluid to ease removal and prevent breakage. Some mechanics use turpentine in a spout-type oil can, which works quite well. After applying the rust penetrant, let it work for a few minutes before trying to loosen the nut or bolt. Badly rusted fasteners may have to be chiseled or sawed off or removed with a special nut breaker, available at tool stores.

If a bolt or stud breaks off in an assembly, it can be drilled and removed with a special tool commonly available for this purpose. Most automotive machine shops can perform this task, as well as other repair procedures, such as the repair of threaded holes that have been stripped out.

Flat washers and lockwashers, when removed from an assembly, should always be replaced exactly as removed. Replace any damaged washers with new ones. Never use a lockwasher on any soft metal surface (such as aluminum), thin sheet metal or plastic.

Fastener sizes

For a number of reasons, automobile manufacturers are making wider and wider use of metric fasteners. Therefore, it is important to be able to tell the difference between standard (sometimes called U.S. or SAE) and metric hardware, since they cannot be interchanged.

All bolts, whether standard or metric, are sized according to diameter, thread pitch and length. For example, a standard 1/2 - 13 x 1 bolt is 1/2 inch in diameter, has 13 threads per inch and is 1 inch long. An M12 - 1.75 x 25 metric bolt is 12 mm in diameter, has a thread pitch of 1.75 mm (the distance between threads) and is 25 mm long. The two bolts are nearly identical, and easily confused, but they are not interchangeable.

In addition to the differences in diameter, thread pitch and length, metric and standard bolts can also be distinguished by examining the bolt heads. To begin with, the distance across the flats on a standard bolt head is measured in inches, while the same dimension on a metric bolt is sized in millimeters (the same is true for nuts). As a result, a standard wrench should not be used on a metric bolt and a metric wrench should not be used on a standard bolt. Also, most standard bolts have slashes radiating out from the center of the head to denote the grade or strength of the bolt, which is an indication of the amount of torque that can be applied to it. The greater the number of slashes, the greater the strength of the bolt. Grades 0 through 5 are commonly used on automobiles. Metric bolts have a property class (grade) number, rather than a slash, molded into their heads to indicate bolt strength. In this case, the higher the number, the stronger the bolt. Property class numbers 8.8, 9.8 and 10.9 are commonly used on automobiles.

Strength markings can also be used to distinguish standard hex nuts from metric hex nuts. Many standard nuts have dots stamped into one side, while metric nuts are marked with a number. The greater the number of

dots, or the higher the number, the greater the strength of the nut.

Metric studs are also marked on their ends according to property class (grade). Larger studs are numbered (the same as metric bolts), while smaller studs carry a geometric code to denote grade.

It should be noted that many fasteners, especially Grades 0 through 2, have no distinguishing marks on them. When such is the case, the only way to determine whether it is standard or metric is to measure the thread pitch or compare it to a known fastener of the same size.

Standard fasteners are often referred to as SAE, as opposed to metric. However, it should be noted that SAE technically refers to a non-metric fine thread fastener only. Coarse thread non-metric fasteners are referred to as USS sizes.

Since fasteners of the same size (both standard and metric) may have different

strength ratings, be sure to reinstall any bolts, studs or nuts removed from your vehicle in their original locations. Also, when replacing a fastener with a new one, make sure that the new one has a strength rating equal to or greater than the original.

Tightening sequences and procedures

Most threaded fasteners should be tightened to a specific torque value (torque is the twisting force applied to a threaded component such as a nut or bolt). Overtightening the fastener can weaken it and cause it to break, while undertightening can cause it to eventually come loose. Bolts, screws and studs, depending on the material they are made of and their thread diameters, have specific torque values, many of which are noted in the Specifications at the beginning of each Chapter. Be sure to follow the torque recommendations closely. For fasteners not assigned a

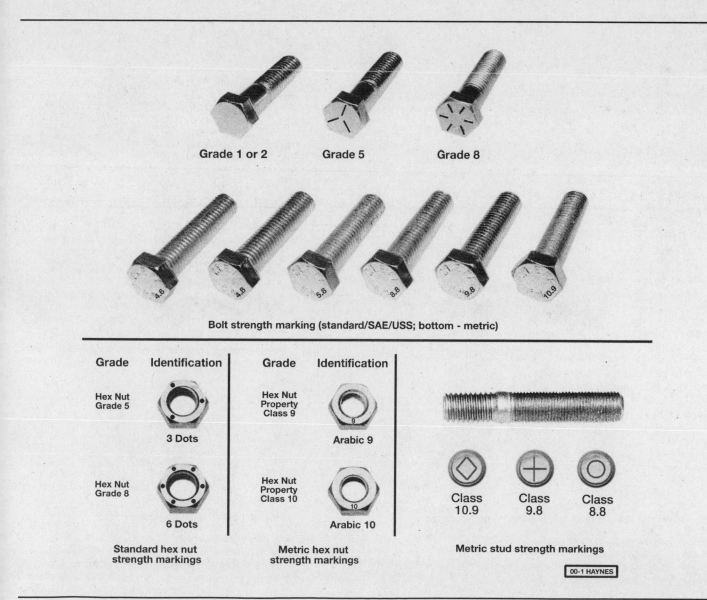

Grade 1 or 2   Grade 5   Grade 8

Bolt strength marking (standard/SAE/USS; bottom - metric)

Grade	Identification
Hex Nut Grade 5	3 Dots
Hex Nut Grade 8	6 Dots

Standard hex nut strength markings

Grade	Identification
Hex Nut Property Class 9	Arabic 9
Hex Nut Property Class 10	Arabic 10

Metric hex nut strength markings

Class 10.9   Class 9.8   Class 8.8

Metric stud strength markings

00-1 HAYNES

specific torque, a general torque value chart is presented here as a guide. These torque values are for dry (unlubricated) fasteners threaded into steel or cast iron (not aluminum). As was previously mentioned, the size and grade of a fastener determine the amount of torque that can safely be applied to it. The figures listed here are approximate for Grade 2 and Grade 3 fasteners. Higher grades can tolerate higher torque values.

Fasteners laid out in a pattern, such as cylinder head bolts, oil pan bolts, differential cover bolts, etc., must be loosened or tightened in sequence to avoid warping the component. This sequence will normally be shown in the appropriate Chapter. If a specific pattern is not given, the following procedures can be used to prevent warping.

Initially, the bolts or nuts should be assembled finger-tight only. Next, they should be tightened one full turn each, in a crisscross or diagonal pattern. After each one has been tightened one full turn, return to the first one and tighten them all one-half turn, following the same pattern. Finally, tighten each of them one-quarter turn at a time until each fastener has been tightened to the proper torque. To loosen and remove the fasteners, the procedure would be reversed.

Component disassembly

Component disassembly should be done with care and purpose to help ensure that

Metric thread sizes	Ft-lbs	Nm
M-6	6 to 9	9 to 12
M-8	14 to 21	19 to 28
M-10	28 to 40	38 to 54
M-12	50 to 71	68 to 96
M-14	80 to 140	109 to 154

Pipe thread sizes		
1/8	5 to 8	7 to 10
1/4	12 to 18	17 to 24
3/8	22 to 33	30 to 44
1/2	25 to 35	34 to 47

U.S. thread sizes		
1/4 - 20	6 to 9	9 to 12
5/16 - 18	12 to 18	17 to 24
5/16 - 24	14 to 20	19 to 27
3/8 - 16	22 to 32	30 to 43
3/8 - 24	27 to 38	37 to 51
7/16 - 14	40 to 55	55 to 74
7/16 - 20	40 to 60	55 to 81
1/2 - 13	55 to 80	75 to 108

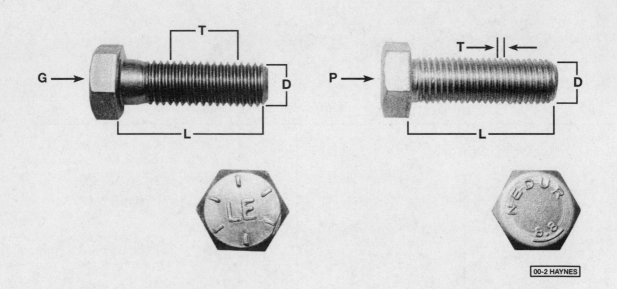

Standard (SAE and USS) bolt dimensions/grade marks

G   Grade marks (bolt strength)
L   Length (in inches)
T   Thread pitch (number of threads per inch)
D   Nominal diameter (in inches)

Metric bolt dimensions/grade marks

P   Property class (bolt strength)
L   Length (in millimeters)
T   Thread pitch (distance between threads in millimeters)
D   Diameter

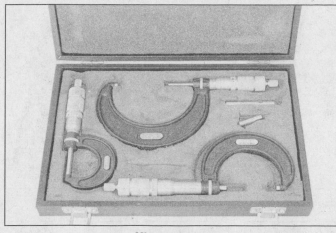

Micrometer set

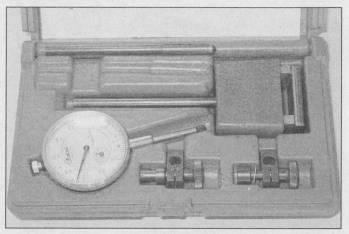

Dial indicator set

the parts go back together properly. Always keep track of the sequence in which parts are removed. Make note of special characteristics or marks on parts that can be installed more than one way, such as a grooved thrust washer on a shaft. It is a good idea to lay the disassembled parts out on a clean surface in the order that they were removed. It may also be helpful to make sketches or take instant photos of components before removal.

When removing fasteners from a component, keep track of their locations. Sometimes threading a bolt back in a part, or putting the washers and nut back on a stud, can prevent mix-ups later. If nuts and bolts cannot be returned to their original locations, they should be kept in a compartmented box or a series of small boxes. A cupcake or muffin tin is ideal for this purpose, since each cavity can hold the bolts and nuts from a particular area (i.e. oil pan bolts, valve cover bolts, engine mount bolts, etc.). A pan of this type is especially helpful when working on assemblies with very small parts, such as the carburetor, alternator, valve train or interior dash and trim pieces. The cavities can be marked with paint or tape to identify the contents.

Whenever wiring looms, harnesses or connectors are separated, it is a good idea to identify the two halves with numbered pieces of masking tape so they can be easily reconnected.

Gasket sealing surfaces

Throughout any vehicle, gaskets are used to seal the mating surfaces between two parts and keep lubricants, fluids, vacuum or pressure contained in an assembly.

Many times these gaskets are coated with a liquid or paste-type gasket sealing compound before assembly. Age, heat and pressure can sometimes cause the two parts to stick together so tightly that they are very difficult to separate. Often, the assembly can be loosened by striking it with a soft-face hammer near the mating surfaces. A regular hammer can be used if a block of wood is placed between the hammer and the part. Do

not hammer on cast parts or parts that could be easily damaged. With any particularly stubborn part, always recheck to make sure that every fastener has been removed.

Avoid using a screwdriver or bar to pry apart an assembly, as they can easily mar the gasket sealing surfaces of the parts, which must remain smooth. If prying is absolutely necessary, use an old broom handle, but keep in mind that extra clean up will be necessary if the wood splinters.

After the parts are separated, the old gasket must be carefully scraped off and the gasket surfaces cleaned. Stubborn gasket material can be soaked with rust penetrant or treated with a special chemical to soften it so it can be easily scraped off. **Caution:** *Never use gasket removal solutions or caustic chemicals on plastic or other composite components.* A scraper can be fashioned from a piece of copper tubing by flattening and sharpening one end. Copper is recommended because it is usually softer than the surfaces to be scraped, which reduces the chance of gouging the part. Some gaskets can be removed with a wire brush, but regardless of the method used, the mating surfaces must be left clean and smooth. If for some reason the gasket surface is gouged, then a gasket sealer thick enough to fill scratches will have to be used during reassembly of the components. For most applications, a non-drying (or semi-drying) gasket sealer should be used.

Hose removal tips

Warning: *If the vehicle is equipped with air conditioning, do not disconnect any of the A/C hoses without first having the system depressurized by a dealer service department or a service station.*

Hose removal precautions closely parallel gasket removal precautions. Avoid scratching or gouging the surface that the hose mates against or the connection may leak. This is especially true for radiator hoses. Because of various chemical reactions, the rubber in hoses can bond itself to the metal spigot that the hose fits over. To remove

a hose, first loosen the hose clamps that secure it to the spigot. Then, with slip-joint pliers, grab the hose at the clamp and rotate it around the spigot. Work it back and forth until it is completely free, then pull it off. Silicone or other lubricants will ease removal if they can be applied between the hose and the outside of the spigot. Apply the same lubricant to the inside of the hose and the outside of the spigot to simplify installation.

As a last resort (and if the hose is to be replaced with a new one anyway), the rubber can be slit with a knife and the hose peeled from the spigot. If this must be done, be careful that the metal connection is not damaged.

If a hose clamp is broken or damaged, do not reuse it. Wire-type clamps usually weaken with age, so it is a good idea to replace them with screw-type clamps whenever a hose is removed.

Tools

A selection of good tools is a basic requirement for anyone who plans to maintain and repair his or her own vehicle. For the owner who has few tools, the initial investment might seem high, but when compared to the spiraling costs of professional auto maintenance and repair, it is a wise one.

To help the owner decide which tools are needed to perform the tasks detailed in this manual, the following tool lists are offered: *Maintenance and minor repair, Repair/overhaul* and *Special.*

The newcomer to practical mechanics should start off with the *maintenance and minor repair* tool kit, which is adequate for the simpler jobs performed on a vehicle. Then, as confidence and experience grow, the owner can tackle more difficult tasks, buying additional tools as they are needed. Eventually the basic kit will be expanded into the *repair and overhaul* tool set. Over a period of time, the experienced do-it-yourselfer will assemble a tool set complete enough for most repair and overhaul procedures and will add tools from the special category when it is felt that the expense is justified by the frequency of use.

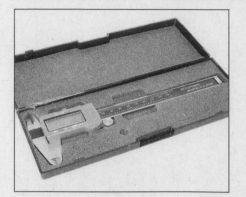

Dial caliper

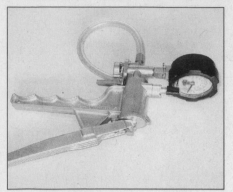

Hand-operated vacuum pump

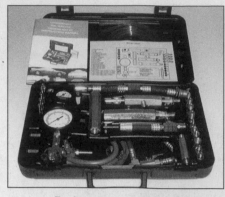

Fuel pressure gauge set

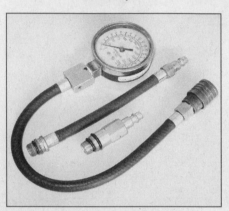

Compression gauge with spark plug hole adapter

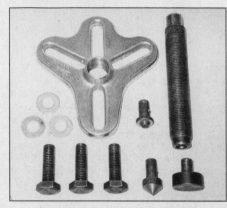

Damper/steering wheel puller

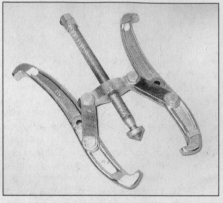

General purpose puller

Hydraulic lifter removal tool

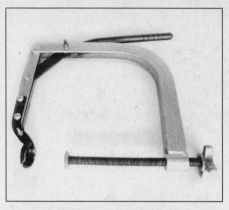

Valve spring compressor

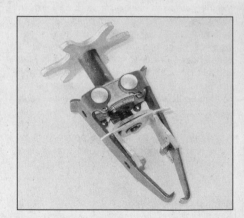

Valve spring compressor

Ridge reamer

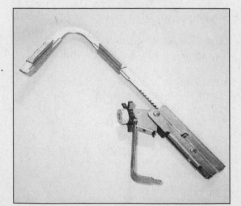

Piston ring groove cleaning tool

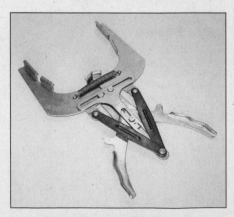

Ring removal/installation tool

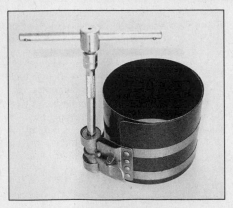

Ring compressor

Cylinder hone

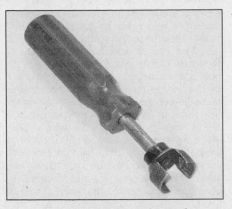

Brake hold-down spring tool

Torque angle gauge

Clutch plate alignment tool

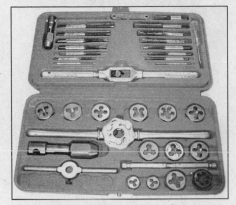

Tap and die set

Maintenance and minor repair tool kit

The tools in this list should be considered the minimum required for performance of routine maintenance, servicing and minor repair work. We recommend the purchase of combination wrenches (box-end and open-end combined in one wrench). While more expensive than open end wrenches, they offer the advantages of both types of wrench.

*Combination wrench set (1/4-inch to
    1 inch or 6 mm to 19 mm)*
Adjustable wrench, 8 inch
Spark plug wrench with rubber insert
Spark plug gap adjusting tool
Feeler gauge set
Brake bleeder wrench
*Standard screwdriver (5/16-inch x
    6 inch)*
Phillips screwdriver (No. 2 x 6 inch)
Combination pliers - 6 inch
Hacksaw and assortment of blades
Tire pressure gauge
Grease gun
Oil can
Fine emery cloth
Wire brush
Battery post and cable cleaning tool
Oil filter wrench
Funnel (medium size)
Safety goggles
Jackstands (2)
Drain pan

Note: *If basic tune-ups are going to be part of routine maintenance, it will be necessary to purchase a good quality stroboscopic timing light and combination tachometer/dwell meter. Although they are included in the list of special tools, it is mentioned here because they are absolutely necessary for tuning most vehicles properly.*

Repair and overhaul tool set

These tools are essential for anyone who plans to perform major repairs and are in addition to those in the maintenance and minor repair tool kit. Included is a comprehensive set of sockets which, though expensive, are invaluable because of their versatility, especially when various extensions and drives are available. We recommend the 1/2-inch drive over the 3/8-inch drive. Although the larger drive is bulky and more expensive, it has the capacity of accepting a very wide range of large sockets. Ideally, however, the mechanic should have a 3/8-inch drive set and a 1/2-inch drive set.

Socket set(s)
Reversible ratchet
Extension - 10 inch
Universal joint
*Torque wrench (same size drive as
    sockets)*
Ball peen hammer - 8 ounce
Soft-face hammer (plastic/rubber)
Standard screwdriver (1/4-inch x 6 inch)

*Standard screwdriver (stubby -
    5/16-inch)*
Phillips screwdriver (No. 3 x 8 inch)
Phillips screwdriver (stubby - No. 2)
Pliers - vise grip
Pliers - lineman's
Pliers - needle nose
Pliers - snap-ring (internal and external)
Cold chisel - 1/2-inch
Scribe
*Scraper (made from flattened copper
    tubing)*
Centerpunch
Pin punches (1/16, 1/8, 3/16-inch)
Steel rule/straightedge - 12 inch
*Allen wrench set (1/8 to 3/8-inch or
    4 mm to 10 mm)*
A selection of files
Wire brush (large)
Jackstands (second set)
Jack (scissor or hydraulic type)

Note: *Another tool which is often useful is an electric drill with a chuck capacity of 3/8-inch and a set of good quality drill bits.*

Special tools

The tools in this list include those which are not used regularly, are expensive to buy, or which need to be used in accordance with their manufacturer's instructions. Unless these tools will be used frequently, it is not very economical to purchase many of them. A consideration would be to split the cost and use between yourself and a friend or friends. In addition, most of these tools can be obtained from a tool rental shop on a temporary basis.

This list primarily contains only those tools and instruments widely available to the public, and not those special tools produced by the vehicle manufacturer for distribution to dealer service departments. Occasionally, references to the manufacturer's special tools are included in the text of this manual. Generally, an alternative method of doing the job without the special tool is offered. However, sometimes there is no alternative to their use. Where this is the case, and the tool cannot be purchased or borrowed, the work should be turned over to the dealer service department or an automotive repair shop.

> *Valve spring compressor*
> *Piston ring groove cleaning tool*
> *Piston ring compressor*
> *Piston ring installation tool*
> *Cylinder compression gauge*
> *Cylinder ridge reamer*
> *Cylinder surfacing hone*
> *Cylinder bore gauge*
> *Micrometers and/or dial calipers*
> *Hydraulic lifter removal tool*
> *Balljoint separator*
> *Universal-type puller*
> *Impact screwdriver*
> *Dial indicator set*
> *Stroboscopic timing light (inductive pick-up)*
> *Hand operated vacuum/pressure pump*
> *Tachometer/dwell meter*
> *Universal electrical multimeter*
> *Cable hoist*
> *Brake spring removal and installation tools*
> *Floor jack*

Buying tools

For the do-it-yourselfer who is just starting to get involved in vehicle maintenance and repair, there are a number of options available when purchasing tools. If maintenance and minor repair is the extent of the work to be done, the purchase of individual tools is satisfactory. If, on the other hand, extensive work is planned, it would be a good idea to purchase a modest tool set from one of the large retail chain stores. A set can usually be bought at a substantial savings over the individual tool prices, and they often come with a tool box. As additional tools are needed, add-on sets, individual tools and a larger tool box can be purchased to expand the tool selection. Building a tool set gradually allows the cost of the tools to be spread over a longer period of time and gives the mechanic the freedom to choose only those tools that will actually be used.

Tool stores will often be the only source of some of the special tools that are needed,

but regardless of where tools are bought, try to avoid cheap ones, especially when buying screwdrivers and sockets, because they won't last very long. The expense involved in replacing cheap tools will eventually be greater than the initial cost of quality tools.

Care and maintenance of tools

Good tools are expensive, so it makes sense to treat them with respect. Keep them clean and in usable condition and store them properly when not in use. Always wipe off any dirt, grease or metal chips before putting them away. Never leave tools lying around in the work area. Upon completion of a job, always check closely under the hood for tools that may have been left there so they won't get lost during a test drive.

Some tools, such as screwdrivers, pliers, wrenches and sockets, can be hung on a panel mounted on the garage or workshop wall, while others should be kept in a tool box or tray. Measuring instruments, gauges, meters, etc. must be carefully stored where they cannot be damaged by weather or impact from other tools.

When tools are used with care and stored properly, they will last a very long time. Even with the best of care, though, tools will wear out if used frequently. When a tool is damaged or worn out, replace it. Subsequent jobs will be safer and more enjoyable if you do.

How to repair damaged threads

Sometimes, the internal threads of a nut or bolt hole can become stripped, usually from overtightening. Stripping threads is an all-too-common occurrence, especially when working with aluminum parts, because aluminum is so soft that it easily strips out.

Usually, external or internal threads are only partially stripped. After they've been cleaned up with a tap or die, they'll still work. Sometimes, however, threads are badly damaged. When this happens, you've got three choices:

1) *Drill and tap the hole to the next suitable oversize and install a larger diameter bolt, screw or stud.*
2) *Drill and tap the hole to accept a threaded plug, then drill and tap the plug to the original screw size. You can also buy a plug already threaded to the original size. Then you simply drill a hole to the specified size, then run the threaded plug into the hole with a bolt and jam nut. Once the plug is fully seated, remove the jam nut and bolt.*
3) *The third method uses a patented thread repair kit like Heli-Coil or Slimsert. These easy-to-use kits are designed to repair*

damaged threads in straight-through holes and blind holes. Both are available as kits which can handle a variety of sizes and thread patterns. Drill the hole, then tap it with the special included tap. Install the Heli-Coil and the hole is back to its original diameter and thread pitch.

Regardless of which method you use, be sure to proceed calmly and carefully. A little impatience or carelessness during one of these relatively simple procedures can ruin your whole day's work and cost you a bundle if you wreck an expensive part.

Working facilities

Not to be overlooked when discussing tools is the workshop. If anything more than routine maintenance is to be carried out, some sort of suitable work area is essential.

It is understood, and appreciated, that many home mechanics do not have a good workshop or garage available, and end up removing an engine or doing major repairs outside. It is recommended, however, that the overhaul or repair be completed under the cover of a roof.

A clean, flat workbench or table of comfortable working height is an absolute necessity. The workbench should be equipped with a vise that has a jaw opening of at least four inches.

As mentioned previously, some clean, dry storage space is also required for tools, as well as the lubricants, fluids, cleaning solvents, etc. which soon become necessary.

Sometimes waste oil and fluids, drained from the engine or cooling system during normal maintenance or repairs, present a disposal problem. To avoid pouring them on the ground or into a sewage system, pour the used fluids into large containers, seal them with caps and take them to an authorized disposal site or recycling center. Plastic jugs, such as old antifreeze containers, are ideal for this purpose.

Always keep a supply of old newspapers and clean rags available. Old towels are excellent for mopping up spills. Many mechanics use rolls of paper towels for most work because they are readily available and disposable. To help keep the area under the vehicle clean, a large cardboard box can be cut open and flattened to protect the garage or shop floor.

Whenever working over a painted surface, such as when leaning over a fender to service something under the hood, always cover it with an old blanket or bedspread to protect the finish. Vinyl covered pads, made especially for this purpose, are available at auto parts stores.

Jacking and towing

Jacking

Warning: *The jack supplied with the vehicle should only be used for changing a tire or placing jackstands under the frame. Never work under the vehicle or start the engine while this jack is being used as the only means of support.*

The vehicle should be on level ground. Place the shift lever in Park, if you have an automatic, or Reverse if you have a manual transmission. Block the wheel diagonally opposite the wheel being changed. Set the parking brake.

Remove the spare tire and jack from stowage. Remove the wheel cover and trim ring (if so equipped) with the tapered end of the lug nut wrench by inserting and twisting the handle and then prying against the back of the wheel cover. Loosen, but do not remove, the lug nuts (one-half turn is sufficient).

Place the scissors-type jack under the vehicle and adjust the jack height until it engages with the proper jacking point. There is a front and rear jacking point on each side of the vehicle **(see illustration)**.

Turn the jack handle clockwise until the tire clears the ground. Remove the lug nuts and pull the wheel off, then install the spare.

Install the lug nuts with the beveled edges facing in. Tighten them snugly. Don't attempt to tighten them completely until the vehicle is lowered or it could slip off the jack. Turn the jack handle counterclockwise to lower the vehicle. Remove the jack and tighten the lug nuts in a diagonal pattern.

Stow the tire, jack and wrench. Unblock the wheels.

Towing

Two-wheel drive models can be towed from the rear with the rear wheels off the ground, using a wheel lift type tow truck. If towed from the front, the rear wheels must be placed on a dolly. All-wheel drive models must be towed with all four wheels off the ground. A sling-type tow truck cannot be used, as body damage will result. The best way to tow the vehicle is with a flat-bed car carrier.

In an emergency the vehicle can be towed a short distance with a cable or chain attached to one of the towing eyelets located under the front or rear bumpers. The driver must remain in the vehicle to operate the steering and brakes (remember that power steering and power brakes will not work with the engine off).

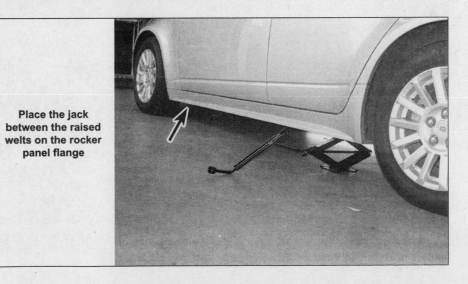

Place the jack between the raised welts on the rocker panel flange

Booster battery (jump) starting

Observe these precautions when using a booster battery to start a vehicle:

a) *Before connecting the booster battery, make sure the ignition switch is in the Off position.*

b) *Turn off the lights, heater and other electrical loads.*

c) *Your eyes should be shielded. Safety goggles are a good idea.*

d) *Make sure the booster battery is the same voltage as the dead one in the vehicle.*

e) *The two vehicles MUST NOT TOUCH each other!*

f) *Make sure the transmission is in Neutral (manual) or Park (automatic).*

g) *If the booster battery is not a maintenance-free type, remove the vent caps and lay a cloth over the vent holes.*

Connect the red jumper cable to the positive (+) terminals of each battery (see illustration). Note: *On 2008 and later models the battery is mounted in the trunk or rear cargo area next to the spare tire. These models are equipped with a remote positive terminal, located in the engine compartment to make jumper cable connection easier* (see illustration).

Connect one end of the black jumper cable to the negative (-) terminal of the booster battery. The other end of this cable should be connected to a good ground on the vehicle to be started, such as a bolt or bracket on the body.

Start the engine using the booster battery, then, with the engine running at idle speed, disconnect the jumper cables in the reverse order of connection.

Connect one end of the black jumper cable to the negative (-) terminal of the booster battery. The other end of this cable should be connected to a good ground on the vehicle to be started, such as a bolt or bracket on the body.

Start the engine using the booster battery, then, with the engine running at idle speed, disconnect the jumper cables in the reverse order of connection.

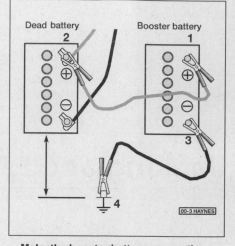

Make the booster battery connections in the numerical order shown (note the negative cable of the booster battery is not attached to the negative terminal of the dead battery) - 2007 and earlier models

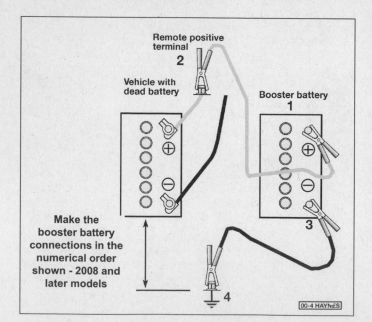

Make the booster battery connections in the numerical order shown - 2008 and later models

Locations of the remote positive terminal (A) and the remote ground terminal (B) - 2008 and later models

Automotive chemicals and lubricants

A number of automotive chemicals and lubricants are available for use during vehicle maintenance and repair. They include a wide variety of products ranging from cleaning solvents and degreasers to lubricants and protective sprays for rubber, plastic and vinyl.

Cleaners

Carburetor cleaner and choke cleaner is a strong solvent for gum, varnish and carbon. Most carburetor cleaners leave a dry-type lubricant film which will not harden or gum up. Because of this film it is not recommended for use on electrical components.

Brake system cleaner is used to remove brake dust, grease and brake fluid from the brake system, where clean surfaces are absolutely necessary. It leaves no residue and often eliminates brake squeal caused by contaminants.

Electrical cleaner removes oxidation, corrosion and carbon deposits from electrical contacts, restoring full current flow. It can also be used to clean spark plugs, carburetor jets, voltage regulators and other parts where an oil-free surface is desired.

Demoisturants remove water and moisture from electrical components such as alternators, voltage regulators, electrical connectors and fuse blocks. They are non-conductive and non-corrosive.

Degreasers are heavy-duty solvents used to remove grease from the outside of the engine and from chassis components. They can be sprayed or brushed on and, depending on the type, are rinsed off either with water or solvent.

Lubricants

Motor oil is the lubricant formulated for use in engines. It normally contains a wide variety of additives to prevent corrosion and reduce foaming and wear. Motor oil comes in various weights (viscosity ratings) from 0 to 50. The recommended weight of the oil depends on the season, temperature and the demands on the engine. Light oil is used in cold climates and under light load conditions. Heavy oil is used in hot climates and where high loads are encountered. Multi-viscosity oils are designed to have characteristics of both light and heavy oils and are available in a number of weights from 0W-20 to 20W-50.

Gear oil is designed to be used in differentials, manual transmissions and other areas where high-temperature lubrication is required.

Chassis and wheel bearing grease is a heavy grease used where increased loads and friction are encountered, such as for wheel bearings, balljoints, tie-rod ends and universal joints.

High-temperature wheel bearing grease is designed to withstand the extreme temperatures encountered by wheel bearings in disc brake equipped vehicles. It usually contains molybdenum disulfide (moly), which is a dry-type lubricant.

White grease is a heavy grease for metal-to-metal applications where water is a problem. White grease stays soft under both low and high temperatures (usually from -100 to +190-degrees F), and will not wash off or dilute in the presence of water.

Assembly lube is a special extreme pressure lubricant, usually containing moly, used to lubricate high-load parts (such as main and rod bearings and cam lobes) for initial start-up of a new engine. The assembly lube lubricates the parts without being squeezed out or washed away until the engine oiling system begins to function.

Silicone lubricants are used to protect rubber, plastic, vinyl and nylon parts.

Graphite lubricants are used where oils cannot be used due to contamination problems, such as in locks. The dry graphite will lubricate metal parts while remaining uncontaminated by dirt, water, oil or acids. It is electrically conductive and will not foul electrical contacts in locks such as the ignition switch.

Moly penetrants loosen and lubricate frozen, rusted and corroded fasteners and prevent future rusting or freezing.

Heat-sink grease is a special electrically non-conductive grease that is used for mounting electronic ignition modules where it is essential that heat is transferred away from the module.

Sealants

RTV sealant is one of the most widely used gasket compounds. Made from silicone, RTV is air curing, it seals, bonds, waterproofs, fills surface irregularities, remains flexible, doesn't shrink, is relatively easy to remove, and is used as a supplementary sealer with almost all low and medium temperature gaskets.

Anaerobic sealant is much like RTV in that it can be used either to seal gaskets or to form gaskets by itself. It remains flexible, is solvent resistant and fills surface imperfections. The difference between an anaerobic sealant and an RTV-type sealant is in the curing. RTV cures when exposed to air, while an anaerobic sealant cures only in the absence of air. This means that an anaerobic sealant cures only after the assembly of parts, sealing them together.

Thread and pipe sealant is used for sealing hydraulic and pneumatic fittings and vacuum lines. It is usually made from a Teflon compound, and comes in a spray, a paint-on liquid and as a wrap-around tape.

Chemicals

Anti-seize compound prevents seizing, galling, cold welding, rust and corrosion in fasteners. High-temperature ant-seize, usually made with copper and graphite lubricants, is used for exhaust system and exhaust manifold bolts.

Anaerobic locking compounds are used to keep fasteners from vibrating or working loose and cure only after installation, in the absence of air. Medium strength locking compound is used for small nuts, bolts and screws that may be removed later. High-strength locking compound is for large nuts, bolts and studs which aren't removed on a regular basis.

Oil additives range from viscosity index improvers to chemical treatments that claim to reduce internal engine friction. It should be noted that most oil manufacturers caution against using additives with their oils.

Gas additives perform several functions, depending on their chemical makeup. They usually contain solvents that help dissolve gum and varnish that build up on carburetor, fuel injection and intake parts. They also serve to break down carbon deposits that form on the inside surfaces of the combustion chambers. Some additives contain upper cylinder lubricants for valves and piston rings, and others contain chemicals to remove condensation from the gas tank.

Miscellaneous

Brake fluid is specially formulated hydraulic fluid that can withstand the heat and pressure encountered in brake systems. Care must be taken so this fluid does not come in contact with painted surfaces or plastics. An opened container should always be resealed to prevent contamination by water or dirt.

Weatherstrip adhesive is used to bond weatherstripping around doors, windows and trunk lids. It is sometimes used to attach trim pieces.

Undercoating is a petroleum-based, tar-like substance that is designed to protect metal surfaces on the underside of the vehicle from corrosion. It also acts as a sound-deadening agent by insulating the bottom of the vehicle.

Waxes and polishes are used to help protect painted and plated surfaces from the weather. Different types of paint may require the use of different types of wax and polish. Some polishes utilize a chemical or abrasive cleaner to help remove the top layer of oxidized (dull) paint on older vehicles. In recent years many non-wax polishes that contain a wide variety of chemicals such as polymers and silicones have been introduced. These non-wax polishes are usually easier to apply and last longer than conventional waxes and polishes.

Conversion factors

Length (distance)

Inches (in)	X	25.4	= Millimeters (mm)	X	0.0394	= Inches (in)
Feet (ft)	X	0.305	= Meters (m)	X	3.281	= Feet (ft)
Miles	X	1.609	= Kilometers (km)	X	0.621	= Miles

Volume (capacity)

Cubic inches (cu in; in^3)	X	16.387	= Cubic centimeters (cc; cm^3)	X	0.061	= Cubic inches (cu in; in^3)
Imperial pints (Imp pt)	X	0.568	= Liters (l)	X	1.76	= Imperial pints (Imp pt)
Imperial quarts (Imp qt)	X	1.137	= Liters (l)	X	0.88	= Imperial quarts (Imp qt)
Imperial quarts (Imp qt)	X	1.201	= US quarts (US qt)	X	0.833	= Imperial quarts (Imp qt)
US quarts (US qt)	X	0.946	= Liters (l)	X	1.057	= US quarts (US qt)
Imperial gallons (Imp gal)	X	4.546	= Liters (l)	X	0.22	= Imperial gallons (Imp gal)
Imperial gallons (Imp gal)	X	1.201	= US gallons (US gal)	X	0.833	= Imperial gallons (Imp gal)
US gallons (US gal)	X	3.785	= Liters (l)	X	0.264	= US gallons (US gal)

Mass (weight)

Ounces (oz)	X	28.35	= Grams (g)	X	0.035	= Ounces (oz)
Pounds (lb)	X	0.454	= Kilograms (kg)	X	2.205	= Pounds (lb)

Force

Ounces-force (ozf; oz)	X	0.278	= Newtons (N)	X	3.6	= Ounces-force (ozf; oz)
Pounds-force (lbf; lb)	X	4.448	= Newtons (N)	X	0.225	= Pounds-force (lbf; lb)
Newtons (N)	X	0.1	= Kilograms-force (kgf; kg)	X	9.81	= Newtons (N)

Pressure

Pounds-force per square inch (psi; lbf/in^2; lb/in^2)	X	0.070	= Kilograms-force per square centimeter (kgf/cm^2; kg/cm^2)	X	14.223	= Pounds-force per square inch (psi; lbf/in^2; lb/in^2)
Pounds-force per square inch (psi; lbf/in^2; lb/in^2)	X	0.068	= Atmospheres (atm)	X	14.696	= Pounds-force per square inch (psi; lbf/in^2; lb/in^2)
Pounds-force per square inch (psi; lbf/in^2; lb/in^2)	X	0.069	= Bars	X	14.5	= Pounds-force per square inch (psi; lbf/in^2; lb/in^2)
Pounds-force per square inch (psi; lbf/in^2; lb/in^2)	X	6.895	= Kilopascals (kPa)	X	0.145	= Pounds-force per square inch (psi; lbf/in^2; lb/in^2)
Kilopascals (kPa)	X	0.01	= Kilograms-force per square centimeter (kgf/cm^2; kg/cm^2)	X	98.1	= Kilopascals (kPa)

Torque (moment of force)

Pounds-force inches (lbf in; lb in)	X	1.152	= Kilograms-force centimeter (kgf cm; kg cm)	X	0.868	= Pounds-force inches (lbf in; lb in)
Pounds-force inches (lbf in; lb in)	X	0.113	= Newton meters (Nm)	X	8.85	= Pounds-force inches (lbf in; lb in)
Pounds-force inches (lbf in; lb in)	X	0.083	= Pounds-force feet (lbf ft; lb ft)	X	12	= Pounds-force inches (lbf in; lb in)
Pounds-force feet (lbf ft; lb ft)	X	0.138	= Kilograms-force meters (kgf m; kg m)	X	7.233	= Pounds-force feet (lbf ft; lb ft)
Pounds-force feet (lbf ft; lb ft)	X	1.356	= Newton meters (Nm)	X	0.738	= Pounds-force feet (lbf ft; lb ft)
Newton meters (Nm)	X	0.102	= Kilograms-force meters (kgf m; kg m)	X	9.804	= Newton meters (Nm)

Vacuum

Inches mercury (in. Hg)	X	3.377	= Kilopascals (kPa)	X	0.2961	= Inches mercury
Inches mercury (in. Hg)	X	25.4	= Millimeters mercury (mm Hg)	X	0.0394	= Inches mercury

Power

Horsepower (hp)	X	745.7	= Watts (W)	X	0.0013	= Horsepower (hp)

Velocity (speed)

Miles per hour (miles/hr; mph)	X	1.609	= Kilometers per hour (km/hr; kph)	X	0.621	= Miles per hour (miles/hr; mph)

Fuel consumption*

Miles per gallon, Imperial (mpg)	X	0.354	= Kilometers per liter (km/l)	X	2.825	= Miles per gallon, Imperial (mpg)
Miles per gallon, US (mpg)	X	0.425	= Kilometers per liter (km/l)	X	2.352	= Miles per gallon, US (mpg)

Temperature

Degrees Fahrenheit = (°C x 1.8) + 32

Degrees Celsius (Degrees Centigrade; °C) = (°F - 32) x 0.56

*It is common practice to convert from miles per gallon (mpg) to liters/100 kilometers (l/100km), where mpg (Imperial) x l/100 km = 282 and mpg (US) x l/100 km = 235

DECIMALS to MILLIMETERS

Decimal	mm	Decimal	mm
0.001	0.0254	0.500	12.7000
0.002	0.0508	0.510	12.9540
0.003	0.0762	0.520	13.2080
0.004	0.1016	0.530	13.4620
0.005	0.1270	0.540	13.7160
0.006	0.1524	0.550	13.9700
0.007	0.1778	0.560	14.2240
0.008	0.2032	0.570	14.4780
0.009	0.2286	0.580	14.7320
0.010	0.2540	0.590	14.9860
0.020	0.5080	0.600	15.2400
0.030	0.7620	0.610	15.4940
0.040	1.0160	0.620	15.7480
0.050	1.2700	0.630	16.0020
0.060	1.5240	0.640	16.2560
0.070	1.7780	0.650	16.5100
0.080	2.0320	0.660	16.7640
0.090	2.2860	0.670	17.0180
0.100	2.5400	0.680	17.2720
0.110	2.7940	0.690	17.5260
0.120	3.0480	0.700	17.7800
0.130	3.3020	0.710	18.0340
0.140	3.5560	0.720	18.2880
0.150	3.8100	0.730	18.5420
0.160	4.0640	0.740	18.7960
0.170	4.3180	0.750	19.0500
0.180	4.5720	0.760	19.3040
0.190	4.8260	0.770	19.5580
0.200	5.0800	0.780	19.8120
0.210	5.3340	0.790	20.0660
0.220	5.5880	0.800	20.3200
0.230	5.8420	0.810	20.5740
0.240	6.0960	0.820	21.8280
0.250	6.3500	0.830	21.0820
0.260	6.6040	0.840	21.3360
0.270	6.8580	0.850	21.5900
0.280	7.1120	0.860	21.8440
0.290	7.3660	0.870	22.0980
0.300	7.6200	0.880	22.3520
0.310	7.8740	0.890	22.6060
0.320	8.1280	0.900	22.8600
0.330	8.3820	0.910	23.1140
0.340	8.6360	0.920	23.3680
0.350	8.8900	0.930	23.6220
0.360	9.1440	0.940	23.8760
0.370	9.3980	0.950	24.1300
0.380	9.6520	0.960	24.3840
0.390	9.9060	0.970	24.6380
0.400	10.1600	0.980	24.8920
0.410	10.4140	0.990	25.1460
0.420	10.6680	1.000	25.4000
0.430	10.9220		
0.440	11.1760		
0.450	11.4300		
0.460	11.6840		
0.470	11.9380		
0.480	12.1920		
0.490	12.4460		

FRACTIONS to DECIMALS to MILLIMETERS

Fraction	Decimal	mm	Fraction	Decimal	mm
1/64	0.0156	0.3969	33/64	0.5156	13.0969
1/32	0.0312	0.7938	17/32	0.5312	13.4938
3/64	0.0469	1.1906	35/64	0.5469	13.8906
1/16	0.0625	1.5875	9/16	0.5625	14.2875
5/64	0.0781	1.9844	37/64	0.5781	14.6844
3/32	0.0938	2.3812	19/32	0.5938	15.0812
7/64	0.1094	2.7781	39/64	0.6094	15.4781
1/8	0.1250	3.1750	5/8	0.6250	15.8750
9/64	0.1406	3.5719	41/64	0.6406	16.2719
5/32	0.1562	3.9688	21/32	0.6562	16.6688
11/64	0.1719	4.3656	43/64	0.6719	17.0656
3/16	0.1875	4.7625	11/16	0.6875	17.4625
13/64	0.2031	5.1594	45/64	0.7031	17.8594
7/32	0.2188	5.5562	23/32	0.7188	18.2562
15/64	0.2344	5.9531	47/64	0.7344	18.6531
1/4	0.2500	6.3500	3/4	0.7500	19.0500
17/64	0.2656	6.7469	49/64	0.7656	19.4469
9/32	0.2812	7.1438	25/32	0.7812	19.8438
19/64	0.2969	7.5406	51/64	0.7969	20.2406
5/16	0.3125	7.9375	13/16	0.8125	20.6375
21/64	0.3281	8.3344	53/64	0.8281	21.0344
11/32	0.3438	8.7312	27/32	0.8438	21.4312
23/64	0.3594	9.1281	55/64	0.8594	21.8281
3/8	0.3750	9.5250	7/8	0.8750	22.2250
25/64	0.3906	9.9219	57/64	0.8906	22.6219
13/32	0.4062	10.3188	29/32	0.9062	23.0188
27/64	0.4219	10.7156	59/64	0.9219	23.4156
7/16	0.4375	11.1125	15/16	0.9375	23.8125
29/64	0.4531	11.5094	61/64	0.9531	24.2094
15/32	0.4688	11.9062	31/32	0.9688	24.6062
31/64	0.4844	12.3031	63/64	0.9844	25.0031
1/2	0.5000	12.7000	1	1.0000	25.4000

Safety first!

Regardless of how enthusiastic you may be about getting on with the job at hand, take the time to ensure that your safety is not jeopardized. A moment's lack of attention can result in an accident, as can failure to observe certain simple safety precautions. The possibility of an accident will always exist, and the following points should not be considered a comprehensive list of all dangers. Rather, they are intended to make you aware of the risks and to encourage a safety conscious approach to all work you carry out on your vehicle.

Essential DOs and DON'Ts

DON'T rely on a jack when working under the vehicle. Always use approved jackstands to support the weight of the vehicle and place them under the recommended lift or support points.

DON'T attempt to loosen extremely tight fasteners (i.e. wheel lug nuts) while the vehicle is on a jack - it may fall.

DON'T start the engine without first making sure that the transmission is in Neutral (or Park where applicable) and the parking brake is set.

DON'T remove the radiator cap from a hot cooling system - let it cool or cover it with a cloth and release the pressure gradually.

DON'T attempt to drain the engine oil until you are sure it has cooled to the point that it will not burn you.

DON'T touch any part of the engine or exhaust system until it has cooled sufficiently to avoid burns.

DON'T siphon toxic liquids such as gasoline, antifreeze and brake fluid by mouth, or allow them to remain on your skin.

DON'T inhale brake lining dust - it is potentially hazardous (see *Asbestos* below).

DON'T allow spilled oil or grease to remain on the floor - wipe it up before someone slips on it.

DON'T use loose fitting wrenches or other tools which may slip and cause injury.

DON'T push on wrenches when loosening or tightening nuts or bolts. Always try to pull the wrench toward you. If the situation calls for pushing the wrench away, push with an open hand to avoid scraped knuckles if the wrench should slip.

DON'T attempt to lift a heavy component alone - get someone to help you.

DON'T *rush or take unsafe shortcuts to finish a job.*

DON'T allow children or animals in or around the vehicle while you are working on it.

DO wear eye protection when using power tools such as a drill, sander, bench grinder, etc. and when working under a vehicle.

DO keep loose clothing and long hair well out of the way of moving parts.

DO make sure that any hoist used has a safe working load rating adequate for the job.

DO get someone to check on you periodically when working alone on a vehicle.

DO carry out work in a logical sequence and make sure that everything is correctly assembled and tightened.

DO keep chemicals and fluids tightly capped and out of the reach of children and pets.

DO remember that your vehicle's safety affects that of yourself and others. If in doubt on any point, get professional advice.

Steering, suspension and brakes

These systems are essential to driving safety, so make sure you have a qualified shop or individual check your work. Also, compressed suspension springs can cause injury if released suddenly - be sure to use a spring compressor.

Airbags

Airbags are explosive devices that can **CAUSE** injury if they deploy while you're working on the vehicle. Follow the manufacturer's instructions to disable the airbag whenever you're working in the vicinity of airbag components.

Asbestos

Certain friction, insulating, sealing, and other products - such as brake linings, brake bands, clutch linings, torque converters, gaskets, etc. - may contain asbestos or other hazardous friction material. Extreme care must be taken to avoid inhalation of dust from such products, since it is hazardous to health. If in doubt, assume that they do contain asbestos.

Fire

Remember at all times that gasoline is highly flammable. Never smoke or have any kind of open flame around when working on a vehicle. But the risk does not end there. A spark caused by an electrical short circuit, by two metal surfaces contacting each other, or even by static electricity built up in your body under certain conditions, can ignite gasoline vapors, which in a confined space are highly explosive. Do not, under any circumstances, use gasoline for cleaning parts. Use an approved safety solvent.

Always disconnect the battery ground (-) cable at the battery before working on any part of the fuel system or electrical system. Never risk spilling fuel on a hot engine or exhaust component. It is strongly recommended that a fire extinguisher suitable for use on fuel and electrical fires be kept handy in the garage or workshop at all times. Never try to extinguish a fuel or electrical fire with water.

Fumes

Certain fumes are highly toxic and can quickly cause unconsciousness and even death if inhaled to any extent. Gasoline vapor falls into this category, as do the vapors from some cleaning solvents. Any draining or pouring of such volatile fluids should be done in a well ventilated area.

When using cleaning fluids and solvents, read the instructions on the container carefully. Never use materials from unmarked containers.

Never run the engine in an enclosed space, such as a garage. Exhaust fumes contain carbon monoxide, which is extremely poisonous. If you need to run the engine, always do so in the open air, or at least have the rear of the vehicle outside the work area.

The battery

Never create a spark or allow a bare light bulb near a battery. They normally give off a certain amount of hydrogen gas, which is highly explosive.

Always disconnect the battery ground (-) cable at the battery before working on the fuel or electrical systems.

If possible, loosen the filler caps or cover when charging the battery from an external source (this does not apply to sealed or maintenance-free batteries). Do not charge at an excessive rate or the battery may burst.

Take care when adding water to a non maintenance-free battery and when carrying a battery. The electrolyte, even when diluted, is very corrosive and should not be allowed to contact clothing or skin.

Always wear eye protection when cleaning the battery to prevent the caustic deposits from entering your eyes.

Household current

When using an electric power tool, inspection light, etc., which operates on household current, always make sure that the tool is correctly connected to its plug and that, where necessary, it is properly grounded. Do not use such items in damp conditions and, again, do not create a spark or apply excessive heat in the vicinity of fuel or fuel vapor.

Secondary ignition system voltage

A severe electric shock can result from touching certain parts of the ignition system (such as the spark plug wires) when the engine is running or being cranked, particularly if components are damp or the insulation is defective. In the case of an electronic ignition system, the secondary system voltage is much higher and could prove fatal.

Hydrofluoric acid

This extremely corrosive acid is formed when certain types of synthetic rubber, found in some O-rings, oil seals, fuel hoses, etc. are exposed to temperatures above 750-degrees F (400-degrees C). The rubber changes into a charred or sticky substance containing the acid. *Once formed, the acid remains dangerous for years. If it gets onto the skin, it may be necessary to amputate the limb concerned.*

When dealing with a vehicle which has suffered a fire, or with components salvaged from such a vehicle, wear protective gloves and discard them after use.

Troubleshooting

Contents

This section provides an easy reference guide to the more common problems which may occur during the operation of your vehicle. These problems and their possible causes are grouped under headings denoting various components or systems, such as Engine, Cooling system, etc. They also refer you to the chapter and/or section which deals with the problem.

Remember that successful troubleshooting is not a mysterious black art practiced only by professional mechanics. It is simply the result of the right knowledge combined with an intelligent, systematic approach to the problem. Always work by a process of elimination, starting with the simplest solution and working through to the most complex - and never overlook the obvious. Anyone can run the gas tank dry or leave the lights on overnight, so don't assume that you are exempt from such oversights.

Finally, always establish a clear idea of why a problem has occurred and take steps to ensure that it doesn't happen again. If the electrical system fails because of a poor connection, check the other connections in the system to make sure that they don't fail as well. If a particular fuse continues to blow, find out why - don't just replace one fuse after another. Remember, failure of a small component can often be indicative of potential failure or incorrect functioning of a more important component or system.

Engine

1 Engine will not rotate when attempting to start

1 Battery terminal connections loose or corroded (Chapter 1).
2 Battery discharged or faulty (Chapters 1 and 5).
3 Automatic transmission not completely engaged in Park (Chapter 7) or clutch pedal not completely depressed (Chapter 6).
4 Broken, loose or disconnected wiring in the starting circuit (Chapters 5 and 12).
5 Starter motor pinion jammed in flywheel/driveplate ring gear (Chapter 5).
6 Starter solenoid faulty (Chapter 5).
7 Starter motor faulty (Chapter 5).
8 Ignition switch faulty (Chapter 12).
9 Starter pinion or flywheel/driveplate teeth worn or broken (Chapter 5).

2 Engine rotates but will not start

1 Fuel tank empty.
2 Battery discharged (engine rotates slowly) (Chapter 5).
3 Battery terminal connections loose or corroded (Chapter 1).
4 Leaking fuel injector(s), faulty fuel pump, pressure regulator, etc. (Chapter 4).
5 Broken timing belt or chain (Chapter 2A, 2B or 2C).

6 Ignition system problem (Chapter 5).
7 Worn, faulty or incorrectly-gapped spark plugs (Chapter 1).
8 Defective crankshaft or camshaft sensor (Chapter 6).

3 Engine hard to start when cold

1 Battery discharged or low (Chapter 1).
2 Malfunctioning fuel system (Chapter 4).
3 Faulty coolant temperature sensor or intake air temperature sensor (Chapter 6).
4 Faulty ignition system (Chapter 5).

4 Engine hard to start when hot

1 Air filter clogged (Chapter 1).
2 Malfunctioning fuel system (Chapter 4).
3 Corroded battery connections (Chapter 1).
4 Faulty coolant temperature sensor or intake air temperature sensor (Chapter 6).

5 Starter motor noisy or excessively rough in engagement

1 Pinion or flywheel/driveplate gear teeth worn or broken (Chapter 5).
2 Starter motor mounting bolts loose or missing (Chapter 5).

6 Engine starts but stops immediately

1 Insufficient fuel reaching the fuel injector(s) (Chapters 1 and 4).
2 Vacuum leak at the gasket between the intake manifold/plenum and throttle body (Chapter 4).

7 Oil puddle under engine

1 Oil pan gasket and/or oil pan drain bolt washer leaking (Chapter 2).
2 Oil pressure sending unit leaking (Chapter 2).
3 Valve cover leaking (Chapter 2).
4 Engine oil seals leaking (Chapter 2).
5 Oil pump housing leaking (Chapter 2).

8 Engine lopes while idling or idles erratically

1 Vacuum leakage (Chapters 2 and 4).
2 Leaking EGR valve (Chapter 6).
3 Air filter clogged (Chapter 1).
4 Malfunction in the fuel injection or engine control system (Chapters 4 and 6).
5 Leaking head gasket (Chapter 2).
6 Timing chain and/or sprockets worn (Chapter 2).
7 Camshaft lobes worn (Chapter 2).

9 Engine misses at idle speed

1 Spark plugs worn or not gapped properly (Chapter 1).
2 Faulty coil(s) (Chapter 1).
3 Vacuum leaks (Chapter 1).
4 Uneven or low compression (Chapter 2).
5 Problem with the fuel injection system (Chapter 4).

10 Engine misses throughout driving speed range

1 Fuel filter clogged and/or impurities in the fuel system (Chapter 4).
2 Low fuel pressure (Chapter 4).
3 Faulty or incorrectly gapped spark plugs (Chapter 1).
4 Faulty emission system components (Chapter 6).
5 Low or uneven cylinder compression pressures (Chapter 2).
6 Weak or faulty ignition system (Chapter 5).
7 Vacuum leak in fuel injection system, intake manifold, air control valve or vacuum hoses (Chapters 4 and 6).

11 Engine stumbles on acceleration

1 Spark plugs fouled (Chapter 1).
2 Problem with fuel injection or engine control system (Chapters 4 and 6).
3 Fuel filter clogged (Chapters 1 and 4).
4 Intake manifold air leak (Chapters 2 and 4).
5 Problem with the emissions control system (Chapter 6).

12 Engine surges while holding accelerator steady

1 Intake air leak (Chapter 4).
2 Fuel pump or fuel pressure regulator faulty (Chapter 4).
3 Problem with the fuel injection system (Chapter 4).
4 Problem with the emissions control system (Chapter 6).

13 Engine stalls

1 Fuel filter clogged and/or water and impurities in the fuel system (Chapter 4).
2 Faulty emissions system components (Chapter 6).
3 Faulty or incorrectly-gapped spark plugs (Chapter 1).
4 Vacuum leak at fuel injector(s), intake manifold or vacuum hoses (Chapters 2 and 4).

14 Engine lacks power

1 Obstructed exhaust system (Chapter 4).
2 Faulty or incorrectly-gapped spark plugs (Chapter 1).
3 Problem with the fuel injection system (Chapter 4).
4 Dirty air filter (Chapter 1).
5 Brakes binding (Chapter 9).
6 Automatic transmission fluid level incorrect (Chapter 1).
7 Clutch slipping (Chapter 8).
8 Fuel filter clogged and/or impurities in the fuel system (Chapters 1 and 4).
9 Emission control system not functioning properly (Chapter 6).
10 Low or uneven cylinder compression pressures (Chapter 2).

15 Engine backfires

1 Emission control system not functioning properly (Chapter 6).
2 Problem with the fuel injection system (Chapter 4).
3 Vacuum leak at fuel injector(s), intake manifold or vacuum hoses (Chapters 2 and 4).
4 Valve sticking (Chapter 2).

16 Pinging or knocking engine sounds during acceleration or uphill

1 Incorrect grade of fuel.
2 Fuel injection system faulty (Chapter 4).
3 Improper or damaged spark plugs or wires (Chapter 1).
4 Knock sensor defective (Chapter 6).
5 EGR valve not functioning (Chapter 6).
6 Vacuum leak (Chapters 2 and 4).

17 Engine runs with oil pressure light on

1 Low oil level (Chapter 1).
2 Idle rpm below specification (Chapter 1).
3 Short in wiring circuit (Chapter 12).
4 Faulty oil pressure sender (Chapter 2).
5 Worn engine bearings and/or oil pump (Chapter 2).

18 Engine continues to run after switching off

1 Defective ignition switch (Chapter 12).
2 Faulty Powertrain Control Module (Chapter 6).
3 Faulty Body Control Module.
4 Leaking fuel injector (Chapter 4).

Engine electrical systems

19 Battery will not hold a charge

1 Drivebelt or tensioner defective (Chapter 1).
2 Battery electrolyte level low (Chapter 1).
3 Battery terminals loose or corroded (Chapter 1).
4 Alternator not charging properly (Chapter 5).
5 Loose, broken or faulty wiring in the charging circuit (Chapter 5).
6 Internally defective battery (Chapters 1 and 5).

20 Alternator light fails to go out

1 Faulty alternator or charging circuit (Chapter 5).
2 Drivebelt or tensioner defective (Chapter 1).

21 Alternator light fails to come on when key is turned on

1 Instrument cluster defective (Chapter 12).
2 Fault in the wiring harness (Chapter 12).

Fuel system

22 Excessive fuel consumption

1 Dirty air filter element (Chapter 1).
2 Emissions system not functioning properly (Chapter 6).
3 Fuel injection system not functioning properly (Chapter 4).
4 Low tire pressure or incorrect tire size (Chapter 1).

23 Fuel leakage and/or fuel odor

1 Leaking fuel line (Chapters 1 and 4).
2 Tank overfilled.
3 Evaporative emissions control system problem (Chapters 1 and 6).
4 Problem with the fuel injection system (Chapter 4).

Cooling system

24 Overheating

1 Insufficient coolant in system (Chapter 1).
2 Water pump drivebelt defective or out of adjustment (Chapter 1).

3 Radiator core blocked or grille restricted (Chapter 3).
4 Thermostat faulty (Chapter 3).
5 Electric coolant fan inoperative or blades broken (Chapter 3).
6 Expansion tank cap not maintaining proper pressure (Chapter 3).

25 Overcooling

1 Faulty thermostat (Chapter 3).
2 Inaccurate temperature gauge sending unit (Chapter 3).

26 External coolant leakage

1 Deteriorated/damaged hoses; loose clamps (Chapters 1 and 3).
2 Water pump defective (Chapter 3).
3 Leakage from radiator core or coolant reservoir (Chapter 3).
4 Engine drain or water jacket core plugs leaking (Chapter 2).

27 Internal coolant leakage

1 Leaking cylinder head gasket (Chapter 2).
2 Cracked cylinder bore or cylinder head (Chapter 2).

28 Coolant loss

1 Too much coolant in reservoir (Chapter 1).
2 Coolant boiling away because of overheating (Chapter 3).
3 Internal or external leakage (Chapter 3).
4 Faulty radiator cap (Chapter 3).

29 Poor coolant circulation

1 Inoperative water pump (Chapter 3).
2 Restriction in cooling system (Chapters 1 and 3).
3 Drivebelt or tensioner defective (Chapter 1).
4 Thermostat sticking (Chapter 3).

Clutch

30 Pedal travels to floor - no pressure or very little resistance

1 Master or release cylinder faulty (Chapter 8).

2   Hose/pipe burst or leaking (Chapter 8).
3   Connections leaking (Chapter 8).
4   No fluid in reservoir (Chapter 8).
5   If fluid level in reservoir rises as pedal is depressed, master cylinder center valve seal is faulty (Chapter 8).
6   If there is fluid on dust seal at master cylinder, piston primary seal is leaking (Chapter 8).
7   Broken release bearing or fork (Chapter 8).
8   Faulty pressure plate diaphragm spring (Chapter 8).

31   Fluid in area of master cylinder dust cover and on pedal

Rear seal failure in master cylinder (Chapter 8).

32   Fluid dripping from transmission bellhousing

Release cylinder seal faulty (Chapter 8).

33   Pedal feels spongy when depressed

Air in system (Chapter 8).

34   Unable to select gears

1   Faulty transmission (Chapter 7A).
2   Faulty clutch disc or pressure plate (Chapter 8).
3   Faulty release lever or release bearing (Chapter 8).
4   Faulty shift lever assembly or linkage (Chapter 8).

35   Clutch slips (engine speed increases with no increase in vehicle speed)

1   Clutch plate worn (Chapter 8).
2   Clutch plate is oil soaked by leaking rear main seal (Chapters 2 and 8).
3   Clutch plate not seated (Chapter 8).
4   Warped pressure plate or flywheel (Chapter 8).
5   Weak diaphragm springs (Chapter 8).
6   Clutch plate overheated. Allow to cool.

36   Grabbing (chattering) as clutch is engaged

1   Oil on clutch plate lining, burned or glazed facings (Chapter 8).

2   Worn or loose engine or transmission mounts (Chapter 2).
3   Worn splines on clutch plate hub (Chapter 8).
4   Warped pressure plate or flywheel (Chapter 8).
5   Burned or smeared resin on flywheel or pressure plate (Chapter 8).

37   Transmission rattling (clicking)

1   Release lever loose (Chapter 8).
2   Clutch plate damper spring failure (Chapter 8).

38   Noise in clutch area

1   Fork shaft improperly installed (Chapter 8).
2   Faulty bearing (Chapter 8).

39   Clutch pedal stays on floor

1   Clutch master cylinder faulty (Chapter 8).
2   Broken release bearing or fork (Chapter 8).

40   High pedal effort

1   Clutch master cylinder faulty (Chapter 8).
2   Pressure plate faulty (Chapter 8).

Manual transmission

41   Knocking noise at low speeds

Worn input shaft bearing (Chapter 7A).*

42   Noise most pronounced when turning

Rear differential gear noise (Chapter 10).*

43   Clunk on acceleration or deceleration

1   Loose engine or transmission mounts (Chapter 2).
2   Worn differential pinion shaft in case.*
3   Worn side gear shaft counterbore in rear differential case (Chapter 10).*

44   Clicking noise in turns

Worn or damaged outboard CV joint (Chapter 8).

45   Vibration

1   Rough wheel bearing (Chapter 10).
2   Damaged drive shaft (Chapter 8).
3   Out-of-round tires (Chapter 1).
4   Tire out of balance (Chapters 1 and 10).
5   Worn driveshaft joints (Chapter 8).

46   Noisy in neutral with engine running

1   Damaged input gear bearing (Chapter 7A).*
2   Damaged clutch release bearing (Chapter 8).

47   Noisy in one particular gear

1   Damaged or worn constant mesh gears (Chapter 7A).*
2   Damaged or worn synchronizers (Chapter 7A).*
3   Bent reverse fork (Chapter 7A).*
4   Damaged fourth/fifth speed gear or output gear (Chapter 7A).*
5   Worn or damaged reverse idler gear or idler bushing (Chapter 7A).*

48   Noisy in all gears

1   Insufficient lubricant (Chapter 7A).
2   Damaged or worn bearings (Chapter 7A).*
3   Worn or damaged input gear shaft and/or output gear shaft (Chapter 7A).*

49   Slips out of gear

1   Worn or improperly adjusted linkage (Chapter 7A).
2   Shift linkage does not work freely, binds (Chapter 7A).
3   Input gear bearing retainer broken or loose (Chapter 7A).*
4   Worn or bent shift fork (Chapter 7A).*

50   Leaks lubricant

1   Excessive amount of lubricant in transmission (Chapters 1 and 7A).
2   Loose or broken input gear shaft bearing retainer (Chapter 7A).*
3   Input gear bearing retainer O-ring and/or lip seal damaged (Chapter 7A).*
4   Output shaft seal worn (Chapter 7A).

51   Locked in gear

Lock pin or interlock pin missing (Chapter 7A).*

Although the corrective action necessary to remedy the symptoms described is beyond the scope of this manual, the above information should be helpful in isolating the cause of the condition so that the owner can communicate clearly with a professional mechanic.

Automatic transmission

Note: *Due to the complexity of the automatic transmission, it is difficult for the home mechanic to properly diagnose and service this component. For problems other than the following, the vehicle should be taken to a dealer or transmission shop.*

52 Fluid leakage

1   Automatic transmission fluid is a deep red color. Fluid leaks should not be confused with engine oil, which can easily be blown onto the transmission by air flow.
2   To pinpoint a leak, first remove all built-up dirt and grime from the transmission housing with degreasing agents and/or steam cleaning. Then drive the vehicle at low speeds so air flow will not blow the leak far from its source. Raise the vehicle and determine where the leak is coming from. Common areas of leakage are:
a) *Transmission oil lines (Chapter 7).*
b) *Speed sensor (Chapter 6).*
c) *Driveshaft rear oil seal (Chapter 7).*

53 Transmission fluid brown or has a burned smell

Transmission fluid overheated (Chapter 1).

54 General shift mechanism problems

1   Chapter 7, Part B, deals with checking and adjusting the shift linkage on automatic transmissions. Common problems which may be attributed to poorly adjusted linkage are:
a) *Engine starting in gears other than Park or Neutral.*
b) *Indicator on shifter pointing to a gear other than the one actually being used.*
c) *Vehicle moves when in Park.*
2   Refer to Chapter 7B for the shift linkage adjustment procedure.

55 Transmission slips, shifts roughly, is noisy or has no drive in forward or reverse gears

There are many probable causes for the above problems, but the home mechanic should be concerned with only one possibility - fluid level. Before taking the vehicle to a repair shop, check the level and condition of the fluid as described in Chapter 1. Correct

the fluid level as necessary or change the fluid and filter if needed. If the problem persists, have a professional diagnose the cause.

Rear driveaxles

56 Clicking noise in turns

Worn or damaged outboard CV joint (Chapter 8).

57 Shudder or vibration during acceleration

1   Excessive toe-in (Chapter 10).
2   Worn or damaged inboard or outboard CV joints (Chapter 8).
3   Sticking inboard CV joint assembly (Chapter 8).

58 Vibration at highway speeds

1   Out-of-balance front wheels and/or tires (Chapters 1 and 10).
2   Out-of-round front tires (Chapters 1 and 10).
3   Worn CV joint(s) (Chapter 8).

Brakes

Note: *Before assuming that a brake problem exists, make sure that:*
a) *The tires are in good condition and properly inflated (Chapter 1).*
b) *The front end alignment is correct.*
c) *The vehicle is not loaded with weight in an unequal manner.*

59 Vehicle pulls to one side during braking

1   Incorrect tire pressures (Chapter 1).
2   Front end out of alignment (have the front end aligned).
3   Front, or rear, tire sizes not matched to one another.
4   Restricted brake lines or hoses (Chapter 9).
5   Malfunctioning caliper assembly (Chapter 9).
6   Loose suspension parts (Chapter 10).
7   Excessive wear of pad material or disc on one side (Chapter 9).
8   Contamination (grease or brake fluid) of brake pad material or disc on one side (Chapter 9).

60 Noise (high-pitched squeal or grinding when the brakes are applied)

Brake pads worn out. Replace pads with new ones immediately (Chapter 9).

61 Brake roughness or chatter (pedal pulsates)

1   Excessive lateral runout (Chapter 9).
2   Uneven pad wear (Chapter 9).
3   Defective disc (Chapter 9).

62 Excessive brake pedal effort required to stop vehicle

1   Malfunctioning power brake booster (Chapter 9).
2   Partial system failure (Chapter 9).
3   Excessively worn pads (Chapter 9).
4   Piston in caliper stuck or sluggish (Chapter 9).
5   Brake pads contaminated with oil or grease (Chapter 9).
6   Brake disc grooved and/or glazed (Chapter 9).

63 Excessive brake pedal travel

1   Partial brake system failure (Chapter 9).
2   Insufficient fluid in master cylinder (Chapters 1 and 9).
3   Air trapped in system (Chapter 9).

64 Dragging brakes

1   Incorrect adjustment of brake light switch (Chapter 9).
2   Master cylinder pistons not returning correctly (Chapter 9).
3   Caliper piston stuck (Chapter 9).
4   Restricted brakes lines or hoses (Chapter 9).
5   Incorrect parking brake adjustment (Chapter 9).

65 Grabbing or uneven braking action

1   Malfunction of proportioning valve (Chapter 9).
2   Contaminated brake linings (Chapter 9).

66 Brake pedal feels spongy when depressed

1   Air in hydraulic lines (Chapter 9).
2   Master cylinder mounting bolts loose (Chapter 9).
3   Master cylinder defective (Chapter 9).

67 Brake pedal travels to the floor with little resistance

1   Little or no fluid in the master cylinder reservoir caused by leaking caliper piston(s) (Chapter 9).
2   Loose, damaged or disconnected brake lines (Chapter 9).

68 Parking brake does not hold

Parking brake improperly adjusted (Chapter 9).

Suspension and steering systems

Note: *Before attempting to diagnose the suspension and steering systems, perform the following preliminary checks:*

a) *Tires for wrong pressure and uneven wear.*
b) *Steering universal joints from the column to the rack and pinion for loose connectors or wear.*
c) *Front and rear suspension and the rack-and-pinion assembly for loose or damaged parts.*
d) *Out-of-round or out-of-balance tires, bent rims and loose and/or rough wheel bearings.*

69 Vehicle pulls to one side

1   Mismatched or uneven tires (Chapter 10).
2   Broken or sagging springs (Chapter 10).
3   Wheel alignment incorrect. Have the wheels professionally aligned.
4   Front brake dragging (Chapter 9).

70 Abnormal or excessive tire wear

1   Wheel alignment out-of-specification. Have the wheels aligned.
2   Sagging or broken springs (Chapter 10).
3   Tire out-of-balance (Chapter 10).
4   Worn shock absorber (Chapter 10).
5   Overloaded vehicle.
6   Tires not rotated regularly.

71 Wheel makes a thumping noise

1   Blister or bump on tire (Chapter 10).
2   Improper shock absorber action (Chapter 10).

72 Shimmy, shake or vibration

1   Tire or wheel out-of-balance or out-of-round (Chapter 10).
2   Loose or worn wheel bearings (Chapter 10).
3   Worn tie-rod ends (Chapter 10).
4   Worn balljoints (Chapters 1 and 10).
5   Excessive wheel runout (Chapter 10).
6   Blister or bump on tire (Chapter 10).

73 Hard steering

1   Worn balljoints and/or tie-rod ends (Chapter 10).
2   Wheel alignment out-of-specifications.

Have the wheels professionally aligned.
3   Low tire pressure(s) (Chapter 1).
4   Worn steering gear (Chapter 10).

74 Poor returnability of steering to center

1   Worn balljoints or tie-rod ends (Chapter 10).
2   Worn steering gear assembly (Chapter 10).
3   Wheel alignment out-of-specifications. Have the wheels professionally aligned.

75 Abnormal noise at the front end

1   Worn balljoints or tie-rod ends (Chapter 10).
2   Damaged shock absorber mounting (Chapter 10).
3   Worn control arm bushings or tie-rod ends (Chapter 10).
4   Loose stabilizer bar (Chapter 10).
5   Loose wheel nuts (Chapter 1).
6   Loose suspension bolts (Chapter 10).

76 Wander or poor steering stability

1   Mismatched or uneven tires (Chapter 10).
2   Lack of lubrication at balljoints and tie-rod ends (Chapters 1 and 10).
3   Worn shock absorber assemblies (Chapter 10).
4   Broken or sagging springs (Chapter 10).
5   Wheels out of alignment. Have the wheels professionally aligned.

77 Erratic steering when braking

1   Wheel bearings worn (Chapter 10).
2   Broken or sagging springs (Chapter 10).
3   Leaking wheel cylinder or caliper (Chapter 10).
4   Excessive brake disc runout (Chapter 9).

78 Excessive pitching and/or rolling around corners or during braking

1   Loose stabilizer bar (Chapter 10).
2   Worn shock absorbers or mountings (Chapter 10).
3   Broken or sagging springs (Chapter 10).
4   Overloaded vehicle.

79 Suspension bottoms

1   Overloaded vehicle.
2   Sagging springs (Chapter 10).

80 Cupped tires

1   Front wheel or rear wheel alignment out-of-specifications. Have the wheels professionally aligned.
2   Worn shock absorbers (Chapter 10).
3   Wheel bearings worn (Chapter 10).
4   Excessive tire or wheel runout (Chapter 10).
5   Worn balljoints (Chapter 10).

81 Excessive tire wear on outside edge

1   Inflation pressures incorrect (Chapter 1).
2   Excessive speed in turns.
3   Wheel alignment incorrect (excessive toe-in). Have professionally aligned.
4   Suspension arm bent (Chapter 10).

82 Excessive tire wear on inside edge

1   Inflation pressures incorrect (Chapter 1).
2   Wheel alignment incorrect (toe-out). Have professionally aligned.
3   Loose or damaged steering components (Chapter 10).

83 Tire tread worn in one place

1   Tires out-of-balance.
2   Damaged wheel. Inspect and replace if necessary.
3   Defective tire (Chapter 1).

84 Excessive play or looseness in steering system

1   Wheel bearing(s) worn (Chapter 10).
2   Tie-rod end loose (Chapter 10).
3   Steering gear loose (Chapter 10).
4   Worn or loose steering intermediate shaft U-joint (Chapter 10).

85 Rattling or clicking noise in steering gear

1   Steering gear loose (Chapter 10).
2   Steering gear defective.

Chapter 1
Tune-up and routine maintenance

Contents

Specifications

Recommended lubricants and fluids

Note: *Listed here are manufacturer recommendations at the time this manual was written. Manufacturers occasionally upgrade their fluid and lubricant specifications, so check with your local auto parts store for current recommendations.*

Engine oil*	
Type	Synthetic Mobil 1, API "certified for gasoline engines"
Viscosity	SAE 5W-30
Automatic transmission fluid	DEXRON-VI
Manual transmission lubricant	
Getrag 5-speed	DEXRON-III or equivalent
Tremec 6-speed	DEXRON-III or equivalent
Aisin AY6 6-speed	GL-5, SAE 75W-90 rear oil
Rear differential lubricant	
2006 and earlier models	GM part no. 12378261 rear axle (synthetic) lubricant, or equivalent
2007 and later models	GM part no. 89021677 rear axle (synthetic) lubricant, or equivalent
Limited slip rear differential additive	GM part# 1052358
Brake fluid	DOT 3 brake fluid
Clutch fluid	
2004 and earlier models	DOT 3 brake fluid
2005 and later models	DOT 4 brake fluid
Engine coolant	50/50 mixture of DEX-COOL coolant and water
Power steering system	GM power steering fluid part# 89021184

*Caution: *Use only oil that has the standard designation "GM 4718M" or possible engine damage can occur and void the vehicle warranty.*

Capacities*

Engine oil (including filter)
  V6 engines
    3.2L.. 5.0 quarts (4.8 liters)
    All others.. 6.0 quarts (5.7 liters)
  V8 engines
    5.7L.. 6.5 quarts (6.151 liters)
    6.0L.. 5.5 quarts (5.2 liters)
    6.2L.. 6.0 quarts (5.7 liters)
Coolant
  V6 engines
    2.8L.. Up to 10.6 quarts (10.0 liters)
    3.0L.. Up to 11.3 quarts (10.7 liters)
    3.2L.. Up to 11.3 quarts (10.7 liters)
    3.6L (LY7)
      2003 through 2007 .... Up to 12.0 quarts (11.3 liters)
      2008 and 2009 .... Up to 9.7 quarts (10.3 liters)
    3.6L (LLT, LFX)
      2009 .... Up to 10.6 quarts (10.0 liters)
      2010 through 2012 .... Up to 11.2 quarts (10.6 liters)
      2013 and later .... Up to 12.3 quarts (11.6 liters)
  V8 engines
    5.7L.. Up to 13.4 quarts (12.7 liters)
    6.0L.. Up to 13.4 quarts (12.7 liters)
    6.2L.. Up to 12.5 quarts (11.8 liters)
    6.2L charger air (intercooler) system .... 2.4 quarts (2.3 liters)
Automatic transmission
  2003 models
    Dry fill .... Up to 9.0 quarts (8.5 liters)
    Pan removed and refill.................................... Up to 5.0 quarts (4.7 liters)
  2004 through 2007 models
    Dry fill .... Up to 9.4 quarts (8.9 liters)
    Pan removed and refill.................................... Up to 7.4 quarts (7.0 liters)
  2008 through 2012 models
    Dry fill .... Up to 11.4 quarts (10.8 liters)
    Pan removed and refill.................................... Up to 6.7 quarts (6.3 liters)
  2013 and later models
    Dry fill
      GL45 (RPO Code MYA) .... Up to 10.3 quarts (9.7 liters)
      GL50 (RPO Code MYB) .... Up to 9.8 quarts (9.3 liters)
      GL90 (RPO Code MYD) .... Up to 13.2 quarts (12.5 liters)
    Pan removed and refill.................................... Up to 6.7 quarts (6.3 liters)
Manual transmission
  GETRAG 5-speed.. 1.32 quarts (1.25 liters)
  Aisin AV6 6-speed .... 1.9 quarts (1.8 liters)
  Tremec 6-speed
    2008 and earlier.. 3.7 quarts (3.5 liters)
    2009 and later... 4.0 quarts (3.8 liters)
Rear differential
  With limited slip differential
    Draining with cover removed .... 1.27 quarts (1.2 liters)
    Using drain plug.. 1.06 quarts (1.0 liters)
  Without limited slip differential
    Draining with cover removed .... 1.3 quarts (1.3 liters)
    Using drain plug.. 1.16 quarts (1.1 liters)
Limited slip differential additive
  Draining with cover removed.............................. 3.38 ounces (100 ml)
  Draining through drain plug................................ 2.37 ounces (70 ml)

All capacities approximate. Add as necessary to bring up to appropriate level.

41743-1-SPECS HAYNES

Cylinder locations - V6 engines

41743-1-A HAYNES

Cylinder locations - V8 engines

Ignition system

Spark plug type and gap
  Type
    V6 engines
      3.2L .... Bosch FGR8KQE0 or equivalent
      2006 and earlier 2.8L .... AC 41-988 or equivalent
      2005 and earlier 3.6L .... AC 41-988 or equivalent
      2006 3.6L .... AC 41-990 or equivalent
      2007 through 2009 (all) .... AC 41-990 or equivalent
      2010 and later (all) .... AC-41-988 or equivalent
    V8 engines
      2004 and earlier .... AC 41-985 or equivalent
      2005 and later .... AC 41-104 or equivalent
  Gap (non adjustable)
    V6 engines
      2004 and earlier .... 0.053 inch (1.35 mm)
      2005 through 2009 .... 0.044 inch (1.10 mm)
      2010 and 2011 .... 0.043 inch (1.1 mm)
      2012 and later .... 0.040 inch (1.02 mm)
    V8 engines .... 0.040 inch (1.02 mm)
Engine firing order
  V6 engines 1-2-3-4-5-6
  V8 engines 1-8-7-2-6-5-4-3

Brakes

Disc brake pad lining thickness (minimum) .... 1/8 inch (3 mm)
Drum brake shoe lining thickness (minimum) .... 1/16 inch (1.5 mm)
Parking brake adjustment .... 3 to 5 clicks

Torque specifications

	Ft-lbs (unless otherwise indicated)	Nm

Note: One foot-pound (ft-lb) of torque is equivalent to 12 inch-pounds (in-lbs) of torque. Torque values below approximately 15 foot-pounds are expressed in inch-pounds, because most foot-pound torque wrenches are not accurate at these smaller values.

	Ft-lbs	Nm
Automatic transmission check/fill plug* (6L45/6L50/6L80/6L90)	18	25
Automatic transmission drain plug* (5L40-E/5L50-E)	15	20
Automatic transmission pan bolts*		
2007 and earlier (5L40-E/5L50-E)	97 in-lbs	11
2008 and later (6L45/6L50/6L80/6L90)	80 in-lbs	9
Drivebelt tensioner bolts		
2003 and 2004 3.2L V6 engines	26	35
2005 through 2012		
V6 and V8 engines	37	50
2013 and later		
V6 engines	18	25
V8 engines	43	58
Engine oil drain plug	18	25
Manual transmission drain and fill plugs		
Getrag 5-speed	26	35
Aisin AY6 6-speed	27	37
Tremec 6-speed		
2008 and earlier	159 in-lbs	18
2009 and later	20	27
Oil filter housing cap (V6 engines)	18	25
Rear differential cover bolts	21	29
Rear differential check/fill plug		
2003 through 2012	29	39
2013 and later	17	23
Spark plugs		
2003 through 2012		
V6 engines	15	20
V8 engines	132 in-lbs	15
2013 and later		
V6 engines	156 in-lbs	18
V8 engines	15	20
Supercharger belt idler pulley bracket bolts	37	50
Supercharger idler pulley bolts	37	50
Supercharger belt tensioner bolts	37	50
Wheel lug nuts		
2007 and earlier	100	140
2008 through 2012	140	190
2013 and later	111	150

* For automatic transmission identification, refer to the "Vehicle Identification Numbers" Section at the front of this manual.

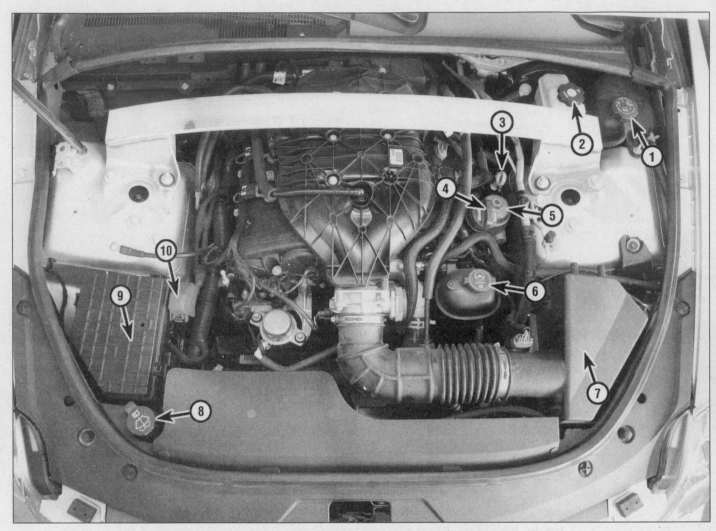

Engine compartment components (3.0L V6 engine shown, other models similar)

1	Coolant expansion tank	6	Power steering fluid reservoir
2	Brake fluid reservoir	7	Air filter housing
3	Engine oil dipstick	8	Windshield washer fluid reservoir
4	Engine oil filler cap	9	Fuse/relay block
5	Oil filter housing	10	Remote battery positive terminal

Typical engine compartment underside components (3.0L V6 engine shown, other models similar)

1   Engine oil drain plug
2   Automatic transmission fluid level check plug
3   Radiator hose
4   Front disc brake caliper
5   Exhaust system
6   Radiator drain fitting

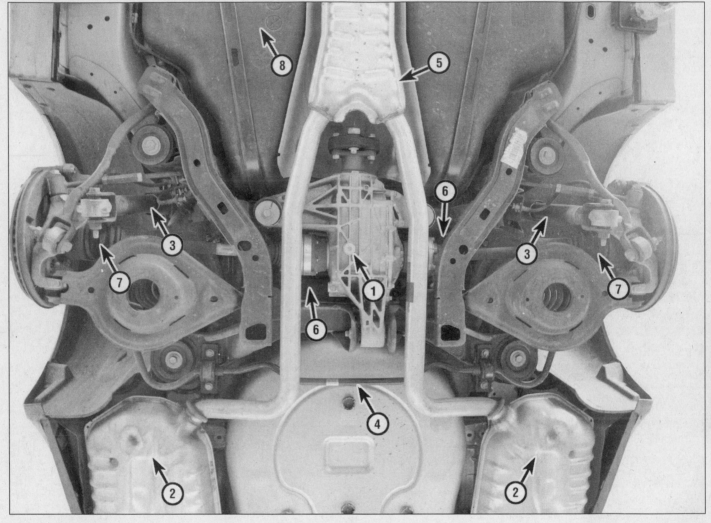

Typical rear underside components

1	Differential drain plug	4	Stabilizer bar	7	Outer CV boot
2	Mufflers	5	Exhaust system hanger	8	Fuel tank
3	Shock absorbers	6	Inner CV boot		

1 Maintenance schedule

The maintenance intervals in this manual are provided with the assumption that you, not the dealer, will be doing the work. These are the minimum maintenance intervals recommended by the factory for vehicles that are driven daily. If you wish to keep your vehicle in peak condition at all times, you may wish to perform some of these procedures even more often. Because frequent maintenance enhances the efficiency, performance and resale value of your car, we encourage you to do so. If you drive in dusty areas, tow a trailer, idle or drive at low speeds for extended periods or drive for short distances (less than four miles) in below freezing temperatures, shorter intervals are also recommended.

When your vehicle is new, it should be serviced by a factory authorized dealer service department to protect the factory warranty. In many cases, the initial maintenance check is done at no cost to the owner.

Every 250 miles or weekly, whichever comes first

Check the engine oil level (Section 4)
Check the engine coolant level (Section 4)
Check the brake and clutch fluid level (Section 4)
Check the windshield washer fluid level (Section 4)
Check the power steering fluid level (Section 4)
Check the tires and tire pressures (Section 5)

Every 3000 miles or 3 months, whichever comes first

All items listed above plus:
Change the engine oil and oil filter (Section 6)

Every 7500 miles or 6 months, whichever comes first

All items listed above plus:
Inspect (and replace, if necessary) the windshield wiper blades (Section 8)
Check and service the battery (Section 9)
Check the cooling system (Section 10)
Rotate the tires (Section 11)
Check the seat belts (Section 12)

Every 15,000 miles or 12 months, whichever comes first

All items listed above plus:
Check all underhood hoses (Section 13)
Inspect the brake system (Section 14)*
Inspect the suspension, steering and driveaxle boots (Section 15)*
Check the fuel system (Section 16)

Check the manual transmission lubricant level (Section 17)
Check the rear differential lubricant level (Section 18)
Check (and replace, if necessary) the air filter (Section 19)*
Replace the cabin air filter (Section 20)

Every 30,000 miles or 24 months, whichever comes first

All items listed above plus:
Check the automatic transmission fluid level (Section 7)
Check the exhaust system (Section 21)
Change the brake fluid (Section 23)
Check/adjust the engine drivebelts (Section 24)

Every 60,000 miles or 48 months, whichever comes first

Replace the automatic transmission fluid and filter (Section 25)**
Replace the manual transmission lubricant (Section 26)**
Replace the rear differential lubricant (Section 27)**
Check (and replace, if necessary) the spark plugs (conventional, non-platinum or iridium type) (Section 28)

Every 100,000 miles

Service the cooling system (drain, flush and refill) (Section 22)
Replace the spark plugs (platinum or iridium type) (Section 28)
This item is affected by "severe" operating conditions as described below. If your vehicle is operated under "severe" conditions, perform all maintenance indicated with an asterisk (*) at 3000 mile/3 month intervals. Severe conditions are indicated if you mainly operate your vehicle under one or more of the following conditions:
Operating in dusty areas
Towing a trailer
Idling for extended periods and/or low speed operation
Operating when outside temperatures remain below freezing and when most trips are less than 4 miles
** *If operated under one or more of the following conditions, change the manual or automatic transmission fluid and differential lubricant every 30,000 miles:*
Operating in dusty areas
In heavy city traffic where the outside temperature regularly reaches 90-degrees F (32-degrees C) or higher
In hilly or mountainous terrain
On flex-fuel models, using E85 fuel more than 50% of the time

2   Introduction

This Chapter is designed to help the home mechanic maintain the Cadillac CTS with the goals of maximum performance, economy, safety and reliability in mind.

Included is a master maintenance schedule, followed by procedures dealing specifically with each item on the schedule. Visual checks, adjustments, component replacement and other helpful items are included. Refer to the accompanying illustrations of the engine compartment and the underside of the vehicle for the locations of various components.

Servicing the vehicle, in accordance with the mileage/time maintenance schedule and the step-by-step procedures will result in a planned maintenance program that should produce a long and reliable service life. Keep in mind that it is a comprehensive plan, so maintaining some items but not others at the specified intervals will not produce the same results.

As you service the vehicle, you will discover that many of the procedures can - and should - be grouped together because of the nature of the particular procedure you're performing or because of the close proximity of two otherwise unrelated components to one another.

For example, if the vehicle is raised for chassis lubrication, you should inspect the exhaust, suspension, steering and fuel systems while you're under the vehicle. When you're rotating the tires, it makes good sense to check the brakes since the wheels are already removed. Finally, let's suppose you have to borrow or rent a torque wrench. Even if you only need it to tighten the spark plugs, you might as well check the torque of as many critical fasteners as time allows.

The first step in this maintenance program is to prepare yourself before the actual work begins. Read through all the procedures you're planning to do, then gather up all the parts and tools needed. If it looks like you might run into problems during a particular job, seek advice from a mechanic or an experienced do-it-yourselfer.

Owner's Manual and VECI label information

Your vehicle owner's manual was written for your year and model and contains very specific information on component locations, specifications, fuse ratings, part numbers, etc. The Owner's Manual is an important resource for the do-it-yourselfer to have; if one was not supplied with your vehicle, it can generally be ordered from a dealer parts department.

Among other important information, the Vehicle Emissions Control Information (VECI) label contains specifications and procedures for applicable tune-up adjustments and, in some instances, spark plugs (see Chapter 6 for more information on the VECI label). The information on this label is the exact maintenance data recommended by the manufacturer. This data often varies by intended oper-

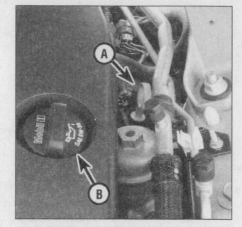

4.2 Engine oil dipstick (A) and oil filler cap (B) locations (3.0L V6 engine shown, other models similar)

ating altitude, local emissions regulations, month of manufacture, etc.

This Chapter contains procedural details, safety information and more ambitious maintenance intervals than you might find in manufacturer's literature. However, you may also find procedures or specifications in your Owner's Manual or VECI label that differ with what's printed here. In these cases, the Owner's Manual or VECI label can be considered correct, since it is specific to your particular vehicle.

3   Tune-up general information

The term tune-up is used in this manual to represent a combination of individual operations rather than one specific procedure.

If, from the time the vehicle is new, the routine maintenance schedule is followed closely and frequent checks are made of fluid levels and high wear items, as suggested throughout this manual, the engine will be kept in relatively good running condition and the need for additional work will be minimized.

More likely than not, however, there will be times when the engine is running poorly due to lack of regular maintenance. This is even more likely if a used vehicle, which has not received regular and frequent maintenance checks, is purchased. In such cases, an engine tune-up will be needed outside of the regular routine maintenance intervals.

The first step in any tune-up or diagnostic procedure to help correct a poor running engine is a cylinder compression check. A compression check (see Chapter 2D) will help determine the condition of internal engine components and should be used as a guide for tune-up and repair procedures. If, for instance, a compression check indicates serious internal engine wear, a conventional tune-up will not improve the performance of the engine and would be a waste of time and money. Because of its importance, the compression check should be done by someone

with the proper equipment and the knowledge to use it properly.

The following procedures are those most often needed to bring a generally poor running engine back into a proper state of tune.

Minor tune-up

Check all engine related fluids (Section 4)
Clean, inspect and test the battery (Section 9)
Check the cooling system (Section 10)
Check all underhood hoses (Section 13)
Check the fuel system (Section 16)
Check the air filter (Section 19)
Check the drivebelt (Section 24)

Major tune-up

All items listed under Minor tune-up, plus . . .

Replace the air filter (Section 19)
Replace the spark plugs (Section 28)

4   Fluid level checks (every 250 miles or weekly)

1   Fluids are an essential part of the lubrication, cooling, brake and windshield washer systems. Because the fluids gradually become depleted and/or contaminated during normal operation of the vehicle, they must be periodically replenished. See *Recommended lubricants and fluids* in this Chapter's Specifications before adding fluid to any of the following components. **Note:** *The vehicle must be on level ground when fluid levels are checked.*

Engine oil

Refer to illustrations 4.2 and 4.4

2   The oil level is checked with a dipstick, which is attached to the engine block **(see illustrations)**. The dipstick extends through a metal tube down into the oil pan.

3   The oil level should be checked before the vehicle has been driven, or about 5 minutes after the engine has been shut off. If the oil is checked immediately after driving the vehicle, some of the oil will remain in the upper part of the engine, resulting in an inaccurate reading on the dipstick.

4   Pull the dipstick out of the tube and wipe all the oil from the end with a clean rag or paper towel. Insert the clean dipstick all the way back into the tube and pull it out again. Note the oil at the end of the dipstick. At its highest point, the level should be between the MIN and MAX marks on the dipstick **(see illustration)**.

5   It takes one quart of oil to raise the level from the MIN mark to the MAX mark on the dipstick. Do not allow the level to drop below the MIN mark or oil starvation may cause engine damage. Conversely, overfilling the engine (adding oil above the MAX mark) may cause oil fouled spark plugs, oil leaks or oil seal failures. Maintaining the oil level above

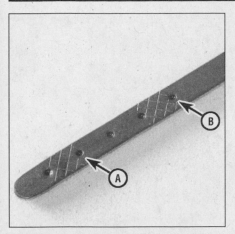

4.4 The oil level should be in the safe range - if it's below the MIN or ADD mark (A), add enough oil to bring it up to or near the MAX or FULL mark (B)

4.8 The cooling system expansion tank is located at the left side of the engine compartment

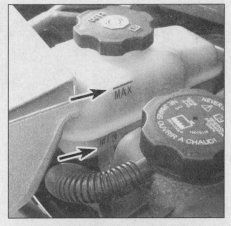

4.15 The brake fluid level should be kept between the MIN and MAX marks on the translucent plastic reservoir

the MAX mark can cause excessive oil consumption.

6   To add oil, remove the filler cap from the valve cover **(see illustration 4.2)**. After adding oil, wait a few minutes to allow the level to stabilize, then pull out the dipstick and check the level again. Add more oil if required. Install the filler cap and tighten it by hand only.

7   Checking the oil level is an important preventive maintenance step. A consistently low oil level indicates oil leakage through damaged seals, defective gaskets or past worn rings or valve guides. If the oil looks milky in color or has water droplets in it, the cylinder head gasket(s) may be blown or the head(s) or block may be cracked. The engine should be checked immediately. The condition of the oil should also be checked. Whenever you check the oil level, slide your thumb and index finger up the dipstick before wiping off the oil. If you see small dirt or metal particles clinging to the dipstick, the oil should be changed (see Section 6).

Engine coolant

Refer to illustration 4.8

Warning: *Do not allow antifreeze to come in contact with your skin or painted surfaces of the vehicle. Flush contaminated areas immediately with plenty of water. Don't store new coolant or leave old coolant lying around where it's accessible to children or pets - they're attracted by its sweet smell. Ingestion of even a small amount of coolant can be fatal! Wipe up garage floor and drip pan spills immediately. Keep antifreeze containers covered and repair cooling system leaks as soon as they're noticed.* **Note:** *To check the coolant level in the charge air cooling system on CTS-V models, refer to Chapter 2C, Section 21.*

8   All vehicles covered by this manual are equipped with a pressurized coolant recovery system. A plastic expansion tank located at

the left rear corner of the engine compartment is connected by hoses to the cooling system **(see illustration)**. As the engine heats up during operation, the expanding coolant fills the tank.

9   The coolant level in the tank should be checked regularly. **Warning:** *Do not remove the expansion tank cap to check the coolant level when the engine is warm!* The level in the tank varies with the temperature of the engine. When the engine is cold, the coolant level should be at the FULL COLD mark on the reservoir. If it isn't, remove the cap from the tank and add a 50/50 mixture of DEX-COOL antifreeze and water.

10   Drive the vehicle, let the engine cool completely then recheck the coolant level. Don't use rust inhibitors or additives. If only a small amount of coolant is required to bring the system up to the proper level, water can be used. However, repeated additions of water will dilute the antifreeze and water solution. In order to maintain the proper ratio of antifreeze and water, always top up the coolant level with the correct mixture. An empty plastic milk jug or bleach bottle makes an excellent container for mixing coolant.

11   If the coolant level drops consistently, there may be a leak in the system. Inspect the radiator, hoses, filler cap, drain plugs and water pump (see Section 10 and Chapter 3). If no leaks are noted, have the expansion tank cap pressure tested by a service station.

12   If you have to remove the expansion tank cap wait until the engine has cooled completely, then wrap a thick cloth around the cap and unscrew it slowly, stopping if you hear a hissing noise. If coolant or steam escapes, let the engine cool down longer, then remove the cap.

13   Check the condition of the coolant as well. If it's brown or rust colored, the system should be drained, flushed and refilled. Even if the coolant appears to be normal, the corrosion inhibitors wear out, so it must be replaced at the specified intervals.

Brake and clutch fluid

Refer to illustration 4.15

14   The brake master cylinder is mounted on the front of the power booster unit in the engine compartment. The hydraulic clutch master cylinder reservoir used on manual transmission vehicles is also in the engine compartment. The clutch master cylinder reservoir is mounted to the driver's side fender on 2007 and earlier models and the firewall, next to the brake booster on 2008 and later models.

15   The brake master cylinder and the clutch master cylinder have their own reservoirs. To check the fluid level of either system, simply look at the MAX and MIN marks on the reservoir **(see illustration)**.

16   If the level is low, wipe the top of the reservoir cover with a clean rag to prevent contamination of the brake system before lifting the cover.

17   Add only the specified brake fluid to the reservoir (refer to *Recommended lubricants and fluids* in this Chapter's Specifications or to your owner's manual). Mixing different types of brake fluid can damage the system. Fill the reservoir only to the MAX line. **Warning:** *Use caution when filling the reservoir - brake fluid can harm your eyes and damage painted surfaces. Do not use brake fluid that is more than one year old or has been left open. Brake fluid absorbs moisture from the air. Excess moisture can cause a dangerous loss of braking.*

18   While the reservoir cap is removed, inspect the master cylinder reservoir for contamination. If deposits, dirt particles or water droplets are present, the system should be drained and refilled.

19   After filling the reservoir to the proper level, make sure the lid is properly seated to prevent fluid leakage.

20   The fluid in the brake master cylinder will drop slightly as the brake pads at each wheel wear down during normal operation. If the

4.22 The windshield/rear window washer fluid reservoir is located in the right front corner of the engine compartment

4.25 The power steering fluid reservoir is located at the left front corner of the engine compartment

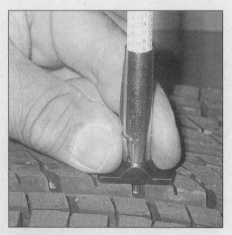

5.2 A tire tread depth indicator should be used to monitor tire wear - they are available at auto parts stores and service stations and cost very little

master cylinder requires repeated replenishing to keep it at the proper level, this is an indication of leakage in the brake or clutch system, which should be corrected immediately. If the brake system shows an indication of leakage check all brake lines and connections, along with the calipers and booster (see Section 14 for more information). If the hydraulic clutch system shows an indication of leakage check all clutch lines and connections, along with the clutch release cylinder (see Chapter 8 for more information).

21   If, upon checking the brake or clutch master cylinder fluid level, you discover the reservoir empty or nearly empty, the systems should be bled (see Chapters 8 and 9).

Windshield washer fluid

Refer to illustration 4.22

22   Fluid for the windshield washer system is stored in a plastic reservoir located at the right front of the engine compartment **(see illustration)**.

23   In milder climates, plain water can be used in the reservoir, but it should be kept no more than 2/3 full to allow for expansion if the water freezes. In colder climates, use windshield washer system antifreeze, available at any auto parts store, to lower the freezing point of the fluid. Mix the antifreeze with water in accordance with the manufacturer's directions on the container. **Caution:** *Do not use cooling system antifreeze - it will damage the vehicle's paint.*

Power steering fluid

Refer to illustration 4.25

24   Check the power steering fluid level periodically to avoid steering system problems, such as damage to the pump. **Caution:** *DO NOT hold the steering wheel against either stop (extreme left or right turn) for more than five seconds. If you do, the power steering pump could be damaged.*

25   The power steering reservoir, located at the left side of the engine compartment **(see illustration)**, is checked with a dipstick located in the cap. For the check, the front wheels should be pointed straight ahead and the engine should be off.

26   Use a clean rag to wipe off the reservoir cap and the area around the cap. This will help prevent any foreign matter from entering the reservoir during the check.

27   Twist off the cap and check the temperature of the fluid at the end of the dipstick with your finger.

28   Wipe off the fluid with a clean rag, reinsert it, then withdraw it and read the fluid level. The level should be at the HOT mark if the fluid was hot to the touch. It should be at the COLD mark if the fluid was cool to the touch.

29   Add small amounts of fluid until the level is correct. **Caution:** *Do not overfill the reservoir. If too much fluid is added, remove the excess with a clean syringe or suction pump.*

30   Check the power steering hoses and connections for leaks and wear.

5   Tire and tire pressure checks (every 250 miles or weekly)

Refer to illustrations 5.2, 5.3, 5.4a, 5.4b and 5.8

1   Periodic inspection of the tires may spare you the inconvenience of being stranded with a flat tire. It can also provide you with vital information regarding possible problems in the steering and suspension systems before major damage occurs.

2   The original tires on this vehicle are equipped with 1/2-inch wide bands that will appear when tread depth reaches 1/16-inch, at which point they can be considered worn out. Tread wear can be monitored with a simple, inexpensive device known as a tread depth indicator **(see illustration)**.

3   Note any abnormal tread wear **(see illustration)**. Tread pattern irregularities such as cupping, flat spots and more wear on one side than the other are indications of front end alignment and/or balance problems. If any of these conditions are noted, take the vehicle to a tire shop or service station to correct the problem.

4   Look closely for cuts, punctures and embedded nails or tacks. Sometimes a tire will hold air pressure for a short time or leak down very slowly after a nail has embedded itself in the tread. If a slow leak persists, check the valve stem core to make sure it is tight **(see illustration)**. Examine the tread for an object that may have embedded itself in the tire or for a plug that may have begun to leak (radial tire punctures are repaired with a plug that is installed in a puncture). If a puncture is suspected, it can be easily verified by spraying a solution of soapy water onto the puncture area **(see illustration)**. The soapy solution will bubble if there is a leak. Unless the puncture is unusually large, a tire shop or service station can usually repair the tire.

5   Carefully inspect the inner sidewall of each tire for evidence of brake fluid leakage. If

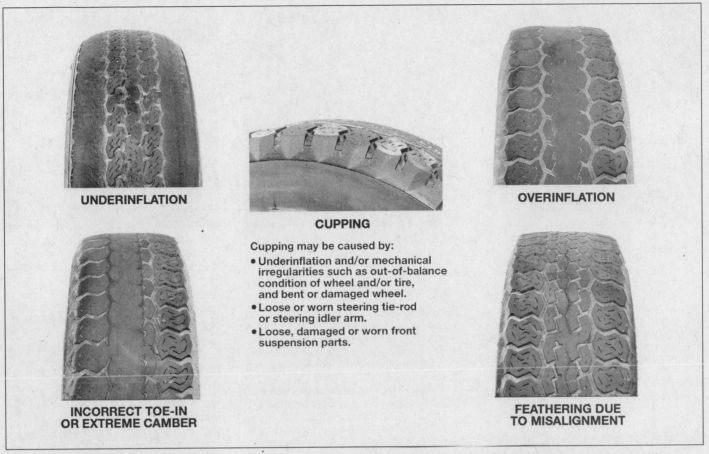

UNDERINFLATION

CUPPING

Cupping may be caused by:

- Underinflation and/or mechanical irregularities such as out-of-balance condition of wheel and/or tire, and bent or damaged wheel.
- Loose or worn steering tie-rod or steering idler arm.
- Loose, damaged or worn front suspension parts.

OVERINFLATION

INCORRECT TOE-IN OR EXTREME CAMBER

FEATHERING DUE TO MISALIGNMENT

5.3 This chart will help you determine the condition of your tires, the probable cause(s) of abnormal wear and the corrective action necessary

you see any, inspect the brakes immediately.

6   Correct air pressure adds miles to the life span of the tires, improves mileage and enhances overall ride quality. Tire pressure cannot be accurately estimated by looking at a tire, especially if it's a radial. A tire pressure gauge is essential. Keep an accurate gauge in the glove compartment. The pressure gauges attached to the nozzles of air hoses at gas stations are often inaccurate.

7   Always check tire pressure when the tires are cold. Cold, in this case, means the vehicle has not been driven over a mile in the three hours preceding a tire pressure check.

A pressure rise of four to eight pounds is not uncommon once the tires are warm.

8   Unscrew the valve cap protruding from the wheel or hubcap and push the gauge firmly onto the valve stem **(see illustration)**. Note the reading on the gauge and compare the figure to the recommended tire pressure

5.4a If a tire loses air on a steady basis, check the valve core first to make sure it's snug (special inexpensive wrenches are commonly available at auto parts stores)

5.4b If the valve core is tight, raise the corner of the vehicle with the low tire and spray a soapy water solution onto the tread as the tire is turned slowly - slow leaks will cause small bubbles to appear

5.8 To extend the life of your tires, check the air pressure at least once a week with an accurate gauge (don't forget the spare!)

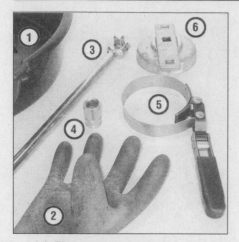

6.2 These tools are required when changing the engine oil and filter

1   **Drain pan** - *It should be fairly shallow in depth, but wide in order to prevent spills*
2   **Rubber gloves** - *When removing the drain plug and filter, it is inevitable that you will get oil on your hands (the gloves will prevent burns)*
3   **Breaker bar** - *Sometimes the oil drain plug is pretty tight and a long breaker bar is needed to loosen it*
4   **Socket** - *To be used with the breaker bar or a ratchet (must be the correct size to fit the drain plug)*
5   **Filter wrench** - *This is a metal band-type wrench, which requires clearance around the filter to be effective*
6. **Filter wrench** - *This type fits on the bottom of the filter and can be turned with a ratchet or breaker bar (different size wrenches are available for different types of filters)*

shown on the tire placard on the driver's side door. Be sure to reinstall the valve cap to keep dirt and moisture out of the valve stem mechanism. Check all four tires and, if necessary, add enough air to bring them up to the recommended pressure.

9   Don't forget to keep the spare tire inflated to the specified pressure (refer to the pressure molded into the tire sidewall).

6   Engine oil and filter change (every 3000 miles or 3 months)

Refer to illustrations 6.2 and 6.7

Note: *These models are equipped with an oil life indicator system that illuminates a light or message on the instrument panel when the system deems it necessary to change the oil. A number of factors are taken into consideration to determine when the oil should be considered worn out. Generally, this system will allow the vehicle to accumulate more miles between oil changes than the traditional 3000-mile interval, but we believe that frequent oil changes are cheap insurance and*

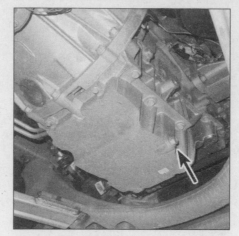

6.7 Oil drain plug location (3.0L V6 engine shown, other models similar)

will prolong engine life. If you do decide not to change your oil every 3000 miles and rely on the oil life indicator instead, make sure you don't exceed 1 year or 7,500 miles before the oil is changed, regardless of what the oil life indicator shows.

1   Frequent oil changes are the most important preventive maintenance procedures that can be done by the home mechanic. As engine oil ages, it becomes diluted and contaminated, which leads to premature engine wear.

2   Make sure that you have all the necessary tools before you begin this procedure **(see illustration)**. You should also have plenty of rags or newspapers handy for mopping up oil spills.

3   Access to the oil drain plug and filter will be improved if the vehicle can be lifted on a hoist, driven onto ramps or supported by jackstands. **Warning:** *Do not work under a vehicle supported only by a jack - always use jackstands!*

4   If you haven't changed the oil on this vehicle before, get under it and locate the oil drain plug and the oil filter. The exhaust components will be warm as you work, so note how they are routed to avoid touching them when you are under the vehicle.

5   Start the engine and allow it to reach normal operating temperature - oil and sludge will flow out more easily when warm. If new oil, a filter or tools are needed, use the vehicle to go get them and warm up the engine/oil at the same time. Park on a level surface and shut off the engine when it's warmed up. Remove the oil filler cap from the valve cover.

6   Raise the vehicle and support it on jackstands. Make sure it is safely supported!

7   Being careful not to touch the hot exhaust components, position a drain pan under the plug in the bottom of the engine, then remove the plug **(see illustration)**. It's a good idea to wear a rubber glove while unscrewing the plug the final few turns to avoid being scalded by hot oil.

8   It may be necessary to move the drain

6.11 Starting from the front, lift the engine cover up and out to release the cover (3.0L V6 engine shown, other models similar)

6.13 Remove the oil filter cap and filter cartridge

pan slightly as oil flow slows to a trickle. Inspect the old oil for the presence of metal particles.

9   After all the oil has drained, wipe off the drain plug with a clean rag. Any small metal particles clinging to the plug would immediately contaminate the new oil.

10   Clean the area around the drain plug opening, reinstall the plug and tighten it to the torque listed in this Chapter's Specifications.

V6 engines

Refer to illustrations 6.11, 6.13 and 6.14

Note: *On 2004 and earlier models, the oil filter housing and cartridge are mounted at the bottom of the engine.*

11   Remove the upper engine cover from the vehicle **(see illustration)**.

12   Using a socket attached to the oil filter housing cap, unscrew the cap by rotating it counterclockwise.

13   Remove the oil filter cartridge and O-ring **(see illustration)**.

14   Clean the threads of the filter cap and

the oil filter housing. Replace the O rings supplied with the new oil filter and apply a small amount of clean engine oil on the threads of the filter cap **(see illustration)**.

15 Install the filter cap and tighten it to the torque listed in this Chapter's Specifications.

V8 engines

Refer to illustration 6.20

16 Move the drain pan into position under the oil filter.

17 Loosen the oil filter by turning it counter-clockwise with a filter wrench. Any standard filter wrench will work.

18 Once the filter is loose, use your hands to unscrew it from the block. Just as the filter is detached from the block, immediately tilt the open end up to prevent the oil inside the filter from spilling out.

19 Using a clean rag, wipe off the mounting surface on the block. Also, make sure that none of the old gasket remains stuck to the mounting surface. It can be removed with a scraper if necessary.

20 Compare the old filter with the new one to make sure they are the same type. Smear some engine oil on the rubber gasket of the new filter and screw it into place **(see illustration)**. Overtightening the filter will damage the gasket, so don't use a filter wrench. Most filter manufacturers recommend tightening the filter by hand only. Normally they should be tightened 3/4-turn after the gasket contacts the block, but be sure to follow the directions on the filter or container.

All models

21 Remove all tools and materials from under the vehicle, being careful not to spill the oil in the drain pan, then lower the vehicle.

22 Add new oil to the engine through the oil filler cap. Use a funnel to prevent oil from spilling onto the top of the engine. Pour four quarts of fresh oil into the engine. Wait a few minutes to allow the oil to drain into the pan, then check the level on the dipstick (see Section 4 if necessary). If the oil level is in the OK range, install the filler cap.

23 Start the engine and run it for about a minute. While the engine is running, look under the vehicle and check for leaks at the oil pan drain plug and around the oil filter. If either one is leaking, stop the engine and tighten the plug or filter slightly.

24 Wait a few minutes, then recheck the level on the dipstick. Add oil as necessary to bring the level into the OK range.

25 During the first few trips after an oil change, make it a point to check frequently for leaks and proper oil level.

26 The old oil drained from the engine cannot be reused in its present state and should be disposed of. Check with your local auto parts store, disposal facility or environmental agency to see if they will accept the oil for recycling. After the oil has cooled it can be drained into a container (capped plastic jugs, topped bottles, milk cartons, etc.) for transport to one of these disposal sites. Don't dispose

6.14 Always replace the O-ring on the filter cap

of the oil by pouring it on the ground or down a drain!

Oil life monitor resetting

Note: *It is possible that driving under the best possible conditions the oil life monitoring system may not indicate the oil needs to be changed. The manufacturer states that the oil and filter must be changed at least once every year and the oil life monitor reset.*

Note: *If the CHANGE ENGINE OIL message comes on when the vehicle is immediately restarted, the oil life monitor was not reset and the reset procedure must be done again.*

With Driver's Information Center (DIC) or base audio systems - 2003 through 2008 models

27 Turn the ignition key to the ON position and press the up and down arrow on the INFO button to display the "XXX% ENGINE OIL LIFE" menu on the driver information center.

28 With ENGINE OIL LIFE highlighted, press and hold the CLR button until the indicator reads "OIL LIFE SET TO 100%," which is approximately a 7,500-mile interval.

29 Turn the ignition key to the OFF position.

Without Driver's Information Center (DIC) - 2005 through 2008 models

30 Turn the ignition key to the RUN position without starting the engine and press the accelerator pedal all the way to the floor and release the pedal, three times within 5 seconds.

31 Turn the ignition key to the OFF position, then start the vehicle.

With Navigation system - 2003 through 2008 models

32 Turn the ignition key to the ON position and turn the navigation system on. Press the information button to access the "information menu," then turn the TUNE/SELECT knob until the engine oil life display is highlighted and press the knob to display the "XXX%

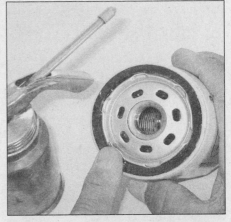

6.20 Lubricate the oil filter gasket with clean engine oil before installing the filter on the engine (V8 models)

ENGINE OIL LIFE" menu.

33 With ENGINE OIL LIFE displayed, press and hold the multi-function button in the upper right corner (next to the RESET button) until the indicator reads "OIL LIFE SET TO 100%."

34 Turn the ignition key to the OFF position.

All 2009 models

35 Turn the ignition key to the ON position and press the SETUP button to display "OIL LIFE XXX%."

36 Press and hold the SET/RESET button for five seconds, then release it. The indicator should now read "OIL LIFE SET TO 100%."

37 Turn the ignition key to the OFF position.

All 2010 and later models

38 Turn the ignition key to the ON/RUN position without starting the engine. Press the accelerator pedal all the way to the floor and release the pedal three times within 5 seconds. The "Change Oil Soon" light will go out if the system is reset.

39 Turn the ignition key to the OFF position, then start the vehicle.

7   Automatic transmission fluid level check (every 30,000 miles or 24 months)

Warning: *Never get underneath the vehicle when it is supported only by a jack. The jack provided with your vehicle is designed solely for raising the vehicle to remove and install a wheel. Always use jackstands to support the vehicle when it becomes necessary to place your body underneath the vehicle.*

Note: *The vehicle must be level to accurately check the automatic transmission fluid, so it will be necessary to raise both the front and rear of the vehicle.*

1 The automatic transmission fluid level should be carefully maintained. Low fluid level can lead to slipping or loss of drive, while

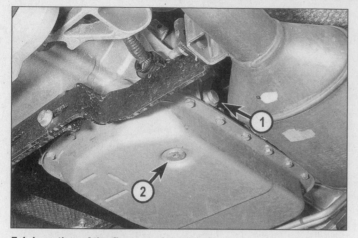

7.4 Location of the five-speed automatic transmission fluid check plug (1) and the drain plug (2) (2007 and earlier models)

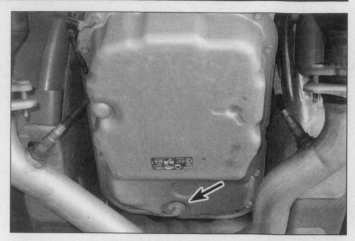

7.6 Location of the six-speed automatic transmission fluid check/ fill plug (2008 and later models)

overfilling can cause foaming, leaking and loss of fluid. **Warning:** *These transmissions do not have a dipstick to check fluid level. Depending on the transmission, the fluid level is checked at a filler plug on the driver's side of the transmission housing, just above the front or rear corner of the transmission pan, or the transmission check plug at the bottom of the transmission pan. To accurately check the fluid level, the engine must be running in Park and the vehicle has to be raised off the ground. There is a risk of personal injury from hot transmission fluid and also from the nearby exhaust system. Therefore if attempting this procedure, wear heat proof gloves and position yourself beneath the vehicle so you are not at risk of being splashed by any transmission fluid. Do not remove the filler plug or check plug unless the engine is running at idle and in Park, as the transmission fluid drains from the torque converter once the engine is switched off and flows back to the transmission pan. If removed with the engine Off, a large amount of transmission fluid will be expelled from the plug hole.*

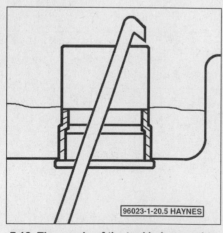

`96023-1-20.5 HAYNES`

7.12 The nozzle of the tool being used to add fluid to the transmission must pass through the check/fill plug opening

2   With the parking brake set, start the engine, then move the shift lever through all the gear ranges, ending in Park. The fluid level must be checked with the vehicle level and the engine running at idle. The automatic transmission must be at operating temperature to obtain an accurate fluid level reading. **Note:** *Incorrect fluid level readings will result if the vehicle has just been driven at high speeds for an extended period, in hot weather in city traffic, or if it has been pulling a trailer. If any of these conditions apply, wait until the fluid has cooled (about 30 minutes).*

3   Raise the vehicle and support it securely on jackstands. **Warning:** *Position your body far enough away from the filler plug hole or oil level check plug hole as hot transmission fluid can cause burns. Also take care as the exhaust is positioned close to the filler plug.*

Fluid level check

2007 and earlier models with 5L40-E or 5L50-E transmissions

Refer to illustration 7.4

4   Make sure the engine is idling in Park, then place a drain pan underneath the filler plug to catch any fluid that may come from the plug, and remove the plug from the driver's side of the transmission **(see illustration)**.

5   Use a small screwdriver as a dipstick to check the level of the fluid. The level is correct if the fluid is level with the bottom of the filler plug hole. If fluid is needed, add it through the filler hole until the level is correct.

2008 and later models with 6L45, 6L50, 6L80 or 6L90 transmissions

Refer to illustration 7.6

6   Make sure the engine is idling in Park and place a drain pan under the transmission oil level check plug to catch any fluid that may come out, then remove the check plug from the transmission pan **(see illustration)**.

7   Allow the fluid to drain until it starts to just drip from the hole. If no fluid comes out when

the oil level check plug is removed, fluid will have to be added until it begins to drip from the pan.

Adding fluid

Models with a fill tube

8   Clean the area off around the fill plug, then use a pair of needle-nose pliers to lift the plug cover and remove the filler plug from the passenger's side of the transmission.

9   Slightly over fill the transmission through the filler plug hole, allowing the excess to drain until fluid only drips out of the oil level check plug hole.

10   Install the oil level check plug into the transmission pan and tighten it to the torque listed in this Chapter's Specifications.

11   Install the filler plug into the transmission and make sure the plug is completely seated into the hole.

Models without a fill tube

Refer to illustration 7.12

12   Using special tools DT 47784 and J 45096-30, fill the transmission through the oil level check plug, then remove the tools and allow the excess to drain until fluid only drips out of the oil level check plug hole. **Note:** *If the special tools are not available, a small fluid pump with a curved hose can be used to fill the transmission through the oil level hole* **(see illustration)**.

13   Install the oil level check plug into the transmission pan and tighten it to the torque listed in this Chapter's Specifications.

All models

14   The condition of the fluid should also be checked along with the level. If the fluid is a dark reddish-brown color, or if the fluid has a burned smell, the fluid should be changed. If you're in doubt about the condition of the fluid, purchase some new fluid and compare the two for color and smell.

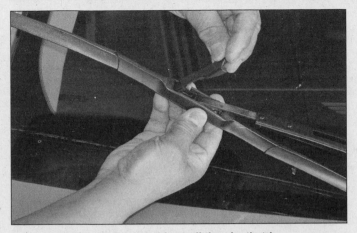

8.4a To release the blade holder, pull the plastic trim cover up . . .

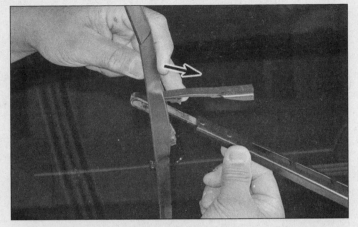

8.4b . . . and pull the wiper blade in the direction of the arrow to separate it from the arm

8 Windshield wiper blade inspection and replacement (every 7500 miles or 6 months)

Refer to illustrations 8.4a and 8.4b

1   The windshield wiper and blade assembly should be inspected periodically for damage, loose components and cracked or worn blade elements.

2   Road film can build up on the wiper blades and affect their efficiency, so they should be washed regularly with a mild detergent solution.

3   If the wiper blade elements are cracked, worn or warped, or no longer clean adequately, they should be replaced with new ones.

4   Lift the arm assembly away from the glass for clearance, pull the trim cover up, then slide the wiper blade assembly out of the hook in the end of the arm **(see illustrations)**.

5   Attach the new wiper to the arm. Connection can be confirmed by an audible click.

9 Battery check, maintenance and charging (every 7500 miles or 6 months)

Refer to illustrations 9.1, 9.6a, 9.6b, 9.7a, 9.7b and 9.8

Warning: *Certain precautions must be followed when checking and servicing the battery. Hydrogen gas, which is highly flammable, is always present in the battery cells, so keep lighted tobacco and all other open flames and sparks away from the battery. The electrolyte inside the battery is actually diluted sulfuric acid, which will cause injury if splashed on your skin or in your eyes. It will also ruin clothes and painted surfaces. When removing the battery cables, always detach the negative cable first and hook it up last!*
Note: *On 2007 and earlier models, the battery is located under the hood. On 2008 and later models, the battery is located in the trunk or rear storage compartment.*

1   A routine preventive maintenance program for the battery in your vehicle is the only way to ensure quick and reliable starts. But before performing any battery maintenance, make sure that you have the proper equipment necessary to work safely around the battery **(see illustration)**.

2   There are also several precautions that should be taken whenever battery maintenance is performed. Before servicing the battery, always turn the engine and all accessories off and disconnect the cables from the negative terminal of the battery (see Chapter 5).

3   The battery produces hydrogen gas, which is both flammable and explosive. Never create a spark, smoke or light a match around the battery. Always charge the battery in a ventilated area.

4   Electrolyte contains poisonous and corrosive sulfuric acid. Do not allow it to get in your eyes, on your skin on your clothes. Never ingest it. Wear protective safety glasses when working near the battery. Keep children away from the battery.

5   Note the external condition of the battery. If the positive terminal and cable clamp on your vehicle's battery is equipped with a

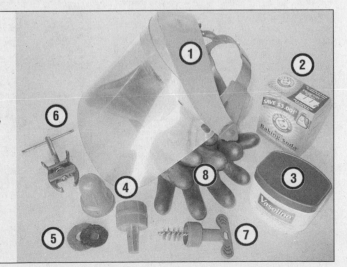

9.1 Tools and materials required for battery maintenance

1   **Face shield/safety goggles** - *When removing corrosion with a brush, the acidic particles can easily fly up into your eyes*

2   **Baking soda** - *A solution of baking soda and water can be used to neutralize corrosion*

3   **Petroleum jelly** - *A layer of this on the battery posts will help prevent corrosion*

4   **Battery post/cable cleaner** - *This wire brush cleaning tool will remove all traces of corrosion from the battery posts and cable clamps*

5   **Treated felt washers** - *Placing one of these on each post, directly under the cable clamps, will help prevent corrosion*

6   **Puller** - *Sometimes the cable clamps are very difficult to pull off the posts, even after the nut/bolt has been completely loosened. This tool pulls the clamp straight up and off the post without damage*

7   **Battery post/cable cleaner** - *Here is another cleaning tool which is a slightly different version of number 4 above, but it does the same thing*

8   **Rubber gloves** - *Another safety item to consider when servicing the battery; remember that's acid inside the battery*

9.6a Battery terminal corrosion usually appears as light, fluffy powder

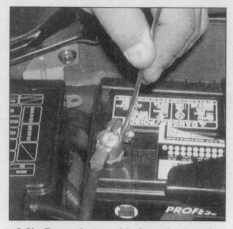

9.6b Removing a cable from the battery post with a wrench - sometimes a pair of special battery pliers are required for this procedure if corrosion has caused deterioration of the nut hex. Always remove the negative (-) cable first and hook it up last!

9.7a When cleaning the cable clamps, all corrosion must be removed (the inside of the clamp is tapered to match the taper on the post, so don't remove too much material)

rubber protector, make sure that it's not torn or damaged. It should completely cover the terminal. Look for any corroded or loose connections, cracks in the case or cover or loose hold-down clamps. Also check the entire length of each cable for cracks and frayed conductors.

6   If corrosion, which looks like white, fluffy deposits **(see illustration)** is evident, particularly around the terminals, the battery should be removed for cleaning. Loosen the cable clamp bolts with a wrench, being careful to remove the ground cable first, and slide them off the terminals **(see illustration)**. Then disconnect the hold-down clamp bolt and nut, remove the clamp and lift the battery from the engine compartment.

7   Clean the cable clamps thoroughly with a battery brush or a terminal cleaner and a solution of warm water and baking soda **(see illustration)**. Wash the terminals and the top of the battery case with the same solution but make sure that the solution doesn't get into the battery. When cleaning the cables, terminals and battery top, wear safety goggles and rubber gloves to prevent any solution from coming in contact with your eyes or hands. Wear old clothes too - even diluted, sulfuric acid splashed onto clothes will burn holes in them. If the terminals have been extensively corroded, clean them up with a terminal cleaner **(see illustration)**. Thoroughly wash all cleaned areas with plain water.

8   Make sure that the battery tray is in good condition and the hold-down clamp fasteners are tight **(see illustration)**. If the battery is removed from the tray, make sure no parts remain in the bottom of the tray when the battery is reinstalled. When reinstalling the hold-down clamp bolts, do not overtighten them.

9   Information on removing and installing the battery can be found in Chapter 5. If you disconnected the cable(s) from the negative and/or positive battery terminals, the power-

train control module (PCM) must relearn its idle and fuel trim strategy for optimum drivability and performance (see Chapter 5 for this procedure). Information on jump starting can be found at the front of this manual. For more detailed battery checking procedures, refer to the *Haynes Automotive Electrical Manual*.

Cleaning

10   Corrosion on the hold-down components, battery case and surrounding areas can be removed with a solution of water and baking soda. Thoroughly rinse all cleaned areas with plain water.

11   Any metal parts of the vehicle damaged by corrosion should be covered with a zinc-based primer, then painted.

Charging

Warning: *When batteries are being charged, hydrogen gas, which is very explosive and flammable, is produced. Do not smoke or*

allow open flames near a charging or a recently charged battery. Wear eye protection when near the battery during charging. Also, make sure the charger is unplugged before connecting or disconnecting the battery from the charger.*

12   Slow-rate charging is the best way to restore a battery that's discharged to the point where it will not start the engine. It's also a good way to maintain the battery charge in a vehicle that's only driven a few miles between starts. Maintaining the battery charge is particularly important in the winter when the battery must work harder to start the engine and electrical accessories that drain the battery are in greater use.

13   It's best to use a one or two-amp battery charger (sometimes called a "trickle" charger). They are the safest and put the least strain on the battery. They are also the least expensive. For a faster charge, you can use a higher amperage charger, but don't use one

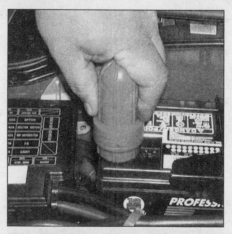

9.7b Regardless of the type of tool used to clean the battery posts, a clean, shiny surface should be the result

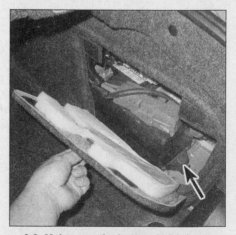

9.8 Make sure the battery hold-down fastener(s) are tight (2008 and later model shown)

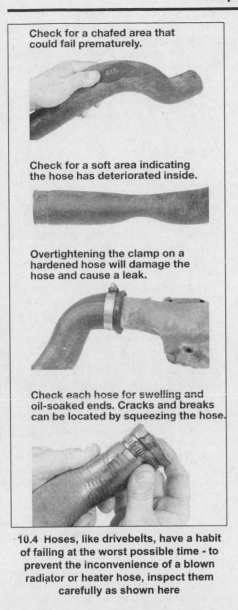

Check for a chafed area that could fail prematurely.

Check for a soft area indicating the hose has deteriorated inside.

Overtightening the clamp on a hardened hose will damage the hose and cause a leak.

Check each hose for swelling and oil-soaked ends. Cracks and breaks can be located by squeezing the hose.

10.4 Hoses, like drivebelts, have a habit of failing at the worst possible time - to prevent the inconvenience of a blown radiator or heater hose, inspect them carefully as shown here

rated more than 1/10th the amp/hour rating of the battery. Rapid boost charges that claim to restore the power of the battery in one to two hours are hardest on the battery and can damage batteries not in good condition. This type of charging should only be used in emergency situations.

14   The average time necessary to charge a battery should be listed in the instructions that come with the charger. As a general rule, a trickle charger will charge a battery in 12 to 16 hours.

10   Cooling system check (every 7,500 miles or 6 months)

Refer to illustration 10.4
Warning: *Wait until the engine is completely cool before beginning this procedure.*
1   Many major engine failures can be caused by a faulty cooling system.
2   The engine must be cold for the cooling

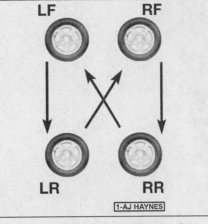

11.2a The recommended tire rotation pattern for non-directional tires

system check, so perform the following procedure before the vehicle is driven for the day or after it has been shut off for at least three hours.
3   Remove the pressure-relief cap from the expansion tank at the right side of the engine compartment. Clean the cap thoroughly, inside and out, with clean water. The presence of rust or corrosion in the expansion tank means the coolant should be changed (see Section 22). The coolant inside the expansion tank should be relatively clean and transparent. If it's rust colored, drain the system and refill it with new coolant.
4   Carefully check the radiator hoses and the smaller diameter heater hoses (see Chapter 3). Inspect each coolant hose along its entire length, replacing any hose which is cracked, swollen or deteriorated **(see illustration)**. Cracks will show up better if the hose is squeezed. Pay close attention to hose clamps that secure the hoses to cooling system components. Hose clamps can pinch and puncture hoses, resulting in coolant leaks.
5   Make sure that all hose connections are tight. A leak in the cooling system will usually show up as white or rust colored deposits on the area adjoining the leak. If wire-type clamps are used on the hoses, it may be a good idea to replace them with screw-type clamps.
6   Clean the front of the radiator and air conditioning condenser with compressed air, if available, or a soft brush. Remove all bugs, leaves, etc. embedded in the radiator fins. Be extremely careful not to damage the cooling fins or cut your fingers on them.
7   If the coolant level has been dropping consistently and no leaks are detectable, have the expansion tank cap and cooling system pressure checked at a service station.

11   Tire rotation (every 7,500 miles or 6 months)

Refer to illustrations 11.2a and 11.2b
1   The tires should be rotated at the specified intervals and whenever uneven wear is

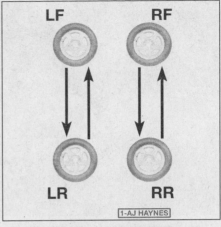

11.2b The recommended tire rotation pattern for directional tires

noticed. Since the vehicle will be raised and the tires removed anyway, check the brakes also (see Section 14).
2   Radial tires must be rotated in a specific pattern **(see illustration)**. Don't include the spare tire in the rotation pattern.
3   Refer to the information in *Jacking and towing* at the front of this manual for the proper procedure to follow when raising the vehicle and changing a tire. If the brakes must be checked, don't apply the parking brake as stated.
4   The vehicle must be raised on a hoist or supported on jackstands to get all four wheels off the ground. Make sure the vehicle is safely supported!
5   After the rotation procedure is finished, check and adjust the tire pressures as necessary and be sure to check the lug nut tightness.

12   Seat belt check (every 7,500 miles or 6 months)

1   Check seat belts, buckles, latch plates and guide loops for obvious damage and signs of wear.
2   See if the seat belt reminder light comes on when the key is turned to the Run or Start position. A chime should also sound.
3   The seat belts are designed to lock up during a sudden stop or impact, yet allow free movement during normal driving. Make sure the retractors return the belt against your chest while driving and rewind the belt fully when the buckle is unlatched.
4   If any of the above checks reveal problems with the seat belt system, replace parts as necessary.

13   Underhood hose check and replacement (every 15,000 miles or 12 months)

Warning: *Replacement of air conditioning hoses must be left to a dealer service department or air conditioning shop that has the equip-*

14.5a You will find an inspection hole like this in each caliper through which you can view the thickness of remaining friction material for the inner pad

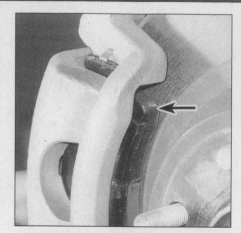

14.5b Be sure to check the thickness of the outer pad material, too

ment to depressurize the system safely. Never remove air conditioning components or hoses until the system has been depressurized.

General

1   High temperatures under the hood can cause deterioration of the rubber and plastic hoses used for engine, accessory and emission systems operation. Periodic inspection should be made for cracks, loose clamps, material hardening and leaks.

2   Information specific to the cooling system hoses can be found in Section 10.

3   Most (but not all) hoses are secured to the fittings with clamps. Where clamps are used, check to be sure they haven't lost their tension, allowing the hose to leak. If clamps aren't used, make sure the hose has not expanded and/or hardened where it slips over the fitting, allowing it to leak.

PCV system hose

4   To reduce hydrocarbon emissions, crankcase blow-by gas are vented through the PCV hoses from the valve cover the intake manifold on most models. The blow-by gases mix with incoming air in the intake manifold before being burned in the combustion chambers.

5   Check the PCV hose(s) for cracks, leaks and other damage. Disconnect it from the valve cover and the intake manifold and check the inside for obstructions. If it's clogged, clean it out with solvent.

Vacuum hoses

6   It's quite common for vacuum hoses, especially those in the emissions system, to be color coded or identified by colored stripes molded into them. Various systems require hoses with different wall thickness, collapse resistance and temperature resistance. When replacing hoses, be sure the new ones are made of the same material.

7   Often the only effective way to check a hose is to remove it completely from the vehicle. If more than one hose is removed, be

sure to label the hoses and fittings to ensure correct installation.

8   When checking vacuum hoses, be sure to include any plastic T-fittings in the check. Inspect the fittings for cracks and the hose where it fits over each fitting for distortion, which could cause leakage.

9   A small piece of vacuum hose (1/4-inch inside diameter) can be used as a stethoscope to detect vacuum leaks. Hold one end of the hose to your ear and probe around vacuum hoses and fittings, listening for the hissing sound characteristic of a vacuum leak. **Warning:** *When probing with the vacuum hose stethoscope, be careful not to come into contact with moving engine components such as drivebelts, the cooling fan, etc.*

Fuel hose

Warning: *Gasoline is flammable, so take extra precautions when you work on any part of the fuel system. Don't smoke or allow open flames or bare light bulbs near the work area, and don't work in a garage where a gas-type appliance (such as a water heater or clothes dryer) is present. Since fuel is carcinogenic, wear fuel-resistant gloves when there's a possibility of being exposed to fuel, and, if you spill any fuel on your skin, rinse it off immediately with soap and water. Mop up any spills immediately and do not store fuel-soaked rags where they could ignite. The fuel system is under constant pressure, so, if any fuel lines are to be disconnected, the fuel pressure in the system must be relieved first (see Chapter 4 for more information). When you perform any kind of work on the fuel system, wear safety glasses and have a Class B type fire extinguisher on hand.*

10   The fuel lines are usually under pressure, so if any fuel lines are to be disconnected be prepared to catch spilled fuel. **Warning:** *Your vehicle is equipped with fuel injection and you must relieve the fuel system pressure before servicing the fuel lines.* Refer to Chapter 4 for the fuel system pressure relief procedure.

11   Check all flexible fuel lines for deterioration and chafing. Check especially for cracks in areas where the hose bends and just before

fittings, such as where the fuel line attaches to the fuel rail.

12   When replacing a hose, use only hose that is specifically designed for your fuel injection system.

13   Some fuel lines use quick-connect fittings, which require a special tool to disconnect. See Chapter 4 for more information on these types of fittings.

Metal lines

14   Sections of metal line are often used for fuel line that runs underneath the vehicle. Check carefully to make sure the line isn't bent, crimped or cracked.

15   If a section of metal fuel line must be replaced, use seamless steel tubing only, since copper and aluminum tubing do not have the strength necessary to withstand vibration caused by the engine.

16   Check the metal brake lines where they enter the master cylinder and brake proportioning unit (if used) for cracks in the lines and loose fittings. Any sign of brake fluid leakage calls for an immediate thorough inspection of the brake system.

14   Brake check (every 15,000 miles or 12 months)

Warning: *Dust created by the brake system is harmful to your health. Never blow it out with compressed air and don't inhale any of it. An approved filtering mask should be worn when working on brakes. Do not, under any circumstances, use petroleum-based solvents to clean brake parts. Use brake system cleaner only!*

1   The brakes should be inspected every time the wheels are removed or whenever a defect is suspected. Indications of a potential brake system problem include the vehicle pulling to one side when the brake pedal is depressed, noises coming from the brakes when they are applied, excessive brake pedal travel, a pulsating pedal and leakage of fluid, usually seen on the inside of the tire or wheel. **Note:** *It is normal for a vehicle equipped with an Anti-lock Brake System (ABS) to exhibit brake pedal pulsations during severe braking conditions.*

Disc brakes

Refer to illustrations 14.5a and 14.5b

2   Disc brakes can be visually checked without removing any parts except the wheels. Remove the hub caps (if applicable) and loosen the wheel lug nuts a quarter turn each.

3   Raise the vehicle and place it securely on jackstands. **Warning:** *Never work under a vehicle that is supported only by a jack!*

4   Remove the wheels. Now visible is the disc brake caliper which contains the pads. There is an outer brake pad and an inner pad. Both must be checked for wear. **Note:** *Usually the inner pad wears faster than the outer pad.*

5   Measure the thickness of the outer pad at each end of the caliper and the inner pad through the inspection hole in the caliper body **(see illustrations)**. Compare the measure-

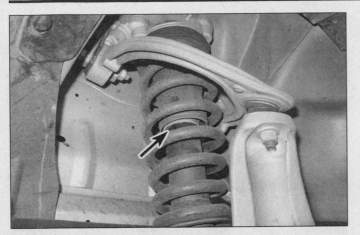

15.6 Check the shocks for leakage at the indicated area

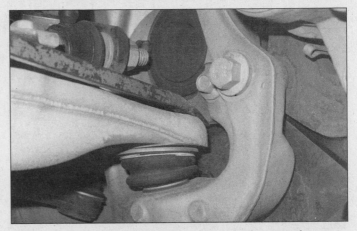

15.11 To check a balljoint for wear, try to pry the control arm up and down to make sure there is no play in the balljoint (if there is, replace it)

ment with the limit given in this Chapter's Specifications; if any brake pad thickness is less than specified, then all brake pads must be replaced (see Chapter 9).

6 If you're in doubt as to the exact pad thickness or quality, remove them for measurement and further inspection (see Chapter 9).

7 Check the disc for score marks, wear and burned spots. If any of these conditions exist, the disc should be removed for servicing or replacement (see Chapter 9).

8 Before installing the wheels, check all the brake lines and hoses for damage, wear, deformation, cracks, corrosion, leakage, bends and twists, particularly in the vicinity of the rubber hoses and calipers.

9 Install the wheels, lower the vehicle and tighten the wheel lug nuts to the torque given in this Chapter's Specifications.

Parking brake

10 Slowly pull up on the parking brake and count the number of clicks you hear until the handle is up as far as it will go. The adjustment is correct if you hear the specified number of clicks (see this Chapter's Specifications). If you hear more or fewer clicks, it's time to adjust the parking brake (see Chapter 9).

11 An alternative method of checking the parking brake is to park the vehicle on a steep hill with the engine running (so you can apply the brakes if necessary) with the parking brake set and the transmission in Neutral. If the parking brake cannot prevent the vehicle from rolling, it needs adjustment (see Chapter 9).

15 Steering, suspension and driveaxle boot check (every 15,000 miles or 12 months)

Note: *For detailed illustrations of the steering and suspension components, refer to Chapter 10.*

Shock absorber check

Refer to illustration 15.6

1 Park the vehicle on level ground, turn the engine off and set the parking brake. Check the tire pressures.

2 Push down at one corner of the vehicle, then release it while noting the movement of the body. It should stop moving and come to rest in a level position within one or two bounces.

3 If the vehicle continues to move up-and-down or if it fails to return to its original position, a worn or weak shock absorber is probably the reason.

4 Repeat the above check at each of the three remaining corners of the vehicle.

5 Raise the vehicle and support it securely on jackstands.

6 Check the shock absorbers for evidence of fluid leakage **(see illustration)**. A light film of fluid is no cause for concern. Make sure that any fluid noted is from the shocks and not from some other source. If leakage is noted, replace the shocks as a set.

7 Check the shocks to be sure that they are securely mounted and undamaged. Check the upper mounts for damage and wear. If damage or wear is noted, replace the shocks as a set (front or rear).

8 If the shocks must be replaced, refer to Chapter 10 for the procedure.

Steering and suspension check

Refer to illustrations 15.11 and 15.12

9 Check the tires for irregular wear patterns and proper inflation. See Section 5 in this Chapter for information regarding tire wear and Chapter 10 for information on wheel bearing replacement.

10 Inspect the universal joint between the steering shaft and the steering gear housing. Check the steering gear housing for lubricant leakage. Make sure that the dust boots are not damaged and that the boot clamps are not loose. Check the tie-rod ends for excessive play. Look for loose bolts, broken or discon-

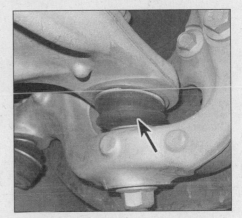

15.12 Check the balljoint boots for damage

nected parts and deteriorated rubber bushings on all suspension and steering components. While an assistant turns the steering wheel from side to side, check the steering components for free movement, chafing and binding. If the steering components do not seem to be reacting with the movement of the steering wheel, try to determine where the slack is located.

11 Check the balljoints for wear by trying to move each control arm up and down with a prybar **(see illustration)** to ensure that its balljoint has no play. If any balljoint does have play, it's worn out. See Chapter 10 for the control arm replacement procedure (the balljoints aren't replaceable separately).

12 Inspect the balljoint boots for damage and leaking grease **(see illustration)**.

13 At the rear of the vehicle, inspect the suspension arm bushings for deterioration. Additional information on suspension components can be found in Chapter 10.

Driveaxle boot check

Refer to illustration 15.15

14 The rear driveaxle boots are very important because they prevent dirt, water and for-

15.15 Flex the driveaxle boots by hand to check for cracks and/or leaking grease

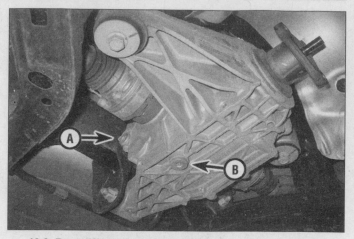

18.2 Rear differential fill/check plug (A) and drain plug (B)

eign material from entering and damaging the constant velocity (CV) joints. Oil and grease can cause the boot material to deteriorate prematurely, so it's a good idea to wash the boots with soap and water.

15   Inspect the boots for tears and cracks as well as loose clamps **(see illustration)**. If there is any evidence of cracks or leaking lubricant, they must be replaced (see Chapter 8).

16   Fuel system check (every 15,000 miles or 12 months)

Warning: *Gasoline is flammable, so take extra precautions when you work on any part of the fuel system. Don't smoke or allow open flames or bare light bulbs near the work area, and don't work in a garage where a gas-type appliance (such as a water heater or clothes dryer) is present. Since fuel is carcinogenic, wear fuel-resistant gloves when there's a possibility of being exposed to fuel, and, if you spill any fuel on your skin, rinse it off immediately with soap and water. Mop up any spills immediately and do not store fuel-soaked rags where they could ignite. When you perform any kind of work on the fuel system, wear safety glasses and have a Class B type fire extinguisher on hand. The fuel system is under constant pressure, so, before any lines are disconnected, the fuel system pressure must be relieved (see Chapter 4).*

1   If you smell gasoline while driving or after the vehicle has been sitting in the sun, inspect the fuel system immediately.

2   Remove the fuel filler cap and inspect if for damage and corrosion. The gasket should have an unbroken sealing imprint. If the gasket is damaged or corroded, install a new cap.

3   Inspect the fuel feed line for cracks. Make sure that the connections between the fuel lines and the fuel injection system and between the fuel lines and the fuel tank (inspect from below) are tight and dry. **Warn-**

ing: *Your vehicle is fuel injected, so you must relieve the fuel system pressure before servicing fuel system components. The fuel system pressure relief procedure is outlined in Chapter 4.*

4   Since some components of the fuel system - the fuel tank and part of the fuel feed line, for example - are underneath the vehicle, they can be inspected more easily with the vehicle raised on a hoist. If that's not possible, raise the vehicle and support it on jackstands.

5   With the vehicle raised and safely supported, inspect the gas tank and filler neck for punctures, cracks and other damage. The connection between the filler neck and the tank is particularly critical. Sometimes a rubber filler neck will leak because of loose clamps or deteriorated rubber. Inspect all fuel tank mounting brackets and straps to be sure that the tank is securely attached to the vehicle. **Warning:** *Do not, under any circumstances, try to repair a fuel tank (except rubber components). A welding torch or any open flame can easily cause fuel vapors inside the tank to explode.*

6   Carefully check all rubber hoses and metal lines leading away from the fuel tank. Check for loose connections, deteriorated hoses, crimped lines and other damage. Repair or replace damaged sections as necessary (see Chapter 4).

17   Manual transmission lubricant level check (every 15,000 miles or 12 months)

1   The manual transmission does not have a dipstick. To check the fluid level, raise the vehicle and support it securely on jackstands. On the side of the transmission housing towards the back you will see a fill plug about half-way up on the transmission case. Remove the plug; if the lubricant level is correct, it should be up to the lower edge of the hole.

2   If the transmission needs more lubricant (if the level is not up to the hole), use a syringe or a gear oil pump to add more. Stop filling the transmission when the lubricant begins to run out of the hole.

3   Install the plug and tighten it to the torque listed in this Chapter's Specifications. Drive the vehicle a short distance, then check for leaks.

18   Rear differential lubricant level check (every 15,000 miles or 12 months)

Refer to illustration 18.2

1   The differential has a filler plug which must be removed to check the lubricant level. If the vehicle is raised to gain access to the plug, be sure to support it safely on jackstands - DO NOT crawl under the vehicle when it's supported only by the jack.

2   Remove the filler plug from the side of the differential **(see illustration)**.

3   The lubricant level should be at the bottom of the plug opening. If not, use a syringe to add the recommended lubricant until it just starts to run out of the opening.

4   Inspect the differential breather hose to make sure it isn't kinked and is securely mounted.

5   Install the plug and tighten it to the torque listed in this Chapter's Specifications.

19   Air filter check and replacement (every 15,000 miles or 12 months)

Refer to illustrations 19.1a and 19.1b

1   The air filter is located inside a housing at the left (driver's) side of the engine compartment. To remove the air filter, remove the fasteners that secure the two halves of the air filter housing together, then separate the

19.1a Remove the air filter cover fasteners . . .

19.1b . . . pull the cover out of the way and lift the element out

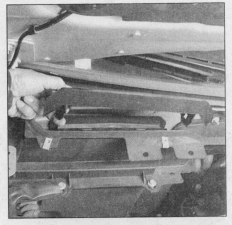

20.3 Pull the tabs on the filter cover outwards to remove the filter cover

cover halves and remove the air filter element **(see illustrations)**. **Note:** *Some models are equipped with side engine covers that must be unclipped and removed to access the air cleaner housing.*

2   Inspect the outer surface of the filter element. If it is dirty, replace it. If it is only moderately dusty, it can be reused by blowing it clean from the back to the front surface with compressed air. Because it is a pleated paper type filter, it cannot be washed or oiled. If it cannot be cleaned satisfactorily with compressed air, discard and replace it. While the cover is off, be careful not to drop anything down into the housing. **Caution:** *Never drive the vehicle with the air filter removed. Excessive engine wear could result and backfiring could even cause a fire under the hood.*

3   Wipe out the inside of the air cleaner housing.

4   Place the new filter into the air cleaner housing, making sure it seats properly.

5   Make sure the top half of the housing is seated properly, then secure it with the clamps.

20   Cabin air filter replacement (every 15,000 miles or 12 months)

Refer to illustrations 20.3 and 20.4

1   Operate the windshield wipers to position them up on the windshield, then turn the ignition key off.

2   Remove the passenger's side cowl panel grille (see Chapter 11).

3   Pull the tabs on each side of the filter housing access cover outwards and lift off the cover **(see illustration)**.

4   Remove the filter from the housing **(see illustration)**.

5   Installation is the reverse of removal.

21   Exhaust system check (every 30,000 miles or 24 months)

Refer to illustration 21.2

1   With the engine cold (at least three hours after the vehicle has been driven), check the

complete exhaust system from the engine to the end of the tailpipe. Ideally, the inspection should be done with the vehicle on a hoist to permit unrestricted access. If a hoist isn't available, raise the vehicle and support it securely on jackstands.

2   Check the exhaust pipes and connections for evidence of leaks, severe corrosion and damage. Make sure that all brackets and hangers are in good condition and tight **(see illustration)**.

3   At the same time, inspect the underside of the body for holes, corrosion, open seams, etc. which may allow exhaust gases to enter the passenger compartment. Seal all body openings with silicone or body putty.

4   Rattles and other noises can often be traced to the exhaust system, especially the mounts and hangers. Try to move the pipes, muffler and catalytic converter. If the components can come in contact with the body or suspension parts, secure the exhaust system with new mounts.

5   Check the running condition of the engine by inspecting inside the end of the tailpipe. The exhaust deposits here are an indi-

20.4 Pull the filter from the housing

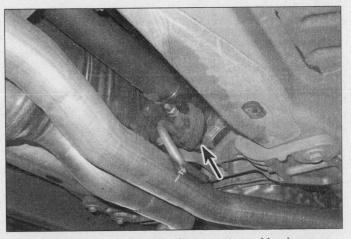

21.2 Be sure to check each exhaust system rubber hanger for damage

22.4 Splash shield fasteners

22.5 The radiator drain fitting is located at the lower right corner of the radiator - before opening the valve, push a short length of rubber hose onto the plastic fitting to prevent the coolant from splashing

cation of engine state-of-tune. If the pipe is black and sooty or coated with white deposits, the engine may need a tune-up, including a thorough fuel system inspection and adjustment.

22   Cooling system servicing (draining, flushing and refilling) (every 100,000 miles or 70 months)

Warning: *Do not allow antifreeze to come in contact with your skin or painted surfaces of the vehicle. Rinse off spills immediately with plenty of water. Antifreeze is highly toxic if ingested. Never leave antifreeze lying around in an open container or in puddles on the floor; children and pets are attracted by its sweet smell and may drink it. Check with local authorities about disposing of used antifreeze. Many communities have collection centers which will see that antifreeze is disposed of safely. Never dump used antifreeze on the ground or pour it into drains.*

Warning: *Wait until the engine is completely cool before beginning this procedure.*

Note: *Non-toxic antifreeze is now manufactured and available at local auto parts stores, but even this type must be disposed of properly.*

Note: *To drain the coolant in the charge air cooling system on CTS-V models, refer to Chapter 2C, Section 16. To refill the charge air cooling system, see Chapter 2C, Section 21.*

1   Periodically, the cooling system should be drained, flushed and refilled to replenish the antifreeze mixture and prevent formation of rust and corrosion, which can impair the performance of the cooling system and cause engine damage. When the cooling system is serviced, all hoses and the expansion tank cap should be checked and replaced if necessary.

Draining

Refer to illustrations 22.4 and 22.5

2   Apply the parking brake and block the wheels. If the vehicle has just been driven,

wait several hours to allow the engine to cool down before beginning this procedure.

3   Once the engine is completely cool, remove the expansion tank cap, then raise the vehicle and support it securely on jackstands.

4   Remove the engine splash shield **(see illustration)** and move a large container under the radiator to catch the coolant.

5   On models with a drain fitting, insert a length of hose through the subframe and attach the hose to the drain fitting to direct the coolant into the container, then open the drain fitting (a pair of pliers may be required to turn it) **(see illustration)**.

6   On models without a drain fitting, loosen the lower radiator hose clamp and slide the clamp back. Slowly remove the lower radiator hose and allow the coolant to drain into the container.

7   While the coolant is draining, check the condition of the radiator hoses, heater hoses and clamps (see Section 10, if necessary). Replace any damaged clamps or hoses.

Flushing

8   Fill the cooling system with clean water, following the *Refilling* procedure (see Step 14).

9   Start the engine and allow it to reach normal operating temperature, then rev up the engine a few times.

10   Turn the engine off and allow it to cool completely, then drain the system as described earlier.

11   Repeat Steps 8 through 10 until the water being drained is free of contaminants.

12   In severe cases of contamination or clogging of the radiator, remove the radiator (see Chapter 3) and have a radiator repair facility clean and repair it if necessary.

13   Many deposits can be removed by the chemical action of a cleaner available at auto parts stores. Follow the procedure outlined in the manufacturer's instructions. **Note:** *When the coolant is regularly drained and the system refilled with the correct antifreeze/water mixture, there should be no need to use chemical cleaners or descalers.*

Refilling

14   Close and tighten the radiator drain or reattach the radiator hose.

15   Place the heater temperature control in the maximum heat position.

16   Slowly add new coolant (a 50/50 mixture of water and DEX-COOL antifreeze) to the expansion tank until the level is at the MAX fill mark on the expansion tank.

17   Install the expansion tank cap and run the engine at idle for two minutes, periodically raising the engine rpm to 2500 to 3000 rpm. **Caution:** *If at any time the engine begins to overheat, or the coolant level falls below the MIN fill line on the expansion tank, turn off the engine, allow it to cool completely, then add coolant to the expansion tank to the MAX fill line.*

18   Turn the engine off and let it cool. Add more coolant mixture to bring the level to the MAX fill mark on the expansion tank.

19   Repeat Steps 16 through 18 as necessary.

20   Start the engine, allow it to reach normal operating temperature and check for leaks. Also, set the heater and blower controls to the maximum setting and check to see that the heater output from the air ducts is warm. This is a good indication that all air has been purged from the cooling system.

21   The remainder of installation is the reverse of removal.

23   Brake fluid change (every 30,000 miles or 24 months)

Warning: *Brake fluid can harm your eyes and damage painted surfaces, so use extreme caution when handling or pouring it. Do not use brake fluid that has been standing open or is more than one year old. Brake fluid absorbs moisture from the air. Excess moisture can cause a dangerous loss of braking effectiveness.*

1   At the specified intervals, the brake fluid should be drained and replaced. Since the

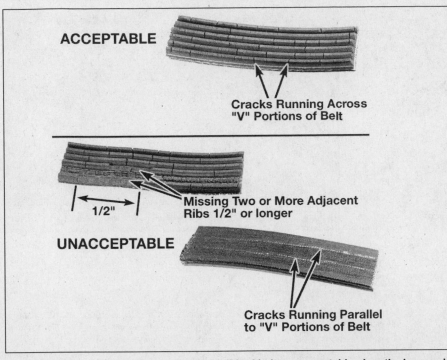

24.5 To remove the drivebelt, insert a 1/2-inch drive ratchet or breaker bar into the square hole and rotate the tensioner arm to relieve belt tension - V6 model shown, other models similar

24.4 Small cracks in the underside of a V-ribbed belt are acceptable - lengthwise cracks, or missing pieces that cause the belt to make noise, are cause for replacement

brake fluid may drip or splash when pouring it, place plenty of rags around the master cylinder to protect any surrounding painted surfaces.

2   Before beginning work, purchase the specified brake fluid (see *Recommended lubricants and fluids* in this Chapter's Specifications).

3   Remove the cap from the master cylinder reservoir.

4   Using a hand suction pump or similar device, withdraw the fluid from the master cylinder reservoir.

5   Add new fluid to the master cylinder until it rises to the base of the filler neck.

6   Bleed the brake system as described in Chapter 9 at all four brakes until new and uncontaminated fluid is expelled from the bleeder screw. Be sure to maintain the fluid level in the master cylinder as you perform the bleeding process. If you allow the master cylinder to run dry, air will enter the system.

7   Refill the master cylinder with fluid and check the operation of the brakes. The pedal should feel solid when depressed, with no sponginess. **Warning:** *Do not operate the vehicle if you are in doubt about the effectiveness of the brake system.*

24 Drivebelt check and replacement (every 30,000 miles or 24 months)

1   The serpentine drivebelt(s) are located at the front of the engine and play an important role in the overall operation of the engine and its components. Depending on the year and engine used several configurations are available ranging from a single belt to multiple belts. Due to its function and material make up, the belts are prone to wear and should be periodically inspected. The serpentine belt or belts drive the alternator, power steering pump, water pump, air conditioning compressor and super charger on later model V8 engines. Although the belts should be inspected at the recommended intervals, replacement may not be necessary for more than 100,000 miles.

Check

Refer to illustrations 24.4

2   The tension of the belt is automatically adjusted by the belt tensioner and does not require any adjustments. Drivebelt wear can be checked visually by inspecting the wear indicator marks located on the front of the tensioner body. Locate the belt tensioner(s) at the front of the engine. If the indicator mark is outside the operating range, the belt should be replaced. Since the drivebelt(s) are located at the front of the engine compartment, it will be necessary to remove the engine cover and air cleaner inlet or outlet duct on V8 models.

3   With the engine stopped, inspect the full length of the drivebelt(s) for cracks and separation of the belt plies. It will be necessary to turn the engine (using a wrench or socket and bar on the crankshaft pulley bolt, working clockwise only) in order to move the belt from the pulleys so that the belt can be inspected thoroughly. Twist the belt between the pulleys so that both sides can be viewed. Also check for fraying, and glazing which gives the belt a shiny appearance. Check the pulleys for nicks, cracks, distortion and corrosion.

4   Note that it is not unusual for a ribbed belt to exhibit small cracks in the edges of the belt ribs, and unless these are extensive or very deep, belt replacement is not essential (see illustration).

Replacement

V6 engines

Refer to illustration 24.5

Note: *Before removing the drivebelts, take a good look and note how the belt is routed on all the pulleys.*

5   On models equipped with a single drivebelt, insert a 1/2-inch drive ratchet or breaker bar into the tensioner hole and rotate the handle clockwise to release the drivebelt tension (see illustration). Once tension has been released, remove the belt from the pulleys. **Note:** *It may be easier to work from under the vehicle to remove the belt.*

6   Install the new drivebelt onto the crankshaft, alternator, power steering pump, and air conditioning compressor pulleys, as applicable, then turn the tensioner back and locate the drivebelt on the pulley. Make sure that the drivebelt is correctly seated in all of the pulley grooves, then release the tensioner.

7   On models equipped with multiple drive belts, start with the outer (water pump/alternator) drivebelt. Insert a 1/2-inch drive ratchet or breaker bar into the tensioner square hole and rotate the handle clockwise to release the drivebelt tension. Once tension has been released, remove the belt from the pulleys.

8   With the outer drivebelt removed, insert a 1/2-inch drive ratchet or breaker bar into the inner (power steering/air conditioning compressor) belt tensioner square hole and rotate the handle clockwise to release the drivebelt tension. Once tension has been released, remove the belt from the pulleys.

9   Starting with the inside belt, install the

24.11 To remove the drivebelt, rotate the tensioner bolt (1) clockwise (2) to relieve belt tension (2007)

24.25 Typical V6 tensioner mounting fastener locations

new drivebelt onto the crankshaft, power steering pump, and air conditioning compressor pulley, then turn the tensioner back and locate the drivebelt on the pulley. Make sure that the drivebelt is correctly seated in all of the pulley grooves, then release the tensioner. Repeat the same procedure for the outer drivebelt.

V8 engines

10   Remove the air filter housing outlet duct (see Chapter 4).

2007 and earlier models

Refer to illustration 24.11

11   Place a socket on to the accessory drivebelt tensioner pulley center bolt and rotate the tensioner clockwise to release the drivebelt tension **(see illustration)**. Once tension has been released, remove the belt from the pulleys.

12   With the outer accessory drivebelt removed, place a socket on the air conditioning compressor drivebelt tensioner pulley center bolt and rotate the tensioner clockwise to release the drivebelt tension. Once tension has been released, remove the belt from the pulleys.

13   Starting with the inside belt, install the new drivebelt onto the crankshaft and air conditioning compressor pulley, then turn the tensioner back and locate the drivebelt on the pulley. Make sure that the drivebelt is correctly seated in all of the pulley grooves, then release the tensioner. Repeat the same procedure for the outer accessory drivebelt and reinstall the air filter duct.

2009 and later model supercharger and accessory drivebelts

14   Start with the outer (supercharger) drivebelt. Insert a 1/2-inch drive ratchet or breaker bar into the tensioner square hole and rotate the handle clockwise to release the drivebelt tension. Once tension has been released, remove the belt from the pulleys.

15   With the outer supercharger drivebelt

removed, insert a 1/2-inch drive ratchet or breaker bar into the accessory tensioner square hole and rotate the handle clockwise to release the drivebelt tension. Once tension has been released, remove the belt from the pulleys.

16   Starting with the accessory belt, install the new drivebelt onto the crankshaft and various pulleys, then turn the tensioner back and locate the drivebelt on the pulley. Make sure that the drivebelt is correctly seated in all of the pulley grooves, then release the tensioner. Repeat the same procedure for the outer supercharger drivebelt and reinstall the air filter duct.

2009 and later model air conditioning compressor drivebelt

Note: *The air conditioning compressor belt doesn't use a tensioner and must be cut to be removed. Make sure you have a new belt before cutting the old belt off.*

17   Remove the supercharger and accessory belts (see Steps 14 and 15).

18   Remove the splash shield **(see illustration 22.4)**.

19   Disconnect the electrical connector to the charge air cooler pump, then remove the pump mounting nuts and the pump (see Chapter 3).

20   Using a pair of diagonal cutters, cut the air conditioning belt to remove it.

21   Place the new belt to the rear of the crankshaft pulley, making sure the belt is fully seated in the pulley grooves.

22   Install the special belt installation tool on to the air conditioning compressor and place the belt over the tool.

23   Rotate the crankshaft pulley and allow the tool to turn and seat the belt on the compressor pulley.

24   The remainder of installation is the reverse of removal.

Drivebelt tensioner

Refer to illustration 24.25

25   On V6 models, remove the bolts secur-

ing the tensioner to the engine, then detach the tensioner from the engine **(see illustration)**.

26   On V8 models, remove two bolts securing accessory tensioner to the engine, then detach the tensioner.

27   On V8 models with superchargers, remove the supercharger tensioner center bolt, then detach the tensioner.

28   Installation is the reverse of removal. Tighten the tensioners bolt(s) to the torque listed in this Chapter's Specifications.

---

25   Automatic transmission fluid and filter change (every 60,000 miles or 48 months)

Refer to illustrations 25.5, 25.8 and 25.9

1   Before beginning work, purchase the specified transmission fluid (see *Recommended lubricants and fluids* in this Chapter's Specifications) and a new filter.

2   Other tools necessary for this job include a floor jack, jackstands to support the vehicle in a raised position, a drain pan capable of holding at least 5 quarts, newspapers and clean rags.

3   Raise the vehicle and support it securely on jackstands. **Note:** *The vehicle must be level.*

4   Place the drain pan underneath the transmission pan. Remove the front and side pan mounting bolts, but only loosen the rear pan bolts approximately four turns. **Note:** *Some early models are equipped with a drain plug in the bottom of the transmission pan. If equipped with a drain plug, drain the fluid from the drain plug before loosening any pan bolts.*

5   Carefully pry the transmission pan loose with a screwdriver, allowing the fluid to drain **(see illustration)**.

6   Remove the remaining bolts, pan and gasket. Carefully clean the gasket surface of

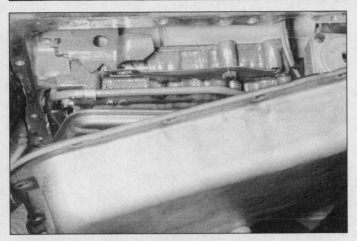

25.5 With the rear bolts in place but loose, pull the front of the pan down to drain the transmission fluid

25.8 Rotate the filter out of the retaining clip, then lower it from the transmission

the transmission to remove all traces of the old gasket and sealant.

7　Drain the fluid from the transmission pan, clean it with solvent and dry it.

8　Pull the filter straight down from the transmission **(see illustration)** do not bend or twist the filter tube neck.

9　If the seal(s) did not come out with the filter, carefully remove it from the transmission **(see illustration)**. Install a new filter and seal(s).

10　Make sure the gasket surface on the transmission pan is clean, then fit a new gasket on the pan. Put the pan in place against the transmission and, working around the pan, tighten each bolt a little at a time until the final torque is reached (see this Chapter's Specifications). Keep in mind that the correct torque to avoid leaks is quite low.

11　Add new fluid to the transmission (see Section 7). Check the specifications in this Chapter for the proper quantity. **Note:** *Using a syringe or hand pump, fill the transmission until it is level with the bottom of the filler plug hole before starting the engine.*

25.9 If necessary, use a screwdriver to remove the seal from the transmission - be careful not to gouge or scratch the aluminum housing

12　With the transmission in Park and the parking brake set, run the engine at a fast idle, but don't race it.

13　Move the gear selector through each range and back to Park. Check the fluid level (see Section 7); it will probably be low.

14　Check under the vehicle for leaks during the first few trips.

15　The old fluid drained from the transmission cannot be reused in its present state and should be disposed of. Check with your local auto parts store, disposal facility or environmental agency to see if they will accept the fluid for recycling. After the fluid has cooled it can be drained into a container (capped plastic jugs, topped bottles, milk cartons, etc.) for transport to one of these disposal sites. Don't dispose of the fluid by pouring it on the ground or down a drain!

26 Manual transmission lubricant change (every 60,000 miles or 48 months)

1　This procedure should be performed after the vehicle has been driven so the lubricant will be warm and therefore flow out of the transmission more easily.

2　Raise the vehicle and support it securely on jackstands. Position a drain pan under the transmission. Remove the transmission fill plug on the front of the case; it's about halfway up on the transmission case.

3　On Getrag and Aisin AY6 models, remove the drain plug at the bottom of the case and allow the lubricant to drain into the pan.

4　On Tremec 6-speed models, disconnect the transmission fluid temperature sensor, then remove the sensor/drain plug and allow the fluid to drain.

5　After the lubricant has drained completely, reinstall the drain or sensor plug and tighten it securely.

6　Using a hand pump, syringe or funnel, fill the transmission with the specified lubricant

until it is level with the lower edge of the filler hole. Using a new sealing washer, reinstall the fill plug and tighten it to the torque listed in this Chapter's Specifications.

7　Lower the vehicle.

8　Drive the vehicle for a short distance, then check the drain and fill plugs for leakage.

9　The old lubricant drained from the transmission cannot be reused in its present state and should be disposed of. Check with your local auto parts store, disposal facility or environmental agency to see if they will accept the lubricant for recycling. After the lubricant has cooled it can be drained into a container (capped plastic jugs, topped bottles, milk cartons, etc.) for transport to one of these disposal sites. Don't dispose of the lubricant by pouring it on the ground or down a drain!

27 Rear differential lubricant change (every 60,000 miles or 48 months)

1　This procedure should be performed after the vehicle has been driven so the lubricant will be warm and therefore flow out of the differential more easily.

2　Raise the vehicle and support it securely on jackstands. Position a drain pan under the differential.

3　Remove the check/fill plug, then remove the drain plug from the differential and allow the lubricant to drain into the pan (see Section 18).

4　After the lubricant has drained completely, install the drain plug and tighten it to the torque listed in this Chapter's Specifications.

5　Using a hand pump, syringe or funnel, fill the differential with the specified lubricant until it begins to leak out through the hole. Install the fill plug and tighten it to the torque listed in this Chapter's Specifications.

6　Lower the vehicle.

7　Drive the vehicle for a short distance, then check the drain and fill plugs for leakage.

28   Spark plug check and replacement (see Maintenance schedule for service intervals)

Refer to illustrations 28.2, 28.5, 28.6, 28.7, 28.8, 28.10, 28.12a and 28.12b

1   On V6 models, the spark plugs are located in the center of the valve covers. On V8 models, the spark plugs are located at the sides of the engine.

2   In most cases, the tools necessary for spark plug replacement include a spark plug socket which fits onto a ratchet (spark plug sockets are padded inside to prevent damage to the porcelain insulators on the new plugs), various extensions and a gap gauge to check the gaps on the new plugs **(see illustration)**. A torque wrench should be used to tighten the new plugs.

3   The best approach when replacing the spark plugs is to purchase the new ones in advance, adjust them to the proper gap and replace the plugs one at a time. When buying the new spark plugs, be sure to obtain the correct plug type for your particular engine. This information can be found in this Chapter's Specifications or in the owner's manual.

4   Allow the engine to cool completely before attempting to remove any of the plugs. These engines are equipped with aluminum cylinder heads, which can be damaged if the spark plugs are removed when the engine is hot. While you are waiting for the engine to cool, check the new plugs for defects and adjust the gaps.

5   The gap is checked by inserting the proper-thickness gauge between the electrodes at the tip of the plug **(see illustration)**. The gap between the electrodes should be the same as the one specified in this Chapter's Specifications. The gauge should just slide between the electrodes with a slight amount of drag.

6   On V6 engines, remove the upper intake manifold (see Chapter 2A or 2B) to gain

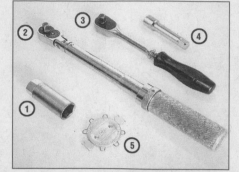

28.2 Tools required for changing spark plugs

*1   **Spark plug socket** - This will have special padding inside to protect the spark plug porcelain insulator*

*2   **Torque wrench** - Although not mandatory, use of this tool is the best way to ensure that the plugs are tightened properly*

*3   **Ratchet** - Standard hand tool to fit the plug socket*

*4   **Extension** - Depending on model and accessories, you may need special extensions and universal joints to reach one or more of the plugs*

*5   **Spark plug gap gauge** - This gauge for checking the gap comes in a variety of styles. Make sure the gap for your engine is included*

access to all of the ignition coils **(see illustration)**.

7   On V6 engines, disconnect the wiring from each ignition coil and, after loosening the retaining bolts, pull the coil from the valve cover **(see illustration)**. **Note:** *On some models the coil bolts are captive bolts. They will remain in the coil housing.*

8   On V8 engines, with the engine cool, remove the spark plug wire from one spark plug. Pull only on the boot at the end of the

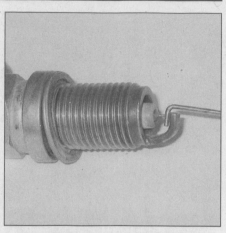

28.5 When checking the spark plug gap, the wire should slide between the electrodes with a slight drag

wire - do not pull on the wire. A plug wire removal tool should be used if available **(see illustration)**.

9   If compressed air is available, use it to blow any dirt or foreign material away from the spark plug hole. The idea here is to eliminate the possibility of debris falling into the cylinder as the spark plug is removed.

10   Place the spark plug socket over the plug and remove it from the engine by turning it in a counterclockwise direction **(see illustration)**.

11   Compare the spark plug to those shown in the photos located on the inside back cover of this book to get an indication of the general running condition of the engine.

12   Apply a small amount of anti-seize compound to the spark plug threads **(see illustration)**. Install one of the new plugs into the hole until you can no longer turn it with your fingers, then tighten it with a torque wrench (if available) or the ratchet. It is a good idea to slip a short length of rubber hose over the end of the plug to use as a tool to thread it into

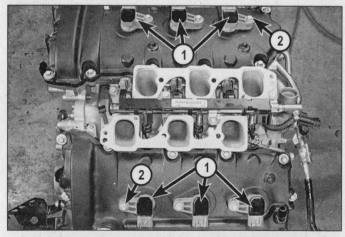

28.6 All V6 engine models are equipped with individual coils which must be removed to access the spark plugs

1   Ignition coils   *2   Ignition coil mounting bolts*

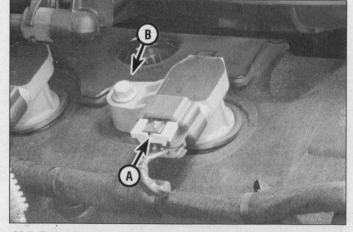

28.7 To remove the coils, depress the tab (A) and disconnect the electrical connector, remove the coil retaining bolt (B), then pull the coil straight up to remove it

28.8 On V8 models, when removing the spark plug wires, pull only on the boot and use a twisting, pulling motion

28.10 Use a ratchet and extension to remove the spark plugs (V6 models shown)

place (see illustration). The hose will grip the plug well enough to turn it, but will start to slip if the plug begins to cross-thread in the hole - this will prevent damaged threads and the accompanying repair costs.

13   Repeat the procedure for the remaining spark plugs.

14   On V6 engine models, install the ignition coil into position, tighten the retaining bolts and connect the wiring connector.

15   Repeat this procedure for the remaining spark plugs, then install the upper intake manifold (see Chapter 2A or 2B).

16   On V8 engine models, before pushing the spark plug wire onto the end of the plug, check the boot and wire for damage. Attach the plug wire to the new spark plug, again using a twisting motion on the boot until it's seated on the spark plug. Repeat this procedure for the remaining spark plugs

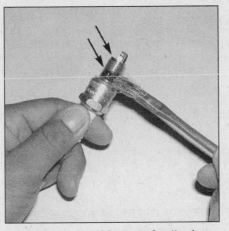

28.12a Apply a thin coat of anti-seize compound to the spark plug threads (be careful not to get any near the electrodes)

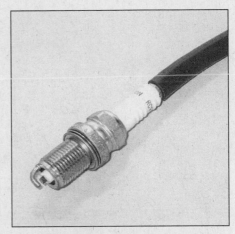

28.12b A length of snug-fitting rubber hose will save time and prevent damaged threads when installing the spark plugs

Notes

Chapter 2 Part A
3.2L V6 engine

Contents

Specifications

General

Engine type	V6
Displacement	195 cubic inches (3.2 liters)
Engine VIN code	N
RPO code	LA3
Firing order	1-2-3-4-5-6
Bore	3.45 inches (87.5 mm)
Stroke	3.47 inches (88 mm)
Compression ratio	10.0: 1
Compression pressure	See Chapter 2D
Oil pressure	See Chapter 2D

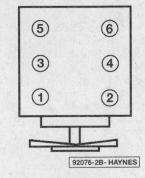

Cylinder locations

Camshafts

Lobe height	
Intake	0.394 inch (10.0 mm)
Exhaust	0.394 inch (10.0 mm)
Bearing journal diameter	1.1000 to 1.1008 inches (27.939 to 27.960 mm)
Endplay	0.001 to 0.002 inch (0.025 to 0.051 mm)

Warpage limits

Cylinder head gasket surfaces (head and block)	0.0010 inch (0.025 mm)
Exhaust manifold	0.0010 inch (0.025 mm)

Oil pump

Driven rotor-to-pump body clearance	0.0039 inch (0.10 mm)
Rotor tip clearance	0.00026 inch (0.07 mm)
Rotor-side clearance	0.0039 inch (0.10 mm)

Torque specifications

	Ft-lbs (unless otherwise indicated)	Nm

Note: *One foot-pound (ft-lb) of torque is equivalent to 12 inch-pounds (in-lbs) of torque. Torque values below approximately 15 foot-pounds are expressed in inch-pounds, because most foot-pound torque wrenches are not accurate at these smaller values.*

	Ft-lbs (unless otherwise indicated)	Nm
Camshaft bearing cap bolts* (in sequence - **see illustrations 11.27a and 11.27b**)		
Step 1	Hand tighten all bolts	
Step 2	71 in-lbs	8
Camshaft sprocket bolts*		
Step 1	37	50
Step 2	Tighten an additional 60-degrees	
Step 3	Tighten an additional 15-degrees	
Crankshaft balancer/pulley bolts	15	20
Crankshaft drive gear bolt (timing belt)		
Step 1	184	250
Step 2	Tighten an additional 45-degrees	
Step 3	Tighten an additional 15-degrees	
Cylinder head bolts* (in sequence - **see illustration 12.28a**)		
Step 1	18	25
Step 2	Tighten an additional 90-degrees	
Step 3	Tighten an additional 90-degrees	
Step 4	Tighten an additional 90-degrees	
Step 5	Tighten an additional 15-degrees	
Drivebelt tensioner bolts	26	35
Engine mount bracket-to-cylinder block bolts	44	60
Engine mount nuts	59	80
Exhaust manifolds		
Nuts	15	20
Studs	22	30
Flywheel/driveplate bolts		
Step 1	48	65
Step 2	Tighten an additional 30-degrees	
Step 3	Tighten an additional 15-degrees	
Intake plenum tuning		
Solenoid bolt	71 in-lbs	8
Valve bolt	71 in-lbs	8
Intake plenum bolts	15	20
Lower intake manifold-to-cylinder head bolts	15	20
Upper intake manifold-to-lower intake manifold bolts	15	20
Oil cooler cover bolts	15	20
Oil cooler supply and return line banjo bolts-to-cylinder block	22	30
Oil cooler supply and return nuts	22	30
Oil cooler pipe fitting-to-oil cooler	22	30
Oil filter adapter bolt	15	20
Oil pan baffle bolts	71 in-lbs	8
Oil pan-to-cylinder block bolts	133 in-lbs	15
Oil pick-up pipe bolt	71 in-lbs	8
Oil pick-up pipe bracket bolt	71 in-lbs	8
Oil pump-to-cylinder block bolts	15	20
Timing belt cover (front and rear) bolts	71 in-lbs	8
Timing belt rear cover threaded pin	89 in-lbs	10
Timing belt idler pulley	30	40
Timing belt tensioner bracket bolts	30	40
Timing belt tensioner pulley nut	15	20
Torque converter bolts*	46	63
Transmission-to-engine bolts		
M10 size bolts	37	50
M12 size bolts	55	75
Valve cover bolts	71 in-lbs	8

*Always replace with new bolts

1 General information

How to use this Chapter

This Part of Chapter 2 is devoted to repair procedures possible while the engine is still installed in the vehicle. Since these procedures are based on the assumption that the engine is installed in the vehicle, if the engine has been removed from the vehicle and mounted on a stand, some of the preliminary removal steps outlined will not apply.

Information concerning engine/transmission removal and replacement and engine overhaul, can be found in Part D of this Chapter.

Engine description

These engines are twenty-four valve, double overhead camshaft (DOHC), V6 type. They incorporate aluminum cylinder heads and a cast iron (one-piece casting) cylinder block.

The four camshafts are driven by a single timing belt, each operating six valves via direct acting hydraulic (non-adjustable) lifters. Each camshaft rotates in four bearings that are line-bored directly in the cylinder head and the (bolted-on) bearing caps. This means that the bearing caps are not available separately from the cylinder head, and must not be interchanged with caps from another engine.

These engines incorporate a stamped steel front and rear timing belt cover. The oil pump housing and oil pan are aluminum, and the crankshaft is supported by four main caps retained by a crankshaft bearing bridge to strengthen the cylinder block. All main bearing caps are replaceable and the number four main bearing is a thrust bearing.

The piston pins are full floating, held in place by locking clips in the piston pin bore. The camshaft bearing cap, cylinder head and connecting rod bolts are non-reusable torque-to-yield bolts.

When working on these engines, note that Torx-type (both male and female heads) and hexagon socket (Allen head) fasteners are widely used. A good selection of sockets, with the necessary adapters, will be required, so that these can be unscrewed without damage and, on reassembly, tightened to the torque wrench settings specified.

Lubrication system

The oil pump is driven from the front of the crankshaft. The pump forces oil through an externally mounted full-flow cartridge-type filter. From the filter, the oil is pumped into a main gallery in the cylinder block/crankcase, from where it is distributed to the crankshaft (main bearings) and cylinder head.

The connecting rod bearings are supplied with oil via internal drillings in the crankshaft. Each piston crown and connecting rod is cooled by a spray of oil.

2 Repair operations possible with the engine in the vehicle

Many major repair operations can be accomplished without removing the engine from the vehicle.

Clean the engine compartment and the exterior of the engine with some type of degreaser before any work is done. It will make the job easier and help keep dirt out of the internal areas of the engine.

Depending on the components involved, it may be helpful to remove the hood to improve access to the engine as repairs are performed (refer to Chapter 11 if necessary). Cover the fenders to prevent damage to the paint. Special pads are available, but an old bedspread or blanket will also work.

If vacuum, exhaust, oil or coolant leaks develop, indicating a need for gasket or seal replacement, the repairs can generally be made with the engine in the vehicle. The intake and exhaust manifold gaskets, oil pan gasket, crankshaft oil seals and cylinder head gasket are all accessible with the engine in place.

Exterior engine components, such as the intake and exhaust manifolds, the oil pan, the oil pump, the water pump, the starter motor, the alternator and the fuel system components can be removed for repair with the engine in place.

Since the camshaft(s) and cylinder head can be removed without pulling the engine, valve component servicing can also be accomplished with the engine in the vehicle. Replacement of the timing chain and sprockets is also possible with the engine in the vehicle.

In extreme cases caused by a lack of necessary equipment, repair or replacement of piston rings, pistons, connecting rods and rod bearings is possible with the engine in the vehicle. However, this practice is not recommended because of the cleaning and preparation work that must be done to the components involved.

3 Top Dead Center (TDC) for number 1 piston - locating

1 Top Dead Center (TDC) is the highest point in the cylinder that each piston reaches as it travels up the cylinder bore. Each piston reaches TDC on the compression stroke and again on the exhaust stroke, but TDC generally refers to piston position on the compression stroke.

2 Positioning the piston(s) at TDC is an essential part of many procedures such as timing chain/sprocket removal.

3 Before beginning this procedure, be sure to place the transmission in Neutral and apply the parking brake or block the rear wheels. Also, disable the ignition system by disconnecting the primary electrical connectors at the ignition coil packs, then remove the spark plugs (see Chapter 1).

4 In order to bring any piston to TDC, the crankshaft must be turned using one of the methods outlined below. When looking at the front of the engine, normal crankshaft rotation is clockwise.

a) *The preferred method is to turn the crankshaft with a socket and ratchet attached to the bolt threaded into the front of the crankshaft. Apply pressure on the bolt in a clockwise direction only. Never turn the bolt counterclockwise.*

b) *A remote starter switch, which may save some time, can also be used. Follow the instructions included with the switch. Once the piston is close to TDC, use a socket and ratchet as described in the previous paragraph.*

c) *If an assistant is available to turn the ignition switch to the Start position in short bursts, you can get the piston close to TDC without a remote starter switch. Make sure your assistant is out of the vehicle, away from the ignition switch, then use a socket and ratchet as described in Paragraph (a) to complete the procedure.*

5 Place your finger partially over the number one spark plug hole and rotate the crankshaft using one of the methods described above until air pressure is felt at the No 1 cylinder spark plug hole. Air pressure at the spark plug hole indicates that the cylinder has started the compression stroke. Once the compression stroke has begun, TDC for the number one cylinder is obtained when the piston reaches the top of the cylinder on the compression stroke.

6 To bring the piston to the top of the cylinder, insert a long screwdriver into the number one spark plug hole until it touches the top of the piston. **Note:** *Make sure to wrap the tip of the screwdriver with tape to avoid scratching the top of the piston and the cylinder walls.* Use the screwdriver (as a feeler gauge) to tell where the top of the piston is located in the cylinder while slowly rotating the crankshaft. As the piston rises the screwdriver will be pushed out. The point at which the screwdriver stops moving outward is TDC. **Note:** *Always hold the screwdriver upright while the engine is being rotated so that the screwdriver will not get wedged as the piston travels upward.*

7 If you go past TDC, rotate the crankshaft counterclockwise until the piston is approximately 2 inches below TDC, then slowly rotate the crankshaft clockwise again until TDC is reached.

8 After the number one piston has been positioned at TDC on the compression stroke, TDC for any of the remaining pistons can be located by repeating the procedure described above and following the firing order.

4   Valve covers - removal and installation

Removal

1   Disconnect the cable from the negative battery terminal (see Chapter 5).
2   Remove the intake manifold covers, if equipped (see Section 6).
3   Remove the individual ignition coil assemblies from the spark plugs (see Chapter 5).
4   Remove the upper intake manifold (see Section 6).
5   On the left side valve cover, disconnect the electrical connectors to the Camshaft Position (CMP) sensor, O2 sensor and knock sensor, then disconnect the vacuum lines from the rear of the cylinder head. Remove the throttle body heater hose retaining fastener from the rear engine lifting bracket and move the hose out of the way.
6   Working progressively, unscrew the valve cover retaining fasteners and withdraw the cover.
7   Discard the cover gasket and O-rings. They must be replaced whenever there disturbed. **Note:** *There are eight O-ring seals located where each retaining fasteners goes through the valve cover. Make sure you locate each of the O-rings; they can stick to the camshaft bearing caps or valve cover, or fall off when the valve cover is removed.*

Installation

8   Clean the cover and cylinder head gasket faces carefully, then install a new gasket onto the valve cover, ensuring that it is located correctly in the valve cover.
9   Lightly coat the new O-rings with clean engine oil and install the O-ring onto the valve cover.
10   Apply a thin bead of RTV sealant to the corners at the front and rear of the gasket and the valve cover.
11   Apply a 1/8-inch (3.0 mm) bead of RTV sealer to the front and rear on the flat sections of the valve cover(s).
12   Install the cover to the cylinder head, ensuring as the cover is tightened that the gasket and O-rings remains seated.
13   Working in a diagonal sequence from the center outwards, first tighten the cover bolts by hand only. Once all the bolts are hand-tight, go around once more in sequence, and tighten the bolts to the torque listed in this Chapter Specifications.
14   Reconnect the battery.
15   Run the engine and check for signs of oil leakage.

5   Intake plenum - removal and installation

Removal

1   Disconnect the air inlet hoses from the throttle body (see Chapter 4).
2   Disconnect the vent tube from the bottom of the throttle body.
3   Remove the throttle body and O-rings from the intake plenum (see Chapter 4).
4   Remove the crankcase vent adapter to the intake plenum mounting fasteners and lift the vent adapter up and off of the plenum. Set the vent adapter to the side.
5   Unclip the PCV hose retaining clip from the fuel line.
6   Remove the power steering fluid reservoir mounting bracket fasteners then set the reservoir and bracket out of the way.
7   Disconnect the electrical connector and the vacuum hose from the switching valve at the rear of the plenum.
8   Remove the throttle body heater inlet hose-to-plenum mounting fastener.
9   Disconnect the brake booster vacuum hose from the fitting.
10   Remove the Engine Control Module (ECM) bracket-to-plenum mounting fasteners and pull the bracket back.
11   Remove the intake plenum mounting fastener cover caps, then remove the intake plenum mounting fasteners.
12   Lift the intake plenum from the upper intake manifold and remove the plenum gaskets.

Installation

13   There are individual gaskets for each of the six ports of the intake plenum. Using new plenum gaskets, install the intake plenum. Tighten the mounting fasteners, working from the center out, to the torque listed in this Chapter's Specifications.
14   Installation is otherwise the reverse of removal.

6   Intake manifolds - removal and installation

Intake manifold covers

Note: *Not all engines are equipped with intake manifold covers.*

Left side

1   Using a small screwdriver, disengage the locking tab on the oil filler spout, then rotate the spout counterclockwise to remove it.
2   Disconnect the brake booster vacuum hose and the vacuum lines from the fittings.
3   Disconnect the electrical connectors for the Camshaft Position (CMP) sensor and the left knock sensor (see Chapter 6).
4   Remove the power steering fluid reservoir mounting bracket fasteners, then set the reservoir and bracket out of the way.
5   Disconnect the electrical connector and the vacuum hose from the switching valve at the rear of the plenum.
6   Lift up and remove the intake manifold cover.
7   Installation is the reverse of removal.

Right side

8   Relieve the fuel system pressure (see Chapter 4)
9   Disconnect and remove the fuel lines to the fuel rail (see Chapter 4).
10   Disconnect the quick-disconnect fitting to the EVAP hose (see Chapter 6).
11   Disconnect the wiring harness fasteners mounting the harness to the Engine Control Module (ECM) bracket.
12   Disconnect the cable from the negative battery terminal (see Chapter 5).
13   Remove the after run coolant pump-to-ECM mounting bracket fasteners and set the pump out of the way.
14   Disconnect and remove the ECM (see Chapter 6).
15   Remove the ECM bracket mounting fasteners from the intake plenum and cylinder head, then remove the bracket.
16   Lift up and remove the intake manifold cover.
17   Installation is the reverse of removal.

Upper intake manifold

Removal

18   Remove the intake manifold covers, if equipped (see Steps 1 through 17).
19   Relieve the fuel system pressure (see Chapter 4)
20   Disconnect the cable from the negative battery terminal (see Chapter 5).
21   Remove the intake plenum (see Section 5).
22   Disconnect and remove the fuel lines to the fuel rail (see Chapter 4).
23   Disconnect the quick-disconnect fitting to the EVAP hose (see Chapter 6).
24   Disconnect the fuel injector's electrical connectors from the main engine harness.
25   Disconnect the vent tube from the fuel pressure regulator. **Note:** *If the upper intake manifold is being replaced, the fuel rail must be removed from the manifold (see Chapter 4).*
26   The intake manifold is secured along the base of the manifold with 6 bolts. Remove the bolts and pull the intake manifold and fuel rail away from the engine.

Installation

27   There are individual gaskets for each of the six ports of the intake manifold. Using new manifold gaskets, install the intake manifold. Tighten the bolts in several stages, working from the center out, to the torque listed in this Chapter's Specifications.
28   Installation is otherwise the reverse of removal.

Lower intake manifold

Removal

29   Remove the upper intake manifold (see Steps 18 through 26).
30   Remove the lower intake manifold-to-cylinder head bolts and remove the manifold from the cylinder heads.

Installation

31   Using new manifold gaskets, install the intake manifold. Tighten the bolts in several stages, working from the center out, to the

torque listed in this Chapter's Specifications.
32   Installation is otherwise the reverse of removal.

---

7   Exhaust manifold - removal and installation

Warning: *Allow the engine to cool completely before beginning this procedure.*

Removal
Left side
1   Remove the air cleaner housing (see Chapter 4).
2   Remove the drivebelt (see Chapter 1).
3   Raise the vehicle and place it securely on jackstands.
4   When the engine has cooled, it will be helpful to soak the manifold retaining nuts with penetrating oil to loosen any rust.
5   Disconnect the air inlet hoses from the throttle body and remove the intake air resonator (see Chapter 4).
6   Disconnect the retainers attaching the engine wiring harness to the A/C pressure hose and the accessory mounting bracket.
7   Remove nuts attaching the power steering hoses to the A/C compressor stud.
8   Remove the power steering pump from the accessory mounting bracket, and tie the pump out of the way (see Chapter 10).
9   Disconnect the vacuum brake booster hose and wiring harness from the side of the power steering reservoir.
10   Remove the power steering fluid reservoir mounting fasteners and set the reservoir to the side.
11   Disconnect the electrical connector from the A/C compressor, then remove the A/C compressor mounting bolts, but do not disconnect the A/C lines (see Chapter 3). Tie the compressor out of the way using a suitable piece of wire; do not allow it to hang unsupported from the flexible hoses. **Warning:** *The air conditioning system is under high pressure. DO NOT loosen any fittings or remove any components until after the system has been discharged. Air conditioning refrigerant should be properly discharged into an EPA-approved container at a dealership service department or an automotive air conditioning facility. Always wear eye protection when disconnecting air conditioning system fittings.*
12   Remove the mounting fasteners attaching the accessory mounting bracket to the engine and remove the bracket from the engine.
13   Unplug the heated oxygen sensor electrical connector and harness connector.
14   Remove the catalytic converter-to-exhaust manifold mounting fasteners and lower the converter from the manifold (see Chapter 4).
15   Remove the exhaust manifold retaining nuts, then remove the exhaust manifold and the old manifold gasket. **Note:** *It may be necessary to remove the oxygen sensor from the*

manifold for easier access and removal (see Chapter 6).
16   Use a stud removal tool or two nuts tightened against each other to remove the old studs from the cylinder head if they are damaged.

Right side
17   Remove the drivebelt and drivebelt tensioner (see Chapter 1).
18   Disconnect the harness clips attaching the engine wiring harness to the Engine Control Module (ECM) bracket and set the harness out of the way.
19   Remove the after run coolant pump-to-ECM mounting bracket fasteners and set the pump out of the way.
20   Remove the starter motor (see Chapter 5).
21   Unplug the heated oxygen sensor electrical connector and harness connector.
22   Remove the catalytic converter-to-exhaust manifold mounting fasteners and lower the converter from the manifold (see Chapter 4).
23   Remove the exhaust manifold retaining nuts, then remove the exhaust manifold and the old manifold gasket. **Note:** *It may be necessary to remove the oxygen sensor from the manifold for easier access and removal (see Chapter 6).*
24   Use a stud removal tool or two nuts tightened against each other to remove the old studs from the cylinder head if they are damaged.

Inspection
25   Inspect the exhaust manifolds for cracks and any other obvious damage. If a manifold is cracked or damaged in any way, replace it.
26   Using a scraper, remove all traces of gasket material from the mating surfaces and inspect them for wear and cracks. **Caution:** *When removing gasket material from any surface, especially aluminum, be very careful not to scratch or gouge the gasket surface. Any damage to the surface may cause an exhaust leak. Gasket removal solvents are available from auto parts stores and may prove helpful.*
27   Using a straightedge and feeler gauge, inspect the exhaust manifold mating surface for warpage. Also check the exhaust manifold surface on the cylinder head. If the warpage on any surface exceeds the limits listed in this Chapter's Specifications, the exhaust manifold and/or cylinder head must be replaced or resurfaced at an automotive machine shop.

Installation
28   If any of the studs are damaged, install new exhaust studs in the cylinder head and install the manifold with a new gasket and new self-locking nuts. **Note:** *Coat the threads of the exhaust manifold studs with an anti-seize compound.* Tighten the nuts in several stages, working from the center out, to the torque listed in this Chapter's Specifications.
29   The remainder of installation is the reverse of removal. Run the engine and check for exhaust leaks.

---

8   Crankshaft pulley - removal and installation

1   Disconnect the air inlet hoses to the throttle body, then the inlet hose to the air filter housing and lift out the air inlet resonator (see Chapter 4). **Note:** *Set the resonator to the side, if the resonator must be completely removed all the electrical connectors must be disconnected.*
2   Remove the drivebelt (see Chapter 1).
3   Remove the crankshaft pulley bolts and remove the pulley.
4   Install the crankshaft pulley and mounting bolts, then tighten the bolts to the torque listed in this Chapter's Specifications.
5   Reinstall all components removed previously.

---

9   Timing belt cover, timing belt and sprockets - removal, inspection, installation and adjustment

Timing belt cover
1   Disconnect the negative battery cable (see Chapter 5).
2   Remove the intake air resonator (see Chapter 4).
3   Remove the intake plenum (see Section 5).
4   Remove the drivebelt and drivebelt tensioner (see Chapter 1).
5   Remove the water pump pulley mounting fasteners and pulley (see Chapter 3).
6   Remove the power steering pump mounting fasteners, then remove the power steering pump from the bracket, and place the pump out of the way.
7   Remove the timing belt cover mounting fasteners and remove the cover from the engine.
8   Installation is the reverse of removal.

Timing belt and sprockets
Warning: *Wait until the engine is completely cool before beginning this procedure.*
Caution: *Do not rotate the crankshaft or camshafts separately during this procedure with the timing belt removed as damage to the valves may occur.*
Note: *Several special tools are required to complete these procedures, so read through the entire Section and obtain the special tools before beginning work.*

Removal
Refer to illustration 9.12
Caution: *The timing system is complex, and severe engine damage will occur if you make any mistakes. Do not attempt this procedure unless you are highly experienced with this type of repair. If you are at all unsure of your abilities, be sure to consult an expert. Double-check all your work and be sure everything is correct before you attempt to start the engine.*
9   Remove the timing belt cover (see Steps 1 through 7).

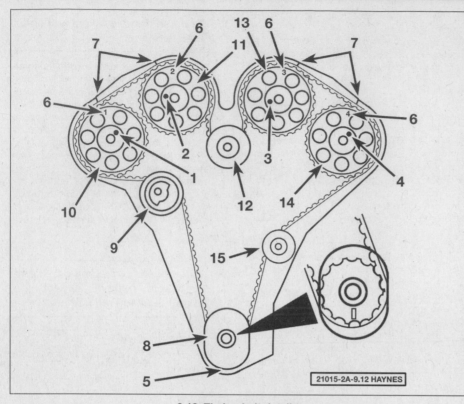

9.12 Timing belt details

1   Exhaust camshaft pin and sprocket numbered mark
2   Intake camshaft pin and sprocket numbered mark
3   Intake camshaft pin and sprocket numbered mark
4   Exhaust camshaft pin and sprocket numbered mark
5   Crankshaft timing mark
6   Camshaft sprocket reference marks
7   Rear timing belt cover notches
8   Crankshaft sprocket

9   Timing belt tensioner
10 Exhaust camshaft sprocket (right cylinder bank)
11 Intake camshaft sprocket (right cylinder bank)
12 Upper idler pulley (with eccentric)
13 Intake camshaft sprocket (left cylinder bank)
14 Exhaust camshaft sprocket (left cylinder bank)
15 Lower idler pulley

10   Remove the crankshaft pulley (see Section 8).

11   Rotate the crankshaft clockwise until the #1 cylinder is at Top Dead Center (TDC) on the compression stroke (see Section 3).

12   The timing marks on the camshaft gears should line up with the notches on the rear timing belt cover, and the mark on the crankshaft sprocket should line up with the mark on the oil pump housing **(see illustration)**. **Note:** *If all marks are aligned, this is TDC for cylinder number one; if the marks are not aligned, rotate the engine 180-degrees.*

13   Install special tool J 42069-10 to prevent the crankshaft from being turned once the engine is at TDC. To install the special tool, rotate the crankshaft counterclockwise 60-degrees and align the mark on the crankshaft sprocket with the index mark on the oil pump cover. Install tool J 42069-10 to the crankshaft sprocket and tighten the mounting fastener to the sprocket. Rotate the crankshaft clockwise until the lever of the special tool contacts the

water pump pulley flange, and lock the tool to the water pump flange.

14   Insert special tool J 42069-1 and J 42069-2 between the camshaft gears on each cylinder head. **Note***: If either special tool does not fit into the teeth of the camshaft gears, it may be necessary to loosen the upper idler pulley mounting fastener and turn the eccentric or rotate the camshaft gears slightly until the tool can be inserted.*

15   Loosen the nut on the timing belt tensioner, then the upper idler pulley mounting fastener.

16   Remove the lower idler pulley mounting fastener, then the pulley and spacer.

17   Remove special tool J 42069-10 from the water pump pulley flange and the crankshaft sprocket (see Step 13, if necessary).

18   Remove the timing belt from the engine, taking care to avoid twisting or kinking it excessively. **Caution:** *Do not rotate the crankshaft or camshafts separately or remove special tools J 42069-1 and J 42069-2 with the*

timing belt removed, as damage to the valves may occur.

19   To remove the camshaft sprocket, rotate the crankshaft 60-degrees counterclockwise (to prevent the valves from possibly hitting the pistons), then remove the camshaft sprocket bolts. Remove the special tool in between the sprockets that you're removing, then remove the sprockets from the end of the camshafts. **Note:** *When the engine is rotated 60-degrees BTDC, the mark on the crankshaft sprocket will line up with the index mark on the oil pump cover. Always replace the camshaft sprocket bolts with new ones.*

Inspection

Refer to illustration 9.21

Caution: *Do not bend, twist or turn the timing belt inside out. Do not allow it to come in contact with oil, coolant or fuel.*

20   Spin the timing belt tensioner pulley and the upper and lower idler pulleys, and check the bearings for smooth operation and excessive play. Also inspect the timing belt sprockets for any obvious damage. Replace all worn parts as necessary. **Note:** *The tensioner cannot be separated from the bracket and is replaced as an assembly.*

21   Examine the belt for evidence of contamination by coolant or lubricant. If this is the case, find the source of the contamination before progressing any further. Check the belt for signs of wear or damage, particularly around the leading edges of the belt teeth **(see illustration)**. The timing belt has index marks and directional arrows printed on the belt to help in installation. If these marks are worn, replace the belt. **Caution:** *If the belt appears to be in good condition and can be re-used, it is essential that it is reinstalled the same way around, otherwise accelerated wear will result, leading to premature failure.*

22   Replace the belt if its condition is in doubt; the cost of belt replacement is negligible compared with potential cost of the engine repairs, should the belt fail in service. Similarly, if the belt is known to have covered more than 60,000 miles, it is prudent to replace it regardless of condition, as a precautionary measure.

Installation

Refer to illustrations 9.31 and 9.32

Caution: *Before starting the engine, carefully rotate the crankshaft by hand through at least two full revolutions (use a socket and breaker bar on the crankshaft pulley center bolt). If you feel any resistance, STOP! There is something wrong - most likely, valves are contacting the pistons. You must find the problem before proceeding. Check your work and see if any updated repair information is available.*

23   Install the camshaft sprockets to the correct camshafts **(see illustration 9.12)**, making sure the camshaft pins are in the same numbered slot on the sprocket as they were removed from.

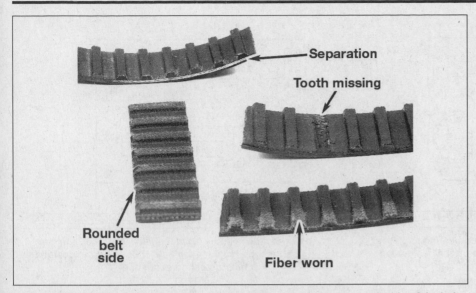

9.21 Check the timing belt for cracked and missing teeth - wear on one side of the belt indicates sprocket misalignment problems

Separation

Tooth missing

Rounded belt side

Fiber worn

24   Install new camshaft sprocket bolts and tighten the bolts to the torque listed in this Chapter's Specifications.

25   Install the tensioner and bracket assembly and upper idler pulley and tighten the fasteners to the torque listed in this Chapter's Specifications, if removed.

26   Make sure the camshaft sprockets marks are still in alignment with the marks on the rear timing belt cover **(see illustration 9.12)**.

27   Loop the timing belt under the crankshaft sprocket and align the parallel marks on the timing belt with the oil pump housing and crankshaft sprocket marks. **Caution:** *Observe the direction of rotation markings on the belt.*

28   Route the belt clockwise while aligning the marks on the belt with the marks on the rear timing belt cover and the sprockets, in this order: around the tensioner pulley, the right side camshaft sprockets, the upper idler pulley, the left side camshaft sprockets. Ensure the belt teeth seat correctly on the sprockets,

especially at the crankshaft sprocket. **Note:** *Slight adjustments to the position of the camshaft sprocket may be necessary to achieve this.*

29   Carefully rotate the crankshaft counterclockwise 3-degrees BTDC, then install the lower idler pulley with spacer and tighten the fastener to the torque listed in this Chapter's Specifications.

30   Rotate the engine back to TDC and verify the marks on the crankshaft sprocket and oil pump housing are in between the parallel marks on the timing belt.

31   Using a wrench on the upper idler pulley eccentric, apply tension to the timing belt using the pulley, by rotating the eccentric until the high point of the eccentric is at the 9 o'clock position **(see illustration)**. Hold the eccentric bolt in this position and temporarily tighten the tensioner pulley fastener securely.

32   Set the timing belt tension, using a Allen wrench to turn the timing belt tensioner eccen-

tric counterclockwise to a full stop, then turn the eccentric back until the reference mark (A) is 0.03 inches (1 mm) over the face **(see illustration)**. Temporarily tighten the timing belt tensioner locking nut securely.

33   Check to make sure all the marks on the belt, sprockets and rear timing cover are aligned, then remove special tools J 42069-1 and J 42069-2 from the camshaft gears.

34   Rotate the crankshaft two complete revolutions, bringing it back to TDC on the compression stroke. Rotate the crankshaft counterclockwise 60-degrees and align the mark on the crankshaft sprocket with the index mark on the oil pump cover. Install special tool J 42069-10 to the crankshaft sprocket and tighten the mounting fastener to the sprocket. Rotate the crankshaft clockwise until the lever of the special tool contacts the water pump pulley flange, and lock the tool to the water pump flange.

35   Install special tool J 42069-20 to the No.3 (left side intake) and No.4 (left side exhaust) camshaft sprockets, then install another special tool J 42069-20 to the No.1 (right side exhaust) and No.2 (right side intake) camshaft sprockets. **Note:** *The special tool kit J 42069 comes with two J 42069-20 special tools.*

36   Check that the marks on the crankshaft sprocket and oil pump housing are aligned, then check that the marks on the camshaft sprockets are aligned with the notches on the rear timing belt cover and the J 42069-20 tools; they must match exactly. **Note:** *The index marks on the timing belt will no longer be aligned with the marks on the camshaft sprockets.*

37   If the marks on all the sprockets are aligned and do not need any adjustment, loosen the timing belt tensioner eccentric lock nut. If the any of the marks are not matched exactly, the belt must be adjusted (see Steps 42 through 51).

38   If the marks are aligned, use an Allan wrench to turn the eccentric counterclockwise to a full stop, then back until the reference mark (A) is 0.118 to 0.157-inches (3 to 4 mm) above the datum line (on a new belt),

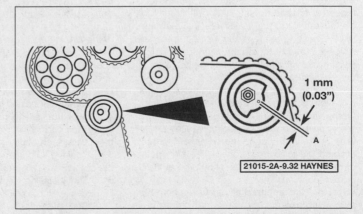

1 mm
(0.03")

A

21015-2A-9.31 HAYNES

21015-2A-9.32 HAYNES

9.31 Using a large wrench on the hex portion of the upper idler pulley eccentric, rotate the eccentric to the 9 o'clock position

9.32 Using an Allen wrench, turn the timing belt tensioner eccentric counterclockwise to a full stop, then turn the eccentric back until the reference mark (A) is 0.03 inches (1 mm) over the face

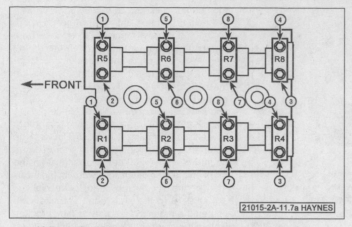

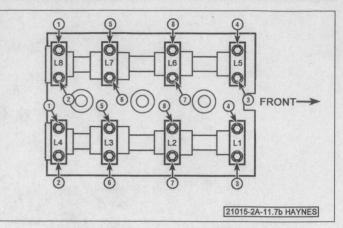

11.7a Left side cylinder head, camshaft and bearing cap loosening sequence - loosen each pair of bolts on the designated bearing cap in sequence

11.7b Right side cylinder head, camshaft and bearing cap loosening sequence - loosen each pair of bolts on the designated bearing cap in sequence

or aligned with the datum line (on a used belt) **(see illustration 9.32)**. Tighten the tensioner locking nut to the torque listed in this Chapter's Specifications.

39   Using a wrench on the upper idler pulley eccentric, hold the eccentric bolt in position and tighten the upper idler pulley fastener to the torque listed in this Chapter's Specifications.

40   Install the timing belt cover.

41   The remainder of installation is the reverse of removal.

Adjustment

Caution: *The following steps are meant to be used in conjunction with the timing belt removal and installation procedure (Steps 9 through 41), and should not be used as a separate repair procedure.*

Note: *It is normal for this procedure to take several tries before the timing belt is installed and adjusted correctly.*

42   Install the two J 42069-20 special tools to the camshaft sprockets (see Step 35).

43   Check the marks on the camshaft sprockets align with the marks on the tools.

44   If the marks on the camshaft sprockets are misaligned to the left of the special tool, loosen the upper idler pulley bolt, then turn the eccentric on the upper idler pulley counterclockwise until the marks on the camshaft sprockets and the tools are aligned. The high point of the idler pulley eccentric should be at the 9 o'clock position.

45   If the marks on camshaft sprockets are misaligned to the right of the special tool, loosen the upper idler pulley bolt, then turn the eccentric on the upper idler pulley clockwise until the marks on the camshaft sprockets and the tools are aligned. The high point of the idler pulley eccentric should be at the 9 o'clock position.

46   Hold the upper idler pulley eccentric in place with a wrench, to prevent it from moving, tighten the upper idler pulley fastener to the torque listed in this Chapter's Specifications, then remove the tool.

47   Rotate the crankshaft clockwise two

complete revolutions, stopping at the 60-degrees BTDC index mark on the oil pump housing, and install special tool J 42069-10 (see Step 13).

48   The marks on the camshaft sprockets should be aligned with the notches on the rear timing belt cover. If they're not aligned, rotate the engine 180-degrees and check again.

49   Install the J 42069-20 tools to the camshaft sprockets and verify that the marks on the camshaft sprockets are aligned with the marks on the tools. If the marks are not aligned, repeat Step 44 or 45.

50   If the camshaft sprockets are properly aligned, adjust the timing belt tensioner as described in Step 38.

51   The remainder of installation is the reverse of removal.

10   Crankshaft front oil seal - replacement

1   Remove the timing belt and crankshaft drive gear (see Section 9).

2   Use a screwdriver or hook tool to carefully pry out the seal. **Note:** *Be careful not to damage the oil pump cover bore where the seal is seated or the nose and sealing surface of the crankshaft.*

3   Another procedure for removing the seal is to drill a small hole on each side of the seal and place a self-tapping screw in each hole. Use these screws as a means of pulling the seal out without having to pry on it.

4   Wipe the sealing surfaces in the oil pump cover and on the crankshaft. Clean and coat them with clean engine oil.

5   Coat the lip of the seal (where it contacts the crankshaft) with clean engine oil.

6   Start installing the new seal by pressing it into the oil pump cover.

7   Once started, use a seal driver or a suitable socket of the correct size to carefully drive the seal squarely into place.

8   The seal should be flush with the engine cover and remain square when installed.

9   Install the crankshaft drive gear and timing belt (see Section 9).

11   Camshafts and lifters - removal, inspection and installation

Removal

Refer to illustrations 11.7a and 11.7b

1   Disconnect the cable from the negative battery terminal (see Chapter 5).

2   Rotate the engine until the #1 cylinder is at Top Dead Center (TDC) on the compression stroke (see Section 3).

3   Remove the valve cover(s) (see Section 4).

4   Remove the timing belt (see Section 9).

5   Rotate the crankshaft 60-degrees counterclockwise, to prevent the valves from possibly hitting the pistons, then remove the camshaft sprocket bolts and sprockets. **Note:** *When the engine is rotated 60-degrees BTDC, the mark on the crankshaft sprocket will line up with the index mark on the oil pump cover.*

6   All the camshaft bearing caps have a double-digit identifying number etched on them. The camshaft bearing caps are numbered from the front of the engine (timing belt) to the rear. On the left cylinder head side, the exhaust camshaft's bearing caps are numbered in sequence from R1 (bottom) front to R4 (bottom) rear; the intake's are numbered from R5 (top) front to R8 (top) rear cap. On the right cylinder head side, the exhaust camshaft's bearing caps are numbered in sequence from L1 (bottom) front to L4 (bottom) rear; the intake's are numbered from L5 (top) front to L8 (top) rear cap. Each cap is to be installed so that its numbered side faces the same direction. If no marks are present, or they are hard to see, make your own - the bearing caps must be reinstalled in their original positions.

7   Working in the sequence shown, loosen the camshaft bearing cap bolts progressively by half a turn at a time **(see illustrations)**. Work only as described, to gradually

11.11 Measure the lifter outside diameter at several points

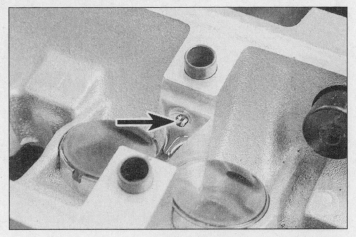

11.14 Check that the camshaft bearing oilways are not blocked with debris

and evenly release the pressure of the valve springs on the caps.

8   Withdraw the caps, noting their markings and the presence of the locating dowels, then remove the camshafts and front oil seals. The intake camshafts are stamped with the letter "G" and the exhaust camshafts are stamped with the letter "J." All stampings are next to the first bearing journal.

9   Obtain twelve small, clean containers (for each cylinder head), and number them 1 to 12. Using a rubber suction tool (such as a valve-lapping tool), withdraw each lifter in turn and place them in the containers. Do not interchange the lifters.

Inspection

Refer to illustrations 11.11 and 11.14

10   With the camshafts and lifters removed, check each for signs of obvious wear (scoring, pitting, etc) and for roundness and replace if necessary.

11   Measure the outside diameter of each lifter - take measurements at the top and bottom of each lifter, then a second set at right-angles to the first; if any measurement is significantly different from the others, the lifter is tapered or oval (as applicable) and must be replaced **(see illustration)**. If the necessary equipment is available, measure the inside diameter of the corresponding cylinder head bore. No manufacturer's specifications were available at the time of writing; if the lifters or the cylinder head bores are excessively worn, new lifters and/or a new cylinder head may be required.

12   If the engine's valve components have sounded noisy, the camshaft lobes or valve lifters may be worn and need to be replaced.

13   Visually examine the camshaft lobes for score marks, pitting, galling (wear due to rubbing) and evidence of overheating (blue, discolored areas). Look for flaking away of the hardened surface layer of each lobe. If any

such signs are evident, replace the component concerned.

14   Examine the camshaft bearing journals and the cylinder head bearing surfaces for signs of obvious wear or pitting. If any such signs are evident, consult an automotive machine shop for advice. Also check that the bearing oilways in the cylinder head are clear **(see illustration)**.

15   Using a micrometer, measure the diameter of each journal at several points. If the diameter of any one journal is less than the specified value, replace the camshaft.

16   To check the bearing journal running clearance, remove the lifters, use a suitable solvent and a clean lint-free rag to carefully clean all bearing surfaces, then install the camshafts and bearing caps with a strand of Plastigage across each journal. Tighten the bearing cap bolts in the proper sequence **(see illustrations 11.27a or 11.27b)** to the specified torque setting (do not rotate the camshafts), then remove the bearing caps and use the scale provided to measure the width of the compressed strands. Scrape off the Plastigage with your fingernail or the edge of a credit card - don't scratch or nick the journals or bearing caps.

17   If the running clearance of any bearing is found to be worn to beyond the specified service limits, install a new camshaft and repeat the check; if the clearance is still excessive, the cylinder head must be replaced.

18   To check camshaft endplay, remove the lifters, clean the bearing surfaces carefully and install the camshafts and bearing caps. Tighten the bearing cap bolts to the specified torque wrench setting, then measure the endplay using a dial indicator mounted on the cylinder head so that its tip bears on the camshaft right-hand end.

19   Tap the camshaft fully towards the gauge, zero the gauge, then tap the camshaft fully away from the gauge and note the gauge reading. If the endplay measured is found to be at or beyond the specified service limit,

install a new camshaft and repeat the check; if the clearance is still excessive, the cylinder head must be replaced.

Installation

Refer to illustrations 11.27a and 11.27b

Note: *The intake camshaft is stamped with the letter "G" and the exhaust camshaft is stamped with the letter "J." All stampings are next to the first bearing journal.*

20   Confirm that the crankshaft is still positioned at 60-degrees BTDC.

21   Liberally oil the cylinder head lifter bores and the lifters. Carefully install the lifters to the cylinder head, ensuring that each lifter is replaced to its original bore.

22   Liberally oil the camshaft bearing surfaces in the cylinder head, taking care not to get any on the camshaft cap mating surface.

23   Ensuring that each camshaft is in its original location, install the camshafts. On the left side cylinder head place the pin on the exhaust camshaft at the 1 o'clock position and the pin on the intake camshaft at the 8 o'clock position. On the right side cylinder head place the pin on the exhaust camshaft at the 11 o'clock position and the pin on the intake camshaft at the 12 o'clock position. **Note:** *When the camshafts are in these positions the spring pressure against the camshafts are at the lowest point.*

24   Apply silicone sealer or equivalent to the forward edge of the front bearing caps (closest to the camshaft seals) and the cylinder head. **Caution:** *Make sure no sealer gets into the oil journals.*

25   Check that all mating surfaces are completely clean, unmarked and free from oil.

26   Apply a little oil to the camshaft journals and lobes, then install each of the camshaft bearing caps to its previously-noted position, so that its numbered side faces outwards **(see illustrations 11.7a or 11.7b)**.

27   Ensure that each cap is kept square to the cylinder head as it is tightened down.

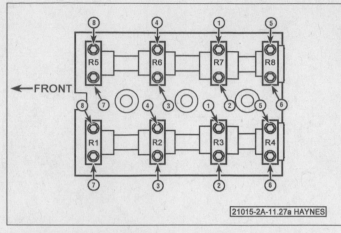

11.27a Left side cylinder head, camshafts and bearing caps tightening sequence - tighten each pair of bolts on the designated bearing cap in sequence

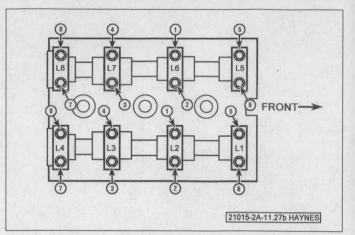

11.27b Right side cylinder head, camshafts and bearing caps tightening sequence - tighten each pair of bolts on the designated bearing cap in sequence

Working in the sequence shown **(see illustrations)**, tighten the camshaft bearing cap bolts slowly and by one turn at a time, until each cap touches the cylinder head. This is the Step 1 torque.

28   Using the same sequence **(see illustrations 11.27a and 11.27b)**, tighten the bearing cap bolts to the Step 2 torque listed in this Chapter's Specifications.

29   Coat the lip of the camshaft seal (where it contacts the camshaft) with clean engine oil.

30   Start installing the new seal by pressing it into the end of the bearing cap.

31   Once started, use a seal driver or a suitable socket of the correct size to carefully drive the seal squarely into place.

32   The seal should be flush with the bearing cap and remain square when installed.

33   Install the camshaft sprockets to the correct camshafts **(see illustration 9.12)**, making sure the camshaft pin is in the same numbered slot on the sprocket it was removed from.

34   Install a new camshaft sprocket bolt and tighten the bolt to the torque listed in this Chapter's Specifications.

35   The remainder of the reassembly procedure, including replacement of the timing belt, is as described in Section 9.

5   Remove the intake plenum (see Section 5) and the intake manifolds (see Section 6).

6   Disconnect the electrical connector to the Engine Coolant Temperature (ECT) sensor.

7   Remove the hose clamps for the throttle body heater and bypass hoses, then disconnect the hoses from the engine crossover pipe.

8   Remove the coolant crossover pipe banjo bolts and upper seals, then remove the crossover pipe and lower seals from the cylinder heads.

9   Disconnect the engine wiring harness from the bracket at the rear of the cylinder head.

10   Remove the timing belt cover and timing belt (see Section 9). Remove the upper two mounting bolts that attach the rear half of the timing belt to the cylinder head.

11   Remove the exhaust camshaft only, unless the cylinder head is going to be replaced (see Section 11).

12   Remove the exhaust manifold (see Section 7).

13   Remove the radiator hose clamp and hose from the coolant outlet pipe, then remove the outlet pipe-to-front engine lift bracket fastener, and remove the outlet pipe (see Chapter 3, if necessary). **Note:** *Always replace the*

O-ring at the end of the coolant outlet pipe.

14   Loosen the eight cylinder head bolts in sequence **(see illustration)**, progressively and by half a turn at a time. **Caution:** *The head bolts are torque-to-yield bolts that must be replaced with new ones on installation.*

15   Lift the cylinder head from the engine compartment.

16   If the head is stuck, be careful how you choose to free it. Remember that the cylinder head is made of aluminum alloy, which is easily damaged. Striking the head with tools carries the risk of damage, and the head is located on two dowels, so its movement will be limited. Do not, under any circumstances, pry the head between the mating surfaces, as this will certainly damage the sealing surfaces for the gasket, leading to leaks. Try rocking the head free to break the seal, taking care not to damage any of the surrounding components.

17   Once the head has been removed, remove and discard the gasket. Check for the presence of locating dowels in the cylinder block and cylinder head. If dowels are present, make sure they are returned to their original locations after cleaning the components.

12   Cylinder heads - removal and installation

Warning: *Wait until the engine is completely cool before beginning this procedure.*

Removal

Refer to illustration 12.14

1   Relieve the fuel pressure (see Chapter 4).

2   Disconnect the cable from the negative battery terminal (see Chapter 5).

3   Drain the cooling system (see Chapter 1).

4   Remove the valve cover(s) (see Section 4).

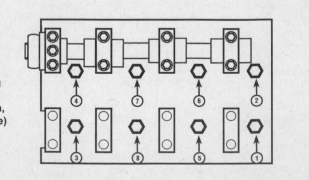

12.14 Cylinder head bolt loosening sequence (left side cylinder head shown, right side is the same)

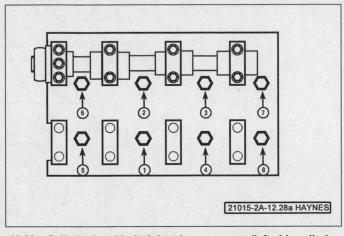

12.28a Cylinder head bolt tightening sequence (left side cylinder head shown, right side is the same)

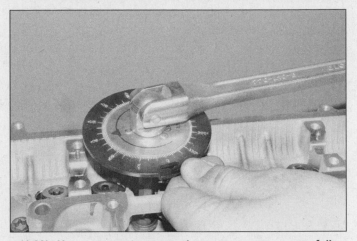

12.28b You can use a torque angle gauge, or you can carefully note the starting and stopping points of the wrench handle

Inspection

18   The mating faces of the cylinder head and cylinder block must be perfectly clean before replacing the head. Use spray-on gasket remover and a hard plastic or wood scraper to remove all traces of gasket and carbon.

19   Take particular care during the cleaning operations, as aluminum alloy is easily damaged. Also, make sure that the carbon is not allowed to enter the oil and water passages - this is particularly important for the lubrication system, as carbon could block the oil supply to the engine's components.

20   To prevent carbon entering the gap between the pistons and bores, smear a little grease in the gap. After cleaning each piston, use a small brush to remove all traces of grease and carbon from the gap, then wipe away the remainder with a clean rag.

21   Check the mating surfaces of the cylinder block and the cylinder head for nicks, deep scratches and other damage. Also check the cylinder head gasket surface and the cylinder block gasket surface with a precision straight-edge and feeler gauges. If either surface exceeds the warpage limit listed in this Chapter's Specifications, the manufacturer states that the component out of specification must be replaced. If the gasket mating surface of your cylinder head or block is out of specification or is severely nicked or scratched, you may want to consult with an automotive machine shop for advice.

Installation

Refer to illustrations 12.28a and 12.28b

22   Wipe clean the mating surfaces of the cylinder head and cylinder block. If equipped, install the alignment dowels into their original locations.

23   The cylinder head bolt holes must be free from oil or water. This is most important, because a hydraulic lock in a cylinder head bolt hole can cause a fracture of the block casting when the bolt is tightened. Note the

location of the cylinder head alignment dowels in the block.

24   Position a new gasket on the cylinder block surface, so that the "TOP" mark is facing up.

25   The cylinder head is a heavy and awkward assembly to install. It is helpful to make up a pair of guide studs; you can use two of the old cylinder head bolts with their heads cut off, and a screwdriver slot cut in one end. Screw these guide studs, screwdriver slot upwards to permit removal, into the bolt holes at diagonally-opposite corners of the cylinder block surface; ensure that approximately 2-1/2 inches of stud protrudes above the gasket.

26   Install the cylinder head, sliding it down the guide studs (if used) and locating it on the dowels. Unscrew the guide studs (if used) when the head is in place.

27   Do not coat the threads with engine oil unless the new bolt manufacturer requires it. Install the new cylinder head bolts and screw them in by hand only until finger-tight. **Note:** *New cylinder head bolts must be used.*

28   Working progressively and in the sequence shown **(see illustration)**, first tighten all the bolts to the specified Step 1 torque setting listed in this Chapter's Specifications. There are five tightening stages; the final four use the angle torque method **(see illustration)**.

29   Replacement of the other components removed is a reversal of removal.

30   Change the engine oil and filter and refill the cooling system (see Chapter 1).

---

13   Oil pan - removal and installation

Removal

1   Raise the vehicle and support it securely on jackstands.

2   Drain the engine oil (see Chapter 1), then clean and install the engine oil drain plug, tightening it to the torque listed in the

Chapter 1 Specifications. Remove and discard the oil filter, so that it can be replaced with the oil.

3   Remove the engine lower splash shield.

4   Support the engine and transmission from above with an engine support fixture (see Chapter 2D).

5   With the engine and transmission supported, remove the front subframe (see Chapter 10).

6   Remove the transmission cooler line bracket fastener and remove the bracket from the cylinder block.

7   Remove the three lower transmission-to-engine mounting bolts.

8   Progressively unscrew the oil pan retaining bolts in the reverse of the tightening sequence **(see illustration 13.12)**. Use a rubber mallet to loosen the oil pan seal, then lower the oil pan. Unfortunately, the use of sealant can make removal of the oil pan more difficult. Be careful when prying between the mating surfaces, otherwise they will be damaged, resulting in leaks when finished. With care, a putty knife can be used to cut through the sealant.

Installation

Refer to illustration 13.12

9   Thoroughly clean and degrease the mating surfaces of the lower engine block/crankcase and oil pan, removing all traces of sealant, then use a clean rag to wipe out the oil pan.

10   Apply a 1/8-inch wide bead of sealant to the oil pan flange so that the bead is approximately 3/16-inch from the outside edge of the flange. Make sure the bead is around the inside edge of the bolt holes. Also apply sealant to the front flange of the oil pan. **Note:** *The oil pan must be installed within 4 minutes of applying the sealant.*

11   Install the oil pan and press the pan towards the rear, then install the oil pan bolts, only tightening them finger tight at this time.

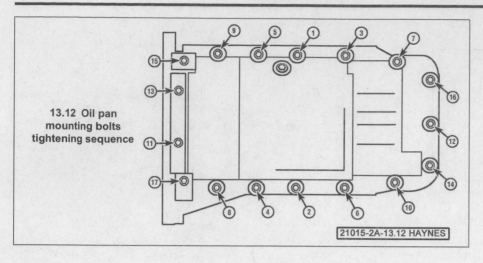

13.12 Oil pan mounting bolts tightening sequence

21015-2A-13.12 HAYNES

12 Tighten the oil pan-to-engine block bolts, a little at a time, working from the center outwards in a criss-cross pattern **(see illustration)**, to the torque listed in this Chapter's Specifications.

13 Install the three transmission-to-engine fasteners and tighten them to the torque listed in this Chapter's Specifications.

14 Install the subframe (see Chapter 10).

15 Lower the vehicle to the ground. Before refilling the engine with oil, wait at least 1 hour for the sealant to cure, or whatever time is indicated by the sealant manufacturer. Trim off the excess sealant with a sharp knife. Install a new oil filter (see Chapter 1).

---

14 Oil pump - removal, inspection and installation

1 Drain the engine oil and remove the oil filter (see Chapter 1).

2 Remove the timing belt and the crankshaft drive gear (see Section 9).

3 Remove the oil pan (see Section 13).

4 Unscrew and remove the oil pressure sending unit (see Chapter 2D).

5 Remove the oil pick-up tube mounting fasteners and the pick-up tube. Remove and replace the O-ring from the groove in the oil pick-up tube.

6 Remove the alternator lower mounting bolt, loosen the upper mounting bolt and pivot the alternator out of the way. Tighten the upper mounting bolt to hold the alternator out of the way. **Note:** *If more space is needed, remove the alternator (see Chapter 5).*

7 Remove the oil pump-to-engine mounting bolts and detach the oil pump from the engine. You may have to pry carefully between the front main bearing cap and the pump body with a screwdriver.

8 Remove the relief valve plug, then slide out the spring, O-ring and the relief valve.

9 Remove the oil pump cover bolts and remove the oil pump cover. Remove the oil pump drive rotor and driven rotor.

Inspection

10 Clean all components with solvent, then inspect them for wear and damage. Check that the oiled relief valve falls easily through its bore without sticking.

11 Check the oil pressure relief valve sliding surface and valve spring. If either the spring or the valve is damaged, they must be replaced as a set.

12 Check the clearance of the following components with a feeler gauge and compare the measurements to this Chapter's Specifications:

a) *Driven rotor-to-oil pump body*
b) *Rotor side clearance*
c) *Rotor tip clearance*

13 Replace any worn parts or replace the entire oil pump assembly.

Installation

14 Pry the old crankshaft seal out of the timing chain cover with a screwdriver.

15 Apply multi-purpose grease or engine oil to the outer edge of the new crank seal and carefully drive it into place with a deep socket and a hammer. Apply multi-purpose grease or engine oil to the seal lip.

16 Apply a coat of petroleum jelly to the pump drive and driven rotors, then place the two rotors into position in the timing chain cover. Make sure that the pump marks (dimples) are facing out, toward the pump cover and away from the timing chain cover.

17 Pack the pump cavity with petroleum jelly (this will help to prime the pump) and install the cover. Tighten the cover bolts to the torque listed in this Chapter's Specifications.

18 Lubricate the oil pressure relief valve with clean engine oil and insert the valve, then the spring, into the pump cover and install the plug.

19 Installation is the reverse of removal, noting the following points:

a) *Replace all gaskets with new ones.*
b) *Tighten the oil pump mounting bolts to the torque listed in this Chapter's Specifications in a criss-cross pattern.*

c) *After installing the oil pan, install a new oil filter and refill the crankcase with oil (see Chapter 1).*
d) *Check for any oil warning lights in the instrument panel after the vehicle has been started and idling.*

---

15 Flywheel/driveplate - removal, inspection and installation

Removal

1 Remove the transmission as described in Chapter 7A or 7B. Now is a good time to check components such as oil seals and replace them if necessary.

2 On manual transmission models, remove the clutch as described in Chapter 8. Now is a good time to check or replace the clutch components and release bearing.

3 Use a center-punch or paint to make alignment marks on the flywheel and crankshaft to make replacement easier - the bolt holes are slightly offset, and will only line up one way, but making a mark eliminates the guesswork (and the flywheel is heavy).

4 Hold the flywheel/driveplate stationary and unscrew the bolts. To prevent the flywheel/driveplate from turning, insert one of the transmission mounting bolts into the cylinder block and have an assistant engage a wide-bladed screwdriver with the starter ring gear teeth while the flywheel or driveplate bolts are loosened.

5 Loosen and remove each bolt in turn and ensure that new replacements are obtained for reassembly. These bolts are subjected to severe stresses and must be replaced, regardless of their apparent condition, whenever they are removed.

6 Remove the retainer and flywheel, remembering that it is very heavy - do not drop it. The driveplate used with automatic transmissions is much lighter.

Inspection

7 Clean the flywheel to remove grease and oil. Inspect the surface for cracks, rivet grooves, burned areas and score marks. Light scoring can be removed with emery cloth. Check for cracked and broken ring gear teeth. Lay the flywheel on a flat surface and use a straight-edge to check for warpage.

8 Clean and inspect the mating surfaces of the flywheel and the crankshaft. If the oil seal is leaking, replace it (see Section 16) before replacing the flywheel. If the engine has high mileage, it may be worth installing a new seal as a matter of course, given the amount of work needed to access it.

9 While the flywheel is removed, carefully clean its inboard face, particularly the recesses that serve as the reference points for the crankshaft speed/position sensor. Clean the sensor's tip and check that the sensor is securely fastened.

Installation

10   Install the flywheel/driveplate on the crankshaft so that all bolt holes align - it will fit only one way - check this using the marks made on removal. Install the retainer and new bolts, tightening them by hand.

11   Lock the flywheel by the method used on disassembly. Working in a diagonal sequence to tighten them evenly and increasing to the final amount in two or three stages, tighten the new bolts to the torque listed in this Chapter's Specifications.

12   The remainder of installation is the reverse of the removal procedure

16   Rear main oil seal - replacement

1   The one-piece rear main oil seal is pressed into the rear of the cylinder block. Remove the transmission (see Chapter 7A or 7B) and the flywheel/driveplate (see Section 15).

2   Use a screwdriver or hook tool to carefully pry out the seal. **Note:** *Be careful not to damage the cylinder block and main bearing bore where the seal is seated or the nose and sealing surface of the crankshaft.*

3   Another procedure for removing the seal is to drill a small hole on each side of the seal and place a self-tapping screw in each hole. Use these screws as a means of pulling the seal out without having to pry on it.

4   Wipe the sealing surfaces in the engine block and main bearing and on the crankshaft.

Clean and coat them with clean engine oil.

5   Coat the lip of the seal (where it contacts the crankshaft) with clean engine oil.

6   Start installing the new seal by pressing it into the cylinder block.

7   Once started, use a seal driver or a suitable socket of the correct size to carefully drive the seal squarely into place.

8   The seal should be flush with the cylinder block and remain square when installed.

9   Install the flywheel/driveplate (see Section 15).

10   The remainder of installation is the reverse of removal.

17   Engine mounts - check and replacement

1   Engine mounts seldom require attention, but broken or deteriorated mounts should be replaced immediately or the added strain placed on the driveline components may cause damage or wear.

Check

2   During the check, the engine must be raised slightly to remove the weight from the mounts.

3   Raise the vehicle and support it securely on jackstands, then position a jack under the engine oil pan. Place a large wood block between the jack head and the oil pan to prevent oil pan damage, then carefully raise the

engine just enough to take the weight off the mounts. **Warning:** *DO NOT place any part of your body under the engine when it's supported only by a jack!*

4   Check the mounts to see if the rubber is cracked, hardened, separated from the bushing in the center of the mount or leaking antifreeze fluid.

5   Check for relative movement between the mount and the engine or chassis. Use a large screwdriver or prybar to attempt to move the mounts. If movement is noted, lower the engine and tighten the mount fasteners.

Replacement

Note: *Refer to Chapter 7 for information on the transmission mount.*

6   Disconnect the cable from the negative terminal of the battery (see Chapter 5), then raise the vehicle and support it securely on jackstands (if not already done).

7   Place a floor jack under the engine with a wood block between the jack head and oil pan and raise the engine slightly to relieve the weight from the mounts.

8   Remove the fasteners and detach the mount from the frame and engine bracket. **Caution:** *Do not disconnect more than one mount at a time, except during engine removal.* **Note:** *It may be necessary to lower the exhaust system to gain access to the right side engine mount nut.*

9   Installation is the reverse of removal. Use thread-locking compound on the mount nuts and be sure to tighten them securely.

Notes

Chapter 2 Part B
2.8L, 3.0L and 3.6L V6 engines

Contents

Specifications

General

2.8L engine

Engine type	V6
Displacement	171 cubic inches (2.8 liters)
Engine VIN code	T
RPO code	LP1
Bore	3.5039 inches (89 mm)
Stroke	2.9449 inches (74.8 mm)
Compression ratio	10.0: 1
Compression pressure	See Chapter 2D
Oil pressure	See Chapter 2D

3.0L engine

Engine type	V6
Displacement	183 cubic inches (3.0 liters)
Engine VIN code/RPO code	
2010	G/LF1
2011	Y/LF1
2012 and later	5/LFW
Bore	3.5039 inches (89 mm)
Stroke	3.1614 inches (80.3 mm)
Compression ratio	11.7: 1
Compression pressure	See Chapter 2D
Oil pressure	See Chapter 2D

General (continued)

3.6L engines

Engine type	V6
Displacement	217 cubic inches (3.6 liters)
Engine VIN code/RPO code	
2004 through 2009	7/LY7
2008 through 2010	V/LLT
2011	D/LLT
2012	3/LFX
Bore	3.7008 inches (94 mm)
Stroke	3.3701 inches (85.6 mm)
Compression ratio	
2004 through 2009 (LY7)	10.2: 1
2008 and later (LLT/LFX)	11.4: 1
Compression pressure	See Chapter 2D
Oil pressure	See Chapter 2D
Cylinder numbers (front-to-rear)	
Left (driver's) side	2-4-6
Right side	1-3-5
Firing order	1-2-3-4-5-6

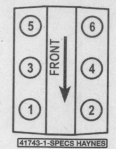

41743-1-SPECS HAYNES

Cylinder locations - V6 engines

Camshafts

2.8L engine
Lobe height	
Intake	1.6687 to 1.6805 inches (42.385 to 42.685 mm)
Exhaust	1.6715 to 1.6833 inches (42.456 to 42.756 mm)
Bearing journal diameter	
Front cylinders	1.3754 to 1.3764 inches (34.936 to 34.960 mm)
Middle and rear cylinders	1.0605 to 1.0614 inches (26.936 to 26.960 mm)

3.0L engine
Lobe height	
Intake	1.6687 to 1.6805 inches (42.385 to 42.685 mm)
Exhaust	1.6715 to 1.6833 inches (42.456 to 42.756 mm)
Bearing journal diameter	
2005 through 2011	
Front cylinders	1.3779 to 1.3787 inches (35.000 to 35.020 mm)
Middle and rear cylinders	1.0630 to 1.0638 inches (27.000 to 27.020 mm)
2012 and later	
Front cylinders	1.3754 to 1.3764 inches (34.936 to 34.960 mm)
Middle and rear cylinders	1.0605 to 1.0614 inches (26.936 to 26.960 mm)

3.6L engine
Lobe height	
Intake	1.6687 to 1.6805 inches (42.385 to 42.685 mm)
Exhaust	1.6703 to 1.6821 inches (42.425 to 42.725 mm)
Bearing journal diameter	
Front cylinders	1.3754 to 1.3764 inches (34.936 to 34.960 mm)
Middle and rear cylinders	1.0605 to 1.0614 inches (26.936 to 26.960 mm)
Endplay (all models)	0.0018 to 0.0085 inch (0.045 to 0.215 mm)

Warpage limits

Cylinder head gasket surfaces (head and block)	0.0010 inch (0.025 mm)
Exhaust manifold	0.0010 inch (0.025 mm)

Oil pump

Rotor-to-pump body (side) clearance	0.0039 to 0.0091 inch (0.100 to 0.230 mm)
Rotor tip clearance	0.0030 to 0.0071 inch (0.075 to 0.180 mm)
Rotor-to-pump cover clearance	0.0012 to 0.0033 inch (0.030 to 0.085 mm)

Torque specifications

Note: *One foot-pound (ft-lb) of torque is equivalent to 12 inch-pounds (in-lbs) of torque. Torque values below approximately 15 foot-pounds are expressed in inch-pounds, because most foot-pound torque wrenches are not accurate at these smaller values.*

	Ft-lbs (unless otherwise indicated)	Nm
Camshaft bearing cap bolts	89 in-lbs	10
Camshaft actuator sprocket bolts	43	58
Camshaft actuator oil control valve bolts	89 in-lbs	10
Camshaft intermediate drive sprocket bolts	43	58
Crankshaft balancer bolt		
Step 1*	74	100
Step 2*	Tighten an additional 150 degrees	

*Use new fastener(s)

Torque specifications (continued)

	Ft-lbs (unless otherwise indicated)	Nm
Cylinder head bolts (in sequence)		
M8 bolts		
Step 1	132 in-lbs	15
Step 2	Tighten an additional 75 degrees	
M11 bolts		
Step 1	22	30
Step 2	Tighten an additional 150 degrees	
Dipstick tube bolt	89 in-lbs	10
Engine mount		
Bracket-to-engine block bolts (M8)		
2008 and earlier models	28	38
2009 and later models	16	22
Bracket-to-engine block bolts (M10)	45	60
Bracket-to-mount nuts	59	80
Nuts-to-frame	59	80
Exhaust manifold bolts	15	20
Exhaust manifold heat shield bolt	89 in-lbs	10
Flywheel/driveplate bolts		
2.8L and 3.6L engines		
Step 1	168 in-lbs	19
Step 2	Tighten an additional 60 degrees	
3.0L engines		
Driveplate bolts (automatic transmission)		
Step 1	22	30
Step 2	Tighten an additional 45 degrees	
Flywheel bolts (manual transmission)	49	67
Fuel rail bolts	89 in-lbs	10
Intake manifold bolts		
2005 through 2011 models		
2.8L and 3.6L engines		
Manifold-to-cylinder head bolts		
2009 and earlier models	17	23
2010 and later models	18	25
Plenum-to-manifold bolts	89 in-lbs	10
3.0L engines		
Lower manifold-to-cylinder head bolts, in sequence	18	25
Upper manifold-to-lower manifold fasteners	18	25
2012 and later models **(see illustration 7.34)**		
Step 1	18	25
Step 2	18	25
Oil filter housing-to-cylinder head bolts (M10)	48	65
Oil filter housing-to-cylinder block bolts (M8)	18	25
Oil pan baffle bolts	89 in-lbs	10
Oil pan drain plug	18	25
Oil pan bolts (M8)		
2009 and earlier models	17	23
2010 and later models	18	25
Oil pickup pipe bolts	89 in-lbs	10
Oil pump cover bolts	115 in-lbs	13
Oil pump mounting bolts		
2009 and earlier models	17	23
2010 and later models	18	25
Rear main oil seal housing bolts	89 in-lbs	10
Timing chain cover bolts		
2005 through 2011 models		
Cover studs (3.0L engines)	132 in-lbs	15
M6 bolts (3.0L engines)	132 in-lbs	15
M8 bolts		
2.8L engines		
Step 1	168 in-lbs	19
Step 2	Tighten an additional 60 degrees	
3.0L engines		
Step 1	168 in-lbs	19
Step 2	168 in-lbs	19
Step 3	Tighten an additional 60 degrees	
3.6L engines	17	23

Torque specifications (continued)

Note: *One foot-pound (ft-lb) of torque is equivalent to 12 inch-pounds (in-lbs) of torque. Torque values below approximately 15 foot-pounds are expressed in inch-pounds, because most foot-pound torque wrenches are not accurate at these smaller values.*

	Ft-lbs (unless otherwise indicated)	**Nm**
Timing chain cover bolts (continued)		
2005 through 2011 models (continued)		
M12 bolts		
2.8L engines		
Step 1	48	65
Step 2	Tighten an additional 60 degrees	
3.0L engines	48	65
2012 and later models		
M6 bolts	132 in-lbs	15
M8 bolts		
Step 1	168 in-lbs	20
Step 2	Tighten an additional 60 degrees	
M12 bolts	48	65
Primary timing chain		
Left guide bolt		
2009 and earlier models	115 in-lbs	13
2010 and later models	18	25
Upper guide bolt		
2009 and earlier models	17	23
2010 and later models	18	25
Tensioner bolt		
2009 and earlier models	17	23
2010 and later models	18	25
Secondary timing chain		
Guide bolt		
2009 and earlier models	17	23
2010 and later models	18	25
Shoe bolt		
2009 and earlier models	17	23
2010 and later models	18	25
Tensioner bolt		
2009 and earlier models	17	23
2010 and later models	18	25
Torque converter bolts	44	60
Valve cover bolts	89 in-lbs	10

1   General information

Warning: *The models covered by this manual are equipped with airbags. Always disable the airbag system before working in the vicinity of the impact sensors, steering column or instrument panel to avoid the possibility of accidental deployment of the airbag(s), which could cause personal injury (see Chapter 12).*

How to use this Chapter

This Part of Chapter 2 is devoted to repair procedures possible while the engine is still installed in the vehicle. Since these procedures are based on the assumption that the engine is installed in the vehicle, if the engine has been removed from the vehicle and mounted on a stand, some of the preliminary removal steps outlined will not apply.

Information concerning engine/transmission removal and installation and engine overhaul, can be found in Part D of this Chapter.

Engine description

The engine utilizes an aluminum block with cast-iron sleeves. The six cylinders are arranged in a "V" shape at a 60-degree angle between the two banks. The cylinder heads utilize a twin overhead camshaft arrangement with four valves per cylinder. Variable cam timing is used on all models via an adjustable camshaft drive sprocket controlled by the engine control system. The engine uses aluminum cylinder heads with powdered metal guides and valve seats. Hydraulic lifters negate the need for valve adjustments and roller rocker arms actuate the valves. The oil pump is mounted at the front of the engine behind the timing chain cover and is driven by the crankshaft. The 3.0L and 3.6L (VIN V) engines also incorporate direct fuel injection, where fuel is delivered into the combustion chamber.

2   Repair operations possible with the engine in the vehicle

Many major repair operations can be accomplished without removing the engine from the vehicle.

Clean the engine compartment and the exterior of the engine with some type of degreaser before any work is done. It will make the job easier and help keep dirt out of the internal areas of the engine.

Depending on the components involved, it may be helpful to remove the hood to improve access to the engine as repairs are

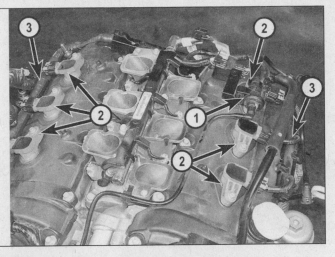

4.4 Disconnect the canister purge solenoid (1) wiring and hoses, the wiring from the ignition coils (2) and the PCV hose (3)

performed (refer to Chapter 11 if necessary). Cover the fenders to prevent damage to the paint. Special pads are available, but an old bedspread or blanket will also work.

If vacuum, exhaust, oil or coolant leaks develop, indicating a need for gasket or seal replacement, the repairs can generally be made with the engine in the vehicle. The intake and exhaust manifold gaskets, oil pan gasket, crankshaft oil seals and cylinder head gasket are all accessible with the engine in place.

Exterior engine components, such as the intake and exhaust manifolds, the oil pan, the oil pump, the water pump, the starter motor, the alternator and the fuel system components can be removed for repair with the engine in place.

Since the camshaft(s) and cylinder head can be removed without pulling the engine, valve component servicing can also be accomplished with the engine in the vehicle. Replacement of the timing chain and sprockets is also possible with the engine in the vehicle.

In extreme cases caused by a lack of necessary equipment, repair or replacement of piston rings, pistons, connecting rods and rod bearings is possible with the engine in the vehicle. However, this practice is not recommended because of the cleaning and preparation work that must be done to the components involved.

3 Top Dead Center (TDC) for number one piston - locating

1 Top Dead Center (TDC) is the highest point in the cylinder that each piston reaches as it travels up the cylinder bore. Each piston reaches TDC on the compression stroke and again on the exhaust stroke, but TDC generally refers to piston position on the compression stroke.

2 Positioning the piston(s) at TDC is an essential part of many procedures such as timing chain/sprocket removal.

3 Before beginning this procedure, be sure to place the transmission in Neutral and apply the parking brake or block the rear wheels. Also, disable the ignition system by disconnecting the primary electrical connectors at the ignition coil packs, then remove the spark plugs (see Chapter 1).

4 In order to bring any piston to TDC, the crankshaft must be turned using one of the methods outlined below. When looking at the front of the engine, normal crankshaft rotation is clockwise.

a) The preferred method is to turn the crankshaft with a socket and ratchet attached to the bolt threaded into the front of the crankshaft. Apply pressure on the bolt in a clockwise direction only. Never turn the bolt counter clockwise.

b) A remote starter switch, which may save some time, can also be used. Follow the instructions included with the switch. Once the piston is close to TDC, use a socket and ratchet as described in the previous paragraph.

c) If an assistant is available to turn the ignition switch to the Start position in short bursts, you can get the piston close to TDC without a remote starter switch. Make sure your assistant is out of the vehicle, away from the ignition switch, then use a socket and ratchet as described in Paragraph (a) to complete the procedure.

5 Place your finger partially over the number one spark plug hole and rotate the crankshaft using one of the methods described above until air pressure is felt at the No 1 cylinder spark plug hole. Air pressure at the spark plug hole indicates that the cylinder has started the compression stroke. Once the compression stroke has begun, TDC for the number one cylinder is obtained when the piston reaches the top of the cylinder on the compression stroke.

6 To bring the piston to the top of the cylinder, insert a long screwdriver into the number one spark plug hole until it touches the top of the piston. **Note:** *Make sure to wrap the tip of the screwdriver with tape to avoid scratching the top of the piston and the cylinder walls.* Use the screwdriver as a feeler gauge to tell where the top of the piston is located in the cylinder while slowly rotating the crankshaft. As the piston rises the screwdriver will be pushed out. The point at which the screwdriver stops moving outward is TDC. **Note:** *Always hold the screwdriver upright while the engine is being rotated so that the screwdriver will not get wedged as the piston travels upward.*

7 If you go past TDC, rotate the crankshaft counter clockwise until the piston is approximately 20 mm below TDC, then slowly rotate the crankshaft clockwise again until TDC is reached.

8 After the number one piston has been positioned at TDC on the compression stroke, TDC for any of the remaining pistons can be located by repeating the procedure described above and following the firing order.

4 Valve covers - removal and installation

Removal

Refer to illustration 4.4

1 Disconnect the negative lead from the battery (see Chapter 5).

2 Remove the front suspension crossbrace from the vehicle (see Chapter 10).

3 Remove the engine covers (see Chapter 1) and the plenum (see Section 7).

4 Disconnect the crankcase ventilation pipe (PCV) hose. Also disconnect the camshaft position sensor electrical connectors, the camshaft actuator valve electrical connectors and the necessary wiring to allow the wiring harnesses connected to the valve covers to be positioned clear of the work area **(see illustration)**. Release the wiring harness plastic sleeves from alongside the valve covers and in front of the engine and position the wiring clear of the work area.

5 Remove the intake manifold (see Section 7).

6 Remove the ignition coils from the valve cover (see Chapter 5).

7 For the right valve cover, disconnect the wiring harness clips from the front of the cover.

8 For the left valve cover, depress the locking tabs and remove the wiring harness from the valve cover.

9 Remove the valve cover bolts, then detach the cover from the cylinder head. **Note:** *If the cover is stuck to the cylinder head, tap one end with a block of wood and a hammer to jar it loose. If that doesn't work, try to slip a flexible putty knife between the cylinder head and cover to break the gasket seal. Don't pry at the cover-to-head joint or damage to the sealing surfaces may occur (leading to oil leaks in the future).*

Installation

Refer to illustrations 4.13 and 4.14

10 The mating surfaces of each cylinder head and valve cover must be perfectly clean when the covers are installed. Use a gasket

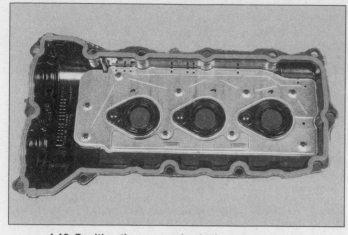

4.13 Position the new gasket in the valve cover lip

4.14 Place some RTV sealant between the timing cover and cylinder head mating face

scraper to remove all traces of sealant and old gasket material, then clean the mating surfaces with lacquer thinner or acetone. If there's sealant or oil on the mating surfaces when the cover is installed, oil leaks may develop.

11   Clean the mounting bolt threads with a die to remove any corrosion and restore damaged threads. Make sure the threaded holes in the cylinder head are clean - run a tap into them to remove corrosion and restore damaged threads.

12   The manufacturer recommends installing tool EN-46101 to the spark plug tube holes to allow the spark plug tube seals to slide over the tubes without tearing. However, after applying a small amount of engine oil to the spark plug tube seal inner faces and with care, the valve cover with the seals attached can slide over the spark plug tubes without the special tools.

13   The gaskets should be mated to the covers before the covers are installed. Position the gasket inside the cover lip **(see illustration)**. If the gasket will not stay in place in the cover lip, apply a thin coat of RTV sealant to the cover flange, and allow the sealant to cure slightly, so the gasket adheres to the cover.

14   Apply a 0.157-inch (4 mm) bead of RTV sealant to the joints between the timing cover and cylinder head mating faces where the valve cover will sit **(see illustration)**.

15   Inspect the valve cover bolt grommets for damage. If the grommets aren't damaged they can be reused. Carefully position the valve cover(s) on the cylinder head and install the bolts and grommets.

16   Tighten the bolts in three or four steps to the torque listed in this Chapter's Specifications.

17   The remainder of installation is the reverse of removal.

18   Start the engine and check carefully for oil leaks as the engine warms up.

---

5   Rocker arms and hydraulic lifters - removal, inspection and installation

---

Removal

Refer to illustration 5.2

1   Detach the valve covers from the cylinder heads (see Section 4).

2   Remove the camshafts **(see illustration and Section 14)**.

3   Place markings on each rocker arm to ensure they are returned to the same position, then lift each one from the engine. Once the rocker arms are removed, the hydraulic lifters can be lifted from the cylinder head. **Note:** *It is important that any rocker arms or lifters being used again must be returned to their original position on the engine.*

Inspection

Refer to illustration 5.4

4   Check each rocker arm for wear, cracks and other damage, especially where the valve stems contact the rocker arm **(see illustration)**.

5   Check the rollers for binding and roughness. If the bearings are worn or damaged, replacement of the entire rocker arm will be

5.2 Camshafts (1), rockers (2) and lifter sockets (3)

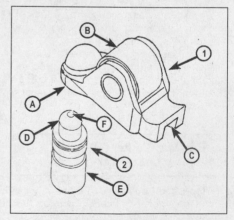

5.4 Rocker arm (1) and hydraulic lifter (2) wear points

A   Lifter socket
B   Roller
C   Valve stem contact point
D   Lifter to rocker contact point
E   Lifter base
F   Lifter oil passage

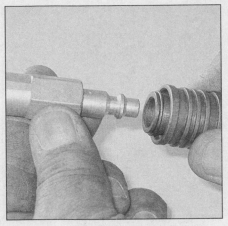

6.4 Thread the air hose adapter into the spark plug hole - adapters are commonly available at auto parts stores

6.5 After compressing the valve spring, remove the keepers with a magnet or needle-nose pliers

6.7a A screwdriver can be used to pry off the valve seals

necessary. **Note:** *Keep in mind that there is no valve adjustment on these engines, so excessive wear or damage in the valve train can easily result in excessive valve clearance, which in turn will cause valve noise when the engine is running.* Also check the rocker arm pivot support pedestal for cracks and other obvious damage.

6   Make sure the oil passage hole in each hydraulic lifter is not blocked, and there are no burrs on the base of the lifter **(see illustration 5.4)**.

Installation

7   Apply some camshaft/lifter pre-lube to the pivot pockets, roller and the slot that contacts the valve on each rocker arm. Apply clean engine oil into the bores for the hydraulic lifters and then install them into the cylinder head. Position the rocker arms onto the lifters.

8   The remainder of installation is the reverse of removal.

9   Before starting and running the engine, change the oil and install a new oil filter (see Chapter 1).

6   Valve springs, retainers and seals - replacement

Refer to illustrations 6.4, 6.5, 6.7a, 6.7b and 6.16

Note: *Broken valve springs and defective valve stem seals can be replaced without removing the cylinder head. Two special tools and a compressed air source are normally required to perform this operation, so read through this Section carefully and rent or buy the tools before beginning the job.*

1   Remove the spark plugs (see Chapter 1).

2   Remove the plenum and intake manifold (see Section 7), valve covers (see Section 4), timing chains (see Section 13), camshafts (see Section 14) and rocker arms (see Section 5).

3   Thread an adapter into the spark plug hole and connect an air hose from a compressed air source to it. Most auto parts stores can supply the air hose adapter. **Note:** *Many cylinder compression gauges utilize a screw-in fitting that may work with your air hose quick-disconnect fitting. If a cylinder compression gauge fitting is used, it will be necessary to remove the Schrader valve from the end of the fitting before using it in this procedure.*

4   Apply compressed air to the cylinder. The valves should be held in place by the air pressure **(see illustration)**.

5   Using a socket and a hammer, gently tap on the top of each valve spring retainer several times (this will break the seal between the valve keeper and the spring retainer and allow the keeper to separate from the valve spring retainer as the valve spring is compressed), then use a valve-spring compressor to compress the spring. Remove the keepers with small needle-nose pliers or a magnet **(see illustration)**. **Note:** *Several different types of tools are available for compressing the valve springs with the head in place. One type grips the lower spring coils and presses on the retainer as the knob is turned, while the lever-type shown here utilizes the rocker arm bolt for leverage. Both types work very well, although the lever type is usually less expensive.*

6   Remove the valve spring and retainer. **Note:** *If air pressure fails to retain the valve in the closed position during this operation, the valve face or seat may be damaged. If so, the cylinder head will have to be removed for repair.*

7   Remove the old valve stem seals, noting differences between the intake and exhaust seals **(see illustrations)**.

8   Wrap a rubber band or tape around the top of the valve stem so the valve won't fall into the combustion chamber, then release the air pressure.

9   Inspect the valve stem for damage. Rotate the valve in the guide and check the

6.7b There is a difference between the intake (1) and exhaust (2) valve seals

end for eccentric movement, which would indicate that the valve is bent.

10   Move the valve up-and-down in the guide and make sure it does not bind. If the valve stem binds, either the valve is bent or the guide is damaged. In either case, the head will have to be removed for repair.

11   Reapply air pressure to the cylinder to retain the valve in the closed position, then remove the tape or rubber band from the valve stem.

12   If you're working on an exhaust valve, install the new exhaust valve seal on the valve stem and press it down over the valve guide to the specified depth. Don't force the seal against the top of the guide. **Note:** *Take this measurement from the steel spring seat to the top edge of the intake and exhaust valve seals, not from the aluminum seat on the head!*

13   If you're working on an intake valve, install a new intake valve stem seal over the valve stem and press it down over the valve guide to the specified depth. Don't force the intake valve seal against the top of the guide. **Caution:** *Do not install an exhaust valve seal on an intake valve.*

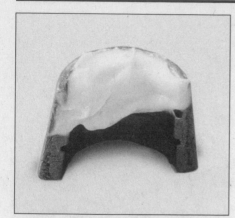

6.16 Apply a small dab of grease to each keeper as shown here before installation - it'll hold them in place on the valve stem as the spring is released

7.6 Throttle control motor connector (1), PCV hose (2), and canister purge solenoid (3) locations

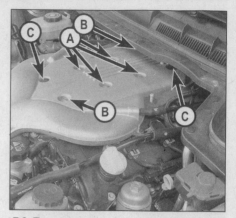

7.9 To remove the plenum from the intake manifold, remove bolts A and B. To remove the plenum chamber and intake manifold as an assembly, remove bolts A and C

14   Install the spring and retainer in position over the valve.

15   Compress the valve spring assembly only enough to reinstall the keepers in the valve stem.

16   Position the keepers in the valve stem groove. Apply a small dab of grease to the inside of each keeper to hold it in place if necessary **(see illustration)**. Remove the pressure from the spring tool and make sure the keepers are seated.

17   Disconnect the air hose and remove the adapter from the spark plug hole.

18   Repeat the above procedure on the remaining cylinders.

19   Reinstall the rocker arm assemblies, camshafts, timing chains and the valve covers (see appropriate Sections).

20   Start the engine, then check for oil leaks and unusual sounds coming from the valve cover area. Allow the engine to idle for at least five minutes before revving the engine.

7   Plenum and intake manifold - removal and installation

Warning: *Wait until the engine is completely cool before beginning this procedure.*

Removal

1   Relieve the fuel system pressure (see Chapter 4).

2   Disconnect the cable from the negative battery terminal (see Chapter 5).

3   Remove the suspension crossbrace from on top of the front struts (see Chapter 10).

4   Remove the engine covers (see Chapter 1).

2005 through 2011 models

2.8L and 3.6L engines

Refer to illustrations 7.6, 7.9 and 7.12

5   Disconnect the wiring from the MAF sensor and remove the air intake duct from between the throttle body and the air filter

(see Chapter 4).

6   Disconnect the wiring from the throttle control motor, then disconnect the throttle control motor wiring harness from the intake manifold. Disconnect the PCV pipe from the hoses on each side of the plenum and disconnect the air pipe from the rear of the left side valve cover **(see illustration)**.

7   Working at the rear of the engine, disconnect the wiring from the barometric pressure (BARO) sensor, the fuel injector harness, EVAP purge solenoid and the variable intake manifold control valve motor. Disconnect the PCV hose from the retaining bracket near the barometric pressure sensor, the purge solenoid line and the vacuum line to the brake booster.

8   Remove the manifold brace bolts and

brace just behind the throttle body.

9   Remove the plenum bolts **(see illustration)**.

10   Lift the plenum from the intake manifold, disconnecting anything still attached to the manifold.

11   Disconnect the fuel line from the rear of the fuel rail (see Chapter 4).

12   Remove the remaining bolts holding the intake manifold to the cylinder heads **(see illustration)**. Lift the intake manifold from the engine with the fuel rail and injectors attached.

13   Remove the bolts holding the fuel rail to the intake manifold. Lift the fuel rail and injectors as an assembly from the manifold.

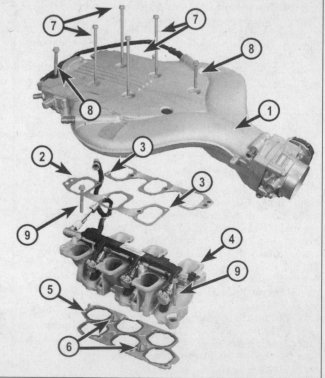

7.12 Intake manifold components - 2.8L and 3.6L engines

1   Plenum

2   Gasket

3   Gasket installation tabs

4   Intake manifold

5   Gasket

6   Gasket installation tabs

7   Plenum to cylinder head bolts

8   Plenum to intake manifold bolts

9   Intake manifold to cylinder head bolts

7.14 Disconnect the brake booster vacuum hose (A), then the
PCV valve (B) (3.0L engines)

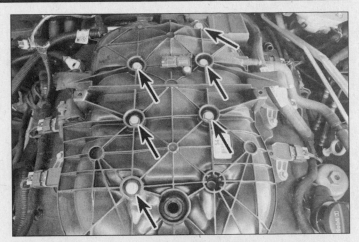

7.17a On 3.0L engines, loosen the intake manifold bolts . . .

3.0L engines

*Refer to illustrations 7.14, 7.17a, 7.17b, 7.18
and 7.19*

14   Disconnect the brake booster vacuum
hose and the PCV valve from the intake manifold **(see illustration)**.
15   Disconnect the EVAP hose from the
EVAP solenoid (see Chapter 6).
16   Disconnect all the electrical connectors
to the intake manifold.
17   Remove the intake manifold bolts **(see
illustrations)**.
18   Remove the intake manifold assembly
from the vehicle **(see illustration)**.
19   Place the intake manifold upside down
on a bench, then remove the gasket and the
lower intake manifold-to-upper intake manifold mounting fasteners **(see illustration)**.

2012 and later models

20   Disconnect the PCV tube from the intake
manifold and the right-side valve cover.
21   Disconnect the EVAP hose from the
EVAP solenoid (see Chapter 6).
22   Working on the rear side of the intake
manifold, remove the fuel rail shield and the
rear noise shield.
23   Disconnect and mark any electrical connectors from the intake manifold.

24   Remove the bolts and lift off the intake
manifold.
25   Remove the intake manifold gasket.

Installation

Refer to illustration 7.31
Note: *The mating surfaces of the cylinder
heads and manifold must be perfectly clean
when the manifold is installed.*
26   Carefully remove all traces of old gasket
material. Note that the intake manifold is made
of a composite material and the cylinder heads
are made of aluminum, therefore aggressive
scraping is not suggested and will damage the
sealing surfaces. After the gasket surfaces are
cleaned and free of any gasket material, wipe
the mating surfaces with a cloth saturated with
solvent. If there is old sealant or oil on the mating surfaces when the manifold is installed, oil
or vacuum leaks may develop. Use a vacuum
cleaner to remove any gasket material that
falls into the intake ports in the heads.

2005 through 2011 models

27   On 3.0L engines, install new gaskets
to the lower intake manifold. Place the lower
intake on the upper intake and tighten the
manifold fasteners to the torque listed in this
Chapter's Specifications.

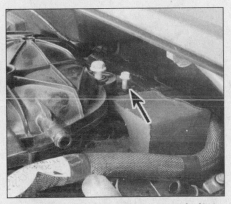

7.17b . . . and the rear support bolt

28   Position the new gaskets on the intake
manifold. Note that the gaskets are equipped
with installation tabs that must snap into place
on the intake manifold **(see illustration 7.12)**.
The words "Manifold Side" may appear on the
gasket. If so, this will ensure proper installation. Make sure the gaskets snap into place
and all intake port openings align.
29   Carefully set the manifold in place.
30   Apply medium-strength thread locking
compound to the threads of the bolts. On 2.8L
and 3.6L engines, install the bolts and tighten

7.18 Remove the intake manifold assembly from the engine

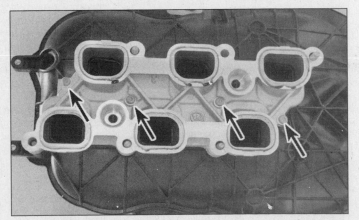

7.19 Remove the lower intake manifold-to-upper intake fasteners

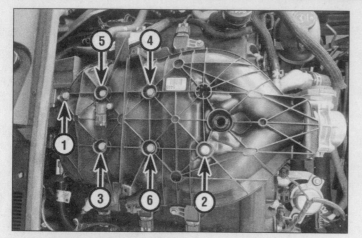

7.31 Intake manifold bolt tightening sequence (3.0L engine)

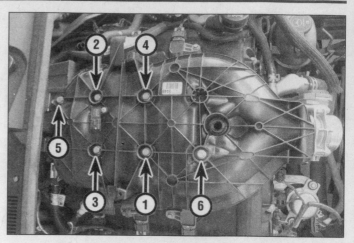

**7.34 Intake manifold bolt tightening sequence
(2012 and later models)**

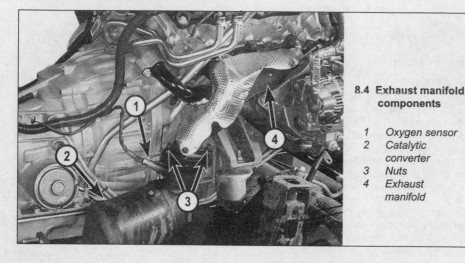

**8.4 Exhaust manifold
components**

1   *Oxygen sensor*
2   *Catalytic
    converter*
3   *Nuts*
4   *Exhaust
    manifold*

**8.8 Remove the nut holding the bottom of
the coolant pipe and push the pipe down
to gain access to the lower manifold bolts**

them, starting with the four long bolts and working toward each end of the manifold, to the torque listed in this Chapter's Specifications. Do not overtighten the bolts or gasket leaks may develop.

31   On 3.0L engines, install the bolts and tighten in sequence (see illustration) to the torque listed in this Chapter's Specifications.

2012 and later models

Refer to illustration 7.34

32   Install the new gaskets onto the engine. Note the location of the installation tabs and make sure they snap into place.

33   Carefully set the manifold into place, then install the bolts.

34   Tighten the intake manifold bolts, following the proper sequence (see illustration), to the torque listed in this Chapter's Specifications.

All models

35   The remainder of installation is the reverse of removal. Check the coolant level, adding as necessary (see Chapter 1). Start the engine and check carefully for vacuum leaks at the intake manifold joints.

8   Exhaust manifolds - removal and installation

Removal

Refer to illustration 8.4

Warning: *Wait until the engine is completely cool before beginning this procedure.*

Warning: *Use caution when working around the exhaust manifolds - the sheetmetal heat shields can be sharp on the edges.*

1   Disconnect the cable from the negative battery terminal (see Chapter 5).

2   Raise the vehicle and support it securely on jackstands.

3   Working under the vehicle, apply penetrating oil to the catalytic converter-to-manifold studs and nuts (they're usually rusty).

4   Remove the nuts retaining the catalytic converter to the manifold (see illustration).

5   Disconnect the electrical connectors for the oxygen sensors and unclip the wiring harness from the engine. Move the harness clear of the work area.

Right side manifold

Refer to illustration 8.8

6   Remove the engine covers.

7   Remove the retaining bolts and remove the outer heat shield. Remove the ground wire from the coolant pipe mounting bracket beneath the manifold.

8   Push the coolant pipe down to access the lower manifold bolts (see illustration). Remove the mounting bolts (see illustration 8.9), starting with the outside bolts and working toward the center of the manifold. Separate the exhaust manifold from the cylinder head. Remove the inner heat shields from the manifold after the manifold has been removed.

Left side manifold

Refer to illustration 8.9

9   Remove the mounting bolts (see illustration), starting with the outside bolts and working toward the center of the manifold. Separate the exhaust manifold from the cylinder head. Remove the inner heat shields from the manifold after the manifold has been removed.

8.9 Exhaust manifold fastener locations (left side shown, right side similar)

9.7 Remove the oil filter housing bolt from the left side cylinder head. There is no need to remove any other oil filter housing bolts (2.8L and 3.6L engines)

Installation

10   Check the manifold for cracks and make sure the bolt threads are clean and undamaged. The manifold and cylinder head mating surfaces must be clean before the manifolds are installed - use a gasket scraper to remove all carbon deposits and gasket material. **Note:** *The cylinder heads are made of aluminum, therefore aggressive scraping is not suggested and will damage the sealing surfaces. Also, if any of the manifold bolts are broken, it indicates a warped manifold. Have the manifold machined at a machine workshop prior to installing the manifold to the vehicle. If this is not done, the manifold may not seal properly and the new manifold bolts will probably break.*

11   Apply an anti-seize compound to the threads of the inner heat shield bolts. Install the inner heat shields, then the bolts and gaskets onto the manifold. Retaining tabs surrounding the gasket bolt holes should hold the assembly together as the manifold is installed.

12   Apply a 1/4-inch (6 mm) wide bead of medium-strength thread locking compound to the threads of the bolts.

13   Place the manifold on the cylinder head and install the mounting bolts finger tight.

14   When tightening the manifold bolts, work from the center to the ends and be sure to use a torque wrench. Tighten the bolts to the torque listed in this Chapter's Specifications. If required, bend the exposed end of the exhaust manifold gasket back against the cylinder head.

15   Apply an anti-seize compound to the threads of the outer heat shield and install the heat shield bolts.

16   The remainder of installation is the reverse of removal.

17   Start the engine and check for exhaust leaks.

9   Cylinder heads - removal and installation

Note: *It will be necessary to purchase a new set of M8 (8 mm) and M11 (11 mm) head bolts to perform this procedure.*

Removal

1   Disconnect the cable from the negative battery terminal (see Chapter 5).

2   Remove the plenum and intake manifold (see Section 7), valve covers (see Section 4), timing cover (see Section 12) and timing chains (see Section 13). Noting its installed position, remove the timing chain sprocket from the crankshaft.

2.8L and 3.6L engines

Refer to illustration 9.7

3   Remove the oil dipstick tube mounting bolt and tube.

4   Disconnect all the electrical connectors and ground straps from the cylinder heads.

5   Disconnect the exhaust pipes from the exhaust manifolds (see Chapter 4); the exhaust manifolds will be removed with the cylinder heads.

6   If removing the left side cylinder head, remove the power steering pump (see Chapter 10).

7   Remove the upper bolt from the oil filter adapter **(see illustration)**.

3.0L engines

8   Remove the fuel pump (see Chapter 4).

9   Remove the oil filter adapter bolts and the adapter.

10   If removing the left side cylinder head, remove the power steering pump and bracket (see Chapter 10).

11   Remove the coolant pipe mounting fasteners and set the pipe out of the way.

12   Detach both exhaust manifolds from the cylinder heads (see Section 8).

13   Disconnect all the electrical connectors and ground straps from the cylinder heads.

All models

14   Loosen the head bolts, in 1/4-turn increments, in the reverse order of the tightening sequence **(see illustrations 9.22a and 9.22b)** until they can be removed by hand. **Note:** *There will be different length and size head bolts for different locations. Make a note of the different sizes and lengths and where they go when removing the bolts to ensure correct installation of the new bolts.*

15   Lift the heads off the engine. If resistance is felt, do not pry between the head and block, as damage to the mating surfaces will result. To dislodge the head, place a pry bar or long screwdriver into the intake port and carefully pry the head off the engine. Store the heads on blocks of wood to prevent damage to the gasket sealing surfaces.

Installation

Refer to illustrations 9.22a and 9.22b

16   The mating surfaces of the cylinder heads and block must be perfectly clean when the heads are installed. Gasket removal solvents are available at auto parts stores and may prove helpful.

17   Use a gasket scraper to remove all traces of carbon and old gasket material, then wipe the mating surfaces with a cloth saturated with lacquer thinner or acetone. **Note:** *The cylinder heads are made of aluminum, therefore aggressive scraping is not suggested and will damage the sealing surfaces. If there is oil on the mating surfaces when the heads are installed, the gaskets may not seal correctly and leaks may develop. When working on the block, use a vacuum cleaner to remove any debris that falls into the cylinders.*

18   Check the block and head mating surfaces for nicks, deep scratches and other

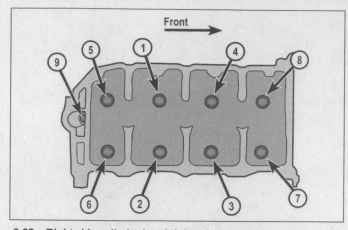

9.22a   Right side cylinder head tightening sequence - bolts 1 to 8 are M11 bolts, bolt 9 is an M8 bolt

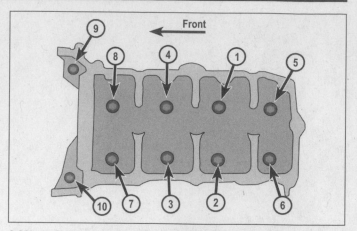

9.22b   Left side cylinder head bolt tightening sequence - bolts 1 to 8 are M11 bolts, bolts 9 and 10 are M8 bolts

damage. If damage is slight, it can be removed with emery cloth. If it is excessive, machining may be the only alternative.

19   Position the new gaskets over the dowels in the block.

20   Carefully position the heads on the block without disturbing the gaskets.

21   Coat the threads of the new 8 mm head bolts with a medium-strength thread locking compound, then install them, (bolt 9 on the right side bolts 9 and 10 on left side cylinder head) finger tight **(see illustration 9.22a and 9.22b)**.

22   Install new 11 mm head bolts (bolts 1 through 8) and tighten them finger tight. Following the recommended sequence **(see illustrations)**, tighten the bolts in four steps to the torque and angle of rotation listed in this Chapter's Specifications. **Warning:** *DO NOT reuse the head bolts - always replace them.*

23   The remainder of installation is the reverse of removal.

24   Add coolant and change the oil and filter (see Chapter 1). Start the engine and check for proper operation and coolant or oil leaks.

10   Crankshaft balancer - removal and installation

Refer to illustrations 10.5, 10.6, 10.9a and 10.9b

Note: *This procedure requires a new crankshaft balancer bolt and a special balancer installation tool that is only available through specialized tool manufacturers. Read through the entire procedure and obtain all tools and materials before proceeding.*

1   Disconnect the cable from the negative battery terminal (see Chapter 5).

2   Raise the front of the vehicle and support it securely on jackstands.

3   Remove the drivebelts (see Chapter 1).

4   Remove the splash shield (see Chapter 1).

5   Remove the starter motor (see Chapter 5). Use a prybar through the rear of the engine block to hold the ring gear teeth on the flywheel/driveplate and loosen the crankshaft pulley center bolt **(see illustration)**.

6   Pull the balancer off the crankshaft with a puller **(see illustration)**. **Caution:** *The jaws*

of the puller must only contact the hub of the balancer - not the outer ring. **Note:** *A long Allen-head bolt should be inserted into the crankshaft nose for the puller's tapered tip to push against to prevent damage to the crankshaft threads.*

7   Lubricate the end of the crankshaft and oil seal with clean engine oil. Position the crankshaft pulley/balancer on the crankshaft and slide it on as far as it will go. Note that the slot (keyway) in the hub must be aligned with the Woodruff key in the end of the crankshaft.

8   Hold the crankshaft steady and use the old crankshaft balancer bolt to press the balancer onto the crankshaft.

9   Install a new crankshaft balancer bolt and tighten it in two steps to the torque and angle of rotation listed in this Chapter's Specifications **(see illustrations)**.

10   The remainder of installation is the reverse of removal.

11   Crankshaft front oil seal - removal and installation

Refer to illustrations 11.2 and 11.5

1   Remove the crankshaft balancer (see Section 10).

2   Note how the seal is installed - the new one must be installed to the same depth and facing the same way. Carefully pry the oil seal out of the cover with a seal puller **(see illustration)**.

3   If the seal is being replaced when the timing chain cover is removed, support the cover on top of two blocks of wood and drive the seal out from the backside with a hammer and punch. **Caution:** *Be careful not to scratch, gouge or distort the area that the seal fits into, or a leak will develop.*

4   Apply clean engine oil or multi-purpose grease to the outer edge of the new seal, then install it in the cover with the lip (spring side) facing IN. Drive the seal into place with a large socket and a hammer (if a large socket isn't available, a piece of pipe will also work). Make sure the seal enters the bore squarely

10.5   Place a prybar between the ring gear teeth and the cylinder block to hold the crankshaft while removing the center bolt

10.6   The use of a three jaw puller will be necessary to remove the crankshaft balancer - always place the puller jaws around the hub, not the outer ring

10.9a Tightening the new crankshaft balancer bolt to the specified torque

10.9b Use a torque angle gauge to finish the tightening sequence

11.2 Another way of removing an old oil seal is to screw a self-tapping screw partially into the seal, then use pliers as a lever to pull it from the engine

and stop when the front face is at the proper depth.

5   Check the surface on the balancer hub that the oil seal rides on. If the surface has been grooved from long-time contact with the seal, a press-on sleeve may be available to replace the sealing surface **(see illustration)**. This sleeve is pressed into place with a hammer and a block of wood and is commonly available at auto parts stores for various applications.

6   Lubricate the balancer hub with clean engine oil and install the crankshaft balancer (see Section 10).

7   The remainder of installation is the reverse of the removal.

12   Timing chain cover - removal and installation

Removal

Refer to illustrations 12.13a and 12.13b

1   Disconnect the cable from the negative battery terminal (see Chapter 5).

2   Remove the suspension crossbrace from on top of the front struts (see Chapter 10).

3   Remove the engine covers (see Chapter 1).

4   Remove the intake manifold (see Section 7).

5   Remove the drivebelts and tensioners, and drain the cooling system (see Chapter 1).

6   Remove the alternator and alternator bracket (see Chapter 5).

7   Remove the valve covers (see Section 4).

8   Remove the air filter and the air intake duct from the engine compartment (see Chapter 4), then remove the upper and lower radiator hoses, coolant recovery hose, cooling fans, drivebelt and coolant outlet pipe (see Chapter 3).

9   Remove the crankshaft balancer (see Section 10).

10   Remove the bolts retaining the power steering pump reservoir and associated brackets. Do not open any of the power steering lines. Position the reservoir and bracket as an assembly clear of the work area. Remove the power steering pump and pump bracket

(see Chapter 10).

11   Remove the bolts retaining the A/C compressor and associated brackets. Do not open any A/C refrigerant lines. Position the compressor and brackets as an assembly clear of the work area.

12   Disconnect the wiring connectors and remove each Camshaft Position (CMP) sensor. Also disconnect the wiring and remove the variable cam timing solenoids from the front of the engine.

13   Remove the timing chain cover mounting bolts, in sequence **(see illustration 12.16)**, with the water pump attached, then separate the timing chain cover from the block **(see illustrations)**. The cover may be stuck; if so, lever only at the points illustrated with a screwdriver. Since the cover is made of aluminum, it can easily be damaged, so DO NOT attempt to pry it off.

Installation

Refer to illustrations 12.14, 12.15 and 12.16

14   Install a new seal to the inside of the timing cover and apply a bead of RTV sealant

11.5 If the sealing surface of the pulley hub has a wear groove from contact with the seal, repair sleeves are available at most auto parts stores

12.13a Use a screwdriver to pry the cover from the engine at the illustrated points

to the faces of the cover that will mate with the engine (see illustration). Slide the timing chain cover over the crankshaft and the two studs, then install the bolts hand tight into the cover.

15   Install two 8 mm studs into the engine block to guide the timing chain cover into the correct position (see illustration).

16   Remove the two 8 mm studs, then tighten the timing chain cover bolts, in sequence (see illustration), to the torque listed in this Chapter's Specifications.

17   The remainder of installation is the reverse of removal.

---

13   Timing chain and camshaft sprockets - removal, inspection and installation

Removal

Caution: *The timing system is complex, and severe engine damage will occur if you make any mistakes. Do not attempt this procedure unless you are highly experienced with this type of repair. If you are at all unsure of your abilities, be sure to consult an expert. Double-check all your work and be sure everything is correct before you attempt to start the engine.*
Note: *This procedure requires special tools to lock the camshafts on each cylinder head into position. There are two different designs for the sprockets and chains. Early models (2005 through mid-2007) use Design 1 which requires special camshaft locking tools (part numbers EN-46105-1 and EN-46105-2, available through SPX tools). Later models (mid-2007 through 2014) are equipped with Design 2 which also requires special camshaft locking tools (part numbers EN-48383-1, EN-48383-2 and EN-48383-3). Design 2 systems incorpo-*

12.13b A 10 x 1.5 mm bolt can be used at the illustrated point, near the water pump to press the center portion of the cover away from the engine.

rate 'inverted tooth' chains for quieter operation, new camshaft position actuators for each bank and a new crankshaft sprocket with 'reverse chain pitch' also for quiet operation. Read through the entire procedure and obtain the tools before proceeding.

1   Remove the timing chain cover (see Section 12).

2005 through mid-2007 models (Design 1)

Refer to illustrations 13.2, 13.3a, 13.3b and 13.5

2   Rotate the crankshaft clockwise until the timing mark on the timing chain sprocket aligns with the mark on the oil pump housing in the 9 o'clock position (see illustration).

3   In this position, the flat segment on the rear of each camshaft on the right-side cylinder head should be facing up and parallel with

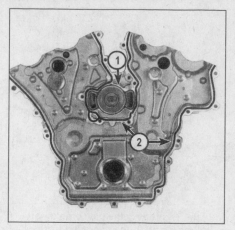

12.14 Install a new seal (1) and apply RTV sealant (2)

the valve cover mating face. If this is not the case, rotate the crankshaft clockwise one full turn and re-align the crankshaft timing marks. Install the special tools to the camshafts of each cylinder head (see illustrations). **Note:** *Tool EN-46105-1 mounts to the right-side cylinder head for disassembly. Tool EN-46105-2 mounts to the left-side cylinder head.*

4   Remove the timing chain tensioner bolts for the right-side cylinder head, then remove the tensioner and discard the gasket. **Note:** *The tensioner is under spring pressure. Use care, as the tensioner can fly apart once the bolts are removed.*

5   Remove the right-side cylinder head timing chain guides and remove the chain (see illustration). Remove the special holding tools from the rear of the camshafts.

6   Repeat the process to remove the lower, or primary timing chain and the timing chain for the left-side cylinder head. **Note:** *The*

12.15 Fabricate two timing cover aligning studs from M8 x 1.25 mm bolts with the heads removed and use the plastic sleeves that were between the original timing cover bolts and the timing cover to ensure the cover is in the correct position.

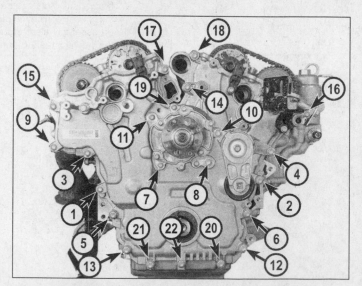

12.16 Timing cover bolt tightening sequence (typical)

13.2 Crankshaft sprocket with timing marks aligned

13.3a Right side cylinder head with camshaft locking tool EN-46105-1 installed

13.3b Left side cylinder head with camshaft locking tool EN-46105-2 installed

camshaft locking tools can remain off while removing the lower and left-side cylinder head timing chains. Use care, as the tensioners are under spring pressure.

7   If necessary, after noting their installed position, remove the center bolt retaining the idler sprockets and remove the sprockets.

8   If necessary, mark the relationship between the camshaft sprockets and their respective camshaft. Hold the camshaft steady with an open ended wrench placed on the hexagonal in the camshaft and remove the camshaft sprocket bolt. Remove the sprocket from the camshaft.

Mid-2007 and later models (Design 2)

9   Rotate the crankshaft clockwise until the timing mark on the timing chain sprocket aligns with the mark on the oil pump housing in the 9 o'clock (or Stage 2) position **(see illustration 13.41)**.

10   In this position, the camshaft locking tool EN-48383-3 will lock the rear of the camshafts on the right cylinder bank and tool EN-48383-2 will lock the camshafts on the left cylinder bank. If this is not the case, rotate the crankshaft clockwise one full turn and re-align the crankshaft timing marks. Install the special tools to the camshafts of each cylinder head.

11   Remove the timing chain tensioner bolts for the right-side cylinder head, then remove the tensioner and discard the gasket. **Note:** *The tensioner is under spring pressure. Use care, as the tensioner can fly apart once the bolts are removed.*

12   Remove the right-side timing chain guide and the right-side pivot arm chain guide bolts and the timing chain guides.

13   Remove the right-side cylinder head timing chain. Remove the special holding tools from the rear of the camshafts.

14   Repeat the process to remove the lower, or primary timing chain and the timing chain for the left-side cylinder head. **Note:** *The camshaft locking tools can remain off while removing the lower and left-side cylinder head timing chains. Use care, as the tensioners are under spring pressure.*

15   If necessary, after noting their installed position, remove the center bolt retaining the idler sprockets and remove the sprockets.

16   If they are to be removed, mark the relationship between the camshaft sprockets and their respective camshaft. Hold the camshaft steady with an open ended wrench placed on the hexagonal in the camshaft and remove the camshaft sprocket bolt. Remove the sprocket from the camshaft.

Inspection

Refer to illustrations 13.20a and 13.20b

17   Inspect the timing chain cover for damage. Remove all old sealant from the cover and the engine block. Remove and discard the seal for the coolant passage from the rear of the housing.

18   Clean all components with solvent and inspect the guides and timing chain sprockets for wear or damage. Any gouges or deformities on the guides or tensioners will require replacement parts to be installed. Ensure the rear face of the tensioner is clean and there are no marks that would affect the sealing quality once reassembled. Remove any old gasket material from the tensioner mating faces with the engine.

19   Inspect the timing chains for wear, stiff or loose rollers and binding.

20   Inspect the tensioners for damage or wear. Reset the tensioner by removing the plunger the rear of the plunger into the plunger shaft using a flat-bladed screwdriver. Install the plunger to the body of the tensioner and, while maintaining pressure on the plunger, insert a paper clip into the hole in the tensioner body to maintain the tensioner in the retracted position **(see illustrations)**. Repeat this on

13.5 Right side cylinder head timing chain tensioner (1), outer guide pivot bolt (2) and inner guide bolts (3)

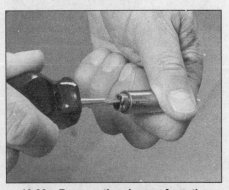

13.20a Remove the plunger from the tensioner and reset it by screwing the bottom of the plunger shaft into the top half of the plunger shaft with a screwdriver

13.20b Slowly push the plunger back into the tensioner body and secure it in place with a paper clip

13.23a Left side cylinder head with camshaft locking tool EN-46105-1 installed

the other two timing chain tensioners. **Note:** *The wire must be inserted into the tensioner to maintain it in the compressed position. If this is not done, the spring pressure will not tension the chain once it is installed to the engine.*

Installation

Caution: *Before starting the engine, carefully rotate the crankshaft by hand through at least two full revolutions (use a socket and breaker bar on the crankshaft pulley center bolt). If you feel any resistance, STOP! There is something wrong - most likely, valves are contacting the pistons. You must find the problem before proceeding.*

Note: *Timing chains must be replaced as a set with the camshaft and crankshaft sprockets. Never put a new chain on old sprockets.*

2005 through mid-2007 models (Design 1)

Refer to illustrations 13.23a, 13.23b, 13.24, 13.28, 13.30, and 13.32

21   Align the crankshaft sprocket with the Woodruff key and slide the sprocket onto the crankshaft. Ensure the timing mark on the sprocket is visible and the timing marks are aligned. If necessary, rotate the crankshaft clockwise and align the crankshaft sprocket mark with the mark on the oil pump housing that is in the 5 o'clock position. **Caution:** *If resistance is encountered, do not force the sprocket onto the crankshaft. It may eventually move onto the shaft, but it may be cracked in the process and fail later, causing extensive engine damage.*

22   Rotate the camshafts for the left-side cylinder head counterclockwise using an open ended wrench on the hexagonal portion of the camshafts until the flats on the rear of the camshaft are parallel to the valve cover gasket face on the rear of the cylinder head.

23   Install the special locking tool EN-46105-1 onto the left-side cylinder head camshafts. Ensure the tool is correctly seated against the camshafts. Rotate the camshafts for the right-side cylinder head in the same way and install tool EN-46105-2 to the right-side cylinder head **(see illustrations)**.

24   Install the left-side cylinder head tim-

ing chain first, aligning the bright chain links with the letter L stamped on the camshaft sprocket **(see illustration)**. Then install the left-side lower idler sprocket onto the chain, ensuring the large sprocket and the markings "LB Front" are facing outward. The bright link on the chain must align with the mark on the outer sprocket **(see illustration 13.28)**. Slide the idler sprocket onto the engine and install the bolt. Tighten the idler sprocket bolt to the torque listed in this Chapter's Specifications and check that all of the timing marks are still aligned correctly.

25   Install the outer left-side timing chain guide that runs between the idler sprocket and the exhaust camshaft, then install the inner left-side timing chain guide to the engine. Tighten the bolts to the torque listed in this Chapter's Specifications. **Note:** *Ensure the inner timing chain guide is not placed on the mounting pad for the tensioner before tightening the bolts.*

26   Using a new gasket, install the tensioner for the left-side timing chain. Ensure the tensioner is aligned with the inner guide and tighten the tensioner bolts to the torque listed

13.23b Right side cylinder head with camshaft locking tool EN-46105-2 installed

13.24 Left side cylinder head timing chain-to-camshaft sprocket aligning marks

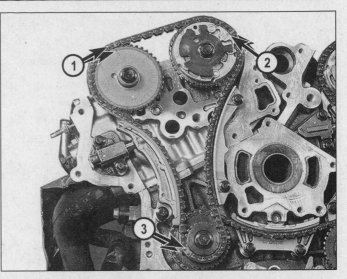

13.28 Lower timing chain sprocket aligning marks (A), tensioner (1), upper timing chain guide (2) and lower timing chain guide (3)

13.30 Right side cylinder head timing chain alignment marks: exhaust camshaft (1), intake camshaft (2), and idler sprocket (3)

in this Chapter's Specifications. Release the pin from the tensioner. Grasp the inner guide and force it into the tensioner. This will allow the tensioner to tension the chain. Check that the timing chain alignment marks are all correct.

27   Install the right-side timing chain idler sprocket to the engine, ensuring that the small sprocket is facing outward along with the markings "RB Front." Tighten the idler sprocket bolt to the torque listed in this Chapter's Specifications.

28   Ensure the crankshaft sprocket is still aligned with the timing mark on the oil pump housing that is in the 5 o'clock position and install the lower, or primary, timing chain. Ensure the shiny chain links align with the arrows on both large idler sprockets and also with the timing mark on the crankshaft sprocket. Install the timing chain guide to the lower chain running between the two idler sprockets, tightening the bolts to the torque listed in this Chapter's Specifications. Using a new gasket, install the tensioner and tighten the tensioner bolts. Remove the pin from the tensioner; force the tensioner guide and pushrod into the tensioner body to unlock it. Allow the tensioner to tension the timing chain. Check that the timing chain alignment marks are all correct. Remove the camshaft special locking tools from the camshafts on both cylinder heads **(see illustration)**.

29   Rotate the crankshaft until the timing mark on the crankshaft sprocket is aligned with the mark on the oil pump housing that is in the 9 o'clock position. Install special locking tool EN-46105-2 onto the left-side cylinder head camshafts. Rotate the camshafts for the right-side cylinder head and install special locking tool EN-46105-1 to the right-side cylinder head. Ensure the tools are correctly seated against the camshafts **(see illustrations 13.3a and 13.3b)**. **Note:** *The camshaft*

flats for the right-side *cylinder head must be parallel to the valve cover gasket face on the rear of the cylinder head.*

30   Install the right-side cylinder head timing chain, aligning the bright chain links with the letter R stamped on the camshaft sprockets. The lower bright link on the chain must align with the hole in the face of the inner idler sprocket. Check that all of the timing marks are still aligned correctly **(see illustration)**.

31   Install the inner right-side timing chain guide that runs between the idler sprocket and the intake camshaft, then install the outer right-side timing chain guide to the engine. Tighten the bolts to the torque listed in this Chapter's Specifications.

32   Using a new gasket, install the tensioner for the right-side timing chain. Ensure the tensioner is aligned with the outer guide, and tighten the tensioner bolts to the torque listed in this Chapter's Specifications. Remove the pin from the tensioner, force the tensioner guide and pushrod into the tensioner body

to unlock it **(see illustration)**. Allow the tensioner to tension the timing chain. Check that the timing chain alignment marks are all correct, then rotate the engine slowly by hand until oil is forced into the three timing chain tensioners. **Note:** *While doing this, ensure that the timing chains don't jump teeth on any of the timing gears.*

33   Remove the special locking tools from the camshafts. The remainder of installation is the reverse of removal.

Mid-2007 and later models – Design 2

Refer to illustrations 13.34, and 13.41

34   Align the crankshaft sprocket with the Woodruff key and slide the sprocket onto the crankshaft. Ensure the timing mark on the sprocket is visible and the timing marks are aligned. If necessary, rotate the crankshaft clockwise and align the crankshaft sprocket mark with the mark on the oil pump housing

13.32 Force the tensioner guide and chain into the tensioner body to unlock the tensioner

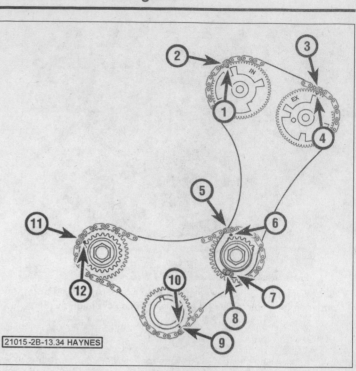

13.34 Stage one position for timing chain installation on the Design 2 system

1 *Left intake camshaft sprocket timing mark (L)*
2 *Left intake camshaft sprocket secondary timing chain colored link*
3 *Left exhaust camshaft sprocket secondary timing chain colored link*
4 *Left exhaust camshaft sprocket timing mark (L)*
5 *Primary chain colored link for left (lower) idler sprocket*
6 *Left idler sprocket timing mark for primary chain*
7 *Left secondary chain colored link and timing mark on left (lower) Idler sprocket*
8 *Left primary camshaft intermediate drive chain timing window*
9 *Primary chain colored link on crankshaft sprocket*
10 *Crankshaft sprocket timing mark for primary chain*
11 *Primary chain colored link for right (lower) idler sprocket*
12 *Right Idler sprocket timing mark for primary chain*

21015-2B-13.34 HAYNES

that is in the 5 o'clock position. This will be the Stage 1 position **(see illustration)**. **Caution:** *If resistance is encountered, do not force the sprocket onto the crankshaft. It may eventually move onto the shaft, but it may be cracked in the process and fail later, causing extensive engine damage.*

35   Rotate the camshafts slightly (not more than 10 degrees) for the left-side cylinder head using an open ended wrench on the hexagonal portion of the camshafts and install camshaft locking tool EN-48383-1 onto the rear of the left bank cylinder head. Ensure the tool is correctly seated against the camshafts.
36   Install the left-side cylinder head timing chain first, aligning the bright chain links with the letter L stamped on the camshaft sprockets **(see illustration 13.34).** Then install the left-side lower idler sprocket, ensuring the large sprocket and the markings are facing outward. The lower bright link on the chain must align with the hole in the face of the idler sprocket (7 o'clock position). Slide the idler sprocket onto the engine and install the bolt. Tighten the idler sprocket bolt to the torque listed in this Chapter's Specifications and check that all of the timing marks are still aligned correctly. **Note:** *Make sure there are 10 links between the colored links on the camshaft sprockets. Do not count the colored links.*
37   Install the outer left-side timing chain guide that runs between the idler sprocket and the exhaust camshaft, then install the inner left-side timing chain guide to the engine. Tighten the bolts to the torque listed in this Chapter's Specifications. **Note:** *Ensure the inner timing chain guide is not placed on the mounting pad for the tensioner before tightening the bolts.*
38   Using a new gasket, install the tensioner

for the left-side timing chain. Ensure the tensioner is aligned with the inner guide and tighten the tensioner bolts to the torque listed in this Chapter's Specifications. Release the pin from the tensioner. Grasp the inner guide and force it into the tensioner. This will allow the tensioner to tension the chain. Check that the timing chain alignment marks are all correct.
39   Install the right-side timing chain idler sprocket to the engine, ensuring that the small sprocket is facing outward along with the markings. Tighten the idler sprocket bolt to the torque listed in this Chapter's Specifications.
40   Ensure the crankshaft sprocket is still aligned with the timing mark on the oil pump housing that is in the 5 o'clock position and install the lower, or primary, timing chain. Ensure the shiny chain links align with the arrows on both large idler sprockets and also with the timing mark on the crankshaft sprocket **(see illustration 13.34)**. First, install the upper and lower timing chain guides between the two idler sprockets, tightening the bolts to the torque listed in this Chapter's Specifications. Using a new gasket, install the tensioner and tighten the tensioner bolts. Remove the pin from the tensioner; force the tensioner guide and pushrod into the tensioner body to unlock it. Allow the tensioner to tension the timing chain. Check that the timing chain alignment marks are all correct **(see illustration 13.34)**. Remove the camshaft special locking tool from the camshafts on the left bank cylinder head.
41   Rotate the crankshaft clockwise until the timing mark on the crankshaft sprocket is aligned with the mark on the oil pump housing that is in the 9 o'clock position (115 degrees clockwise). Install special locking tool

EN-48383-2 onto the left-side cylinder head camshafts. Rotate the camshafts for the right-side cylinder head and install special locking tool EN-48383-3 to the right-side cylinder head. Ensure the tools are correctly seated against the camshafts. This will be referred to as Stage 2 position **(see illustration)**.
42   Install the right-side cylinder head timing chain, aligning the bright chain links with the letter R stamped on the camshaft sprockets. The lower bright link on the chain must align with the hole in the face of the inner idler sprocket. Check that all of the timing marks are still aligned correctly **(see illustration 3.41)**.
43   Install the inner right-side timing chain guide that runs between the idler sprocket and the intake camshaft, then install the outer right-side timing chain guide to the engine. Tighten the bolts to the torque listed in this Chapter's Specifications. **Note:** *Make sure there are 10 links between the colored links on the camshaft sprockets. Do not count the colored links.*
44   Using a new gasket, install the tensioner for the right-side timing chain. Ensure the tensioner is aligned with the outer guide, and tighten the tensioner bolts to the torque listed in this Chapter's Specifications. Remove the pin from the tensioner, force the tensioner guide and pushrod into the tensioner body to unlock it. Allow the tensioner to tension the timing chain. Check that the timing chain alignment marks are all correct, then rotate the engine slowly by hand until oil is forced into the three timing chain tensioners. **Note:** *While doing this, ensure that the timing chains don't jump teeth on any of the timing gears.*
45   Remove the special locking tools from the camshafts. The remainder of installation is the reverse of removal.

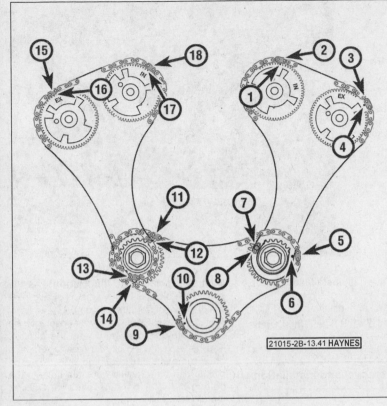

13.41 Stage two position for timing chain installation on the Design 2 system

1   Left intake camshaft sprocket timing mark (L)
2   Left intake camshaft sprocket secondary timing chain colored link
3   Left exhaust camshaft sprocket secondary timing chain colored link
4   Left exhaust camshaft sprocket timing mark (L)
5   Primary chain colored link for left (lower) idler sprocket
6   Left idler sprocket timing mark for primary chain
7   Left primary chain sprocket timing window
8   Left secondary chain colored link and timing mark on left (lower) Idler sprocket
9   Primary chain colored link on crankshaft sprocket
10 Crankshaft sprocket timing mark for primary chain
11 Primary chain colored link for right (lower) idler sprocket
12 Right Idler sprocket timing mark for primary chain
13 Right secondary chain colored link for right (lower) idler sprocket
14 Right secondary chain timing mark on right (lower) idler sprocket
15 Right exhaust sprocket secondary timing chain colored link
16 Right exhaust camshaft sprocket timing mark (R)
17 Right intake camshaft sprocket timing mark (R)
18 Right Intake secondary timing chain colored link

14   Camshafts - removal and installation

Note: *The camshaft should always be thoroughly inspected before installation and camshaft endplay should always be checked prior to camshaft removal.*
Note: *If the camshaft is being replaced, always install new rocker arms and hydraulic lifters as well. Do not use old rockers and lifters on a new camshaft.*
Note: *The camshaft bearing caps are marked with a number and letter and a raised arrow. The number signifies the bearing journal (cylinder number) position from the front of the engine. The letter indicates whether it originates from the intake camshaft (I), or the exhaust (E) camshaft, and the arrow should always point toward the front of the engine.*

Removal

1   Remove the plenum and intake manifold (see Section 7), valve covers (see Section 4), CMP sensors and camshaft actuators (see Chapter 6), timing cover (see Section 12), timing chains and camshaft sprockets (see Section 13).
2   Check the camshaft endplay by mounting a dial indicator to the front of the engine with the plunger bearing against the end of the camshaft. Using a prybar wrapped in a rag, pry the camshaft toward the rear of the

engine and zero the dial gauge. Then pry the camshaft toward the front of the engine and note the dial gauge. This is the camshaft endplay. Compare with Specifications and repeat the test on the remaining camshafts. Any camshaft with excessive endplay will have to be replaced. **Note:** *Use care not to damage the lobes on the camshaft when prying it. The camshaft can easily be damaged.*
3   Before removing the bearing caps and lifters, arrange to store them in a clearly labeled box to ensure that they're installed in their original locations.
4   Remove the camshaft bearing cap bolts and bearing caps and lift the camshafts from the cylinder head.
5   After the camshaft has been removed from the engine, cleaned with solvent and dried, inspect the bearing journals for uneven wear, pitting and evidence of seizure; if you suspect a problem, take the camshafts to a machine shop and have it inspected. **Note:** *If the journals are damaged, the bearing inserts in the block are probably damaged as well. Both the camshaft and bearings will have to be replaced by an automotive machine shop.*

Installation

Refer to illustration 14.6, 14.8, 14.9 and 14.10
6   Ensure the sealing rings on the front of the camshafts are in place and lubricate the camshaft bearing journals and cam lobes with camshaft assembly lube **(see illustration)**.

7   Working on the right side cylinder head, lubricate the bearing journals and place the camshafts onto the bearing journals. Position the camshafts so the flat portions on the rear of the camshaft are parallel to the valve cover gasket face on the top of the cylinder head. **Note:** *It should be possible to install camshaft lock tool EN-48383-1 (used when removing the timing chains and sprockets).*
8   Apply engine oil to the inside of the bearing caps, then install the front bearing

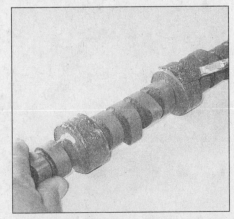

14.6 Be sure to apply camshaft assembly lube to the cam lobes and bearing journals before installing the camshaft

14.8 The camshafts are in the correct position if special tool EN-46105-1 (1) can be installed to the rear of the camshafts. The camshaft bearing journals should have the tang (2) facing toward the center of the cylinder head and the number (3) signifies the cylinder No for that mating journal and the letter next to the number indicates whether it is for the intake camshaft (I) or exhaust camshaft (E)

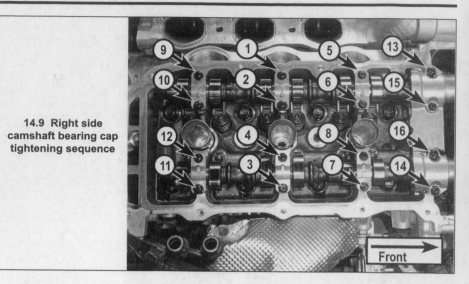

14.9 Right side camshaft bearing cap tightening sequence

cap first, ensuring the thrust face is correctly positioned. Install the remaining bearing caps and hand tighten the bolts **(see illustration)**. **Note:** *Ensure the bearing caps are returned to their original position and the arrows face the center of the cylinder head.*

9   Tighten the bearing cap bolts for both camshafts in sequence **(see illustration)** to the torque listed in this Chapter's Specifications. Once the torque procedure is complete, loosen the bolts labeled 1, 2, 3 and 4 and re-torque them.

10   Repeat Steps 7 through 9 to install the left side cylinder head camshafts **(see illustration)**.

11   The remainder of installation is the reverse of removal.

12   Change the oil and install a new oil filter (see Chapter 1). Run the engine and check for leaks.

15   Oil pan - removal and installation

Removal

Refer to illustration 15.4

1   Disconnect the cable from the negative battery terminal (see Chapter 5).

2   Remove the plenum and intake manifold (see Section 7), valve covers (see Section 4) and timing chain cover (see Section 12).

3   With the engine supported on a suitable engine stand, remove the long bolts retaining the oil pan to the rear main oil seal housing.

4   Remove the remaining bolts holding the oil pan to the timing cover and engine block. Pry the oil pan from the engine block at the

illustrated points **(see illustration)**. As the seal to the block is broken, the oil pickup pipe will disconnect from the oil pump.

5   If necessary, the oil level sensor can be removed by unscrewing it from the oil pan. The baffle inside the oil pan can be removed after removing the retaining bolts. The oil pickup can be removed once the bolts in the bottom of the oil pan are removed. Discard the oil pickup oil seal.

Installation

Refer to illustration 15.11

6   Thoroughly clean the mounting surfaces of the oil pan and engine block of old gasket material and sealer. Wipe the gasket surfaces clean with a rag soaked in lacquer thinner, acetone or brake system cleaner.

7   Check the oil pump pickup for cracks or signs of leakage. Ensure the screen in the bottom of the pickup is not blocked or damaged.

8   Install a new oil seal to the oil pump

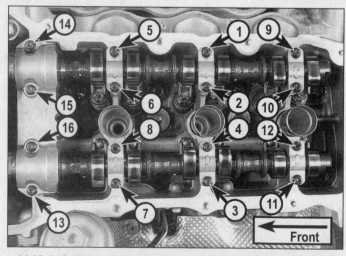

14.10 Left side cylinder head bearing cap tightening sequence

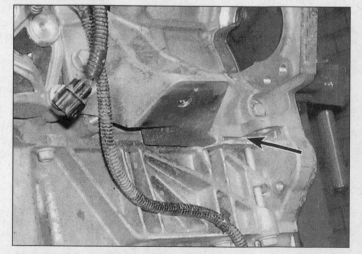

15.4 Arrow indicates a prying point to break the seal between the oil pan and cylinder block. There is another one at the front on the opposite side of the engine

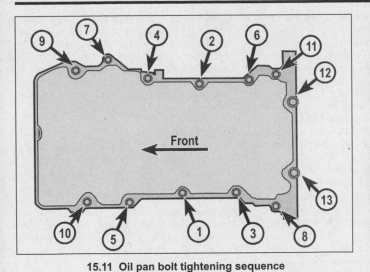

15.11 Oil pan bolt tightening sequence

16.2 Oil pump retaining bolts

pickup. Install the oil pickup and tighten the bolts in the bottom of the oil pan. Install the baffle to the inside of the oil pan, tightening the retaining bolts.

9   Fabricate two aligning studs from M8 x 1.25 mm bolts with the heads removed and screw them into the oil pan bolt holes labeled 1 and 2 to allow for correct oil pan alignment **(see illustration 15.11).**

10   Apply a 1/8-inch (3 mm) wide bead of oxygen sensor safe RTV sealant to the oil pan mating surface with the engine block. Also apply some sealant to the corners of the block where the front cover and the rear cover meet the engine block. Install the oil pan and tighten the bolts finger-tight.

11   Remove the threaded dowel pins before tightening the oil pan bolts in the order shown to the torque listed in this Chapter's Specifications **(see illustration). Note:** *Check Specifications for the correct torque. The two bolts holding the oil pan to the rear main oil seal housing are a different torque than the remaining bolts.*

12   The remainder of installation is the reverse of removal.

13   Add the proper type and quantity of oil (see Chapter 1), start the engine and check for leaks before placing the vehicle back in service.

16   Oil pump - removal, inspection and installation

Removal

Refer to illustration 16.2

1   Remove the plenum and intake manifold (see Section 7), valve covers (see Section 4), timing cover (see Section 12) and timing chains (see Section 13). After noting the installed position, remove the timing chain sprocket from the crankshaft.

2   Remove the oil pump retaining bolts and

slide the pump off the end of the crankshaft **(see illustration)**.

Inspection

3   Remove the timing chain guide from the oil pump housing, remove the oil pump cover and withdraw the rotors from the pump body. Remove the snap-ring from the side of the pump housing and withdraw the cap, spring and plunger from the oil pump housing. These components are the oil pressure relief valve assembly. Clean the components with solvent, dry them thoroughly and inspect for any obvious damage. Also check the bolt holes for damaged threads and the splined surfaces on the crankshaft sprocket for any apparent damage. If any of the components are scored, scratched or worn, replace the entire oil pump assembly. There are no serviceable parts currently available.

Installation

4   If re-using the oil pump, assemble the pressure relief valve components and the rotors to the oil pump housing. Prior to installing the cover, prime the pump by pouring

18.4 Rear main oil seal housing bolts

clean engine oil between the rotors. Install the cover and tighten the retaining bolts.

5   Position the oil pump over the end of the crankshaft and align the teeth on the crankshaft sprocket with the teeth on the oil pump drive gear. Make sure the pump is fully seated against the block.

6   Install the oil pump mounting bolts and tighten them to the torque listed in this Chapter's Specifications.

7   The remainder of installation is the reverse of removal.

8   Add oil and coolant as necessary. Run the engine and check for oil and coolant leaks; also check the oil pressure (see Chapter 2D).

17   Flywheel/driveplate - removal and installation

The flywheel/driveplate removal for the 2.8L, 3.0L and 3.6L V6 engine is identical to the flywheel/driveplate removal procedure for the 3.2L V6 engine. Refer to Chapter 2A for the procedure and use the torque figures in this Chapter's Specifications. **Note:** *New bolts must be used when re-installing the flywheel/ driveplate assembly.*

18   Rear main oil seal - replacement

Refer to illustrations 18.4 and 18.7

1   Disconnect the cable from the negative battery terminal (see Chapter 5).

2   Remove the transmission (see Chapter 7A or 7B).

3   Remove the flywheel/driveplate (see Section 17) and the oil pan (see Section 15).

4   Remove the retaining bolts and remove the seal housing from the engine **(see illustration). Caution:** *Use care not to scratch the machined faces of the cylinder block, rear main seal housing or oil pan when scraping old gasket material from components.*

18.7 Alignment dowels installed to the rear main oil seal housing bolt holes

5   Thoroughly clean the mounting surfaces of the oil pan, rear main oil seal housing and engine block of old gasket material and sealer. Wipe the gasket surfaces clean with a rag soaked in lacquer thinner, acetone or brake cleaner.

6   If the seal is supplied separately from the seal housing, note the installed position of the old seal before tapping it out using a small punch or a seal removal tool. Lubricate the outside diameter of the seal and install the seal over the seal housing. Make sure the lip of the seal points toward the engine. Preferably, a seal installation tool (available at most auto parts stores) should be used to press the new seal back into place. If a seal installation tool is unavailable, use a large socket, section of pipe or a blunt tool and carefully drive the new seal squarely into the seal bore to the same position that the original seal held.

7   Install two threaded dowel pins to the cylinder block to allow for correct rear main oil seal housing alignment **(see illustration)**.

8   Apply a 1/8-inch (3mm) wide bead of RTV sealant around the mating face of the rear main oil seal housing, without going into the bolt holes. Slide the seal over the crankshaft and the dowel pins and tighten the upper bolts finger-tight. **Note:** *Most new rear main oil seals and housing assembly are supplied with a seal protector on the inside running face of the oil seal. Leave this in place until the housing is in position.*

9   Remove the dowel pins and install the remaining rear main oil seal housing bolts. Tighten the bolts to the torque listed in this Chapter's Specifications, then remove the seal protector.

10   Install the oil pan (see Section 15) and flywheel/driveplate (see Section 17).

11   The remainder of installation is the reverse of removal.

12   Add oil, run the engine and check for oil leaks.

19   Engine mounts - check and replacement

1   Engine mounts seldom require attention, but broken or deteriorated mounts should be replaced immediately or the added strain placed on the driveline components may cause damage.

Check

2   During the check, the engine must be raised slightly to remove the weight from the mounts.

3   Raise the vehicle and support it securely on jackstands, then position the jack under the engine oil pan. Place a large block of wood between the jack head and the oil pan, then carefully raise the engine just enough to take the weight off the mounts. Do not use the jack to support the entire weight of the engine.

4   Check the mounts to see if the rubber is cracked, hardened or separated from the metal plates. Sometimes the rubber will split right down the center.

5   Check for relative movement between the mount plates and the engine or subframe (use a large screwdriver or pry bar to attempt to move the mounts). If movement is noted, check the tightness of the mount fasteners first before condemning the mounts. Usually when engine mounts are broken, they are very obvious as the engine will easily move away from the mount when pried or under load.

Replacement

Warning: *The air conditioning system is under high pressure. DO NOT loosen any fittings or remove any components until after the system has been discharged. Air conditioning refrigerant must be properly discharged into an EPA-approved container at a dealer service department or an automotive air conditioning repair facility. Always wear eye protection when disconnecting air conditioning system fittings.*

6   Have the air conditioning refrigerant discharged at a dealer service department or air conditioning shop.

7   Disconnect the cable from the negative battery terminal (see Chapter 5).

8   Remove the shock tower crossbrace (see Chapter 10).

9   Remove the air conditioning lines to the compressor to access the mount top nut.

10   Working below the vehicle, remove the engine mount to front suspension subframe nut and then the engine mount to engine bracket nut.

11   Attach an engine holding fixture or engine hoist to the top of the engine for lifting; do not use a jack under the oil pan to support the entire weight of the engine or the oil pump pick-up could be damaged.

12   Raise the engine slightly until the engine mount can be moved by hand. Unbolt the engine bracket from the engine block and remove it and the engine mount from the vehicle. Separate the mount from the engine bracket.

13   Installation is the reverse of removal. Tighten all fasteners to the torque listed in this Chapter's Specifications.

Chapter 2 Part C
5.7L, 6.0L and 6.2L V8 engines

Contents

Specifications

General

5.7L engine

Engine type	V8
Displacement	346 cubic inches (5.7 liters)
Engine VIN code	S
RPO code	LS6
Bore	3.897 inches (99 mm)
Stroke	3.622 inches (92.0 mm)
Compression ratio	10.5: 1

6.0L engine

Engine type	V8
Displacement	364 cubic inches (6.0 liters)
Engine VIN code	U
RPO code	LS2
Bore	4.0007 inches (101.618 mm)
Stroke	3.622 inches (92.0 mm)
Compression ratio	10.9: 1

6.2L engines

Engine type	V8
Displacement	376 cubic inches (6.2 liters)
Engine VIN code	P
RPO code	LSA
Bore	4.0065 inches (103.241 mm)
Stroke	3.622 inches (92.0 mm)
Compression ratio	9.1:1
Supercharger boost compression ratio	10.1:1
Compression pressure	See Chapter 2D
Oil pressure	See Chapter 2D
Firing order	1-8-7-2-6-5-4-3
Cylinder numbers (drivebelt end-to-transmission end)	
Left bank	2-4-6-8
Right bank	1-3-5-7

24017-1-B HAYNES

Cylinder numbering

Camshafts

5.7L engine
  Lobe height
    Intake .... 0.324 inch (8.24 mm)
    Exhaust .... 0.322 inch (8.19 mm)
  Bearing journal diameter .... 2.1678 to 2.1688 inches (55.063 to 55.088 mm)
6.0L engine
  Lobe height
    Intake .... 0.306 inch (7.78 mm)
    Exhaust .... 0.305 inch (7.77 mm)
  Bearing journal diameter .... 2.164 to 2.166 inches (54.99 to 55.04 mm)
6.2L engine
  Lobe height
    Intake .... 0.283 inch (7.2 mm)
    Exhaust .... 0.283 inch (7.2 mm)
  Bearing journal diameter .... 2.164 to 2.166 inches (54.99 to 55.04 mm)
Endplay (all models) .... 0.001 to 0.012 inch (0.025 to 0.305 mm)

Warpage limits

Cylinder head gasket surfaces (head and block) .... 0.003 inch (0.08 mm)
Intake manifold (head) .... 0.003 inch (0.08 mm)
Exhaust manifold (head) .... 0.004 inch (0.08 mm)
Intake manifold .... 0.02 inch (0.10 mm)

Torque specifications

Note: *One foot-pound (ft-lb) of torque is equivalent to 12 inch-pounds (in-lbs) of torque. Torque values below approximately 15 foot-pounds are expressed in inch-pounds, because most foot-pound torque wrenches are not accurate at these smaller values.*

	Ft-lbs (unless otherwise indicated)	Nm
Camshaft retainer bolts		
5.7L engines	18	25
6.0L engines		
Hex head bolts	18	25
Torx head bolts	132 in-lbs	15
6.2L engines (Torx head bolts)	132 in-lbs	15
Camshaft sprocket bolts		
5.7L engines	26	35
6.0L engines		
Step 1	66	90
Step 2	Tighten an additional 40 degrees	
6.2L engines		
Step 1	55	75
Step 2	Tighten an additional 50 degrees	
Coolant air bleed pipe bolts	106 in-lbs	12
Crankshaft balancer-to-crankshaft bolt		
5.7L and 6.0L engines		
Step 1 (use old bolt to fully seat)	240	330
Step 2 (replace old bolt and install new bolt)	37	50
Step 3	Tighten an additional 140 degrees	
6.2L engines		
Step 1	111	150
Step 2	Loosen 360 degrees	
Step 3		
2004 through 2012	37	50
2013 and later	59	80
Step 4		
2004 through 2012	Tighten an additional 230 degrees	
2013 and later	Tighten an additional 200 degrees	
Crankshaft rear oil seal housing bolts	22	30
Cylinder head bolts, in sequence **(see illustration 9.16)**		
5.7L engines with first design bolts		
Step 1 all M11 bolts	22	30
Step 2 all M11 bolts	Tighten an additional 90 degrees	
Step 3 M11 long bolts	Tighten an additional 90 degrees	
Step 3 M11 short bolts (front/rear cylinder head)	Tighten an additional 50 degrees	
5.7L engines with second design bolts, and all 6.0L engines		
Step 1 all M11 bolts	22	30
Step 2 all M11 bolts	Tighten an additional 90 degrees	
Step 3 all M11 bolts	Tighten an additional 70 degrees	
Step 4 M8 bolts	22	30

Torque specifications

	Ft-lbs (unless otherwise indicated)	Nm
Cylinder head bolts, in sequence (see illustration 9.16) (continued)		
6.2L engines		
Step 1 all M11 bolts	37	50
Step 2 all M11 bolts	Tighten an additional 80 degrees	
Step 3 all M11 bolts	Tighten an additional 55 degrees	
Step 4 M8 bolts	22	30
Exhaust manifold-to-cylinder head bolts/studs		
Step 1	132 in-lbs	15
Step 2		
2004 through 2012	18	25
2013 and later	15	20
Exhaust manifold heat shield bolts		
2007 and earlier models	80 in-lbs	9
2009 and later models	106 in-lbs	12
Flywheel bolts*		
Step 1	37	50
Step 2	Tighten an additional 45 degrees	
Driveplate-to-crankshaft bolts *		
Step 1	15	20
Step 2	37	50
Step 3	74	100
Front cover bolts		
5.7L and 6.0L engines	18	25
6.2L engines	22	30
Intake manifold-to-cylinder head bolts, in sequence (5.7L and 6.0L engines)		
Step 1	44 in-lbs	5
Step 2	89 in-lbs	10
Engine mount bracket-to-block bolts	44	60
Engine mount bracket-to-frame bolts/nuts (5.7L engines)	59	80
Engine mount bracket-to-frame stud (5.7L engines)	59	80
Engine mount-to-mount bracket nuts		
5.7L engines	59	80
6.0L and 6.2L engines	74	100
Engine mount-to-frame nut		
5.7L engines	59	80
6.0L and 6.2L engines	74	100
Oil pan-to-block and front cover bolts (M8)	18	25
Oil pan-to-rear cover bolts (M6)	106 in-lbs	12
Oil pan baffle bolts	106 in-lbs	12
Oil pump relief valve plug	106 in-lbs	12
Oil filter adapter-to-oil pump bolts	17 to 22	24 to 30
Oil pump-to-engine block bolts	18	25
Oil pump cover-screws	106 in-lbs	12
Oil pump pick-up tube		
Bolt	106 in-lbs	12
Nut	18	25
Rocker arm pivot bolts	22	30
Supercharger (6.2L engines)		
Idler pulley bolt		
2005 through 2012	37	50
2013 and later	43	58
Drivebelt tensioner bolt		
2005 through 2012	37	50
2013 and later	43	58
Front cover assembly*		
Step 1	20	27
Step 2 Bolts 1 and 2	20	27
Supercharger-to-cylinder head bolts, in sequence (see illustrations 16.22)		
Step 1	44 in-lbs	5
Step 2	89 in-lbs	10
Charge air cooler cover bolts, in sequence (see illustrations 16.25)		
Step 1	44 in-lbs	5
Step 2	89 in-lbs	10
Timing chain guide bolts (5.7L engines)	26	35
Timing chain tensioner bolt (6.0L engines)	18	25
Timing chain tensioner bolts (6.2L engines)	22	30
Valve cover bolts	106 in-lbs	12
Valley cover bolts	18	25

*Use new bolts

1   General information

Warning: *The models covered by this manual are equipped with airbags. Always disable the airbag system before working in the vicinity of the impact sensors, steering column or instrument panel to avoid the possibility of accidental deployment of the airbag(s), which could cause personal injury (see Chapter 12).*

How to use this Chapter

This Part of Chapter 2 is devoted to repair procedures possible while the engine is still installed in the vehicle. Since these procedures are based on the assumption that the engine is installed in the vehicle, if the engine has been removed from the vehicle and mounted on a stand, some of the preliminary removal steps outlined will not apply.

Information concerning engine/transmission removal and installation and engine overhaul can be found in Part D of this Chapter.

Engine description

This Part of Chapter 2 is devoted to in-vehicle repair procedures for the 5.7L, 6.0L and 6.2L supercharged V8 engines. The main difference between the three types of engines covered is bore size and the supercharger used on 6.2L engines. All information concerning engine removal and installation and engine block and cylinder head overhaul on these engines can be found in Part D of this Chapter.

Since the repair procedures included in this Part are based on the assumption the engine is still in the vehicle, if they are being used during a complete engine overhaul (with the engine already out of the vehicle and on a stand) many of the Steps included here will not apply.

The Specifications included in this Part of Chapter 2 apply only to the procedures found here. The specifications necessary for rebuilding the block and cylinder heads are included in Part D.

The engine utilizes an aluminum block with cast-iron sleeves. The eight cylinders are arranged in a "V" shape at a 90-degree angle between the two banks. The cylinder heads utilize an overhead valve arrangement. The engine uses aluminum cylinder heads with powdered metal guides and valve seats. Hydraulic roller lifters actuate the valves through tubular pushrods and rocker arms. The oil pump is mounted at the front of the engine behind the timing chain cover and is driven by the crankshaft.

2   Repair operations possible with the engine in the vehicle

Many major repair operations can be accomplished without removing the engine from the vehicle.

Clean the engine compartment and the exterior of the engine with some type of degreaser before any work is done. It will make the job easier and help keep dirt out of the internal areas of the engine.

Depending on the components involved, it may be helpful to remove the hood to improve access to the engine as repairs are performed (refer to Chapter 11 if necessary). Cover the fenders to prevent damage to the paint. Special pads are available, but an old bedspread or blanket will also work.

If vacuum, exhaust, oil or coolant leaks develop, indicating a need for gasket or seal replacement, the repairs can generally be made with the engine in the vehicle. The intake and exhaust manifold gaskets, oil pan gasket, crankshaft oil seals and cylinder head gasket are all accessible with the engine in place.

Exterior engine components, such as the intake and exhaust manifolds, the oil pan, the oil pump, the water pump, the starter motor, the alternator and the fuel system components can be removed for repair with the engine in place.

Since the camshaft(s) and cylinder head can be removed without pulling the engine, valve component servicing can also be accomplished with the engine in the vehicle. Replacement of the timing chain and sprockets is also possible with the engine in the vehicle.

In extreme cases caused by a lack of necessary equipment, repair or replacement of piston rings, pistons, connecting rods and rod bearings is possible with the engine in the vehicle. However, this practice is not recommended because of the cleaning and preparation work that must be done to the components involved.

3   Top Dead Center (TDC) for number one piston - locating

Refer to illustration 3.6

1   Top Dead Center (TDC) is the highest point in the cylinder that each piston reaches as it travels up the cylinder bore. Each piston reaches TDC on the compression stroke and again on the exhaust stroke, but TDC generally refers to piston position on the compression stroke.

2   Positioning the piston(s) at TDC is an essential part of many procedures such as distributor and timing chain/sprocket removal.

3   Before beginning this procedure, be sure to place the transmission in Neutral and apply the parking brake or block the rear wheels. Also, disable the ignition system by disconnecting the primary electrical connectors at the ignition coil packs, then remove the spark plugs (see Chapter 1).

4   In order to bring any piston to TDC, the crankshaft must be turned using one of the methods outlined below. When looking at the front of the engine, normal crankshaft rotation is clockwise.

a)   *The preferred method is to turn the crankshaft with a socket and ratchet attached to the bolt threaded into the front of the crankshaft. Apply pressure on the bolt in a clockwise direction only. Never turn the bolt counter clockwise.*

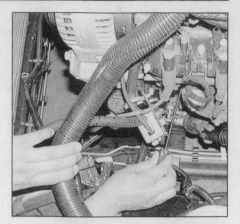

3.6 A long screwdriver inserted in the number one spark plug hole can be used to determine the highest point reached by that piston - make sure to wrap the tip of the screwdriver with tape to avoid scratching the top of the piston or the cylinder walls

b)   *A remote starter switch, which may save some time, can also be used. Follow the instructions included with the switch. Once the piston is close to TDC, use a socket and ratchet as described in the previous paragraph.*

c)   *If an assistant is available to turn the ignition switch to the Start position in short bursts, you can get the piston close to TDC without a remote starter switch. Make sure your assistant is out of the vehicle, away from the ignition switch, then use a socket and ratchet as described in Paragraph (a) to complete the procedure.*

5   Place your finger partially over the number one spark plug hole and rotate the crankshaft using one of the methods described above until air pressure is felt at the spark plug hole. Air pressure at the spark plug hole indicates that the cylinder has started the compression stroke. Once the compression stroke has begun, TDC for the number one cylinder is obtained when the piston reaches the top of the cylinder on the compression stroke.

6   To bring the piston to the top of the cylinder, insert a long screwdriver into the number one spark plug hole until it touches the top of the piston. **Note:** *Make sure to wrap the tip of the screwdriver with tape to avoid scratching the top of the piston and the cylinder walls.* Use the screwdriver (as a feeler gauge) to tell where the top of the piston is located in the cylinder while slowly rotating the crankshaft **(see illustration)**. As the piston rises the screwdriver will be pushed out. The point at which the screwdriver stops moving outward is TDC. **Note:** *Always hold the screwdriver upright while the engine is being rotated so that the screwdriver will not get wedged as the piston travels upward.*

7   If you go past TDC, rotate the crankshaft counter clockwise until the piston is approximately 1/2-inch below TDC, then slowly rotate

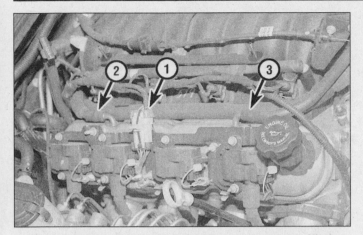

4.4 Disconnect the coil main wiring harness connector (1), the PCV hose (2) and the fresh air hose (3) from the valve cover (right side shown)

4.7 Using the quick release tool, remove the fuel line (1), then disconnect the EVAP purge valve and line (2) and coil main wiring harness (3) (left side shown)

the crankshaft clockwise again until TDC is reached.

8   After the number one piston has been positioned at TDC on the compression stroke, TDC for any of the remaining pistons can be located by repeating the procedure described above and following the firing order.

4   Valve covers - removal and installation

Removal

Refer to illustrations 4.4, 4.7 and 4.9

1   Disconnect the cable from the negative battery terminal (see Chapter 5).

2   Remove the engine top front cover fasteners, then remove the cover. Remove the rear cover fasteners, lift the rear cover up and remove it from the vehicle.

3   Remove the air filter and resonator assembly to allow access to the front of the engine (see Chapter 4).

Right side

4   Unclip the wiring harness from the ignition coil bracket and lay it aside. Remove the fresh air hose and PCV hose from the valve cover **(see illustration)**.

5   Remove the ignition coils from the valve

cover (see Chapter 5). Be sure each plug wire is labeled before removal to ensure correct installation.

6   Remove the valve cover bolts **(see illustration 4.9)**, then remove the cover from the cylinder head. **Note:** *If the cover is stuck to the cylinder head, bump one end with a block of wood and a hammer to jar it loose. If that doesn't work, try to slip a flexible putty knife between the cylinder head and cover to break the gasket seal. Don't pry at the cover-to-head joint or damage to the sealing surfaces may occur (leading to oil leaks in the future).*

Left side

7   Relieve the fuel system pressure. Remove the fuel feed and return lines from the fuel rail and the vapor purge valve **(see illustration)** (see Chapter 4). Unclip the wiring harness from the ignition coil bracket and lay it aside.

8   Remove the ignition coil assembly from the valve cover (see Chapter 5). Be sure each plug wire is labeled before removal to ensure correct installation.

9   Remove the valve cover bolts **(see illustration)**, then remove the cover from the cylinder head. **Note:** *If the cover is stuck to the cylinder head, bump one end with a block of wood and a hammer to jar it loose. If that doesn't work, try to slip a flexible putty knife*

between the cylinder head and cover to break the gasket seal. Don't pry at the cover-to-head joint or damage to the sealing surfaces may occur (leading to oil leaks in the future).

Installation

Refer to illustration 4.12

10   The mating surfaces of each cylinder head and valve cover must be perfectly clean when the covers are installed. Use a gasket scraper to remove all traces of sealant and old gasket material, then clean the mating surfaces with lacquer thinner or acetone. If there's sealant or oil on the mating surfaces when the cover is installed, oil leaks may develop.

11   Clean the mounting bolt threads with a die to remove any corrosion and restore damaged threads. Make sure the threaded holes in the cylinder head are clean - run a tap into them to remove corrosion and restore damaged threads.

12   The gaskets should be mated to the covers before the covers are installed. Position the gasket inside the cover lip **(see illustration)**. If the gasket will not stay in place in the cover lip, apply a thin coat of RTV sealant to the cover flange, and allow the sealant to set up so the gasket adheres to the cover.

4.9 Valve cover mounting bolts - arrow to the far right indicates location of the PCV valve (left valve cover shown)

4.12 Position the new gasket in the valve cover lip

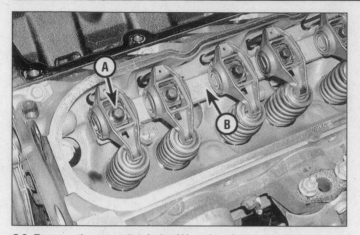

5.2 Remove the mounting bolts (A) and rocker arms, then remove the pivot support pedestal (B)

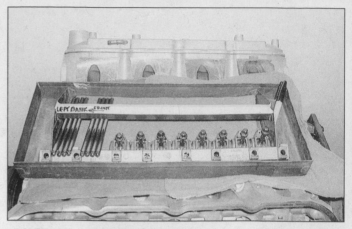

5.3 Store the pushrods and rocker arms in order to ensure they are installed in their original locations - note the arrow indicating the front of the engine

13   Inspect the valve cover bolt grommets for damage. If the grommets aren't damaged they can be reused. Carefully position the valve cover(s) on the cylinder head and install the bolts and grommets.

14   Tighten the bolts in three or four steps to the torque listed in this Chapter's Specifications.

15   The remainder of installation is the reverse of removal.

16   Start the engine and check carefully for oil leaks.

5   Rocker arms and pushrods - removal, inspection and installation

Removal

Refer to illustrations 5.2 and 5.3

1   Remove the valve covers from the cylinder heads (see Section 4).

2   Loosen the rocker arm pivot bolts one at a time and remove the rocker arms and bolts,

then remove the pivot support pedestal **(see illustration)**. Keep track of the rocker arm positions, since they must be returned to the same locations. Store each set of rocker components separately in a marked plastic bag to ensure that they're installed in their original locations.

3   Remove the pushrods and store them separately to make sure they don't get mixed up during installation **(see illustration)**.

Inspection

Refer to illustration 5.4

4   Check each rocker arm for wear, cracks and other damage, especially where the pushrods and valve stems contact the rocker arm **(see illustration)**.

5   Check the pivot bearings for binding and roughness. If the bearings are worn or damaged, replacement of the entire rocker arm will be necessary. **Note:** *Keep in mind that there is no valve adjustment on these engines, so excessive wear or damage in the valve train can easily result in excessive valve clearance, which in turn will cause valve noise when the*

engine is running. Also check the rocker arm pivot support pedestal for cracks and other obvious damage.

6   Make sure the hole at the pushrod end of each rocker arm is open.

7   Inspect the pushrods for cracks and excessive wear at the ends, also check that the oil hole running through each pushrod is not clogged. Roll each pushrod across a piece of plate glass to see if it's bent (if it wobbles, it's bent).

Installation

Refer to illustration 5.9

8   Lubricate the lower end of each pushrod with clean engine oil or engine assembly lube and install them in their original locations. Make sure each pushrod seats completely in the lifter socket.

9   Apply engine assembly lube to the ends of the valve stems and to the upper ends of the pushrods to prevent damage to the mating surfaces on initial start-up **(see illustration)**. Also apply clean engine oil to the pivot shaft and bearing of each rocker arm and install the rocker arms loosely in their original locations. DO NOT tighten the bolts at this time!

10   Rotate the crankshaft until the number one piston is at TDC (see Section 3). With the number one piston is at TDC, tighten the intake valve rocker arms for the Number 1, 3, 4 and 5 cylinders and the exhaust rocker arms for the Number 1, 2, 7 and 8 cylinders. Tighten each of the specified rocker arm bolts to the torque listed in this Chapter's Specifications.

11   Rotate the crankshaft 360 degrees. Tighten the intake valve rocker arms for the Number 2, 6, 7 and 8 cylinders and the exhaust rocker arms for the Number 3, 4, 5 and 6 cylinders. Tighten each of the rocker arm bolts to the torque listed in this Chapter's Specifications.

12   Install the valve covers (see Section 4). Start the engine, listen for unusual valve train noises and check for oil leaks at the valve cover gaskets.

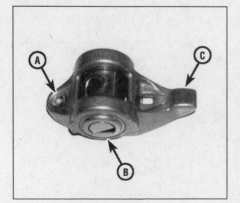

5.4 Rocker arm wear points

A   Pushrod socket
B   Pivot bearings
C   Valve stem contact point

5.9 Lubricate the pushrod ends and the valve stems with engine assembly lube before installing the rocker arms

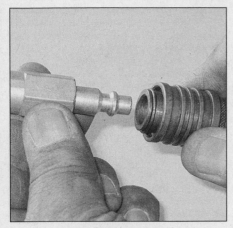

6.5 Thread the air hose adapter into the spark plug hole - adapters are commonly available from auto parts stores

6.8 Once the spring is depressed, the keepers can be removed with a small magnet or needle-nose pliers (a magnet is preferred to prevent dropping the keepers)

6.10 Use a pair of needle-nose pliers to remove the valve seals

6   Valve springs, retainers and seals - replacement

Refer to illustrations 6.5, 6.8, 6.10 and 6.18

Note: *Broken valve springs and defective valve stem seals can be replaced without removing the cylinder head. Two special tools and a compressed air source are normally required to perform this operation, so read through this Section carefully and rent or buy the tools before beginning the job.*

1   Remove the spark plugs (see Chapter 1).
2   Remove the valve covers (see Section 4).
3   Rotate the crankshaft until the number one piston is at Top Dead Center on the compression stroke (see Section 3).
4   Remove the rocker arms for the number 1 piston (see Section 5).
5   Thread an adapter into the spark plug hole and connect an air hose from a compressed air source to it **(see illustration)**. Most auto parts stores can supply the air hose adapter. **Note:** *Many cylinder compression gauges utilize a screw-in fitting that may work with your air hose quick-disconnect fitting. If a cylinder compression gauge fitting is used, it will be necessary to remove the Schrader valve from the end of the fitting before using it in this procedure.*
6   Apply compressed air to the cylinder. The valves should be held in place by the air pressure. **Warning:** *If the cylinder isn't exactly at TDC, air pressure may force the piston down, causing the engine to quickly rotate. DO NOT leave a wrench on the crankshaft balancer bolt or you may be injured by the tool.*
7   Stuff shop rags into the cylinder head holes around the valves to prevent parts and tools from falling into the engine.
8   Using a socket and a hammer gently tap on the top of each valve spring retainer several times (this will break the seal between the valve keeper and the spring retainer and allow

the keeper to separate from the valve spring retainer as the valve spring is compressed), then use a valve-spring compressor to compress the spring. Remove the keepers with small needle-nose pliers or a magnet **(see illustration)**. **Note:** *Several different types of tools are available for compressing the valve springs with the head in place. One type grips the lower spring coils and presses on the retainer as the knob is turned, while the lever-type shown here utilizes the rocker arm bolt for leverage. Both types work very well, although the lever type is usually less expensive.*
9   Remove the valve spring and retainer. **Note:** *If air pressure fails to retain the valve in the closed position during this operation, the valve face or seat may be damaged. If so, the cylinder head will have to be removed for repair.*
10   Remove the old valve stem seals, noting differences between the intake and exhaust seals **(see illustration)**.
11   Wrap a rubber band or tape around the top of the valve stem so the valve won't fall into the combustion chamber, then release the air pressure.
12   Inspect the valve stem for damage. Rotate the valve in the guide and check the end for eccentric movement, which would indicate that the valve is bent.
13   Move the valve up-and-down in the guide and make sure it does not bind. If the valve stem binds, either the valve is bent or the guide is damaged. In either case, the head will have to be removed for repair.
14   Reapply air pressure to the cylinder to retain the valve in the closed position, then remove the tape or rubber band from the valve stem.
15   Install the new valve stem seals, carefully pressing them over the ends of the intake and exhaust valve guides.
16   Install the spring and retainer in position over the valve.

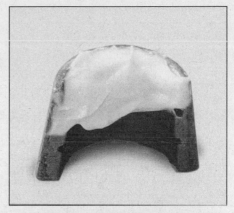

6.18 Apply small dab of grease to each keeper as shown here before installation - it'll hold them in place on the valve stem as the spring is released

17   Compress the valve spring assembly only enough to install the keepers in the valve stem.
18   Position the keepers in the valve stem groove. Apply a small dab of grease to the inside of each keeper to hold it in place if necessary **(see illustration)**. Remove the pressure from the spring tool and make sure the keepers are seated.
19   Disconnect the air hose and remove the adapter from the spark plug hole.
20   Repeat the above procedure on the remaining cylinders, following the firing order sequence (see this Chapter's Specifications). Bring each piston to TDC on the compression stroke before applying air pressure (see Section 3).
21   Install the rocker arm assemblies and the valve covers (see Sections 4 and 5).
22   Start the engine, then check for oil leaks and unusual sounds coming from the valve cover area. Allow the engine to idle for at least five minutes before accelerating the engine.

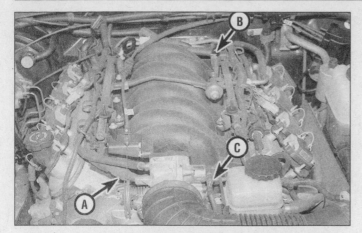

7.7 Locations of the fresh air hose (A), power brake booster vacuum hose (B) and the TPS connector (C) to the throttle body

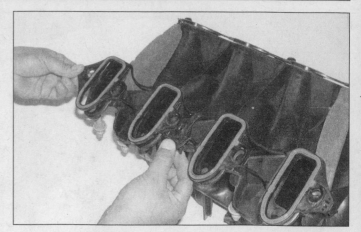

7.13 Align the tabs on the intake gaskets with the tabs on the manifold and snap the gasket into place

7   Intake manifold (5.7L and 6.0L engines) - removal and installation

Warning: Wait until the engine is completely cool before starting this procedure.

Removal

Refer to illustration 7.7

1   Disconnect the cable from the negative battery terminal (see Chapter 5).
2   Remove the engine top front cover fasteners, then remove the cover. Remove the rear cover fasteners, lift the rear cover up and remove it from the vehicle. Disconnect the electrical connector to the throttle body.
3   Remove the air filter and the air intake assembly, then relieve the fuel system pressure (see Chapter 4).
4   Disconnect the electrical connectors from the fuel injectors.
5   Disconnect the electrical connectors

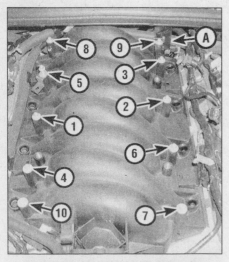

7.15 Intake manifold bolt tightening sequence - (A) is the fuel stop bracket

from the EVAP solenoid, the MAP sensor and the sensors on the throttle body. Label each connector clearly to aid in the reassembly process. Disconnect the knock sensor electrical connectors and remove the ground straps at the rear of the left cylinder head. Remove any remaining wiring harness brackets from the top of the intake manifold and lay the harness aside.
6   Remove the fuel rails and injectors as an assembly (see Chapter 4). The two fuel rails can be pulled straight up with the injectors still attached, but it will take some force to dislodge the injectors from the intake manifold. **Note:** This Step is not absolutely necessary, but it will help prevent subsequent damage to the fuel injectors as the intake manifold is removed.
7   Disconnect the coolant hoses from the throttle body. Disconnect any vacuum hoses attached to the intake manifold or throttle body, such as the power brake booster, the PCV and the EVAP purge control valve **(see illustration)**.
8   Disconnect any remaining electrical connectors or vacuum hoses connected to the intake manifold or throttle body.
9   Loosen the intake manifold mounting bolts in 1/4-turn increments in the reverse order of the tightening sequence **(see illustration 7.15)** until they can be removed by hand. The manifold will probably be stuck to the cylinder heads and force may be required to break the gasket seal. A prybar can be positioned between the front of the manifold and the valley tray to break the bond made by the gasket. **Caution:** Do not pry between the manifold and the heads or damage to the gasket sealing surfaces may result and vacuum leaks could develop. Also, don't use too much force - the manifold is made of a plastic composite and could crack.
10   Remove the intake manifold. As the manifold is lifted from the engine, check for and disconnect anything still attached to the manifold.

Installation

Refer to illustrations 7.13 and 7.15

Note: The mating surfaces of the cylinder heads, block and manifold must be perfectly clean when the manifold is installed.
11   Carefully remove all traces of old gasket material. Note that the intake manifold is made of a composite material and the cylinder heads are made of aluminum, therefore aggressive scraping is not suggested and will damage the sealing surfaces. After the gasket surfaces are cleaned and free of any gasket material wipe the mating surfaces with a cloth saturated with safety solvent. If there is old sealant or oil on the mating surfaces when the manifold is installed, oil or vacuum leaks may develop. Use a vacuum cleaner to remove any gasket material that falls into the intake ports in the heads.
12   Use a tap of the correct size to chase the threads in the bolt holes, then use compressed air (if available) to remove the debris from the holes. **Warning:** Wear safety glasses or a face shield to protect your eyes when using compressed air.
13   Position the new gaskets on the intake manifold **(see illustration)**. Note that the gaskets are equipped with installation tabs that must snap into place on the intake manifold. The words "Manifold Side" may appear on the gasket. If so, this will ensure proper installation. Make sure the gaskets snap into place and all intake port openings align.
14   Carefully set the manifold in place.
15   Apply medium-strength thread locking compound to the threads of the bolts. Install the bolts and tighten them following the recommended sequence **(see illustration)** to the torque listed in this Chapter's Specifications. Do not overtighten the bolts or gasket leaks may develop.
16   The remainder of installation is the reverse of removal. Check the coolant level, adding as necessary (see Chapter 1). Start the engine and check carefully for vacuum leaks at the intake manifold joints.

8   Exhaust manifolds - removal and installation

Removal

Refer to illustrations 8.4, 8.7 and 8.9

Warning: *Use caution when working around the exhaust manifolds - the sheetmetal heat shields can be sharp on the edges. Also, the engine should be cold when this procedure is followed.*

1   Disconnect the cable from the negative battery terminal (see Chapter 5).
2   Raise the vehicle and support it securely on jackstands.
3   Working under the vehicle, apply penetrating oil to the exhaust pipe-to-manifold studs and nuts (they're usually rusty). Disconnect the electrical connector for the oxygen sensor.
4   Remove the nuts retaining the exhaust pipe(s) to the manifold(s) **(see illustration)**.
5   Remove the engine top front cover fasteners, then remove the cover. Remove the rear cover fasteners, lift the rear cover up and remove it from the vehicle.
6   Remove the spark plug wires and remove the spark plugs from the side being worked on (see Chapter 1). If both manifolds are being removed, remove all the spark plug wires and remove all the spark plugs.
7   For the right side manifold, remove the oil dipstick, unbolt the dipstick tube bracket and remove the dipstick tube **(see illustration)**.
8   For the left side manifold, disconnect the steering shaft from the steering gear (see Chapter 10) and set the shaft to the side.
9   Remove the mounting bolts and separate the exhaust manifold from the cylinder head **(see illustration)**. Remove the heat shields from the manifold after the manifold has been removed.

Installation

10   Check the manifold for cracks and make sure the bolt threads are clean and undam-

aged. The manifold and cylinder head mating surfaces must be clean before the manifolds are installed - use a gasket scraper to remove all carbon deposits and gasket material. **Note:** *The cylinder heads are made of aluminum, therefore aggressive scraping is not suggested and will damage the sealing surfaces.*
11   Install the heat shields, then the bolts and gaskets onto the manifold. Retaining tabs surrounding the gasket bolt holes should hold the assembly together as the manifold is installed.
12   Starting at the fourth thread, apply a small amount of medium-strength thread locking compound to the threads of the bolts. **Note:** *The manufacturer recommends not applying thread locking compound on the first three threads.*
13   Place the manifold on the cylinder head and install the mounting bolts finger tight.
14   When tightening the mounting bolts, work from the center to the ends and be sure to use a torque wrench. Tighten the bolts in two steps to the torque listed in this Chapter's Specifications. If required, bend the exposed end of the exhaust manifold gasket back against the cylinder head.
15   The remainder of installation is the reverse of removal.
16   Start the engine and check for exhaust leaks.

9   Cylinder heads - removal and installation

Note: *It will be necessary to purchase a new set of head bolts to perform this procedure.*

Removal

Refer to illustration 9.8

1   Disconnect the cable from the negative battery terminal (see Chapter 5).
2   On 5.7L and 6.0L engines, remove the intake manifold (see Section 7) and the cool-

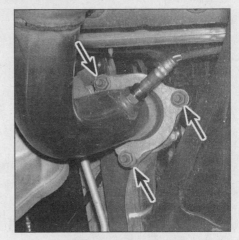

8.4   Remove the exhaust pipe-to-manifold nuts

ant bleed pipe mounting bolts and pipe. On 6.2L engines, remove the supercharger (see Section 16).
3   Remove the valve covers (see Section 4).
4   Remove both exhaust manifolds from the cylinder heads (see Section 8) and the oil dipstick tube from the right side.
5   Remove the rocker arms and pushrods (see Section 5). **Caution:** *Keep all the parts in order so they are reinstalled in the same location.*
6   Disconnect the wiring from the back of the alternator. Remove the power steering pump and the power steering pump rear mounting bracket from the left cylinder head. Lay the pump and brackets aside without disconnecting the lines from the steering pump (see Chapter 10).
7   Loosen the head bolts in 1/4-turn increments in the reverse order of the tightening sequence **(see illustration 9.16)** until they can be removed by hand. **Note:** *There will be different length and size head bolts for different locations. Make a note of the different*

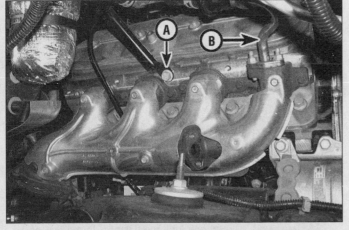

8.7   Remove the oil dipstick tube mounting bolt (A) and tube - (B) indicates the secondary air injection check valve and pipe assembly on the right manifold

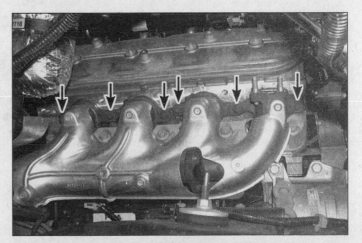

8.9   Exhaust manifold fastener locations (right side shown, left side similar)

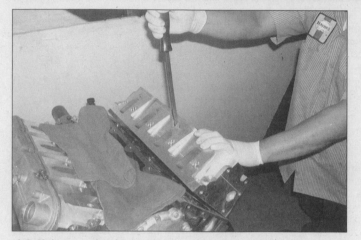

9.8 Using a prybar inserted into an intake port to break the head loose - do not use excessive force or damage to the head may result

9.13 Position the head gasket over the dowels at each end of the cylinder head with the mark facing the front of the vehicle

sizes and lengths and where they go when removing the bolts to ensure correct installation of the new bolts.

8   Lift the heads off the engine. If resistance is felt, do not pry between the head and block as damage to the mating surfaces will result. To dislodge the head, place a prybar or long screwdriver into the intake port and carefully pry the head off the engine **(see illustration)**. Store the heads on blocks of wood to prevent damage to the gasket sealing surfaces.

Installation

Refer to illustrations 9.13 and 9.16

9   The mating surfaces of the cylinder head and the block must be perfectly clean before installing the cylinder head. Clean the surfaces with a scraper, but be careful not to gouge the aluminum. **Caution:** *Be very careful when scraping on aluminum engine parts. Aluminum is soft and gouges easily. Severely gouged parts may require replacement.*

10   Check the mating surfaces of the block and the cylinder head for nicks, deep scratches, and other damage. If slight, they can be removed carefully with a file; if exces-

sive, machining may be the only alternative to replacement.

11   If you suspect warpage of the cylinder head gasket surface, use a straightedge to check it for distortion. If the gasket mating surface of your cylinder head or block is out of specification or is severely nicked or scratched, consult an automotive machine shop for advice.

12   Clean the mating surfaces of the cylinder head and block with a clean shop towel and brake system cleaner. Use a wire brush to remove the thread locking compound from the 8 mm head bolts. Corrosion, sealant and damaged threads will affect torque readings, so be sure the threads are clean.

13   Position the new gaskets over the dowels in the block **(see illustration)**.

14   Carefully position the heads on the block without disturbing the gaskets.

15   Before installing the 8 mm head bolts (bolts 11 through 15), coat the threads with a medium-strength thread locking compound, then install them finger tight.

16   Install new 11 mm head bolts (bolts 1 through 10) and tighten them finger tight. Following the recommended sequence **(see**

illustration), tighten the bolts in four steps to the torque and angle of rotation listed in this Chapter's Specifications. **Warning:** *DO NOT reuse 11 mm head bolts - always replace them with new ones.*

17   Install the coolant bleed pipe, using new O-rings, onto the cylinder heads. Tighten the bolts to the torque listed in this Chapter's Specifications.

18   The remainder of installation is the reverse of removal.

19   Add coolant and change the oil and filter (see Chapter 1). Start the engine and check for proper operation and coolant or oil leaks.

---

10   Crankshaft balancer - removal and installation

Refer to illustrations 10.5a, 10.5b and 10.6
Note: *This procedure requires a new crankshaft balancer bolt and special balancer installation tools J 41665 and EN-47812 (available through specialized tool manufacturers only). Read through the entire procedure and obtain all tools and materials before proceeding.*

1   Disconnect the cable from the negative battery terminal (see Chapter 5).

2   Raise the front of the vehicle and support it securely on jackstands, then apply the parking brake.

3   Remove the splash shield and the drivebelt (see Chapter 1).

4   Working under the vehicle, remove the transmission oil cooler lines and the power steering cooler lines from the radiator (if equipped).

5   Use a strap wrench around the crankshaft pulley to hold it while using a breaker bar and socket to remove the crankshaft pulley center bolt **(see illustration)**. Measure the distance from the balancer to the end of the crankshaft snout for installation **(see illustration)**.

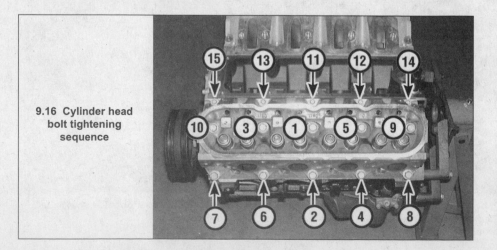

9.16 Cylinder head bolt tightening sequence

10.5a Use a strap wrench to hold the crankshaft balancer while removing the center bolt (a chain-type wrench may be used if you wrap a section of old drivebelt or rag around the balancer first)

10.5b Before the new crankshaft bolt is installed and tightened, the balancer must be measured for proper depth - it should match the original measurement taken before removal

6   Pull the balancer off the crankshaft with a puller **(see illustration)** and remove the washer from the end of the balancer, if equipped **Caution:** *The jaws of the puller must only contact the hub of the balancer - not the outer ring.* **Note:** *A long Allen-head bolt should be inserted into the crankshaft nose for the puller's tapered tip to push against to prevent damage to the crankshaft threads.*

7   Install the balancer washer to the end of the balancer, position the crankshaft pulley/balancer on the crankshaft and slide it on as far as it will go. Note that the slot (keyway) in the hub must be aligned with the Woodruff key in the end of the crankshaft.

8   Using the specialized crankshaft balancer installation tool, press the crankshaft pulley/balancer onto the crankshaft.

9   Install the old crankshaft balancer bolt and tighten the crankshaft bolt to Step 1 of the torque listed in this Chapter's Specifications. Remove the old bolt and make sure the distance from the end of the crankshaft snout and the balancer is the same as mea-

sured in Step 5 **(see illustration 10.5b)**. If the measurement is incorrect, install the balancer installation tool and press the balancer on the crankshaft until the measurement is correct.

10   Install a new crankshaft balancer bolt and tighten it in two steps to the torque and angle of rotation listed in this Chapter's Specifications. **Note:** *Some models are equipped with balance weights that need to transferred from the old balancer to the replacement unit.*

11   The remainder of installation is the reverse of removal.

11   Crankshaft front oil seal - removal and installation

Refer to illustrations 11.2 and 11.4

1   Remove the crankshaft balancer (see Section 10).

2   Note how the seal is installed - the new one must be installed to the same depth and facing the same way. Carefully pry the oil seal out of the cover with a seal puller or a large

screwdriver **(see illustration)**. Be very careful not to distort the cover or scratch the crankshaft! Wrap electrical tape around the tip of the screwdriver to avoid damage to the crankshaft.

3   If the seal is being replaced with the timing chain cover removed, support the cover on top of two blocks of wood and drive the seal out from the backside with a hammer and punch. **Caution:** *Be careful not to scratch, gouge or distort the area that the seal fits into, or a leak will develop.*

4   Apply clean engine oil or multi-purpose grease to the outer edge of the new seal, then install it in the cover with the lip (spring side) facing IN. Drive the seal into place **(see illustration)** with a large socket and a hammer (if a large socket isn't available, a piece of pipe will also work). Make sure the seal enters the bore squarely and stop when the front face is at the proper depth.

5   Check the surface on the balancer hub that the oil seal rides on. If the surface has been grooved from long-time contact with the seal the balancer will need to be replaced.

10.6 The use of a three jaw puller will be necessary to remove the crankshaft balancer - always place the puller jaws around the hub, not the outer ring

11.2 Carefully pry the old seal out of the timing chain cover - don't damage the crankshaft in the process

11.4 Drive the new seal into place with a large socket and hammer

12.8 Timing chain cover mounting bolts

12.11 Timing chain alignment marks - when properly aligned, the crankshaft gear should be in the 12 o'clock position, the camshaft gear should be in the 6 o'clock position and the number one piston should be at TDC

6   Lubricate the balancer hub with clean engine oil and install the crankshaft balancer (see Section 10).
7   The remainder of installation is the reverse of the removal.

12   Timing chain - removal, inspection and installation

Removal and inspection

Refer to illustrations 12.8, 12.11 and 12.14

1   Disconnect the cable from the negative battery terminal (see Chapter 5).
2   Remove the front engine cover fasteners, then remove the cover. Remove the rear cover fasteners, lift the rear cover up and remove it from the vehicle.
3   Drain the cooling system and engine oil, and remove the drivebelt (see Chapter 1).
4   Remove the air filter and the air intake resonator from the engine compartment (see

Chapter 4), then remove the upper and lower radiator hoses, the cooling fans, and the water pump (see Chapter 3).
5   Remove the crankshaft balancer (see Section 10) and, on 6.0L and 6.2L engines, the Camshaft Position (CMP) sensor (see Chapter 6).
6   Remove the oil pan (see Section 14).
7   Remove the alternator, the alternator bracket mounting bolts and bracket (see Chapter 5).
8   Remove the timing chain cover mounting bolts and separate the timing chain cover from the block **(see illustration)**. The cover may be stuck; if so, use a putty knife to break the gasket seal. Since the cover is made of aluminum it can easily be damaged, so DO NOT attempt to pry it off.
9   Remove the oil pick-up tube and the oil pump (see Section 15).
10   Inspect the gears, chain and dampener for wear, cracks or deep grooves; replace if any of these are found.
11   Loosen the camshaft sprocket bolts one

turn, then screw the crankshaft balancer bolt into the end of the crankshaft. Rotate the crankshaft in the normal direction of rotation (clockwise) until the timing marks align **(see illustration)**. Verify that the number one piston is at TDC.
12   Remove the bolts from the end of the camshaft, then remove the camshaft sprocket and chain as an assembly.
13   Inspect the camshaft and crankshaft sprockets for damage or wear.
14   If replacement of the timing chain is necessary, remove the sprocket on the crankshaft with a two-or three-jaw puller, but be careful not to damage the threads in the end of the crankshaft **(see illustration)**.

Installation

Refer to illustrations 12.17, 12.21 and 12.22

Note: *Timing chains must be replaced as a set with the camshaft and crankshaft sprockets. Never put a new chain on old sprockets.*
15   Use a gasket scraper to remove all traces of old gasket material and sealant from the cover and engine block.
16   Align the crankshaft sprocket with the Woodruff key and press the sprocket onto the crankshaft (if removed) with the crankshaft balancer bolt, a large socket and some washers, or tap it gently into place, until it is completely seated. **Caution:** *If resistance is encountered, do not hammer the sprocket onto the crankshaft. It may eventually move onto the shaft, but it may be cracked in the process and fail later, causing extensive engine damage.*
17   Loop the new chain over the camshaft sprocket, then turn the sprocket until the timing mark is at the bottom **(see illustration)**. Mesh the chain with the crankshaft sprocket and position the crankshaft sprocket on the end of the camshaft. If necessary, turn the camshaft so the dowel in the camshaft fits into the hole in the sprocket with the timing mark in the 6 o'clock position **(see illustration 12.11)**. When the chain is installed, the timing marks MUST align as shown.

12.14 The sprocket on the crankshaft can be removed with a two or three-jaw puller

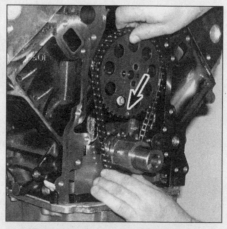

12.17 Slip the chain and camshaft sprocket in place over the crankshaft sprocket with the camshaft sprocket timing mark at the bottom

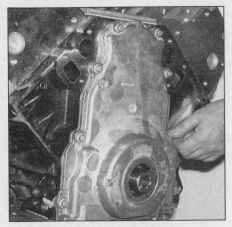

12.21 LOOSELY install the front cover with a new gasket onto the engine block - the cover must be aligned properly before final installation

12.22 With the crankshaft balancer in place and the front cover bolts installed LOOSELY, measure the distance between the oil pan rail and the front cover sealing surface on each side - then adjust the cover so the measurements are even on both sides before tightening the cover bolts

18   Apply a thread locking compound to the camshaft sprocket bolt threads and tighten the bolts to the torque listed in this Chapter's Specifications.

19   Lubricate the chain with clean engine oil.

20   Install the oil pump and the oil pick-up tube onto the engine (see Section 15). Now would be a good time to replace the crankshaft front oil seal (see Section 11).

21   Loosely install the timing chain cover on the engine, using a new gasket **(see illustration)**.

22   The manufacturer states that a front cover alignment tool must be used when installing the front cover; however, this tool is very difficult to find, even from tool rental companies. If the tool is not available, follow the alternate procedure outlined below:

a) *Install the crankshaft balancer on the engine (see Section 10). This Step will align the front oil seal with the balancer hub.*

b) *Place a straightedge on the engine block oil pan rail. Measure the distance on*

each side of the block from the oil pan rail to the timing chain cover with a feeler gauge **(see illustration)**. *This Step measures the difference between the sealing surface of the oil pan and the sealing surface of the timing chain cover in relationship to each other.*

c) *Tilt the front timing cover as necessary to achieve an even measurement on each side. This Step properly aligns the front timing cover to oil pan sealing surfaces. Typically, 0 to 0.0098 inch (0.25 mm) is an acceptable tolerance.* **Note:** *Ideally the timing chain cover should be flush with the oil pan rail, but because of the differences in seal thickness, this may not always be obtainable. That is why there is a tolerance 0 to 0.0098 inch (0.25 mm). Always let the front seal center itself around the crankshaft balancer*

hub and tilt the cover from side to side to even up the measurement at both oil pan rails. Never push downward on the front timing cover in an attempt to make the oil pan sealing surface flush, as this will distort the front oil seal and eventually lead to an oil leak!

d) *With the timing chain cover properly aligned, tighten the cover bolts to the torque listed in this Chapter's Specifications.*

23   Apply a thin layer of RTV sealant to the areas where the timing chain cover and cylinder block meet, then install the oil pan as described in Section 14.

24   The remainder of installation is the reverse of removal. Add coolant and oil to the engine (see Chapter 1). Run the engine and check for oil and coolant leaks.

13 Camshaft and lifters - removal and installation

Note: *If the camshaft is being replaced, always install new lifters as well. Do not use old lifters on a new camshaft.*

Removal

Refer to illustrations 13.2a, 13.2b and 13.4

1   Refer to the appropriate Sections and remove the intake manifold or supercharger, valve covers, rocker arms, pushrods, timing chain and cylinder heads. Also remove the radiator and air conditioning condenser (see Chapter 3) and, on 6.0L and 6.2L engines, the Camshaft Position (CMP) sensor (see Chapter 6).

2   Before removing the lifters, arrange to store them in a clearly labeled box to ensure that they're installed in their original locations. Remove the lifter retainers and lifters and store them where they won't get dirty **(see illustrations)**. DO NOT attempt to withdraw the camshaft with the lifters in place.

13.2a The roller lifters are held in place by retainers - remove the retainer bolts, then remove the retainers and the lifters as an assembly. Note that each retainer houses four individual lifters and they must be reinstalled back in their original locations if they're going to be reused

13.2b Once the lifters and retainers are removed from the block they can be marked (for location and installation purposes) and inspected

13.4 Remove the bolts and remove the camshaft retainer plate, noting which side faces the block

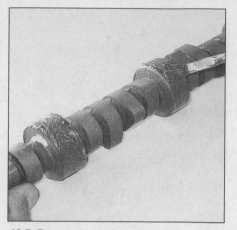

13.7 Be sure to apply camshaft assembly lube to the cam lobes and bearing journals before installing the camshaft

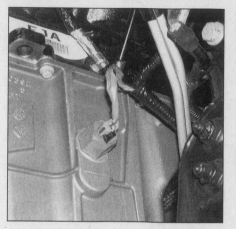

14.5 The oil level sensor is located on the right side of the oil pan

3   If the lifters are built up with gum and varnish they may not come out with the retainer. If so, there are several ways to extract the lifters from the bores. A special tool designed to grip and remove lifters is manufactured by many tool companies and is widely available, but it may not be required in every case. On newer engines without a lot of varnish buildup, the lifters can often be removed with a small magnet or even with your fingers. **Caution:** *Don't use pliers to remove the lifters unless you intend to replace them. The pliers will damage the precision machined and hardened lifters, rendering them useless.*

4   Remove the bolts and the camshaft retainer plate, noting which direction faces the block **(see illustration)**.

5   Thread three long bolts into the camshaft sprocket bolt holes to use as a handle when removing the camshaft from the block.

6   Carefully pull the camshaft out. Support the cam near the block so the lobes don't nick or gouge the bearings as it's withdrawn.

Installation

Refer to illustration 13.7

7   Lubricate the camshaft bearing journals and cam lobes with camshaft and lifter assembly lube **(see illustration)**.

8   Slide the camshaft into the engine. Support the cam near the block and be careful not to scrape or nick the bearings.

9   Turn the camshaft until the dowel pin is in the 3 o'clock position, and install the camshaft retainer plate, tighten the bolts to the torque listed in this Chapter's Specifications. Make sure the gasket surface on the camshaft retainer plate and the engine block are free from oil and dirt.

10   Install the timing chain and sprockets (see Section 12). On 6.0L and 6.2L engines, install the CMP sensor (see Chapter 6).

11   Lubricate the lifters with clean engine oil and install them in the lifter retainers. Be sure to align the flats on the lifters with the flats in the lifter retainers. Install the retainer and lifters into the engine block as an assembly. If

the original lifters are being installed, be sure to return them to their original locations. If a new camshaft is being installed, install new lifters as well. Tighten the lifter retainer bolts to the torque listed in this Chapter's Specifications.

12   The remainder of installation is the reverse of removal. Before starting and running the engine, change the oil and install a new oil filter (see Chapter 1).

---

14   Oil pan - removal and installation

Removal

Refer to illustration 14.5

1   Disconnect the cable from the negative battery terminal (see Chapter 5).

2   Raise the vehicle and support it securely on jackstands. Drain the engine oil and remove the oil filter (see Chapter 1), then remove the air filter housing and the air intake resonator (see Chapter 4).

3   Disconnect the front exhaust Y pipe from the engine and the exhaust system and remove it from the vehicle. This step is not absolutely necessary, but it will help facilitate removal of the oil pan.

4   Remove the starter motor (see Chapter 5) and the plastic covers on each side of the bellhousing.

5   Remove any wiring harness brackets connected to the oil pan and the brackets on the passenger side of the oil pan securing the transmission oil cooler lines (if equipped). Also disconnect the electrical connector from the oil level sensor **(see illustration)**.

6   Attach a support fixture to the engine from above and raise the engine slightly to allow removal of the engine mount through-bolts or the engine mount-to-subframe bolts (see Section 20).

7   Raise the engine approximately 1/2-inch.
Caution: *When lifting the engine, check that no upper engine components or wiring harnesses are hitting the edge of the cowl.*

8   Unbolt the shock absorbers from the lower control arms, then loosen the steering shaft coupler from the steering gear (see Chapter 10). Loosen the front suspension subframe bolts four to five turns. This will lower the front suspension subframe away from the body and will allow clearance for removal of the oil pan. **Caution:** *Do not loosen the front suspension subframe bolts more than five turns without the use of floor jack or jackstands to support the subframe, or injury may occur.*

9   Remove the transmission-to-oil pan bolts.

10   If the vehicle is equipped with an engine oil cooler, remove the engine oil cooler lines and adapter from the driver's side of the oil pan.

11   Remove the access plugs covering the nuts at the rear of the oil pan (if equipped).

12   Remove all the oil pan bolts, then lower the oil pan from the engine. The oil pan will probably stick to the engine, so strike the oil pan with a rubber mallet until it breaks the gasket seal. **Caution:** *Before using force on the oil pan, be sure all the bolts have been removed. Carefully slide the oil pan down and out, to the rear.*

Installation

Refer to illustration 14.16

13   Remove the old gasket. Wash out the oil pan with solvent.

14   Thoroughly clean the mounting surfaces of the oil pan and engine block of old gasket material and sealer. Wipe the gasket surfaces clean with a rag soaked in lacquer thinner, acetone or brake system cleaner.

15   Apply a 0.2 inch (5 mm) wide bead of RTV sealant to the corners of the block where the front cover and the rear cover meet the engine block. Then attach the new gasket to the oil pan, install the oil pan and tighten the bolts finger-tight. Be sure the oil gallery passages in the oil pan and the gasket are aligned properly.

16   The alignment of the rear face of the aluminum oil pan to the rear of the block is

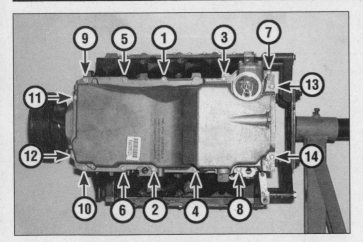

14.16 Oil pan bolt tightening sequence

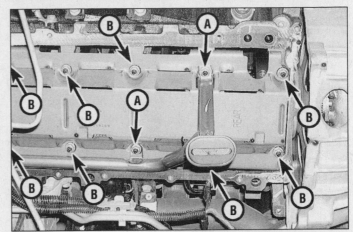

15.2a Remove the oil pick-up tube-to-main stud retaining nuts (A), then remove the remaining oil deflector nuts (B)

important. Measure between the rear face of the oil pan and the front face of the transmission bellhousing with feeler gauges. Clearance should be flush, never past. If the clearance is OK, tighten the oil pan bolts/studs in sequence (see illustration) to the torque listed in this Chapter's Specifications. If the clearance is not acceptable, install the two lower oil pan-to-bellhousing bolts and tighten them finger tight. This should draw the oil pan flush with the bellhousing.

17 The remainder of installation is the reverse of removal. Refill the engine oil (see Chapter 1), start the engine and check for leaks before driving the vehicle.

---

15 Oil pump - removal, inspection and installation

Removal

Refer to illustrations 15.2a, 15.2b and 15.4

1 Remove the timing chain cover (see Section 12).

2 Remove the oil pump pick-up tube mounting nuts and bolts and lower the pick-up tube and screen assembly from the vehicle (see illustrations).

3 On 6.0L and 6.2L engines, remove the remaining crankshaft oil deflector nuts and remove the deflector.

4 Remove the oil pump retaining bolts and slide the pump off the end of the crankshaft (see illustration).

Inspection

Refer to illustration 15.5

5 Remove the oil pump cover and withdraw the rotors from the pump body (see illustration). Clean the components with solvent, dry them thoroughly and inspect for any obvious damage. Also check the bolt holes for damaged threads and the splined surfaces on the crankshaft sprocket for any apparent damage. If any of the components are scored, scratched or worn, replace the entire oil pump assembly. There are no serviceable parts currently available.

15.2b Remove the bolt securing the oil pick-up tube to the oil pump and remove it from the engine

15.4 Oil pump mounting bolts

15.5 Oil pump cover-to-oil pump housing mounting bolts

15.9 Always install a new O-ring on the oil pump pick-up tube

Installation

Refer to illustration 15.9

6   Prime the pump by pouring clean engine oil into the pick-up tube hole, while turning the pump by hand.

7   Position the oil pump over the end of the crankshaft and align the teeth on the crankshaft sprocket with the teeth on the oil pump drive gear. Make sure the pump is fully seated against the block.

8   Install the oil pump mounting bolts and tighten them to the torque listed in this Chapter's Specifications.

9   Install a new O-ring on the oil pump pick-up tube, then fasten it to the oil pump and the engine block main studs **(see illustration)**. **Caution:** *Be absolutely certain that the pick-up tube-to-oil pump bolts are properly tightened so that no air can be sucked into the oiling system at this connection.*

10   Install the timing chain cover (see Section 12), then the oil pan (see Section 14).

11   The remainder of installation is the reverse of removal. Add oil and coolant as necessary. Run the engine and check for oil and coolant leaks, then check the oil pressure (see Chapter 2D).

16   Supercharger (6.2L engine) - removal and installation

Warning: *Wait until the engine is completely cool before beginning this procedure.*

Removal

1   Disconnect the cable from the negative battery terminal (see Chapter 5).

2   Remove the front engine cover fasteners, then remove the cover. Remove the rear cover fasteners, lift the rear cover up and remove it from the vehicle.

3   Raise the vehicle and support it securely on jackstands and remove the splash shield.

4   Remove the charge air cooler reservoir cap. Place a drain pan under the charge air cooler radiator, then loosen the drain plug and drain the system. **Note:** *The charge air cooler (intercooler) drain plug is located on the passenger's side lower corner of the cooler, in front of the radiator.*

5   Disconnect the PCV vent tube from the air filter outlet duct.

6   Disconnect the air filter outlet duct clamps and remove the duct from the air filter housing and the throttle body.

7   Remove the supercharger drivebelt (see Chapter 1).

8   Remove the barometric pressure (BARO) sensor (see Chapter 6).

9   Remove the throttle body, fuel rail and injectors as an assembly (see Chapter 4). **Note:** *This Step is not absolutely necessary unless you are servicing one of the individual components; if not, leave them installed and remove them as an assembly with the supercharger.*

10   Disconnect the charge air cooler coolant inlet and outlet line clamps and remove the hoses from the rear of the cooler and the cooler pipe.

11   Disconnect the electrical connectors to the charge air cooler cover.

12   Remove the charge air cooler cover bolts in the reverse order of the tightening sequence **(see illustration 16.25)** and remove the cover and gasket. **Note:** *Do not reuse the charge air cooler cover gasket.*

13   Remove the charge air cooler insulator

from the supercharger and cover the opening to prevent dirt from getting on the rotors.

14   Remove the supercharger-to-cylinder head bolts in the reverse order of the tightening sequence **(see illustration 16.22)**. Install special tool EN-48898 to the supercharger, then attach an engine hoist to the special tool and remove the supercharger. **Note:** *The special tool is used to keep even pressure on the supercharger when removing it from the engine.*

15   Remove the supercharger gasket and rivet from the cylinder heads.

Installation

Refer to illustrations 16.22 and 16.25

16   The mating surfaces of the supercharger and the block must be perfectly clean before installing the supercharger. Clean the surfaces with a scraper, but be careful not to gouge the aluminum. **Caution:** *Be very careful when scraping on aluminum engine parts. Aluminum is soft and gouges easily. Severely gouged parts may require replacement.*

17   If you suspect warpage of the supercharger gasket surface, consult an automotive machine shop for advice.

18   Clean the mating surfaces of the supercharger and block with a clean shop towel and brake system cleaner.

19   Place the supercharger gasket on the cylinder head and install the gasket rivets to hold it in place

20   Install special tool EN-48898 to the supercharger, then attach an engine hoist to the special tool. Lower the supercharger to the engine, aligning the dowel at the passenger's side front corner with the supercharger.

21   Apply a 0.2 inch (5 mm) bead of GM thread locker or equivalent to the supercharger bolts and install the bolts finger tight.

22   Tighten the supercharger bolts in sequence **(see illustration)** to the torque listed in this Chapter's Specifications.

23   Remove the rag used to cover the insulator opening and install the insulator.

24   Install a new charge air cooler cover gasket to the supercharger.

25   Install the charge air cooler cover and cover bolts, then tighten the bolts in sequence

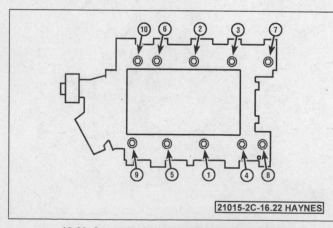

16.22   Supercharger bolt tightening sequence

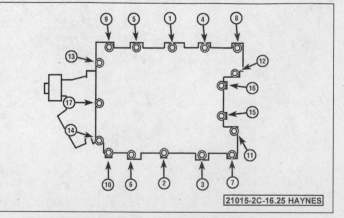

16.25   Charge air cooler cover bolt tightening sequence

18.3 Carefully pry the old seal out with a screwdriver at the notches provided in the rear cover

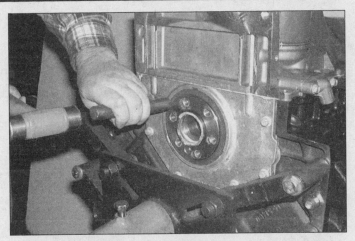

18.4 The rear oil seal can be pressed into place with a seal installation tool, a section of pipe or a blunt object (shown here) - in any case be sure the seal is installed squarely into the seal bore and flush with the rear cover

(see illustration) to the torque listed in this Chapter's Specifications.

26   Refill and bleed the charge air cooler system (see Section 21).

27   The remainder of installation is the reverse of removal, noting the following points:

a) Clean the engine of any excess coolant.
b) Start the engine and check for proper operation and coolant leaks.
c) Install the engine covers.

17   Flywheel/driveplate - removal and installation

The flywheel/driveplate removal for all V8 engines is identical to the flywheel/driveplate removal and installation procedure for V6 engines. Refer to Chapter 2A for the procedure, but use the torque figures in this Chapter's Specifications.

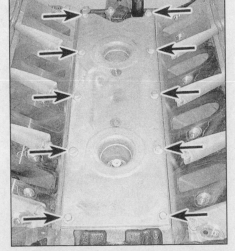

19.3 Valley cover mounting bolt locations

18   Rear main oil seal - replacement

Refer to illustrations 18.3 and 18.4

Note: *If you're installing a new rear seal during a complete engine overhaul, refer to the procedure in Chapter 2D.*

1   Remove the transmission (see Chapter 7).

2   Remove the flywheel/driveplate (see Section 17).

3   Pry the oil seal from the rear cover with a screwdriver **(see illustration)**. Be careful not to nick or scratch the crankshaft or the seal bore. Note how far it's recessed into the housing bore before removal so the new seal can be installed to the same depth. Thoroughly clean the seal bore in the block with a shop towel. Remove all traces of oil and dirt.

4   Lubricate the outside diameter of the seal and install the seal over the end of the crankshaft. Make sure the lip of the seal points toward the engine. Preferably, a seal installation tool (available at most auto parts store) should be used to press the new seal back into place. If the proper seal installation tool is unavailable, use a large socket, section

of pipe or a blunt tool and carefully drive the new seal squarely into the seal bore and flush with the rear cover **(see illustration)**.

5   Install the flywheel/driveplate (see Section 17).

6   Install the transmission (see Chapter 7).

19   Valley cover - removal and installation

Refer to illustrations 19.3 and 19.4

1   Remove the intake manifold (see Section 7) or the supercharger (see Section 16).

2   On 5.7L engines, pry up the rubber grommet to expose the knock sensor electrical connectors and unscrew the sensors (see Chapter 6).

3   Remove the valley cover bolts, valley cover and gasket **(see illustration)**.

4   On 5.7L engines, install new knock sensor oil seals on the bottom of the valley cover **(see illustration)**.

5   Carefully remove all traces of old gasket material.

6   Position the new gaskets on the cylin-

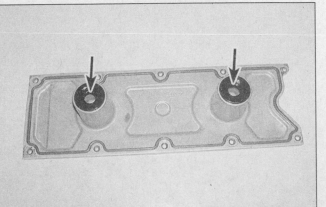

19.4 Install a new valley cover gasket and, on 5.7L engines, install new knock sensor oil seals to the valley cover

der block and carefully set the valley cover in place.

7   Install the bolts and tighten them to the torque listed in this Chapter's Specifications. Do not over-tighten the bolts, or gasket leaks may develop.

8   The remainder of installation is the reverse of removal.

20   Engine mounts - check and replacement

1   Engine mounts seldom require attention, but broken or deteriorated mounts should be replaced immediately or the added strain placed on the driveline components may cause damage.

Check

2   During the check, the engine must be raised slightly to remove the weight from the mounts.

3   Raise the vehicle and support it securely on jackstands, then position the jack under the engine oil pan. Place a large block of wood between the jack head and the oil pan, then carefully raise the engine just enough to take the weight off the mounts. Do not use the jack to support the entire weight of the engine.

4   Check the mounts to see if the rubber is cracked, hardened or separated from the metal plates. Sometimes the rubber will split right down the center. Rubber preservative or WD-40 can be applied to the mounts to slow deterioration.

5   Check for relative movement between the mount plates and the engine or frame (use a large screwdriver or prybar to attempt to move the mounts). If movement is noted, check the tightness of the mount fasteners first before condemning the mounts. Usually when engine mounts are broken, they are very obvious as the engine will easily move away from the mount when pried or under load.

Replacement

6   Disconnect the cable from the negative battery terminal (see Chapter 5).

5.7L and 6.0L engines

7   Remove the air filter housing and the air intake resonator from the engine compartment (see Chapter 4).

8   If you're removing the driver's side mount, remove the engine mount heat shield from the engine compartment. If you're removing the passenger's side mount, disconnect the oil level sensor electrical connector from the oil pan, remove the starter and disconnect the negative battery cable from the engine block (see Chapter 5).

9   Attach an engine hoist to the top of the engine for lifting; do not use a jack under the oil pan to support the entire weight of the engine or the oil pump pick-up could be damaged.

10   From below the engine, remove the engine mount bracket-to-engine block bolts.

11   From above the engine, remove the engine mount bracket-to-subframe bolts.

12   From below the engine, remove the engine mount bracket-to-subframe nuts and unscrew the studs from the bracket.

13   Raise the engine slightly until the engine mount can be removed.

14   Installation is the reverse of removal. Use non-hardening thread-locking compound on the mount bolts and tighten them to the torque listed in this Chapter's Specifications.

6.2L engines

15   Have the air conditioning refrigerant discharged at a dealer service department or air conditioning shop.

16   Remove the shock tower crossbrace (see Chapter 10).

17   Remove the air conditioning lines to the compressor to access the mount top nut.

18   Working below the vehicle, remove the engine mount-to-front suspension subframe nut, then the engine mount-to-engine bracket nut.

19   Attach an engine holding fixture or engine hoist to the top of the engine for lifting; do not use a jack under the oil pan to support the entire weight of the engine or the oil pump pick-up could be damaged.

20   Raise the engine slightly until the engine mount can be moved by hand. Unbolt the engine bracket from the engine block and remove it and the engine mount from the vehicle **(see illustration)**. Separate the mount from the engine bracket.

21   Installation is the reverse of removal. Tighten all bolts and nuts to the torque listed in this Chapter's Specifications.

22   Have the air conditioning system evacuated, recharged and leak tested by the shop that discharged it.

21   Charge air cooler refilling/ bleeding

1   Refill and bleed the charge air cooler by loosening the bleed screw at the top driver's side corner of the charge air cooler radiator. Add a 50/50 coolant and water mixture to the charge air cooler reservoir until coolant flows out of the bleeder, then tighten the bleeder screw.

2   Add more 50/50 coolant mixture until the coolant reaches the reservoir full mark.

3   Install the reservoir cap and turn the ignition key to the "RUN" position, then let the coolant pump run for a few seconds. Turn the key to the "OFF" position, then to the "RUN" position for a few seconds, and turn it off again.

4   Remove the reservoir cap and check for bubbles. Wait fifteen minutes and refill as necessary, then install the reservoir cap.

5   Repeat this procedure until the reservoir is full and no more bubbles are present.

Chapter 2 Part D
General engine overhaul procedures

Contents

Specifications

General

Cylinder compression	Lowest cylinder must be within 70% of the highest cylinder
Minimum	
V6 engines...	140 psi (965 kPa)
V8 engines...	100 psi (690 kPa)
Oil pressure (minimum)	
3.2L V6 engines, warm, at idle..	21.7 psi (150 kPa)
2.8L, 3.0L and 3.6L engines, warm	
At idle...	10 psi (69 kPa)
At 2,000 rpm	
2005 through 2012	20 psi (138 kPa)
2013 and later	30 psi (207 kPa)
5.7L, 6.0L and 6.2L V8 engines	
2005 through 2012	
At 1,000 rpm..	6 psi (41 kPa)
At 2,000 rpm..	18 psi (124 kPa)
2013 and later	
At 1,000 rpm..	24 psi (165 kPa)
At 2,000 rpm..	35 psi (241 kPa)
At 3,000 rpm..	38 psi (262 kPa)

Torque specifications

Note: *One foot-pound (ft-lb) of torque is equivalent to 12 inch-pounds (in-lbs) of torque. Torque values below approximately 15 foot-pounds are expressed in inch-pounds, because most foot-pound torque wrenches are not accurate at these smaller values.*

	Ft-lbs (unless otherwise indicated)	Nm
Connecting rod bolts		
3.2L V6 engines		
Step 1	26	35
Step 2	Tighten an additional 45 degrees	
Step 3	Tighten an additional 15 degrees	
2.8L, 3.0L and 3.6L V6 engines		
Step 1	22	30
Step 2	Loosen bolts completely	
Step 3	18	25
Step 4	Tighten an additional 110 degrees	
5.7L, 6.0L and 6.2L V8 engines		
Step 1	15	20
Step 2	Tighten an additional 85 degrees	

Torque specifications

Note: *One foot-pound (ft-lb) of torque is equivalent to 12 inch-pounds (in-lbs) of torque. Torque values below approximately 15 foot-pounds are expressed in inch-pounds, because most foot-pound torque wrenches are not accurate at these smaller values.*

	Ft-lbs (unless otherwise indicated)	Nm
Crankshaft bearing bridge (3.2L V6 engines)		
Bolts	15	20
Adjusting sleeve	15	20
Main bearing bolts (in sequence, **see illustration 10.19a)**		
3.2L V6 engines		
Step 1	37	50
Step 2	Tighten an additional 60 degrees	
Step 3	Tighten an additional 15 degrees	
2.8L, 3.0L and 3.6L V6 engines (in sequence, **see illustration 10.19b)**		
Inner bolt (1 through 8)		
Step 1	15	20
Step 2	Tighten an additional 80 degrees	
Outer bolt (9 through 16)		
Step 1	120 to 132 in-lbs	15
Step 2	Tighten an additional 110 degrees	
Side bolt (18 through 24)		
Step 1	22	30
Step 2	Tighten an additional 60 degrees	
5.7L, 6.0L and 6.2L V8 engines (in sequence, **see illustration 10.19c)**		
Inner M10 bolts (bolts 1 through 10)		
Step 1	15	20
Step 2	Tighten an additional 80 degrees	
Outer M10 studs (bolts 11 through 20)		
Step 1	15	20
Step 2		
2005 and earlier models	Tighten an additional 53 degrees	
2006 and later models	Tighten an additional 51 degrees	
Side M8 bolts (bolts 21 through 30)	18	25

1.1 An engine block being bored. An engine rebuilder will use special machinery to recondition the cylinder bores

1.2 If the cylinders are bored, the machine shop will normally hone the engine on a machine like this

1   General information - engine overhaul

Refer to illustrations 1.1, 1.2, 1.3, 1.4, 1.5 and 1.6

Included in this portion of Chapter 2 are general information and diagnostic testing procedures for determining the overall mechanical condition of your engine.

The information ranges from advice concerning preparation for an overhaul and the purchase of replacement parts and/or components to detailed, step-by-step procedures covering removal and installation.

The following Sections have been written to help you determine whether your engine needs to be overhauled and how to remove and install it once you've determined it needs to be rebuilt. For information concerning in-vehicle engine repair, see Chapter 2A, 2B or 2C.

The Specifications included in this Part are general in nature and include only those necessary for testing the oil pressure and checking the engine compression. Refer to Chapter 2A, 2B or 2C for additional engine Specifications.

It's not always easy to determine when, or if, an engine should be completely overhauled, because a number of factors must be considered.

High mileage is not necessarily an indication that an overhaul is needed, while low mileage doesn't preclude the need for an overhaul. Frequency of servicing is probably the most important consideration. An engine that's had regular and frequent oil and filter changes, as well as other required maintenance, will most likely give many thousands of miles of reliable service. Conversely, a neglected engine may require an overhaul very early in its service life.

Excessive oil consumption is an indication that piston rings, valve seals and/or valve guides are in need of attention. Make sure that oil leaks aren't responsible before deciding that the rings and/or guides are bad. Per-

form a cylinder compression check to determine the extent of the work required (see Section 3). Also check the vacuum readings under various conditions (see Section 4).

Check the oil pressure with a gauge installed in place of the oil pressure sending unit and compare it to this Chapter's Specifications (see Section 2). If it's extremely low, the bearings and/or oil pump are probably worn out.

Loss of power, rough running, knocking or metallic engine noises, excessive valve train noise and high fuel consumption rates may also point to the need for an overhaul, especially if they're all present at the same time. If a complete tune-up doesn't remedy the situation, major mechanical work is the only solution.

An engine overhaul involves restoring the internal parts to the specifications of a new engine. During an overhaul, the piston rings are replaced and the cylinder walls are reconditioned (rebored and/or honed) **(see illustrations 1.1 and 1.2)**. If a rebore is done by an automotive machine shop, new oversize pistons will also be installed. The main bearings, connecting rod bearings and camshaft bearings are generally replaced

with new ones and, if necessary, the crankshaft may be reground to restore the journals **(see illustration 1.3)**. Generally, the valves are serviced as well, since they're usually in less-than-perfect condition at this point. While the engine is being overhauled, other components, such as the starter and alternator, can be rebuilt or replaced as well. The end result should be similar to a new engine that will give many trouble free miles. **Note:** *Critical cooling system components such as the hoses, drivebelts, thermostat and water pump should be replaced with new parts when an engine is overhauled. The radiator should be checked carefully to ensure that it isn't clogged or leaking (see Chapter 3). If you purchase a rebuilt engine or short block, some rebuilders will not warranty their engines unless the radiator has been professionally flushed. Also, we don't recommend overhauling the oil pump - always install a new one when an engine is rebuilt.*

Overhauling the internal components on today's engines is a difficult and time-consuming task which requires a significant amount of specialty tools and is best left to a professional engine rebuilder **(see illustrations 1.4,**

1.3 A crankshaft having a main bearing journal ground

1.4 A machinist checks for a bent connecting rod, using specialized equipment

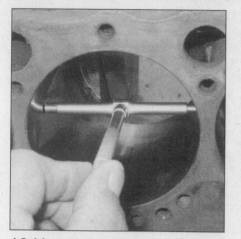

1.5 A bore gauge being used to check the main bearing bore

1.6 Uneven piston wear like this indicates a bent connecting rod

2.2a On 2005 and later V6 engines, the oil pressure sending unit is located on the front of the engine block behind the air conditioning compressor (3.0L V6 shown)

1.5 and 1.6). A competent engine rebuilder will handle the inspection of your old parts and offer advice concerning the reconditioning or replacement of the original engine, never purchase parts or have machine work done on other components until the block has been thoroughly inspected by a professional machine shop. As a general rule, time is the primary cost of an overhaul, especially since the vehicle may be tied up for a minimum of two weeks or more. Be aware that some engine builders only have the capability to rebuild the engine you bring them while other rebuilders have a large inventory of rebuilt exchange engines in stock. Also be aware that many machine shops could take as much as two weeks time to completely rebuild your engine depending on shop workload. Sometimes it makes more sense to simply exchange your engine for another engine that's already rebuilt to save time.

2   Oil pressure check

Refer to illustrations 2.2a, 2.2b and 2.3

1   Low engine oil pressure can be a sign of an engine in need of rebuilding. A low oil pressure indicator (often called an "idiot light") is not a test of the oiling system. Such indicators only come on when the oil pressure is dangerously low. Even a factory oil pressure gauge in the instrument panel is only a relative indication, although much better for driver information than a warning light. A better test is with a mechanical (not electrical) oil pressure gauge.

2   Locate the oil pressure sending unit on the engine:

a) 3.2L V6 engines, the sending unit is located at the front of the engine, on the oil pump cover, near the crankshaft pulley.

b) On 2.8L, 3.0L and 3.6L V6 engines, the sending unit is located on the oil filter housing (see illustration).

c) On V8 engines, the sending unit is located at the top rear of the engine, on the left side (see illustration).

3   Unscrew the oil pressure sending unit and screw in the hose for your oil pressure gauge (see illustration). If necessary, install an adapter fitting. Use Teflon tape or thread sealant on the threads of the adapter and/or the fitting on the end of your gauge's hose. **Note:** *On V8 models, the manufacturer recommends removing the oil filter and installing special adapter tool J 21867 (5.7L models) or EN 4791 (6.0L and 6.2L models) in place of the oil filter, before attaching the oil pressure gauge to the adapter for a more accurate pressure reading.*

4   Connect an accurate tachometer to the engine, according to the tachometer manufacturer's instructions.

2.2b V8 engine oil pressure sending unit location (5.7L shown, other engines similar)

2.3 The oil pressure can be checked by removing the sending unit and installing a pressure gauge in its place

3.6 Use a compression gauge with a threaded fitting for the spark plug hole, not the type that requires hand pressure to maintain the seal

4.4 A simple vacuum gauge can be handy in diagnosing engine condition and performance

5   Check the oil pressure with the engine running (normal operating temperature) at the specified engine speed, and compare it to this Chapter's Specifications. If it's extremely low, the bearings and/or oil pump are probably worn out.

3   Cylinder compression check

Refer to illustration 3.6

1   A compression check will tell you what mechanical condition the upper end of your engine (pistons, rings, valves, head gaskets) is in. Specifically, it can tell you if the compression is down due to leakage caused by worn piston rings, defective valves and seats or a blown head gasket. **Note:** *The engine must be at normal operating temperature and the battery must be fully charged for this check.*

2   Begin by cleaning the area around the ignition coils before you remove them (compressed air should be used, if available). The idea is to prevent dirt from getting into the cylinders as the compression check is being done.

3   Remove the ignition coil packs or coil assemblies (see Chapter 5). Remove all of the spark plugs from the engine (see Chapter 1).

4   Remove the air intake duct from the throttle body, then block the throttle wide open.

5   Remove the fuse for the ignition system (see Chapter 12) and fuel pump relay (see Chapter 4, Section 2).

6   Install a compression gauge in the spark plug hole (**see illustration**).

7   Crank the engine over at least seven compression strokes and watch the gauge. The compression should build up quickly in a healthy engine. Low compression on the first

stroke, followed by gradually increasing pressure on successive strokes, indicates worn piston rings. A low compression reading on the first stroke, which doesn't build up during successive strokes, indicates leaking valves or a blown head gasket (a cracked head could also be the cause). Deposits on the undersides of the valve heads can also cause low compression. Record the highest gauge reading obtained.

8   Repeat the procedure for the remaining cylinders and compare the results to this Chapter's Specifications.

9   Add some engine oil (about three squirts from a plunger-type oil can) to each cylinder, through the spark plug hole, and repeat the test.

10   If the compression increases after the oil Is added, the piston rings arc definitely worn. If the compression doesn't increase significantly, the leakage is occurring at the valves or head gasket. Leakage past the valves may be caused by burned valve seats and/or faces or warped, cracked or bent valves.

11   If two adjacent cylinders have equally low compression, there's a strong possibility that the head gasket between them is blown. The appearance of coolant in the combustion chambers or the crankcase would verify this condition.

12   If one cylinder is slightly lower than the others, and the engine has a slightly rough idle, a worn lobe on the camshaft could be the cause.

13   If the compression is unusually high, the combustion chambers are probably coated with carbon deposits. If that's the case, the cylinder head(s) should be removed and decarbonized.

14   If compression is way down or varies greatly between cylinders, it would be a good idea to have a leak-down test performed by an automotive repair shop. This test will pinpoint exactly where the leakage is occurring

and how severe it is.

15   After performing the test, don't forget to unblock the throttle plate.

4   Vacuum gauge diagnostic checks

Refer to illustrations 4.4 and 4.6

1   A vacuum gauge provides inexpensive but valuable information about what is going on in the engine. You can check for worn rings or cylinder walls, leaking head or intake manifold gaskets, incorrect carburetor adjustments, restricted exhaust, stuck or burned valves, weak valve springs, improper ignition or valve timing and ignition problems.

2   Unfortunately, vacuum gauge readings are easy to misinterpret, so they should be used in conjunction with other tests to confirm the diagnosis.

3   Both the absolute readings and the rate of needle movement are important for accurate interpretation. Most gauges measure vacuum in inches of mercury (in-Hg). The following references to vacuum assume the diagnosis is being performed at sea level. As elevation increases (or atmospheric pressure decreases), the reading will decrease. For every 1,000 foot increase in elevation above approximately 2,000 feet, the gauge readings will decrease about one inch of mercury.

4   Connect the vacuum gauge directly to the intake manifold vacuum, not to ported (throttle body) vacuum (**see illustration**). Be sure no hoses are left disconnected during the test or false readings will result.

5   Before you begin the test, allow the engine to warm up completely. Block the wheels and set the parking brake. With the transmission in Park, start the engine and allow it to run at normal idle speed. **Warning:** *Keep your hands and the vacuum gauge clear of the fans.*

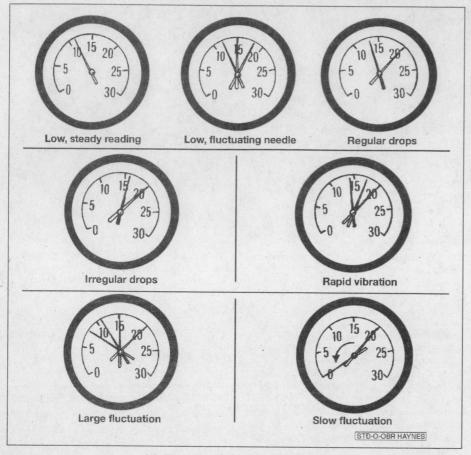

Low, steady reading   Low, fluctuating needle   Regular drops

Irregular drops   Rapid vibration

Large fluctuation   Slow fluctuation

STD-O-OBR HAYNES

4.6 Typical vacuum gauge readings

6   Read the vacuum gauge; an average, healthy engine should normally produce about 17 to 22 in-Hg with a fairly steady needle **(see illustration)**. Refer to the following vacuum gauge readings and what they indicate about the engine's condition:

7   A low steady reading usually indicates a leaking gasket between the intake manifold and cylinder head(s) or throttle body, a leaky vacuum hose, late ignition timing or incorrect camshaft timing. Check ignition timing with a timing light and eliminate all other possible causes, utilizing the tests provided in this Chapter before you remove the timing chain cover to check the timing marks.

8   If the reading is three to eight inches below normal and it fluctuates at that low reading, suspect an intake manifold gasket leak at an intake port or a faulty fuel injector.

9   If the needle has regular drops of about two-to-four inches at a steady rate, the valves are probably leaking. Perform a compression check or leak-down test to confirm this.

10   An irregular drop or down-flick of the needle can be caused by a sticking valve or an ignition misfire. Perform a compression check or leak-down test and read the spark plugs.

11   A rapid vibration of about four in-Hg vibration at idle combined with exhaust smoke indicates worn valve guides. Perform a leak-

down test to confirm this. If the rapid vibration occurs with an increase in engine speed, check for a leaking intake manifold gasket or head gasket, weak valve springs, burned valves or ignition misfire.

12   A slight fluctuation, say one inch up and down, may mean ignition problems. Check all the usual tune-up items and, if necessary, run the engine on an ignition analyzer.

13   If there is a large fluctuation, perform a compression or leak-down test to look for a weak or dead cylinder or a blown head gasket.

14   If the needle moves slowly through a wide range, check for a clogged PCV system, incorrect idle fuel mixture, throttle body or intake manifold gasket leaks.

15   Check for a slow return after revving the engine by quickly snapping the throttle open until the engine reaches about 2,500 rpm and let it shut. Normally the reading should drop to near zero, rise above normal idle reading (about 5 in-Hg over) and then return to the previous idle reading. If the vacuum returns slowly and doesn't peak when the throttle is snapped shut, the rings may be worn. If there is a long delay, look for a restricted exhaust system (often the muffler or catalytic converter). An easy way to check this is to temporarily disconnect the exhaust ahead of the suspected part and redo the test.

5   Engine rebuilding alternatives

The do-it-yourselfer is faced with a number of options when purchasing a rebuilt engine. The major considerations are cost, warranty, parts availability and the time required for the rebuilder to complete the project. The decision to replace the engine block, piston/connecting rod assemblies and crankshaft depends on the final inspection results of your engine. Only then can you make a cost effective decision whether to have your engine overhauled or simply purchase an exchange engine for your vehicle.

Some of the rebuilding alternatives include:

Individual parts - If the inspection procedures reveal that the engine block and most engine components are in reusable condition, purchasing individual parts and having a rebuilder rebuild your engine may be the most economical alternative. The block, crankshaft and piston/connecting rod assemblies should all be inspected carefully by a machine shop first.

Short block - A short block consists of an engine block with a crankshaft and piston/connecting rod assemblies already installed. All new bearings are incorporated and all clearances will be correct. The existing camshafts, valve train components, cylinder head and external parts can be bolted to the short block with little or no machine shop work necessary.

Long block - A long block consists of a short block plus an oil pump, oil pan, cylinder head, valve cover, camshaft and valve train components, timing sprockets and chain or gears and timing cover. All components are installed with new bearings, seals and gaskets incorporated throughout. The installation of manifolds and external parts is all that's necessary.

Low mileage used engines - Some companies now offer low mileage used engines which are a very cost effective way to get your vehicle up and running again. These engines often come from vehicles which have been totaled in accidents or come from other countries which have a higher vehicle turn over rate. A low mileage used engine also usually has a similar warranty like the newly remanufactured engines.

Give careful thought to which alternative is best for you and discuss the situation with local automotive machine shops, auto parts dealers and experienced rebuilders before ordering or purchasing replacement parts.

6   Engine removal - methods and precautions

Refer to illustrations 6.1, 6.2, 6.3 and 6.4

If you've decided that an engine must be removed for overhaul or major repair work, several preliminary steps should be taken. Read all removal and installation procedures

6.1 After tightly wrapping water-vulnerable components, use a spray cleaner on everything, with particular concentration on the greasiest areas, usually around the valve cover and lower edges of the block. If one section dries out, apply more cleaner

6.2 Depending on how dirty the engine is, let the cleaner soak in according to the directions and then hose off the grime and cleaner. Get the rinse water down into every area you can get at; then dry important components with a hair dryer or paper towels

carefully prior to committing to this job. These engines are removed by lowering the engine to the floor, along with the transmission, and then raising the vehicle sufficiently to slide the assembly out; this will require a vehicle hoist as well as an engine hoist. Make sure the engine hoist is rated in excess of the combined weight of the engine and transmission. A transmission jack is also very helpful. Safety is of primary importance, considering the potential hazards involved in removing the engine from the vehicle.

Locating a suitable place to work is extremely important. Adequate work space, along with storage space for the vehicle, will be needed. If a shop or garage isn't available, at the very least a flat, level, clean work surface made of concrete or asphalt is required.

Cleaning the engine compartment and engine before beginning the removal procedure will help keep tools clean and organized **(see illustrations 6.1 and 6.2)**.

If you're a novice at engine removal, get at least one helper. One person cannot easily do all the things you need to do to remove a big heavy engine and transmission assembly from the engine compartment. Also helpful is to seek advice and assistance from someone who's experienced in engine removal.

Plan the operation ahead of time. Arrange for or obtain all of the tools and equipment you'll need prior to beginning the job **(see illustrations 6.3 and 6.4)**. Some of the equipment necessary to perform engine removal and installation safely and with relative ease are (in addition to a vehicle hoist and an engine hoist) a heavy duty floor jack (preferably fitted with a transmission jack head adapter), complete sets of wrenches and sockets as described in the front of this manual, wooden blocks, plenty of rags and cleaning solvent for mopping up spilled oil, coolant and gasoline.

Plan for the vehicle to be out of use for quite a while. A machine shop can do the

6.3 Get an engine stand sturdy enough to firmly support the engine while you're working on it. Stay away from three-wheeled models: they have a tendency to tip over more easily, so get a four-wheeled unit

work that is beyond the scope of the home mechanic. Machine shops often have a busy schedule, so before removing the engine, consult the shop for an estimate of how long it will take to rebuild or repair the components that may need work.

7 Engine - removal and installation

Warning: *The models covered by this manual are equipped with Supplemental Restraint systems (SRS), more commonly known as airbags. Always disable the airbag system before working in the vicinity of airbag system components to avoid the possibility of accidental deployment of the airbag, which could cause personal injury (see Chapter 12).*
Warning: *Gasoline is extremely flammable, so take extra precautions when you work on*

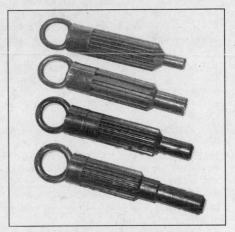

6.4 A clutch alignment tool is necessary if you plan to install a rebuilt engine mated to a manual transmission

any part of the fuel system. Don't smoke or allow open flames or bare light bulbs near the work area, and don't work in a garage where a gas-type appliance (such as a water heater or clothes dryer) is present. Since gasoline is carcinogenic, wear fuel-resistant gloves when there's a possibility of being exposed to fuel, and, if you spill any fuel on your skin, rinse it off immediately with soap and water. Mop up any spills immediately and do not store fuel-soaked rags where they could ignite. The fuel system is under constant pressure, so, if any fuel lines are to be disconnected, the fuel pressure in the system must be relieved first (see Chapter 4 for more information). When you perform any kind of work on the fuel system, wear safety glasses and have a Class B type fire extinguisher on hand.
Warning: *The engine must be completely cool before beginning this procedure.*
Note: *Engine removal on these models is a difficult job, especially for the do-it-yourself mechanic working at home. Because of the*

vehicle's design, the manufacturer states that the front suspension, engine and transmission have to be removed as a unit from the bottom of the vehicle, not the top. With a floor jack and jackstands the vehicle can't be raised high enough and supported safely enough for the suspension, engine/transmission assembly to slide out from underneath. The manufacturer recommends that removal of the suspension, engine/transmission assembly only be performed on a vehicle hoist.

Removal

1   Have the air conditioning system discharged by an automotive air conditioning technician.

2   Park the vehicle on a frame-contact type vehicle hoist. The pads of the hoist arms must contact the body welt along each side of the vehicle.

3   Relieve the fuel system pressure (see Chapter 4), then disconnect the negative cable from the battery (see Chapter 5).

4   Place protective covers on the fenders and cowl and remove the hood (see Chapter 11).

5   Turn the steering wheel so that the front wheels are facing straight and lock the steering wheel. **Caution:** *Damage to the clockspring may occur if the steering wheel is turned when the intermediate shaft is disconnected from the steering gear.*

6   Remove the shift lever assembly (see Chapter 7A or 7B).

7   Remove the crossbrace (see Chapter 10).

8   Remove the engine top front cover fasteners, then remove the cover. Remove the top rear cover fasteners, lift the rear cover up and remove it from the vehicle.

9   Remove the air cleaner and resonator assembly to allow access to the front of the engine (see Chapter 4).

10   Drain the cooling system (see Chapter 1) and disconnect the heater hoses from the engine. On 6.2L engines, drain the charge air cooler and remove the supercharger (see Chapter 2C).

11   Disconnect the coolant line to the throttle body (if equipped).

12   Using a quick disconnect tool, disconnect the air conditioning lines to the evaporator at the firewall and the shock tower (see Chapter 3).

13   Remove the master cylinder nuts from the brake booster (see Chapter 10) and separate the master cylinder from the booster, but do not disconnect the brake lines. Secure the brake master cylinder to the engine with a length of wire. **Caution:** *Do not bend or kink the brake lines to the master cylinder.*

14   Detach all wiring harnesses and hoses from between the engine/transmission and the chassis. Mark all connectors to facilitate reassembly.

15   Disconnect the fuel lines from the rear of the engine (see Chapter 4).

16   Disconnect the EVAP hoses from the rear of the engine.

17   On 2007 and earlier models, remove the battery from the engine compartment (see Chapter 5).

18   Loosen the front wheel lug nuts then raise the vehicle on the hoist. Drain the cooling system and engine oil, and remove the drivebelts (see Chapter 1).

19   Clearly label, then disconnect all vacuum lines, coolant and emissions hoses, wiring harness connectors, ground straps and fuel lines. Masking tape and/or a touch up paint applicator work well for marking items **(see illustration)**. Take instant photos or sketch the locations of components and brackets.

20   Remove the power steering oil cooler mounting fasteners and remove the cooler. **Note:** *Do not disconnect the oil cooler lines.*

21   Remove the engine cooling fan, radiator and air conditioning condenser (see Chapter 3).

22   Remove the inner fender liners (see Chapter 11).

23   Using wire, secure the air conditioning hoses and power steering hoses to the engine.

24   Remove the windshield washer reservoir brace fasteners from the subframe.

25   Detach the steering column shaft from the steering gear (see Chapter 10).

26   Disconnect and plug the two rear brake lines from the Brake Pressure Modulator Valve (BPMV) and secure the lines to the body.

27   Remove the PCM (see Chapter 6) and secure the harness to the engine.

28   Detach the exhaust pipe(s) from the exhaust manifold(s) (see Chapter 4).

29   Remove the driveshaft (see Chapter 8).

30   On V8 models, remove the transmission (see Chapter 7A or 7B).

31   Detach all wiring harnesses and hoses from between the engine/transmission and the chassis. Mark all connectors to facilitate reassembly.

32   On V6 models, remove the shock modules from both sides (see Chapter 10).

33   On 2008 and earlier V8 models, remove the shock and upper control arm assembly bolts from both sides (see Chapter 10); secure the assemblies away from the body.

34   On 2009 and later V8 models, disconnect the lower balljoint from the steering knuckle and remove the shock absorber lower mounting bolt from the lower control arm (see Chapter 10). Remove the stabilizer links from the control arm (see Chapter 10). Remove the steering gear mounting bolts and the tie-rod ends (see Chapter 10). Secure the steering gear to the engine using wire.

35   Attach a lifting sling or chain to the engine. Position an engine hoist and connect the sling to it. If no lifting hooks or brackets are present, fasten the chains or slings to some substantial part of the engine - ones that are strong enough to take the weight, but in locations that will provide good balance. Take up the slack until there is slight tension on the sling or chain. Position the chain on the hoist so it balances the engine or engine and transmission level with the vehicle.

36   Mark the position of each corner of the subframe to the chassis. Support the subframe with two floor jacks, then remove the fasteners. On 2009 and later V8 models,

remove the subframe (see Chapter 10).

37   Recheck to be sure nothing except the mounts are still connecting the engine to the vehicle. Disconnect and label anything still remaining.

38   On 2008 and earlier V8 models, slowly lower the engine and subframe as a unit from the vehicle. **Note:** *Placing a sheet of hardboard or paneling between the subframe and the floor makes moving the powertrain easier.*

39   On V6 models, slowly lower the engine/transmission and subframe as a unit from the vehicle. **Note:** *Placing a sheet of hardboard or paneling between the subframe and the floor makes moving the powertrain easier.*

40   Once the engine is on the floor, disconnect the engine lifting hoist and raise the vehicle hoist until the powertrain can be slid out from underneath. **Note:** *A helper will be needed to move the powertrain.*

41   Remove the transmission on V6 models (see Chapter 7A or 7B). Connect the engine lifting hoist to the engine and raise the engine slightly. Disconnect the engine mounts from the subframe and mount the engine on a stand.

Installation

Note: *The manufacturer recommends replacing all subframe and suspension fasteners with new ones whenever they are loosened or removed.*

42   Installation is the reverse of removal, noting the following points:

a) *Check the engine/transmission mounts. If they're worn or damaged, replace them.*

b) *Attach the transmission to the engine following the procedure described in Chapter 7.*

c) *Add coolant, oil, power steering and transmission fluids as needed (see Chapter 1).*

d) *Align the subframe reference marks before tightening the bolts.*

e) *Tighten the subframe mounting fasteners to the torque listed in the Chapter 10 Specifications.*

f) *Reconnect the negative battery cable (see Chapter 5).*

g) *Run the engine and check for proper operation and leaks. Shut off the engine and recheck fluid levels.*

h) *Have the air conditioning system recharged and leak tested by the shop that discharged it.*

8   Engine overhaul - disassembly sequence

1   It's much easier to remove the external components if it's mounted on a portable engine stand. A stand can often be rented quite cheaply from an equipment rental yard. Before the engine is mounted on a stand, the flywheel/driveplate should be removed from the engine.

2   If a stand isn't available, it's possible to remove the external engine components with it blocked up on the floor. Be extra careful not to tip or drop the engine when working without a stand.

3   If you're going to obtain a rebuilt engine, all external components must come off first, to be transferred to the replacement engine. These components include:

Clutch and flywheel (models with manual transmission)
Driveplate (models with automatic transmission)
Emissions-related components
Engine mounts and mount brackets
Intake/exhaust manifolds
Fuel injection components
Oil filter
Ignition coils and spark plugs
Thermostat and housing assembly
Water pump

Note: When removing the external components from the engine, pay close attention to details that may be helpful or important during installation. Note the installed position of gaskets, seals, spacers, pins, brackets, washers, bolts and other small items.

4   If you're going to obtain a short block (assembled engine block, crankshaft, pistons and connecting rods), remove the timing belt, cylinder head, oil pan, oil pump pick-up tube, oil pump and water pump from your engine so that you can turn in your old short block to the rebuilder as a core. See Engine rebuilding alternatives for additional information regarding the different possibilities to be considered.

9   Pistons and connecting rods - removal and installation

Removal

Refer to illustrations 9.1, 9.3 and 9.4

Note: Prior to removing the piston/connecting rod assemblies, remove the cylinder head and oil pan (see Chapter 2A, 2B or 2C).

1   Use your fingernail to feel if a ridge has formed at the upper limit of ring travel (about 1/4-inch down from the top of each cylinder).

9.1 Before you try to remove the pistons, use a ridge reamer to remove the raised material (ridge) from the top of the cylinders

If carbon deposits or cylinder wear have produced ridges, they must be completely removed with a special tool **(see illustration)**. Follow the manufacturer's instructions provided with the tool. Failure to remove the ridges before attempting to remove the piston/connecting rod assemblies may result in piston breakage. Using a permanent marker or paint, mark each piston with a number and an arrow pointing to the front of the engine. **Caution:** Do not stamp or center punch the pistons or damage may occur to the connecting rod.

2   After the cylinder ridges have been removed, turn the engine so the crankshaft is facing up.

3   Before the main bearing caps and connecting rods are removed, check the connecting rod endplay with feeler gauges. Slide them between the first connecting rod and the crankshaft throw until the play is removed **(see illustration)**. Repeat this procedure for each connecting rod. The endplay is equal to the thickness of the feeler gauge(s). Check with an automotive machine shop for the endplay service limit (a typical end play limit should measure between 0.005 to 0.015 inch [0.127 to 0.381 mm]). If the play exceeds the service

9.3 Checking the connecting rod endplay (side clearance)

limit, new connecting rods will be required. If new rods (or a new crankshaft) are installed, the endplay may fall under the minimum allowable. If it does, the rods will have to be machined to restore it. If necessary, consult an automotive machine shop for advice.

4   Check the connecting rods and caps for identification marks. If they aren't plainly marked, use a permanent marker or paint to clearly identify each rod and cap (1, 2, 3, etc., depending on the cylinder they're associated with) and make an arrow pointing to the front of the engine **(see illustration)**. **Caution:** Do not stamp or center punch the pistons or damage may occur to the connecting rod.

5   Loosen each of the connecting rod cap bolts 1/2-turn at a time until they can be removed by hand. **Note:** New connecting rod cap bolts and bearings must be used when reassembling the engine, but save the old bolts for use when checking the connecting rod bearing oil clearance.

6   Remove the number one connecting rod cap and bearing insert. Don't drop the bearing insert out of the cap.

7   Remove the bearing insert and push the connecting rod/piston assembly out through the top of the engine. Use a wooden or plastic hammer handle to push on the upper bearing surface in the connecting rod. If resistance is felt, double-check to make sure that all of the ridge was removed from the cylinder.

8   Repeat the procedure for the remaining cylinders.

9   After removal, reassemble the connecting rod caps and bearing inserts in their respective connecting rods and install the cap bolts finger tight. Leaving the old bearing inserts in place until reassembly will help prevent the connecting rod bearing surfaces from being accidentally nicked or gouged. **Note:** On V6 engines, once the connecting rod has been removed, new bearing inserts must be installed.

10   The pistons and connecting rods are now ready for inspection and overhaul at an automotive machine shop.

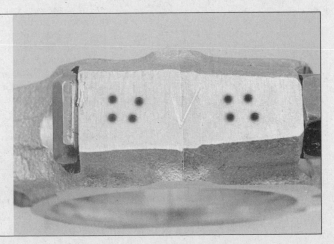

9.4 If the connecting rods and caps are not marked, use permanent ink or paint to mark the caps to the rods by cylinder number (for example, this would be the No. 4 connecting rod) and an arrow on the piston top pointing toward the timing chain end of the engine

9.13 Install the piston ring into the cylinder then push it down into position using a piston so the ring will be square in the cylinder

9.14 With the ring square in the cylinder, measure the ring end gap with a feeler gauge

9.15 If the ring end gap is too small, clamp a file in a vise as shown and file the piston ring ends - be sure to remove all raised material

Piston ring installation

Refer to illustrations 9.13, 9.14, 9.15, 9.19a, 9.19b and 9.22

11   Before installing the new piston rings, the ring end gaps must be checked. It's assumed that the piston ring side clearance has been checked and verified correct.

12   Lay out the piston/connecting rod assemblies and the new ring sets so the ring sets will be matched with the same piston and cylinder during the end gap measurement and engine assembly.

13   Insert the top (number one) ring into the first cylinder and square it up with the cylinder walls by pushing it in with the top of the piston **(see illustration)**. The ring should be near the bottom of the cylinder, at the lower limit of ring travel.

14   To measure the end gap, slip feeler gauges between the ends of the ring until a gauge equal to the gap width is found **(see illustration)**. The feeler gauge should slide between the ring ends with a slight amount

of drag. A typical ring gap should fall between 0.010 and 0.020 inch (0.25 to 0.50 mm) for compression rings and up to 0.030 inch (0.76 mm) for the oil ring steel rails. If the gap is larger or smaller than specified, double-check to make sure you have the correct rings before proceeding.

15   If the gap is too small, it must be enlarged or the ring ends may come in contact with each other during engine operation, which can cause serious damage to the engine. If necessary, increase the end gaps by filing the ring ends very carefully with a fine file. Mount the file in a vise equipped with soft jaws, slip the ring over the file with the ends contacting the file face and slowly move the ring to remove material from the ends. When performing this operation, file only by pushing the ring from the outside end of the file towards the vise **(see illustration)**.

16   Excess end gap isn't critical unless it's greater than 0.040 inch (1.01 mm). Again, double-check to make sure you have the correct ring type.

17   Repeat the procedure for each ring that will be installed in the first cylinder and for each ring in the remaining cylinders. Remember to keep rings, pistons and cylinders matched up.

18   Once the ring end gaps have been checked/corrected, the rings can be installed on the pistons.

19   The oil control ring (lowest one on the piston) is usually installed first. It's composed of three separate components. Slip the spacer/expander into the groove **(see illustration)**. If an anti-rotation tang is used, make sure it's inserted into the drilled hole in the ring groove. Next, install the upper side rail in the same manner **(see illustration)**. Don't use a piston ring installation tool on the oil ring side rails, as they may be damaged. Instead, place one end of the side rail into the groove between the spacer/expander and the ring land, hold it firmly in place and slide a finger around the piston while pushing the rail into the groove. Finally, install the lower side rail.

20   After the three oil ring components have been installed, check to make sure that both the upper and lower side rails can be rotated smoothly inside the ring grooves.

21   The number two (middle) ring is installed next. It's usually stamped with a mark which must face up, toward the top of the piston. Do not mix up the top and middle rings, as they have different cross-sections. **Note:** *Always follow the instructions printed on the ring package or box - different manufacturers may require different approaches.*

22   Use a piston ring installation tool and make sure the identification mark is facing the top of the piston, then slip the ring into the middle groove on the piston **(see illustration)**. Don't expand the ring any more than necessary to slide it over the piston.

23   Install the number one (top) ring in the same manner. Make sure the mark is facing up. Be careful not to confuse the number one and number two rings.

24   Repeat the procedure for the remaining pistons and rings.

9.19a Installing the spacer/expander in the oil ring groove

9.19b DO NOT use a piston ring installation tool when installing the oil control side rails

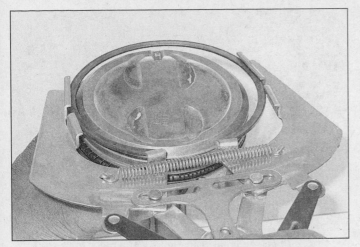

9.22 Use a piston ring installation tool to install the number 2 and the number 1 (top) rings - be sure the directional mark on the piston ring(s) is facing toward the top of the piston

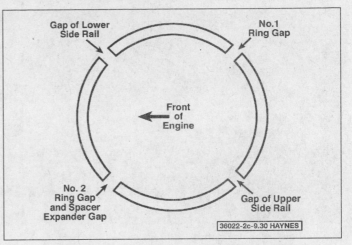

9.30 Position the piston ring end gaps as shown

Installation

25 Before installing the piston/connecting rod assemblies, the cylinder walls must be perfectly clean, the top edge of each cylinder bore must be chamfered, and the crankshaft must be in place.

26 Remove the cap from the end of the number one connecting rod (refer to the marks made during removal). Remove the original bearing inserts and wipe the bearing surfaces of the connecting rod and cap with a clean, lint-free cloth. They must be kept spotlessly clean.

Connecting rod bearing oil clearance check

Refer to Illustrations 9.30, 9.35, 9.37 and 9.41

27 Clean the back side of the new upper bearing insert, then lay it in place in the connecting rod.

28 Make sure the tab on the bearing fits into the recess in the rod. Don't hammer the bearing insert into place and be very careful not to nick or gouge the bearing face. Don't lubricate the bearing at this time.

29 Clean the back side of the other bearing insert and install it in the rod cap. Again, make sure the tab on the bearing fits into the recess in the cap, and don't apply any lubricant. It's critically important that the mating surfaces of the bearing and connecting rod are perfectly clean and oil free when they're assembled.

30 Position the piston ring gaps at 90-degree intervals around the piston as shown **(see illustration)**.

31 Lubricate the piston and rings with clean engine oil and attach a piston ring compressor to the piston. Leave the skirt protruding about 1/4-inch to guide the piston into the cylinder. The rings must be compressed until they're flush with the piston.

32 Rotate the crankshaft until the number one connecting rod journal is at BDC (bottom dead center) and apply a liberal coat of engine oil to the cylinder walls.

33 With the mark on top of the piston facing the front (timing belt or chain end) of the engine, gently insert the piston/connecting rod assembly into the number one cylinder bore and rest the bottom edge of the ring compressor on the engine block.

34 Tap the top edge of the ring compressor to make sure it's contacting the block around its entire circumference.

35 Gently tap on the top of the piston with the end of a wooden or plastic hammer handle **(see illustration)** while guiding the end of the connecting rod into place on the crankshaft journal. The piston rings may try to pop out of the ring compressor just before entering the cylinder bore, so keep some downward pressure on the ring compressor. Work slowly, and if any resistance is felt as the piston enters the cylinder, stop immediately. Find out what's hanging up and fix it before proceeding. Do not, for any reason, force the piston into the cylinder - you might break a ring and/or the piston.

36 Once the piston/connecting rod assembly is installed, the connecting rod bearing oil

clearance must be checked before the rod cap is permanently installed.

37 Cut a piece of the appropriate size Plastigage slightly shorter than the width of the connecting rod bearing and lay it in place on the number one connecting rod journal, parallel with the journal axis **(see illustration)**.

38 Clean the connecting rod cap bearing face and install the rod cap. Make sure the mating mark on the cap is on the same side as the mark on the connecting rod **(see illustration 9.4)**.

39 Install the old rod bolts, at this time, and tighten them to the torque listed in this Chapter's Specifications. **Note:** Use a thin-wall socket to avoid erroneous torque readings that can result if the socket is wedged between the rod cap and the bolt head. If the socket tends to wedge itself between the fastener and the cap, lift up on it slightly until it no longer contacts the cap. DO NOT rotate the crankshaft at any time during this operation.

40 Remove the fasteners and detach the rod cap, being very careful not to disturb the Plastigage.

9.35 Use a plastic or wooden hammer handle to push the piston into the cylinder

9.37 Place Plastigage on each connecting rod bearing journal parallel to the crankshaft centerline

2D-12 Chapter 2 Part D General engine overhaul procedures

9.41 Use the scale on the Plastigage package to determine the bearing oil clearance - be sure to measure the widest part of the Plastigage and use the correct scale; it comes with both standard and metric scales

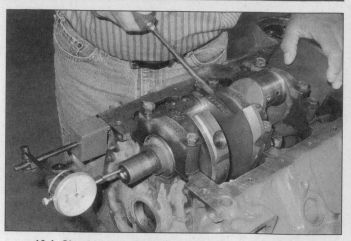

10.1 Checking crankshaft endplay with a dial indicator

41   Compare the width of the crushed Plasti-gage to the scale printed on the Plastigage envelope to obtain the oil clearance **(see illustration)**. The connecting rod oil clear-ance is usually about 0.001 to 0.002 inch (0.025 to 0.05 mm). Consult an automotive machine shop for the clearance specified for the rod bearings on your engine. On the cov-ered vehicles, code numbers on the block and crankshaft are used to select the proper bear-ings, using a chart at a dealership service/parts department.

42   If the clearance is not as specified, the bearing inserts may be the wrong size (which means different ones will be required). Before deciding that different inserts are needed, make sure that no dirt or oil was between the bearing inserts and the connecting rod or cap when the clearance was measured. Also, recheck the journal diameter. If the Plasti-gage was wider at one end than the other, the journal may be tapered. If the clearance still exceeds the limit specified, the bearing will have to be replaced with an undersize bear-ing. **Caution:** *When installing a new crank-shaft always use a standard size bearing.*

Final installation

43   Carefully scrape all traces of the Plasti-gage material off the rod journal and/or bear-ing face. Be very careful not to scratch the bearing - use your fingernail or the edge of a plastic card.

44   Make sure the bearing faces are per-fectly clean, then apply a uniform layer of clean moly-base grease or engine assembly lube to both of them. You'll have to push the piston into the cylinder to expose the face of the bearing insert in the connecting rod.

45   Slide the connecting rod back into place on the journal, install the rod cap, install the new bolts and tighten them to the torque listed in this Chapter's Specifications. **Caution:** *Install new connecting rod cap bolts. Do NOT reuse old bolts - they have stretched and can-not be reused.* Again, work up to the torque in three steps.

46   Repeat the entire procedure for the remaining pistons/connecting rods.

47   The important points to remember are:

a) *Keep the back sides of the bearing inserts and the insides of the connect-ing rods and caps perfectly clean when assembling them.*

b) *Make sure you have the correct piston/rod assembly for each cylinder.*

c) *Align the marks that were made in Step 4 towards the front of the engine.*

d) *Lubricate the cylinder walls liberally with clean oil.*

e) *Lubricate the bearing faces when install-ing the rod caps after the oil clearance has been checked.*

48   After all the piston/connecting rod assemblies have been correctly installed, rotate the crankshaft a number of times by hand to check for any obvious binding.

49   As a final step, check the connecting rod endplay, as described in Step 3. If it was cor-rect before disassembly and the original crank-shaft and rods were reinstalled, it should still be correct. If new rods or a new crankshaft were installed, the endplay may be inadequate. If so, the rods will have to be removed and taken to an automotive machine shop for resizing.

---

10   Crankshaft - removal and installation

Removal

Refer to illustrations 10.1 and 10.3

Note: *The crankshaft can be removed only after the engine has been removed from the vehicle. It's assumed that the flywheel or driveplate, crankshaft pulley, timing chain, oil pan, oil pump body, oil filter and piston/con-necting rod assemblies have already been removed. The rear main oil seal retainer must be unbolted and separated from the block before proceeding with crankshaft removal.*

1   Before the crankshaft is removed, mea-sure the endplay. Mount a dial indicator with the indicator in line with the crankshaft and just touching the end of the crankshaft as shown **(see illustration)**.

2   Pry the crankshaft all the way to the rear and zero the dial indicator. Next, pry the crank-shaft to the front as far as possible and check the reading on the dial indicator. The distance traveled is the endplay. A typical crankshaft endplay will fall between 0.003 to 0.010 inch (0.076 to 0.254 mm). If it is greater than that, check the crankshaft thrust surfaces for wear after it's removed. If no wear is evident, new main bearings should correct the endplay.

3   If a dial indicator isn't available, feeler gauges can be used. Gently pry the crank-shaft all the way to the front of the engine. Slip feeler gauges between the crankshaft and the front face of the thrust bearing or washer to determine the clearance **(see illustration)**.

4   Remove the main bearing bridge (outer) bolts and loosen the main bearing cap (inner) bolts (2.6L and 3.2L engines) or main bearing cap bolts (all others) 1/4-turn at a time each,

10.3 Checking the crankshaft endplay with feeler gauges at the thrust bearing journal

10.17 Place the Plastigage onto the crankshaft bearing journal as shown

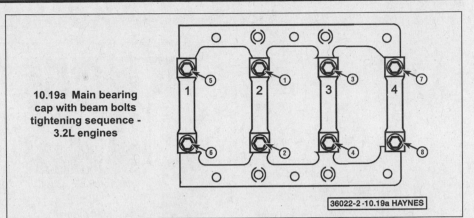

10.19a Main bearing cap with beam bolts tightening sequence - 3.2L engines

until they can be removed by hand. Loosen the bolts in the reverse of the tightening sequence **(see illustration 10.19a, 10.19b or 10.19c)**. **Note:** *On 3.2L engines, use a screwdriver to back out the adjuster sleeve on the main bearing bridge.*

5   Remove the main bearing caps and try not to drop the bearing inserts if they come out with the assembly.

6   Carefully lift the crankshaft out of the engine. It may be a good idea to have an assistant available, since the crankshaft is quite heavy and awkward to handle. With the bearing inserts in place inside the engine block and main bearing caps or lower cylinder block, reinstall the main bearing caps or lower cylinder block onto the engine block and tighten the bolts finger tight.

Installation

7   Crankshaft installation is the first step in engine reassembly. It's assumed at this point that the engine block and crankshaft have been cleaned, inspected and repaired or reconditioned.

8   Position the engine block with the bottom facing up.

9   Remove the bolts and lift off the support

beam, main bearing caps or lower cylinder block, as applicable.

10   If they're still in place, remove the original bearing inserts. Wipe the bearing surfaces of the block and main bearing cap assembly with a clean, lint-free cloth. They must be kept spotlessly clean; this is critical for determining the correct bearing oil clearance.

Main bearing oil clearance check

Refer to illustrations 10.17, 10.19a, 10.19b, 10.91c and 10.21

Note: *New main bearing cap bolts must be used when reassembling the engine, but save the old bolts for use when checking the main bearing oil clearance.*

11   Without mixing them up, clean the back sides of the new upper main bearing inserts (with grooves and oil holes) and lay one in each main bearing saddle in the engine block. Each upper bearing (engine block) has an oil groove and oil hole in it. **Caution:** *The oil holes in the block must line up with the oil holes in the upper bearing inserts.* Clean the back sides of the lower main bearing inserts and lay them in the corresponding location in the main bearing caps. Make sure the tab on the bearing insert fits into its corresponding recess. **Caution:** *Do not hammer the bearing insert into place and don't nick or gouge the bearing faces. DO NOT*

apply any lubrication at this time.

12   Clean the faces of the bearing inserts in the block and the crankshaft main bearing journals with a clean, lint-free cloth.

13   Check or clean the oil holes in the crankshaft, as any dirt here can go only one way - straight through the new bearings.

14   Once you're certain the crankshaft is clean, carefully lay it in position in the cylinder block.

15   Before the crankshaft can be permanently installed, the main bearing oil clearance must be checked.

16   Cut several strips of the appropriate size of Plastigage. They must be slightly shorter than the width of the main bearing journal.

17   Place one piece on each crankshaft main bearing journal, parallel with the journal axis as shown **(see illustration)**.

18   Clean the faces of the bearing inserts in the main bearing caps or the lower cylinder block. Hold the bearing inserts in place and install the caps or the lower cylinder block onto the crankshaft and cylinder block. DO NOT disturb the Plastigage.

19   Apply clean engine oil to all the old bolt threads prior to installation, then install all bolts finger-tight. Tighten the bolts in the sequence shown **(see illustrations)** progressing in steps, to the torque listed in this Chapter's Specifications. DO NOT rotate the

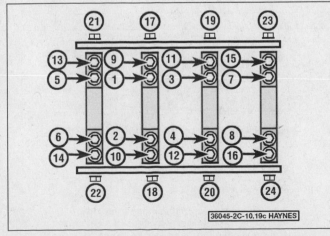

10.19b Main bearing cap bolt tightening sequence - 2.8L, 3.0L and 3.6L V6 engines

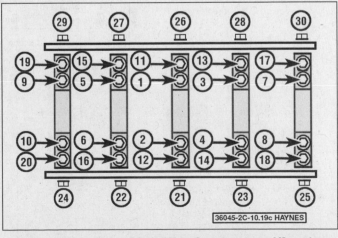

10.19c Main bearing cap bolt tightening sequence - V8 engines

ENGINE BEARING ANALYSIS

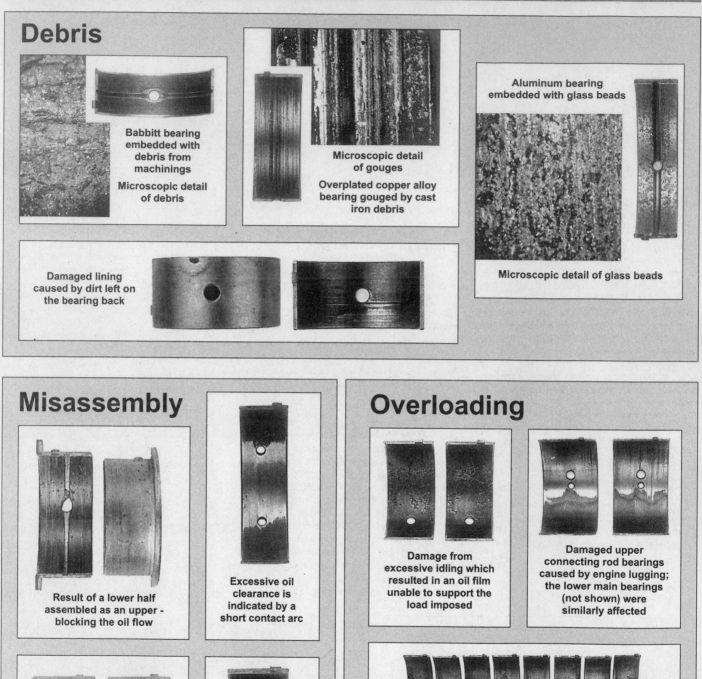

Debris

Babbitt bearing embedded with debris from machinings

Microscopic detail of debris

Microscopic detail of gouges

Overplated copper alloy bearing gouged by cast iron debris

Aluminum bearing embedded with glass beads

Microscopic detail of glass beads

Damaged lining caused by dirt left on the bearing back

Misassembly

Result of a lower half assembled as an upper - blocking the oil flow

Excessive oil clearance is indicated by a short contact arc

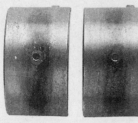

Polished and oil-stained backs are a result of a poor fit in the housing bore

Result of a wrong, reversed, or shifted cap

Overloading

Damage from excessive idling which resulted in an oil film unable to support the load imposed

Damaged upper connecting rod bearings caused by engine lugging; the lower main bearings (not shown) were similarly affected

The damage shown in these upper and lower connecting rod bearings was caused by engine operation at a higher-than-rated speed under load

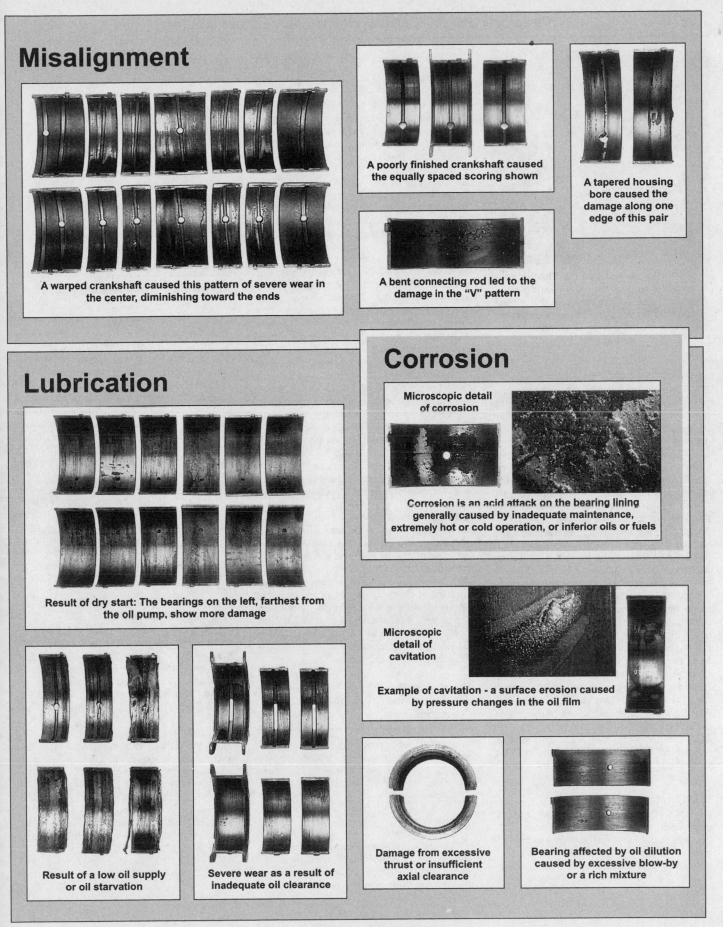

Misalignment

A poorly finished crankshaft caused the equally spaced scoring shown

A tapered housing bore caused the damage along one edge of this pair

A warped crankshaft caused this pattern of severe wear in the center, diminishing toward the ends

A bent connecting rod led to the damage in the "V" pattern

Lubrication

Result of dry start: The bearings on the left, farthest from the oil pump, show more damage

Result of a low oil supply or oil starvation

Severe wear as a result of inadequate oil clearance

Corrosion

Microscopic detail of corrosion

Corrosion is an acid attack on the bearing lining generally caused by inadequate maintenance, extremely hot or cold operation, or inferior oils or fuels

Microscopic detail of cavitation

Example of cavitation - a surface erosion caused by pressure changes in the oil film

Damage from excessive thrust or insufficient axial clearance

Bearing affected by oil dilution caused by excessive blow-by or a rich mixture

10.21 Use the scale on the Plastigage package to determine the bearing oil clearance - be sure to measure the widest part of the Plastigage and use the correct scale; it comes with both standard and metric scales

crankshaft at any time during this operation.

20   Remove the bolts in the *reverse* order of the tightening sequence and carefully lift the caps or the lower cylinder block straight up and off the block. Do not disturb the Plastigage or rotate the crankshaft.

21   Compare the width of the crushed Plastigage on each journal to the scale printed on the Plastigage envelope to determine the main bearing oil clearance **(see illustration)**. Check with an automotive machine shop for the oil clearance for your engine.

22   If the clearance is not as specified, the bearing inserts may be the wrong size (which means different ones will be required). Before deciding if different inserts are needed, make sure that no dirt or oil was between the bearing inserts and the cap assembly or block when the clearance was measured. If the Plastigage was wider at one end than the other, the crankshaft journal may be tapered. If the clearance still exceeds the limit specified, the bearing insert(s) will have to be replaced with an undersize bearing insert(s). **Caution:** *When installing a new crankshaft always install a standard bearing insert set.*

23   Carefully scrape all traces of the Plastigage material off the main bearing journals and/or the bearing insert faces. Be sure to remove all residue from the oil holes. Use your fingernail or the edge of a plastic card - don't nick or scratch the bearing faces.

Final installation

24   Carefully lift the crankshaft out of the cylinder block.

25   Clean the bearing insert faces in the cylinder block, then apply a thin, uniform layer of moly-base grease or engine assembly lube to each of the bearing surfaces. Coat the thrust

faces as well as the journal face of the thrust bearing.

26   Make sure the crankshaft journals are clean, then lay the crankshaft back in place in the cylinder block.

27   Clean the bearing insert faces and apply the same lubricant to them. Clean the engine block and the bearing caps/lower cylinder block thoroughly. The surfaces must be free of oil residue.

28   Install the main bearing caps in their proper locations, with the arrows or marks on the caps facing the front of the engine. **Note:** *On 3.2L engines, apply sealer to the grooves on the side of the rear (fourth) main bearing cap.*

29   Prior to installation, apply clean engine oil to all bolt threads wiping off any excess, then on all models except 3.2L engines, install all new bolts finger-tight. On 3.2L engines, install the crankshaft bearing bridge to the top of the main bearings caps and install the new main bearing bolts finger-tight. **Note:** *Make sure all the crankshaft bridge adjusting sleeves are backed out and the sleeves do not contact the engine block.*

30   Tighten the caps, following the correct torque sequence **(see illustration 10.19a, 10.19b or 10.19c)**. Torque the bolts to the Specifications listed in this Chapter.

31   On 3.2L engines, tighten the crankshaft bridge adjustment sleeves to the torque listed in this Chapters Specification's. Install the crankshaft bridge bolts and tighten the bolts to the torque listed in this Chapters Specification's.

32   Recheck the crankshaft endplay with a feeler gauge or a dial indicator. The endplay should be correct if the crankshaft thrust faces aren't worn or damaged and if new bearings have been installed.

33   Rotate the crankshaft a number of times by hand to check for any obvious binding. It should rotate with a running torque of 50 in-lbs or less. If the running torque is too high, correct the problem at this time.

34   Install a new rear main oil seal (see Chapter 2A, 2B or 2C).

11   Engine overhaul - reassembly sequence

1   Before beginning engine reassembly, make sure you have all the necessary new parts, gaskets and seals as well as the following items on hand:

   Common hand tools
   A 1/2-inch drive torque wrench
   New engine oil
   Gasket sealant
   Thread locking compound

2   If you obtained a short block it will be necessary to install the cylinder head, the oil pump and pick-up tube, the oil pan, the water

pump, the timing belt and timing cover, and the valve cover (see Chapter 2A, 2B or 2C). In order to save time and avoid problems, the external components must be installed in the following general order:

   Thermostat and housing cover
   Water pump
   Intake and exhaust manifolds
   Fuel injection components
   Emission control components
   Spark plugs
   Ignition coils
   Oil filter
   Engine mounts and mount brackets
   Clutch and flywheel (manual transmission)
   Driveplate (automatic transmission)

12   Initial start-up and break-in after overhaul

Warning: *Have a fire extinguisher handy when starting the engine for the first time.*

1   Once the engine has been installed in the vehicle, double-check the engine oil and coolant levels.

2   With the spark plugs out of the engine and the fuel pump disabled (see Chapter 4, Section 3), crank the engine until oil pressure registers on the gauge or the light goes out.

3   Install the spark plugs, hook up the plug wires and restore the ignition system and fuel pump functions.

4   Start the engine. It may take a few moments for the fuel system to build up pressure, but the engine should start without a great deal of effort.

5   After the engine starts, it should be allowed to warm up to normal operating temperature. While the engine is warming up, make a thorough check for fuel, oil and coolant leaks.

6   Shut the engine off and recheck the engine oil and coolant levels.

7   Drive the vehicle to an area with minimum traffic, accelerate from 30 to 50 mph, then allow the vehicle to slow to 30 mph with the throttle closed. Repeat the procedure 10 or 12 times. This will load the piston rings and cause them to seat properly against the cylinder walls. Check again for oil and coolant leaks.

8   Drive the vehicle gently for the first 500 miles (no sustained high speeds) and keep a constant check on the oil level. It is not unusual for an engine to use oil during the break-in period.

9   At approximately 500 to 600 miles, change the oil and filter.

10   For the next few hundred miles, drive the vehicle normally. Do not pamper it or abuse it.

11   After 2,000 miles, change the oil and filter again and consider the engine broken in.

COMMON ENGINE OVERHAUL TERMS

B

Backlash - The amount of play between two parts. Usually refers to how much one gear can be moved back and forth without moving the gear with which it's meshed.

Bearing Caps - The caps held in place by nuts or bolts which, in turn, hold the bearing surface. This space is for lubricating oil to enter.

Bearing clearance - The amount of space left between shaft and bearing surface. This space is for lubricating oil to enter.

Bearing crush - The additional height which is purposely manufactured into each bearing half to ensure complete contact of the bearing back with the housing bore when the engine is assembled.

Bearing knock - The noise created by movement of a part in a loose or worn bearing.

Blueprinting - Dismantling an engine and reassembling it to EXACT specifications.

Bore - An engine cylinder, or any cylindrical hole; also used to describe the process of enlarging or accurately refinishing a hole with a cutting tool, as to bore an engine cylinder. The bore size is the diameter of the hole.

Boring - Renewing the cylinders by cutting them out to a specified size. A boring bar is used to make the cut.

Bottom end - A term which refers collectively to the engine block, crankshaft, main bearings and the big ends of the connecting rods.

Break-in - The period of operation between installation of new or rebuilt parts and time in which parts are worn to the correct fit. Driving at reduced and varying speed for a specified mileage to permit parts to wear to the correct fit.

Bushing - A one-piece sleeve placed in a bore to serve as a bearing surface for shaft, piston pin, etc. Usually replaceable.

C

Camshaft - The shaft in the engine, on which a series of lobes are located for operating the valve mechanisms. The camshaft is driven by gears or sprockets and a timing chain. Usually referred to simply as the cam.

Carbon - Hard, or soft, black deposits found in combustion chamber, on plugs, under rings, on and under valve heads.

Cast iron - An alloy of iron and more than two percent carbon, used for engine blocks and heads because it's relatively inexpensive and easy to mold into complex shapes.

Chamfer - To bevel across (or a bevel on) the sharp edge of an object.

Chase - To repair damaged threads with a tap or die.

Combustion chamber - The space between the piston and the cylinder head, with the piston at top dead center, in which air-fuel mixture is burned.

Compression ratio - The relationship between cylinder volume (clearance volume) when the piston is at top dead center and cylinder volume when the piston is at bottom dead center.

Connecting rod - The rod that connects the crank on the crankshaft with the piston. Sometimes called a con rod.

Connecting rod cap - The part of the connecting rod assembly that attaches the rod to the crankpin.

Core plug - Soft metal plug used to plug the casting holes for the coolant passages in the block.

Crankcase - The lower part of the engine in which the crankshaft rotates; includes the lower section of the cylinder block and the oil pan.

Crank kit - A reground or reconditioned crankshaft and new main and connecting rod bearings.

Crankpin - The part of a crankshaft to which a connecting rod is attached.

Crankshaft - The main rotating member, or shaft, running the length of the crankcase, with offset throws to which the connecting rods are attached; changes the reciprocating motion of the pistons into rotating motion.

Cylinder sleeve - A replaceable sleeve, or liner, pressed into the cylinder block to form the cylinder bore.

D

Deburring - Removing the burrs (rough edges or areas) from a bearing.

Deglazer - A tool, rotated by an electric motor, used to remove glaze from cylinder walls so a new set of rings will seat.

E

Endplay - The amount of lengthwise movement between two parts. As applied to a crankshaft, the distance that the crankshaft can move forward and back in the cylinder block.

F

Face - A machinist's term that refers to removing metal from the end of a shaft or the face of a larger part, such as a flywheel.

Fatigue - A breakdown of material through a large number of loading and unloading cycles. The first signs are cracks followed shortly by breaks.

Feeler gauge - A thin strip of hardened steel, ground to an exact thickness, used to check clearances between parts.

Free height - The unloaded length or height of a spring.

Freeplay - The looseness in a linkage, or an assembly of parts, between the initial application of force and actual movement. Usually perceived as slop or slight delay.

Freeze plug - See Core plug.

G

Gallery - A large passage in the block that forms a reservoir for engine oil pressure.

Glaze - The very smooth, glassy finish that develops on cylinder walls while an engine is in service.

H

Heli-Coil - A rethreading device used when threads are worn or damaged. The device is installed in a retapped hole to reduce the thread size to the original size.

I

Installed height - The spring's measured length or height, as installed on the cylinder head. Installed height is measured from the spring seat to the underside of the spring retainer.

J

Journal - The surface of a rotating shaft which turns in a bearing.

K

Keeper - The split lock that holds the valve spring retainer in position on the valve stem.

Key - A small piece of metal inserted into matching grooves machined into two parts fitted together - such as a gear pressed onto a shaft - which prevents slippage between the two parts.

Knock - The heavy metallic engine sound, produced in the combustion chamber as a result of abnormal combustion - usually detonation. Knock is usually caused by a loose or worn bearing. Also referred to as detonation, pinging and spark knock. Connecting rod or main bearing knocks are created by too much oil clearance or insufficient lubrication.

L

Lands - The portions of metal between the piston ring grooves.

Lapping the valves - Grinding a valve face and its seat together with lapping compound.

Lash - The amount of free motion in a gear train, between gears, or in a mechanical assembly, that occurs before movement can begin. Usually refers to the lash in a valve train.

Lifter - The part that rides against the cam to transfer motion to the rest of the valve train.

M

Machining - The process of using a machine to remove metal from a metal part.

Main bearings - The plain, or babbit, bearings that support the crankshaft.

Main bearing caps - The cast iron caps, bolted to the bottom of the block, that support the main bearings.

O

O.D. - Outside diameter.

Oil gallery - A pipe or drilled passageway in the engine used to carry engine oil from one area to another.

Oil ring - The lower ring, or rings, of a piston; designed to prevent excessive amounts of oil from working up the cylinder walls and into the combustion chamber. Also called an oil-control ring.

Oil seal - A seal which keeps oil from leaking out of a compartment. Usually refers to a dynamic seal around a rotating shaft or other moving part.

O-ring - A type of sealing ring made of a special rubberlike material; in use, the O-ring is compressed into a groove to provide the sealing action.

Overhaul - To completely disassemble a unit, clean and inspect all parts, reassemble it with the original or new parts and make all adjustments necessary for proper operation.

P

Pilot bearing - A small bearing installed in the center of the flywheel (or the rear end of the crankshaft) to support the front end of the input shaft of the transmission.

Pip mark - A little dot or indentation which indicates the top side of a compression ring.

Piston - The cylindrical part, attached to the connecting rod, that moves up and down in the cylinder as the crankshaft rotates. When the fuel charge is fired, the piston transfers the force of the explosion to the connecting rod, then to the crankshaft.

Piston pin (or wrist pin) - The cylindrical and usually hollow steel pin that passes through the piston. The piston pin fastens the piston to the upper end of the connecting rod.

Piston ring - The split ring fitted to the groove in a piston. The ring contacts the sides of the ring groove and also rubs against the cylinder wall, thus sealing space between piston and wall. There are two types of rings: Compression rings seal the compression pressure in the combustion chamber; oil rings scrape excessive oil off the cylinder wall.

Piston ring groove - The slots or grooves cut in piston heads to hold piston rings in position.

Piston skirt - The portion of the piston below the rings and the piston pin hole.

Plastigage - A thin strip of plastic thread, available in different sizes, used for measuring clearances. For example, a strip of plastigage is laid across a bearing journal and mashed as parts are assembled. Then parts are disassembled and the width of the strip is measured to determine clearance between journal and bearing. Commonly used to measure crankshaft main-bearing and connecting rod bearing clearances.

Press-fit - A tight fit between two parts that requires pressure to force the parts together. Also referred to as drive, or force, fit.

Prussian blue - A blue pigment; in solution, useful in determining the area of contact between two surfaces. Prussian blue is commonly used to determine the width and location of the contact area between the valve face and the valve seat.

R

Race (bearing) - The inner or outer ring that provides a contact surface for balls or rollers in bearing.

Ream - To size, enlarge or smooth a hole by using a round cutting tool with fluted edges.

Ring job - The process of reconditioning the cylinders and installing new rings.

Runout - Wobble. The amount a shaft rotates out-of-true.

S

Saddle - The upper main bearing seat.

Scored - Scratched or grooved, as a cylinder wall may be scored by abrasive particles moved up and down by the piston rings.

Scuffing - A type of wear in which there's a transfer of material between parts moving against each other; shows up as pits or grooves in the mating surfaces.

Seat - The surface upon which another part rests or seats. For example, the valve seat is the matched surface upon which the valve face rests. Also used to refer to wearing into a good fit; for example, piston rings seat after a few miles of driving.

Short block - An engine block complete with crankshaft and piston and, usually, camshaft assemblies.

Static balance - The balance of an object while it's stationary.

Step - The wear on the lower portion of a ring land caused by excessive side and back-clearance. The height of the step indicates the ring's extra side clearance and the length of the step projecting from the back wall of the groove represents the ring's back clearance.

Stroke - The distance the piston moves when traveling from top dead center to bottom dead center, or from bottom dead center to top dead center.

Stud - A metal rod with threads on both ends.

T

Tang - A lip on the end of a plain bearing used to align the bearing during assembly.

Tap - To cut threads in a hole. Also refers to the fluted tool used to cut threads.

Taper - A gradual reduction in the width of a shaft or hole; in an engine cylinder, taper usually takes the form of uneven wear, more pronounced at the top than at the bottom.

Throws - The offset portions of the crankshaft to which the connecting rods are affixed.

Thrust bearing - The main bearing that has thrust faces to prevent excessive endplay, or forward and backward movement of the crankshaft.

Thrust washer - A bronze or hardened steel washer placed between two moving parts. The washer prevents longitudinal movement and provides a bearing surface for thrust surfaces of parts.

Tolerance - The amount of variation permitted from an exact size of measurement. Actual amount from smallest acceptable dimension to largest acceptable dimension.

U

Umbrella - An oil deflector placed near the valve tip to throw oil from the valve stem area.

Undercut - A machined groove below the normal surface.

Undersize bearings - Smaller diameter bearings used with re-ground crankshaft journals.

V

Valve grinding - Refacing a valve in a valve-refacing machine.

Valve train - The valve-operating mechanism of an engine; includes all components from the camshaft to the valve.

Vibration damper - A cylindrical weight attached to the front of the crankshaft to minimize torsional vibration (the twist-untwist actions of the crankshaft caused by the cylinder firing impulses). Also called a harmonic balancer.

W

Water jacket - The spaces around the cylinders, between the inner and outer shells of the cylinder block or head, through which coolant circulates.

Web - A supporting structure across a cavity.

Woodruff key - A key with a radiused backside (viewed from the side).

Chapter 3
Cooling, heating and air conditioning systems

Contents

Specifications

General

Cooling system capacity..	See Chapter 1
Refrigerant type	R-134a
Refrigerant capacity...	Refer to HVAC specification tag

Torque specifications

Note: *One foot-pound (ft-lb) of torque is equivalent to 12 inch-pounds (in-lbs) of torque. Torque values below approximately 15 foot-pounds are expressed in inch-pounds, because most foot-pound torque wrenches are not accurate at these smaller values.*

	Ft-lbs (unless otherwise indicated)	Nm
Condenser inlet and outlet nuts...	71 in-lbs	8
Engine coolant outlet pipe bolt (3.2L V6 engines)...................................	15	20
Engine coolant pipe bolts		
2.8L and 3.6L V6 engines		
To thermostat housing	89 in-lbs	10
To cylinder head..	37	50
3.0L V6 engines		
To thermostat housing	16	22
To cylinder head		
Bolt..	43	58
Stud bolt...	16	22

Torque specifications

	Ft-lbs (unless otherwise indicated)	Nm

Note: *One foot-pound (ft-lb) of torque is equivalent to 12 inch-pounds (in-lbs) of torque. Torque values below approximately 15 foot-pounds are expressed in inch-pounds, because most foot-pound torque wrenches are not accurate at these smaller values.*

	Ft-lbs (unless otherwise indicated)	Nm
Thermostat housing bolts		
3.2L V6 engines	15	20
2.8L, 3.0L and 3.6L V6 engines		
Cover-to-housing bolts	89 in-lbs	10
Housing-to-block bolts	15	20
5.7L, 6.0L and 6.2L V8 engines	132 in-lbs	15
Water pump fasteners		
3.2L V6 engines	18	25
2.8L, 3.0L and 3.6L V6 engines		
2005 through 2012		
Step 1	106 in-lbs	12
Step 2	106 in-lbs	12
2013 and later		
Step 1	89 in-lbs	10
Step 2	89 in-lbs	10
5.7L 6.0L and 6.2L V8 engines		
Step 1	132 in-lbs	15
Step 2	22	30
6.2L V8 engines	22	30
Water pump pulley bolts		
3.2L V6 engines	71 in-lbs	8
2.8L and 3.6L V6 engines	106 in-lbs	12

1   General information

Warning: *Do not allow antifreeze to come in contact with your skin or painted surfaces of the vehicle. Rinse off spills immediately with plenty of water. Antifreeze is highly toxic if ingested. Never leave antifreeze lying around in an open container or in puddles on the floor; children and pets are attracted by it's sweet smell and may drink it. Check with local authorities about disposing of used antifreeze. Many communities have collection centers which will see that antifreeze is disposed of safely. Never dump used antifreeze on the ground or pour it into drains.*

Engine cooling system

All modern vehicles employ a pressurized engine cooling system with thermostatically controlled coolant circulation. The cooling system consists of a radiator, an expansion tank or coolant reservoir, a pressure cap (located on the expansion tank or radiator), a thermostat, a cooling fan, and a water pump.

The water pump circulates coolant through the engine. The coolant flows around each cylinder and around the intake and exhaust ports, near the spark plug areas and in close proximity to the exhaust valve guides.

A thermostat controls engine coolant temperature. During warm up, the closed thermostat prevents coolant from circulating through the radiator. As the engine nears normal operating temperature, the thermostat opens and allows hot coolant to travel through the radiator, where it's cooled before returning to the engine.

Heating system

The heating system consists of a blower fan and heater core located in a housing under the dash, the hoses connecting the heater core to the engine cooling system and the heater/air conditioning control head on the dashboard. Hot engine coolant is circulated through the heater core. When the heater mode is activated, a flap door in the housing opens to expose the heater core to the passenger compartment through air ducts. A fan switch on the control head activates the blower motor, which forces air through the core, heating the air.

Air conditioning system

The air conditioning system consists of a condenser mounted in front of the radiator, an evaporator mounted adjacent to the heater core, a compressor mounted on the engine, a receiver-drier or accumulator and the plumbing connecting all of the above components.

A blower fan forces the warmer air of the passenger compartment through the evaporator core (sort of a radiator-in-reverse), transferring the heat from the air to the refrigerant. The liquid refrigerant boils off into low pressure vapor, taking the heat with it when it leaves the evaporator.

2.2 The cooling system pressure tester is connected in place of the pressure cap, then pumped up to pressurize the system

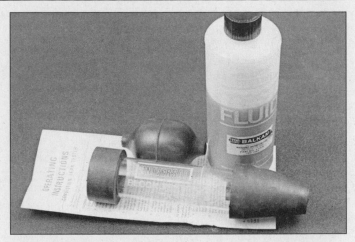

2.5a The combustion leak detector consists of a bulb, syringe and test fluid

2   Troubleshooting

Coolant leaks

Refer to illustration 2.2

1   A coolant leak can develop anywhere in the cooling system, but the most common causes are:

a) *A loose or weak hose clamp*
b) *A defective hose*
c) *A faulty pressure cap*
d) *A damaged radiator*
e) *A bad heater core*
f) *A faulty water pump*
g) *A leaking gasket at any joint that carries coolant*

2   Coolant leaks aren't always easy to find. Sometimes they can only be detected when the cooling system is under pressure. Here's where a cooling system pressure tester comes in handy. After the engine has cooled completely, the tester is attached in place of the pressure cap, then pumped up to the pressure value equal to that of the pressure cap rating **(see illustration)**. Now, leaks that only exist when the engine is fully warmed up will become apparent. The tester can be left connected to locate a nagging slow leak.

Coolant level drops, but no external leaks

Refer to illustrations 2.5a and 2.5b

3   If you find it necessary to keep adding coolant, but there are no external leaks, the probable causes include:

a) *A blown head gasket*
b) *A leaking intake manifold gasket (only on engines that have coolant passages in the manifold)*
c) *A cracked cylinder head or cylinder block*

4   Any of the above problems will also usually result in contamination of the engine oil, which will cause it to take on a milkshake-like

2.5b Place the tester over the cooling system filler neck and use the bulb to draw a sample into the tester

appearance. A bad head gasket or cracked head or block can also result in engine oil contaminating the cooling system.

5   Combustion leak detectors (also known as block testers) are available at most auto parts stores. These work by detecting exhaust gases in the cooling system, which indicates a compression leak from a cylinder into the coolant. The tester consists of a large bulb-type syringe and bottle of test fluid **(see illustration)**. A measured amount of the fluid is added to the syringe. The syringe is placed over the cooling system filler neck and, with the engine running, the bulb is squeezed and a sample of the gases present in the cooling system are drawn up through the test fluid **(see illustration)**. If any combustion gases are present in the sample taken, the test fluid will change color.

6   If the test indicates combustion gas is present in the cooling system, you can be sure that the engine has a blown head gasket or a crack in the cylinder head or block, and will require disassembly to repair.

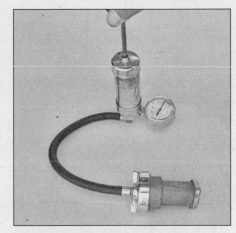

2.8 Checking the cooling system pressure cap with a cooling system pressure tester

Pressure cap

Refer to illustration 2.8

Warning: *Wait until the engine is completely cool before beginning this check.*

7   The cooling system is sealed by a spring-loaded cap, which raises the boiling point of the coolant. If the cap's seal or spring are worn out, the coolant can boil and escape past the cap. With the engine completely cool, remove the cap and check the seal; if it's cracked, hardened or deteriorated in any way, replace it with a new one.

8   Even if the seal is good, the spring might not be; this can be checked with a cooling system pressure tester **(see illustration)**. If the cap can't hold a pressure within approximately 1-1/2 lbs of its rated pressure (which is marked on the cap), replace it with a new one.

9   The cap is also equipped with a vacuum relief spring. When the engine cools off, a vacuum is created in the cooling system. The vacuum relief spring allows air back into the system, which will equalize the pressure and

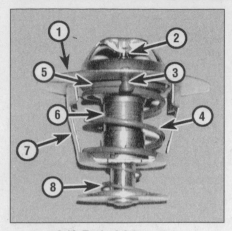

2.10 Typical thermostat:

1 *Flange*
2 *Piston*
3 *Jiggle valve*
4 *Main coil spring*
5 *Valve seat*
6 *Valve*
7 *Frame*
8 *Secondary coil spring*

prevent damage to the radiator (the radiator tanks could collapse if the vacuum is great enough). If, after turning the engine off and allowing it to cool down you notice any of the cooling system hoses collapsing, replace the pressure cap with a new one.

Thermostat

Refer to illustration 2.10

10 Before assuming the thermostat **(see illustration)** is responsible for a cooling system problem, check the coolant level (see Chapter 1), drivebelt tension (see Chapter 1) and temperature gauge (or light) operation.

11 If the engine takes a long time to warm up (as indicated by the temperature gauge or heater operation), the thermostat is probably stuck open. Replace the thermostat with a new one.

12 If the engine runs hot or overheats, a thorough test of the thermostat should be performed.

13 Definitive testing of the thermostat can only be made when it is removed from the vehicle. If the thermostat is stuck in the open position at room temperature, it is faulty and must be replaced. **Caution:** *Do not drive the vehicle without a thermostat. The computer may stay in open loop and emissions and fuel economy will suffer.*

14 To test a thermostat, suspend the (closed) thermostat on a length of string or wire in a pot of cold water.

15 Heat the water on a stove while observing thermostat. The thermostat should fully open before the water boils.

16 If the thermostat doesn't open and close as specified, or sticks in any position, replace it.

2.28 The water pump weep hole is generally located on the underside of the pump

Cooling fan
Electric cooling fan

17 If the engine is overheating and the cooling fan is not coming on when the engine temperature rises to an excessive level, unplug the fan motor electrical connector(s) and connect the motor directly to the battery with fused jumper wires. If the fan motor doesn't come on, replace the motor.

18 If the radiator fan motor is okay, but it isn't coming on when the engine gets hot, the fan relay might be defective. A relay is used to control a circuit by turning it on and off in response to a control decision by the Powertrain Control Module (PCM). These control circuits are fairly complex, and checking them should be left to a qualified automotive technician. Sometimes, the control system can be fixed by simply identifying and replacing a bad relay.

19 Locate the fan relays in the engine compartment fuse/relay box.

20 Test the relay (see Chapter 12).

21 If the relay is okay, check all wiring and connections to the fan motor. Refer to the wiring diagrams at the end of Chapter 12. If no obvious problems are found, the problem could be the Engine Coolant Temperature (ECT) sensor or the Powertrain Control Module (PCM). Have the cooling fan system and circuit diagnosed by a dealer service department or repair shop with the proper diagnostic equipment.

Belt-driven cooling fan

22 Disconnect the cable from the negative terminal of the battery and rock the fan back and forth by hand to check for excessive bearing play.

23 With the engine cold (and not running), turn the fan blades by hand. The fan should turn freely.

24 Visually inspect for substantial fluid leakage from the clutch assembly. If problems are noted, replace the clutch assembly.

25 With the engine completely warmed up, turn off the ignition switch and disconnect the negative battery cable from the battery. Turn

the fan by hand. Some drag should be evident. If the fan turns easily, replace the fan clutch.

Water pump

26 A failure in the water pump can cause serious engine damage due to overheating.

Drivebelt-driven water pump

Refer to illustration 2.28

27 There are two ways to check the operation of the water pump while it's installed on the engine. If the pump is found to be defective, it should be replaced with a new or rebuilt unit.

28 Water pumps are equipped with weep (or vent) holes **(see illustration)**. If a failure occurs in the pump seal, coolant will leak from the hole.

29 If the water pump shaft bearings fail, there may be a howling sound at the pump while it's running. Shaft wear can be felt with the drivebelt removed if the water pump pulley is rocked up and down (with the engine off). Don't mistake drivebelt slippage, which causes a squealing sound, for water pump bearing failure.

Timing chain or timing belt-driven water pump

30 Water pumps driven by the timing chain or timing belt are located underneath the timing chain or timing belt cover.

31 Checking the water pump is limited because of where it is located. However, some basic checks can be made before deciding to remove the water pump. If the pump is found to be defective, it should be replaced with a new or rebuilt unit.

32 One sign that the water pump may be failing is that the heater (climate control) may not work well. Warm the engine to normal operating temperature, confirm that the coolant level is correct, then run the heater and check for hot air coming from the ducts.

33 Check for noises coming from the water pump area. If the water pump impeller shaft or bearings are failing, there may be a howling sound at the pump while the engine is running. **Note:** *Be careful not to mistake drivebelt noise (squealing) for water pump bearing or shaft failure.*

34 It you suspect water pump failure due to noise, wear can be confirmed by feeling for play at the pump shaft. This can be done by rocking the drive sprocket on the pump shaft up and down. To do this you will need to remove the tension on the timing chain or belt as well as access the water pump.

All water pumps

35 In rare cases or on high-mileage vehicles, another sign of water pump failure may be the presence of coolant in the engine oil. This condition will adversely affect the engine in varying degrees. **Note:** *Finding coolant in the engine oil could indicate other serious issues besides a failed water pump, such as a blown head gasket or a cracked cylinder head or block.*

36 Even a pump that exhibits no outward signs of a problem, such as noise or leakage, can still be due for replacement. Removal for close examination is the only sure way to tell. Sometimes the fins on the back of the impeller can corrode to the point that cooling efficiency is diminished significantly.

Heater system

37 Little can go wrong with a heater. If the fan motor will run at all speeds, the electrical part of the system is okay. The three basic heater problems fall into the following general categories:

a) *Not enough heat*
b) *Heat all the time*
c) *No heat*

38 If there's not enough heat, the control valve or door is stuck in a partially open position, the coolant coming from the engine isn't hot enough, or the heater core is restricted. If the coolant isn't hot enough, the thermostat in the engine cooling system is stuck open, allowing coolant to pass through the engine so rapidly that it doesn't heat up quickly enough. If the vehicle is equipped with a temperature gauge instead of a warning light, watch to see if the engine temperature rises to the normal operating range after driving for a reasonable distance.

39 If there's heat all the time, the control valve or the door is stuck wide open.

40 If there's no heat, coolant is probably not reaching the heater core, or the heater core is plugged. The likely cause is a collapsed or plugged hose, core, or a frozen heater control valve. If the heater is the type that flows coolant all the time, the cause is a stuck door or a broken or kinked control cable.

Air conditioning system

41 If the cool air output is inadequate:

a) *Inspect the condenser coils and fins to make sure they're clear.*
b) *Check the compressor clutch for slippage.*
c) *Check the blower motor for proper operation.*
d) *Inspect the blower discharge passage for obstructions.*
e) *Check the system air intake filter for clogging.*

42 If the system provides intermittent cooling air:

a) *Check the circuit breaker, blower switch and blower motor for a malfunction.*
b) *Make sure the compressor clutch isn't slipping.*
c) *Inspect the plenum door to make sure it's operating properly.*
d) *Inspect the evaporator to make sure it isn't clogged.*
e) *If the unit is icing up, it may be caused by excessive moisture in the system, incorrect super heat switch adjustment or low thermostat adjustment.*

43 If the system provides no cooling air:

a) *Inspect the compressor drivebelt. Make sure it's not loose or broken.*
b) *Make sure the compressor clutch engages. If it doesn't, check for a blown fuse.*
c) *Inspect the wire harness for broken or disconnected wires.*
d) *If the compressor clutch doesn't engage, bridge the terminals of the A/C pressure switch(es) with a jumper wire; if the clutch now engages, and the system is properly charged, the pressure switch is bad.*
e) *Make sure the blower motor is not disconnected or burned out.*
f) *Make sure the compressor isn't partially or completely seized.*
g) *Inspect the refrigerant lines for leaks.*
h) *Check the components for leaks.*
i) *Inspect the receiver-drier/accumulator or expansion valve/tube for clogged screens.*

44 If the system is noisy:

a) *Look for loose panels in the passenger compartment.*
b) *Inspect the compressor drivebelt. It may be loose or worn*
c) *Check the compressor mounting bolts. They should be tight.*
d) *Listen carefully to the compressor. It may be worn out.*
e) *Listen to the idler pulley and bearing and the clutch. Either may be defective.*
f) *The winding in the compressor clutch coil or solenoid may be defective.*
g) *The compressor oil level may be low.*
h) *The blower motor fan bushing or the motor itself may be worn out.*
i) *If there is an excessive charge in the system, you'll hear a rumbling noise in the high pressure line, a thumping noise in the compressor, or see bubbles or cloudiness in the sight glass.*
j) *If there's a low charge in the system, you might hear hissing in the evaporator case at the expansion valve, or see bubbles or cloudiness in the sight glass.*

3 Air conditioning and heating system - check and maintenance

Air conditioning system

Warning: *The air conditioning system is under high pressure. Do not loosen any hose fittings or remove any components until after the system has been discharged. Air conditioning refrigerant should be properly discharged into an EPA-approved recovery/recycling unit at a dealer service department or an automotive air conditioning repair facility. Always wear eye protection when disconnecting air conditioning system fittings.*
Caution: *All models covered by this manual use environmentally friendly R-134a. This refrigerant (and its appropriate refrigerant oils) are not compatible with R-12 refrigerant system components and must never be mixed or the components will be damaged.*
Caution: *When replacing entire components, additional refrigerant oil should be added equal to the amount that is removed with the component being replaced. Read the can before adding any oil to the system, to make sure it is compatible with the R-134a system.*

1 The following maintenance checks should be performed on a regular basis to ensure that the air conditioning continues to operate at peak efficiency.

a) *Inspect the condition of the compressor drivebelt. If it is worn or deteriorated, replace it (see Chapter 1).*
b) *Check the drivebelt tension (see Chapter 1).*
c) *Inspect the system hoses. Look for cracks, bubbles, hardening and deterioration. Inspect the hoses and all fittings for oil bubbles or seepage. If there is any evidence of wear, damage or leakage, replace the hose(s).*
d) *Inspect the condenser fins for leaves, bugs and any other foreign material that may have embedded itself in the fins. Use a fin comb or compressed air to remove debris from the condenser.*
e) *Make sure the system has the correct refrigerant charge.*
f) *If you hear water sloshing around in the dash area or have water dripping on the carpet, check the evaporator housing drain tube and insert a piece of wire into the opening to check for blockage.*

2 It's a good idea to operate the system for about ten minutes at least once a month. This is particularly important during the winter months because long term non-use can cause hardening, and subsequent failure, of the seals. Note that using the Defrost function operates the compressor.

3 If the air conditioning system is not working properly, proceed to Step 6 and perform the general checks outlined below.

4 Because of the complexity of the air conditioning system and the special equipment necessary to service it, in-depth troubleshooting and repairs beyond checking the refrigerant charge and the compressor clutch operation are not included in this manual. However, simple checks and component replacement procedures are provided in this Chapter. For more complete information on the air conditioning system, refer to the *Haynes Automotive Heating and Air Conditioning Manual.*

5 The most common cause of poor cooling is simply a low system refrigerant charge. If a noticeable drop in system cooling ability occurs, one of the following quick checks will help you determine if the refrigerant level is low.

Checking the refrigerant charge

Refer to illustration 3.9

6 Warm the engine up to normal operating temperature.

7 Place the air conditioning temperature selector at the coldest setting and put the blower at the highest setting.

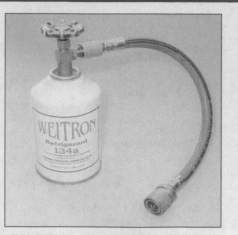

**3.9 Insert a thermometer in the center
vent, turn on the air conditioning system
and wait for it to cool down; depending on
the humidity, the output air should be 35
to 40 degrees cooler than the ambient
air temperature**

**3.11 R-134a automotive air conditioning
charging kit**

**3.13 Location of the low-side
charging port**

8   After the system reaches operating temperature, feel the larger pipe exiting the evaporator at the firewall. The outlet pipe should
be cold (the tubing that leads back to the
compressor). If the evaporator outlet pipe is
warm, the system probably needs a charge.

9   Insert a thermometer in the center air
distribution duct **(see illustration)** while operating the air conditioning system at its maximum setting - the temperature of the output
air should be 35 to 40 degrees F below the
ambient air temperature (down to approximately 40 degrees F). If the ambient (outside)
air temperature is very high, say 110 degrees
F, the duct air temperature may be as high
as 60 degrees F, but generally the air conditioning is 35 to 40 degrees F cooler than the
ambient air.

10   Further inspection or testing of the system requires special tools and techniques and
is beyond the scope of the home mechanic.

Adding refrigerant

Refer to illustrations 3.11 and 3.13

Caution: *Make sure any refrigerant, refrigerant oil or replacement component you
purchase is designated as compatible with
R-134a systems.*

11   Purchase an R-134a automotive charging kit at an auto parts store **(see illustration)**. A charging kit includes a can of refrigerant, a tap valve and a short section of hose
that can be attached between the tap valve
and the system low side service valve. **Caution:** *Never add more than one can of refrigerant to the system. If more refrigerant than
that is required, the system should be evacuated and leak tested.*

12   Back off the valve handle on the charging
kit and screw the kit onto the refrigerant can,
making sure first that the O-ring or rubber seal
inside the threaded portion of the kit is in place.
Warning: *Wear protective eyewear when dealing with pressurized refrigerant cans.*

13   Remove the dust cap from the low-side
charging port and attach the hose's quick-
connect fitting to the port **(see illustration)**.
Warning: *DO NOT hook the charging kit hose
to the system high side!* The fittings on the
charging kit are designed to fit **only** on the
low side of the system.

14   Warm up the engine and turn On the air
conditioning. Keep the charging kit hose away
from the fan and other moving parts. **Note:**
*The charging process requires the compres-
sor to be running. If the clutch cycles off, you
can put the air conditioning switch on High and
leave the car doors open to keep the clutch
on and compressor working. The compressor
can be kept on during the charging by removing the connector from the pressure switch
and bridging it with a paper clip or jumper wire
during the procedure.*

15   Turn the valve handle on the kit until the
stem pierces the can, then back the handle
out to release the refrigerant. You should be
able to hear the rush of gas. Keep the can
upright at all times, but shake it occasionally.
Allow stabilization time between each addition. **Note:** *The charging process will go faster
if you wrap the can with a hot-water-soaked
rag to keep the can from freezing up.*

16   If you have an accurate thermometer,
you can place it in the center air conditioning duct inside the vehicle and keep track of
the output air temperature. A charged system
that is working properly should cool down to
approximately 40 degrees F. If the ambient
(outside) air temperature is very high, say 110
degrees F, the duct air temperature may be
as high as 60 degrees F, but generally the air
conditioning is 35 to 40 degrees F cooler than
the ambient air.

17   When the can is empty, turn the valve
handle to the closed position and release the
connection from the low-side port. Reinstall
the dust cap.

18   Remove the charging kit from the can
and store the kit for future use with the pierc-

ing valve in the UP position, to prevent inad-
vertently piercing the can on the next use.

Heating systems

19   If the carpet under the heater core is
damp, or if antifreeze vapor or steam is coming through the vents, the heater core is leaking. Remove it (see Section 12) and install a
new unit (most radiator shops will not repair a
leaking heater core).

20   If the air coming out of the heater vents
isn't hot, the problem could stem from any of
the following causes:

a) *The thermostat is stuck open, preventing the engine coolant from warming up
   enough to carry heat to the heater core.
   Replace the thermostat (see Section 4).*

b) *There is a blockage in the system, preventing the flow of coolant through the
   heater core. Feel both heater hoses at
   the firewall. They should be hot. If one
   of them is cold, there is an obstruction in
   one of the hoses or in the heater core, or
   the heater control valve is shut. Detach
   the hoses and back flush the heater core
   with a water hose. If the heater core is
   clear but circulation is impeded, remove
   the two hoses and flush them out with a
   water hose.*

c) *If flushing fails to remove the blockage
   from the heater core, the core must be
   replaced (see Section 12).*

Eliminating air conditioning odors

Refer to illustration 3.24

21   Unpleasant odors that often develop in
air conditioning systems are caused by the
growth of a fungus, usually on the surface of
the evaporator core. The warm, humid envi-
ronment there is a perfect breeding ground for
mildew to develop.

22   The evaporator core on most vehicles
is difficult to access, and factory dealerships

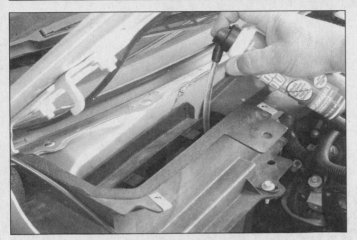

3.24 Insert the nozzle of the disinfectant can into the cabin filter housing

4.12a Coolant pipe front mounting fastener

have a lengthy, expensive process for eliminating the fungus by opening up the evaporator case and using a powerful disinfectant and rinse on the core until the fungus is gone. You can service your own system at home, but it takes something much stronger than basic household germ-killers or deodorizers.

23　Aerosol disinfectants for automotive air conditioning systems are available in most auto parts stores, but remember when shopping for them that the most effective treatments are also the most expensive. The basic procedure for using these sprays is to start by running the system in the RECIRC mode for ten minutes with the blower on its highest speed. Use the highest heat mode to dry out the system and keep the compressor from engaging by disconnecting the wiring connector at the compressor.

24　The disinfectant can usually comes with a long spray hose. Insert the nozzle into an intake port inside the cabin, and spray according to the manufacturer's recommendations **(see illustration)**. Try to cover the whole surface of the evaporator core, by aiming the spray up, down and sideways. Follow the manufacturer's recommendations for the length of spray and waiting time between applications.

25　Once the evaporator has been cleaned, the best way to prevent the mildew from coming back again is to make sure your evaporator housing drain tube is clear.

Automatic heating and air conditioning systems

26　Some vehicles are equipped with an optional automatic climate control system. This system has its own computer that receives inputs from various sensors in the heating and air conditioning system. This computer, like the PCM, has self-diagnostic capabilities to help pinpoint problems or faults within the system. Vehicles equipped with automatic heating and air conditioning

systems are very complex and considered beyond the scope of the home mechanic. Vehicles equipped with automatic heating and air conditioning systems should be taken to dealer service department or other qualified facility for repair.

4　Thermostat - replacement

Warning: *Wait until the engine is completely cool before performing this procedure.*
1　Disconnect the cable from the negative battery terminal (see Chapter 5).
2　Drain the cooling system (see Chapter 1). If the coolant is relatively new and still in good condition, save it and reuse it.

Removal
3.2L V6 engine models
3　Loosen the radiator hose-to-thermostat outlet pipe hose clamp, then detach the hose from the outlet pipe. If it's stuck, grasp it near the end with a pair of adjustable pliers and twist it to break the seal, then pull it off. If the hose is old or if it has deteriorated, cut it off and install a new one.
4　Remove the bolt holding the outlet pipe, oil dipstick tube and engine lifting bracket then pull the outlet pipe and O-rings from the thermostat housing. Always replace the O-rings on the outlet pipe.
5　Remove the intake manifold (see Chapter 2A).
6　Remove the thermostat housing fasteners and detach the thermostat housing cover and thermostat. If the cover is stuck, tap it with a soft-face hammer to jar it loose. Be prepared for some coolant to spill as the gasket seal is broken.
7　Press down on the thermostat and rotate the thermostat until the tabs clear the locking ears on the housing **(see illustration 4.14)**.
8　Remove the thermostat from the housing.

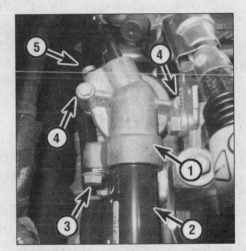

4.12b Thermostat housing details (3.0L V6 engine shown, other models similar)

1　Thermostat housing
2　Coolant inlet pipe
3　Coolant pipe-to-thermostat housing mounting fastener
4　Thermostat housing bolts
5　Coolant outlet pipe mounting fastener

2.8L, 3.0L and 3.6L V6 engine models
Refer to illustrations 4.12a, 4.12b and 4.14
9　Remove the intake manifold (see Chapter 2B).
10　Disconnect the coolant expansion tank hose from the thermostat housing.
11　Remove the coolant pipe-to-thermostat housing fasteners **(see illustration 4.12b)**.
12　Remove the coolant pipe front and rear fasteners then remove the pipe to thermostat housing fasteners and remove the pipes from the thermostat housing **(see illustrations)**.
13　Remove the thermostat cover fasteners and detach the thermostat cover and thermostat. If the cover is stuck, tap it with a soft-face hammer to jar it loose. Be prepared for some

4.14 Thermostat details (3.0L V6 engine shown, other models similar)

4.18 Remove the lower radiator hose (A) and the thermostat housing bolts (B) (5.7L V8 engine shown, other V8 models similar)

1	*Thermostat*	3	*Thermostat housing ears*
2	*Thermostat housing*	4	*Thermostat tabs*

coolant to spill as the O-ring seal is broken.
14   Press down on the thermostat and rotate the thermostat until the tabs clear the locking ears on the housing **(see illustration)**.
15   Remove the thermostat from the housing.

5.7L, 6.0L and 6.2L V8 engine models

Refer to illustration 4.18

Note: *On 5.7L and 6.0L engines, the thermostat and O-ring seal are integral with the housing and must be replaced as an assembly.*
16   Remove the cooling fan assembly (see Section 5).
17   Disconnect the radiator hose clamp from the thermostat housing and remove the hose.
18   Remove the bolts and lift the thermostat housing off **(see illustration)**. It may be necessary to tap it with a soft-face hammer to break the gasket seal. On 6.2L engines, remove the thermostat from the housing.

4.23 Install a new rubber seal around the perimeter of the thermostat (3.0L V6 engine shown, other models similar)

Installation

19   Clean the sealing surfaces. Inspect the hoses, replacing them as necessary.

3.2L V6 engine models

20   Insert the pin at the end of the thermostat into the center recess of the housing. Depress the tabs on the sides of the thermostat and turn the thermostat until the tabs are aligned with the ears on the housing.
21   Install the thermostat housing using a new gasket, then install the housing. Tighten the bolts to the torque listed in this Chapter's Specifications.
22   Install new O-rings to the outlet pipe and install the pipe into the thermostat housing.

2.8L, 3.0L and 3.6L V8 engine models

Refer to illustration 4.23

23   Depress the tabs on the sides of the thermostat and rotate the thermostat until the tabs are aligned with the ears on the housing. Install a new rubber gasket or O-ring on the thermostat **(see illustration)**, then install the thermostat in the lower housing, spring-end first.
24   Install the thermostat housing cover and bolts, then tighten the bolts to the torque listed in this Chapter's Specifications.
25   Install a new O-ring onto the coolant tube and insert the tube into the housing. Tighten the bolts to the torque listed in this Chapter's Specifications.

5.7L V8 engine models

26   Carefully position the cover and install the bolts. Tighten the bolts to the torque listed in this Chapter's Specifications - do not over-tighten them or the cover may crack or become distorted.

All models

27   Installation is the reverse of removal.
28   Refill the cooling system (see Chapter 1).

29   Start the engine and allow it to reach normal operating temperature, then check for leaks and proper thermostat operation.

5   Engine cooling fans - check, removal and installation

Warning: *To avoid possible injury or damage, DO NOT operate the engine with a damaged fan. Do not attempt to repair fan blades - replace a damaged fan with a new one.*
Warning: *The electric fans can start at any time; keep hands, clothes and tools away from the fan until the battery is disconnected to avoid possible injury or damage.*

Check

1   If the engine is overheating and the cooling fan is not coming on when the engine temperature rises to an excessive level, see Section 2. Check the fan relays in the underhood fuse/relay box.
2   If the relays are okay, check all wiring and connections to the fan motor. Refer to the wiring diagrams at the end of Chapter 12. If no obvious problems are found, the problem could be the Engine Coolant Temperature (ECT) sensor or the Powertrain Control Module (PCM). Have the cooling fan system and circuit diagnosed by a dealer service department or repair shop with the proper diagnostic equipment.

Removal and installation

Refer to illustrations 5.12, 5.14 and 5.15
Warning: *Wait until the engine is completely cool before performing this procedure.*
Warning: *These models have an airbag sensor mounted near the radiator support bracket. It will be necessary to disarm the system prior to performing any work around the radiator, fans or other components in this area (see Chapter 12).*

5.12 Typical fan shroud-to-radiator mounting fastener locations

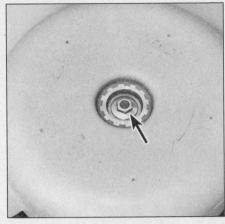

5.14 Hold the fan blade and remove the mounting nut

3   Disconnect the cable from the negative battery terminal (see Chapter 5).

4   Raise the vehicle and support it securely on jackstands. Remove the splash shield and drain the cooling system (see Chapter 1). If the coolant is relatively new and still in good condition, save it and reuse it. Detach the upper radiator hose from the radiator and position it aside.

5   Remove the air filter housing and inlet air resonator (see Chapter 4).

6   Disconnect and plug the expansion tank hose from the top of the radiator.

7   Remove the fastener for the air conditioning line mounting clip that secures the A/C lines to the fan shroud, and move the clip away from the shroud.

9   Remove the auxiliary water pump and any hoses, if equipped.

10   Disconnect the fan motor electrical connector(s).

11   Detach the wire harness clips from the fan shroud and move the harness away from the shroud.

12   Remove the fan shroud-to-radiator mounting bolts **(see illustration)**.

13   Lift the fan/shroud assembly from the vehicle.

14   To detach the fan blade from the motor, remove the nut from the motor shaft **(see illustration)**. Remove the fan blade from the motor.

15   To detach the motor from the shroud, remove the retaining bolts and disconnect the electrical connector **(see illustration)**.

16   Installation is the reverse of removal.

Note: *When reinstalling the fan assembly, make sure the rubber air shields around the shroud are still in place - without them, the cooling system may not work efficiently.*

17   Reconnect the battery. Refill the cooling system (see Chapter 1).

18   Start the engine and allow it to reach normal operating temperature, then check for leaks and proper operation.

---

6   Coolant expansion tank - removal and installation

Warning: *Wait until the engine is completely cool before beginning this procedure.*

1   Drain the cooling system (see Chapter 1).

2007 and earlier models

2   Remove the left side cowl panel (see Chapter 11).

3   Disconnect the hoses.

4   On models equipped with a manual transmission, unbolt the clutch master cylinder reservoir and set it out of the way.

5   Remove the master cylinder mounting nuts, slide the master cylinder forward without disconnecting the brake lines and carefully position it out of the way.

6   Remove the surge tank mounting fasteners and remove the tank.

2008 and later models

Refer to illustration 6.8

7   Remove the fasteners securing the expansion tank to the fender.

8   Lift the tank up enough to disconnect the hoses **(see illustration)**. Disconnect the fluid level sensor, if equipped.

All models

9   Clean out the tank with soapy water and a brush to remove any deposits inside. Inspect

5.15 Disconnect the fan motor electrical connector (A) and remove the fan motor mounting bolts

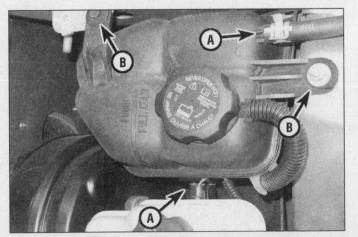

6.8 Disconnect the expansion tank hoses (A), then remove the mounting fasteners (B)

7.5 Remove the bolts to remove the upper radiator support (one per side)

7.6 Remove the bolts securing the condenser to the radiator - bumper cover removed to show upper and lower mounting bolt locations

the reservoir carefully for cracks. If you find a crack, replace the reservoir.

10   Installation is the reverse of removal.

7   Radiator - removal and installation

Warning: *Wait until the engine is completely cool before beginning this procedure.*

Warning: *These models have a an airbag sensor mounted near the radiator support. It will be necessary to disarm the airbag system prior to performing any work around the radiator, fans or other components in this area (see Chapter 12)*

Removal

Refer to illustrations 7.5 and 7.6

1   Disconnect the cable from the negative battery terminal (see Chapter 5).

2   Raise the vehicle and support it securely on jackstands. Remove the lower splash shield.

3   Drain the cooling system (see Chapter 1). If the coolant is relatively new and in good condition, save it and reuse it. Detach the radiator hoses from the bottom and top of the radiator.

4   Disconnect the expansion tank hose from the radiator.

5   Remove the radiator support bracket mounting bolts and brackets from the top of the radiator **(see illustration)**.

6   Remove the condenser upper mounting bolts from the top of the radiator **(see illustration)**. On 2008 models, the remove the condenser upper bolts and brackets from the radiator.

7   Remove the cooling fans (see Section 6).

8   Using a quick disconnect tool #J-44827 or equivalent disconnect the transmission cooler lines from the bottom of the radiator.

9   Remove the condenser lower mounting bolts **(see illustration 7.6)**.

10   Disconnect the push-pins from the sides

of the radiator and remove the side seal panels.

11   Carefully lift out the radiator. Don't spill coolant on the vehicle or scratch the paint. Make sure the rubber radiator insulators that fit on the bottom of the radiator and into the sockets in the body remain in place in the body for proper reinstallation of the radiator.

12   Remove bugs and dirt from the radiator with compressed air and a soft brush. Don't bend the cooling fins. Inspect the radiator for leaks and damage. If it needs repair, have a radiator shop or a dealer service department do the work.

Installation

13   Inspect the rubber insulators in the lower crossmember for cracks and deterioration. Make sure that they're free of dirt and gravel. When installing the radiator, make sure that it's correctly seated on the insulators before fastening the top brackets.

14   Installation is otherwise the reverse of the removal procedure. After installation, fill the cooling system with the correct mixture of antifreeze and water (see Chapter 1).

15   Start the engine and check for leaks. Allow the engine to reach normal operating temperature, indicated by the upper radiator hose becoming hot. Recheck the coolant level and add more if required.

16   If you're working on an automatic transaxle-equipped vehicle, check and add fluid as needed.

Charge air cooler radiator (6.2L V8 engine models)

Note: *The charge air cooler is mounted to the front of the condenser on all supercharged V8 models and is a completely separate system from the engine cooling system.*

Removal

17   Disconnect the cable from the negative battery terminal (see Chapter 5).

18   Raise the vehicle and support it securely on jackstands. Remove the lower splash shield.

19   Drain the charge air cooling system (see Chapter 2C, Section 16). If the coolant is relatively new and in good condition, save it and reuse it.

20   Remove the front bumper cover (see Chapter 11).

21   Disconnect the clamps and remove the charge air cooler pump to radiator hoses.

22   Disconnect and plug the power steering cooler hoses.

23   Remove the charge air cooler radiator-to-condenser mounting bolts and lower the radiator out of the vehicle.

Installation

24   Installation is the reverse of the removal procedure. After installation, fill the charge air cooling system with the correct mixture of antifreeze and water, then bleed the charge air cooling system (see Chapter 2C, Section 21). Top-up the power steering fluid (see Chapter 1).

25   Start the engine and check for leaks. Allow the engine to reach normal operating temperature, indicated by the upper radiator hose becoming hot. Recheck the coolant level and add more if required. Check for power steering fluid leaks and add fluid as needed.

8   Water pump - replacement

Warning: *Wait until the engine is completely cool before beginning this procedure.*

Removal

1   Disconnect the cable from the negative battery terminal (see Chapter 5).

2   Raise the vehicle and support it securely on jackstands. Remove the lower splash shield.

3   Drain the cooling system (see Chapter 1). If the coolant is relatively new and in good condition, save it and reuse it.

4   Remove the water pump drivebelt (see Chapter 1).

5   Remove the air filter housing and inlet air resonator (see Chapter 4).

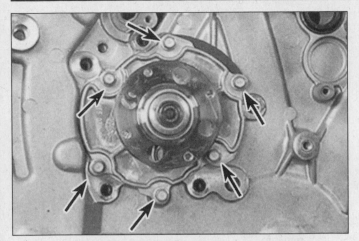

8.7 Typical water pump bolt locations (V6 engine models)

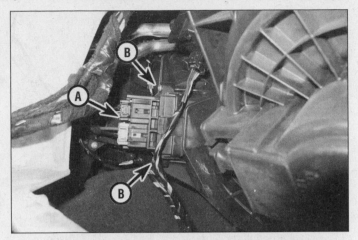

10.2 Unplug the blower motor resistor connectors (A), then remove the mounting screws (B)

V6 models

Refer to illustration 8.7

6   Use a pin spanner or strap wrench to hold the water pump pulley from turning, and remove the pulley mounting bolts and pulley.

7   Remove the bolts attaching the water pump to the engine cover and remove the pump from the engine **(see illustration)**. If the water pump is stuck, gently tap it with a soft-faced hammer to break the seal.

8   Clean the bolt threads and the threaded holes in the engine and remove all corrosion and sealant. Remove all traces of old gasket material from the sealing surfaces.

V8 models

Note: *On V8 engine models, the water pump pulley is not removable.*

9   Remove the engine covers.

10   Disconnect all of the hoses from the water pump. Secure them out of the way.

11   Remove the supercharger drivebelt, tensioner and bracket (see Chapter 1).

12   Disconnect and remove the hoses to the water pump

13   Unbolt and remove the water pump from the front of the engine. It may be necessary to tap the pump with a soft-face hammer to break the gasket seal.

Installation

14   Compare the new pump to the old one to make sure that they're identical.

15   Apply a thin film of RTV sealant to hold the new gasket in place during installation. O-rings should be coated with clean coolant. **Caution:** *Make sure that the gasket is correctly positioned on the water pump and the mating surfaces are clean and free of old gasket material.* Carefully mate the pump to the water pump housing.

16   Install the water pump bolts and tighten them in a criss-cross pattern to the torque listed in this Chapter's Specifications.

17   The remainder of installation is the reverse of removal. Refill the cooling system (see Chapter 1).

18   Operate the engine to check for leaks.

9   Coolant temperature sending unit - check and replacement

Warning: *Wait until the engine is completely cool before beginning this procedure.*

The coolant temperature indicator system consists of a warning light or a temperature gauge on the dash and a coolant temperature sending unit mounted on the engine. On the models covered by this manual, the Engine Coolant Temperature (ECT) sensor is an information sensor for the Powertrain Control Module (PCM) and also functions as the coolant temperature sending unit for the temperature gauge. Information on the ECT sensor can be found in Chapter 6.

10   Blower motor control module and blower motor - replacement

Warning: *The models covered by this manual are equipped with Supplemental Restraint Systems (SRS), more commonly known as airbags. Always disable the airbag system before working in the vicinity of any airbag system component to avoid the possibility of accidental deployment of the airbag, which could cause personal injury (see Chapter 12).*

Blower motor control module

Refer to illustration 10.2

1   Remove the lower trim panel and the glovebox (see Chapter 11).

2   Disconnect the electrical connector from the blower motor control module **(see illustration)**.

3   Remove the blower motor control module mounting screws and remove the control module from the evaporator housing.

4   Installation is the reverse of removal.

Blower motor

Refer to illustration 10.6

5   Remove the lower trim panel and the glovebox (see Chapter 11).

6   Disconnect the blower motor electrical connector **(see illustration)**.

7   Remove the blower motor mounting screws and remove the blower motor.

8   Installation is the reverse of removal.

10.6 Location of the blower motor electrical connector (A) and the blower motor mounting screws (B)

11.6 Pry out the center trim panel/control assembly

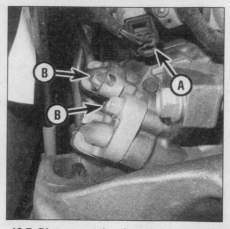

13.7 Disconnect the electrical connector (A) and remove the bolt (B) securing the refrigerant pipes to the compressor (V6 model shown, V8 similar)

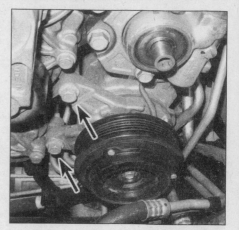

13.8 Compressor mounting bolts (rear two bolts not visible here; power steering pulley removed for clarity (V6 model shown, V8 similar)

11   Heater/air conditioner control assembly - removal and installation

Refer to illustration 11.6

Warning: *The models covered by this manual are equipped with Supplemental Restraint Systems (SRS), more commonly known as airbags. Always disable the airbag system before working in the vicinity of any airbag system component to avoid the possibility of accidental deployment of the airbag, which could cause personal injury (see Chapter 12).*

1   Disconnect the cable from the negative battery terminal (see Chapter 5).
2   Remove the center floor console shifter trim plate (see Chapter 11).
3   Remove the center and right side trim applique panels (see Chapter 11).
4   Remove the upper center trim cover panel (see Chapter 11).
5   Remove the screws at the bottom of the center trim panel/air control panel (see Chapter 12).
6   Use a plastic trim tool to pry the center trim panel/control assembly from its retaining clips **(see illustration)**.
7   Disconnect the electrical connectors at the module.
8   Remove the heater/air conditioner control assembly retaining screws on the back of the panel.
9   Installation is the reverse of removal.

12   Heater core - replacement

Warning: *The models covered by this manual are equipped with Supplemental Restraint Systems (SRS), more commonly known as airbags. Always disarm the airbag system before working in the vicinity of any airbag system component to avoid the possibility of accidental deployment of the airbag, which could cause personal injury (see Chapter 12).*
Warning: *The air conditioning system is under high pressure - have a dealer service depart-*

ment or service station evacuate the system and recover the refrigerant before disconnecting any of the hoses or fittings.
Warning: *Wait until the engine is completely cool before beginning this procedure.*
Note: *This is a difficult procedure for the home mechanic, involving numerous hard-to-find fasteners, clips and electrical connectors.*
1   Have the air conditioning system discharged by an automotive air conditioning technician (see **Warning** above).
2   Disconnect the cable from the negative battery terminal (see Chapter 5).
3   Drain the cooling system (see Chapter 1). Disconnect the heater hoses from the heater core inlet and outlet pipes at the firewall, then disconnect the thermal expansion valve and the two refrigerant pipes.
4   Remove the instrument panel (see Chapter 11).
5   Tag and disconnect the cables (if equipped) and electrical connectors from the HVAC unit. Remove the mounting fasteners.
6   The heater core is in the right half of the HVAC unit, above the blower motor housing. Remove the heater core cover screws and pull the heater core out of the housing.
7   Installation is the reverse of removal. Reconnect the heater core inlet and outlet hoses at the firewall. Use a new gasket where the two air conditioning pipes meet the expansion valve at the firewall.
8   Refill the cooling system (see Chapter 1). Have the system evacuated, recharged and leak tested by the shop that discharged it.

13   Air conditioning compressor - removal and installation

Warning: *The air conditioning system is under high pressure. DO NOT loosen any fittings or remove any components until after the system has been discharged. Air conditioning refrigerant must be properly discharged into an EPA-approved container at a dealer service department or an automotive air conditioning repair*

facility. Always wear eye protection when disconnecting air conditioning system fittings.
Caution: *If the compressor is being replaced due to failure, the rest of the system should be flushed by a technician to remove particles or contaminants.*

Removal

Refer to illustrations 13.7 and 13.8

1   Have the air conditioning system discharged by an automotive air conditioning technician (see **Warning** above).
2   Disconnect the cable from the negative battery terminal (see Chapter 5).
3   Raise the vehicle and support it securely on jackstands. Remove the lower splash shield and inner fender splash shield (see Chapter 11).
4   Remove the drivebelt (see Chapter 1).
5   Remove the air filter housing and inlet air resonator (see Chapter 4).
6   Disconnect the electrical connector from the compressor clutch field coil.
7   Remove the compressor inlet and outlet line mounting bolts **(see illustration)** and remove the lines from the compressor. Remove and discard the old O-rings. **Note:** *On some models, the power steering line support bracket must be removed and the lines moved out of the way to access the compressor line bolts.*
8   Remove the compressor mounting bolts **(see illustration)** and remove the compressor.

Installation

9   If a new compressor is being installed, follow the directions that came with the compressor regarding the draining of excess oil prior to installation.
10   The clutch may have to be transferred from the original to the new compressor.
11   Before reconnecting the inlet and outlet lines to the compressor, replace all O-rings and lubricate them with refrigerant oil.
12   Installation is otherwise the reverse of removal.

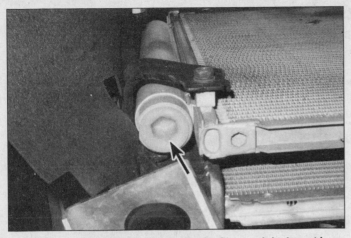

14.2 Remove the plug, then remove the filter and desiccant bag from the condenser

14.4 Typical condenser details

1 Pressure cycling switch electrical connector
2 Inlet refrigerant pipe
3 Outlet refrigerant pipe
4 Power steering cooler lines

13   Have the system evacuated, recharged and leak tested by the shop that discharged it.

14   Air conditioning condenser - removal and installation

Refer to illustrations 14.2 and 14.4

Warning: *The air conditioning system is under high pressure. DO NOT loosen any fittings or remove any components until after the system has been discharged. Air conditioning refrigerant must be properly discharged into an EPA-approved container at a dealer service department or an automotive air conditioning repair facility. Always wear eye protection when disconnecting air conditioning system fittings.*

1   Have the air conditioning system discharged by an automotive air conditioning technician (see **Warning** above).
2   At the bottom right of the condenser, there is a replaceable desiccant bag inside the condenser that is accessible by removing a threaded plug on the bottom of the condenser on the left end **(see illustration)**.
3   On supercharged 6.2L V8 models, remove the charge air cooler radiator (see Section 7).
4   Disconnect the pressure cycling switch and the refrigerant inlet and outlet pipes from the condenser **(see illustration)**. Remove the bolt or nut securing the pipes to the block that is part of the condenser. Cap the lines to prevent contamination.
5   Remove the fastener for the air conditioning line mounting clip that secures the A/C lines to the fan shroud, and move the clip away from the shroud.
6   Remove the condenser mounting bolts and remove the condenser **(see illustration 7.6)**. If you're going to reinstall the same condenser, store it with the line fittings facing up to prevent oil from draining out.
7   If installing a new condenser, pour one

ounce of refrigerant oil of the correct type into it prior to installation.
8   Before reconnecting the refrigerant lines to the condenser, coat a pair of new O-rings with refrigerant oil, install them in the refrigerant line fittings and tighten the condenser inlet and outlet nuts to the torque listed in this Chapter's Specifications.
9   Installation is otherwise the reverse of removal.
10   Have the system evacuated, recharged and leak tested by the shop that discharged it.

15   Air conditioning pressure cycling switch - replacement

Warning: *The air conditioning system is under high pressure. DO NOT loosen any fittings or remove any components until after the system has been discharged. Air conditioning refrigerant must be properly discharged into an EPA-approved container at a dealer service department or an automotive air conditioning repair facility. Always wear eye protection when disconnecting air conditioning system fittings.*

1   The pressure cycling switch is located on top of the hard line from the condenser to the air conditioning thermostatic expansion valve (TXV). The pressure cycling switch detects low refrigerant line pressure, and switches the A/C system off, then back on again to provide higher pressure. If the pressure increases too high, the pressure cut-off switch, located in the high pressure side of the system, shuts the system off.
2   Have the air conditioning system discharged by an automotive air conditioning technician (see **Warning** above).
3   Unplug the electrical connector from the pressure cycling switch **(see illustration 14.4)**.
4   Unscrew the pressure cycling switch.
5   Lubricate the switch O-ring with clean refrigerant oil of the correct type.

6   Screw the new switch into place until hand tight, then tighten it securely.
7   Reconnect the electrical connector.
8   Have the system evacuated, recharged and leak tested by the shop that discharged it.

16   Air conditioning thermostatic expansion valve (TXV) - general information

Warning: *The air conditioning system is under high pressure. DO NOT loosen any hose fittings or remove any components until the system has been discharged. Air conditioning refrigerant must be properly discharged into an EPA-approved recovery/recycling unit by a dealer service department or an automotive air conditioning repair facility. Always wear eye protection when disconnecting air conditioning system fittings.*

There are several ways that air conditioning systems convert the high-pressure liquid refrigerant from the compressor to lower-pressure vapor. The conversion takes place at the air conditioning evaporator; the evaporator is chilled as the refrigerant passes through, cooling the airflow through the evaporator for delivery to the vents. The conversion is usually accomplished by a sudden change in the tubing size. Many vehicles have a removable controlled orifice in one of the AC pipes at the firewall.

The models covered by this manual use a thermostatic expansion valve (TXV) that accomplishes the same purpose as a controlled orifice. To remove the TXV, have the air conditioning system discharged by a licensed air conditioning technician, then remove the evaporator core and disconnect the refrigerant lines from the TXV. Remove the two bolts securing the valve, then remove the valve. Installation is the reverse of removal. Have the system evacuated, recharged and leak tested by the shop that discharged it.

Notes

Chapter 4
Fuel and exhaust systems

Contents

Specifications

Fuel pressure (key on, engine off, except where indicated)

V6 engines
2003 models	49 to 55 psi (337 to 380 kPa)
2004 through 2008 models	55 to 60 psi (380 to 414 kPa)

2009 models
VIN V	50 to 60 psi (344 to 414 kPa)
VIN 7	56 to 62 psi (386 to 427 kPa)

2010 and later models
Key on, engine off	50 to 100 psi (344 to 690 kPa)
Idle	43 to 58 psi (296 to 400 kPa)

V8 engines
2004 through 2007 models	55 to 62 psi (380 to 427 kPa)
2009 and later models	55 to 76 psi (380 to 524 kPa)

Torque specifications

Note: *One foot-pound (ft-lb) of torque is equivalent to 12 inch-pounds (in-lbs) of torque. Torque values below approximately 15 foot-pounds are expressed in inch-pounds, because most foot-pound torque wrenches are not accurate at these smaller values.*

	Ft-lbs (unless otherwise indicated)	Nm
Fuel pressure sensor		
V6 engines	25	33
V8 engines	89 in-lbs	10
High-pressure fuel pump fasteners	132 in-lbs	15
High pressure fuel line fittings (to high-pressure fuel pump and fuel rails)		
2003 through 2012		
Step 1	144 in-lbs	16
Step 2	24	32
2013 and later	20	28
Fuel rail mounting bolts		
2.8L V6 engine	89 in-lbs	10
3.0L V6 engine, in sequence		
Step 1	106 in-lbs	12
Step 2	17	23
3.2L V6 engine	71 in-lbs	8
3.6L V6 engines		
2004 through 2009	89 in-lbs	10
2010 and later, in sequence		
Step 1	106 in-lbs	12
Step 2	17	23
5.7L and 6.0L V8 engines		
6.2L V8 engine	89 in-lbs	10
Fuel tank strap bolts	37	50
Throttle body mounting fasteners		
3.2L engine	71 in-lbs	8
2.8L, 3.0L, 3.6 and 6.2L engines	89 in-lbs	10
5.7L and 6.0L engines	106 in-lbs	12

Fuel system components (3.0L V6 engine shown, other V6 models similar)

1   Engine compartment fuse and relay box
    (fuel pump fuse and fuel pump relay)
2   Air filter housing

3   Air intake duct
4   Throttle body
5   Upper intake manifold

6   Fuel injectors (under upper intake
    manifold)
7   Fuel pressure test port

2.2 On 2008 and later models, the fuel pump fuse is located in the luggage compartment fuse box (the location of the fuse may vary with model and year - refer to the guide on the underside of the fuse box cover and the guide in your owner's manual)

2.9 An automotive stethoscope is used to listen to the fuel injectors in operation

1   General information

Fuel system warnings

Gasoline is extremely flammable and repairing fuel system components can be dangerous. Consider your automotive repair knowledge and experience before attempting repairs which may be better suited for a professional mechanic.

- Don't smoke or allow open flames or bare light bulbs near the work area
- Don't work in a garage with a gas-type appliance (water heater, clothes dryer)
- Use fuel-resistant gloves. If any fuel spills on your skin, wash it off immediately with soap and water
- Clean up spills immediately
- Do not store fuel-soaked rags where they could ignite
- Prior to disconnecting any fuel line, you must relieve the fuel pressure (see Section 3)
- Wear safety glasses
- Have a proper fire extinguisher on hand

Fuel system

The fuel system consists of the fuel tank, electric fuel pump/fuel level sending unit (located in the fuel tank), fuel rail and fuel injectors. The fuel injection system is a multi-port system; multi-port fuel injection uses timed impulses to inject the fuel directly into the intake port of each cylinder. The Powertrain Control Module (PCM) controls the injectors. The PCM monitors various engine parameters and delivers the exact amount of fuel required into the intake ports.

Fuel is circulated from the fuel pump to the fuel rail through fuel lines running along the underside of the vehicle. Various sections of the fuel line are either rigid metal or nylon, or flexible fuel hose. The various sections of the fuel hose are connected either by quick-connect fittings or threaded metal fittings.

Exhaust system

The exhaust system consists of the exhaust manifold(s), catalytic converter(s), muffler(s), tailpipe and all connecting pipes, flanges and clamps. The catalytic converters are an emission control device added to the exhaust system to reduce pollutants.

2   Troubleshooting

Fuel pump

Refer to illustration 2.2

1   The fuel pump is located inside the fuel tank. Sit inside the vehicle with the windows closed, turn the ignition key to ON (not START) and listen for the sound of the fuel pump as it's briefly activated. You will only hear the sound for a second or two, but that sound tells you that the pump is working. Alternatively, have an assistant listen at the fuel filler cap.

2   If the fuel pump does not come on, check the fuel pump fuse and, on later V8 models, the FSCM fuse (refer to the legend on the underside of the fuse block cover for fuse and relay locations).

a) On 2003 through 2007 models, the fuel pump fuse is located in the right rear fuse block, located under the right rear seat.

b) On 2008 and later models, the fuel pump fuse is located in the right rear fuse block, located in the trunk/luggage compartment (see illustration).

If the fuse is good, the relay might be faulty. If the fuse and relay are both ok, check the wiring back to the fuel pump. If no problems are found, the fuel pump module is probably defective.

Fuel injection system

Refer to illustration 2.9

Note: The following procedure is based on the assumption that the fuel pump is working and the fuel pressure is adequate (see Section 4).

3   Check all electrical connectors that are related to the system. Check the ground wire connections for tightness.

4   Verify that the battery is fully charged (see Chapter 5).

5   Inspect the air filter element (see Chapter 1).

6   Check all fuses related to the fuel system (see Chapter 12).

7   Check the air induction system between the throttle body and the intake manifold for air leaks. Also inspect the condition of all vacuum hoses connected to the intake manifold and to the throttle body.

8   Remove the air intake duct from the throttle body and look for dirt, carbon, varnish, or other residue in the throttle body, particularly around the throttle plate. If it's dirty, clean it with carb cleaner, a toothbrush and a clean shop towel.

9   With the engine running, place an automotive stethoscope against each injector, one at a time, and listen for a clicking sound that indicates operation (see illustration). Warning: Stay clear of the drivebelt and any rotating or hot components.

10   If you can hear the injectors operating, but the engine is misfiring, the electrical circuits are functioning correctly, but the injectors might be dirty or clogged. Try a commercial injector cleaning product (available at auto parts stores). If cleaning the injectors doesn't help, replace the injectors.

11   If an injector is not operating (it makes no sound), disconnect the injector electrical connector and measure the resistance across the injector terminals with an ohmmeter. Compare this measurement to the other injectors. If the resistance of the non-operational injector is quite different from the other injectors, replace it.

12   If the injector is not operating, but the resistance reading is within the range of resistance of the other injectors, the PCM or the circuit between the PCM and the injector might be faulty.

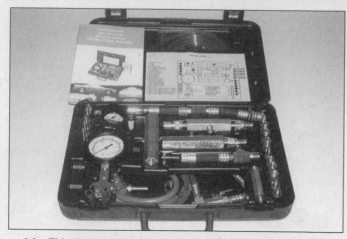

4.1a This fuel pressure testing kit contains all the necessary fittings and adapters, along with the fuel pressure gauge, to test most automotive systems

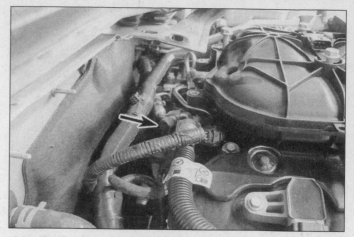

4.1b The fuel pressure test port is located on the fuel supply line to the fuel rail on 2.8L, 3.0L. 3.6L V6 and 6.2L V8 engines (3.0L model shown)

3   Fuel pressure relief procedure

Warning: *Gasoline is extremely flammable. See **Fuel system warnings** in Section 1.*
Warning: *The fuel delivery system on 2008 and later 3.6L (except VIN 7) and all 3.0L V6 models is made up of a low-pressure system and a high-pressure system. Once the pressure on the low-pressure side of the system has been relieved, wait at least two hours before loosening any fuel line fittings in the engine compartment.*

1 Remove the fuel filler cap to relieve any pressure built-up in the fuel tank.
2 Remove the fuel pump fuse (see Section 2, Step 2).
3 Attempt to start the engine; it should immediately stall. Crank the engine several more times to ensure the fuel system has been completely relieved. Disconnect the cable from the negative terminal of the battery before working on the fuel system.
4 It's a good idea to cover any fuel connection to be disassembled with rags to absorb the residual fuel that may leak out. Properly dispose of the rags.

4   Fuel pressure - check

Refer to illustrations 4.1a and 4.1b
Warning: *Gasoline is extremely flammable. See **Fuel system warnings** in Section 1.*
Note: *The following procedure assumes that the fuel pump is receiving voltage and runs.*
1 Locate the fuel pressure test port; on 3.2L V6 and 5.7L and 6.0L V8 engines the test port is on the fuel rail. On 2.8L, 3.0L and 3.6L V6 engines and 6.2L V8 it is located on the fuel supply line. Unscrew the cap and connect a fuel pressure gauge **(see illustrations)**.
2 Turn the ignition key to the On position. Note the gauge reading as soon as the pressure stabilizes, and compare it with the pres-

sure listed in this Chapter's Specifications.
3 If the fuel pressure is not within specifications, check the following:
 a) *Check for a restriction in the fuel system (kinked fuel line, plugged fuel pump inlet strainer or clogged fuel filter). If no restrictions are found, replace the fuel pump module (see Section 7).*
 b) *If the fuel pressure is higher than specified, replace the fuel pump module (see Section 7).*
4 Turn off the engine. Fuel pressure should not fall more than 5 psi in one minute. If it does, the problem could be a leaky fuel injector, fuel line leak, or faulty fuel pump module.
5 Relieve the fuel system pressure (see Section 3), then disconnect the fuel pressure gauge. Wipe up any spilled gasoline.

5   Fuel lines and fittings - general information and disconnection

Warning: *Gasoline is extremely flammable. See **Fuel system warnings** in Section 1.*
1 Relieve the fuel pressure before servicing fuel lines or fittings (see Section 3), then disconnect the cable from the negative battery terminal (see Chapter 5) before proceeding.
2 The fuel supply line connects the fuel pump in the fuel tank to the fuel rail on the engine. The Evaporative Emission (EVAP) system lines connect the fuel tank to the EVAP canister and connect the canister to the intake manifold.
3 Whenever you're working under the vehicle, be sure to inspect all fuel and evaporative emission lines for leaks, kinks, dents and other damage. Always replace a damaged fuel or EVAP line immediately.
4 If you find signs of dirt in the lines during disassembly, disconnect all lines and blow them out with compressed air. Inspect the fuel strainer on the fuel pump pick-up unit for damage and deterioration.

Steel tubing

5 It is critical that the fuel lines be replaced with lines of equivalent type and specification.
6 Some steel fuel lines have threaded fittings. When loosening these fittings, hold the stationary fitting with a wrench while turning the tube nut.

Plastic tubing

7 When replacing fuel system plastic tubing, use only original equipment replacement plastic tubing. **Caution:** *When removing or installing plastic fuel line tubing, be careful not to bend or twist it too much, which can damage it. Also, plastic fuel tubing is NOT heat resistant, so keep it away from excessive heat.*

Flexible hoses

8 When replacing fuel system flexible hoses, use only original equipment replacements.
9 Don't route fuel hoses (or metal lines) within four inches of the exhaust system or within ten inches of the catalytic converter. Make sure that no rubber hoses are installed directly against the vehicle, particularly in places where there is any vibration. If allowed to touch some vibrating part of the vehicle, a hose can easily become chafed and it might start leaking. A good rule of thumb is to maintain a minimum of 1/4-inch clearance around a hose (or metal line) to prevent contact with the vehicle underbody.

6   Exhaust system servicing - general information

Refer to illustration 6.1
Warning: *Allow exhaust system components to cool before inspection or repair. Also, when working under the vehicle, make sure it is securely supported on jackstands.*
1 The exhaust system consists of the exhaust manifolds, catalytic converter, muffler, tailpipe and all connecting pipes, flanges

Disconnecting Fuel Line Fittings

Two-tab type fitting; depress both tabs with your fingers, then pull the fuel line and the fitting apart

On this type of fitting, depress the two buttons on opposite sides of the fitting, then pull it off the fuel line

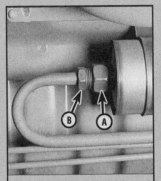

Threaded fuel line fitting; hold the stationary portion of the line or component (A) while loosening the tube nut (B) with a flare-nut wrench

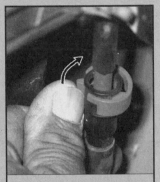

Plastic collar-type fitting; rotate the outer part of the fitting

Metal collar quick-connect fitting; pull the end of the retainer off the fuel line and disengage the other end from the female side of the fitting . . .

. . . Insert a fuel line separator tool into the female side of the fitting, push it into the fitting and pull the fuel line off the pipe

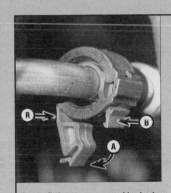

Some fittings are secured by lock tabs. Release the lock tab (A) and rotate it to the fully-opened position, squeeze the two smaller lock tabs (B) . . .

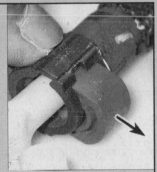

. . . then push the retainer out and pull the fuel line off the pipe

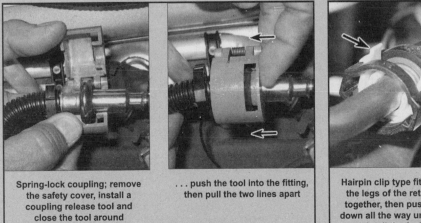

Spring-lock coupling; remove the safety cover, install a coupling release tool and close the tool around the coupling . . .

. . . push the tool into the fitting, then pull the two lines apart

Hairpin clip type fitting: push the legs of the retainer clip together, then push the clip down all the way until it stops and pull the fuel line off the pipe

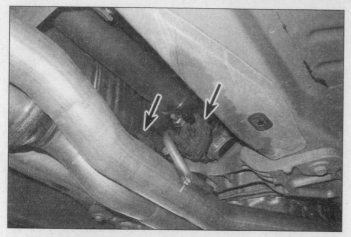

6.1 Typical exhaust system hangers. Inspect regularly and replace at the first sign of damage or deterioration

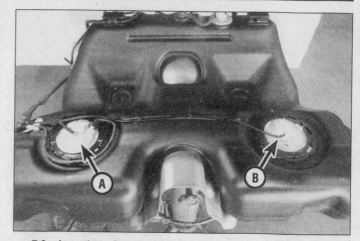

7.3a Location of the primary fuel pump module (A) and the secondary fuel pump module (B)

7.3b Fuel pump module electrical connector (A) and fuel supply line quick-connect fitting (B)

7.4 Using pliers, rotate the locking ring counterclockwise to remove it

7.5 Lift the module out at an angle and disconnect the transfer tube

and clamps. The exhaust system is isolated from the vehicle body and from chassis components by a series of rubber hangers **(see illustration)**. Periodically inspect these hangers for cracks or other signs of deterioration, replacing them as necessary.

2   Conduct regular inspections of the exhaust system to keep it safe and quiet. Look for any damaged or bent parts, open seams, holes, loose connections, excessive corrosion or other defects which could allow exhaust fumes to enter the vehicle. Do not repair deteriorated exhaust system components; replace them with new parts.

3   If the exhaust system components are extremely corroded, or rusted together, a cutting torch is the most convenient tool for removal. Consult a properly-equipped repair shop. If a cutting torch is not available, you can use a hacksaw, or if you have compressed air, there are special pneumatic cutting chisels that can also be used. Wear safety goggles to protect your eyes from metal chips and wear work gloves to protect your hands.

4   Here are some simple guidelines to follow when repairing the exhaust system:

a) *Work from the back to the front when removing exhaust system components.*
b) *Apply penetrating oil to the exhaust system component fasteners to make them easier to remove.*
c) *Use new gaskets, hangers and clamps.*
d) *Apply anti-seize compound to the threads of all exhaust system fasteners during reassembly.*
e) *Be sure to allow sufficient clearance between newly installed parts and all points on the underbody to avoid overheating the floor pan and possibly damaging the interior carpet and insulation. Pay particularly close attention to the catalytic converter and heat shield.*

7   Fuel pump module - removal and installation

Fuel pump module

Refer to illustrations 7.3a, 7.3b, 7.4 and 7.5
Warning: *Gasoline is extremely flammable. See* **Fuel system warnings** *in Section 1.*
Note: *There are two fuel pump modules.*

The primary module includes the fuel pump, a fuel level sending unit, a fuel filter and, on mechanical returnless pumps, a fuel pressure regulator. The secondary module includes a fuel level sending unit and the fuel pick up. On electronic returnless pumps, there is no regulator; fuel pressure is regulated by a Fuel Pump Flow Control Module (FPFCM). None of these components are separately serviceable

1   Disconnect the cable from the negative battery terminal (see Chapter 5). Relieve the fuel system pressure (see Section 3).
2   Remove the fuel tank (see Section 9).
3   Disconnect the electrical connector and the fuel supply line quick-connect fitting from the fuel pump module **(see illustrations)**.
4   Using pliers against the locking ring and the module, rotate the lock ring counterclockwise to remove it **(see illustration)**.
5   Carefully pull the fuel pump module out of the tank and disconnect the transfer tube that connects the modules **(see illustration)**. Angle it as necessary to protect the fuel level sensor float arm and remove it from the tank.
6   Inspect the O-ring and replace it if it shows any sign of deterioration.
7   Installation is the reverse of removal.

8.7 High-pressure fuel line connections

8.9 Remove the high-pressure pump mounting bolts (one of two bolts shown) and discard the bolts

Fuel Pump Flow Control Module (FPFCM)

Note: *On vehicles equipped with an electronic returnless fuel system, the fuel pump module speed, and therefore the output and pressure, is controlled by the FPFCM, which is located in the left rear part of the trunk/luggage compartment.*

8   On sedan and coupe models, remove the carpet trim from the left rear part of the trunk. On wagon models, remove the rear floor storage compartment.

9   Disconnect the electrical connector from the FPFCM.

10   Remove the pin-type retainers and remove the FPFCM.

11   Installation is the reverse of removal.

8   High pressure fuel pump - removal and installation

Refer to illustrations 8.7 and 8.9

Note: *This procedure applies to 2008 and later 3.6L (except VIN 7) and all 3.0L V6 engines.*

Warning: *Gasoline is extremely flammable. See **Fuel system warnings** in Section 1.*

Warning: *The fuel delivery system on 2008 and later 3.6L (except VIN 7) and all 3.0L V6 models is made up of a low-pressure system and a high-pressure system. Once the pressure on the low-pressure side of the system has been relieved, wait at least two hours before loosening any fuel line fittings in the engine compartment.*

1   Remove the engine covers. Remove the suspension crossbrace (see Chapter 10).

2   Relieve the fuel system pressure (see Section 3).

3   Disconnect the cable from the negative battery terminal (see Chapter 5).

4   Remove the cowl panel (see Chapter 11) and the wiper motor and linkage (see Chapter 12).

5   Remove the high-pressure fuel pump line shield fasteners and shield. **Note:** *If necessary for additional working space, remove the intake manifold (see Chapter 2B) and both fuel rails (see Section 13).*

6   Disconnect the low pressure feed line to the pump.

7   Using a flare-nut wrench, unscrew the high-pressure line fittings **(see illustration)**. **Caution:** *The manufacturer states that the pipe must be replaced if it has been removed.*

8   Disconnect the electrical connector from the high-pressure fuel pump.

9   Remove the high-pressure fuel pump bolts **(see illustration)** and remove the pump. Always replace the bolts and O-ring.

10   With the pump removed, rotate the engine by hand and make sure the camshaft lobe is at its base circle before trying to install the pump.

11   Lubricate the pump roller with engine oil and install the gasket and bolts.

12   Set the pump in to the cylinder head and tighten the bolts evenly. **Note:** *As the pump bolts are tightened, it will get harder to tighten the bolts until the spring in the pump is compressed.*

13   Tighten the bolts to the torque listed in this Chapter's Specifications.

14   The remainder of installation is the reverse of removal. Clean the high pressure fuel line fittings on the fuel rails, then apply a little clean engine oil to the threads. Install the new high-pressure fuel line, tightening the fittings to the torque listed in this Chapter's Specifications.

15   Reconnect the cable to the negative battery terminal (see Chapter 5), then start the engine and check for fuel leaks.

9   Fuel tank - removal and installation

Warning: *Gasoline is extremely flammable. See **Fuel system warnings** in Section 1.*

Warning: *The following procedure is much easier to perform if the fuel tank is empty.*

1   Remove the fuel tank filler cap to relieve fuel tank pressure.

2   Relieve the fuel system pressure (see Section 3).

3   Disconnect the cable from the negative battery terminal (see Chapter 5).

4   Raise the rear of the vehicle and support it securely on jackstands.

5   Remove the exhaust system (see Section 6).

6   Remove the driveshaft (see Chapter 8).

7   Drain the fuel tank. On 2007 and earlier models, disconnect the fuel line from the filter (see Section 14) and attach the siphon to the line. On 2008 and later models, insert a hose through the filler neck and into the bottom of the tank. Siphon or hand pump the fuel from the tank into an approved gasoline container. **Warning:** *Do not start the siphoning action by mouth. Use a siphoning pump (available at most auto parts stores).*

2007 and earlier models

Caution: *It is advisable to have an assistant to help with this procedure.*

8   Disconnect the electrical connector and fuel supply line quick-connect fitting from the fuel pump module (see Section 7).

9   Loosen the hose clamps and disconnect the fuel filler neck hose and EVAP system breather hose from the tank.

10   Using two floor jacks, raise the lower control arms enough to take the load from the shock absorbers. Remove the shock absorber lower mounting bolt from each side and slowly lower the jacks.

11   Reposition the floor jacks under the front of the subframe on each side, then remove the bolts from the front of the subframe.

12   Slowly lower the subframe assembly about two inches. **Caution:** *Do not lower it any more than two inches or the brake lines may be damaged.*

13   Support the fuel tank securely, then remove the fuel tank retaining strap bolts and carefully bend the straps enough to allow the tank to be removed.

14   Carefully lower the fuel tank. **Note:** *Make sure that none of the hoses or electrical con-*

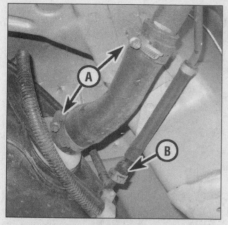

9.18a Disconnect the fuel filler hose clamps (A), and the filler tube quick disconnect line (B)

9.18b To disconnect the quick disconnect lines, pull out the lock . . .

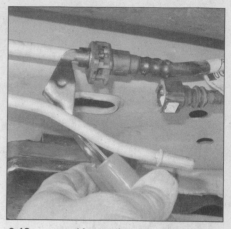

9.18c . . . and insert the release tool, then separate the lines

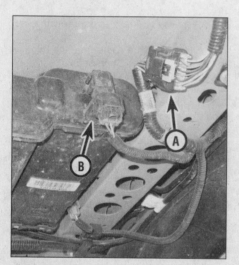

9.19 Disconnect the fuel tank connector (A), then the EVAP canister electrical connector (B)

nectors are being caught when the tank is being lowered.

15   Installation is the reverse of removal. Be sure to tighten the fuel tank strap bolts securely.

16   Reconnect the cable to the negative battery terminal (see Chapter 5), then start the engine and check for fuel leaks.

2008 and later models

Refer to illustrations 9.18a, 9.18b, 9.18c, 9.19, 9.20a and 9.20b

17   Remove the rear subframe and suspension (see Chapter 10).

18   Disconnect the filler hose clamp, then pull the plastic locks down on the vent tube and fuel lines. Insert the quick disconnect tool into the line and separate the lines and the vent tube quick disconnects **(see illustrations)**.

19   Disconnect the fuel tank and EVAP electrical connectors and **(see illustration)** and EVAP canister hoses (see Chapter 6).

20   Support the fuel tank securely, then remove the fuel tank retaining strap bolts **(see illustration)**. Remove the straps and carefully

lower the fuel tank **(see illustration)**.

21   Installation is the reverse of removal. Tighten the fuel tank strap bolts securely.

22   Reconnect the cable to the negative battery terminal (see Chapter 5), then start the engine and check for fuel leaks.

10   Air filter housing - removal and installation

1   Remove the engine covers.

Air intake duct

3.2L V6 models

2   Loosen the clamp at the Mass Air Flow (MAF) housing and remove the first end of the air intake duct.

3   Remove the mounting fastener that secures the air duct/resonator to the fan shroud.

4   Loosen the clamps at the air ducts and the throttle body and remove the air intake ducts from the throttle body.

9.20a Remove the fuel tank strap bolts, making sure all harnesses and fuel lines are out of the way . . .

9.20b . . . then carefully lower the tank from the vehicle

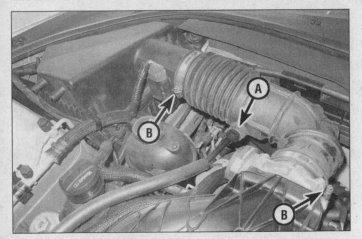

10.8 Disconnect the PCV fresh air hose (A), then remove the intake duct clamps (B) (3.0L V6 shown, other models similar)

10.13 Location of the air filter housing fastener (3.0L V6 shown, other models similar)

5   Lift the air intake duct/resonator up out of its mount, disconnect the vacuum lines and harness fasteners, then remove the duct.

6   Installation is the reverse of removal.

All except 3.2L models

Refer to illustration 10.8

7   Disconnect the PCV fresh air hose from the air intake duct.

8   Loosen the clamps at the air filter housing and the throttle body and remove the air intake duct **(see illustration)**.

9   On 5.7L and 6.0L engines, loosen the clamps at the air filter housing and the throttle body, then lift the duct up from the air filter housing side enough to disconnect the electrical connectors. Remove the duct.

10   Installation is the reverse of removal.

Air filter housing

Refer to illustration 10.13

11   Remove the air intake duct (see Steps 2 through 5 or 7 through 9).

12   Disconnect the electrical connector from the MAF sensor (see Chapter 6).

13   Remove the air filter housing fastener(s) and maneuver the housing out from the body **(see illustration)**.

14   Inspect the condition of the filter housing mounting grommets. If they're cracked, torn or deteriorated, replace them.

15   Installation is the reverse of removal.

---

11   Throttle body - removal and installation

Warning: *Wait until the engine is completely cool before beginning this procedure.*

1   Disconnect the cable from the negative battery terminal (see Chapter 5). Remove the engine covers.

2   Remove the air intake ducts (see Section 10).

3.2L V6 engine

3   Clamp off the coolant hoses connected to the throttle body.

4   Disconnect the vent tube from the throttle body.

5   Disconnect the coolant lines from the throttle body.

6   Disconnect the electrical connector from the throttle body.

7   Remove the throttle body mounting fasteners and detach the throttle body from the intake manifold.

2.8L, 3.0L and 3.6L V6 engines

Refer to illustration 11.10

8   Disconnect the throttle body electrical connector.

9   If equipped, rotate the wiring harness holder down and off of the throttle body.

10   Remove the throttle body mounting fasteners **(see illustration)** and detach the throttle body from the intake manifold.

5.7L V8 engine

11   Clamp off the coolant hoses connected to the throttle body.

12   Disconnect the throttle body and the air control valve electrical connectors.

13   Disconnect the crankcase vent hose.

14   Disconnect the coolant lines from the throttle body.

15   Remove the throttle body mounting fasteners and detach the throttle body from the intake manifold.

6.0L and 6.2L V8 engines

16   Disconnect the throttle body electrical connector.

17   If equipped, rotate the wiring harness holder down and off of the throttle body.

18   Remove the throttle body mounting fasteners and detach the throttle body from the intake manifold.

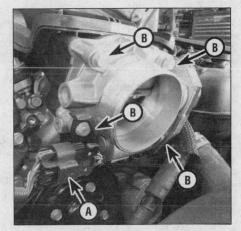

11.10 Disconnect the throttle body electrical connector (A) and remove the mounting fasteners (B)

All models

19   Discard the gasket; it should be replaced with a new one. Cover the intake manifold opening with a clean shop towel.

20   Installation is the reverse of removal. Install a new gasket, tighten the throttle body fasteners to the torque listed in this Chapter's Specifications and perform the idle relearn procedure. On 3.2L V6 or 5.7L V8 engines, check the coolant level, adding as necessary (see Chapter 1).

Idle relearn procedure

21   Start the engine and allow it to idle for three minutes. **Note:** *If a scanner is available, connect the scanner and view or record the actual engine idle speeds.*

22   After the three minutes, the PCM will start to learn the new idle patterns and begin adjusting the idle speed. The engine idle should begin to slow to almost normal.

23   When that happens, turn the engine off for one minute, then start the engine and allow it to idle again for three minutes. At the end of the second three minute cycle, the idle should

12.6 Disconnect the electrical connector from the fuel pressure sensor - intake manifold removed for clarity (3.0L V6 engine shown)

13.22 Remove the foam insulator covering the injector rails

be normal. **Note:** *If the check engine light comes on during the cycles, clear the codes after the second three minute cycle ends.*

24   If the engine does not idle properly after the relearn procedure, drive the vehicle above 44 mph, then decelerate and accelerate several times, allowing it to idle in between. Stop the vehicle and turn the engine off for one minute; the engine should now idle normally.

25   Clear any codes that are present.

12   Fuel pressure sensor - replacement

Warning: *Gasoline is extremely flammable. See* **Fuel system warnings** *in Section 1.*

1   Remove the fuel tank filler cap to relieve fuel tank pressure.

2   Relieve the fuel system pressure (see Section 3).

3   Disconnect the cable from the negative battery terminal (see Chapter 5).

3.0L and 3.6L V6 engines

Refer to illustration 12.6

Warning: *The manufacturer states that the fuel pressure sensor must be replaced with a new one whenever it is removed.*

4   Remove the engine covers. Remove the suspension crossbrace (see Chapter 10).

5   On 3.6L models, remove the intake manifold (see Chapter 2B) and remove the foam insulator.

6   Disconnect the electrical connector from the sensor **(see illustration)**.

7   Unscrew the sensor from the fuel rail. **Note:** *Have rags ready to catch any fuel that is remaining in the fuel rail.*

8   Installation is the reverse of removal. Tighten the sensor to the torque listed in this Chapter's Specifications.

6.2L V8 engines

9   Raise the rear of the vehicle and support it securely on jackstands. Block the front wheels to keep the vehicle from rolling.

10   Locate the sensor in the fuel line to the

right of the tank. Disconnect the electrical connector from the sensor.

11   Wrap a rag around the sensor and unscrew the sensor from the fuel line.

12   Apply a small amount of engine oil to the new O-ring, then install the O-ring and sensor. Tighten the sensor to the torque listed in this Chapter's Specifications.

13   Fuel rail and injectors - removal and installation

Warning: *Gasoline is extremely flammable. See* **Fuel system warnings** *in Section 1.*
Note: *Even if you only removed the fuel rail assembly to replace a single injector or a leaking O-ring, it's a good idea to remove all of the injectors from the fuel rail and replace all of the O-rings at the same time.*

1   Relieve the fuel system pressure (see Section 3).

2   Disconnect the cable from the negative battery terminal (see Chapter 5).

3   Disconnect the fuel supply line at the fuel rail (see *Disconnecting Fuel Line Fittings* on page 4-5).

3.2L V6 engine

4   Remove the upper intake manifold (see Chapter 2A).

5   Remove the fuel rail support bolt and disconnect the electrical connectors from each fuel injector, then remove the harness from the fuel rail and set out it of the way.

6   Disconnect the vent hose from the regulator. Remove the fuel rail-to-intake manifold mounting bolts, then remove the fuel rail and injectors as a single assembly.

7   Release the fuel injector retaining clip and remove each injector from its bore in the fuel rail.

8   Remove the upper and lower injector O-rings from each injector and discard them.

9   Coat the new O-rings with clean engine oil and slide them into place on each of the fuel injectors. Insert each injector into its bore

in the fuel rail. Secure the injectors to the fuel rail with the injector retaining clips.

10   Attach the fuel rail assembly to the intake manifold and carefully press the injectors into the manifold. Tighten the bolts to the torque listed in this Chapter's Specifications.

11   The remainder of installation is the reverse of removal.

2.8L and 2004 through 2009 3.6L (VIN 7) V6 engines

12   Remove the upper and lower intake manifolds (see Chapter 2B).

13   Disconnect the electrical connector from each fuel injector.

14   Remove the fuel rail mounting bolts, then remove the fuel rail and injectors as a single assembly.

15   Release the fuel injector retaining clips and remove each injector from its bore in the fuel rail.

16   Remove the upper and lower injector O-rings from each injector and discard them.

17   Coat the new O-rings with clean engine oil and slide them into place on each of the fuel injectors. Insert each injector into its bore in the fuel rail. Secure the injectors to the fuel rail with the injector retaining clips.

18   Remove the intake manifold gaskets and install new ones (see Chapter 2B).

19   Attach the fuel rail assembly to the intake manifold, tightening the bolts to the torque listed in this Chapter's Specifications. Install the fuel rail and intake manifold as a single assembly (see Chapter 2B).

20   The remainder of installation is the reverse of removal.

3.0L and 2008 and later 3.6L (VINS V, D and 3) V6 engines

Refer to illustrations 13.22, 13.25a, 13.25b, 13.27, 13.28, 13.29, 13.34, 13.35, 13.36a, 13.36b, 13.37 and 13.41

Caution: *The manufacturer recommends having the injectors rebuilt every time they are removed from the cylinder head.*

13.25a With the outer bolts removed and the inner bolts loosened, evenly pry the injectors out of the cylinder head . . .

13.25b . . . and remove the fuel rail and injectors as an assembly

21   Remove the intake manifold (see Chapter 2B).

22   Remove the foam insulator **(see illustration)**.

23   Remove the fuel pressure sensor (see Section 12). Also remove the high-pressure fuel line from the pump and fuel rails **(see Illustration 8.7)**.

24   Remove the mounting bolts from both fuel rails in reverse of the tightening sequence **(see illustration 12.30)**.

25   Install the center bolts, leaving several threads exposed, then evenly pry the Bank 2 (driver's side) fuel rail and injectors out of the cylinder head **(see illustrations)**. Repeat the same procedure for the Bank 1 fuel rail.

26   Disconnect the injector harness from the injectors.

27   Using external snap-ring pliers, carefully spread the retaining clip open then remove the clip **(see illustration)**.

28   Remove each injector from its bore in the fuel rail **(see illustration)**.

29   Remove the old combustion chamber Teflon sealing ring and the upper O-ring and support ring from each injector **(see illustration)**.

Caution: *Be extremely careful not to damage the groove for the seal or the rib in the floor of the groove. If you damage the groove or the rib, you must replace the injector.*

30   Before installing the new Teflon seal on each injector, thoroughly clean the groove for the seal and the injector shaft. Remove all combustion residue and varnish with a clean shop rag.

Teflon seal installation using the special tools

31   The manufacturer recommends that you use the tools included in the special injector tool set described above to install the Teflon lower seals on the injectors: Install the special seal assembly cone on the injector, install the special sleeve on the injector and use the sleeve to push on the assembly cone, which pushes the Teflon seal into place on its groove. Do NOT use any lubricants to do so.

32   Pushing the Teflon seal into place in its groove expands it slightly. There are three sizing sleeves in the special tool set with progressively smaller inside diameters. Using

13.27 Use pliers to open up the retaining clip, then remove it

a clockwise rotating motion of about 180 degrees, install the slightly larger sleeve onto the injector and over the Teflon seal until the sleeve hits its stop, then carefully turn the sleeve counterclockwise as you pull it off the

13.28 Remove the injectors from the fuel rail

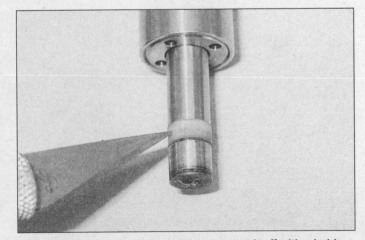

13.29 To remove the Teflon sealing ring, cut it off with a hobby knife (be careful not to scratch the injector groove)

13.34 Slide the new Teflon seal onto the end of a socket that's the same diameter as the end of the fuel injector . . .

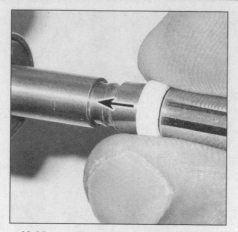

13.35 . . . align the socket with the end of the injector and slide the seal onto the injector and into its mounting groove

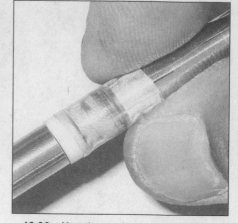

13.36a Use the socket to push a short section of plastic tubing onto the end of the injector and over the new seal . . .

injector. Use the slightly smaller sizing sleeve the same way, followed by the smallest sizing ring. The seal is now sized. Repeat this step for each injector.

13.36b . . . then leave the plastic tubing in place for several hours to compress the new seal

Teflon seal installation without special tools

33   If you don't have the special injector tool set, the Teflon seal can be installed using this method: First, find a socket that is equal or very close in diameter to the diameter of the end of the fuel injector.

34   Work the new Teflon seal onto the end of the socket **(see illustration)**.

35   Place the socket against the end of the injector **(see illustration)** and slide the seal from the socket onto the injector. Do NOT use any lubricants to do so. Continue pushing the seal onto the injector until it seats into its mounting groove.

36   Because the inside diameter of the seal has to be stretched open to fit over the bore of the socket and the injector, its outside diameter is now slightly too large - it is no longer flush with the surface of the injector. It must be shrunk it back to its original size. To do so, push a piece of plastic tubing with an interference fit onto the end of the socket; a plastic straw that fits tightly on the injector will work. After pushing the plastic tubing onto the

socket about an inch, snip off the rest of the tubing, then use the socket to push the tubing onto the end of the injector **(see illustration)** and slide it onto the injector until it completely covers the new seal **(see illustration)**. Leave the tubing on for a few hours, then remove it. The seal should now be shrunk back its original outside diameter, or close to it.

Injector and fuel rail installation

37   Install the new support ring at the upper end of the injector. Lubricate the new upper O-ring with clean engine oil and install it on the injector. Do NOT oil the new Teflon seal. Note that the seal is installed *above* the spacer **(see illustration)**.

38   Thoroughly clean the injector bores with a small nylon brush.

39   Install the new compensation element and retaining ring to the bottom of each injector.

40   Install the fuel injectors in the cylinder head (NOT in the fuel rail). You should be able to push each assembled injector into its bore in the cylinder head. The bore is slightly tapered, so you will encounter some resistance as the Teflon seal nears the bottom of the bore. Press the injector into its bore until it stops, making sure to properly align the injector.

41   Install a new spring steel retainer on each injector. Install the fuel rail, starting with the front injector and working toward the rear, then install the mounting bolts (outer bolts first, then the inner bolts). Tighten the bolts in sequence **(see illustration)** to the torque listed in this Chapter's Specifications.

42   The remainder of installation is the reverse of removal. Clean the high pressure fuel line fittings on the fuel rails, then apply a little clean engine oil to the threads. Install the new high-pressure fuel line, tightening the fittings to the torque listed in this Chapter's Specifications. Install a new fuel pressure sensor (see Section 12).

13.37 Note that the upper O-ring (1) is installed *above* the support ring (2)

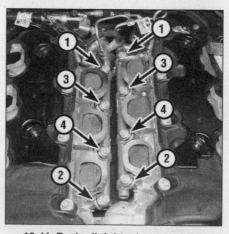

13.41 Fuel rail tightening sequence

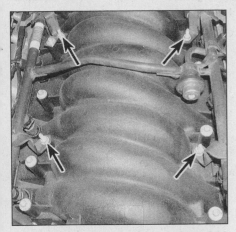

13.45 On 5.7L V8 models, remove the fuel rail mounting stud bolts and remove the rail

5.7L and 6.0L V8 engines

Refer to illustration 13.45

43   Clean debris and dirt from around the fuel injectors and the ports. Remove the engine trim covers.

44   Disconnect the wiring from all of the fuel injectors. Disconnect the fuel feed line.

45   Remove the plastic caps from the heads of the bolts which secure the fuel rail to the manifold **(see illustration)**. Remove the bolts and the fuel rail with the fuel injectors.

46   To remove the injectors from the fuel rail, slide the injector retaining clip and pull the injector from the fuel rail. Spread open the end of the injector clip slightly and remove it from the fuel rail, then extract the injector.

47   Coat the new O-rings with clean engine oil and slide them into place on each of the fuel injectors then insert each injector into its bore in the fuel rail. Secure the injectors to the fuel rail with the injector retaining clips.

48   Install the injectors on the fuel rail and secure the injectors with the retainer clips.

49   The remainder of installation is the reverse of removal.

6.2L V8 engine

50   Disconnect the fuel supply line at the fuel rail (see "Disconnecting Fuel Line Fittings" on page 4-5).

51   Remove the front and rear intake manifold covers (see Chapter 2C).

52   Disconnect the electrical connector from each fuel injector.

53   Disconnect the BARO sensor, intake temperature sensor, outlet pressure sensor and MAF sensor connectors (see Chapter 6).

54   Disconnect all the ignition coil electrical connectors (see Chapter 5).

55   Remove the fuel rail fasteners which secure the fuel rail to the supercharger. **Note:** *Remove the fuel injector harness with the fuel rail.*

56   To remove the fuel injectors, slide the injector retaining clip and pull the injector from the fuel rail. Spread open the end of the injector clip slightly and remove it from the fuel rail, then extract the injector.

57   Coat the new O-rings with clean engine oil and slide them into place on each of the fuel injectors. Insert each injector into its bore in the fuel rail. Secure the injectors to the fuel rail with the injector retaining clips.

58   The remainder of installation is the reverse of removal.

59   Reconnect the cable to the negative battery terminal (see Chapter 5), then turn the ignition switch to ON (but don't operate the starter). This activates the fuel pump for about two seconds, which builds up fuel pressure in the fuel lines and the fuel rail. Repeat this step two or three times, then check the fuel lines, fuel rails and injectors for fuel leaks.

14   Fuel filter (2007 and earlier models) - replacement

Warning: *Gasoline is extremely flammable. See* **Fuel system warnings** *in Section 1.*

Note: *On 2008 and later models, the fuel filter is integral with fuel pump module and is designed to last the life of the vehicle; no service is required.*

1   Relieve the fuel system pressure (see Section 3).

2   Disconnect the cable from the negative battery terminal (see Chapter 5).

3   Raise the vehicle and support it securely on jackstands.

4   The fuel filter is located below the driver's side door. Using the quick-disconnect tools disconnect the fuel line from the fuel filter.

5   Using a wrench (and backup wrench to prevent the filter from turning), unscrew the threaded fuel line fitting.

6   Slide the filter out of the mounting bracket and discard the O-ring.

7   Installation is the reverse of removal. Be sure to replace the O-ring with a new one and tighten the fuel line fitting securely.

Notes

Chapter 5
Engine electrical systems

Contents

1 General information and precautions

General information

Ignition system

The electronic ignition system consists of the Crankshaft Position (CKP) sensor, the Camshaft Position (CMP) sensor, the Knock Sensor (KS), the Powertrain Control Module (PCM), the ignition switch, the battery, the individual ignition coils or a coil pack, and the spark plugs. For more information on the CKP, CMP and KS sensors, as well as the PCM, refer to Chapter 6.

Charging system

The charging system includes the alternator (with an integral voltage regulator), the Powertrain Control Module (PCM), the Body Control Module (BCM), a charge indicator light on the dash, the battery, a fuse or fusible link and the wiring connecting all of these components. The charging system supplies electrical power for the ignition system, the lights, the radio, etc. The alternator is driven by a drivebelt.

Starting system

The starting system consists of the battery, the ignition switch, the starter relay, the Powertrain Control Module (PCM), the Body Control Module (BCM), the transmission Internal Mode Switch (IMS) (automatic transmission) or Clutch Pedal Position switch (manual transmission), the starter motor and solenoid assembly, and the wiring connecting all of the components.

Precautions

Always observe the following precautions when working on the electrical system:

a) Be extremely careful when servicing engine electrical components. They are easily damaged if checked, connected or handled improperly.
b) Never leave the ignition switched on for long periods of time when the engine is not running.
c) Never disconnect the battery cables while the engine is running.
d) Maintain correct polarity when connecting battery cables from another vehicle during jump starting - see the "Booster battery (jump) starting" Section at the front of this manual.
e) Always disconnect the cable from the negative battery terminal before working on the electrical system, but read the battery disconnection procedure first (see Section 3).

It's also a good idea to review the safety-related information regarding the engine electrical systems located in the *Safety first!* Section at the front of this manual before beginning any operation included in this Chapter.

2 Troubleshooting

Ignition system

1 If a malfunction occurs in the ignition system, do not immediately assume that any particular part is causing the problem. First, check the following items:

a) Make sure that the cable clamps at the battery terminals are clean and tight.
b) Test the condition of the battery (see Steps 21 through 24). If it doesn't pass all the tests, replace it.
c) Check the ignition coil or coil pack connections.
d) Check any relevant fuses in the engine compartment fuse and relay box (see Chapter 12). If they're burned, determine the cause and repair the circuit.

Check

Refer to illustration 2.3

Warning: *Because of the high voltage generated by the ignition system, use extreme care when performing a procedure involving ignition components.*
Note: *The ignition system components on these vehicles are difficult to diagnose. In the event of ignition system failure that you can't diagnose, have the vehicle tested at a dealer service department or other qualified auto repair facility.*
Note: *You'll need a spark tester for the follow-*

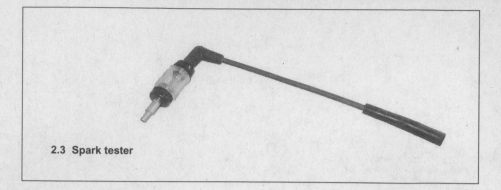

2.3 Spark tester

ing test. Spark testers are available at most auto supply stores.

2   If the engine turns over but won't start, verify that there is sufficient ignition voltage to fire the spark plugs as follows.

3   On models with a coil-over-plug type ignition system, remove a coil and install the tester between the boot at the lower end of the coil and the spark plug **(see illustration)**. On models with spark plug wires, disconnect a spark plug wire from a spark plug and install the tester between the spark plug wire boot and the spark plug.

4   Crank the engine and note whether or not the tester flashes. **Caution:** *Do NOT crank the engine or allow it to run for more than five seconds; running the engine for more than five seconds may set a Diagnostic Trouble Code (DTC) for a cylinder misfire.*

Models with a coil-over-plug type ignition system

5   If the tester flashes during cranking, the coil is delivering sufficient voltage to the spark plug to fire it. Repeat this test for each cylinder to verify that the other coils are OK.

6   If the tester doesn't flash, remove a coil from another cylinder and swap it for the one being tested. If the tester now flashes, you know that the original coil is bad. If the tester still doesn't flash, the PCM or wiring harness is probably defective. Have the PCM checked out by a dealer service department or other qualified repair shop (testing the PCM is beyond the scope of the do-it-yourselfer because it requires expensive special tools).

7   If the tester flashes during cranking but a misfire code (related to the cylinder being tested) has been stored, the spark plug could be fouled or defective.

Models with spark plug wires

8   If the tester flashes during cranking, sufficient voltage is reaching the spark plug to fire it.

9   Repeat this test on the remaining cylinders.

10   Proceed on this basis until you have verified that there's a good spark from each spark plug wire. If there is, then you have verified that the coils in the coil pack are functioning correctly and that the spark plug wires are OK.

11   If there is no spark from a spark plug wire, then either the coil is bad, the plug wire is bad or a connection at one end of the plug wire is loose. Assuming that you're using new plug wires or known good wires, then the coil is probably defective. Also inspect the coil pack electrical connector. Make sure that it's clean, tight and in good condition.

12   If all the coils are firing correctly, but the engine misfires, then one or more of the plugs might be fouled. Remove and check the spark plugs or install new ones (see Chapter 1).

13   No further testing of the ignition system is possible without special tools. If the problem persists, have the ignition system tested by a dealer service department or other qualified repair shop.

Charging system

14   If a malfunction occurs in the charging system, do not automatically assume the alternator is causing the problem. First check the following items:

a)   *Check the drivebelt tension and condition, as described in Chapter 1. Replace it if it's worn or deteriorated.*

b)   *Make sure the alternator mounting bolts are tight.*

c)   *Inspect the alternator wiring harness and the connectors at the alternator and voltage regulator. They must be in good condition, tight and have no corrosion.*

d)   *Check the fusible link (if equipped) or main fuse in the underhood fuse/relay box. If it is burned, determine the cause, repair the circuit and replace the link or fuse (the vehicle will not start and/or the accessories will not work if the fusible link or main fuse is blown).*

e)   *Start the engine and check the alternator for abnormal noises (a shrieking or squealing sound indicates a bad bearing).*

f)   *Check the battery. Make sure it's fully charged and in good condition (one bad cell in a battery can cause overcharging by the alternator).*

g)   *Disconnect the battery cables (negative first, then positive). Inspect the battery posts and the cable clamps for corrosion. Clean them thoroughly if necessary (see Chapter 1). Reconnect the cables (positive first, negative last).*

Alternator - check

15   Use a voltmeter to check the battery voltage with the engine off. It should be at least 12.6 volts **(see illustration 2.21)**.

16   Start the engine and check the battery voltage again. It should now be approximately 13.5 to 15 volts.

17   If the voltage reading is more or less than the specified charging voltage, the voltage regulator is probably defective, which will require replacement of the alternator (the voltage regulator is not replaceable separately). Remove the alternator and have it bench tested (most auto parts stores will do this for you).

18   The charging system (battery) light on the instrument cluster lights up when the ignition key is turned to ON, but it should go out when the engine starts.

19   If the charging system light stays on after the engine has been started, there is a problem with the charging system. Before replacing the alternator, check the battery condition, alternator belt tension and electrical cable connections.

20   If replacing the alternator doesn't restore voltage to the specified range, have the charging system tested by a dealer service department or other qualified repair shop.

Battery - check

Refer to illustrations 2.21 and 2.23

21   Check the battery state of charge. Visually inspect the indicator eye on the top of the battery (if equipped with one); if the indicator eye is black in color, charge the battery as described in Chapter 1. Next perform an open circuit voltage test using a digital voltmeter. **Note:** *The battery's surface charge must be removed before accurate voltage measurements can be made. Turn on the high beams for ten seconds, then turn them off and let the vehicle stand for two minutes.* With the engine and all accessories Off, touch the negative probe of the voltmeter to the negative terminal of the battery and the positive probe to the positive terminal of the battery **(see illustration)**. The battery voltage should be 12.6 volts or slightly above. If the battery is less than the specified voltage, charge the battery before proceeding to the next test. Do not proceed with the battery load test unless the battery charge is correct.

22   Disconnect the negative battery cable, then the positive cable from the battery.

23   Perform a battery load test. An accurate check of the battery condition can only be performed with a load tester **(see illustration)**. This test evaluates the ability of the battery to operate the starter and other accessories during periods of high current draw. Connect the load tester to the battery terminals. Load test the battery according to the tool manufacturer's instructions. This tool increases the load demand (current draw) on the battery.

24   Maintain the load on the battery for 15 seconds and observe that the battery voltage does not drop below 9.6 volts. If the battery condition is weak or defective, the tool will

2.21 To test the open circuit voltage of the battery, touch the black probe of the voltmeter to the negative terminal and the red probe to the positive terminal of the battery; a fully charged battery should be at least 12.6 volts

2.23 Connect a battery load tester to the battery and check the battery condition under load following the tool manufacturer's instructions

indicate this condition immediately. **Note:** *Cold temperatures will cause the minimum voltage reading to drop slightly. Follow the chart given in the manufacturer's instructions to compensate for cold climates. Minimum load voltage for freezing temperatures (32 degrees F) should be approximately 9.1 volts.*

Starting system

The starter rotates, but the engine doesn't

25   Remove the starter (see Section 8). Check the overrunning clutch and bench test the starter to make sure the drive mechanism extends fully for proper engagement with the flywheel ring gear. If it doesn't, replace the starter.

26   Check the flywheel ring gear for missing teeth and other damage. With the ignition turned off, rotate the flywheel so you can check the entire ring gear.

The starter is noisy

27   If the solenoid is making a chattering noise, first check the battery (see Steps 21 through 24). If the battery is okay, check the cables and connections.

28   If you hear a grinding, crashing metallic sound when you turn the key to Start, check for loose starter mounting bolts. If they're tight, remove the starter and inspect the teeth on the starter pinion gear and flywheel ring gear. Look for missing or damaged teeth.

29   If the starter sounds fine when you first turn the key to Start, but then stops rotating the engine and emits a zinging sound, the problem is probably a defective starter drive that's not staying engaged with the ring gear. Replace the starter.

The starter rotates slowly

30   Check the battery (see Steps 21 through 24).

31   If the battery is okay, verify all connections (at the battery, the starter solenoid and

motor) are clean, corrosion-free and tight. Make sure the cables aren't frayed or damaged.

32   Check that the starter mounting bolts are tight so it grounds properly. Also check the pinion gear and flywheel ring gear for evidence of a mechanical bind (galling, deformed gear teeth or other damage).

The starter does not rotate at all

33   Check the battery (see Steps 21 through 24).

34   If the battery is okay, verify all connections (at the battery, the starter solenoid and motor) are clean, corrosion-free and tight. Make sure the cables aren't frayed or damaged.

35   Check all of the fuses in the underhood fuse/relay box.

36   Check that the starter mounting bolts are tight so it grounds properly.

37   Check for voltage at the starter solenoid "S" terminal when the ignition key is turned to the start position. If voltage is present, replace the starter/solenoid assembly. If no voltage is present, the problem could be the starter relay, the transmission Internal Mode Switch (automatic transmission) or clutch start switch (see Chapter 8), or with an electrical connector somewhere in the circuit (see the wiring diagrams at the end of Chapter 12). Also, on many modern vehicles, the Powertrain Control Module (PCM) and the Body Control Module (BCM) control the voltage signal to the starter solenoid; on such vehicles a special scan tool is required for diagnosis.

---

3   Battery - disconnection and reconnection

Caution: *Always disconnect the cable from the negative battery terminal FIRST and hook it up LAST or the battery may be shorted by the tool being used to loosen the cable clamps.*

Warning: *On vehicles equipped with OnStar, make absolutely sure the ignition key is in the Off position and Retained Accessory Power (RAP) has been depleted before disconnecting the cable from the negative battery terminal. Also, never remove the OnStar fuse with the ignition key in any position other than Off. If these precautions are not taken, the OnStar system's back-up battery will be activated, and remain activated, until it goes dead. If this happens, the OnStar system will not function as it should in the event that the main vehicle battery power is cut off (as might happen during a collision).*

Note: *To disconnect the battery for service procedures requiring power to be cut from the vehicle, first open the driver's door to disable Retained Accessory Power (RAP), then loosen the cable end bolt and disconnect the cable from the negative battery terminal. Isolate the cable end to prevent it from coming into accidental contact with the battery terminal.*

Some vehicle systems (radio, alarm system, power door locks, power windows etc.) require battery power all the time, either to enable their operation or to maintain control unit memory (Powertrain Control Module, automatic transmission control module, etc.), which would be lost if the battery were to be disconnected. So before you disconnect the battery, note the following points:

a) *Before connecting or disconnecting the cable from the negative battery terminal, make sure that you turn the ignition key and the lighting switch to their OFF positions. Failure to do so could damage semiconductor components.*

b) *On a vehicle with power door locks, it is a wise precaution to remove the key from the ignition and to keep it with you, so that it does not get locked inside if the power door locks should engage accidentally when the battery is reconnected!*

4.2a On 2008 and later models, open the rear side trim panel

4.2b Depress the tab on the positive cable cover

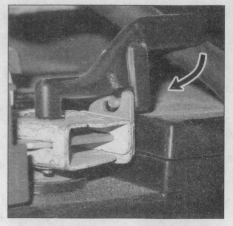

4.2c Rotate the cable handle clockwise to release the cable end

c) *After the battery has been disconnected, then reconnected (or a new battery has been installed) on vehicles with an automatic transaxle, the Transaxle Control Module (TCM) will need some time to relearn its adaptive strategy. As a result, shifting might feel firmer than usual. This is a normal condition and will not adversely affect the operation or service life of the transaxle. Eventually, the TCM will complete its adaptive learning process and the shift feel of the transaxle will return to normal.*

d) *The engine management system's PCM has some learning capabilities that allow it to adapt or make corrections in response to minor variations in the fuel system in order to optimize drivability and idle characteristics. However, the PCM might lose some or all of this information when the battery is disconnected. The PCM must go through a relearning process before it can regain its former drivability and performance characteristics. Until it relearns this lost data, you might notice a difference in drivability, idle and/ or (if you have an automatic) shift feel. To facilitate this relearning process, refer to "Enabling the PCM to relearn" below.*

e) *The power window system must be recalibrated before the windows will properly open and close To facilitate this calibration process, refer to "Power window calibration" below.*

On 2007 and earlier models, the battery is located in the engine compartment. To disconnect the battery for service procedures requiring power to be cut from the vehicle, loosen the cable end bolt and disconnect the cable from the negative battery terminal. Isolate the cable end to prevent it from coming into accidental contact with the battery terminal.

On 2008 and later models, the battery is located in the trunk or rear hatch, behind the rear side trim panel. To disconnect the battery for service procedures that require battery disconnection, simply disconnect the cable

from the negative battery terminal. Make sure that you isolate the cable to prevent it from coming into contact with the battery negative terminal.

Memory savers

Devices known as memory savers (typically, small 9-volt batteries) can be used to avoid some of the above problems. A memory saver is usually plugged into the cigarette lighter, and then you can disconnect the vehicle battery from the electrical system. The memory saver will deliver sufficient current to maintain security alarm codes and - maybe, but don't count on it! - PCM memory. It will also run unswitched (always on) circuits such as the clock and radio memory, while isolating the car battery in the event that a short circuit occurs while the vehicle is being serviced. **Warning:** *If you're going to work around any airbag system components, disconnect the battery and do not use a memory saver. If you do, the airbag could accidentally deploy and cause personal injury.* **Caution:** *Because memory savers deliver current to operate unswitched circuits when the battery is disconnected, make sure that the circuit that you're going to service is actually open before working on it!*

Enabling the PCM to relearn

After the battery has been reconnected, perform the following procedure in order to facilitate PCM relearning:

1   Start the engine and allow it to warm up to its normal operating temperature.

2   Drive the vehicle at part-throttle, under moderate acceleration and idle conditions, until normal performance returns.

3   Park the vehicle and apply the parking brake with the engine running.

4   On vehicles equipped with a manual transaxle, put the shift lever in NEUTRAL. On vehicles equipped with an automatic transaxle, put the shift lever in DRIVE.

5   Allow the engine to idle for about two minutes or until the idle stabilizes. Make sure that the engine is at its normal operating temperature.

Power window calibration

After the battery has been reconnected, perform the following procedure on each window in order to calibrate the power windows:

1   Turn the ignition switch to the "RUN" position.

2   Using the individual window switches, press the window switch down position until the window is completely down and hold the switch down for an additional three seconds.

3   Using the same individual window switch, press the window switch up position until the window is completely up and hold the switch for an additional three seconds.

4   Check to see that the window goes all the way up and down, then repeat this procedure for the remaining windows.

---

4   Battery - removal and installation

Refer to illustrations 4.2a, 4.2b, 4.2c and 4.3

Note: *The battery on 2008 and later models is located in the trunk or rear hatch, behind the rear side trim panel.*

1   On 2007 and earlier models, loosen the cable end nut and disconnect the cable from the negative battery terminal first, then disconnect the cable from the positive battery terminal.

2   On 2008 and later models, remove the rear side trim panel **(see illustration)**, then rotate the negative battery cable handle clockwise to release the cable end from the battery post. To access the positive battery cable end, depress the tab **(see illustration)** on the terminal cover and remove the cover to access the cable handle **(see illustration)**.

3   Remove the battery hold-down clamps **(see illustration)**.

4   Lift out the battery. Be careful - it's heavy.

Note: *Battery straps and handlers are available at most auto parts stores for reasonable prices. They make it easier to remove and carry the battery.*

5   If you are replacing the battery, make sure you get one that's identical, with the same dimensions, amperage rating, cold

cranking rating, etc. Also, be sure to remove the heat shield from the old battery and install it on the new battery.
6   Installation is the reverse of removal. Connect the positive cable first and the negative cable last.

5   Battery cables - replacement

1   When removing the cables, always disconnect the cable from the negative battery terminal first and hook it up last, or you might accidentally short out the battery with the tool you're using to loosen the cable clamps. Even if you're only replacing the cable for the positive terminal, disconnect the negative cable from the battery first.
2   Disconnect the old cables from the battery, then trace each of them to their opposite ends and disconnect them. Note the routing of each cable before disconnecting it to ensure correct installation.
3   If you are replacing any of the old cables, take them with you when buying new cables. It is vitally important that you replace the cables with identical parts.
4   Clean the threads of the solenoid or ground connection with a wire brush to remove rust and corrosion. Apply a light coat of battery terminal corrosion inhibitor or petroleum jelly to the threads to prevent future corrosion.
5   Attach the cable to the solenoid or ground connection and tighten the mounting nut/bolt securely.
6   Before connecting a new cable to the battery, make sure that it reaches the battery post without having to be stretched.
7   Connect the cable to the positive battery terminal first, *and then* connect the ground cable to the negative battery terminal.

6   Ignition coils - replacement

1   Disconnect the cable from the negative battery terminal (see Section 3).

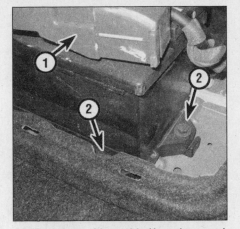

4.3 Battery positive cable (1, under cover) and hold-down bolts (2) (2008 and later models)

V6 engines

Refer to illustration 6.2

Note: *To access the ignition coils on the Bank 1 side, the intake manifold must be removed (see Chapter 2A or 2B).*
2   Remove the engine covers (see Chapter 1), then disconnect the electrical connector from the ignition coil **(see illustration)**. **Note:** *On 3.0L and 3.6L engines, the EVAP solenoid must be removed to access the rear two ignition coils on the Bank 2 side (see Chapter 6).*
3   Remove the mounting fastener from the ignition coil.
4   Grasp the coil firmly and pull it off the spark plug.
5   Installation is the reverse of removal.

V8 engines

Refer to illustrations 6.8 and 6.9

Note: *The ignition coils can be removed individually or as an assembly.*
6   Remove the engine covers from the front and rear of the engine.
7   The ignition coils may be removed from each cylinder bank as a complete assembly

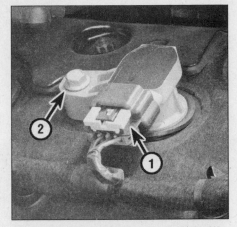

6.2 Ignition coil electrical connector (1) and mounting fastener (2) (3.0L V6 engine shown, other V6 engines similar)

or removed from the mounting bracket individually.
8   If removing the complete assembly, disconnect the ignition coil main electrical connector. Disconnect the spark plug wires from the spark plugs. Remove the ignition coil bracket mounting nuts/bolts and remove the assembly from the engine **(see illustration)**.
9   If removing an individual coil, disconnect the spark plug wire from the coil. Remove the ignition coil mounting screws and remove the ignition coil from the bracket **(see illustration)**.
10   Installation is the reverse of removal.

7   Alternator - removal and installation

1   Disconnect the cable from the negative battery terminal (see Section 3).
2   Raise the vehicle and support it securely on jackstands. Remove the under-vehicle splash shield.
3   Remove the drivebelt (see Chapter 1).

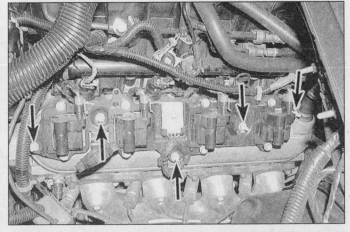

6.8 Remove the ignition coil bracket bolts (5.7L V8 engine shown, other V8 engines similar)

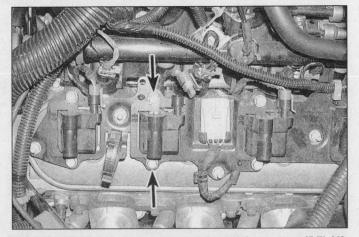

6.9 Remove the individual ignition coil mounting screws (5.7L V8 engine shown, other V8 engines similar)

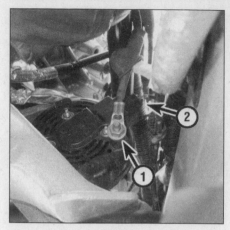

7.14 Alternator battery terminal (1) and electrical connector (2) (2010 3.0L V6 shown, other engines similar)

7.15 Alternator mounting bolt locations (2010 3.0L V6 shown, other engines similar)

8.9 Starter motor mounting bolts (3.0L V6 model shown, other models similar)

3.2L V6 engines

4   Remove the intake air duct mounting fasteners (see Chapter 4).

5   Remove the alternator mounting fasteners.

6   Remove the alternator from the mounting bracket and disconnect the alternator B+ terminal nut and electrical connector.

7   Remove the alternator.

2.8L, 3.0L and 3.6L V6 engines

2007 and earlier models

8   Install an engine support fixture or engine hoist (see Chapter 2D).

9   Push back the protective cover from the alternator's battery terminal, remove the nut and disconnect the battery cable from the alternator. Disconnect the electrical connector from the alternator.

10   Disconnect the electrical connector to the Electronic Brake Control Module (EBCM) and place the connector out of the way.

11   With the engine supported, remove the engine mount lower nuts (see Chapter 2B).

12   Remove the alternator lower mounting bolts and raise the engine enough to access the upper mounting bolt.

13   Remove the upper mounting bolt and remove the alternator.

2008 and later models

Refer to illustrations 7.14 and 7.15

14   Push back the protective cover from the alternator's battery terminal, remove the nut and disconnect the battery cable from the alternator **(see illustration)**. Disconnect the electrical connector from the alternator.

15   Remove the alternator mounting bolts **(see illustration)** and remove the alternator.

V8 engines

16   Remove the air filter housing (see Chapter 4).

17   Remove the radiator cooling fan (see Chapter 3).

18   Remove the power steering pressure

hose bracket fastener, if equipped.

19   Remove the alternator mounting fasteners.

20   Push back the protective cover from the alternator's battery terminal, remove the nut and disconnect the battery cable from the alternator. Disconnect the electrical connector from the alternator.

21   Remove the alternator mounting bolts and remove the alternator.

All models

22   If you're replacing the alternator, take the old one with you when purchasing the replacement unit. Make sure that the new/rebuilt unit looks identical to the old alternator. Look at the electrical terminals on the backside of the alternator. They should be the same in number, size and location as the terminals on the old alternator. Finally, look at the identification numbers. They will be stamped into the housing or printed on a tag attached to the housing. Make sure that the ID numbers are the same on both alternators.

23   Many new/rebuilt alternators DO NOT have a pulley installed, so you might have to swap the pulley from the old unit to the new/rebuilt one. When buying an alternator, find out the store's policy regarding pulley swaps. Some stores perform this service free of charge. If your local auto parts store doesn't offer this service, you'll have to purchase a puller for removing the pulley and do it yourself.

24   Installation is the reverse of removal. Tighten the alternator mounting bolts securely.

25   Reconnect the cable to the negative terminal of the battery. Check the charging voltage (see Section 2) to verify that the alternator is operating correctly.

8   Starter motor - removal and installation

1   Detach the cable from the negative terminal of the battery (see Section 3).

2   Raise the vehicle and support it securely on jackstands. Remove the underbody cover.

3.2L V6 engines

3   Remove the passenger's side catalytic converter (see Chapter 4) then remove the heat shield fasteners and shield.

4   Remove the heat shield mounting bracket fasteners and remove the bracket.

5   Support the engine and remove the right side engine mount (see Chapter 2A).

6   Disconnect the starter motor solenoid wire nut and the starter motor battery cable nut and disconnect both wires from the starter.

7   Installation is the reverse of removal. Tighten the starter mounting stud and bolt securely.

2.8L, 3.0L and 3.6L V6 engines

Refer to illustration 8.9

8   Remove the starter motor solenoid wire nut and the starter motor battery cable nut, then disconnect both wires from the starter motor. **Note:** *Some models are equipped with a starter heat shield; if the engine is equipped with a heat shield, the passenger's side catalytic converter must be disconnected and removed.*

9   Remove the starter motor mounting fasteners **(see illustration)** and remove the starter motor.

10   Installation is the reverse of removal.

V8 engines

11   Remove the passenger's side catalytic converter (see Chapter 4).

12   Remove the starter motor solenoid wire nut and the starter motor battery cable nut, then disconnect both wires from the starter.

13   Remove the starter motor mounting fasteners and remove the starter motor.

14   Installation is the reverse of removal.

Chapter 6
Emissions and engine control systems

Contents

Specifications

Torque specifications

Note: *One foot-pound (ft-lb) of torque is equivalent to 12 inch-pounds (in-lbs) of torque. Torque values below approximately 15 foot-pounds are expressed in inch-pounds, because most foot-pound torque wrenches are not accurate at these smaller values.*

	Ft-lbs (unless otherwise indicated)	Nm
Engine Coolant Temperature (ECT) sensor		
3.0L V6 engine	15	20
3.2L V6 engine	156 in-lbs	18
2.8 and 3.6L V6 engines	16	22
V8 engines	15	20
Knock sensor mounting bolt		
All V6 engines except 3.2L	15	20
3.2L V6 engines	17	23
V8 engines	15	20
Oxygen sensor	35	47

1 General information

To prevent pollution of the atmosphere from incompletely burned and evaporating gases, and to maintain good drivability and fuel economy, a number of emission control systems are incorporated. They include the:

Catalytic converter

A catalytic converter is an emission control device in the exhaust system that reduces certain pollutants in the exhaust gas stream. There are two types of converters: oxidation converters and reduction converters.

Oxidation converters contain a monolithic substrate (a ceramic honeycomb) coated with the semi-precious metals platinum and palladium. An oxidation catalytic converter reduces unburned hydrocarbons (HC) and carbon monoxide (CO) by adding oxygen to the exhaust stream as it passes through the substrate, which, in the presence of high temperature and the catalytic converter materials, converts the HC and CO to water vapor (H_2O) and carbon dioxide (CO_2).

Reduction converters contain a monolithic substrate coated with platinum and rhodium. A reduction catalytic converter reduces oxides of nitrogen (NOx) by removing oxygen, which in the presence of high temperature and the catalytic converter material produces nitrogen (N) and carbon dioxide (CO_2).

Catalytic converters that combine both types of catalytic converters in one assembly are known as "three-way catalytic converters" or TWCs. A TWC can reduce all three pollutants.

Evaporative Emissions Control (EVAP) system

The Evaporative Emissions Control (EVAP) system prevents fuel system vapors (which contain unburned hydrocarbons) from escaping into the atmosphere. On warm days, vapors trapped inside the fuel tank expand until the pressure reaches a certain threshold. Then the fuel vapors are routed from the fuel tank through the fuel vapor vent valve and the fuel vapor control valve to the EVAP canister, where they're stored temporarily until the next time the vehicle is operated. When the conditions are right (engine warmed up, vehicle up to speed, moderate or heavy load on the engine, etc.) the PCM opens the canister purge valve, which allows fuel vapors to be drawn from the canister into the intake manifold. Once in the intake manifold, the fuel vapors mix with incoming air before being drawn through the intake ports into the combustion chambers where they're burned up with the rest of the air/fuel mixture. The EVAP system is complex and virtually impossible to troubleshoot without the right tools and training.

Powertrain Control Module (PCM)

The Powertrain Control Module (PCM) is the brain of the engine management system. It also controls a wide variety of other vehicle systems. In order to program the new PCM, the dealer needs the vehicle as well as the new PCM. If you're planning to replace the PCM with a new one, there is no point in trying to do so at home because you won't be able to program it yourself.

Positive Crankcase Ventilation (PCV) system

The Positive Crankcase Ventilation (PCV) system reduces hydrocarbon emissions by scavenging crankcase vapors, which are rich in unburned hydrocarbons. A PCV valve or orifice regulates the flow of gases into the intake manifold in proportion to the amount of intake vacuum available.

The PCV system generally consists of the fresh air inlet hose, the PCV valve or orifice and the crankcase ventilation hose (or PCV hose). The fresh air inlet hose connects the air intake duct to a pipe on the valve cover. The crankcase ventilation hose (or PCV hose) connects the PCV valve or orifice in the valve cover to the intake manifold.

Emissions and engine control components (3.0L V6 engine shown):

1   *Accelerator Pedal Position (APP) sensor (at the top of accelerator pedal assembly)*
2   *Exhaust Camshaft Position (CMP) sensor (front of cylinder head)*
3   *Intake Camshaft Position (CMP) sensor (front of cylinder head)*
4   *Positive Crankcase Ventilation (PCV) hose (on top of intake manifold)*
5   *Engine Coolant Temperature (ECT) sensor (on coolant passage at left end of engine, behind water pump)*

6   *Knock sensors (lower left rear sides of engine block)*
7   *Camshaft position actuator solenoid valve (exhaust)*
8   *Camshaft position actuator solenoid valve (intake)*
9   *Upstream oxygen sensor (in exhaust manifold)*
10 *EVAP canister purge solenoid valve (right corner of the intake manifold)*
11 *Barometric pressure (BARO) sensor (air filter housing)*

12 *Mass Air Flow/Intake Air Temperature (MAF/IAT) sensor (air inlet duct, or air filter housing)*
13 *Powertrain Control Module (PCM) (behind and below the battery box)*
14 *Manifold Absolute Pressure (MAP) sensor*
15 *Crankshaft Position (CKP) sensor (lower right rear corner of block, near crankshaft pulley)*

Information Sensors

Accelerator Pedal Position (APP) sensor - as you press the accelerator pedal, the APP sensor alters its voltage signal to the PCM in proportion to the angle of the pedal, and the PCM commands a motor inside the throttle body to open or close the throttle plate accordingly

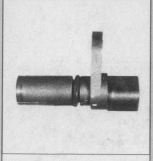

Camshaft Position (CMP) sensor - produces a signal that the PCM uses to identify the number 1 cylinder and to time the firing sequence of the fuel injectors

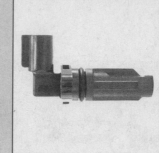

Crankshaft Position (CKP) sensor - produces a signal that the PCM uses to calculate engine speed and crankshaft position, which enables it to synchronize ignition timing with fuel injector timing, and to detect misfires

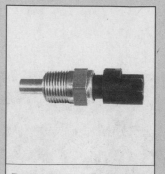

Engine Coolant Temperature (ECT) sensor - a thermistor (temperature-sensitive variable resistor) that sends a voltage signal to the PCM, which uses this data to determine the temperature of the engine coolant

Fuel tank pressure sensor - measures the fuel tank pressure and controls fuel tank pressure by signaling the EVAP system to purge the fuel tank vapors when the pressure becomes excessive

Intake Air Temperature (IAT) sensor - monitors the temperature of the air entering the engine and sends a signal to the PCM to determine injector pulse-width (the duration of each injector's on-time) and to adjust spark timing (to prevent spark knock)

Knock sensor - a piezoelectric crystal that oscillates in proportion to engine vibration which produces a voltage output that is monitored by the PCM. This retards the ignition timing when the oscillation exceeds a certain threshold

Manifold Absolute Pressure (MAP) sensor - monitors the pressure or vacuum inside the intake manifold. The PCM uses this data to determine engine load so that it can alter the ignition advance and fuel enrichment

Mass Air Flow (MAF) sensor - measures the amount of intake air drawn into the engine. It uses a hot-wire sensing element to measure the amount of air entering the engine

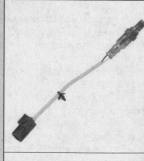

Oxygen sensors - generates a small variable voltage signal in proportion to the difference between the oxygen content in the exhaust stream and the oxygen content in the ambient air. The PCM uses this information to maintain the proper air/fuel ratio. A second oxygen sensor monitors the efficiency of the catalytic converter

Throttle Position (TP) sensor - a potentiometer that generates a voltage signal that varies in relation to the opening angle of the throttle plate inside the throttle body. Works with the PCM and other sensors to calculate injector pulse width (the duration of each injector's on-time)

Photos courtesy of Wells Manufacturing, except APP and MAF sensors.

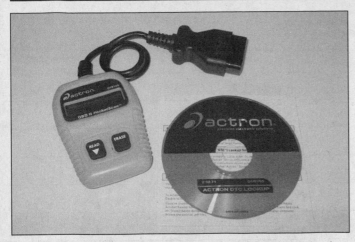

2.4a Simple code readers are an economical way to extract trouble codes when the CHECK ENGINE light comes on

2.4b Hand-held scan tools like these can extract computer codes and also perform diagnostics

2   On Board Diagnosis (OBD) system

General description

1   All models are equipped with the second generation OBD-II system. This system consists of an on-board computer known as the Powertrain Control Module (PCM), and information sensors, which monitor various functions of the engine and send data to the PCM. This system incorporates a series of diagnostic monitors that detect and identify fuel injection and emissions control system faults and store the information in the computer memory. This system also tests sensors and output actuators, diagnoses drive cycles, freezes data and clears codes.

2   The PCM is the brain of the electronically controlled fuel and emissions system. It receives data from a number of sensors and other electronic components (switches, relays, etc.). Based on the information it receives, the PCM generates output signals to control various relays, solenoids (fuel injectors) and other actuators. The PCM is specifically calibrated to optimize the emissions, fuel economy and drivability of the vehicle.

3   It isn't a good idea to attempt diagnosis or replacement of the PCM or emission control components at home while the vehicle is under warranty. Because of a federally-mandated warranty which covers the emissions system components and because any owner-induced damage to the PCM, the sensors and/or the control devices may void this warranty, take the vehicle to a dealer service department if the PCM or a system component malfunctions.

Scan tool information

Refer to illustrations 2.4a and 2.4b

4   Because extracting the Diagnostic Trouble Codes (DTCs) from an engine management system is now the first step in troubleshooting many computer-controlled systems and components, a code reader, at the very least, will be required **(see illustration)**. More powerful scan tools can also perform many of the diagnostics once associated with expensive factory scan tools **(see illustration)**. If you're planning to obtain a generic scan tool for your vehicle, make sure that it's compatible with OBD-II systems. If you don't plan to purchase a code reader or scan tool and don't have access to one, you can have the codes extracted by a dealer service department or an independent repair shop. **Note:** *Some auto parts stores even provide this service.*

3   Obtaining and clearing Diagnostic Trouble Codes (DTCs)

All models covered by this manual are equipped with on-board diagnostics. When the PCM recognizes a malfunction in a monitored emission or engine control system, component or circuit, it turns on the Malfunction Indicator Light (MIL) on the dash. The PCM will continue to display the MIL until the problem is fixed and the Diagnostic Trouble Code (DTC) is cleared from the PCM's memory. You'll need a scan tool to access any DTCs stored in the PCM.

Before outputting any DTCs stored in the PCM, thoroughly inspect ALL electrical connectors and hoses. Make sure that all electrical connections are tight, clean and free of corrosion. And make sure that all hoses are correctly connected, fit tightly and are in good condition (no cracks or tears).

Accessing the DTCs

Refer to illustration 3.1

1   The Diagnostic Trouble Codes (DTCs) can only be accessed with a code reader or scan tool. Professional scan tools are expensive, but relatively inexpensive generic code readers or scan tools **(see illustrations 2.4a and 2.4b)** are available at most auto parts stores. Plug the connector of the scan tool into the diagnostic connector **(see illustration)**, then follow the instructions included with the scan tool to extract the DTCs.

2   Once you have outputted all of the stored DTCs, look them up on the accompanying DTC chart.

3   After troubleshooting the source of each DTC, make any necessary repairs or replace the defective component(s).

Clearing the DTCs

4   Clear the DTCs with the code reader or scan tool in accordance with the instructions provided by the tool's manufacturer.

Diagnostic Trouble Codes

5   The accompanying tables are a list of the Diagnostic Trouble Codes (DTCs) that can be accessed by a do-it-yourselfer working at home (there are many, many more DTCs available to professional mechanics with proprietary scan tools and software, but those codes cannot be accessed by a generic scan tool). If, after you have checked and repaired the connectors, wire harness and vacuum hoses (if applicable) for an emission-related system, component or circuit, the problem persists, have the vehicle checked by a dealer service department or other qualified repair shop.

3.1 The Data Link Connector (DLC) is located at the lower edge of the dash, below the steering column

OBD-II trouble codes (continued)

Note: *Not all trouble codes apply to all models.*

Code	Probable cause
P000A	Intake camshaft position system slow response (Bank 1)
P000B	Exhaust camshaft position system slow response (Bank 1)
P000C	Intake camshaft position system slow response (Bank 2)
P000D	Exhaust camshaft position system slow response (Bank 2)
P0008	Engine position system performance problem (Bank 1)
P0009	Engine position system performance problem (Bank 2)
P0010	Intake camshaft position (CMP) actuator solenoid control circuit (Bank 1)
P0011	Intake camshaft position system performance problem (Bank 1)
P0013	Exhaust camshaft position (CMP) actuator solenoid control (Bank 1)
P0014	Exhaust camshaft position system performance problem (Bank 1)
P0016	Crankshaft position - intake camshaft position (CMP) correlation (Bank 1)
P0017	Crankshaft position - exhaust camshaft position (CMP) correlation (Bank 1)
P0018	Crankshaft position - intake camshaft position (CMP) correlation (Bank 2)
P0019	Crankshaft position - exhaust camshaft position (CMP) correlation (Bank 2)
P0030	Oxygen sensor heaters control circuit (Bank 1, Sensor 1)
P0031	Oxygen sensor heaters control circuit, low voltage (Bank 1, Sensor 1)
P0032	Oxygen sensor heaters control circuit, high voltage (Bank 1, Sensor 1)
P0033	Supercharger bypass valve solenoid control circuit problem
P0036	Oxygen sensor heaters control circuit (Bank 1, Sensor 2)
P0037	Oxygen sensor heaters control circuit, low voltage (Bank 1, Sensor 2)
P0038	Oxygen sensor heaters control circuit, high voltage (Bank 1, Sensor 2)
P0050	Oxygen sensor heaters control circuit (Bank 2, Sensor 1)
P0051	Oxygen sensor heaters control circuit, low voltage (Bank 2, Sensor 1)
P0052	Oxygen sensor heaters control circuit, high voltage (Bank 2, Sensor 1)
P0053	Oxygen sensor heaters resistance (Bank 1, Sensor 1)
P0054	Oxygen sensor heaters resistance (Bank 1, Sensor 2)
P0056	Oxygen sensor heaters control circuit (Bank 2, Sensor 2)
P0057	Oxygen sensor heaters control circuit, low voltage (Bank 2, Sensor 2)
P0058	Oxygen sensor heaters heater control circuit, high voltage (Bank 2, Sensor 2)
P0059	Oxygen sensor heaters heater resistance (Bank 2, Sensor 1)

Code	Probable cause
P0060	Oxygen sensor heaters heater resistance (Bank 2, Sensor 2)
P0068	Throttle body airflow performance problem
P006D	Barometric sensor (BARO) – supercharger inlet pressure correlation inaccuracy
P0087	Fuel rail low pressure
P0088	Fuel rail high pressure
P0089	Fuel pressure regulator performance problem
P0090	Fuel pressure regulator control circuit open
P0091	Fuel pressure regulator control circuit, low voltage
P0092	Fuel pressure regulator control circuit, high voltage
P0096	Intake air temperature (IAT) sensor 2 performance problem
P0097	Intake air temperature (IAT) sensor 2 circuit, low voltage
P0098	Intake air temperature (IAT) sensor 2 circuit, high voltage
P00C6	Fuel rail pressure low during engine cranking
P00C8	Fuel pressure regulator high control circuit
P00C9	Fuel pressure regulator high control circuit, low voltage
P00CA	Fuel pressure regulator high control circuit, high voltage
P0100	Mass air flow (MAF) sensor circuit problem
P0101	Mass air flow (MAF) sensor circuit, performance problem
P0102	Mass air flow (MAF) sensor circuit, low frequency
P0103	Mass air flow (MAF) sensor circuit, high frequency
P0106	Manifold absolute pressure (MAP) sensor performance problem
P0107	Manifold absolute pressure (MAP) sensor circuit, low voltage
P0108	Manifold absolute pressure (MAP) sensor circuit, high voltage
P0111	Intake air temperature (IAT) sensor circuit, performance problem
P0112	Intake air temperature (IAT) sensor circuit, low voltage
P0113	Intake air temperature (IAT) sensor circuit, high voltage
P0114	Intake air temperature (IAT) sensor circuit, intermittent
P0116	Engine coolant temperature (ECT) sensor performance problem
P0117	Engine coolant temperature (ECT) sensor circuit, low voltage
P0118	Engine coolant temperature (ECT) sensor circuit, high voltage
P0119	Engine coolant temperature (ECT) sensor circuit, intermittent
P0120	Throttle position (TP) sensor 1 circuit malfunction

OBD-II trouble codes (continued)

Note: *Not all trouble codes apply to all models.*

Code	Probable cause
P0121	Throttle position sensor performance problem
P0122	Throttle position sensor 1 circuit, low voltage
P0123	Throttle position sensor 1 circuit, high voltage
P0128	Engine coolant temperature (ECT) below thermostat regulating temperature
P012B	Supercharger inlet pressure sensor performance
P012C	Supercharger inlet pressure sensor circuit, low voltage
P012D	Supercharger inlet pressure sensor circuit, high voltage
P0130	Oxygen sensor heaters signal circuit, shorted to heater circuit (Bank 1, Sensor 1)
P0131	Oxygen sensor heaters circuit, low voltage (Bank 1, Sensor 1)
P0132	Oxygen sensor heaters circuit, high voltage (Bank 1, Sensor 1)
P0133	Oxygen sensor heaters slow response (Bank 1, Sensor 1)
P0134	Oxygen sensor heaters circuit, insufficient activity (Bank 1, Sensor 1)
P0135	Oxygen sensor heaters heater performance (Bank 1, Sensor 1)
P0137	Oxygen sensor heaters circuit, low voltage (Bank 1, Sensor 2)
P0138	Oxygen sensor heaters circuit, high voltage (Bank 1, Sensor 2)
P013A	Oxygen sensor heaters slow response rich to lean (Bank 1, Sensor 2)
P013B	Oxygen sensor heaters slow response lean to rich (Bank 1, Sensor 2)
P013C	Oxygen sensor heaters slow response rich to lean (Bank 2, Sensor 2)
P013D	Oxygen sensor heaters slow response lean to rich (Bank 2, Sensor 2)
P013E	Oxygen sensor heaters delayed response rich to lean (Bank 1, Sensor 2)
P0140	Oxygen sensor heaters circuit, insufficient activity (Bank 1, Sensor 2)
P0141	Oxygen sensor heaters heater performance (Bank 1, Sensor 2)
P014A	Oxygen sensor heaters delayed response rich to lean (Bank 2, Sensor 2)
P014B	Oxygen sensor heaters delayed response lean to rich (Bank 2, Sensor 2)
P0150	Oxygen sensor heaters signal circuit, shorted to heater circuit (Bank 2, Sensor 1)
P0151	Oxygen sensor heaters circuit, low voltage (Bank 2, Sensor 1)
P0152	Oxygen sensor heaters circuit, high voltage (Bank 2, Sensor 1)
P0153	Oxygen sensor heaters slow response (Bank 2, Sensor 1)
P0154	Oxygen sensor heaters circuit, insufficient activity (Bank 2, Sensor 1)
P0155	Oxygen sensor heaters heater performance (Bank 2, Sensor 1)

Code	Probable cause
P0157	Oxygen sensor heaters circuit, low voltage (Bank 2, Sensor 2)
P0158	Oxygen sensor heaters circuit, high voltage (Bank 2, Sensor 2)
P015A	Oxygen sensors delayed response rich to lean (Bank 1 Sensor 1)
P015B	Oxygen sensors delayed response lean to rich (Bank 1 Sensor 1)
P015C	Oxygen sensors delayed response rich to lean (Bank 2 Sensor 1)
P015D	Oxygen sensors delayed response lean to rich (Bank 2 Sensor 1)
P0160	Oxygen sensor heaters circuit, insufficient activity (Bank 2, Sensor 2)
P0161	Oxygen sensor heaters heater performance problem (Bank 2, Sensor 2)
P0171	Fuel trim system lean (Bank 1)
P0172	Fuel trim system rich (Bank 1)
P0174	Fuel trim system lean (Bank 2)
P0175	Fuel trim system rich (Bank 2)
P018B	Fuel pressure sensor performance problem
P018C	Fuel pressure sensor circuit, low voltage
P018D	Fuel pressure sensor circuit, high voltage
P0191	Fuel rail pressure sensor performance problem
P0192	Fuel rail pressure sensor circuit, low voltage
P0193	Fuel rail pressure sensor circuit, high voltage
P0201	Cylinder 1 injector control circuit malfunction
P0202	Cylinder 2 injector control circuit malfunction
P0203	Cylinder 3 injector control circuit malfunction
P0204	Cylinder 4 injector control circuit malfunction
P0205	Cylinder 5 injector control circuit malfunction
P0206	Cylinder 6 injector control circuit malfunction
P0207	Cylinder 7 injector control circuit malfunction
P0208	Cylinder 8 injector control circuit malfunction
P0220	Throttle position sensor 2 circuit problem
P0221	Throttle position sensor 2 performance problem
P0222	Throttle position sensor 2 circuit, low voltage
P0223	Throttle position sensor 2 circuit, high voltage
P0230	Fuel pump relay control circuit

OBD-II trouble codes (continued)

Note: *Not all trouble codes apply to all models.*

Code	Probable cause
P0231	Fuel pump control circuit, low voltage
P0232	Fuel pump control circuit, high voltage
P023A	Charge air cooler (CAC) coolant pump relay control circuit
P023F	Fuel pump control circuit
P025A	Fuel pump control module enable circuit
P0261	Cylinder 1 injector control circuit, low voltage
P0262	Cylinder 1 injector control circuit, high voltage
P0264	Cylinder 2 injector control circuit, low voltage
P0265	Cylinder 2 injector control circuit, high voltage
P0267	Cylinder 3 injector control circuit, low voltage
P0268	Cylinder 3 injector control circuit, high voltage
P0270	Cylinder 4 injector control circuit, low voltage
P0271	Cylinder 4 injector control circuit, high voltage
P0273	Cylinder 5 injector control circuit, low voltage
P0274	Cylinder 5 injector control circuit, high voltage
P0276	Cylinder 6 injector control circuit, low voltage
P0277	Cylinder 6 injector control circuit, high voltage
P029D	Cylinder 1 injector leak detected
P02A1	Cylinder 2 injector leak detected
P02A5	Cylinder 3 injector leak detected
P02A9	Cylinder 4 injector leak detected
P02AD	Cylinder 5 injector leak detected
P02B1	Cylinder 6 injector leak detected
P0300	Engine misfire detected
P0301	Cylinder 1 misfire detected
P0302	Cylinder 2 misfire detected
P0303	Cylinder 3 misfire detected
P0304	Cylinder 4 misfire detected
P0305	Cylinder 5 misfire detected

Code	Probable cause
P0306	Cylinder 6 misfire detected
P0307	Cylinder 7 misfire detected
P0308	Cylinder 8 misfire detected
P0315	Crankshaft position system variation not learned
P0324	Knock sensor module performance problem
P0325	Knock sensor circuit (Bank 1)
P0326	Knock sensor performance problem (Bank 1)
P0327	Knock sensor circuit, low voltage (Bank 1)
P0328	Knock sensor circuit, high voltage (Bank 1)
P0330	Knock sensor circuit (Bank 2)
P0331	Knock sensor performance problem (Bank 2)
P0332	Knock sensor circuit, low voltage (Bank 2)
P0333	Knock sensor circuit, high voltage (Bank 2)
P0335	Crankshaft position sensor circuit malfunction
P0336	Crankshaft position sensor performance problem
P0338	Crankshaft position sensor circuit, high duty cycle
P0340	Intake camshaft position sensor circuit (Bank 1)
P0341	Intake camshaft position sensor performance problem (Bank 1)
P0342	Intake camshaft position sensor circuit, low voltage (Bank 1)
P0343	Intake camshaft position sensor circuit, high voltage (Bank 1)
P0345	Intake camshaft position sensor circuit (Bank 2)
P0346	Intake camshaft position sensor performance problem (Bank 2)
P0347	Intake camshaft position sensor circuit, low voltage (Bank 2)
P0348	Intake camshaft position sensor circuit, high voltage (Bank 2)
P0351	Ignition coil 1 control circuit malfunction
P0352	Ignition coil 2 control circuit malfunction
P0353	Ignition coil 3 control circuit malfunction
P0354	Ignition coil 4 control circuit malfunction
P0355	Ignition coil 5 control circuit malfunction
P0356	Ignition coil 6 control circuit malfunction
P0357	Ignition coil 7 control circuit malfunction
P0358	Ignition coil 8 control circuit malfunction

OBD-II trouble codes (continued)

Note: *Not all trouble codes apply to all models.*

Code	Probable cause
P0365	Exhaust camshaft position sensor circuit (Bank 1)
P0366	Exhaust camshaft position sensor performance problem (Bank 1)
P0367	Exhaust camshaft position sensor circuit, low voltage (Bank 1)
P0368	Exhaust camshaft position sensor circuit, high voltage (Bank 1)
P0390	Exhaust camshaft position sensor circuit (Bank 2)
P0391	Exhaust camshaft position sensor performance problem (Bank 2)
P0392	Exhaust camshaft position sensor circuit, low voltage (Bank 2)
P0393	Exhaust camshaft position sensor circuit, high voltage (Bank 2)
P0420	Catalytic converter system low efficiency (Bank 1) - right side
P0430	Catalytic converter system low efficiency (Bank 2) - left side
P0442	Evaporative emission (EVAP) system small leak detected
P0443	Evaporative emission (EVAP) purge solenoid control circuit,
P0446	Evaporative emissions (EVAP) vent system performance problem
P0449	Evaporative emission (EVAP) vent solenoid control circuit,
P0450	Fuel tank pressure (FTP) sensor circuit
P0451	Fuel tank pressure (FTP) sensor performance problem
P0452	Fuel tank pressure (FTP) sensor circuit, low voltage
P0453	Fuel tank pressure (FTP) sensor circuit, high voltage
P0454	Fuel tank pressure (FTP) sensor intermittent
P0455	Evaporative emission (EVAP) system large leak detected
P0458	Evaporative emission (EVAP) purge solenoid control circuit, low voltage
P0459	Evaporative emission (EVAP) purge solenoid control circuit, high voltage
P0496	Evaporative emission system flow during non-purge
P0497	Evaporative emission (EVAP) system no flow during purge
P0498	Evaporative emission (EVAP) vent solenoid valve control circuit, low voltage
P0499	Evaporative emission (EVAP) vent solenoid valve control circuit, high voltage
P0506	Idle speed low
P0507	Idle speed high
P050A	Cold start idle air control system performance problem
P050D	Cold start rough idle

Code	Probable cause
P0601	Control module read only memory performance
P0602	Control module not programmed
P0603	Control module long term memory reset
P0604	Control module random access memory performance
P0606	Control module processor performance
P0607	Control module performance
P060D	Control module accelerator pedal position (APP) system circuitry, performance
P0627	Fuel pump enable circuit
P0628	Fuel pump enable circuit, low voltage
P0629	Fuel pump enable circuit, high voltage
P062B	Control module fuel injector control performance
P062F	Control module long term memory performance
P0630	VIN not programmed or mismatched - engine control module (ECM)
P0638	Throttle actuator control (TAC) command performance
P0641	5 volt reference 1 circuit
P0642	5 volt reference 1 circuit, low voltage
P0643	5 volt reference 1 circuit, high voltage
P064A	Fuel pump control module performance
P0650	Malfunction indicator lamp (MIL) control circuit,
P0651	5 volt reference 2 circuit
P0652	5 volt reference 2 circuit, low voltage
P0653	5 volt reference 2 circuit, high voltage
P0685	Engine controls ignition relay control circuit
P0686	Engine controls ignition relay control circuit, low voltage
P0687	Engine controls ignition relay control circuit, high voltage
P0689	Engine controls ignition relay feedback circuit, low voltage
P0690	Engine controls ignition relay feedback circuit, high voltage
P0697	5 volt reference 3 circuit
P0698	5 volt reference 3 circuit, low voltage
P0699	5 volt reference 3 circuit, high voltage

OBD-II trouble codes (continued)
Note: *Not all trouble codes apply to all models.*

Code	Probable cause
P069E	Fuel pump control module requested MIL illumination
P06A3	5 volt reference 4 circuit
P06A6	5 volt reference performance
P06B6	Control module knock sensor processor 1 performance problem
P06B7	Control module knock sensor processor 2 performance problem
P0700	Transmission control module (TCM) requested MIL illumination
P0856	Traction control torque request circuit

4   Accelerator Pedal Position (APP) sensor - replacement

Refer to illustration 4.2

1   Remove the knee bolster trim panel and the knee bolster (see Chapter 11, Section 24).
2   Disconnect the electrical connector from the upper end of the APP sensor assembly **(see illustration)**.
3   Remove the accelerator pedal/APP sensor assembly mounting nuts and remove the assembly.
4   Installation is the reverse of removal.

5   Camshaft Position (CMP) sensor(s) - replacement

1   Disconnect the cable from the negative battery terminal (see Chapter 5).

3.2L V6 models

Note: *The CMP sensor is located at the top corner of the valve cover, above the left end of the exhaust camshaft.*

2   Disconnect the CMP sensor electrical connector.
3   Remove the CMP sensor mounting bolt and remove the CMP sensor from the top of the valve cover.
4   Inspect the condition of the CMP sensor O-ring. If it's cracked, torn or deteriorated, replace it.
5   Installation is the reverse of removal.

All other V6 models

Refer to illustration 5.8

Note: *There are four CMP sensors, one for the intake camshaft and one for the exhaust on each cylinder head.*

6   If you're removing the CMP sensors from the right side (Bank 1), remove the air filter housing (see Chapter 4).
7   If you're removing the CMP sensors from the left side (Bank 2), remove the engine mount bracket (see Chapter 2B).
8   Disconnect the CMP sensor electrical connector **(see illustration)**.
9   Remove the CMP sensor mounting bolt and remove the CMP sensor.
10   Remove the CMP sensor O-ring and inspect its condition. If it's cracked, torn or otherwise deteriorated, replace it.
11   Lubricate the sensor O-ring with clean engine oil. Installation is otherwise the reverse of removal.

5.7L V8 models

Note: *The sensor is located at the rear of the cylinder block, between the two cylinder banks.*

12   Remove the intake manifold (see Chapter 2C).
13   Disconnect the CMP sensor electrical connector.
14   Remove the CMP sensor mounting bolt and remove the CMP sensor.
15   Remove the CMP sensor O-ring and

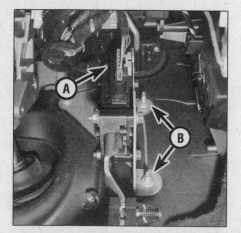

4.2 APP sensor electrical connector (A) and mounting nuts (B)

5.8 The CMP sensors are located at the front of each cylinder head (3.0L V6 engine shown, others similar)

1   *Intake camshaft position sensor (Bank 1)*
2   *Exhaust camshaft position sensor (Bank 1)*

6.8 CKP sensor location - on the right rear of engine (V6 engines shown)

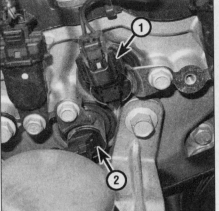

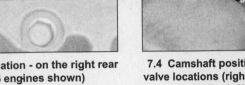

7.4 Camshaft position actuator solenoid valve locations (right side shown, left side [Bank 2] identical)

1   *Intake camshaft position actuator solenoid valve (Bank 1)*
2   *Exhaust camshaft position actuator solenoid valve (Bank 1)*

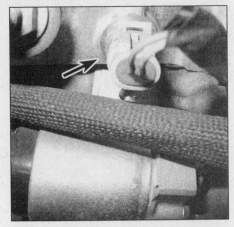

8.4 ECT sensor location (3.0L V6 engines)

inspect its condition. If it's cracked, torn or otherwise deteriorated, replace it.
16   Lubricate the sensor O-ring with clean engine oil. Installation is otherwise the reverse of removal.

6.0L and 6.2L V8 models
17   Remove the drivebelts and idler pulley (see Chapter 1).
18   Remove the crankshaft pulley/balancer (see Chapter 2C).
19   Remove the sensor and jumper harness assembly mounting bolts from the front cover.
20   Disconnect the engine harness electrical connector from the jumper harness connector, then disconnect the sensor from the jumper harness connector.
21   Remove the CMP sensor O-ring and inspect its condition. If it's cracked, torn or otherwise deteriorated, replace it.
22   Lubricate the sensor O-ring with clean engine oil. Installation is otherwise the reverse of removal.

6   Crankshaft Position (CKP) sensor - replacement

1   Disconnect the cable from the negative battery terminal (see Chapter 5).
2   Raise the front of the vehicle and support it securely on jackstands.

3.2L V6 engine models
3   The sensor is located at the left rear of the engine block. Remove the CKP sensor retaining bolt and remove the sensor.
4   Remove and inspect the sensor O-ring. If it's cut, torn or otherwise deteriorated, replace it.
5   Follow the harness to the top of the engine and disconnect the electrical connector from the CKP sensor.
6   Installation is otherwise the reverse of removal. **Note:** *From above, feed the sensor down through the engine, then install the sensor to the engine.*

All other models
Refer to illustration 6.8

7   On V8 models, remove the starter motor (see Chapter 5).
8   From under the right side of the vehicle, disconnect the electrical connector from the CKP sensor **(see illustration)**. **Note:** *On V6 models, remove the exhaust manifold heat shield for easier access to the sensor.*
9   Remove the CKP sensor mounting bolt and remove the CKP sensor.
10   Remove and inspect the sensor O-ring. If it's cut, torn or otherwise deteriorated, replace it.
11   Lubricate the sensor O-ring with clean engine oil. Installation is otherwise the reverse of removal.

7   Camshaft position actuator solenoid valve - replacement

Refer to illustration 7.4
Warning: *Wait until the engine has cooled completely before beginning this procedure.*
Note: *This Section applies to all V6 engines, except 3.2L models.*
1   Disconnect the cable from the negative battery terminal (see Chapter 5).
2   If you're removing the camshaft position actuator solenoid valve from the right side (Bank 1), remove the Engine Control Module (ECM) bracket.
3   If you're removing the camshaft position actuator solenoid valve from the left side (Bank 2), remove the power steering reservoir (see Chapter 10) but do not disconnect the lines.
4   Disconnect the solenoid valve electrical connector **(see illustration)**.

5   Remove the solenoid valve mounting bolt and remove the camshaft position actuator solenoid valve.
6   Remove the solenoid valve O-ring and inspect its condition. If it's cracked, torn or otherwise deteriorated, replace it.
7   Lubricate the O-ring with clean engine oil. Installation is otherwise the reverse of removal.

8   Engine Coolant Temperature (ECT) sensor - replacement

Warning: *Wait until the engine has cooled completely before beginning this procedure.*
1   Partially drain the engine coolant (see Chapter 1).
2   Disconnect the cable from the negative battery terminal (see Chapter 5).

Removal
3.0L V6 models
Refer to illustration 8.4
3   Remove the engine covers.
4   Disconnect the electrical connector from the ECT sensor located on the left rear cylinder head just above the starter **(see illustration)**.
5   Unscrew the sensor from the cylinder head.

3.2L V6 models
6   Remove the cowl panel (see Chapter 11) and the windshield wiper motor and linkage (see Chapter 12).
7   Disconnect the electrical connector from the ECT sensor.
8   Unscrew the sensor from the water cross over at the rear of the engine.

2.8L and 3.6L V6 models
9   Disconnect the electrical connector from the ECT sensor located on the left side cylinder head just behind the oil filter housing.
10   Unscrew the sensor from the cylinder head.

8.11 The ECT sensor on V8 engines is located on the side of the left cylinder head, near the front

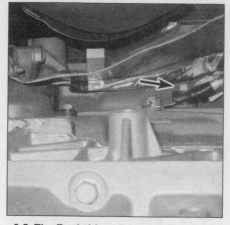

9.5 The Bank 1 knock sensor is located on the right side of the engine block (V6 engines)

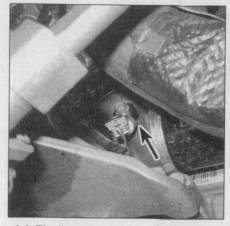

9.6 The Bank 2 knock sensor is located on the left side of the engine block, just in front of the starter (V6 engines)

V8 models

Refer to illustration 8.11

11   Disconnect the electrical connector from the ECT sensor (**see illustration**).
12   Unscrew the sensor from the cylinder head.

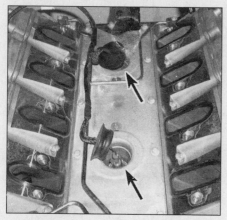

9.10 5.7L V8 engine knock sensor locations

10.2 The MAP sensor is located on top of the intake manifold (3.0L V6 engine shown)

Installation

13   Wrap the threads of the new sensor with Teflon tape to prevent leakage and thread corrosion.
14   Install the sensor and tighten it to the torque listed in this Chapter's Specifications.
15   Refill the cooling system (see Chapter 1).

9   Knock sensors - replacement

Removal

1   Disconnect the cable from the negative battery terminal (see Chapter 5).
2   Raise the vehicle and support it securely on jackstands. Remove the engine compartment under-cover.

V6 engines

Refer to illustrations 9.5 and 9.6

3   3.2L engines: To remove the Bank 1 knock sensor, remove the alternator (see Chapter 5).
4   3.2L engines: To remove the Bank 2 knock sensor, remove the power steering pump and bracket (see Chapter 10).
5   All other V6 engines: The Bank 1 knock sensor is located on the right side of the engine block, just below the exhaust manifold (**see illustration**).**Note:** *On late model V6 engines, it will be necessary to remove the right-side catalytic converter to access the knock sensor.*
6   All other V6 engines: The Bank 2 knock sensor is located on the left side of the engine block, just in front of the starter (**see illustration**).
7   Disconnect the electrical connector from the knock sensor.
8   Remove the bolt in the center of the knock sensor and remove the knock sensor.

5.7L V8 engines

Refer to illustration 9.10

9   Remove the intake manifold (see Chapter 2C).
10   Detach the grommets from the valley

cover, pull the grommets up and disconnect the electrical connectors from the knock sensors (**see illustration**). Remove the wiring harness.
11   Unscrew the knock sensors from the engine block.

6.0L and 6.2L V8 engines

12   The Bank 1 knock sensor is located on the left side of the engine block, just in front of the oil filter housing.
13   The Bank 2 knock sensor is located on the right side of the engine block, just in front of the starter.
14   Disconnect the electrical connector from the knock sensor.
15   Remove the bolt in the center of the knock sensor and remove the knock sensor.

Installation

16   Installation is the reverse of removal. Tighten the knock sensor bolt to the torque listed in this Chapter's Specifications.

10   Manifold Absolute Pressure (MAP) sensor - replacement

Refer to illustration 10.2

Note: *This Section applies to 2010 and later V6 models and 5.7L and 6.0L V8 models only.*
1   Disconnect the cable from the negative battery terminal (see Chapter 5).
2   Disconnect the electrical connector from the MAP sensor (**see illustration**).
3   Remove the MAP sensor retaining bolt and remove the sensor.
4   Installation is the reverse of removal.

11   Mass Air Flow/Intake Air Temperature (MAF/IAT) sensor - replacement

Refer to illustration 11.2

1   Remove the air intake duct (see Chapter 4, Section 10). **Note:** *On 2.8 and 3.6L V6 engines, the sensor is inside the duct mounted*

11.2 The MAF/IAT sensor is located on the air filter housing cover (3.0L V6 engine shown, other engines similar)

12.1 The BARO sensor is located on the air filter housing cover (3.0L V6 engine)

to the air filter housing and is replaced as a unit.

2   Disconnect the electrical connector from the MAF/IAT sensor **(see illustration)**.

3   Remove the MAF/IAT sensor mounting fasteners and remove the sensor from the air filter housing or duct.

4   Installation is the reverse of removal.

12   Barometric pressure (BARO) sensor - replacement

Refer to illustration 12.1

1   On 2007 and earlier 2.8L and 3.6L V6 models, and all 6.2L V8 engines, the sensor is located on the left side of the intake manifold. On 2010 and later 3.0L engines, the sensor is on top of the air filter housing **(see illustration)**.

2   Disconnect the electrical connector from the sensor.

3   Remove the sensor mounting fasteners and remove the sensor from the intake manifold/air filter housing.

4   Installation is the reverse of removal.

13   Oxygen sensors - replacement

Note: *Because it is installed in the exhaust manifold or pipe, both of which contract when cool, an oxygen sensor might be very difficult to loosen when the engine is cold. Rather than risk damage to the sensor or its mounting threads, start and run the engine for a minute or two, then shut it off. Be careful not to burn yourself during the following procedure.*

1   Be particularly careful when servicing an oxygen sensor:

a) *Oxygen sensors have a permanently attached pigtail and an electrical connector that cannot be removed. Damaging or removing the pigtail or electrical connector will render the sensor useless.*

13.4a Upstream oxygen sensor location (left cylinder bank exhaust manifold flange-to-converter pipe shown, right side similar) (3.0L V6 engine shown)

b) *Keep grease, dirt and other contaminants away from the electrical connector and the louvered end of the sensor.*

c) *Do not use cleaning solvents of any kind on an oxygen sensor.*

d) *Oxygen sensors are extremely delicate. Do not drop a sensor or handle it roughly.*

e) *Make sure that the silicone boot on the sensor is installed in the correct position. Otherwise, the boot might melt and it might prevent the sensor from operating correctly.*

Replacement

Refer to illustrations 13.4a, 13.4b and 13.5

Note: *This procedure applies to upstream and downstream sensors.*

Note: *The upstream sensors are installed in the exhaust manifolds, or upper part of the exhaust manifold flange and catalytic*

13.4b Downstream oxygen sensor locations (3.0L V6 engine shown, other engines similar)

converter assembly. There is an upstream sensor in each exhaust manifold on all models.

Note: *The downstream oxygen sensors are located in the lower end of the exhaust manifold/catalytic converter assembly or on the short section of exhaust pipe, just below the catalytic converter. There is a downstream oxygen sensor in each exhaust pipe on all models.*

2   Disconnect the cable from the negative battery terminal (see Chapter 5).

3   To access downstream sensors on all models, and the upstream sensor on the exhaust manifold for the rear cylinder head on V6 models, raise the front of the vehicle and support it securely on jackstands. Remove the engine under-cover.

4   Locate the oxygen sensor **(see illustrations)**, then trace the sensor's electrical lead to its electrical connector and disconnect the connector. Disengage any harness clips.

5   Using a wrench or an oxygen sensor

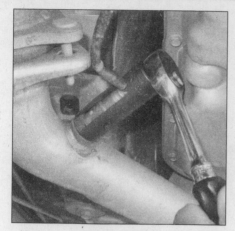

13.5 Use a slotted socket to remove the oxygen sensors

16.2 To release the PCM electrical connector harness locking tabs, pull the connector lever up and over

socket, unscrew the sensor **(see illustration)**.

6   If you're going to install the old sensor, apply anti-seize compound to the threads of the sensor to facilitate future removal. If you're going to install a new oxygen sensor, it's not necessary to apply anti-seize compound to the threads; the threads on new sensors already have anti-seize compound on them.

7   Installation is the reverse of removal. Tighten the oxygen sensor to the torque listed in this Chapter's Specifications.

14   Throttle Position (TP) sensor - replacement

The TP sensor is an integral component of the electronic throttle body, and is not separately serviceable. If you need to replace the TP sensor, you must replace the throttle body (see Chapter 4).

15   Vehicle Speed Sensor (VSS) - replacement

Manual transmission

Note: *The VSS is located on the right rear side of the transmission.*

1   Raise the vehicle and support it securely on jackstands. Remove the engine undercover.

2   Disconnect the electrical connector from the VSS.

3   Remove the VSS mounting bolt and remove the VSS.

4   Remove and discard the old VSS O-ring.

5   Installation is the reverse of removal; use a new O-ring.

Automatic transmission

6   The speed sensors on the automatic transmissions are internally mounted to the valve body and should not be replaced at home.

16   Powertrain Control Module (PCM) - removal and installation

Caution: *To avoid electrostatic discharge damage to the PCM, handle the PCM only by its case. Do not touch the electrical terminals during removal and installation. If available, ground yourself to the vehicle with an anti-static ground strap, available at computer supply stores.*

Note: *This procedure applies only to disconnecting, removing and installing the PCM that is already installed in your vehicle. If the PCM is defective and has to be replaced, it must be programmed with new software and calibrations. This procedure requires the use of GM's TECH-2 scan tool and GM's latest PCM-programming software, so you WILL NOT BE ABLE TO REPLACE THE PCM AT HOME.*

1   Disconnect the battery (see Chapter 5).

2007 and earlier V6 models

Refer to illustration 16.2

Note: *The PCM is mounted on the right side of the engine.*

2   Disconnect the two electrical connector locking tabs from the PCM **(see illustration)**.

3   Remove the PCM mounting bolts and remove the PCM.

4   Installation is the reverse of removal.

2008 and later V6 models and 6.2L V8 engine models

Refer to illustration 16.5

Note: *On 2008 and 2009 V6 models, the PCM is located on the right side of the vehicle, just below the power distribution box in the engine compartment.*

Note: *On 2010 and later V6 models, the PCM is located on the left side of the vehicle under the headlight housing.*

Note: *On 6.2L V8 models, the PCM is located on the right side of the vehicle in the engine compartment.*

5   Depress the tabs and slide the PCM out of the plastic holding bracket **(see illustration 16.2 and the accompanying illustration)**.

6   Disconnect the three electrical connector locking tabs from the PCM.

7   Installation is the reverse of removal.

5.7L and 6.0L V8 engine models

Note: *The PCM is located under the left side of the vehicle forward of the front wheel.*

8   Raise the vehicle and support it securely on jackstands. Remove the engine splash shield.

9   From under the left side of the engine compartment, remove the PCM cover fastener and push the outside cover back to release the retaining tab.

10   Rotate the cover to remove it. Remove the PCM housing.

11   Remove the screw in the center of the PCM connectors and disconnect the connector from the PCM

12   Installation is the reverse of removal.

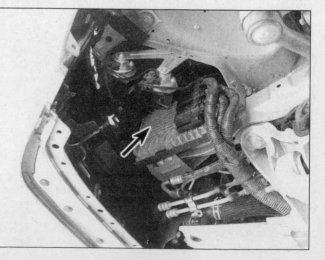

16.5 Powertrain Control Module (PCM) location (2010 and later 3.0L V6 engines)

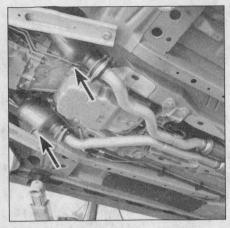

17.6 Catalytic converter locations

17   Catalytic converter - replacement

Refer to illustration 17.6

Warning: *Wait until the engine has cooled completely before beginning this procedure.*

1   Raise the front of the vehicle and support it securely on jackstands. Remove the engine under-cover.

2   Locate the upstream and downstream oxygen sensors, trace their electrical leads to their respective connectors and disconnect them. Remove both oxygen sensors (see Section 13).

3   If the catalytic converter and/or exhaust manifold is equipped with a heat shield, remove the heat shield bolts and remove the heat shield from the exhaust manifold.

4   Remove the fasteners that secure the heat shield mounting bracket and remove the bracket.

5   Remove the fasteners that secure the catalytic converter's upper mounting flange to the exhaust manifold. If the threads are severely damaged or rusted, apply some penetrant to the threads and wait awhile before loosening them.

6   Remove the fasteners that secure the lower mounting flange to the exhaust pipe **(see illustration)**. If the threads are severely damaged or rusted, apply some penetrant to the threads and wait awhile before loosening them.

7   Pull the exhaust pipe down far enough to clear the lower end of the catalytic converter.

8   Remove the catalytic converter from the exhaust manifolds.

9   Remove and discard the old gaskets between the exhaust manifold flange and the upper catalytic converter flange and, if equipped, between the lower catalytic converter flange and the exhaust pipe flange.

10   Installation is the reverse of removal. Use new flange gaskets.

18   Evaporative emissions control (EVAP) system - component replacement

Note: *See Chapter 4 for information on quick-connect fittings.*

1   Disconnect the cable from the negative battery terminal (see Chapter 5).

2   Open the fuel filler cap to relieve the fuel pressure in the tank.

3   Remove the engine covers.

EVAP canister purge valve

3.2L V6 engines

4   Disconnect the EVAP canister purge valve vacuum line from the top of the intake manifold.

5   Disconnect the coil pack electrical connector (see Chapter 5).

6   Disconnect the electrical connector from the canister purge valve.

7   Disconnect the EVAP line quick-connect fittings.

8   Remove the purge valve and mounting bracket as a single assembly, then remove the purge valve from the mounting bracket.

9   Installation is the reverse of removal.

All 2009 and earlier models except 3.2L V6 engines

10   Disconnect the purge line quick-connect fittings from the purge valve.

11   Disconnect the electrical connector from the canister purge valve.

12   Loosen the mounting bracket and remove the purge valve.

13   Installation is the reverse of removal.

2010 and later models

Refer to illustration 18.14

14   Disconnect the electrical connector from the canister purge valve **(see illustration)**.

15   Disconnect the EVAP line quick-connect fittings.

16   Remove the canister purge valve mounting bolt and remove the valve from the manifold.

17   Installation is the reverse of removal.

EVAP canister

Refer to illustration 18.20

Note: *The EVAP canister is located under the vehicle, above the rear suspension and subframe.*

18   Raise the vehicle and support it securely on jackstands.

19   Remove the rear subframe and suspension (see Chapter 10).

20   Disconnect the electrical connector and the vapor hose quick-connect fitting from the EVAP canister vent solenoid **(see illustration)**.

21   Disconnect the two EVAP line quick-connect fittings from the EVAP canister.

22   Remove the mounting fasteners that secure the canister and remove the canister.

23   Installation is the reverse of removal.

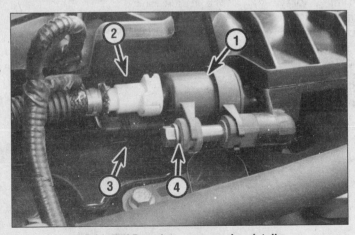

18.14 EVAP canister purge valve details (2010 and later V6 engines)

1   *EVAP canister purge valve*
2   *EVAP line quick-connect fitting*
3   *Electrical connector*
4   *Mounting bolt*

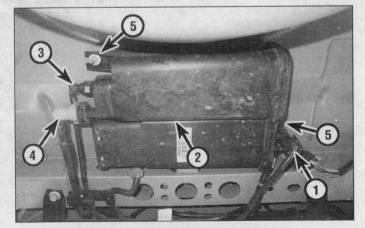

18.20 Typical EVAP canister details:

1   *EVAP canister vent solenoid electrical connector*
2   *EVAP canister*
3   *Quick-connect fitting*
4   *Quick-connect fitting*
5   *EVAP canister mounting nuts*

18.25 EVAP canister vent solenoid location

20.2 PCV hose layout (3.0L V6 engines)

1   PCV hose
2   PCV-to-intake manifold connection
3   PCV-to-valve cover connection

EVAP canister vent solenoid

Refer to illustration 18.24

24   Remove the rear subframe and suspension (see Chapter 10).
25   Disconnect the canister vent solenoid electrical connector **(see illustration)**.
26   Rotate the valve counterclockwise and remove the valve from the canister
27   Installation is the reverse of removal.

19   Intake manifold runner control solenoid (2008 and earlier V6 engines) - replacement

1   Disconnect the cable from the negative battery terminal (see Chapter 5).
2   Remove the plenum and intake manifold together (see Chapter 2B). **Caution:** *Do not separate the plenum for the manifold while the intake manifold runner control solenoid is removed or damage may occur to the runner control.*
3   Disconnect the electrical connector to the intake manifold runner control solenoid.
4   Remove the intake manifold runner control solenoid fasteners.
5   Slide the intake manifold runner control solenoid out of the manifold.
6   Installation is the reverse of removal.

20   Positive Crankcase Ventilation (PCV) hose - replacement

Refer to illustration 20.2
Note: *On all models, the PCV valve or orifice is mounted in the PCV hose. On 2.8L, 3.2L and 3.6L V6 engines, the PCV hoses are connected to the rear of each valve cover. On 3.0L V6 engines, the PCV hose is connected to the right rear valve cover only. On 5.7L V8 engines, the PCV hose is connected to the right rear valve cover. On 6.0L V8 engines, the PCV hoses are connected to the front of each valve cover. On 6.2L V8 engines, the PCV hoses are connected to the rear of the right valve cover and the front of the right valve cover.*
1   Remove the engine covers.
2   Disconnect the PCV hose(s) from the connections **(see illustration)**.
3   Installation is the reverse of removal.

21   Variable Valve Timing (VVT) system - description

1   The VVT system controls intake valve timing to increase engine torque in the low and mid-speed range and to increase horsepower in the high-speed range.

2   The VVT system consists of the PCM-controlled camshaft position actuator solenoid valves (see Section 7), which are mounted to the front of the cylinder heads and the VVT actuators (camshaft sprockets), mounted to the ends of the camshafts (see Chapter 2B).
3   The camshaft position actuator solenoid valve varies the oil pressure in the VVT actuator, which continually varies the timing of the intake and exhaust camshafts.
4   Refer to Chapter 2 for component replacement procedures for the VVT actuators.

22   Supercharger air pressure sensors (6.2L V8 engine) - replacement

1   The inlet pressure sensor is located on the right side of the charge air cooler cover. The outlet pressure sensor is located on the left side of the charge air cooler cover.
2   Disconnect the electrical connector from the pressure sensor.
3   Remove the sensor mounting fastener and remove the sensor from the cover.
4   Installation is the reverse of removal.

Chapter 7 Part A
Manual transmission

Contents

Specifications

General
Transmission oil type .... See Chapter 1
Transmission oil capacity .... See Chapter 1

Torque specifications

	Ft-lbs	Nm
Transmission-to-engine mounting bolts		
Getrag M35, 5-speed		
M10 x 1.5	37	50
M12 x 1.75	55	75
Aisin AY6, 6-speed	37	50
Tremec 6-speed	37	50
Transmission, drain and fill plug		
Getrag M35 5-speed	26	35
Aisin AY6 6-speed	27	37
Tremec 6-speed		
2008 and earlier	159 in-lbs	18
2009 and later	20	27
Crossmember-to-subframe bolts	141	191
Transmission rear mount bolts		
2007 and earlier models	44	60
2008 and later models	43	58
Transmission rear mount travel restrictor bolt (2008 and later models)	66	90
Transmission rear mount support-to-body bolts	60	40

1 General information

The vehicles covered by this manual are equipped with either a Getrag M35 5-speed manual, a Aisin AY6 6-speed manual, a Tremec 6-speed manual or a 5- or 6-speed automatic transmission. This Part of Chapter 7 contains information on the manual transmission. Service procedures for the automatic transmission are contained in Part B.

The transmission is contained in a cast-aluminum alloy casing bolted to the rear of the engine and gears are fully synchronized. All transmissions use control rods to shift the transmissions instead of shift cables. The transmission unit type is stamped on a plate attached to the transmission.

Transmission overhaul

Because of the complexity of the assembly, possible unavailability of replacement parts and special tools necessary, internal repair procedures for the transmission are not recommended for the home mechanic. The bulk of the information in this Chapter is devoted to removal and installation procedures.

2 Shift knob - removal and installation

1   Apply the parking brake. Place the shift lever in Neutral.
2   Using a trim tool, release the tabs around the shift console trim. Lift up the shifter trim panel with the shifter boot.
3   Disconnect any electrical connectors, then pull the shift knob (with boot and shifter trim panel) straight up and off. **Note:** *The knob is held in place by a blind clip and will require some effort to pull off.*
4   Installation is the reverse of removal.

3 Shift control assembly - removal and installation

Warning: *These models are equipped with a Supplemental Restraint System (SRS), more commonly known as airbags. Always disable the airbag system before working in the vicinity of any airbag system component to avoid the possibility of accidental deployment of the airbag(s), which could cause personal injury (see Chapter 12). Do not use a memory saving device to preserve the PCM or radio memory when working on or near airbag system components.*

1   Raise the front of the vehicle and support it securely on jackstands.
2   Remove the exhaust system (see Chapter 4).
3   Remove the driveshaft (see Chapter 8).
4   Support the transmission with an approved transmission jack and remove the

transmission support bolts (see Section 6).

5   Remove the shift knob (see Section 2).

6   Remove the floor center console (see Chapter 11).

2004 and earlier models

7   Lift up and remove the foam sound insulator.

8   Remove the transmission control rod mounting plate fasteners and plate.

9   Lower the rear of the transmission enough to access the top of the transmission.

10   Using a small screwdriver, pry the control rod pin retaining clips off and remove the clips.

11   Remove the two control rod pins and disconnect the rods from the transmission.

12   Remove the shift control rod assembly up and out of the vehicle through the access hole in the floor.

13   Installation is the reverse of removal.

2005 and later models

14   Remove the transmission control rod mounting plate fasteners and plate.

15   Lower the rear of the transmission enough to access the top of the transmission.

16   Using a small screwdriver, rotate the left side control rod pin retaining clips upwards and remove the clips. Rotate the right side control rod pin retaining clips downwards and remove the clips.

17   Using a small screwdriver, pry the center control rod pin retaining clips up and remove the clips.

18   Slide out the left and right side control rod pins, then slide out the center control rod pin.

19   Remove the shift control rod assembly by lifting it up and out of the vehicle through the access hole in the floor.

20   Installation is the reverse of removal. Lock the control rod pin clips in place.

---

4   Manual transmission - removal and installation

Removal

1   Turn the steering wheel so that the front wheels are facing straight and lock the steering wheel. **Caution:** *Damage to the clockspring may occur if the steering wheel is turned when the intermediate shaft is disconnected from the steering gear.*

2   Disconnect the battery (see Chapter 5).

3   Raise the front of the vehicle and support it securely on jackstands. Be sure you're able to raise the vehicle high enough so the transmission can be pulled out from under the vehicle. Sometimes, raising the rear of the vehicle as well provides greater safety, since the vehicle is level. Above all, make sure you have solid, safe support!

4   Remove the exhaust system (see Chapter 4).

5   Remove the driveshaft (see Chapter 8).

6   Disconnect the electrical connectors for the Vehicle Speed Sensor (VSS) and backup light switch.

7   Remove the clutch hydraulic line retaining clip to the release cylinder, pull the line out of the housing and plug the line. **Caution:** *Don't allow brake fluid to come into contact with the paint, as it will damage the finish.*

2004 and earlier models

Note: *This is a difficult procedure, requiring the use of a floor jack and a powertrain platform jack large enough to support loosening and lowering the vehicle front subframe, and/or a transmission jack.*

8   Remove both downstream oxygen sensors (see Chapter 6).

9   Support the transmission with an approved transmission jack and remove the transmission support bolts.

10   Lower the rear of the transmission enough to access the top of the transmission and remove the control rods (see Section 3).

11   Remove the intermediate shaft-to-steering gear retaining bolt and disconnect the shaft from the gear (see Chapter 10).

12   Using a floor jack, support the rear of the front subframe.

13   Loosen the front two subframe bolts, remove the rear two bolts, and lower the jack about 1-1/2 inches.

14   Remove the three upper engine-to-transmission mounting bolts and disconnect any wiring harness retaining clips.

15   Remove the remaining transmission-to-engine bolts.

16   Move the transmission away from the engine while slightly to the right to disengage it from the engine block dowel pins. Carefully lower the transmission jack to the floor and remove the transmission.

2005 and later models

17   Remove the shift knob (see Section 2) and the shift control rod assembly (see Section 3).

18   Support the transmission with an approved transmission jack.

19   Lower the rear of the transmission enough to remove the engine-to-transmission mounting bolts and disconnect any wiring harness retaining clips.

20   Move the transmission away to disengage it from the engine block dowel pins. Carefully lower the transmission jack to the floor and remove the transmission.

Installation

21   Lubricate the input shaft with a light coat of high-temperature grease. With the transmission secured to the jack, raise it into position behind the engine and carefully slide it forward, engaging the input shaft with the clutch. Do not use excessive force to install the transmission - if the input shaft won't slide into place, readjust the angle of the transmission or turn the input shaft so the splines engage properly with the clutch.

22   Once the transmission is flush with the engine, install the transmission-to-engine bolts. Tighten the bolts to the torque listed in this Chapter's Specifications. **Caution:** *Don't use the bolts to force the transmission and engine together.*

23   The remainder of installation is the reverse of removal, noting the following points:

a)   *Tighten the suspension crossmember mounting bolts to the torque values listed in this Chapter's Specifications.*

b)   *Lock the control rod pin retainers in place.*

c)   *Fill the transmission with the correct type and amount of transmission fluid as described in Chapter 1.*

d   *Fill and bleed the clutch system (see Chapter 8).*

---

5   Manual transmission overhaul - general information

1   Overhauling a manual transmission is a difficult job for the do-it-yourselfer. It involves the disassembly and reassembly of many small parts. Numerous clearances must be precisely measured and, if necessary, changed with select-fit spacers and snap-rings. As a result, if transmission problems arise, it can be removed and installed by a competent do-it-yourselfer, but overhaul should be left to a transmission repair shop. Rebuilt transmissions may be available - check with your dealer parts department and auto parts stores. At any rate, the time and money involved in an overhaul is almost sure to exceed the cost of a rebuilt unit.

2   Nevertheless, it's not impossible for an inexperienced mechanic to rebuild a transmission if the special tools are available and the job is done in a deliberate step-by-step manner so nothing is overlooked.

3   The tools necessary for an overhaul include internal and external snap-ring pliers, a bearing puller, a slide hammer, a set of pin punches, a dial indicator and possibly a hydraulic press. In addition, a large, sturdy workbench and a vise or transmission stand will be required.

4   During disassembly of the transmission, make careful notes of how each piece comes off, where it fits in relation to other pieces and what holds it in place.

5   Before taking the transmission apart for repair, it will help if you have some idea what area of the transmission is malfunctioning. Certain problems can be closely tied to specific areas in the transmission, which can make component examination and replacement easier. Refer to the "Troubleshooting" Section at the front of this manual for information regarding possible sources of trouble.

Chapter 7 Part B
Automatic transmission

Contents

Specifications

General

Fluid type and capacity .... See Chapter 1

Torque specifications

Ft-lbs (unless otherwise indicated)   Nm

Note: *One foot-pound (ft-lb) of torque is equivalent to 12 inch-pounds (in-lbs) of torque. Torque values below approximately 15 foot-pounds are expressed in inch-pounds, because most foot-pound torque wrenches are not accurate at these smaller values.*

	Ft-lbs (unless otherwise indicated)	Nm
Fluid pan bolts		
5L40-E and 5L50-E	97 in-lbs	11
6L50/6L80/6L90	80 in-lbs	9
Torque converter-to-driveplate nuts	46	63
Transmission-to-engine mounting bolts		
5L40-E and 5L50-E		
M10 x 1.5	37	50
M12 x 1.75	55	75
6L50/6L80/6L90	37	50

1 General information

All information on the automatic transmissions is included in this Part of Chapter 7. Information for the manual transmission can be found in Part A of this Chapter.

Because of the complexity of the automatic transmissions and the specialized equipment necessary to perform most service operations, this Chapter contains only those procedures related to general diagnosis, routine maintenance, adjustment and removal and installation.

If the transmission requires major repair work, it should be left to a dealer service department or an automotive or transmission repair shop. Once properly diagnosed you can, however, remove and install the transmission yourself and save the expense, even if the repair work is done by a transmission shop.

2 Diagnosis - general

1 Automatic transmission malfunctions may be caused by five general conditions:

a) *Poor engine performance*
b) *Improper adjustments*
c) *Hydraulic malfunctions*
d) *Mechanical malfunctions*
e) *Malfunctions in the computer or its signal network*

2   Diagnosis of these problems should always begin with a check of the easily repaired items: fluid level and condition (see Chapter 1), shift cable adjustment and shift lever installation. Next, perform a road test to determine if the problem has been corrected or if more diagnosis is necessary. If the problem persists after the preliminary tests and corrections are completed, additional diagnosis should be performed by a dealer service department or other qualified transmission repair shop. On modern electronically-controlled automatic transmissions, a scan tool is helpful in retrieving trouble codes relating to the transmission. Refer to the "Troubleshooting" Section at the front of this manual for information on symptoms of transmission problems.

Preliminary checks

3   Drive the vehicle to warm the transmission to normal operating temperature.
4   Check the fluid level as described in Chapter 1:

a) *If the fluid level is unusually low, add enough fluid to bring the level within the designated area of the dipstick, then check for external leaks (see following).*
b) *If the fluid level is abnormally high, drain off the excess, then check the drained fluid for contamination by coolant. The presence of engine coolant in the automatic transmission fluid indicates that a failure has occurred in the internal radiator oil cooler walls that separate the coolant from the transmission fluid (see Chapter 3).*
c) *If the fluid is foaming, drain it and refill the transmission, then check for coolant in the fluid, or a high fluid level.*

5   Check the engine idle speed. **Note:** *If the engine is malfunctioning, do not proceed with the preliminary checks until it has been repaired and runs normally.*
6   Check and adjust the shift cable, if necessary (see Section 4).
7   If hard shifting is experienced, inspect the shift cable under the steering column and at the manual lever on the transmission (see Section 4).

Fluid leak diagnosis

8   Most fluid leaks are easy to locate visually. Repair usually consists of replacing a seal or gasket. If a leak is difficult to find, the following procedure may help.
9   Identify the fluid. Make sure it's transmission fluid and not engine oil or brake fluid (automatic transmission fluid is a deep red color).
10   Try to pinpoint the source of the leak. Drive the vehicle several miles, then park it over a large sheet of cardboard. After a minute or two, you should be able to locate the leak by determining the source of the fluid dripping onto the cardboard.
11   Make a careful visual inspection of the

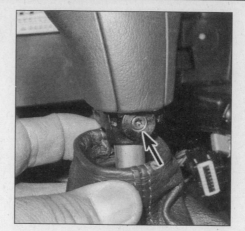

3.2 Pull down the shift boot, then remove the screw

suspected component and the area immediately around it. Pay particular attention to gasket mating surfaces. A mirror is often helpful for finding leaks in areas that are hard to see.
12   If the leak still cannot be found, clean the suspected area thoroughly with a degreaser or solvent, then dry it thoroughly.
13   Drive the vehicle for several miles at normal operating temperature and varying speeds. After driving the vehicle, visually inspect the suspected component again.
14   Once the leak has been located, the cause must be determined before it can be properly repaired. If a gasket is replaced but the sealing flange is bent, the new gasket will not stop the leak. The bent flange must be straightened.
15   Before attempting to repair a leak, check to make sure that the following conditions are corrected or they may cause another leak. **Note:** *Some of the following conditions cannot be fixed without highly specialized tools and expertise. Such problems must be referred to a qualified transmission shop or a dealer service department.*

Gasket leaks

16   Check the pan periodically. Make sure the bolts are tight, no bolts are missing, the gasket is in good condition and the pan is flat (dents in the pan may indicate damage to the valve body inside).
17   If the pan gasket is leaking, the fluid level or the fluid pressure may be too high, the vent may be plugged, the pan bolts may be too tight, the pan sealing flange may be warped, the sealing surface of the transmission housing may be damaged, the gasket may be damaged or the transmission casting may be cracked or porous. If sealant instead of gasket material has been used to form a seal between the pan and the transmission housing, it may be the wrong type of sealant.

Seal leaks

18   If a transmission seal is leaking, the fluid level or pressure may be too high, the vent may be plugged, the seal bore may be

damaged, the seal itself may be damaged or improperly installed, the surface of the shaft protruding through the seal may be damaged or a loose bearing may be causing excessive shaft movement.
19   Make sure the dipstick tube seal is in good condition and the tube is properly seated. Periodically check the area around the sensors for leakage. If transmission fluid is evident, check the seals for damage.

Case leaks

20   If the case itself appears to be leaking, the casting is porous and will have to be repaired or replaced.
21   Make sure the oil cooler hose fittings are tight and in good condition.

Fluid comes out vent pipe or fill tube

22   If this condition occurs the possible causes are: the transmission is overfilled; there is coolant in the fluid; the case is porous; the dipstick is incorrect; the vent is plugged or the drain-back holes are plugged.

---

3   Shift lever - replacement

Warning: *These models are equipped with a Supplemental Restraint System (SRS), more commonly known as airbags. Always disable the airbag system before working in the vicinity of any airbag system component to avoid the possibility of accidental deployment of the airbag(s), which could cause personal injury (see Chapter 12).*

Shift knob

Refer to illustration 3.2

1   Use a plastic trim tool to separate the shift boot from the shift knob.
2   Pull down the shift boot, then remove the screw in the knob assembly and remove the knob **(see illustration)**.
3   Installation is the reverse of the removal procedure.

Shift lever assembly

Refer to illustrations 3.9 and 3.10

4   Disconnect the cable from the negative battery terminal (see Chapter 5). Wait at least two minutes before proceeding. **Note:** *Prior to removal of the shift lever, check the adjustment of the shift linkage (see Section 4).*
5   Remove the shift knob (see Steps 1 and 2).
6   Using a plastic trim tool, carefully pry the tabs inwards at the base of the boot and remove the shift lever boot.
7   Remove the floor console (see Chapter 11).
8   Raise the front of the vehicle and support it securely on jackstands.
9   Remove the shift lever control linkage adjustment nut and separate the linkage rod from the shifter **(see illustration)**.

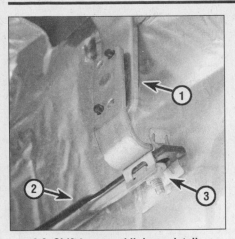

3.9 Shift lever and linkage details

1 Shift lever control linkage
2 Linkage rod
3 Adjustment nut

3.10 To remove the shifter assembly, remove the four mounting nuts

5.21a Remove the torque converter cover plug . . .

10 Disconnect any electrical connectors and remove the four mounting nuts **(see illustration)**. Remove the shift assembly from the floor.

11 Installation is the reverse of removal. The shift linkage should be adjusted anytime it has been disconnected (see Section 4).

---

4   Shift linkage - adjustment

1   Place the shifter in the Park position.

2   Raise the front of the vehicle and support it securely on jackstands.

3   Loosen the shift control linkage adjustment nut **(see illustration 3.9)** enough to allow the linkage rod to move.

4   Push the selector lever towards the stop (rear of the vehicle) and hold it in this position to prevent any play.

5   Tighten the shift control linkage adjustment nut securely.

6   Apply the parking brake, and operate the vehicle in each range to verify the adjustment is correct. If the linkage is difficult to shift or the vehicle does not start properly, adjust the linkage again.

---

5   Automatic transmission - removal and installation

Removal

1   Disconnect the battery (see Chapter 5).

2   Raise the front of the vehicle and support it securely on jackstands. Be sure you're able to raise the vehicle high enough so the transmission can be pulled out from under the vehicle. Sometimes, raising the rear of the vehicle as well provides greater safety, since the vehicle is level. Above all, make sure you have solid, safe support!

3   Remove the lower splash shield (see Chapter 1).

4   Remove the manual shift shaft nut, disconnect the linkage and manually place the transmission in Neutral. **Note:** *To place the transmission in the Neutral position, rotate the transmission shift shaft two clicks clockwise.*

5   Remove the exhaust system (see Chapter 4) and the bracket for the catalytic converter hanger.

6   Remove the driveshaft (see Chapter 8).

7   Disconnect the wiring harness to the transmission.

8   Place a drain pan under the transmission cooler lines and disconnect the lines from the transmission. Plug the cooler lines to prevent dirt getting into the lines.

2007 and earlier models (with the 5L40-E/L50-E transmissions)

9   On 3.6L engines, remove the thermostat (see Chapter 3) for access to the upper transmission-to-engine mounting bolts.

10   On 3.2L engines, remove the torque converter cover plug and mark the torque converter to the driveplate for installation.

11   On 3.2L engines, remove the torque converter bolt access plug just below the starter motor.

12   On 3.6L engines, remove the close out cover studs and cover and the starter motor (see Chapter 5) to access the torque converter bolts.

13   Remove the torque converter-to-driveplate bolts. At the front of the engine, place a socket and ratchet on the crankshaft center bolt, then rotate the engine to access and remove the remaining bolts.

14   Support the transmission with a jack - preferably a transmission jack made for this purpose (available at most tool rental yards). Safety chains will help steady the transmission on the jack. Remove the transmission support-to-body bolts.

15   Remove the transmission mount-to-support nuts and bolts and remove the support.

16   On 3.6L engines, use a floor jack to support the rear of the front subframe. With the jack supporting the subframe, loosen the rear

5.21b . . . and mark the relationship of the torque converter to the driveplate

two subframe bolts a few turns and lower the subframe enough to access and remove the three upper engine-to-transmission mounting bolts.

17   Lower the rear of the transmission and remove the engine-to-transmission mounting bolts, disconnecting any wiring harness retaining clips. Move the transmission away to disengage it from the engine block dowel pins. Carefully lower the transmission jack to the floor and remove the transmission.

2008 and later models (with the 6L50/6L80/6L90 transmissions)

Refer to illustrations 5.21a, 5.21b and 5.22

18   On 3.6L models, remove the thermostat housing (see Chapter 3) for access to the upper transmission-to-engine mounting bolts.

19   Disconnect the vent hose retaining clips and place the hose out of the way.

20   Remove the oxygen sensor wiring harness connector from the side of the transmission.

21   Remove the torque converter cover and mark the relationship of the torque converter to the driveplate **(see illustrations)**.

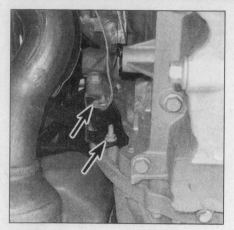

5.22 Remove the ground strap nut then remove the close out cover studs

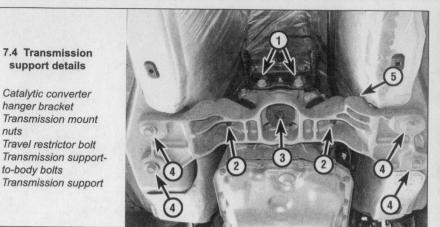

7.4 Transmission support details

1   *Catalytic converter hanger bracket*
2   *Transmission mount nuts*
3   *Travel restrictor bolt*
4   *Transmission support-to-body bolts*
5   *Transmission support*

22   Remove the ground strap nut, the close out cover studs **(see illustration)** and starter motor (see Chapter 5) to access the torque converter bolts. Remove the torque converter-to-driveplate bolts. Place a socket and ratchet on the crankshaft center bolt; then rotate the engine to access and remove the remaining converter bolts.
23   Support the transmission with a floorjack and remove the transmission mount-to-support nuts/bolts, then remove the support **(see illustration 7.4)**.
24   Lower the rear of the transmission enough to remove the engine-to-transmission mounting bolts and disconnect any wiring harness retaining clips. Move the transmission away to disengage it from the engine block dowel pins. Carefully lower the transmission jack to the floor and remove the transmission.

Installation

25   Installation of the transmission is a reversal of the removal procedure, but note the following points:

a) *As the torque converter is reinstalled, ensure that the drive tangs at the center of the torque converter hub engage with the recesses in the automatic transmission fluid pump inner gear. This can be confirmed by turning the torque converter while pushing it towards the trans-*
mission. If it isn't fully engaged, it will clunk into place.
b) *When installing the transmission, make sure the matchmarks you made on the torque converter and driveplate line up.*
c) *Install all of the driveplate-to-torque converter nuts before tightening any of them.*
d) *Tighten the driveplate-to-torque converter nuts to the specified torque.*
e) *Tighten the transmission mounting bolts to the specified torque.*
f) *Tighten the suspension crossmember mounting bolts to the torque values listed in this Chapter's Specifications.*
g) *Fill the transmission with the correct type and amount of fluid (see Chapter 1).*
h) *Adjust the shift linkage (see Section 4).*

6   Automatic transmission overhaul - general information

In the event of a problem occurring, it will be necessary to establish whether the fault is electrical, mechanical or hydraulic in nature, before repair work can be contemplated. Diagnosis requires detailed knowledge of the transmission's operation and construction, as well as access to specialized test equipment, and so is deemed to be beyond the scope of this manual. It is therefore essential that problems with the automatic transmission

are referred to a dealer service department or other qualified repair facility for assessment.

Note that a faulty transmission should not be removed before the vehicle has been diagnosed by a knowledgeable technician equipped with the proper tools, as troubleshooting must be performed with the transmission installed in the vehicle.

7   Transmission mount - replacement

Refer to illustration 7.4

1   Raise the front of the vehicle and support it securely on jackstands.
2   Insert a large screwdriver or prybar between the mount and the transmission and pry up.
3   The transmission should not move excessively away from the mount. If it does, replace the mount.
4   Support the transmission with a floorjack and remove the transmission support bolts **(see illustration)**.
5   Remove the mount travel restrictor bolt, if equipped.
6   Remove the mount-to-transmission support nuts/bolts and remove the mount. **Note:** *2008 and later model use two individual transmission mounts that are replaced separately.*
7   Installation is the reverse of removal.

Chapter 8
Clutch and driveline

Contents

Specifications

Clutch fluid type .... See Chapter 1

Torque specifications

Ft-lbs (unless otherwise indicated) **Nm**

Note: *One foot-pound (ft-lb) of torque is equivalent to 12 inch-pounds (in-lbs) of torque. Torque values below approximately 15 foot-pounds are expressed in inch-pounds, because most foot-pound torque wrenches are not accurate at these smaller values.*

Clutch

2007 and earlier models

	Ft-lbs	Nm
Clutch pressure plate-to-flywheel bolts	21	28
Clutch release cylinder mounting bolt	15	20
Clutch fluid reservoir mounting bolt	27	36

2008 through 2012 models (except 2012 CTS-V)

Clutch pressure plate-to-flywheel bolts (in sequence - **see illustration 6.18**)

	Ft-lbs	Nm
Step 1	132 in-lbs	15
Step 2	22	30
Step 3	33	45
Step 4 (bolts 1, 2 and 3)	Loosen 180-degrees	
Step 5 (bolts 1, 2 and 3)	22	30
Step 6 (bolts 1, 2 and 3)	Tighten an additional 20-degrees	
Step 7 (bolts 4, 5 and 6)	Loosen 180-degrees	
Step 8 (bolts 4, 5 and 6)	22	30
Step 9 (bolts 4, 5 and 6)	Tighten an additional 20-degrees	

2012 CTS-V and all 2013 and later models

Clutch pressure plate-to-flywheel bolts (in sequence **see illustration 6.18b)***

	Ft-lbs	Nm
Step 1 bolts 1 and 2	Finger tight	
Step 2 bolts 1 and 2	Tighten an additional 360 degrees	
Step 3 bolts 3 and 4	Finger tight	
Step 4 bolts 3 and 4	Tighten an additional 360 degrees	
Step 5 bolts 5 and 6	Finger tight	
Step 6 bolts 5 and 6	Tighten an additional 360 degrees	
Step 7 bolts 1 and 2	Tighten an additional 360 degrees	
Step 8 bolts 3 and 4	Tighten an additional 360 degrees	
Step 9 bolts 5 and 6	Tighten an additional 360 degrees	
Step 10 repeat Steps 7, 8 and 9 until the pressure plate is flat against the flywheel		
Step 11 remove the clutch alignment tool		
Step 12 follow the correct sequence and torque the bolts	52	70
Clutch release cylinder mounting bolts	15	20
Clutch release cylinder quick-disconnect line bolt	89 in-lbs	10

• *Use new bolts*

Torque specifications

Note: *One foot-pound (ft-lb) of torque is equivalent to 12 inch-pounds (in-lbs) of torque. Torque values below approximately 15 foot-pounds are expressed in inch-pounds, because most foot-pound torque wrenches are not accurate at these smaller values.*

	Ft-lbs (unless otherwise indicated)	Nm
Rear differential		
Differential cover bolts	21	29
Differential mounting bracket bolts	21	29
Differential mounting front bolts	129	175
Differential mounting rear nut	162	220
Drain and filler plug		
2003 through 2012	29	39
2013 and later	17	23
Differential pinion nut	181	245
Driveaxles		
Driveaxle/hub nut		
2007 and earlier models	118	160
2008 and later models	158	215
Inner joint-to-stub shaft bolts (2008 and later models)	59	80
Driveshafts		
Driveshaft rubber coupler-to-flange bolts	63	85
Driveshaft rubber coupler flange-to-transmission/differential bolts	63	85
Driveshaft center support bearing nuts	37	50
Driveshaft heat shield fasteners	71 in-lbs	8

1   General information

The information in this Chapter deals with the components from the rear of the engine to the rear drive wheels.

Since nearly all the procedures covered in this Chapter involve working under the vehicle, make sure it's securely supported on sturdy jackstands or on a hoist where the vehicle can be easily raised and lowered.

2   Clutch - description and check

1   All vehicles with a manual transmission have a single dry plate, diaphragm spring-type clutch. The clutch disc has a splined hub which allows it to slide along the splines of the transmission input shaft. The clutch and pressure plate are held in contact by spring pressure exerted by the diaphragm in the pressure plate.

2   The clutch release system is operated by hydraulic pressure. The hydraulic release system consists of the clutch pedal, a master cylinder with a remote reservoir, a release (or slave) cylinder that is mounted to the front of the transmission and incorporates the release bearing and the hydraulic line connecting the two components.

3   When the clutch pedal is depressed, a pushrod pushes against brake fluid inside the master cylinder, applying hydraulic pressure to the release cylinder, which pushes the release bearing against the diaphragm fingers of the clutch pressure plate.

4   Terminology can be a problem when discussing the clutch components because common names are in some cases different from those used by the manufacturer. For example, the driven plate is also called the clutch plate or disc, the clutch release bearing is sometimes called a throwout bearing, the release cylinder is sometimes called the slave cylinder.

5   Unless you're replacing components with obvious damage, perform these preliminary checks to diagnose clutch problems:

a) *The first check should be of the fluid level in the clutch master cylinder. If the fluid level is low, add fluid as necessary and inspect the hydraulic system for leaks. If the master cylinder reservoir is dry, bleed the system as described in Section 5 and recheck the clutch operation.*

b) *To check clutch spin-down time, run the engine at normal idle speed with the transmission in Neutral (clutch pedal up - engaged). Disengage the clutch (pedal down), wait several seconds and shift the transmission into Reverse. No grinding noise should be heard. A grinding noise would most likely indicate a bad pressure plate or clutch disc.*

c) *To check for complete clutch release, run the engine (with the parking brake applied to prevent vehicle movement) and hold the clutch pedal approximately 1/2-inch from the floor. Shift the transmission between 1st gear and Reverse several times. If the shift is rough, component failure is indicated.*

d) *Visually inspect the pivot bushing at the top of the clutch pedal to make sure there's no binding or excessive play.*

3   Clutch master cylinder - removal and installation

Removal

1   Remove the driver's side insulation panel (see Chapter 11).

2   Disconnect the clutch pedal position sensor electrical connector.

3   Using a small screwdriver, disconnect the master cylinder pushrod from the clutch pedal pin.

4   Remove the clutch reservoir mounting bolt and remove reservoir from the fender.

5   Remove the expansion tank mounting fasteners (see Chapter 3) and set the expansion tank to the side.

6   On 2008 and later models, remove the power brake booster (see Chapter 9).

7   Clamp a pair of locking pliers onto the

clutch fluid feed hose, a couple of inches downstream of the brake fluid reservoir (the clutch master cylinder is supplied with fluid from the clutch fluid reservoir). The pliers should be just tight enough to prevent fluid flow when the hose is disconnected. Pull the hydraulic clutch line retaining clip up from the clutch master and remove the clutch hose. **Caution:** *Don't allow brake fluid to come into contact with the paint, as it will damage the finish.*

8   Rotate the clutch master cylinder clockwise 1/8-turn and pull the cylinder from the firewall.

Installation

9   Place the master cylinder with the connection of the fluid reservoir pointing at the two o'clock position, then insert the cylinder in firewall aligning the slots on the clutch master with the tabs on the clutch pedal bracket.

10   Seat the clutch master cylinder to the firewall by rotating the cylinder 1/8-turn counterclockwise. **Note:** *The master cylinder reservoir connection should be facing the twelve o'clock position when properly seated.*

11   Connect the hydraulic line fitting to the clutch master cylinder and insert the locking pin.

12   Attach the fluid feed hose from the reservoir to the clutch master cylinder. Remove the locking pliers.

13   Install the clutch reservoir and tighten the mounting bolt securely.

14   Working under the dash, push the pushrod on to the clutch pedal pin and connect the clutch pedal position sensor electrical connector.

15   Fill the reservoir with brake fluid conforming to DOT 3 specifications and bleed the clutch system (see Section 5).

16   Installation is the reverse of removal.

---

4   Clutch release cylinder - removal and installation

Removal

Note: *The release bearing and release cylinder are an assembly and can't be replaced separately.*

1   Remove the transmission (see Chapter 7A).

2   Remove the release cylinder quick-disconnect line bolt.

3   Remove the release cylinder mounting bolts.

4   Remove the release cylinder assembly and O-ring.

Installation

5   Install a new O-ring then install the release cylinder, making sure the quick disconnect line lock into place.

6   Install the release cylinder mounting bolts and tighten them to the torque listed in this Chapter's Specifications.

7   Install the release cylinder quick-discon-

nect bolt and tighten it to the torque listed in this Chapter's Specifications.

8   Install the transmission (see Chapter 7A).

9   Check the fluid level in the brake fluid reservoir, adding brake fluid conforming to DOT 3 specifications until the level is correct.

10   Bleed the system (see Section 5), then recheck the brake fluid level.

---

5   Clutch hydraulic system - bleeding

1   Bleed the hydraulic system whenever any part of the system has been removed or the fluid level has fallen so low that air has been drawn into the master cylinder. The bleeding procedure is very similar to bleeding a brake system.

2   Fill the brake master cylinder reservoir with new brake fluid conforming to DOT 3 specifications. **Caution:** *Do not re-use any of the fluid coming from the system during the bleeding operation or use fluid which has been inside an open container for an extended period of time.*

3   Have an assistant depress the clutch pedal and hold it. Open the bleeder valve on the release cylinder, allowing fluid and any air to escape. Close the bleeder valve when the flow of fluid (and bubbles) ceases. Once closed, have your assistant release the pedal.

4   Continue this process until all air is evacuated from the system, indicated by a solid stream of fluid being ejected from the bleeder valve each time with no air bubbles. Keep a close watch on the fluid level inside the brake master cylinder reservoir - if the level drops too far, air will get into the system and you'll have to start all over again. **Note:** *Wash the area with water to remove any excess brake fluid.*

5   Check the brake fluid level again, and add some, if necessary, to bring it to the appropriate level. Check carefully for proper operation before placing the vehicle into normal service.

---

6   Clutch components - removal, inspection and installation

Warning: *Dust produced by clutch wear is hazardous to your health. DO NOT blow it out with compressed air and DO NOT inhale it. DO NOT use gasoline or petroleum-based solvents to remove the dust. Brake system cleaner should be used to flush the dust into a drain pan. After the clutch components are wiped clean with a rag, dispose of the contaminated rags and cleaner in a covered, marked container.*

Removal

Refer to illustration 6.5

1   Access to the clutch components is normally accomplished by removing the trans-

6.5 Mark the relationship of the pressure plate to the flywheel (if you're planning to re-use the old pressure plate)

mission, leaving the engine in the vehicle. If the engine is being removed for major overhaul, check the clutch for wear and replace worn components as necessary. However, the relatively low cost of the clutch components compared to the time and trouble spent gaining access to them warrants their replacement anytime the engine or transmission is removed, unless they are new or in near-perfect condition. The following procedures are based on the assumption the engine will stay in place.

2   Remove the transmission from the vehicle (see Chapter 7A). Support the engine while the transmission is out. An engine support fixture or a hoist should be used to support it from above.

3   The clutch release cylinder assembly can remain attached to the transmission for the time being.

4   To support the clutch disc during removal, install a clutch alignment tool through the clutch disc hub.

5   Carefully inspect the flywheel and pressure plate for indexing marks. The marks are usually an X, an O or a white letter. If they cannot be found, scribe or paint marks yourself so the pressure plate and the flywheel will be in the same alignment during installation **(see illustration)**.

6   Turning each bolt a little at a time, loosen the pressure plate-to-flywheel bolts. Work in a criss-cross pattern until all spring pressure is relieved. Then hold the pressure plate securely and completely remove the bolts, followed by the pressure plate and clutch disc.

Inspection

Refer to illustrations 6.9, 6.11a and 6.11b

7   Ordinarily, when a problem occurs in the clutch, it can be attributed to wear of the clutch driven plate assembly (clutch disc). However, all components should be inspected at this time.

8   Inspect the flywheel for cracks, heat checking, grooves and other obvious defects. If the imperfections are slight, a machine shop can machine the surface flat and smooth, which is highly recommended regardless of the surface appearance. Refer to Chapter 2 for the flywheel removal and installation procedure.

9   Inspect the lining on the clutch disc. There should be at least 1/16-inch of lining above the rivet heads. Check for loose rivets, distortion, cracks, broken springs and other obvious damage **(see illustration)**. As mentioned above, ordinarily the clutch disc is routinely replaced, so if in doubt about the condition, replace it with a new one.

10   The release cylinder assembly should also be replaced along with the clutch disc (see Section 4).

11   Check the machined surfaces and the diaphragm spring fingers of the pressure plate **(see illustrations)**. If the surface is grooved or otherwise damaged, replace the pressure plate. Also check for obvious damage, distortion, cracking, etc. Light glazing can be removed with emery cloth or sandpaper. If a new pressure plate is required, new and re-manufactured units are available.

12   Check the pilot bushing in the end of the crankshaft for excessive wear, scoring, dryness, roughness and any other obvious damage. If any of these conditions are noted,

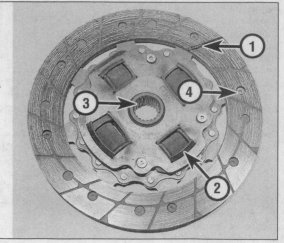

6.9 The clutch disc

1   **Lining** - this will wear down in use
2   **Springs or dampers** - check for cracking and deformation
3   **Splined hub** - the splines must not be worn and should slide smoothly on the transmission input shaft splines
4   **Rivets** - these secure the lining and will damage the flywheel or pressure plate if allowed to contact the surfaces

replace the bushing (see Section 7).

13   Removal can be accomplished with a slide hammer and puller attachment, which are available at most auto parts stores or tool rental yards.

Installation

Refer to illustration 6.16, 6.18a and 6.18b

14   Install the flywheel (see Chapter 2).

15   Before installation, clean the flywheel and pressure plate machined surfaces with

brake cleaner, lacquer thinner or acetone. It's important that no oil or grease is on these surfaces or the lining of the clutch disc. Handle the parts only with clean hands.

16   Position the clutch disc and pressure plate against the flywheel with the clutch held in place with an alignment tool **(see illustration)**. Make sure the disc is installed properly (most replacement clutch discs will be marked "flywheel side" or something similar - if not marked, install the clutch disc with the damper springs toward the transmission).

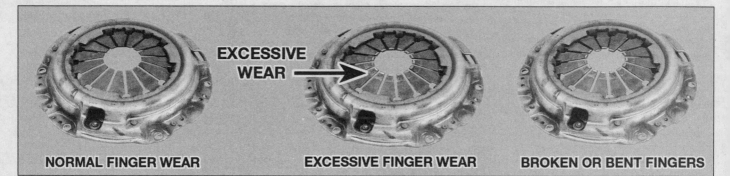

NORMAL FINGER WEAR   **EXCESSIVE WEAR** →   **EXCESSIVE FINGER WEAR**   **BROKEN OR BENT FINGERS**

6.11a Replace the pressure plate if excessive wear or damage are noted

6.11b Inspect the pressure plate surface for excessive score marks, cracks and signs of overheating

6.16 Center the clutch disc in the pressure plate with a clutch alignment tool

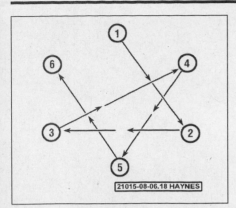

6.18a Clutch pressure plate-to-flywheel bolt tightening sequence (2012 and earlier except 2012 CTS-V)

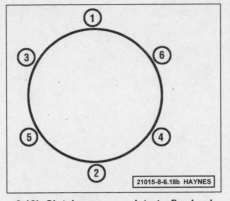

6.18b Clutch pressure plate-to-flywheel bolt tightening sequence (2012 CTS-V and all 2013 and later models)

7.5 A small slide-hammer is handy for removing the pilot bushing

17   Tighten the pressure plate-to-flywheel bolts only finger tight, working around the pressure plate.

18   Center the clutch disc by ensuring the alignment tool extends through the splined hub and into the pilot bearing in the crankshaft. Wiggle the tool up, down or side-to-side as needed to center the disc. Tighten the pressure plate-to-flywheel bolts a little at a time, working in a criss-cross pattern to prevent distorting the cover. After all of the bolts are snug, tighten them in sequence **(see illustrations)** and to the torque listed in this Chapter's Specifications. Remove the alignment tool.

19   Using high-temperature grease, place a small amount of grease on the release lever contact areas and the transmission input shaft bearing retainer.

20   If removed, install the clutch release cylinder assembly (see Section 4).

21   Install the transmission and all components removed previously.

7   Pilot bushing - replacement

Caution: *There is a steel plug directly behind the pilot bushing that seals pressurized oil in the crankshaft. Be extremely careful not to dislodge this plug during removal and installa-* *tion of the pilot bushing.*

1   The clutch pilot bushing is an oil-impregnated type bush which is pressed into the rear of the crankshaft. Its purpose is to support the front of the transmission input shaft. It should be inspected whenever the clutch components are removed from the engine. Due to its inaccessibility, if you are in doubt as to its condition, replace it. **Note:** *If the engine has been removed from the vehicle, disregard the following steps which don't apply.*

2   Remove the transmission (see Chapter 7A).

3   Remove the clutch components (see Section 6).

4   Inspect for any excessive wear, scoring, lack of grease, dryness or obvious damage. If any of these conditions are noted, the bushing should be replaced. A flashlight will be helpful to direct light into the recess.

5   Removal can be accomplished with a small slide-hammer and puller attachment, which are available at auto parts stores and tool supply outlets **(see illustration)**.

6   Once the bushing is removed, clean the bore and the area behind it, in the crankshaft recess. Carefully inspect for any signs of oil leakage from the plug in the crankshaft.

7   To install a new pilot bushing, lightly lubricate the outside surface with lithium-

based grease, then drive it into the recess with a hammer and a bushing driver or socket **(see illustration)**. Most new bushings come already lubricated, but, if it is dry, apply a thin coat of high-temperature grease to it.

8   Install the clutch components, transmission and all other components removed previously, tightening all fasteners securely.

8   Driveshaft - removal and installation

Refer to illustrations 8.3, 8.4a, 8.4b and 8.7

Warning: *There two types of driveshaft coupler flange bolts used. The first design bolts are completely threaded and the second design has a shoulder and threads half way up the bolt. The first design must be replaced with the second design any time the coupler bolts are removed. If the first design is reused, damage to the driveshaft shaft couplers may occur.*

1   Raise the vehicle and support it securely on jackstands. Place the shift lever in Neutral.

2   Remove the exhaust pipes and mufflers (see Chapter 4).

3   Remove the heat shield from the driveshaft tunnel insulator **(see illustration)**.

4   Use chalk or a scribe to mark the rela-

7.7 Tap the bushing into place with a bushing driver or a socket that is slightly smaller than the outside diameter of the bushing

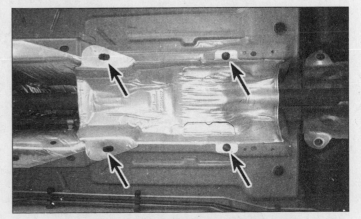

8.3 Remove the heat shield mounting fasteners

8.4a Mark the rear driveshaft and coupler to the pinion yoke

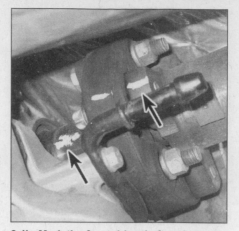

8.4b Mark the front driveshaft and coupler to the transmission yoke

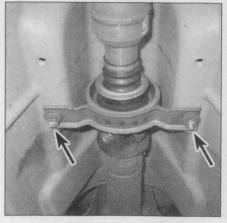

8.7 Center support bearing mounting fasteners

tionship of the driveshaft couplers to the differential pinion yoke and the transmission **(see illustrations)**. This ensures correct alignment when the driveshaft is reinstalled.

5 Remove the bolts securing the driveshaft rear couplers to the differential pinion yoke.

6 Working at the front of the driveshaft, remove the bolts securing the driveshaft couplers to the transmission.

7 Remove the bolts securing the center support bearings **(see illustration)**. **Caution:** *Some models are equipped with shims or rubber spacers between the mounting bracket and center support bearing that must be reused to maintain proper driveshaft angle.*

8 With help from an assistant, carefully remove the driveshaft from the vehicle.

9 Installation is the reverse of removal. Make sure the universal joint caps are properly placed in the flange seat. Tighten the fasteners to the torque listed in this Chapter's Specifications.

9   Rear driveaxles - removal and installation

Warning: *Wait until the engine is completely cool before beginning this procedure.*

Removal

Refer to illustrations 9.2 and 9.8

1 Block the front wheels to prevent the vehicle from rolling. Loosen the wheel lug nuts, raise the rear of the vehicle and support it securely on jackstands. Remove the wheels.

2 Break the driveaxle/hub nut loose with a socket and large breaker bar **(see illustration)**.

3 Remove and discard the driveaxle/hub nut, then push the driveaxle in slightly.

4 Disconnect the ABS sensor electrical connector and remove the parking brake cable bracket fasteners and bracket.

5 While supporting the lower control arm with a jack, unbolt the upper arm from the

steering knuckle, the trailing arm, tie-rod and the shock absorber lower bolt.

6 Unbolt the stabilizer link end from the lower control arm.

7 On 2007 and earlier models, carefully pry the inner end of the driveaxle out of the differential. **Caution:** *The driveaxle oil seals can be easily damaged when removing the driveaxle.* **Caution:** *Take care not to damage the differential seal with the driveaxle splines. It is recommended to use a plastic seal protector (manufacturer tool #J-44394-A).*

8 On 2008 and later models, mark the relationship of the inner joint to the stub shaft **(see illustration)**. Remove the mounting bolts and spacers and pry the inner end of the driveaxle out of the stub shafts.

9 Push the driveaxle out of the hub. If the driveaxle splines are frozen, free them by tapping the end of the driveaxle with a soft-faced hammer or a hammer and brass punch, or use a puller to push the driveaxle out of the hub and remove the driveaxle.

Installation

10 On 2007 and earlier models, apply a light film of grease to the area on the inner CV joint

stub shaft where the seal rides, then insert the splined end of the inner CV joint into the differential. Make sure the spring clip locks in its groove. **Caution:** *Take care not to damage the differential seal with the driveaxle splines. It is recommended to use a plastic seal protector (manufacturer tool #J-44394-A).*

11 Apply a light film of grease to the outer CV joint splines, pry the knuckle and insert the outer end of the driveaxle into the hub.

12 On 2008 and later models, set the inner joint of the driveaxle onto the stub shaft, align the marks, then install the spacers and bolts. Tighten the driveaxle inner joint bolts to the torque listed in this Chapter's Specifications

13 The remainder of installation is the reverse of removal.

14 Install a ***new*** driveaxle/hub nut. Tighten the hub nut securely, but don't try to tighten it to the actual torque specification until the vehicle has been lowered to the ground.

15 Install the wheel and lug nuts, then lower the vehicle. Tighten the lug nuts to the torque listed in the Chapter 1 Specifications.

16 Tighten the driveaxle/hub nut to the torque listed in this Chapter's Specifications. Install the wheel cover or hub cap.

9.2 Place a prybar between two wheel studs while you loosen the driveaxle nut

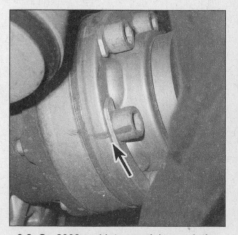

9.8 On 2008 and later models, mark the relationship between the inner joint and the stub shaft

10   Rear driveaxle boot - replacement

1   Remove the driveaxle (see Section 9).
2   Mount the driveaxle in a vise. The jaws of the vise should be lined with wood or rags to prevent damage to the driveaxle.

All outer CV joint boots and 2007 and earlier inner CV joint boots

Removal

3   Remove the boot clamps.
4   If equipped, cut the swage ring off using side cutters **Note:** *2007 and earlier models are equipped with a swage ring that must be pressed in place using manufacturer tool #J-41048 or equivalent. If this tool is unavailable, take the driveaxle to a machine shop to have the ring pressed on to the CV joint.*
5   Slide the boot back to access the outer joint retaining snap-ring.
6   Using snap-ring pliers, spread open the retaining snap ring and slide the CV joint boot off the axleshaft.

Inspection

7   Thoroughly clean all components with solvent until the old grease is completely removed. Inspect the bearing surfaces of the chrome alloy balls and joint cage for cracks, pitting, scoring, and other signs of wear. If any part of the CV joint is worn, you must replace the entire driveaxle assembly (inner CV joint, axleshaft and outer CV joint).

Installation

Refer to illustrations 10.12a, 10.12b, 10.12c and 10.15

8   Install a new clamp or new swage ring onto the outer end of the sealing boot and slide the sealing boot onto the axleshaft.
9   Push the boot on until the end of the boot rests over the third groove in the axleshaft.
10   Using manufacturer tool #J-41048 or equivalent, compress the swage ring, if

10.12a Pack the outer CV joint assembly with CV grease . . .

10.12b . . . then apply grease to the inside of the boot . . .

equipped.
11   Install a new snap-ring and bearing retainer clip onto the axleshaft.
12   Place half the grease provided in the sealing boot kit into the outer CV joint assembly housing **(see illustration)**. Put the remaining grease into the sealing boot **(see illustrations)**.
13   Align the splines on the axleshaft with the splines on the CV joint assembly and, using a soft-faced hammer, gently drive the CV joint onto the axleshaft until the CV joint is seated to the axleshaft.
14   Position the CV joint mid-way through its travel, then equalize the pressure in the boot.
15   Tighten the boot clamps **(see illustration)**.
16   Install the driveaxle (see Section 9).

2008 and later inner CV joint boots

Removal

17   Cut off the boot clamps.
18   Using a hammer and brass punch, carefully drive the end cap off of the CV joint.
19   Clean the face of the joint and remove

the snap ring using snap ring pliers.
20   Slide the boot back and use a hammer and brass punch or drift to drive the inner joint off of the axleshaft.
21   Slide the boot off of the axleshaft.
22   Using snap-ring pliers, spread open the retaining snap ring and slide the CV joint boot off the axleshaft.

Inspection

23   Clean the old grease from the outer race and the tri-pod bearing assembly. Carefully disassemble each section of the tri-pod assembly, one at a time so as not to mix up the parts. Clean the needle bearings with solvent.
24   Inspect the rollers, tri-pod, bearings and outer race for scoring, pitting or other signs of abnormal wear, which will warrant the replacement of the inner CV joint.

Installation

25   Slide the clamps and boot onto the axleshaft. It's a good idea to wrap the axleshaft splines with tape to prevent damaging the boot.
26   Place the tri-pod inside of the joint housing and slide the joint on the shaft.

10.12c . . . until the level is up to the end of the axle

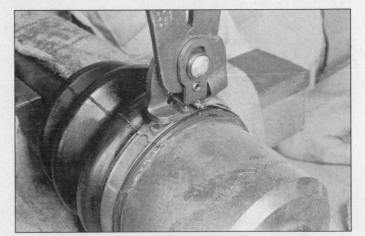

10.15 To install crimp-type boot clamps, you'll need a pair of special crimping pliers (available at most auto parts stores)

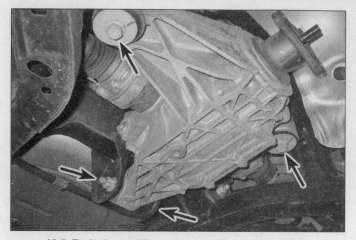

12.5 Typical rear differential mounting bolt locations

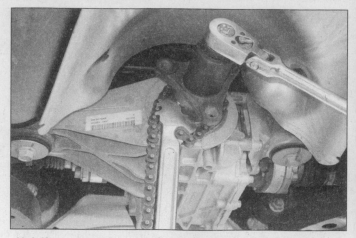

13.4 If you don't have a special holding tool, use a chain wrench to hold the pinion flange from turning while you remove the nut

27   Use a hammer and brass drift to drive the joint on the axleshaft.

28   Install a retaining snap-ring and seat the ring in its groove.

29   Apply CV joint grease to the tri-pod assembly, the inside of the joint housing and the inside of the boot.

30   Slide the boot into place, then equalize the pressure in the boot.

31   Tighten the boot clamps **(see illustration 10.15)**.

32   Using a hammer and brass punch, evenly drive the end cap to the CV joint.

33   Install the driveaxle assembly (see Section 9).

11   Rear driveaxle oil seals - replacement

1   Raise the rear of the vehicle and support it securely on jackstands. Place the transmission in Neutral with the parking brake off. Block the front wheels to prevent the vehicle from rolling.

2   Remove the driveaxle(s) (see Section 9).

3   On 2008 and later models, use a slide hammer to pull the rear driveaxle flanges out from the differential.

4   Carefully pry out the driveaxle oil seal with a seal removal tool or a large screwdriver. Be careful not to damage or scratch the seal bore.

5   Using a seal installer or a large deep socket as a drift, install the new oil seal. Drive it into the bore squarely and make sure it's completely seated.

6   Lubricate the lip of the new seal with multi-purpose grease, then install the drive-axle flange, making sure it is properly seated in the differential. Be careful not to damage the lip of the new seal.

7   Install the rear driveaxle(s) (see Section 9).

8   Check the differential lubricant level and add some, if necessary, to bring it to the appropriate level (see Chapter 1).

12   Rear differential - removal and installation

Refer to illustration 12.5

Warning: *The differential is heavy and can cause injury. Use a jack designed for the purpose and work carefully.*

1   Raise the rear of the vehicle and support it securely on jackstands. Block the front wheels to prevent the vehicle from rolling.

2   Remove the driveshaft (see Section 8).

3   Remove the driveaxles (see Section 9).

4   There are three rear differential mounting points securing the differential to the subframe, one at either side at the front of the assembly and one at the rear.

5   Support the rear of the differential with an approved jack. Remove the two bolts on each front bracket **(see illustration)**.

6   Remove the through bolt and nut securing the differential to the rear mounting bracket.

7   Lower the differential with the jack.

8   Installation is the reverse of removal. Tighten all fasteners to the torque listed in this Chapter's Specifications.

13   Rear differential pinion oil seal - replacement

Refer to illustration 13.4

1   Loosen the wheel lug nuts. Raise the rear of the vehicle and support it securely on

jackstands. Block the opposite set of wheels to keep the vehicle from rolling off the stands. Remove the wheels.

2   Disconnect the driveshaft from the differential companion flange and fasten it out of the way (see Section 8).

3   Mark the relationship of the pinion flange to the shaft, then count and write down the number of exposed threads on the shaft.

4   A flange holding tool will be required to keep the companion flange from moving while the self-locking pinion nut is loosened. A chain wrench will also work **(see illustration)**.

5   Remove the pinion nut.

6   Withdraw the flange. It may be necessary to use a two-jaw puller engaged behind the flange to draw it off. Do not attempt to pry or hammer behind the flange or hammer on the end of the pinion shaft.

7   Pry out the old seal and discard it.

8   Lubricate the lips of the new seal and fill the space between the seal lips with wheel bearing grease, then tap it evenly into position with a seal installation tool or a large socket. Make sure it enters the housing squarely and is tapped in to its full depth.

9   Install the pinion flange, lining up the marks made in Step 3. If necessary, tighten the pinion nut to draw the flange into place. Do not try to hammer the flange into position.

10   Install a new pinion nut, then tighten it to the torque listed in this Chapter's Specifications.

11   The remainder of installation is the reverse of removal.

Chapter 9 Brakes

Contents

Specifications

General
Brake fluid type... See Chapter 1

Disc brakes
Minimum pad lining thickness	See Chapter 1
Disc lateral runout limit	0.002 inch (0.06 mm)
Disc minimum thickness	Cast into disc

Torque specifications

Ft-lbs (unless otherwise indicated) **Nm**

Note: *One foot-pound (ft-lb) of torque is equivalent to 12 inch-pounds (in-lbs) of torque. Torque values below approximately 15 foot-pounds are expressed in inch-pounds, because most foot-pound torque wrenches are not accurate at these smaller values.*

	Ft-lbs	Nm
Brake line banjo bolt		
2007 and earlier		
Equipped with GM caliper code JE5 or JL9	37	50
Equipped with GM caliper code J56 (CTS-V)	25	34
2008 and later	36	49
Brake rotor-to-hub attaching screw	124 in-lbs	14
Caliper mounting bracket bolts		
Front		
2007 and earlier	96	130
2008	166	225
2009 and later	170	230
Rear		
2007 and earlier	88	120
2008	96	130
2009 and later	100	135

Torque specifications

Note: *One foot-pound (ft-lb) of torque is equivalent to 12 inch-pounds (in-lbs) of torque. Torque values below approximately 15 foot-pounds are expressed in inch-pounds, because most foot-pound torque wrenches are not accurate at these smaller values.*

	Ft-lbs (unless otherwise indicated)	Nm
Caliper mounting bolts		
Front		
2007 and earlier		
Equipped with GM caliper code JE5	25	34
Equipped with GM caliper code JL9	46	63
Equipped with GM caliper code J56 (CTS-V)	96	130
2008		
Equipped with GM caliper code JE5	20	27
Equipped with GM caliper code J55	48	65
Equipped with GM caliper code J56 (CTS-V)	96	130
2009 and later		
Equipped with GM caliper code JE5 or J55	46	63
Equipped with GM caliper code J56 (CTS-V)	129	175
Rear		
All except models equipped with GM caliper code J56 (CTS-V)		
2007 and earlier	44	60
2008	20	27
2009 and later	44	60
Models equipped with GM caliper code J56 (CTS-V)		
2008 and earlier	88	120
2009 and later	96	130
Caliper bridge pin bolts (2009 and later CTS-V models [J56])	24	33
Master cylinder fluid reservoir pin bolts (2009 and later models)	71 in-lbs	8
Master cylinder mounting nuts	18	24
Wheel lug nuts	See Chapter 1	

1   General information

The vehicles covered by this manual are equipped with hydraulically operated front and rear brake systems. The front and rear brakes are disc type. Both the front and rear brakes are self adjusting. The disc brakes automatically compensate for pad wear.

Hydraulic system

The hydraulic system consists of two separate circuits. The master cylinder has separate reservoirs for the two circuits, and, in the event of a leak or failure in one hydraulic circuit, the other circuit will remain operative. A dual proportioning valve on the firewall provides brake balance between the front and rear brakes.

Power brake booster

The power brake booster, utilizing engine manifold vacuum and atmospheric pressure to provide assistance to the hydraulically operated brakes, is mounted on the firewall in the engine compartment.

Parking brake

The parking brake operates the rear brakes only, through cable actuation. It's activated by either a foot pedal mounted on the driver's side with a release handle or an electronic parking brake that has a switch in the center console. The switch takes the place of the manual foot pedal and release handle and activates a control module that operates the cable.

Service

After completing any operation involving disassembly of any part of the brake system, always test drive the vehicle to check for proper braking performance before resuming normal driving. When testing the brakes, perform the tests on a clean, dry, flat surface. Conditions other than these can lead to inaccurate test results.

Test the brakes at various speeds with both light and heavy pedal pressure. The vehicle should stop evenly without pulling to one side or the other. Avoid locking the brakes, because this slides the tires and diminishes braking efficiency and control of the vehicle.

Tires, vehicle load and wheel alignment are factors which also affect braking performance.

Precautions

There are some general cautions and warnings involving the brake system on this vehicle:

a) Use only brake fluid conforming to DOT 3 specifications.

b) The brake pads contain fibers which are hazardous to your health if inhaled. Whenever you work on brake system components, clean all parts with brake system cleaner. Do not allow the fine dust to become airborne. Also, wear an approved filtering mask.

c) Safety should be paramount whenever any servicing of the brake components is performed. Do not use parts or fasteners which are not in perfect condition, and be sure that all clearances and torque specifications are adhered to. If you are at all unsure about a certain procedure, seek professional advice. Upon completion of any brake system work, test the brakes carefully in a controlled area before putting the vehicle into normal service. If a problem is suspected in the brake system, don't drive the vehicle until it's fixed.

2   Troubleshooting

PROBABLE CAUSE	CORRECTIVE ACTION

No brakes - pedal travels to floor

1 Low fluid level	1 and 2 Low fluid level and air in the system are symptoms of another problem -
2 Air in system	a leak somewhere in the hydraulic system. Locate and repair the leak
3 Defective seals in master cylinder	3 Replace master cylinder
4 Fluid overheated and vaporized due to heavy braking	4 Bleed hydraulic system (temporary fix). Replace brake fluid (proper fix)

Brake pedal slowly travels to floor under braking or at a stop

1 Defective seals in master cylinder	1 Replace master cylinder
2 Leak in a hose, line, caliper or wheel cylinder	2 Locate and repair leak
3 Air in hydraulic system	3 Bleed the system, inspect system for a leak

Brake pedal feels spongy when depressed

1 Air in hydraulic system	1 Bleed the system, inspect system for a leak
2 Master cylinder or power booster loose	2 Tighten fasteners
3 Brake fluid overheated (beginning to boil)	3 Bleed the system (temporary fix). Replace the brake fluid (proper fix)
4 Deteriorated brake hoses (ballooning under pressure) them if	4 Inspect hoses, replace as necessary (it's a good idea to replace all of one hose shows signs of deterioration)

Brake pedal feels hard when depressed and/or excessive effort required to stop vehicle

1 Power booster faulty	1 Replace booster
2 Engine not producing sufficient vacuum, or hose to booster clogged, collapsed or cracked	2 Check vacuum to booster with a vacuum gauge. Replace hose if cracked or clogged, repair engine if vacuum is extremely low
3 Brake linings contaminated by grease or brake fluid	3 Locate and repair source of contamination, replace brake pads or shoes
4 Brake linings glazed	4 Replace brake pads or shoes, check discs and drums for glazing, service as necessary
5 Caliper piston(s) or wheel cylinder(s) binding or frozen	5 Replace calipers or wheel cylinders
6 Brakes wet	6 Apply pedal to boil-off water (this should only be a momentary problem)
7 Kinked, clogged or internally split brake hose or line	7 Inspect lines and hoses, replace as necessary

Excessive brake pedal travel (but will pump up)

1 Drum brakes out of adjustment	1 Adjust brakes
2 Air in hydraulic system	2 Bleed system, inspect system for a leak

Excessive brake pedal travel (but will not pump up)

1 Master cylinder pushrod misadjusted	1 Adjust pushrod
2 Master cylinder seals defective	2 Replace master cylinder
3 Brake linings worn out	3 Inspect brakes, replace pads and/or shoes
4 Hydraulic system leak	4 Locate and repair leak

Brake pedal doesn't return

1 Brake pedal binding	1 Inspect pivot bushing and pushrod, repair or lubricate
2 Defective master cylinder	2 Replace master cylinder

Troubleshooting (continued)

PROBABLE CAUSE

CORRECTIVE ACTION

Brake pedal pulsates during brake application

1 Brake drums out-of-round	1 Have drums machined by an automotive machine shop
2 Excessive brake disc runout or disc surfaces out-of-parallel	2 Have discs machined by an automotive machine shop
3 Loose or worn wheel bearings	3 Adjust or replace wheel bearings
4 Loose lug nuts	4 Tighten lug nuts

Brakes slow to release

1 Malfunctioning power booster	1 Replace booster
2 Pedal linkage binding	2 Inspect pedal pivot bushing and pushrod, repair/lubricate
3 Malfunctioning proportioning valve	3 Replace proportioning valve
4 Sticking caliper or wheel cylinder	4 Repair or replace calipers or wheel cylinders
5 Kinked or internally split brake hose	5 Locate and replace faulty brake hose

Brakes grab (one or more wheels)

1 Grease or brake fluid on brake lining	1 Locate and repair cause of contamination, replace lining
2 Brake lining glazed	2 Replace lining, deglaze disc or drum

Vehicle pulls to one side during braking

1 Grease or brake fluid on brake lining	1 Locate and repair cause of contamination, replace lining
2 Brake lining glazed	2 Deglaze or replace lining, deglaze disc or drum
3 Restricted brake line or hose	3 Repair line or replace hose
4 Tire pressures incorrect	4 Adjust tire pressures
5 Caliper or wheel cylinder sticking	5 Repair or replace calipers or wheel cylinders
6 Wheels out of alignment	6 Have wheels aligned
7 Weak suspension spring	7 Replace springs
8 Weak or broken shock absorber	8 Replace shock absorbers

Brakes drag (indicated by sluggish engine performance or wheels being very hot after driving)

1 Brake pedal pushrod incorrectly adjusted	1 Adjust pushrod
2 Master cylinder pushrod (between booster and master cylinder) incorrectly adjusted	2 Adjust pushrod
3 Obstructed compensating port in master cylinder	3 Replace master cylinder
4 Master cylinder piston seized in bore	4 Replace master cylinder
5 Contaminated fluid causing swollen seals throughout system	5 Flush system, replace all hydraulic components
6 Clogged brake lines or internally split brake hose(s)	6 Flush hydraulic system, replace defective hose(s)
7 Sticking caliper(s) or wheel cylinder(s)	7 Replace calipers or wheel cylinders
8 Parking brake not releasing	8 Inspect parking brake linkage and parking brake mechanism, repair as required
9 Improper shoe-to-drum clearance	9 Adjust brake shoes
10 Faulty proportioning valve	10 Replace proportioning valve

Troubleshooting (continued)

PROBABLE CAUSE | **CORRECTIVE ACTION**

Brakes fade (due to excessive heat)

PROBABLE CAUSE	CORRECTIVE ACTION
1 Brake linings excessively worn or glazed	1 Deglaze or replace brake pads and/or shoes
2 Excessive use of brakes	2 Downshift into a lower gear, maintain a constant slower speed (going down hills)
3 Vehicle overloaded	3 Reduce load
4 Brake drums or discs worn too thin	4 Measure drum diameter and disc thickness, replace drums or discs as required
5 Contaminated brake fluid	5 Flush system, replace fluid
6 Brakes drag	6 Repair cause of dragging brakes
7 Driver resting left foot on brake pedal	7 Don't ride the brakes

Brakes noisy (high-pitched squeal)

PROBABLE CAUSE	CORRECTIVE ACTION
1 Glazed lining	1 Deglaze or replace lining
2 Contaminated lining (brake fluid, grease, etc.)	2 Repair source of contamination, replace linings
3 Weak or broken brake shoe hold-down or return spring	3 Replace springs
4 Rivets securing lining to shoe or backing plate loose	4 Replace shoes or pads
5 Excessive dust buildup on brake linings	5 Wash brakes off with brake system cleaner
6 Brake drums worn too thin	6 Measure diameter of drums, replace if necessary
7 Wear indicator on disc brake pads contacting disc	7 Replace brake pads
8 Anti-squeal shims missing or installed improperly	8 Install shims correctly

Note: Other remedies for quieting squealing brakes include the application of an anti-squeal compound to the backing plates of the brake pads, and lightly chamfering the edges of the brake pads with a file. The latter method should only be performed with the brake pads thoroughly wetted with brake system cleaner, so as not to allow any brake dust to become airborne.

Brakes noisy (scraping sound)

PROBABLE CAUSE	CORRECTIVE ACTION
1 Brake pads or shoes worn out; rivets, backing plate or brake shoe metal contacting disc or drum	1 Replace linings, have discs and/or drums machined (or replace)

Brakes chatter

PROBABLE CAUSE	CORRECTIVE ACTION
1 Worn brake lining	1 Inspect brakes, replace shoes or pads as necessary
2 Glazed or scored discs or drums	2 Deglaze discs or drums with sandpaper (if glazing is severe, machining will be required)
3 Drums or discs heat checked	3 Check discs and/or drums for hard spots, heat checking, etc. Have discs/drums machined or replace them
4 Disc runout or drum out-of-round excessive	4 Measure disc runout and/or drum out-of-round, have discs or drums machined or replace them
5 Loose or worn wheel bearings	5 Adjust or replace wheel bearings
6 Loose or bent brake backing plate (drum brakes)	6 Tighten or replace backing plate
7 Grooves worn in discs or drums	7 Have discs or drums machined, if within limits (if not, replace them)
8 Brake linings contaminated (brake fluid, grease, etc.)	8 Locate and repair source of contamination, replace pads or shoes
9 Excessive dust buildup on linings	9 Wash brakes with brake system cleaner
10 Surface finish on discs or drums too rough after machining (especially on vehicles with sliding calipers)	10 Have discs or drums properly machined
11 Brake pads or shoes glazed	11 Deglaze or replace brake pads or shoes

Troubleshooting (continued)

PROBABLE CAUSE	CORRECTIVE ACTION

Brake pads or shoes click

PROBABLE CAUSE	CORRECTIVE ACTION
1 Shoe support pads on brake backing plate grooved or excessively worn	1 Replace brake backing plate
2 Brake pads loose in caliper	2 Loose pad retainers or anti-rattle clips
3 Also see items listed under Brakes chatter	

Brakes make groaning noise at end of stop

PROBABLE CAUSE	CORRECTIVE ACTION
1 Brake pads and/or shoes worn out	1 Replace pads and/or shoes
2 Brake linings contaminated (brake fluid, grease, etc.)	2 Locate and repair cause of contamination, replace brake pads or shoes
3 Brake linings glazed	3 Deglaze or replace brake pads or shoes
4 Excessive dust buildup on linings	4 Wash brakes with brake system cleaner
5 Scored or heat-checked discs or drums	5 Inspect discs/drums, have machined if within limits (if not, replace discs or drums)
6 Broken or missing brake shoe attaching hardware	6 Inspect drum brakes, replace missing hardware

Rear brakes lock up under light brake application

PROBABLE CAUSE	CORRECTIVE ACTION
1 Tire pressures too high	1 Adjust tire pressures
2 Tires excessively worn	2 Replace tires
3 Defective proportioning valve	3 Replace proportioning valve

Brake warning light on instrument panel comes on (or stays on)

PROBABLE CAUSE	CORRECTIVE ACTION
1 Low fluid level in master cylinder reservoir (reservoirs with fluid level sensor)	1 Add fluid, inspect system for leak, check the thickness of the brake pads and shoes
2 Failure in one half of the hydraulic system	2 Inspect hydraulic system for a leak
3 Piston in pressure differential warning valve not centered	3 Center piston by bleeding one circuit or the other (close bleeder valve as soon as the light goes out)
4 Defective pressure differential valve or warning switch	4 Replace valve or switch
5 Air in the hydraulic system	5 Bleed the system, check for leaks
6 Brake pads worn out (vehicles with electric wear sensors - small probes that fit into the brake pads and ground out on the disc when the pads get thin)	6 Replace brake pads (and sensors)

Brakes do not self adjust

Disc brakes

PROBABLE CAUSE	CORRECTIVE ACTION
1 Defective caliper piston seals	1 Replace calipers. Also, possible contaminated fluid causing soft or swollen seals (flush system and fill with new fluid if in doubt)
2 Corroded caliper piston(s)	2 Same as above

Rapid brake lining wear

PROBABLE CAUSE	CORRECTIVE ACTION
1 Driver resting left foot on brake pedal	1 Don't ride the brakes
2 Surface finish on discs or drums too rough	2 Have discs or drums properly machined
3 Also see Brakes drag	

3   Anti-lock Brake System (ABS) - general information

General information

1   The anti-lock brake system - in conjunction with the engine drag control (EDC), dynamic rear proportioning (DRP), traction control system (TCS), vehicle stability enhancement system (VSES) or vehicle electronic stability (VES) - is designed to maintain vehicle steerability, directional stability and optimum deceleration under severe braking conditions on most road surfaces. It does so by monitoring the rotational speed of each wheel and controlling the brake line pressure to each wheel during braking. This prevents the wheels from locking up.

2   The ABS system has three main components - the wheel speed sensors, the electronic control unit (ECU) and the hydraulic unit. Four wheel-speed sensors - one at each wheel - send a variable voltage signal to the control unit, which monitors these signals, compares them to its program and determines whether a wheel is about to lock up. When a wheel is about to lock up, the control unit signals the hydraulic unit to reduce hydraulic pressure (or not increase it further) at that wheel's brake caliper. Pressure modulation is handled by electrically-operated solenoid valves.

3   If a problem develops within the system, an "ABS" warning light will glow on the dashboard. Sometimes, a visual inspection of the ABS system can help you locate the problem. Carefully inspect the ABS wiring harness. Pay particularly close attention to the harness and connections near each wheel. Look for signs of chafing and other damage caused by incorrectly routed wires. If a wheel sensor harness is damaged, the sensor must be replaced. **Warning:** *Do NOT try to repair an ABS wiring harness. The ABS system is sensitive to even the smallest changes in resistance. Repairing the harness could alter resistance values and cause the system to malfunction. If the ABS wiring harness is damaged in any way, it must be replaced.* **Caution:** *Make sure the ignition is turned off before unplugging or reattaching any electrical connections.*

Diagnosis and repair

4   If a dashboard warning light comes on and stays on while the vehicle is in operation, the ABS system requires attention. Although special electronic ABS diagnostic testing tools are necessary to properly diagnose the system, you can perform a few preliminary checks before taking the vehicle to a dealer service department.

   a) *Check the brake fluid level in the reservoir.*
   b) *Verify that the computer electrical connectors are securely connected.*
   c) *Check the electrical connectors at the hydraulic control unit.*
   d) *Check the fuses.*

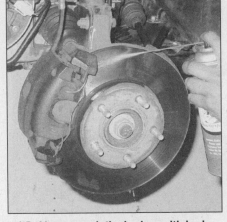

4.5 Always wash the brakes with brake cleaner before disassembling anything

   e) *Follow the wiring harness to each wheel and verify that all connections are secure and that the wiring is undamaged.*

5   If the above preliminary checks do not rectify the problem, the vehicle should be diagnosed by a dealer service department or other qualified repair shop. Due to the complex nature of this system, all actual repair work must be done by a qualified automotive technician.

Wheel speed sensor - removal and installation

2007 and earlier models

6   On these models, the wheel speed sensors are integral with the hub and bearing assemblies. Refer to Chapter 10 for the removal procedure.

2008 and later models

7   Loosen the wheel lug nuts, raise the vehicle and support it securely on jackstands. Remove the wheel.

8   Make sure the ignition key is turned to the Off position.

9   Trace the wiring back from the sensor, detaching all brackets and clips while noting its correct routing, then disconnect the electrical connector.

10   Remove the mounting bolt and carefully pull the sensor out from the knuckle.

11   Installation is the reverse of the removal procedure. Tighten the mounting bolt securely.

12   Install the wheel and lug nuts, tightening them securely. Lower the vehicle and tighten the lug nuts to the torque listed in the Chapter 1 Specifications.

4   Disc brake pads - replacement

Refer to illustrations 4.5, 4.6a through 4.6l and 4.7a through 4.7i

Warning: *Disc brake pads must be replaced on both front or both rear wheels at the same*

4.6a Depress the piston into the bottom of its bore in the caliper with large C-clamp to make room for the new pads - make sure the fluid in the master cylinder reservoir doesn't overflow

time - never replace the pads on only one wheel. Also, the dust created by the brake system is harmful to your health. Never blow it out with compressed air and don't inhale any of it. An approved filtering mask should be worn when working on the brakes. Do not, under any circumstances, use petroleum-based solvents to clean brake parts. Use brake system cleaner only! **Note:** *On models equipped with an electronic parking brake, the cable tension must be released before any work can be performed on the rear disc brake (see Section 11).*

All models except CTS-V with GM designation J56 calipers

1   Remove the cap from the brake fluid reservoir.

2   Loosen the wheel lug nuts, raise the end of the vehicle you're working on and support it securely on jackstands. Block the wheels at the opposite end.

3   Remove the wheels. Work on one brake assembly at a time, using the assembled brake for reference if necessary.

4   Inspect the brake disc carefully as outlined in Section 6. If machining is necessary, follow the information in that Section to remove the disc, at which time the pads can be removed as well.

5   Before disassembling the brake, wash it thoroughly with brake system cleaner and allow it to dry **(see illustration)**. Position a drain pan under the brake to catch the residue - DO NOT use compressed air to blow off the brake dust.

6   Follow the accompanying photos **(illustrations 4.6a through 4.6l)** for the actual pad replacement procedure. Be sure to stay in order and read the caption under each illustration.

7   For the rear brake pad replacement sequence, follow Steps 1 through 5, then depress the piston into the bottom of its bore

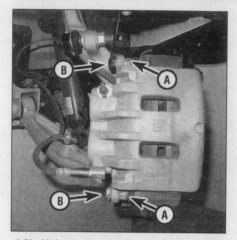

4.6b Using two wrenches, hold the guide pins (A) while loosening the caliper mounting bolts (B)

4.6c Remove the upper caliper mounting bolt and allow the caliper to rotate down on the mounting bracket

4.6d Remove the inner brake pad

4.6e Remove the outer brake pad

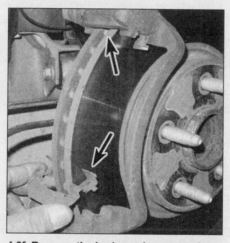

4.6f Remove the brake pad support plates from the caliper bracket

4.6g Remove the remaining caliper bolt and secure the caliper to the suspension with a length of wire

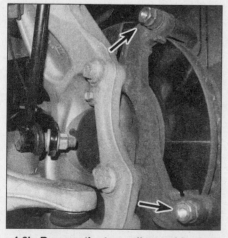

4.6h Remove the two caliper guide pins

4.6i Pull out the caliper guide pins and clean them, then apply a coat of high-temperature grease to the pins and reinstall the pins in the caliper bracket

4.6j Clean the support plates and lubricate the wear points with high-temp brake grease, then reinstall on the caliper mounting bracket

in the caliper with a large C-clamp to make room for the new pads, making sure the fluid in the master cylinder reservoir doesn't overflow **(see illustration 4.6a)**. Follow **illustrations 4.7a through 4.7i** for the remainder of the procedure.

8   When reinstalling the caliper, be sure to tighten the mounting bolts to the torque listed in this Chapter's Specifications. After the job has been completed, firmly depress the brake pedal a few times to bring the pads into contact with the disc. Check the level of the brake fluid, adding some if necessary. Check the operation of the brakes carefully before placing the vehicle into normal service.

4.6k Place the pads in the caliper mounting bracket

4.6l Install the caliper and tighten the caliper mounting bolts to the torque listed in this Chapter's Specifications

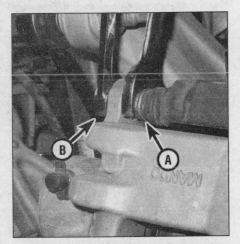

4.7a Using two wrenches, hold the guide pins (A) while loosening the caliper mounting bolts (B)

4.7b Remove the upper caliper mounting bolt and allow the caliper to rotate down on the mounting bracket

4.7c Remove the inner brake pad

4.7d Remove the outer brake pad

4.7e Remove the brake pad support plates from the caliper bracket, then remove the remaining caliper bolt and secure the caliper to the suspension with a length of wire

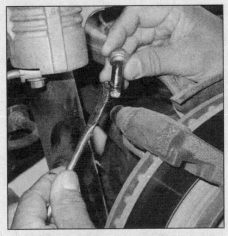

4.7f Pull out the caliper guide pins and clean them, then apply a coat of high-temperature grease to the pins and reinstall the pins in the caliper bracket

4.7g Clean the support plates and lubricate the wear points with a small amount of high-temp brake grease, then reinstall them on the caliper mounting bracket

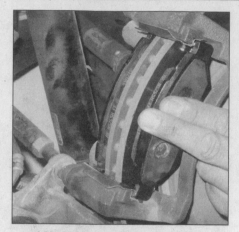

4.7h Place the pads in the caliper mounting bracket

4.7i Install the caliper and tighten the caliper mounting bolts to the torque listed in this Chapter's Specifications

CTS-V with GM designation J56 calipers

Note: *GM J56 calipers are standard equipment on CTS-V models. They can be identified by looking through the front wheel. The name J56 will be cast into the caliper.*

9   Review the **Warning** and **Note** at the beginning of this Section.

10   Perform Steps 1 through 5.

11   While holding the lower end of the spring-steel pad retainer down, use a punch and hammer to drive the lower caliper guide pin inward, toward the center of the vehicle, then remove it from the caliper. Rotate the pad retainer up and remove it from the caliper.

12   Drive the upper caliper guide pin inward, toward the center of the vehicle and remove it from the caliper.

13   On 2009 and later model front calipers, remove the caliper pin bridge bolt, then slide the caliper bridge pin out.

14   Using needle-nose pliers, pull the inboard (inner) brake pad from the caliper. **Note:** *Remove only one pad during this step.*

15   Using a pair of prybars or screwdrivers, slowly push the caliper pistons into the bores on the inboard side. There are two pistons on each side of the caliper for a total of four. **Caution:** *One piston can be forced out of the caliper bore while the other is being pushed in on the same side. Use a small piece of wood or another tool to keep one piston from coming out while the other is being pushed in.* As the pistons are depressed to the bottom of the caliper bores, the fluid in the master cylinder reservoir will rise. Continue to make sure that it doesn't overflow.

16   Prepare each new brake pad by using a very small amount of copper-based brake paste on the edges of the pad's metal back plate that contacts the caliper. **Warning:** *Do not get any lubricant on the pad material.*

17   Position the new inboard brake pad into the caliper.

18   Using needle-nose pliers, pull the outboard (outer) brake pad from the caliper.

19   Repeat Step 15 on the outboard side of the caliper.

20   Position the new outboard brake pad into the caliper.

21   On 2009 and later model front calipers, install the caliper bridge pin and bridge pin bolt, tightening it to the torque listed in this Chapter's Specification.

22   Install the upper guide pin and place the spring-steel pad retainer in position.

23   Press the bottom end of the retainer and install the lower guide pin.

24   After the job is done, firmly depress the brake pedal a few times to bring the new pads into contact with the disc. Check the level of the brake fluid, adding some if necessary. Check the operation of the brakes carefully before placing the vehicle into normal service.

---

5   Disc brake caliper - removal and installation

Warning: *Dust created by the brake system is harmful to your health. Never blow it out with compressed air and don't inhale any of it. An approved filtering mask should be worn when working on the brakes. Do not, under any circumstances, use petroleum-based solvents to clean brake parts. Use brake system cleaner only.*

Note: *If replacement is indicated (usually because of fluid leakage), it is recommended that the calipers be replaced, not overhauled. New and factory rebuilt units are available on an exchange basis, which makes this job quite easy. Always replace the calipers in pairs - never replace just one of them.*

Note: *On models equipped with electronic parking brake, the cable tension must be released before any work can be performed on the rear disc brakes, see Section 11.*

Removal

Refer to illustration 5.2

1   Loosen the wheel lug nuts, raise the vehicle (front or rear) and place it securely on jackstands. Remove the wheels.

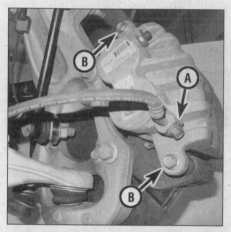

5.2 Remove the brake line banjo bolt (A), then remove the caliper mounting bolts (B) (typical front caliper shown, rear calipers similar)

2   Remove the banjo fitting bolt and disconnect the brake hose from the caliper **(see illustration)**. Discard the sealing washers from each side of the hose fitting. Plug the brake hose to keep contaminants out of the brake system and to prevent losing any more brake fluid than is necessary. **Note:** *If the caliper is being removed for access to another component, don't disconnect the hose.*

3   On all except CTS-V models, refer to **illustration 4.6b** (front) or **4.7a** (rear) for the caliper removal procedure. If the caliper is being removed just to access another component, use a piece of wire to securely hang it out of the way **(see illustration 4.6g)**. **Caution:** *Do not let the caliper hang by the brake hose.*

4   On CTS-V models, remove the caliper-to-steering knuckle bolts (front) or caliper-to-rear knuckle bolts (rear) and detach the caliper from the knuckle.

Installation

5   Install the caliper by reversing the removal procedure, tightening the mounting bolts to the torque listed in this Chapter's

6.3 The brake pads on this vehicle were obviously neglected, as they wore down completely and cut deep grooves into the disc - wear this severe means the disc must be replaced

6.4a To check disc runout, mount a dial indicator as shown and rotate the disc

Specifications. Use new sealing washers and tighten the banjo fitting bolt to the torque listed in this Chapter's Specifications.

6   Bleed the brake circuit (see Section 9). Make sure there are no leaks from the hose connections. Test the brakes carefully before returning the vehicle to normal service.

6   Brake disc - inspection, removal and installation

Inspection

Refer to illustrations 6.3, 6.4a, 6.4b, 6.5a and 6.5b

1   Loosen the wheel lug nuts, raise the vehicle and support it securely on jackstands.

2   Remove the brake caliper (see Section 5). It isn't necessary to disconnect the brake hose. After removing the caliper bolts, suspend the caliper out of the way with a piece of wire **(see illustration 4.6g)**.

3   Visually inspect the disc surface for score marks and other damage. Light scratches and shallow grooves are normal after use and may

not always be detrimental to brake operation, but deep scoring requires disc removal and refinishing by an automotive machine shop. Be sure to check both sides of the disc **(see illustration)**. If pulsating has been noticed during application of the brakes, suspect disc runout.

4   To check disc runout, reinstall the lug nuts (inverted) and place a dial indicator at a point about 1/2-inch from the outer edge of the disc **(see illustration)**. Set the indicator to zero and turn the disc. The indicator reading should not exceed the specified allowable runout limit. If it does, the disc should be refinished by an automotive machine shop. **Note:** *If the brake pads are being replaced, the discs should be resurfaced regardless of the dial indicator reading, as this will impart a smooth finish and ensure a perfectly flat surface, eliminating any brake pedal pulsation or other undesirable symptoms related to questionable discs. At the very least, if you elect not to have the discs resurfaced, remove the glaze from the surface with emery cloth or sandpaper, using a swirling motion* **(see illustration)**.

5   It's absolutely critical that the disc not be machined to a thickness under the specified

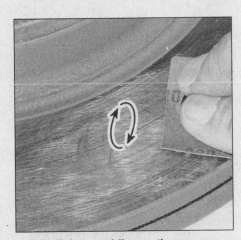

6.4b Using a swirling motion, remove the glaze from the disc surface with sandpaper or emery cloth

minimum thickness. The minimum (or discard) thickness is cast or stamped into the disc **(see illustration)**. The disc thickness can be checked with a micrometer **(see illustration)**.

6.5a The minimum thickness dimension is stamped into the outer edges of the disc

6.5b Use a micrometer to measure disc thickness

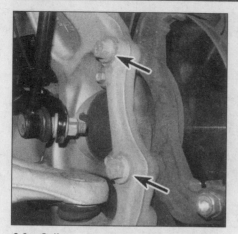

6.6a Caliper mounting bracket-to-knuckle bolts (typical front caliper shown, rear caliper similar)

6.6b A screw secures the disc to the hub (rear disc shown, front disc identical)

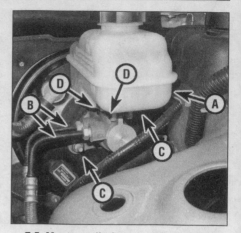

7.5 Master cylinder mounting details

A   *Fluid level warning switch connector*
B   *Brake line fittings*
C   *Mounting nuts*
D   *Reservoir retaining fasteners*

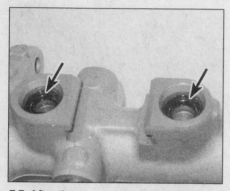

7.7 After the reservoir has been removed, replace the O-rings with new ones

Removal

Refer to illustrations 6.6a and 6.6b

Note: *On models equipped with an electronic parking brake, the cable tension must be released before any work can be performed on the rear disc brakes (see Section 11).*

6   Remove the caliper mounting bracket (non-CTS-V models, **see illustration**) or caliper (CTS-V models). Also remove the lug nuts, if they were reinstalled for the runout check. Remove the screw that secure the disc to the hub, then remove the disc (**see illustration**).

Installation

7   While the disc is off, wire-brush the backside of the center portion that contacts the wheel hub. Also clean off any rust or dirt on the hub face.
8   Apply small dots of high-temperature anti-seize around the circumference of the hub, and around the raised center portion.
9   Place the disc in position over the threaded studs. Install the disc retaining screw, tightening the screw to the torque values listed in this Chapter's Specifications.
10   Install the caliper mounting bracket and caliper, tightening the bolts to the torque values listed in this Chapter's Specifications.

11   Install the wheel, then lower the vehicle to the ground. Tighten the lug nuts to the torque listed in the Chapter 1 Specifications. Depress the brake pedal a few times to bring the brake pads into contact with the disc. Bleeding won't be necessary unless the brake hose was disconnected from the caliper. Check the operation of the brakes carefully before driving the vehicle.
12   Check the operation of the brakes carefully before driving the vehicle.

7   Master cylinder - removal and installation

Removal

Refer to illustrations 7.5 and 7.7

1   The master cylinder is located in the engine compartment, mounted to the power brake booster.
2   Remove as much fluid as you can from the reservoir with a syringe, such as an old turkey baster. **Warning:** *If a baster is used, never again use it for the preparation of food.*
3   Place rags under the fluid fittings and prepare caps or plastic bags to cover the ends of the lines once they are disconnected. **Caution:** *Brake fluid will damage paint. Cover all body parts and be careful not to spill fluid during this procedure.*
4   Disconnect the electrical connector at the brake fluid level switch on the master cylinder reservoir.
5   Loosen the fittings at the ends of the brake lines where they enter the master cylinder (**see illustration**). To prevent rounding off the corners on these nuts, the use of a flare-nut wrench, which wraps around the nut, is preferred. Pull the brake lines slightly away from the master cylinder and plug the ends to prevent contamination.
6   Remove the nuts attaching the master cylinder to the power booster. Pull the master cylinder off the studs and out of the engine

compartment. Again, be careful not to spill the fluid as this is done.
7   If a new master cylinder is being installed and does not come with a reservoir, remove the retaining fasteners and reservoir from the old master cylinder, then transfer it to the new master cylinder. **Note:** *Install new seals when transferring the reservoir* (**see illustration**).

Installation

Refer to illustrations 7.9 and 7.14

8   Bench bleed the new master cylinder before installing it. Mount the master cylinder in a vise, with the jaws of the vise clamping on the mounting flange.
9   Attach a pair of master cylinder bleeder tubes to the outlet ports of the master cylinder (**see illustration**).
10   Fill the reservoir with brake fluid of the recommended type (see Chapter 1).

7.9 The best way to bleed air from the master cylinder before installing it on the vehicle is with a pair of bleeder tubes that direct brake fluid into the reservoir during bleeding

7.14 Install a new O-ring onto the master cylinder sleeve

11   Slowly push the pistons into the master cylinder (a large Phillips screwdriver can be used for this) - air will be expelled from the pressure chambers and into the reservoir. Because the tubes are submerged in fluid, air can't be drawn back into the master cylinder when you release the pistons.

12   Repeat the procedure until no more air bubbles are present.

13   Remove the bleed tubes, one at a time, and install plugs in the open ports to prevent fluid leakage and air from entering. Install the reservoir cap.

14   Install the master cylinder over the studs on the power brake booster and tighten the attaching nuts only finger tight at this time. **Note:** *Install a new seal into the groove of the master cylinder* **(see illustration).**

15   Thread the brake line fittings into the master cylinder. Since the master cylinder is still a bit loose, it can be moved slightly in order for the fittings to thread in easily. Do not strip the threads as the fittings are tightened.

16   Tighten the mounting nuts to the torque listed in this Chapter's Specifications, then tighten the brake line fittings securely.

17   Fill the master cylinder reservoir with fluid, then bleed the master cylinder and the brake system (see Section 9). To bleed the cylinder on the vehicle, have an assistant depress the brake pedal and hold the pedal to the floor. Loosen the fitting to allow air and fluid to escape. Repeat this procedure on both fittings until the fluid is clear of air bubbles. **Caution:** *Have plenty of rags on hand to catch the fluid - brake fluid will ruin painted surfaces. After the bleeding procedure is completed, rinse the area under the master cylinder with clean water.*

18   Test the operation of the brake system carefully before placing the vehicle into normal service. **Warning:** *Do not operate the vehicle if you are in doubt about the effectiveness of the brake system. It is possible for air to become trapped in the anti-lock brake system hydraulic control unit, so, if the pedal continues to feel spongy after repeated bleedings or the BRAKE or ANTI-LOCK light stays on, have the vehicle towed to a dealer service department or other qualified shop to be bled with the aid of a scan tool.*

8   Brake hoses and lines - inspection and replacement

1   About every six months, with the vehicle raised and placed securely on jackstands, the flexible hoses which connect the steel brake lines with the front and rear brake assemblies should be inspected for cracks, chafing of the outer cover, leaks, blisters and other damage. These are important and vulnerable parts of the brake system and inspection should be complete. A light and mirror will be needed for a thorough check. If a hose exhibits any of the above defects, replace it with a new one.

Flexible hoses

Refer to illustrations 8.3a and 8.3b

2   Clean all dirt away from the ends of the hose.

3   To remove a brake hose, unscrew the tube nut with a flare-nut wrench, if available, to prevent rounding-off the corners of the nut, then remove the bolt(s) or clip(s) securing the hose to the body (and any suspension components) **(see illustrations)**.

4   Disconnect the hose from the caliper, discarding the sealing washers on either side of the fitting.

5   Using new sealing washers, attach the new brake hose to the caliper. Tighten the banjo fitting bolt to the torque listed in this Chapter's Specifications.

6   Reverse the removal procedure to install the hose, making sure it isn't twisted.

7   Carefully check to make sure the suspension or steering components don't make contact with the hose. Have an assistant push down on the vehicle and also turn the steering wheel lock-to-lock during inspection.

8   Bleed the brake system (see Section 9).

Metal brake lines

9   When replacing brake lines, be sure to use the correct parts. Don't use copper tubing for any brake system components. Purchase steel brake lines from a dealer parts department or auto parts store.

10   Prefabricated brake line, with the tube ends already flared and fittings installed, is available at auto parts stores and dealer parts departments. These lines can be bent to the proper shapes using a tubing bender.

11   When installing the new line make sure it's well supported in the brackets and has plenty of clearance between moving or hot components.

12   After installation, check the master cylinder fluid level and add fluid as necessary. Bleed the brake system as outlined in Section

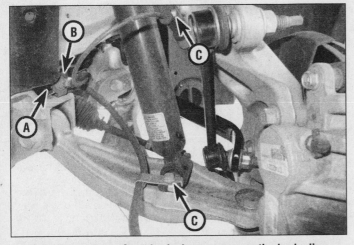

8.3a To remove a front brake hose, unscrew the brake line fitting (A) while holding the fitting block (B) with another wrench, remove the mounting bolts (C), then unscrew the banjo bolt (see illustration 5.2) and detach the hose from the caliper

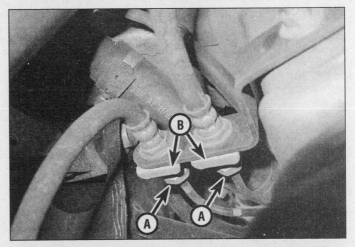

8.3b To remove a rear brake hose, unscrew the brake line fitting (A) while holding the bracket with a pair of pliers, remove the clip (B), then unscrew the banjo bolt and detach the hose from the caliper

9.8 When bleeding the brakes, a hose is connected to the bleed screw at the caliper and submerged in brake fluid - air will be seen as bubbles in the tube and container (all air must be expelled before moving to the next wheel)

9 and test the brakes carefully before placing the vehicle into normal operation.

9   Brake hydraulic system - bleeding

Refer to illustration 9.8

Warning: *If air has found its way into the hydraulic control unit, the system must be bled with the use of a scan tool. If the brake pedal feels spongy even after bleeding the brakes, or the ABS light on the instrument panel does not go off, or if you have any doubts whatsoever about the effectiveness of the brake system, have the vehicle towed to a dealer service department or other repair shop equipped with the necessary tools for bleeding the system.*

Warning: *Wear eye protection when bleeding the brake system. If the fluid comes in contact with your eyes, immediately rinse them with water and seek medical attention.*

Note: *Bleeding the brake system is necessary to remove any air that's trapped in the system when it's opened during removal and installation of a hose, line, caliper, wheel cylinder or master cylinder.*

1   It will probably be necessary to bleed the system at all four brakes if air has entered the system due to low fluid level, or if the brake lines have been disconnected at the master cylinder.

2   If a brake line was disconnected only at a wheel, then only that caliper or wheel cylinder must be bled.

3   If a brake line is disconnected at a fitting located between the master cylinder and any of the brakes, that part of the system served by the disconnected line must be bled.

4   Remove any residual vacuum (or hydraulic pressure) from the brake power booster by applying the brake several times with the engine off.

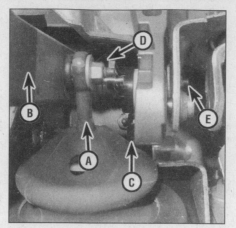

10.8 Brake booster pushrod details (2008 and later models)

A   Brake booster pushrod
B   Brake pedal
C   Brake pedal position sensor electrical connector
D   Brake pedal pushrod-to-brake pedal mounting nut
E   Brake pedal sensor mounting fastener

5   Remove the master cylinder reservoir cap and fill the reservoir with brake fluid. Reinstall the cap. **Note:** *Check the fluid level often during the bleeding operation and add fluid as necessary to prevent the fluid level from falling low enough to allow air bubbles into the master cylinder.*

6   Have an assistant on hand, as well as a supply of new brake fluid, an empty clear plastic container, a length of plastic, rubber or vinyl tubing to fit over the bleeder valve and a wrench to open and close the bleeder valve.

7   Beginning at the right rear wheel, loosen the bleeder screw slightly, then tighten it to a point where it's snug but can still be loosened quickly and easily.

8   Place one end of the tubing over the bleeder screw fitting and submerge the other end in brake fluid in the container **(see illustration)**.

9   Have the assistant slowly depress the brake pedal and hold it in the depressed position.

10   While the pedal is held depressed, open the bleeder screw just enough to allow a flow of fluid to leave the valve. Watch for air bubbles to exit the submerged end of the tube. When the fluid flow slows after a couple of seconds, tighten the screw and have your assistant release the pedal.

11   Repeat Steps 9 and 10 until no more air is seen leaving the tube, then tighten the bleeder screw and proceed to the left rear wheel, the right front wheel and the left front wheel, in that order, and perform the same procedure. Be sure to check the fluid in the master cylinder reservoir frequently.

12   Never use old brake fluid. It contains moisture which can boil, rendering the brake system inoperative.

13   Refill the master cylinder with fluid at the

end of the operation.

14   Check the operation of the brakes. The pedal should feel solid when depressed, with no sponginess. If necessary, repeat the entire process. **Warning:** *Do not operate the vehicle if you are in doubt about the effectiveness of the brake system. It is possible for air to become trapped in the anti-lock brake system hydraulic control unit, so, if the pedal continues to feel spongy after repeated bleedings or the BRAKE or ANTI-LOCK light stays on, have the vehicle towed to a dealer service department or other qualified shop to be bled with the aid of a scan tool.*

10   Power brake booster - check, removal and installation

Operating check

1   Depress the brake pedal several times with the engine off and make sure that there is no change in the pedal reserve distance.

2   Depress the pedal and start the engine. If the pedal goes down slightly, operation is normal.

Airtightness check

3   Start the engine and turn it off after one or two minutes. Depress the brake pedal several times slowly. If the pedal goes down farther the first time but gradually rises after the second or third depression, the booster is airtight.

4   Depress the brake pedal while the engine is running, then stop the engine with the pedal depressed. If there is no change in the pedal reserve travel after holding the pedal for 30 seconds, the booster is airtight.

Removal and installation

Refer to illustrations 10.8 and 10.15

5   Disassembly of the power unit requires special tools and is not ordinarily performed by the home mechanic. If a problem develops, it's recommended that a new or factory rebuilt unit be installed.

6   Working inside the vehicle, remove the driver's side insulator panel (see Chapter 11).

7   Disconnect the electrical connector to the Brake Pedal Position (BPP) sensor **(see illustration 10.8)**.

8   Remove the booster pushrod retaining clip (2007 and earlier models) or pushrod nut (2008 and later models) **(see illustration)** from under the instrument panel. Disconnect the pushrod from the brake pedal.

9   Remove the crossbrace from the engine compartment, if equipped (see Chapter 11).

10   On manual transmission models, remove the clutch master cylinder (see Chapter 8).

11   Remove the coolant expansion tank (see Chapter 3) and set the tank out of the way. **Note:** *It is not necessary to drain the cooling system.*

12   Remove the master cylinder from the booster (see Section 7).

13   Remove the cowl panel (see Chapter 11) to access the locking tab on the brake booster.

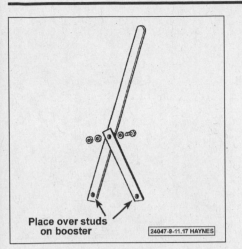

10.15 A tool can be fabricated out of strap steel to enable you to unlock the booster from its bracket

14 Disconnect the brake booster check valve and vacuum hose where it attaches to the booster.

15 Install special tool J-22805-B or equivalent, to the brake booster studs and lock the tool in place using the master cylinder mounting nuts **(see illustration)**. **Note:** *If the special tool is not available, drill two holes in a flat bar or pipe and mount the bar to the booster studs. Lock it in place using the master cylinder mounting nuts.*

16 Using a screwdriver, depress the locking tab on the side of the booster to release it from the mounting flange, while rotating the booster counterclockwise using the special tool or equivalent.

17 Once the locking tab is free of the mounting flange, carefully pull the booster forward from the mounting flange until the end of the booster is visible.

18 While supporting the booster, push the foam seal inwards at the end of the booster to expose the pushrod retaining clip.

19 The pushrod retaining clip has a long and short side - lift and hold the longer side of the clip up and separate the pushrod from the booster. **Note:** *On 2008 and later models, the pushrod retaining clip must be removed to separate the pushrod from the booster.*

20 Carefully lift the booster unit away from the firewall and out of the engine compartment.

21 To install the booster, place it into position and insert the pushrod until the pushrod retaining clip clicks in place. **Note:** *Check to see if the pushrod is properly seated by pulling on the pushrod; if the pushrod can't be pulled out, the booster is properly seated.*

22 Using the special tool J-22805-B or equivalent, rotate the booster clockwise until the locking tab locks into the mounting flange.

23 Install the master cylinder. Reconnect the vacuum hose and check valve.

24 Install the booster pushrod, retaining clip and washer or nut to the brake pedal.

25 The remainder of installation is the reverse of removal.

26 Carefully test the operation of the brakes before placing the vehicle in normal service.

12.4a Rear parking brake assembly details

A *Parking brake shoe adjuster spring*
B *Parking brake shoe hold down spring and pins*
C *Parking brake shoe adjuster*
D *Parking brake shoe return spring*
E *Parking brake shoes*
F *Parking brake actuator*

11 Electronic parking brake cable - tension release

1 Block the rear wheels to prevent the vehicle from rolling.

2 Turn the ignition key to the RUN position without starting the engine and place the transmission in the Park (automatic) or Neutral (manual) position.

3 Depress the brake pedal and hold it down, then press the electronic parking brake switch for 5 seconds until the parking brake light on the instrument cluster starts flashing.

4 Once the parking brake light starts flashing, immediately release the electronic parking brake switch, then press the switch again and release it. The cable tension should be fully released and the brake pedal can be released.

12 Parking brake shoes - replacement

Refer to illustrations 12.4a through 12.4n and 12.5

Warning: *Parking brake shoes must be replaced on both wheels at the same time - never replace the shoes on only one wheel.*

12.4b Remove the parking brake shoe adjuster spring

Also, the dust created by the brake system is harmful to your health. Never blow it out with compressed air and don't inhale any of it. An approved filtering mask should be worn when working on the brakes. Do not, under any circumstances, use petroleum-based solvents to clean brake parts. Use brake system cleaner only!

Note: *On models equipped with an electronic parking brake, the cable tension must be released before any work can be performed on the rear disc brakes (see Section 11).*

1 Loosen the wheel lug nuts, raise the rear of the vehicle and support it securely on jackstands. Block the front wheels to keep the vehicle from rolling.

2 Release the parking brake.

3 Remove the wheel and the screw that secures the disc/drum to the hub, then remove the disc **(see illustration 6.6b)**. **Note:** *All four parking brake shoes must be replaced at the same time, but to avoid mixing up parts, work on only one brake assembly at a time.*

4 Follow **Illustrations 12.4a through 12.4n** for the parking brake shoe replacement procedure. Be sure to stay in order and read the caption under each illustration. **Note:** *If the brake disc/drum cannot be easily removed, make sure the parking brake is completely*

12.4c Remove the parking brake shoe adjuster from the ends of the parking brake shoes

12.4d With locking pliers, remove one end of the parking brake shoe return spring, then remove the spring from the shoe

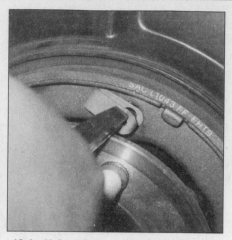

12.4e Using pliers, rotate the hold-down spring retaining pin

12.4f Release the hold-down springs and remove them from the shoes

12.4g Remove the shoes from the backing plate

12.4h Clean the backing plate with brake cleaner and lightly lube the shoe contact points with brake grease

12.4i If necessary, disconnect the parking brake cable from the back side of the backing plate at the parking brake actuator, then unclip the actuator from the backing plate

12.4j With the parking brake actuator installed, insert the brake shoes into the actuator

12.4k Install the pins and shoe hold down springs, locking the pins to the springs

12.4l Install the parking brake shoe return spring to the shoes

12.4m Clean and lube the threads of the adjuster and reinstall it between the shoes

12.4n Install the adjuster spring, then adjust the shoes by turning the star wheel (the drum should just be able to slide over the shoes)

12.5 The maximum diameter is cast into the inside face of the drum side of the brake rotor

13   Brake light switch (2003 models only) - replacement

1   Remove the insulation panel under the knee bolster (see Chapter 11).
2   Disconnect the electrical connector from the switch.
3   Depress the retaining clip on the switch and pull the switch from the brake pedal.
4   Install the sensor to the pedal, then pull up on the brake pedal and connect the electrical connector.
5   Apply the brake pedal, release the pedal and verify that the brake lights go off when the pedal is released.

14   Brake Pedal Position (BPP) sensor - replacement

Warning: *The Brake Pedal Position (BPP) sensor must be calibrated after the sensor is removed or replaced using a factory scan tool.*
1   Remove the insulation panel and the knee bolster (see Chapter 11).
2   Disconnect the electrical connector at the sensor.
3   Remove the BPP sensor mounting fastener **(see illustration 10.8)** and remove the sensor from the bracket.
4   Install the sensor to the bracket and tighten the sensor mounting fastener securely.
5   Connect the electrical connector to the sensor and calibrate the sensor using a factory type scan tool. **Caution:** *Do not touch the brake pedal during the sensor calibration procedure; any movement of the sensor or brake pedal will cause the calibration procedure to fail.*

released, and use a small hammer to tap the hub surface between the wheel studs to shock the disc/drum free.
5   Before reinstalling the rear disc, the drum portion of the disc should be checked for cracks, score marks, deep scratches and hard spots, which will appear as small discolored areas. If the hard spots cannot be removed with fine emery cloth or if any of the other conditions listed above exist, the disc must be taken to an automotive machine shop to have it resurfaced. **Note:** *Professionals recommend resurfacing the drum portion each time a brake job is done. Resurfacing will eliminate the possibility of out-of-round drums. If the drum portions are worn so much that they can't be resurfaced without exceeding the maximum allowable diameter (cast into the drum), then new discs will be required* **(see illustration)**. *At the very least, if you elect not to have them resurfaced, remove the glaze from the surface with emery cloth using a swirling motion.*

6   Install the brake disc/drum on the axle flange; the parking brake shoes should lightly touch the drum. Apply the parking brake a couple of times, then turn the disc and listen for the sound of the shoes rubbing.
7   Install the caliper bracket, rear brake pads and caliper.
8   Install the wheel and lug nuts and check to see if the wheel rotates freely. Apply the parking brake; the wheel should not be able to turn. If it does, apply the parking brake three times and check it again. **Note:** *The parking brake is adjusted automatically by applying the park brake at least three times.*
9   Lower the vehicle and tighten the lug nuts to the torque listed in the Chapter 1 Specifications.
10   Check the operation of the brakes carefully before driving the vehicle. After driving the vehicle, check the operation of the parking brake and if necessary, apply the parking brake to adjust the brakes until satisfactory action is obtained.

Notes

Chapter 10
Suspension and steering systems

Contents

Specifications

Torque specifications

	Ft-lbs (unless otherwise indicated)	Nm
Front suspension		
Upper control arm		
Pivot bolts/nuts	Not available	
Upper balljoint-to-steering knuckle		
Pinch bolt (2007 and earlier models)	44	60
Ballstud nut (2008 and later models)	44	60
Lower control arm		
Lower balljoint-to-knuckle nut		
Step 1	30	40
Step 2	Tighten an additional 120-degrees	
Lower control arm-to-subframe bolt		
2007 and earlier models	100	135
2008 and later models		
Front bolt	148	200
Rear bolt	236	320
Stabilizer bar		
Bracket bolts		
2007 and earlier models	44	60
2008 and later models	48	65
Link nuts		
2007 and earlier models	37	50
2008 and later models		
Bar to link nut	74	100
Knuckle to link nut	92	125

Torque specifications (continued)

	Ft-lbs (unless otherwise indicated)	Nm
Front suspension (continued)		
Shock absorber/coil spring assembly		
Upper mounting bolts	83	112
Shock absorber-to-lower control arm bolt	18	25
Shock absorber piston rod nut	18	25
Hub and bearing assembly mounting bolts	100	135
Subframe		
Front subframe		
Subframe-to-frame mounting bolts	141	191
Subframe-to-body mounting bolts (rear)	180	250
Rear subframe		
2008 and earlier models		
Front mounting bolts	195	265
Rear mounting bolts	141	191
2009 through 2012 models		
Front mounting bolts	180	250
Rear mounting bolts	141	191
2013 and later models		
Front mounting bolts		
Step 1	148	200
Step 2	Tighten an additional 65-degrees	
Rear mounting bolts		
Step 1	74	100
Step 2	Tighten an additional 90-degrees	
Rear suspension		
Shock absorber		
Upper mounting nuts	18	25
Lower mounting bolt/nut	111	150
Upper suspension arm		
Inner nut/bolt		
2007 and earlier models	129	175
2008 and later models	88	120
Outer nut		
Step 1	15	20
Step 2	Tighten an additional 210-degrees	
Lower arm		
2007 and earlier models		
Outer bolt-to-knuckle	129	175
Inner bolt-to-body	111	150
2008 and later models		
Outer bolt-to-knuckle	118	160
Inner bolt-to-body	122	165
Trailing arm		
2007 and earlier models		
Arm-to-body nut/bolt	66	90
Arm-to-knuckle bolt	129	175
2008 and later models		
Arm-to-body nut/bolt	111	150
Arm-to-knuckle bolt	125	170
Toe-link arm		
2007 and earlier models	129	175
2008 and later models		
Inner bolt	125	170
Outer bolt	118	160
Stabilizer bar		
Bracket bolts	44	60
Link nuts		
2007 and earlier	37	50
2008 and later	49	66
Hub and bearing assembly mounting bolts		
2007 and earlier models	92	125
2008 and later models	103	140

Steering

	Ft-lbs	Nm
Intermediate shaft bolt	35	49
Power steering pump mounting bolts		
3.2L engines	26	35
2006 and earlier V6 engines (except 3.2L engines)	17	22
2007 V6 engines	18	25
2008 and later V6 engines	17	23
V8 engines	18	25
Power steering pump mounting bracket bolts		
V6 engines	37	50
V8 engines	18	25

Torque specifications

	Ft-lbs (unless otherwise indicated)	Nm
Steering column mounting bolts/nuts		
2007 and earlier models	18	25
2008 and later models (in sequence, **see illustration 16.4**)		
Step 1 mounting nut 3	20	27
Step 2 mounting nut 4	20	27
Step 3 mounting bolt 1	20	27
Step 4 mounting bolt 2	20	27
Steering wheel nut/bolt		
2007 and earlier models (nut)	30	41
2008 through 2012 (bolt)	30	41
2013 and later models	22	30
Steering gear mounting bolts		
2006 and earlier models	70	95
2007 models	30	40
2008 and later models	63	85
Tie-rod end-to-steering knuckle nut		
2007 and earlier models	52	70
2008 and later models		
Step 1	26	35
Step 2	Tighten an additional 110-degrees	

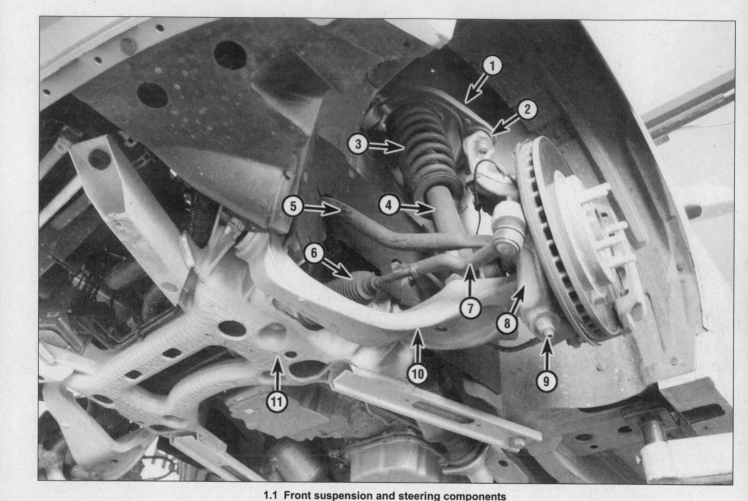

1.1 Front suspension and steering components

1	Upper control arm	5	Stabilizer bar	9	Lower balljoint
2	Upper balljoint	6	Steering gear boot	10	Lower control arm
3	Coil spring	7	Tie-rod end	11	Front subframe
4	Shock absorber	8	Steering knuckle		

1   General information

Refer to illustrations 1.1 and 1.2

The front suspension is made up of lower and upper control arms, steering knuckle/hub assemblies; coil-over shock absorbers and a stabilizer bar **(see illustration)**.

The rear suspension employs two trailing arms, upper and lower control arms, a knuckle, a coil spring and shock absorber per side, and an adjustable toe-link that permits toe setting adjustment for each rear wheel **(see illustration)**.

The rack-and-pinion steering gear is located under the engine assembly on the front suspension subframe and actuates the tie-rods, which are attached to the steering knuckles. The inner ends of the tie-rods are protected by rubber boots which should be inspected periodically for secure attachment, tears and leaking lubricant (which would indicate a failed rack seal).

The power assist system on most models consists of a belt-driven pump and associated lines and hoses. The fluid level in the power steering pump reservoir should be checked periodically (see Chapter 1). 2005 and later models are equipped with a variable effort steering system (VES), which controls the amount of power assistance depending on driving conditions. The VES system uses inputs from the steering wheel position sensor and wheel speed sensors, and the brake control module sends a signal to the electromagnetic actuator in the steering gear to control the power steering fluid pressure to maintain even steering effort during all speeds.

The steering wheel operates the steering shaft, which actuates the steering gear through universal joints. Looseness in the steering can be caused by wear in the steering shaft universal joints, the steering gear, the tie-rod ends and loose retaining bolts.

Precautions

Frequently, when working on the suspension or steering system components, you may

1.2 Rear suspension components

1	Shock absorber	5	Toe adjuster link
2	Upper suspension arm	6	Knuckle
3	Trailing arm	7	Lower suspension arm
4	Subframe		

come across fasteners which seem impossible to loosen. These fasteners on the underside of the vehicle are continually subjected to water, road grime, mud, etc., and can become rusted or frozen, making them extremely difficult to remove. In order to unscrew these stubborn fasteners without damaging them (or other components), be sure to use lots of penetrating oil and allow it to soak in for a while. Using a wire brush to clean exposed threads will also ease removal of the nut or bolt and prevent damage to the threads. Sometimes a sharp blow with a hammer and punch will break the bond between a nut and bolt threads, but care must be taken to prevent the punch from slipping off the fastener and ruin-

ing the threads. Heating the stuck fastener and surrounding area with a torch sometimes helps too, but isn't recommended because of the obvious dangers associated with fire. Long breaker bars and extension, or cheater, pipes will increase leverage, but never use an extension pipe on a ratchet - the ratcheting mechanism could be damaged. Sometimes tightening the nut or bolt first will help to break it loose. Fasteners that require drastic measures to remove should always be replaced with new ones.

Since most of the procedures dealt with in this Chapter involve jacking up the vehicle and working underneath it, a good pair of jackstands will be needed. A hydraulic floor

jack is the preferred type of jack to lift the vehicle, and it can also be used to support certain components during various operations. **Warning:** *Never, under any circumstances, rely on a jack to support the vehicle while working on it. Whenever any of the suspension or steering fasteners are loosened or removed they must be inspected and, if necessary, replaced with new ones of the same part numberoroforiginalequipmentqualityanddesign. Torque specifications must be followed for proper reassembly and component retention. Never attempt to heat or straighten any suspension or steering components. Instead, replace any bent or damaged part with a new one.*

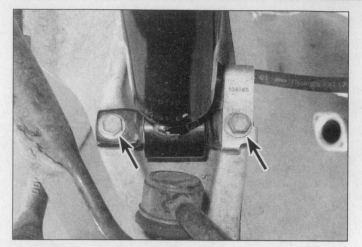

2.2 Remove the lower shock absorber mounting bolts and reposition the brake hose bracket

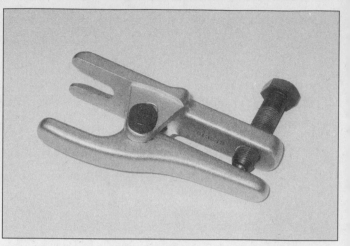

2.4a You'll need a balljoint separator tool like this to separate the balljoint from the steering knuckle without damaging the balljoint boot

2.4b Using hand tools only, hold the ballstud with an Allen wrench and loosen the ballstud nut with a wrench

2   Shock absorber/coil spring assembly (front) - removal, inspection and installation

Removal

Refer to illustrations 2.2, 2.4a, 2.4b, 2.5, 2.7 and 2.8

1 Loosen the wheel lug nuts, raise the vehicle and support it securely on jackstands. Remove the wheel.

2 Remove the brake hose bracket and lower shock absorber mounting bolts **(see illustration)**.

3 On 2007 and earlier models, remove the upper balljoint pinch bolt and separate the balljoint from the steering knuckle.

4 On 2008 and later models, remove the upper balljoint nut and separate the upper balljoint from the steering knuckle using a balljoint separator **(see illustration)**. Do not allow the ballstud to turn with the nut; use an Allen wrench to hold the stud **(see illustration)**. **Caution:** *Do not use an impact wrench to remove the ballstud nut; damage to the ballstud or steering knuckle may occur.*

5 Remove the crossbrace fasteners and remove the crossbrace, if equipped **(see illustration)**. **Note:** *On 2007 and earlier models, remove the air conditioning line bracket fastener and bracket from the shock tower.*

6 Support the steering knuckle with a floor jack.

7 Support the shock absorber assembly, then remove the upper mounting fasteners **(see illustration)**.

8 Lower the knuckle, being careful not to strain the brake hose, and remove the assembly **(see illustration)**.

Inspection

9 Check the shock body for leaking fluid, dents, cracks and other obvious damage which would warrant replacement.

2.5 Crossbrace mounting fastener locations

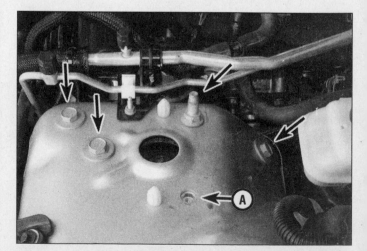

2.7 Shock absorber assembly upper mounting fastener locations. On models without a crossbrace, there is an additional fastener located at point (A)

2.8 Carefully remove the shock absorber assembly from the vehicle

4.2 Disconnect the stabilizer bar link from the bar

10   Check the coil spring for chips or cracks in the spring coating (this will cause premature spring failure due to corrosion). Inspect the spring seat for cuts, hardness and general deterioration.

11   If any undesirable conditions exist, proceed to the shock absorber/coil spring disassembly procedure (see Section 3).

Installation

12   Guide the assembly up into the fenderwell and insert the upper aligning studs through the holes in the body. Once the studs protrude, install the bolts (except for the one that secures the crossbrace). This is most easily accomplished with the help of an assistant, as the assembly is quite heavy and awkward. Tighten the bolts to the torque listed in this Chapter's Specifications.

13   Install the upper balljoint to the steering knuckle and tighten the pinch bolt (2007 and earlier models) or ballstud nut (2008 and later models). Do not allow the ballstud to turn with the nut, use an Allen wrench to hold the stud **(see illustration 2.4)**. Tighten the bolt or nut to the torque value listed in this Chapter's Specifications. **Caution:** *Do not use an impact wrench to remove the ballstud nut; damage to the ballstud or steering knuckle may occur.*

14   Align the bottom of the shock absorber assembly so that the bolts can be inserted to secure it to the lower control arm. Tighten the bolts to the torque listed in this Chapter's Specifications.

15   Install the crossbrace and fasteners, then tighten the fasteners to the torque value listed in this Chapter's Specifications.

16   Install the wheel and lug nuts, then lower the vehicle and tighten the lug nuts to the torque listed in the Chapter 1 Specifications.

17   Drive the vehicle to an alignment shop to have the front end alignment checked, and if necessary, adjusted.

3   Shock absorber/coil spring assembly (front) - replacement

It is possible to replace the shock absorbers or coil springs individually, but the units will have to be disassembled by a qualified repair shop with the proper equipment. You can compare the cost of replacing the complete assemblies with rebuilt units to the cost of having individual components replaced at a shop. **Caution:** *Whenever replacing shock absorbers or coil springs, always replace them in pairs; never just replace one side.*

4   Stabilizer bar, bushings and links (front) - removal and installation

Removal

Refer to illustrations 4.2 and 4.3

1   Loosen the front wheel lug nuts. Raise the front of the vehicle and support it securely on jackstands. Apply the parking brake and block the rear wheels to keep the vehicle from rolling off the stands. Remove the front wheels.

2   Disconnect the wheel speed sensor harness from the stabilizer bar link, then detach the stabilizer bar links from the bar **(see illustration)** and the knuckle. If the ballstud turns with the nut, use a wrench to hold the stud.

3   Unbolt the stabilizer bar bushing brackets **(see illustration)**. Guide the stabilizer bar out from between the subframe and the body.

4   While the stabilizer bar is off the vehicle, slide off the retainer bushings and inspect them. If they're cracked, worn or deteriorated, replace them.

5   Clean the bushing area of the stabilizer bar with a stiff wire brush to remove any rust or dirt.

Installation

6   Lubricate the inside and outside of the new bushing with vegetable oil (used in cook-

4.3 Stabilizer bar bracket bolts

ing) to simplify reassembly. **Caution:** *Don't use petroleum or mineral-based lubricants or brake fluid - they will lead to deterioration of the bushings.* The slits of the bushings must face the rear of the vehicle.

7   Installation is the reverse of removal. Tighten the fasteners to the torque values listed in this Chapter's Specifications.

5   Control arms (front) - removal, inspection and installation

Removal

Lower arm

Refer to illustrations 5.5 and 5.6

1   Loosen the wheel lug nuts, raise the vehicle and support it securely on jackstands. Remove the wheel and splash shield.

2   On 2008 and later models, remove the front wheel speed sensor.

3   Remove the stabilizer bar link from the control arm (see Section 4). Also unbolt the lower end of the shock absorber from the con-

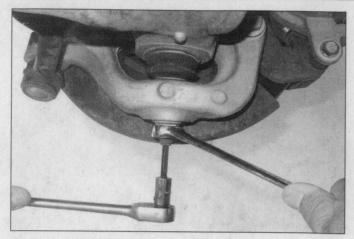

5.5 Using hand tools only, hold the ballstud with an Allen wrench and loosen the ballstud nut with a wrench

5.6 Lower control arm mounting fastener locations

5.10 Upper control arm mounting fastener locations

trol arm (see Section 2).

4   Disconnect the outer tie-rod ends (see Section 17) and loosen the steering gear mounting bolts (see Section 19), raising the steering gear slightly to aid in bolt removal.

5   Loosen the lower balljoint nut, then install a balljoint removal tool to separate the ball-stud from the knuckle. Do not allow the ball-stud to turn with the nut, use an Allen wrench to hold the stud **(see illustration)**. **Caution:** *Do not use an impact wrench to remove the ballstud nut; damage to the ballstud or steering knuckle may occur.*

6   Remove the arm-to-subframe mounting bolts **(see illustration)**.

7   Remove the lower control arm.

Upper arm

Refer to illustration 5.10

8   The upper control arm is attached to the top of the steering knuckle with a balljoint, and to two positions on the shock absorber upper mount with pivot bolts.

9   Remove the shock absorber assembly (see Section 2).

10   Remove the upper arm mounting nuts and bolts **(see illustration)**.

Inspection

11   Check the control arm for distortion and the bushings for wear, replacing parts as necessary. Do not attempt to straighten a bent control arm.

Installation

12   Installation is the reverse of removal. Tighten all of the fasteners to the torque values listed in this Chapter's Specifications. **Note:** *Before tightening the pivot nuts/bolts, raise the outer end of the lower arm to simulate normal ride height.*

13   Install the wheel and lug nuts, lower the vehicle and tighten the lug nuts to the torque listed in the Chapter 1 Specifications.

14   It's a good idea to have the front wheel alignment checked and, if necessary, adjusted after this job has been performed.

---

6   Steering knuckle - removal and installation

Warning: *Dust created by the brake system is harmful to your health. Never blow it out with compressed air and don't inhale any of it. Do not, under any circumstances, use petroleum-based solvents to clean brake parts. Use brake system cleaner only.*

Removal

1   Loosen the wheel lug nuts, raise the vehicle and support it securely on jackstands, then remove the wheel and splash shield.

2   Remove the front wheel speed sensor.

3   Remove the stabilizer link from the control arm (see Section 4).

4   Remove the brake caliper (don't disconnect the hose), the caliper mounting bracket and the brake disc (see Chapter 9). Disconnect the brake hose from the strut. Hang the caliper from the coil spring with a piece of wire - don't let it hang by the brake hose.

5   If you're working on a 2007 or earlier model, disconnect the wheel speed sensor electrical connector and free the harness from any retaining clips. If you're working on a 2008 or later model, remove the wheel speed sensor from the steering knuckle (see Chapter 9).

6   Separate the tie-rod end from the steering knuckle arm (see Section 17).

7   Separate the lower control arm balljoint from the steering knuckle (see Section 5).

8   Separate the upper control arm balljoint from the steering knuckle (see Section 5) and remove the knuckle and hub assembly.

Installation

9   Guide the knuckle and hub assembly into position connect the balljoints to the knuckle and tighten the nuts to the torque listed in this Chapter's Specifications.

10   Attach the tie-rod end to the steering knuckle arm (see Section 17) and the stabilizer link to the control arm (see Section 4). Tighten the nuts to the torque listed in this Chapter's Specifications.

11   Place the brake disc on the hub, install the disc-locating screw, and install the caliper (see Chapter 9).

12   Install the wheel and lug nuts. Lower the vehicle and tighten the lug nuts to the torque listed in the Chapter 1 Specifications.

13   Have the front-end alignment checked and, if necessary, adjusted.

---

7   Hub and bearing assembly (front) - removal and installation

Refer to illustration 7.4

Warning: *Dust created by the brake system is harmful to your health. Never blow it out with compressed air and don't inhale any of it. Do not, under any circumstances, use petroleum-based solvents to clean brake parts. Use brake system cleaner only.*

Note: *The hub and wheel bearing are press-fit together and removed as an assembly. The assembly can be removed and taken to an automotive repair facility for service.*

1   Loosen the wheel lug nuts, raise the vehicle and support it securely on jackstands, then remove the wheel.

2   Remove the brake disc (see Chapter 9).

3   If you're working on a 2007 or earlier model, disconnect the wheel speed sensor electrical connector and free the harness from any retaining clips. If you're working on a 2008 or later model, remove the wheel speed sensor from the steering knuckle (see Chapter 9).

4   Remove the three hub mounting bolts from the back side of the steering knuckle **(see illustration)**.

5   Remove the hub and bearing assembly from the knuckle.

6   Installation is the reverse of removal, noting the following points:

  a) *Make sure the mating surfaces on the knuckle and the hub and bearing assembly are clean before installation.*

  b) *Tighten the mounting bolts to the torque listed in this Chapter's Specifications.*

  c) *Install the brake disc (see Chapter 9).*

  d) *Install the brake caliper (see Chapter 9), tightening the mounting bolts to the torque listed in the Chapter 9 Specifications.*

  e) *Install the wheel and wheel lug nuts. Lower the vehicle and tighten the nuts to the torque listed in the Chapter 1 Specifications.*

8   Shock absorber (rear) - removal and installation

Refer to illustrations 8.4 and 8.5

1   Loosen the wheel lug nuts, raise the vehicle and support it securely on jackstands. Block the front wheels to prevent the vehicle from rolling. Remove the wheel.

2   Support the rear lower control arm with a floor jack positioned under the spring pocket. **Warning:** *The jack must remain in this position throughout the entire procedure.*

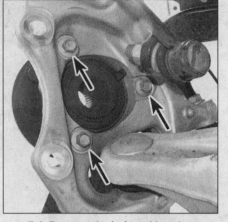

7.4 Remove the hub and bearing assembly mounting fasteners

3   Open the rear hatch or trunk and remove the trunk liner or seat back (see Chapter 11).

4   Remove the lower shock mounting bolt **(see illustration)**.

5   Remove the nuts securing the upper shock mount to the body **(see illustration)**.

6   Maneuver the shock out of the vehicle. If new shocks are to be installed, swap the bracket to the top of the new shock.

7   Installation is the reverse of the removal procedure. **Caution:** *New shock absorbers are gas-filled and come compressed and retained with a fiberglass strap. Do NOT remove the strap until the shock is installed.*

8   Tighten the mounting fasteners to the torque listed in this Chapter's Specifications. **Note:** *Before tightening the lower mounting fasteners, raise the lower arm to simulate normal ride height.*

9   Suspension arms (rear) - removal and installation

1   Loosen the wheel lug nuts, raise the vehicle and support it securely on jackstands. Block the front wheels to prevent the vehicle from rolling. Remove the wheel.

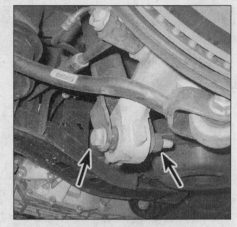

8.4 Remove the rear shock lower mounting nut and bolt

Upper suspension arm

Refer to illustration 9.6

2   Remove the brake caliper and caliper mounting bracket.

3   Remove the rear shock absorber (see Section 8). **Warning:** *Be sure to support the lower control arm with a floor jack positioned under the spring pocket. The jack must remain in this position throughout the entire procedure.*

4   Remove the upper balljoint nut. Install a balljoint removal tool to separate the ballstud from the knuckle.

5   Support the rear differential and subframe with a floor jack. Loosen the subframe bolts enough to allow access to the upper control arm mounting nut/bolts. **Note:** *Some items will need to be removed in order to lower the subframe, but it is not necessary to completely remove the subframe (see Section 13).*

6   Remove the mounting nut/bolts from the inner end of the arm **(see illustration)**. Remove the arm from the vehicle.

7   Installation is the reverse of removal. Tighten the fasteners to the torque listed in this Chapter's Specifications. **Note:** *Before*

8.5 Remove the shock mount-to-body nuts

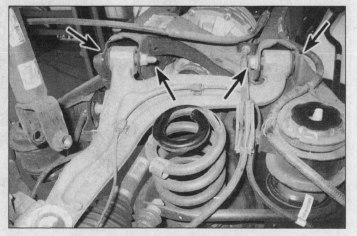

9.6 Upper suspension arm mounting nut/bolt locations

9.12 Trailing arm mounting fastener locations

9.17 Toe-link arm outer mounting bolt location

tightening the inner pivot bolts/nuts, raise the lower arm to simulate normal ride height.

Lower suspension arm

8   Remove the coil spring (see Section 10).
9   Remove the lower arm inner nut/bolt and remove the arm from the vehicle (see Section 10).
10   Installation is the reverse of removal. Tighten the fasteners to the torque listed in this Chapter's Specifications. **Note:** *Before tightening any pivot bolts/nuts, raise the lower arm to simulate normal ride height.*

Trailing arm

Refer to illustration 9.12

11   Support the lower control arm with a floor jack.
12   Remove the trailing arm-to-knuckle nut/bolt **(see illustration)**.
13   Remove the trailing arm-to-subframe nut/bolt and remove the arm.
14   Installation is the reverse of removal. Tighten the fasteners to the torque listed in this Chapter's Specifications.

Toe-link arm

Refer to illustration 9.17

15   On 2008 and later models, it may be necessary to support, unbolt and lower the front of the subframe (see Section 13) to access the inner toe-link bolt.
16   Remove the inner toe-link nut/bolt.
17   Remove the outer toe-link bolt **(see illustration),** then remove the link arm.
18   Installation is the reverse of removal. Tighten the fasteners to the torque listed in this Chapter's Specifications.

10   Coil spring (rear) - removal and installation

Refer to illustrations 10.8 and 10.9

Warning: *Always replace the springs as a set - never replace just one of them.*

1   Loosen the wheel lug nuts, raise the rear of the vehicle and support it securely on jackstands. Block the front wheels to prevent the vehicle from rolling. Remove the wheel.
2   Support the lower control arm with a floor

jack positioned underneath the coil spring pocket.
3   If removing the right side coil spring, remove the brake line mounting bracket nuts and bolts, and remove the bracket.
4   Remove the shock absorber lower mounting bolt **(see illustration 8.4),** then slowly lower the arm and remove the bolt.
5   Loosen the driveaxle/hub nut until it reaches the end of the threads, then push the driveaxle into the hub enough to just loosen the splines.
6   Detach the stabilizer bar link from the lower control arm (see Section 14).
7   Detach the trailing arm and toe-link arm from the knuckle (see Section 9).
8   Loosen the lower control arm inner pivot bolt and remove the outer bolt **(see illustration)**.
9   Pull the steering knuckle outward while pushing the driveaxle into the hub (an assistant would be helpful), then slowly lower the jack to extend the coil spring. Once there is no more load on the spring, remove it from the control arm **(see illustration). Caution:** *Be careful not to overextend the inner CV joint of the driveaxle.*
10   If you're working on a 2007 or earlier model, and you can't lower the control arm far enough to allow the spring to fully extend, support the subframe with another floor jack on the side from which the spring is being removed. Remove the subframe bolts **(see illustration 13.27)** on that side and slowly lower the subframe an adequate amount to allow spring extension.
11   Mark the position of the coil spring to the spring insulators.
12   Check the spring for cracks and chips, replacing the springs as a set if any defects are found. Also check the insulators for damage and deterioration, replacing it if necessary.
13   Installation is the reverse of removal. Be sure to properly orient the lower end of the spring with the insulator. Connect all suspension components before tightening any fasteners. **Note:** *Before tightening any pivot bolts/ nuts, raise the lower arm to simulate normal ride height.*

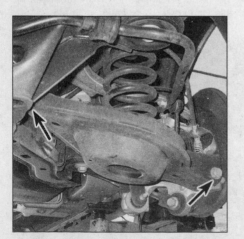

10.8 Lower suspension arm mounting fastener locations

10.9 Slowly lower the floor jack until the coil spring is fully extended, then remove the spring

14   Install a new driveaxle/hub nut and tighten it to the torque listed in the Chapter 8 Specifications. Install the wheel and lug nuts, then lower the vehicle and tighten the lug nuts to the torque listed in the Chapter 1 Specifications.

15   Have the wheel alignment checked and, if necessary, adjusted.

11   Hub and bearing assembly (rear) - removal and installation

1   Loosen the wheel lug nuts and driveaxle/hub nut. Raise the vehicle and support it securely on jackstands, then remove the wheel.

2   Unbolt and set aside the caliper and caliper mounting bracket. Do not let the caliper hang by the brake hose; wire the caliper to the spring or shock absorber with mechanic's wire.

3   Remove the brake disc (see Chapter 9).

4   Remove the driveaxle/hub nut.

5   If you're working on a 2007 or earlier model, disconnect the wheel speed sensor electrical connector and free the harness from any retaining clips. If you're working on a 2008 or later model, remove the wheel speed sensor from the knuckle (see Chapter 9).

6   Remove the three hub mounting bolts from the back side of the rear knuckle. **Note:** *It might be necessary to push the outer end of the driveaxle into the hub to allow bolt removal.*

7   Remove the hub nut and slide the hub and bearing assembly from the rear knuckle. If the driveaxle splines stick in the hub splines, use a two- or three-jaw puller to push the driveaxle from the hub as the hub is removed from the knuckle.

8   Installation is the reverse of removal. Tighten the fasteners to the proper torque specifications. Use a new driveaxle/hub nut and tighten it to the torque listed in the Chapter 8 Specifications. Tighten the brake component fasteners to the torque values listed in the Chapter 9 Specifications. Install the wheel and lug nuts, then lower the vehicle and tighten the lug nuts to the torque listed in the Chapter 1 Specifications.

12   Rear knuckle and hub - removal and installation

Warning: *Dust created by the brake system is harmful to your health. Never blow it out with compressed air and don't inhale any of it. Do not, under any circumstances, use petroleum-based solvents to clean brake parts. Use brake system cleaner only.*
Warning: *Always support the lower control arm before removing the lower shock mounting bolts, because the lower control arm will drop about 3 inches.*

Removal

1   Loosen the wheel lug nuts, raise the vehicle and support it securely on jackstands,

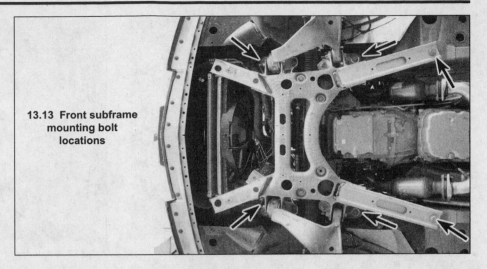

13.13 Front subframe mounting bolt locations

then remove the wheel. Loosen the driveaxle/hub nut (see Chapter 8)

2   Remove the brake caliper (don't disconnect the hose), the caliper mounting bracket and the brake disc (see Chapter 9). Disconnect the brake hose from the strut. Hang the caliper from the coil spring with a piece of wire - don't let it hang by the brake hose.

3   If you're working on a 2007 or earlier model, disconnect the wheel speed sensor electrical connector and free the harness from any retaining clips. If you're working on a 2008 or later model, remove the wheel speed sensor from the knuckle (see Chapter 9).

4   Disconnect the parking brake bracket and cable.

5   Support the lower control arm with a floor jack placed under the spring pocket. **Warning:** *The jack must remain in this position throughout the entire procedure.*

6   Separate the upper control arm balljoint from the knuckle (see Section 9).

7   Detach the toe-link arm from the knuckle (see Section 9).

8   Remove the shock absorber lower mounting bolt (see Section 8).

9   Remove the lower control arm to knuckle bolt/nut (see Section 9).

10   Remove the trailing arm to knuckle bolt/nut (see Section 9).

11   Remove the driveaxle/hub nut and push the driveaxle from the hub while removing the knuckle and hub assembly. Support the end of the driveaxle with a piece of wire and remove the knuckle.

Installation

12   Guide the knuckle and hub assembly into position, inserting the driveaxle into the hub.

13   Connect the upper balljoint to the knuckle, but don't tighten the fasteners yet.

14   Reconnect the shock absorber (see Section 8), lower control arm, trailing arm and the toe-link arm (see Section 9). Raise the suspension to simulate normal ride height, then tighten the suspension fasteners to the torque values listed in this Chapter's Specifications.

15   Place the brake disc on the hub, install

the disc-locating fastener, and install the caliper (see Chapter 9).

16   Install the driveaxle/hub nut and tighten it to the torque listed in the Chapter 8 Specifications.

17   Install the wheel and lug nuts. Lower the vehicle and tighten the lug nuts to the torque listed in the Chapter 1 Specifications.

18   Have the wheel alignment checked and, if necessary, adjusted.

13   Subframe - removal and installation

Front

Refer to illustration 13.13

1   Raise the vehicle and support it securely on jackstands, then remove the wheels.

2   Remove the engine splash shield and covers.

3   Install an engine support fixture or engine hoist.

4   Remove the electrical harness connectors and remove the harness from the subframe.

5   Remove the brake lines from the frame.

6   Disconnect the ABS modulator valve from the frame.

7   Using metal wire, tie the radiator and air conditioning condenser to the body.

8   Disconnect the lower stabilizer bar link (see Section 4).

9   Remove the power steering gear mounting bolts (see Section 19) and tie the gear to the body with a wire.

10   Disconnect the lower balljoint (see Section 5) and tie rod ends from the knuckle (see Section 17).

11   Remove the shock absorber lower mounting bolts from the lower control arm (see Section 2).

12   Remove the engine mount lower mounting nuts.

13   Support the subframe with a transmission jack and remove the subframe mounting bolts **(see illustration)**.

14   Raise the engine and transmission

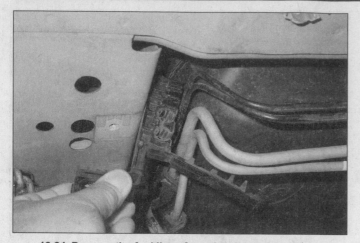

13.24 Remove the fuel lines from the clips on the frame

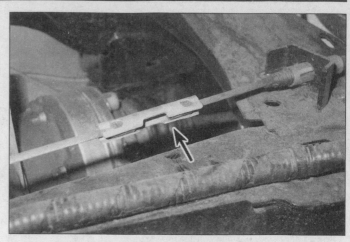

13.26 Disconnect the rear parking brake bable from the front

slightly using the engine support fixture or hoist.

15   Slowly lower the transmission jack and subframe.

16   Disconnect and remove the stabilizer bar and lower control arms from the subframe.

17   With the help of an assistant, remove the subframe from under the vehicle.

Rear

Refer to illustrations 13.24, 13.26, 13.27 and 13.28

18   Loosen the rear wheel lug nuts. Raise the rear of the vehicle and support it securely on jackstands. Block the front wheels to keep the vehicle from rolling off the stands. Remove the rear wheels.

19   Remove the exhaust system (see Chapter 4).

20   Remove the driveshaft (see Chapter 8).

21   Support the subframe and rear differential assembly using a large transmission jack.

22   Support the lower control arm with a floor jack positioned under the coil spring pocket, then remove the shock absorber lower mount-

ing bolt. Slowly lower the floor jack. Repeat this on the other side.

23   Disconnect the rear wheel speed sensor connectors.

24   Remove the fuel lines from the mounting clips running down the body **(see illustration)**.

25   If the rear crossmember is being lowered to access the EVAP canister or fuel tank, disconnect the rear brake line bracket mounting nuts and pull the brake line bracket off the studs. If the crossmember is being replaced, disconnect and plug the brake lines (see Chapter 9).

26   Disconnect the parking brake cable from the front parking brake cable connector **(see illustration)**.

27   With the subframe fully supported by the transmission jack, remove the subframe mounting bolts **(see illustration)**.

28   Lower the subframe from the vehicle **(see illustration)**.

29   Installation is the reverse of removal. If the brake lines were disconnected, bleed the brake system (see Chapter 9).

14   Stabilizer bar, bushings and links (rear) - removal and installation

Removal

Refer to illustrations 14.2 and 14.4

1   Loosen the rear wheel lug nuts. Raise the rear of the vehicle and support it securely on jackstands. Block the front wheels to keep the vehicle from rolling off the stands. Remove the rear wheels.

2   Detach the stabilizer bar links from the lower control arm and stabilizer bar. If the ball-stud turns with the nut, use an Allen wrench to hold the stud **(see illustration)**.

3   On 2008 and later models, support the rear mufflers with a jack. Remove the muffler hangers (see Chapter 4) and lower the rear exhaust.

4   Remove the stabilizer bar bracket bolts **(see illustration)**. Guide the stabilizer bar out from between the exhaust and the body.

5   While the stabilizer bar is off the vehicle, slide off the bushings and inspect them. If

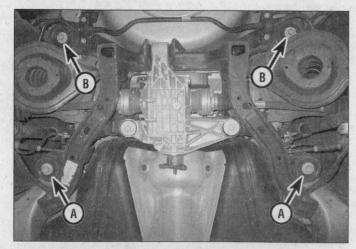

13.27 Rear subframe front (A) and rear (B) mounting bolts

13.28 Use a suitable transmission jack to remove the rear subframe/suspension assembly

14.2 Hold the ball stud using a Allen wrench and loosen the stabilizer link nut with a wrench

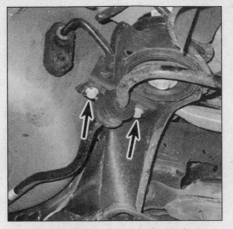

14.4 Stabilizer bar bracket bolts

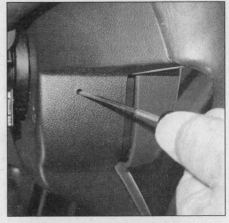

15.2 Depress the clips through the holes on each side of the steering wheel to release the airbag (2008 and later model shown)

they're cracked, worn or deteriorated, replace them.

6   Clean the bushing area of the stabilizer bar with a stiff wire brush to remove any rust or dirt.

Installation

7   Lubricate the inside and outside of the new bushing with vegetable oil (used in cooking) to simplify reassembly. **Caution:** *Don't use petroleum or mineral-based lubricants or brake fluid - they will lead to deterioration of the bushings.* The slits of the bushings must face the front of the vehicle.

8   Installation is the reverse of removal. Tighten the fasteners to the torque values listed in this Chapter's Specifications.

15 Steering wheel - removal and installation

Warning: *These models are equipped with a Supplemental Restraint System (SRS), more*

commonly known as airbags. Always disable the airbag system before working in the vicinity of any airbag system component to avoid the possibility of accidental deployment of the airbag(s), which could cause personal injury (see Chapter 12).

Warning: *Do not use a memory saving device to preserve the PCM or radio memory when working on or near airbag system components.*

Removal

Refer to illustrations 15.2, 15.3, 15.6 and 15.8

1   Turn the ignition key to Off, then disconnect the cable from the negative terminal of the battery. Wait at least two minutes before proceeding.

2   On 2007 and earlier models, turn the steering wheel so that the slots on the back side of the steering wheel are at the top and bottom. Insert special tool #J-44298 and push the tool apart to release the spring loaded airbag module clips. On 2008 and later models, use a small screwdriver through the holes in

the backside of the steering wheel to release the airbag module clips **(see illustration)**. Gently pull the airbag module away from the wheel on the side you have released, then repeat this Step on the other side of the wheel.

3   Pry up the connector locks and disconnect the airbag module electrical connectors **(see illustration)**.

4   If turned in Step 2, turn the steering wheel so the wheels are pointing straight ahead and remove the key.

5   Remove the airbag and set the airbag module in a safe, isolated area. **Warning:** *Carry the airbag module with the trim side facing away from you, and set the airbag module down with the trim side facing up. Don't place anything on top of the airbag module.*

6   Make match marks on the wheel and the steering shaft, then remove the steering wheel mounting nut or bolt **(see illustration)**. Rock the wheel lightly to remove it from the shaft.

7   Feed the wires and connectors through the steering wheel as you remove it.

15.3 Pry up the locking tabs, then disconnect the airbag connectors

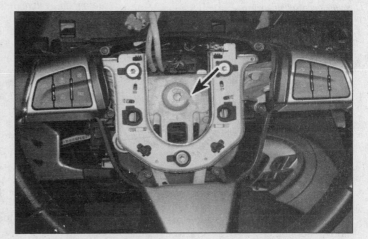

15.6 Mark the position of the steering wheel to the shaft, then use a socket to loosen the steering wheel nut or bolt

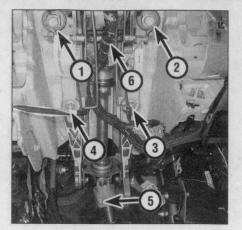

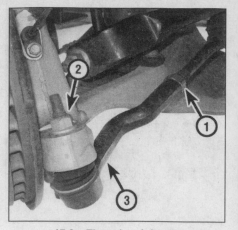

15.8 Apply a piece of tape to the clockspring to prevent it from rotating

16.4 Steering column details

1   *Steering column mounting bolt (1)*
2   *Steering column mounting bolt (2)*
3   *Steering column mounting nut (3)*
4   *Steering column mounting nut (4)*
5   *Intermediate steering shaft bolt*
6   *Steering column wiring harness*

17.2a Tie-rod end details

1   *Jam nut*
2   *Locking nut*
3   *Tie-rod end*

17.2b Mark the position of the tie-rod end in relation to the threads

8   Tape the clockspring so that it cannot rotate **(see illustration)**. **Caution:** *Do not rotate the steering shaft at any time while the wheel and airbag are removed or the clockspring could be damaged.*
9   If the clockspring is to be removed, remove the steering column covers (see Chapter 11), unplug its connectors and remove the mounting screws.

Installation

10   If the clockspring was removed, install it now, then center it (even if it was not removed, but if the inner rotor has turned, it must be centered).

a) *Rotate the inner rotor of the clockspring counterclockwise until you feel resistance.* **Caution:** *Don't apply too much force.*
b) *Turn the rotor clockwise approximately 2 to 2-1/4 turns, placing the electrical connector in the 12 o'clock position.*

11   To install the wheel, feed the wiring and airbag connectors through the wheel and place the steering wheel on the steering shaft, aligning the match marks you made.

12   Tighten the steering wheel nut to the torque listed in this Chapter's Specifications.
13   The remainder of installation is the reverse of removal. **Caution:** *Make sure the connectors fit correctly on the airbag module (with the safety tabs still UP). When connecting the two airbag connectors, follow the color-coding. The orange connector goes to the orange connection on the airbag. Do not push the connectors on if the clips are down. After the clips are secured, push the airbag module down toward the wheel until the retaining clips lock.*

---

16   Steering column - removal and installation

Warning: *These models are equipped with a Supplemental Restraint System (SRS), more commonly known as airbags. Always disable the airbag system before working in the vicinity of any airbag system component to avoid the possibility of accidental deployment of the airbag(s), which could cause personal injury (see Chapter 12).*
Warning: *Do not use a memory saving device to preserve the PCM or radio memory when working on or near airbag system components.*

Removal

Refer to illustration 16.4

1   Park the vehicle with the wheels pointing straight ahead. Disconnect the cable from the negative terminal of the battery (see Chapter 5).
2   Remove the steering wheel (see Section 15)
3   Remove the steering column covers, then tape the airbag clockspring to prevent

it from turning. **Caution:** *If this is not done, the airbag clockspring could be damaged.* Remove the knee bolster trim panel and knee bolster (see Chapter 11, Section 24).
4   Remove the intermediate shaft upper bolt and disconnect the steering shaft from the steering column **(see illustration)**.
5   Disconnect the electrical connectors for the multi-function switch (see Chapter 12).
6   Remove the steering column mounting fasteners **(see illustration 16.4)**. Lower the column and pull it to the rear, making sure nothing is still connected, then remove the column.

Installation

7   Guide the steering column into position, engaging the U-joint with the bottom of the steering shaft. Install the steering column mounting fasteners and tighten them to the torque listed in this Chapter's Specifications. **Note:** *An assistant will be very helpful during this procedure.*
8   Connect the U-joint to the intermediate shaft. Install a New intermediate shaft bolt, tightening it to the torque listed in this Chapter's Specifications.
9   The remainder of installation is the reverse of removal.

---

17   Tie-rod ends - removal and installation

Removal

Refer to illustrations 17.2a, 17.2b and 17.4

1   Loosen the front wheel lug nuts. Apply the parking brake, raise the front of the vehicle and support it securely on jackstands. Remove the front wheel.
2   Hold the tie-rod with a pair of locking pliers or wrench, and loosen the jam nut enough to mark the position of the tie-rod end in relation to the threads **(see illustrations)**.

17.4 Disconnect the tie-rod end from the steering knuckle arm with a puller

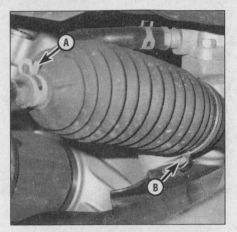

18.3 The outer ends of the steering gear boots are secured by band-type clamps (A); they're easily released with a pair of pliers. The inner ends of the steering gear boots are retained by boot clamps (B) which must be cut off and discarded

3   Loosen (but don't remove) the locking nut on the tie-rod end stud.

4   Disconnect the tie-rod end from the steering knuckle arm with a puller **(see illustration)**. Remove the nut and detach the tie-rod end.

5   Unscrew the tie-rod end from the tie-rod.

Installation

6   Thread on the tie-rod end to the marked position and insert the stud into the steering knuckle arm. Tighten the jam nut securely.

7   Install the locking nut on the stud and tighten it to the torque listed in this Chapter's Specifications.

8   Install the wheel and lug nuts. Lower the vehicle and tighten the lug nuts to the torque listed in the Chapter 1 Specifications.

9   Have the alignment checked and, if necessary, adjusted.

18   Steering gear boots - replacement

Refer to illustration 18.3

1   Loosen the lug nuts, raise the vehicle and support it securely on jackstands. Remove the wheel.

2   Remove the tie-rod end and jam nut (see Section 17).

3   Remove the outer steering gear boot clamp with a pair of pliers **(see illustration)**. Cut off the inner boot clamp with a pair of diagonal cutters. Slide off the boot.

4   Before installing the new boot, wrap the threads and serrations on the end of the steering rod with a layer of tape so the small end of the new boot isn't damaged.

5   Slide the new boot into position on the steering gear until it seats in the groove in the steering rod and install new clamps.

6   Remove the tape and install the tie-rod end (see Section 17).

7   Install the wheel and lug nuts. Lower the vehicle and tighten the lug nuts to the torque listed in the Chapter 1 Specifications.

19   Steering gear - removal and installation

Warning: *These models are equipped with airbags. Always disable the airbag system before working in the vicinity of airbag system components (see Chapter 12). Make sure the steering column shaft is not turned while the steering gear is removed or you could damage the airbag system clockspring. To prevent the shaft from turning, turn the ignition key to the lock position before beginning work, and run the seat belt through the steering wheel and clip it into its latch.*

Removal

1   Disconnect the cable from the negative terminal of the battery (see Chapter 5).

2   From inside the vehicle under the instrument panel, remove and discard the intermediate shaft pinch bolt and remove the shaft (see Section 15).

3   Loosen the front wheel lug nuts. Raise the vehicle and place it securely on jackstands. Remove both front wheels.

4   Detach the tie-rod ends from the steering knuckles (see Section 17).

5   Remove the splash shield.

2007 and earlier models

6   Disconnect the VES electrical connector from the steering gear.

7   Disconnect the stabilizer bar and links (see Section 4).

8   Place a drain pan under the steering gear and detach the power steering pressure and return lines **(see illustration)**. Cap the ends to prevent excessive fluid loss and contamination. **Note:** *Some models have a sheetmetal shield (secured by two bolts) that must be removed for access to the fittings.*

9   Remove the steering gear mounting bolts and slide the steering gear out the driver's side wheel opening.

2008 and later models

10   Attach an engine support fixture or engine hoist to the engine.

11   Disconnect the lower control arms from the steering knuckles (see Section 5).

12   Disconnect the engine mounts from the subframe.

13   Disconnect any wiring harnesses that may be connected to the subframe.

14   Support the rear of the subframe with jackstands.

15   Support the front of the subframe with a floor jack. Loosen the rear subframe mounting fasteners and remove the front subframe fasteners.

16   Slightly raise the engine, then lower the front of the subframe with the jack. Continue raising the engine and lowering the front of the subframe until the steering gear can be removed.

17   Remove the steering gear mounting bolts.

18   Remove the steering gear from the vehicle.

Installation

19   Installation is the reverse of removal, noting the following points:

a)   *When connecting the steering gear input shaft to the intermediate shaft U-joint, be sure to align the matchmarks, and install a new pinch bolt.*

b)   *Use new subframe mounting fasteners.*

c)   *Use a new banjo bolt and sealing washers for the power steering pressure line.*

d)   *Tighten all fasteners to the torque values listed in this Chapter's Specifications.*

e)   *Tighten the lug nuts to the torque listed in the Chapter 1 Specifications.*

f)   *Fill the power steering reservoir with the recommended fluid (see Chapter 1). Bleed the power steering hydraulic system (see Section 21).*

g)   *Have the front end alignment checked and, if necessary, adjusted.*

20   Power steering pump - removal and installation

Removal

Refer to illustrations 20.8 and 20.9

1   Disconnect the cable from the negative battery terminal (see Chapter 5).

2   Remove the engine cover, the air filter housing and inlet air resonator (see Chapter 4).

3   Using a large syringe or suction gun, siphon as much fluid out of the power steering fluid reservoir as possible. Place a drain pan under the vehicle to catch any fluid that spills out when the hoses are disconnected. On models with a remote fluid reservoir, remove the power steering fluid reservoir.

4   Remove the drivebelt (see Chapter 1).

20.8 Install a power steering pulley removal tool onto the pulley and press the pulley off of the pump

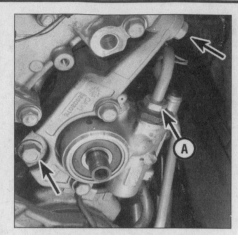

20.9 Once the pulley is removed, disconnect the line from the pump (A), and remove the mounting bolts (two of three shown) - typical 3.0L engine model

5   Disconnect the electrical connector at the power steering pump.

6   Disconnect the supply and pressure hoses from the power steering pump. **Note:** *On some models, all of the lines can't be removed until the pulley has been removed.*

7   On 3.2L engines, rotate the pump pulley and remove the front mounting bolts through the holes in the pulley.

8   On all other models, install a power steering pump pulley removal tool and remove the pulley **(see illustration)**.

9   Remove the pump mounting bolts and remove the power steering pump **(see illustration)**.

10   Unscrew and remove the mounting bolts, and withdraw the power steering pump from the engine.

Installation

11   Installation is the reverse of removal, noting the following points:

a) *Press the power steering pulley onto the pump to the same depth.*

b) *Tighten the mounting bolts to the torque listed in this Chapter's Specifications.*

c) *Fill the power steering reservoir with the recommended fluid (see Chapter 1). Bleed the power steering hydraulic system (see Section 21).*

21   Power steering system - bleeding

1   The power steering system must be bled whenever a line is disconnected. Bubbles can be seen in power steering fluid that has air in it and the fluid will often have a tan or milky appearance. Low fluid level can cause air to mix with the fluid, resulting in a noisy pump as well as foaming of the fluid.

2   Open the hood and check the fluid level in the reservoir, adding the specified fluid necessary to bring it up to the proper level (see Chapter 1).

3   Start the engine and slowly turn the steering wheel several times from left-to-right

and back again. Do not turn the wheel completely from lock-to-lock. Check the fluid level, topping it up as necessary until it remains steady and no more bubbles are visible.

22   Power steering fluid cooler - removal and installation

1   Remove the engine covers.

2   Raise the vehicle and support it securely on jackstands. Remove the splash shield.

3   Place a drain pan under the power steering cooler.

V6 engines

2007 and earlier models

4   On 3.2L engines, remove the air intake duct (see Chapter 4). On 3.6L engines,

remove the radiator (see Chapter 3).

5   Disconnect the cooler hose clamps, then the hoses, and allow the fluid to drain.

6   Remove the cooler-to-frame fasteners and remove the cooler.

2008 and later models

7   Loosen the front bumper cover enough to access the cooler bracket top fasteners (see Chapter 11).

8   Loosen the cooler hose clamps, disconnect the lines from the cooler and allow the fluid to drain.

9   Remove the cooler bracket fasteners, then remove the cooler and bracket from under the vehicle.

V8 engines

10   On 2008 and later models, remove the front bumper cover (see Chapter 11).

11   Loosen the cooler hose clamps, disconnect the lines from the cooler and allow the fluid to drain.

12   Remove the cooler bracket mounting fasteners, then remove the cooler and bracket from the vehicle.

All models

13   Installation is the reverse of removal.

14   Fill the power steering reservoir with the recommended fluid (see Chapter 1). Bleed the power steering hydraulic system (see Section 21).

23   Wheels and tires - general information

Refer to illustration 23.1

1   All vehicles covered by this manual are equipped with metric-sized fiberglass or steel belted radial tires **(see illustration)**. Use of

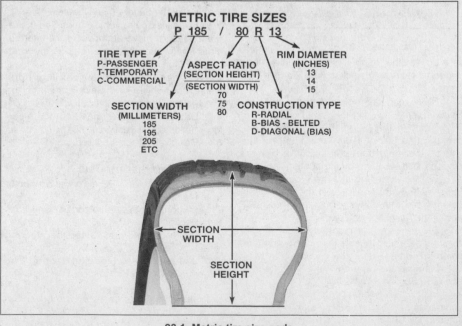

23.1 Metric tire size code

other size or type of tires may affect the ride and handling of the vehicle. Don't mix different types of tires, such as radials and bias belted, on the same vehicle as handling may be seriously affected. It's recommended that tires be replaced in pairs on the same axle, but if only one tire is being replaced, be sure it's the same size, structure and tread design as the other.

2   Because tire pressure has a substantial effect on handling and wear, the pressure on all tires should be checked at least once a month or before any extended trips (see Chapter 1).

3   Wheels must be replaced if they are bent, dented, leak air, have elongated bolt holes, are heavily rusted, out of vertical symmetry or if the lug nuts won't stay tight. Wheel repairs that use welding or peening are not recommended.

4   Tire and wheel balance is important in the overall handling, braking and performance of the vehicle. Unbalanced wheels can adversely affect handling and ride characteristics as well as tire life. Whenever a tire is installed on a wheel, the tire and wheel should be balanced by a shop with the proper equipment.

24   Wheel alignment - general information

Refer to illustration 24.1

A wheel alignment refers to the adjustments made to the wheels so they are in proper angular relationship to the suspension and the ground. Wheels that are out of proper alignment not only affect vehicle control, but also increase tire wear. The front end angles normally measured are camber, caster and toe-in **(see illustration)**. Toe-in and camber are adjustable; if the caster is not correct, check for bent components. Rear toe-in is also adjustable.

Getting the proper wheel alignment is a very exacting process, one in which complicated and expensive machines are necessary to perform the job properly. Because of this, you should have a technician with the proper equipment perform these tasks. We will, however, use this space to give you a basic idea of what is involved with a wheel alignment so you can better understand the process and deal intelligently with the shop that does the work.

Toe-in is the turning in of the wheels. The purpose of a toe specification is to ensure parallel rolling of the wheels. In a vehicle with zero toe-in, the distance between the front edges of the wheels will be the same as the distance between the rear edges of the wheels. The actual amount of toe-in is normally only a fraction of an inch. On the front end, toe-in is

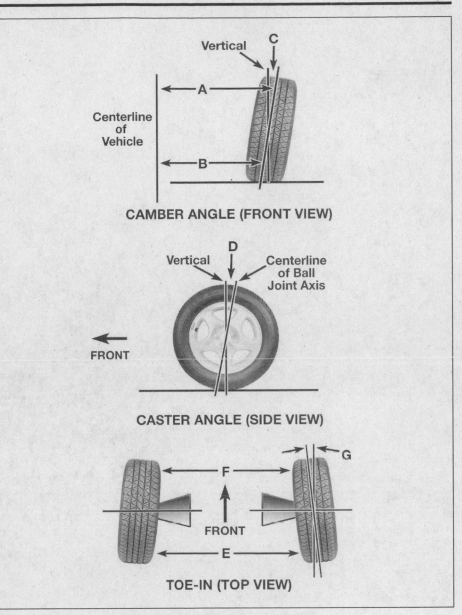

24.1 Camber, caster and toe-in angles

A minus B = C (degrees camber)
D = degrees caster

E minus F = toe-in (measured in inches)
G = toe-in (expressed in degrees)

controlled by the tie-rod end position on the tie-rod. On the rear end, it's controlled by a threaded toe-link. Incorrect toe-in will cause the tires to wear improperly by making them scrub against the road surface.

Camber is the tilting of the wheels from vertical when viewed from one end of the vehicle. When the wheels tilt out at the top, the camber is said to be positive (+). When the wheels tilt in at the top the camber is negative (-). The amount of tilt is measured in degrees from vertical and this measurement is called

the camber angle. This angle affects the amount of tire tread which contacts the road and compensates for changes in the suspension geometry when the vehicle is cornering or traveling over an undulating surface.

Caster is the tilting of the front steering axis from the vertical. A tilt toward the rear is positive caster and a tilt toward the front is negative caster. On the front end, caster can only be adjusted by installing a new upper control arm with offset bushings. On the rear end, caster isn't adjustable.

Notes

Chapter 11 Body

Contents

1   General information

Warning: *The models covered by this manual are equipped with Supplemental Restraint Systems (SRS), more commonly known as airbags. Always disable the airbag system before working in the vicinity of any airbag system components to avoid the possibility of accidental deployment of the airbags, which could cause personal injury (see Chapter 12).*

Certain body components are particularly vulnerable to accident damage and can be unbolted and repaired or replaced. Among these parts are the hood, doors, tailgate, liftgate, bumpers and front fenders.

Only general body maintenance practices and body panel repair procedures within the scope of the do-it-yourselfer are included in this Chapter.

Make sure the damaged area is perfectly clean and rust free. If the touch-up kit has a wire brush, use it to clean the scratch or chip. Or use fine steel wool wrapped around the end of a pencil. Clean the scratched or chipped surface only, not the good paint surrounding it. Rinse the area with water and allow it to dry thoroughly

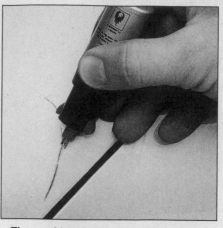

Thoroughly mix the paint, then apply a small amount with the touch-up kit brush or a very fine artist's brush. Brush in one direction as you fill the scratch area. Do not build up the paint higher than the surrounding paint

2   Repair of minor paint scratches

No matter how hard you try to keep your vehicle looking like new, it will inevitably be scratched, chipped or dented at some point. If the metal is actually dented, seek the advice of a professional. But you can fix minor scratches and chips yourself. Buy a touch-up paint kit from a dealer service department or an auto parts store. To ensure that you get the right color, you'll need to have the specific make, model and year of your vehicle and, ideally, the paint code, which is located on a special metal plate under the hood or in the door jamb.

3   Body repair - minor damage

Plastic body panels

The following repair procedures are for minor scratches and gouges. Repair of more serious damage should be left to a dealer service department or qualified auto body shop. Below is a list of the equipment and materials necessary to perform the following repair procedures on plastic body panels.

> Wax, grease and silicone removing
>   solvent
> Cloth-backed body tape
> Sanding discs
> Drill motor with three-inch disc holder
> Hand sanding block
> Rubber squeegees
> Sandpaper
> Non-porous mixing palette
> Wood paddle or putty knife
> Curved-tooth body file
> Flexible parts repair material

Flexible panels (bumper trim)

1   Remove the damaged panel, if necessary or desirable. In most cases, repairs can be carried out with the panel installed.

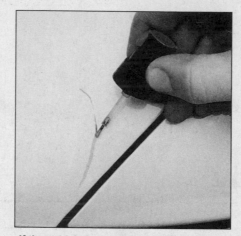

If the vehicle has a two-coat finish, apply the clear coat after the color coat has dried

2   Clean the area(s) to be repaired with a wax, grease and silicone removing solvent applied with a water-dampened cloth.
3   If the damage is structural, that is, if it extends through the panel, clean the backside of the panel area to be repaired as well. Wipe dry.
4   Sand the rear surface about 1-1/2 inches beyond the break.
5   Cut two pieces of fiberglass cloth large enough to overlap the break by about 1-1/2 inches. Cut only to the required length.
6   Mix the adhesive from the repair kit according to the instructions included with the kit, and apply a layer of the mixture approximately 1/8-inch thick on the backside of the panel. Overlap the break by at least 1-1/2 inches.
7   Apply one piece of fiberglass cloth to the adhesive and cover the cloth with additional adhesive. Apply a second piece of fiberglass cloth to the adhesive and immediately cover the cloth with additional adhesive in sufficient quantity to fill the weave.

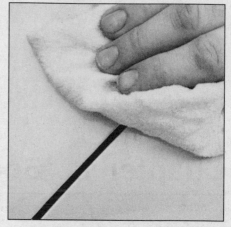

Wait a few days for the paint to dry thoroughly, then rub out the repainted area with a polishing compound to blend the new paint with the surrounding area. When you're happy with your work, wash and polish the area

8   Allow the repair to cure for 20 to 30 minutes at 60-degrees to 80-degrees F.
9   If necessary, trim the excess repair material at the edge.
10   Remove all of the paint film over and around the area(s) to be repaired. The repair material should not overlap the painted surface.
11   With a drill motor and a sanding disc (or a rotary file), cut a "V" along the break line approximately 1/2-inch wide. Remove all dust and loose particles from the repair area.
12   Mix and apply the repair material. Apply a light coat first over the damaged area; then continue applying material until it reaches a level slightly higher than the surrounding finish.
13   Cure the mixture for 20 to 30 minutes at 60-degrees to 80-degrees F.
14   Roughly establish the contour of the area being repaired with a body file. If low areas or

pits remain, mix and apply additional adhesive.

15   Block sand the damaged area with sandpaper to establish the actual contour of the surrounding surface.

16   If desired, the repaired area can be temporarily protected with several light coats of primer. Because of the special paints and techniques required for flexible body panels, it is recommended that the vehicle be taken to a paint shop for completion of the body repair.

Steel body panels

See photo sequence

Repair of dents

17   When repairing dents, the first job is to pull the dent out until the affected area is as close as possible to its original shape. There is no point in trying to restore the original shape completely as the metal in the damaged area will have stretched on impact and cannot be restored to its original contours. It is better to bring the level of the dent up to a point that is about 1/8-inch below the level of the surrounding metal. In cases where the dent is very shallow, it is not worth trying to pull it out at all.

18   If the backside of the dent is accessible, it can be hammered out gently from behind using a soft-face hammer. While doing this, hold a block of wood firmly against the opposite side of the metal to absorb the hammer blows and prevent the metal from being stretched.

19   If the dent is in a section of the body which has double layers, or some other factor makes it inaccessible from behind, a different technique is required. Drill several small holes through the metal inside the damaged area, particularly in the deeper sections. Screw long, self-tapping screws into the holes just enough for them to get a good grip in the metal. Now pulling on the protruding heads of the screws with locking pliers can pull out the dent.

20   The next stage of repair is the removal of paint from the damaged area and from an inch or so of the surrounding metal. This is easily done with a wire brush or sanding disk in a drill motor, although it can be done just as effectively by hand with sandpaper. To complete the preparation for filling, score the surface of the bare metal with a screwdriver or the tang of a file or drill small holes in the affected area. This will provide a good grip for the filler material. To complete the repair, see the Section on filling and painting.

Repair of rust holes or gashes

21   Remove all paint from the affected area and from an inch or so of the surrounding metal using a sanding disk or wire brush mounted in a drill motor. If these are not available, a few sheets of sandpaper will do the job just as effectively.

22   With the paint removed, you will be able to determine the severity of the corrosion and decide whether to replace the whole panel, if possible, or repair the affected area. New body panels are not as expensive as most people think and it is often quicker to install a new panel than to repair large areas of rust.

23   Remove all trim pieces from the affected area except those which will act as a guide to the original shape of the damaged body, such as headlight shells, etc. Using metal snips or a hacksaw blade, remove all loose metal and any other metal that is badly affected by rust. Hammer the edges of the hole in to create a slight depression for the filler material.

24   Wire-brush the affected area to remove the powdery rust from the surface of the metal. If the back of the rusted area is accessible, treat it with rust inhibiting paint.

25   Before filling is done, block the hole in some way. This can be done with sheet metal riveted or screwed into place, or by stuffing the hole with wire mesh.

26   Once the hole is blocked off, the affected area can be filled and painted. See the following subsection on filling and painting.

Filling and painting

27   Many types of body fillers are available, but generally speaking, body repair kits which contain filler paste and a tube of resin hardener are best for this type of repair work. A wide, flexible plastic or nylon applicator will be necessary for imparting a smooth and contoured finish to the surface of the filler material. Mix up a small amount of filler on a clean piece of wood or cardboard (use the hardener sparingly). Follow the manufacturer's instructions on the package, otherwise the filler will set incorrectly.

28   Using the applicator, apply the filler paste to the prepared area. Draw the applicator across the surface of the filler to achieve the desired contour and to level the filler surface. As soon as a contour that approximates the original one is achieved, stop working the paste. If you continue, the paste will begin to stick to the applicator. Continue to add thin layers of paste at 20-minute intervals until the level of the filler is just above the surrounding metal.

29   Once the filler has hardened, the excess can be removed with a body file. From then on, progressively finer grades of sandpaper should be used, starting with a 180-grit paper and finishing with 600-grit wet-or-dry paper. Always wrap the sandpaper around a flat rubber or wooden block, otherwise the surface of the filler will not be completely flat. During the sanding of the filler surface, the wet-or-dry paper should be periodically rinsed in water. This will ensure that a very smooth finish is produced in the final stage.

30   At this point, the repair area should be surrounded by a ring of bare metal, which in turn should be encircled by the finely feathered edge of good paint. Rinse the repair area with clean water until all of the dust produced by the sanding operation is gone.

31   Spray the entire area with a light coat of primer. This will reveal any imperfections in the surface of the filler. Repair the imperfections with fresh filler paste or glaze filler and once more smooth the surface with sandpaper. Repeat this spray-

and-repair procedure until you are satisfied that the surface of the filler and the feathered edge of the paint are perfect. Rinse the area with clean water and allow it to dry completely.

32   The repair area is now ready for painting. Spray painting must be carried out in a warm, dry, windless and dust free atmosphere. These conditions can be created if you have access to a large indoor work area, but if you are forced to work in the open, you will have to pick the day very carefully. If you are working indoors, dousing the floor in the work area with water will help settle the dust that would otherwise be in the air. If the repair area is confined to one body panel, mask off the surrounding panels. This will help minimize the effects of a slight mismatch in paint color. Trim pieces such as chrome strips, door handles, etc., will also need to be masked off or removed. Use masking tape and several thickness of newspaper for the masking operations.

33   Before spraying, shake the paint can thoroughly, then spray a test area until the spray painting technique is mastered. Cover the repair area with a thick coat of primer. The thickness should be built up using several thin layers of primer rather than one thick one. Using 600-grit wet-or-dry sandpaper, rub down the surface of the primer until it is very smooth. While doing this, the work area should be thoroughly rinsed with water and the wet-or-dry sandpaper periodically rinsed as well. Allow the primer to dry before spraying additional coats.

34   Spray on the top coat, again building up the thickness by using several thin layers of paint. Begin spraying in the center of the repair area and then, using a circular motion, work out until the whole repair area and about two inches of the surrounding original paint is covered. Remove all masking material 10 to 15 minutes after spraying on the final coat of paint. Allow the new paint at least two weeks to harden, then use a very fine rubbing compound to blend the edges of the new paint into the existing paint. Finally, apply a coat of wax

4   Body repair - major damage

1   Major damage must be repaired by an auto body shop specifically equipped to perform body and frame repairs. These shops have the specialized equipment required to do the job properly.

2   If the damage is extensive, the frame must be checked for proper alignment or the vehicle's handling characteristics may be adversely affected and other components may wear at an accelerated rate.

3   Due to the fact that all of the major body components (hood, fenders, etc.) are separate and replaceable units, any seriously damaged components should be replaced rather than repaired. Sometimes the components can be found in a wrecking yard that specializes in used vehicle components, often at considerable savings over the cost of new parts.

These photos illustrate a method of repairing simple dents. They are intended to supplement *Body repair - minor damage* in this Chapter and should not be used as the sole instructions for body repair on these vehicles.

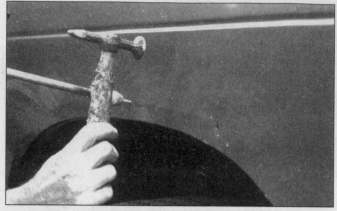

1 If you can't access the backside of the body panel to hammer out the dent, pull it out with a slide-hammer-type dent puller. Tap with a hammer near the edge of the dent to help 'pop' the metal back to its original shape, about 1/8-inch below the surface of the surrounding metal

2 Using coarse-grit sandpaper, remove the paint down to the bare metal. Clean the repair area with wax/silicone remover.

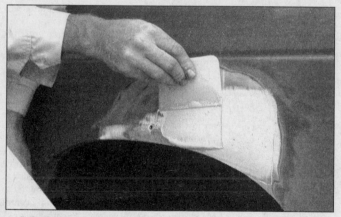

3 Following label instructions, mix up a batch of plastic filler and hardener, then quickly press it into the metal with a plastic applicator. Work the filler until it matches the original contour and is slightly above the surrounding metal

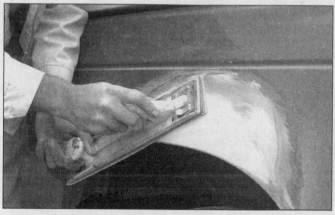

4 Let the filler harden until you can just dent it with your fingernail. File, then sand the filler down until it's smooth and even. Work down to finer grits of sandpaper - always using a board or block - ending up with 360 or 400 grit

5 When the area is smooth to the touch, clean the area and mask around it. Apply several layers of primer to the area. A professional-type spray gun is being used here, but aerosol spray primer works fine

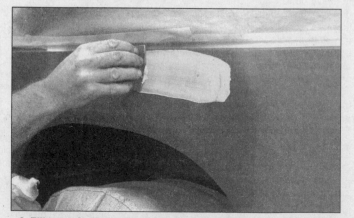

6 Fill imperfections or scratches with glazing compound. Sand with 360 or 400-grit and re-spray. Finish sand the primer with 600 grit, clean thoroughly, then apply the finish coat. Don't attempt to rub out or wax the repair area until the paint has dried completely (at least two weeks)

5   Upholstery, carpets and vinyl trim - maintenance

Upholstery and carpets

1   Every three months remove the floormats and clean the interior of the vehicle (more frequently if necessary). Use a stiff whiskbroom to brush the carpeting and loosen dirt and dust, then vacuum the upholstery and carpets thoroughly, especially along seams and crevices.

2   Dirt and stains can be removed from carpeting with basic household or automotive carpet shampoos available in spray cans. Follow the directions and vacuum again, then use a stiff brush to bring back the "nap" of the carpet.

3   Most interiors have cloth or vinyl upholstery, either of which can be cleaned and maintained with a number of material-specific cleaners or shampoos available in auto supply stores. Follow the directions on the product for usage, and always spot-test any upholstery cleaner on an inconspicuous area (bottom edge of a backseat cushion) to ensure that it doesn't cause a color shift in the material.

4   After cleaning, vinyl upholstery should be treated with a protectant. **Note:** *Make sure the protectant container indicates the product can be used on seats - some products may make a seat too slippery.* **Caution:** *Do not use protectant on vinyl-covered steering wheels.*

5   Leather upholstery requires special care. It should be cleaned regularly with saddle-soap or leather cleaner. Never use alcohol, gasoline, nail polish remover or thinner to clean leather upholstery.

6   After cleaning, regularly treat leather upholstery with a leather conditioner, rubbed in with a soft cotton cloth. Never use car wax on leather upholstery.

7   In areas where the interior of the vehicle is subject to bright sunlight, cover leather seating areas of the seats with a sheet if the vehicle is to be left out for any length of time.

Vinyl trim

8   Don't clean vinyl trim with detergents, caustic soap or petroleum-based cleaners. Plain soap and water works just fine, with a soft brush to clean dirt that may be ingrained. Wash the vinyl as frequently as the rest of the vehicle.

9   After cleaning, application of a high-quality rubber and vinyl protectant will help prevent oxidation and cracks. The protectant can also be applied to weather-stripping, vacuum lines and rubber hoses, which often fail as a result of chemical degradation, and to the tires.

6   Fastener and trim removal

Refer to illustration 6.4

1   There is a variety of plastic fasteners used to hold trim panels, splash shields and other parts in place in addition to typical screws, nuts and bolts. Once you are familiar with them, they can usually be removed without too much difficulty.

2   The proper tools and approach can prevent added time and expense to a project by minimizing the number of broken fasteners and/or parts.

3   The following illustration shows various types of fasteners that are typically used on most vehicles and how to remove and install them **(see illustration)**. Replacement fasteners are commonly found at most auto parts stores, if necessary.

Fasteners

This tool is designed to remove special fasteners. A small pry tool used for removing nails will also work well in place of this tool

A Phillips head screwdriver can be used to release the center portion, but light pressure must be used because the plastic is easily damaged. Once the center is up, the fastener can easily be pried from its hole

Here is a view with the center portion fully released. Install the fastener as shown, then press the center in to set it

This fastener is used for exterior panels and shields. The center portion must be pried up to release the fastener. Install the fastener with the center up, then press the center in to set it

This type of fastener is used commonly for interior panels. Use a small blunt tool to press the small pin at the center in to release it . . .

. . . the pin will stay with the fastener in the released position

Reset the fastener for installation by moving the pin out. Install the fastener, then press the pin flush with the fastener to set it

This fastener is used for exterior and interior panels. It has no moving parts. Simply pry the fastener from its hole like the claw of a hammer removes a nail. Without a tool that can get under the top of the fastener, it can be very difficult to remove

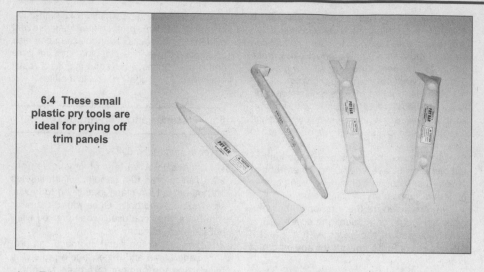

6.4 These small plastic pry tools are ideal for prying off trim panels

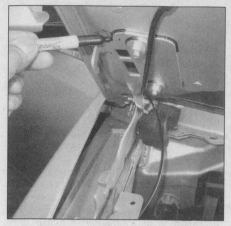

7.2 Draw alignment marks around the hood hinges to ensure proper alignment of the hood when it's reinstalled

4   Trim panels are typically made of plastic and their flexibility can help during removal. The key to their removal is to use a tool to pry the panel near its retainers to release it without damaging surrounding areas or breaking-off any retainers. The retainers will usually snap out of their designated slot or hole after force is applied to them. Stiff plastic tools designed for prying on trim panels are available at most auto parts stores **(see illustration)**. Tools that are tapered and wrapped in protective tape, such as a screwdriver or small pry tool, are also very effective when used with care.

7   Hood - removal, installation and adjustment

Note: *The hood is awkward to remove and install; at least two people should perform this procedure.*

Removal and installation

Refer to illustrations 7.2 and 7.3

1   Open the hood, then place blankets or pads over the fenders and cowl area of the body. This will protect the body and paint as the hood is lifted off.
2   Make marks around the hood hinge to ensure proper alignment during installation **(see illustration)**.
3   Have an assistant support one side of the hood. Grasp the lower corner of the hood and use your shoulder to brace the hood **(see illustration)**. Disconnect the hood strut and take turns removing the hinge-to-hood bolts and lift off the hood.
4   Installation is the reverse of removal. Align the hinge bolts with the marks made in Step 2.

Adjustment

Refer to illustration 7.8

5   Fore-and-aft and side-to-side adjustment of the hood is done by moving the hinges after loosening the hinge-to-body bolts.
6   Loosen the bolts and move the hood into correct alignment. Move it only a little at a time. Tighten the hinge bolts and carefully lower the hood to check the position.
7   The hood can also be adjusted vertically so that it's flush with the fenders.
8   Turn each cushion clockwise to lower the

hood or counterclockwise to raise the hood **(see illustration)**.
9   The hood latch assembly, as well as the hinges, should be periodically lubricated with white, lithium-base grease to prevent binding and wear.

8   Hood latch and release cable - removal and installation

Hood latch

Refer to illustrations 8.1 and 8.2

1   Open the hood and scribe a line around the latch to aid alignment when installing. Remove the retaining bolts securing the hood latch to the radiator support **(see illustration)**. Remove the latch.
2   Squeeze the cable retainer to release the cable from the latch assembly, then disengage the cable end plug from the latch **(see illustration)**.
3   Installation is the reverse of removal.

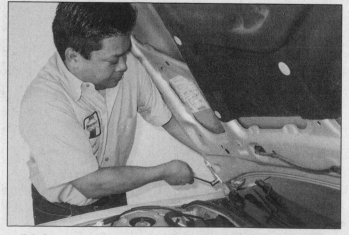

7.3 Support the hood with your shoulder while removing the hood bolts

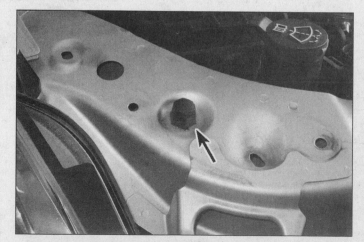

7.8 There are two vertical height adjustment cushions on the radiator support adjacent to the front fenders

8.1 Hood latch assembly bolts

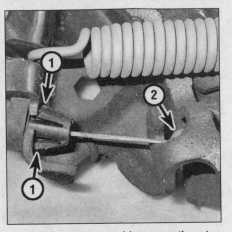

8.2 Hood release cable connection at latch assembly:

1   Retainer fingers
2   Cable end plug

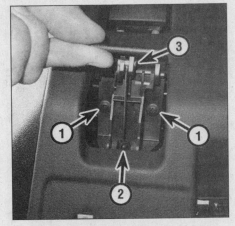

8.9 Hood release cable and release handle details:

1   Release handle mounting bolts
2   Release cable retainer
3   Release cable end plug

Release cable

Refer to illustration 8.9

4   Working in the engine compartment, remove the hood latch and disconnect the hood release cable from the latch (see Steps 1 and 2).
5   Detach the two release cable clips from the radiator grille opening panel reinforcement.
6   Loosen the wheel lug nuts. Raise the vehicle and support it securely on jackstands. Remove the left front wheel. Remove the inner fender splash shield (see Section 10).
7   Open the two release cable clips in the upper part of the fender opening and detach the release cable from the clips.
8   Disengage the release cable clip from the wiring harness.
9   Remove the two hood release handle mounting bolts **(see illustration)** and pull out the handle. Disengage the release cable from the release handle and pull the release cable through the firewall.
10   Installation is the reverse of removal.

9   Bumper covers - removal and installation

Note: *Refer to Section 6 for fastener and trim removal.*

Front bumper cover

2007 and earlier models

1   Carefully pull up and remove the radiator support trim panel.
2   Loosen the front wheel lug nuts, raise the vehicle and support it securely on jackstands. Remove the front wheels and splash shield.
3   Disconnect the electrical connectors from the fog lamps, if equipped (see Chapter 12).
4   Remove the fasteners that secure the inner fender splash shields to the bumper cover.
5   Remove the push-pin retainers across the upper edge of the bumper cover.
6   Remove the bumper cover lower fasteners that secure the upper rear edges of the bumper cover to the fender.

7   Using a flashlight, do a final inspection and verify that the bumper cover is completely detached, all electrical connectors are disconnected and all wiring harnesses are safely out of the way.
8   With an assistant's help, remove the front bumper cover.
9   Installation is the reverse of removal.

2008 and later models

Refer to illustrations 9.10, 9.12 and 9.15

10   Remove the engine compartment weather strip and radiator support trim panel fasteners and remove the panel **(see illustration)**.
11   Loosen the front wheel lug nuts, raise the vehicle and support it securely on jackstands. Remove the front wheels.
12   Remove the fasteners that secure the inner fender splash shields to the bumper cover **(see illustration)**.
13   Disconnect the electrical connectors from the fog lamps, if equipped (see Chapter 12).

9.10 Radiator support trim panel fasteners

9.12 Inner fender splash shield-to-bumper cover fasteners

9.15 Bumper cover lower fasteners

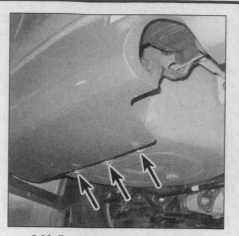

9.32 Rear bumper lower pin-type fastener locations

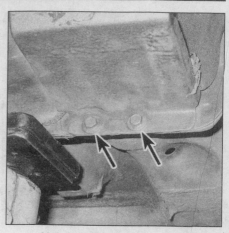

10.7 Front fender lower bolts

14   Remove the bumper cover air deflector plastic retainers, then unclip and remove the air deflector. **Note:** *There are approximately twenty of the plastic retainers.*
15   Remove the bumper cover lower fasteners **(see illustration)**.
16   Remove the bumper cover upper fasteners.
17   Disengage the clips that secure the upper rear edges of the bumper cover to the fender.
18   Using a flashlight, do a final inspection and verify that the bumper cover is completely detached, all electrical connectors are disconnected and all wiring harnesses are safely out of the way.
19   With an assistant's help, remove the front bumper cover.
20   Installation is the reverse of removal.

Rear bumper cover

21   Loosen the rear wheel lug nuts, raise the vehicle and support it securely on jackstands. Remove the rear wheels.

2007 and earlier models

22   To access the rear bumper cover screws, remove the pin-type retainers from the rear part of the wheel well splash shield and push the shields aside.
23   Cut off or drill out the three push-type retainers from the underside center of the bumper cover.
24   Open the trunk and remove the rear sill panel fasteners and sill panel.
25   Remove the four rear nuts from inside the trunk.
26   Remove the bolts from under each corner of the bumper.
27   Using a flashlight, do a final inspection and verify that the bumper cover is completely detached.
28   With an assistant's help, remove the rear bumper cover.
29   Installation is the reverse of removal. Again, get help when putting the bumper

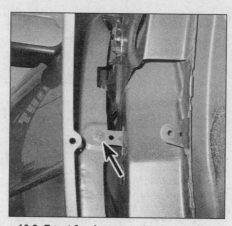

10.9 Front fender mounting nut (inside rear part of the wheel well)

cover back into position.

2008 and later models

Refer to illustration 9.32

30   To access the rear bumper cover screws, remove the wheel well splash shield and push the shields aside.
31   Remove the screw from the underside of each upper front corner of the bumper cover.
32   Remove the pin-type fasteners from the underside of the rear bumper cover **(see illustration)**.
33   Disconnect the rear fog light electrical connector and the tire pressure indicator receiver.
34   Remove the taillight housings (see Chapter 12). On wagon models, insert a screwdriver between the bumper cover and the cover fasteners. Slide a small screwdriver into the bumper cover opening and push in the tabs one at a time, then pull up on the cover at the same time to gradually release the cover.
35   Using a flashlight, do a final inspection

and verify that the bumper cover is completely detached, all electrical connectors are disconnected and all wiring harnesses are safely out of the way.
36   With an assistant's help, remove the rear bumper cover.
37   Installation is the reverse of removal. Again, get help when putting the bumper cover back into position.

10   Front fender - removal and installation

Refer to illustrations 10.7, 10.9 and 10.10
Note: *Refer to Section 6 for fastener and trim removal.*
1   Remove the headlight housing (see Chapter 12).
2   Loosen the front wheel lug nuts. Raise the vehicle, support it securely on jackstands and remove the front wheel.
3   Remove the fasteners that secure the inner fender splash shield **(see illustration 9.12)** and remove the splash shield.
4   Remove the front bumper cover (see Section 9).
5   Using a trim tool, disengage the front rocker panel clips and remove the rocker panel. On wagon models, remove the push-pin clips at the front and rear of the rocker panel, then disengage the remaining panel clips.
6   On 2007 and earlier models, remove the mounting fasteners on the front side of the fender.
7   Remove the two lower fender bolts **(see illustration)**.
8   Open the front door, then remove the rear fender bolt from inside the doorjamb.
9   Remove the front fender mounting nut from inside the back part of the front wheel well **(see illustration)**.
10   Remove the fender upper bolts and the

10.10 Front fender upper mounting bolts

12.2 Upper right side cowl panel fastener locations (2008 and later models, other models similar)

inner rear fender bolt (**see illustration**), then lift off the fender. It's a good idea to have an assistant support the fender while it's being moved away from the vehicle to prevent damage to the surrounding body panels.

11   Installation is the reverse of removal. Check the alignment of the fender to the hood and front edge of the door before tightening the bolts.

11   Radiator grille - removal and installation

1   Remove the front bumper cover (see Section 9).

2007 and earlier models

2   Remove the push-pin type retainers along the outer edge of the grille.
3   Remove the grille from the bumper cover.
4   Installation is the reverse of removal.

2008 and later models

5   From the back side of the bumper cover, squeeze the lower and side retainers out from the tabs on the bumper cover using pliers.
6   Pull the grille away from the bumper cover to disengage the upper clips, then remove the grille.
7   Installation is the reverse of removal.

12   Cowl panels - removal and installation

Note: *Refer to Section 6 for fastener and trim removal techniques.*

Upper cowl panel

Refer to illustrations 12.2 and 12.3
1   Remove the wiper arms (see Chapter 12, Section 18).
2   Remove the screws from the right side upper cowl panel (**see illustration**) and remove the panel.
3   Remove the screws, pin-type retainers

and any retainer clips from the left side upper cowl panel (**see illustration**).
4   Remove the upper cowl panel.
5   Installation is the reverse of removal.

Lower cowl panel

Refer to illustration 12.7
6   Remove the upper cowl panels (see Steps 1 through 4).
7   Remove the nuts/bolts from the lower cowl panel (**see illustration**) and remove the lower cowl panel.
8   Installation is the reverse of removal.

13   Door trim panel - removal and installation

Caution: *Wear gloves when working inside the door openings to protect against sharp metal edges.*
Note: *This procedure applies to both front and rear door trim panels.*

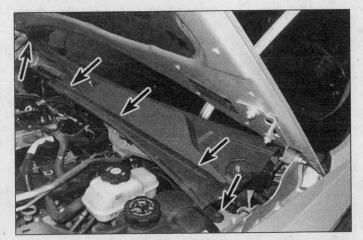

12.3 Upper left side cowl panel fastener locations (2008 and later models, other models similar)

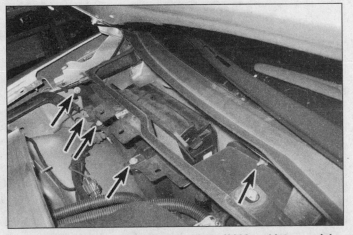

12.7 Lower cowl panel fastener locations (2008 and later models, other models similar)

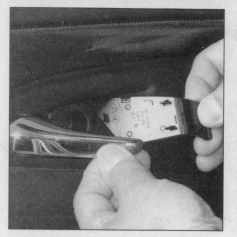

13.8 Remove the trim cover from the inside door handle

13.9 Remove the trim cover from the armrest

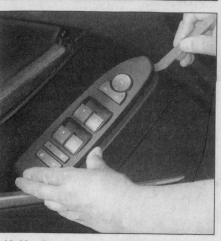

13.10a Pry the power window switch out of the armrest . . .

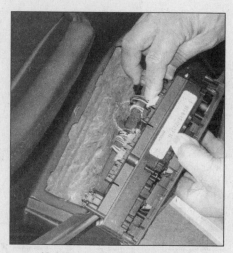

13.10b . . . then disconnect the electrical connectors

Note: *Refer to Section 6 for fastener and trim removal.*

1   Disconnect the cable from the negative battery terminal (see Chapter 5).

2007 and earlier models

2   Lower the window and unlock the door.

3   Insert a screwdriver into the opening in the door lock knob, disconnect the retaining clip and remove the knob.

4   Remove the trim cover from inside door handle bezel and pull the bezel outwards. Use a screwdriver to release the tabs and remove the bezel from the panel.

5   Pry the trim cap out from under the pull handle of the armrest and remove the screws.

6   To detach the door trim panel from its mounting clips, work your way around the periphery of the trim panel, carefully prying loose the clips with a suitable door trim removal tool **(see illustration 13.13)**, then pull off the panel and disconnect any electrical connectors.

7   Installation is the reverse of removal.

2008 and later models

Refer to illustrations 13.8, 13.9, 13.10a, 13.10b, 13.11, 13.12, 13.13, 13.14 and 13.15

8   Remove the trim cover from the inside door handle bezel **(see illustration)**.

9   Pry the trim cover from the armrest **(see illustration)**.

10   Carefully pry the back end of the switch, lift up the panel and disconnect the electrical connectors from the power window switch **(see illustrations)**.

11   Pry out the trunk release and disconnect the electrical connector **(see illustration)**.

12   Remove the door trim panel screws from the armrest and from the bezel **(see illustration)**.

13   To detach the door trim panel from its mounting clips, work your way around the edge of the trim panel, carefully prying loose the clips with a suitable door trim removal tool **(see illustration)**, then pull off the panel and disconnect any electrical connectors.

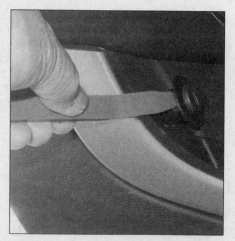

13.11 Pry the trunk release switch out of the door panel

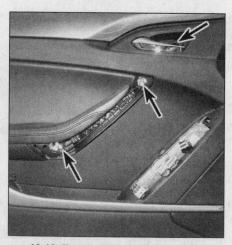

13.12 Remove the door trim panel mounting screws

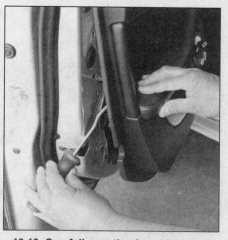

13.13 Carefully pry the door trim panel loose from its mounting clips

13.14 Disconnect the inside door handle cable from the handle

13.15 Disengage the window frame trim panel

14   Disconnect the actuator cable from the inside door handle **(see illustration)**.
15   Carefully pry off the window frame trim, if equipped **(see illustration)**.
16   Installation is the reverse of removal.

14   Door - removal, installation and adjustment

Warning: *The models covered by this manual are equipped with Supplemental Restraint Systems (SRS), more commonly known as airbags. Always disable the airbag system before working in the vicinity of any airbag system component to avoid the possibility of accidental deployment of the airbag, which could cause personal injury (see Chapter 12).*

Removal and installation

Refer to illustrations 14.4 and 14.5

Note: *The door is heavy and somewhat awkward to remove - at least two people should perform this procedure.*

Note: *This procedure applies to front and rear doors.*
1   Raise the window completely in the door.
2   Disconnect the cable from the negative battery terminal (see Chapter 5).
3   Open the door all the way and support it with a jack or blocks covered with rags to prevent damaging the outer surface.
4   Pull off the rubber conduit **(see illustration)** that protects the door's wiring harness, then disconnect the connector.
5   Remove the door stop strut mounting bolt **(see illustration)**.
6   Mark around the door hinges with a pen or a scribe to facilitate realignment during installation.
7   With an assistant holding the door to steady it, remove the hinge-to-door bolts and lift off the door.
8   Installation is the reverse of removal.

Adjustment

Refer to illustration 14.12

9   Correct door-to-body alignment is a critical part of a well-functioning door assembly.

First check the door hinge pins for excessive play. Fully open the door and lift up and down on the door without lifting the body. If a door has 1/16-inch or more excessive play, replace the hinges.
10   If you need to adjust or replace the hinges for a front door, remove the front fender (see Section 10).
11   Make door-to-body alignment adjustments by loosening the hinge-to-body bolts or hinge-to-door bolts and moving the door. When body alignment is correct, the top of each door is parallel with the roof section, the front door is flush with the fender, the rear door is flush with the rear quarter panel and the bottom of each door is aligned with the lower rocker panel. If you're unable to adjust the door correctly, you might be able to obtain body alignment shims that are inserted behind the hinges to correctly align the door.
12   To adjust the door-closed position, scribe a line or mark around the striker plate to provide a reference point, then verify that the door latch is contacting the center of the

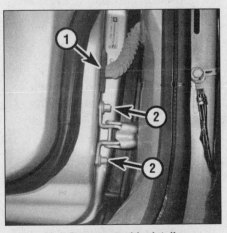

14.4 Door assembly details:

1   *Wiring harness rubber conduit*
2   *Door hinge mounting bolts*

14.5 Door stop strut bolt

14.12 Adjust the door latch striker by loosening the mounting screws and gently tapping the striker in the desired direction

15.6 Remove the trim cap for the outside door handle retaining screw

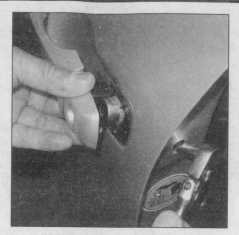

15.7 Remove the outside door handle cover

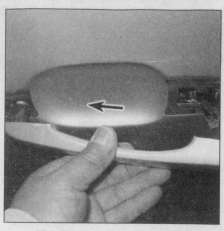

15.8 To disengage the outside door handle lever from the handle reinforcement inside the door, pull it out of the door and to the rear

striker. If not, adjust the up and down position first. To move the striker, tap it gently with a small hammer **(see illustration)**.

13   Once the door latch is contacting the center of the striker, adjust the latch striker sideways position, so that the door panel is flush with the center pillar or rear quarter panel and provides positive engagement with the latch mechanism.

---

15   Door latch, lock cylinder and handles - removal and installation

---

Outside door handle lever

2007 and earlier models

1   Raise the window all the way up then remove the door trim panel and watershield (see Section 13).

2   Remove the anti-theft shield fasteners from the door jamb. Remove the anti-theft shield push-pin to the door handle fastener

and remove the shield from inside the door, if equipped.

3   Pry open the plastic clip for the lock cylinder rod-to-door latch and the handle rod, then disconnect the rods from the latch assembly.

4   Remove the watershield, then remove the door handle nuts. Remove the handle and rods from outside the door.

5   Installation is the reverse of removal.

2008 and later models

Refer to illustrations 15.6, 15.7 and 15.8

Note: *This procedure only applies to the outside door handle lever. If you need to replace the outside door handle reinforcement (the actual mechanism for the outside door handle) and lock, you will need to remove it along with the door latch as a single assembly, then disconnect it from the latch (see Steps 17 through 22).*

6   Remove the trim cap for the outside handle retaining screw **(see illustration)** and remove the screw.

7   Remove the watershield, then remove

the cover from the outside handle **(see illustration)**.

8   To remove the outside door handle, pull it out of the door and to the rear to disengage it from the handle reinforcement inside the door **(see illustration)**.

9   Remove and inspect the outside door handle seals. If the seals are cracked, torn or otherwise deteriorated, replace them.

10   Installation is the reverse of removal.

Inside door handle

2007 and earlier models

11   Remove the door trim panel (see Section 13).

12   Remove the inside door handle retaining bolt and detach the handle assembly from the door.

13   Disconnect the actuator rod from the inside door handle, then remove the handle.

14   Installation is the reverse of removal.

2008 and later models

15   Remove the door trim panel (see Section 13), disconnect the actuator cable from the inside door handle **(see illustration 13.14)**, then remove the handle from the door panel.

16   Installation is the reverse of removal.

Door latch or outside door handle reinforcement (2008 and later models)

Refer to illustration 15.18, 15.19, 15.20, 15.21a, 15.21b and 15.22

17   Remove the outside door handle lever (see Steps 6 through 8), then remove the door trim panel (see Section 13).

18   Remove the trim cap for the outside door handle reinforcement retaining screw **(see illustration)** and remove the screw.

19   Remove the outside door handle reinforcement exterior retaining screw **(see illustration)** and remove the reinforcement.

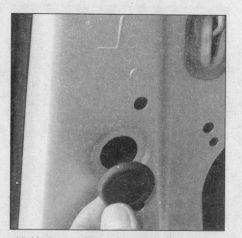

15.18 Remove the trim cap to access the outside door handle reinforcement interior retaining screw

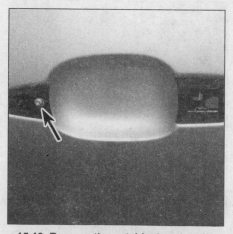

15.19 Remove the outside door handle reinforcement exterior retaining screw

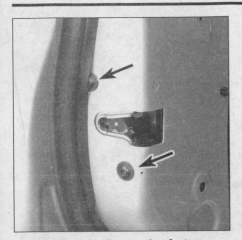

15.20 Door latch mounting fasteners

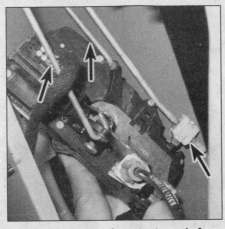

15.21a Disconnect the actuator rods from the door latch

15.21b Rotate the latch electrical connector lock to disengage the wiring

20 Remove the latch mounting fasteners **(see illustration)**.

21 Pull out the latch and rods from the door as a single assembly, then disconnect the rods and electrical connector **(see illustrations)** from the latch if you haven't already done so. Disconnect the inside door handle actuator cable from the latch (for help, **see illustration 13.14**; it's the same setup at both ends of the cable).

22 Place the latch and outside door handle reinforcement on a clean workbench, then disconnect the outside handle and lock cylinder actuator rods from the latch or from the outside door handle reinforcement **(see illustration)**.

23 Installation is the reverse of removal.

Door lock cylinder

24 On 2007 and earlier models, remove the door latch and outside door handle (see Steps 1 through 4).

25 On 2008 and later models, remove the door latch and outside door handle reinforcement (see Steps 17 through 22).

26 On 2008 and later models, remove the E-clip and rod arm from the lock cylinder

27 Press the release button and remove the lock cylinder.

28 When installing the lock cylinder, push it all the way into the outside door handle reinforcement until it clicks into place.

29 Installation is otherwise the reverse of removal.

16 Door window glass - removal and installation

Refer to illustrations 16.2 and 16.3

1 Remove the door trim panel (see Section 13).

2 Remove the watershield **(see illustration)**.

3 Raise the window glass until the glass clamp bolts are accessible through the access holes **(see illustration)**. Loosen (but don't remove) both glass clamp bolts, then secure the window in place with tape so that it won't go down. **Note:** *If the door window regulator motor is broken or disconnected, you'll have to remove it (see Section 17) and move the window glass manually.*

15.22 To disconnect the actuator rods from the outside door handle reinforcement, angle the reinforcement as necessary to disengage each rod

4 Lower the window regulator, then guide the window up and tilt it outward to remove it through the window opening.

5 Installation is the reverse of removal.

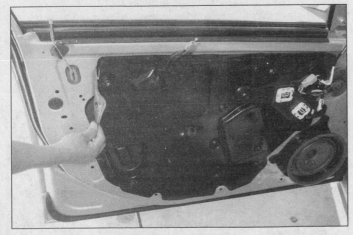

16.2 Remove the watershield

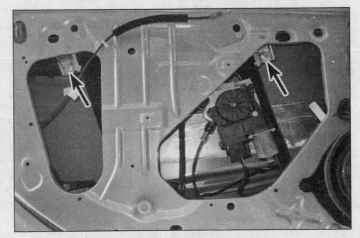

16.3 Front window glass clamp bolts

17.4 Power window regulator motor mounting screws

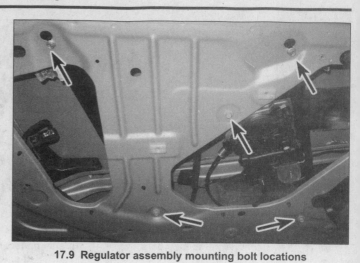

17.9 Regulator assembly mounting bolt locations

17   Door window regulator and motor - removal and installation

Regulator motor

Refer to illustration 17.4

1   Remove the door trim panel (see Section 13).
2   Partially open the window, if possible, then disconnect the electrical connector from the regulator motor.
3   Secure the window in place with tape.
4   Remove the three regulator motor mounting screws **(see illustration)**, then remove the motor.
5   Installation is the reverse of removal.

Regulator assembly

Refer to illustration 17.9

6   Remove the door trim panel (see Section 13).
7   Remove the watershield and remove the window glass (see Section 16).
8   Lower the window regulator mechanism until it is three quarters of the way down.
9   Remove the regulator assembly mount-

ing bolts **(see illustration)**, then remove the regulator and disconnect the electrical connectors.
10   Installation is the reverse of removal.

18   Mirrors - removal and installation

Side view mirror

Refer to illustration 18.3

1   Remove the door trim panel (see Section 13).
2   Remove the window frame trim panel **(see illustration 13.15)**. If the mirror cover is equipped with a speaker, disconnect the speaker electrical connector.
3   Disconnect the electrical connector from the mirror and remove the mirror mounting nuts **(see illustration)** and mirror.
4   Installation is the reverse of removal.

Mirror glass replacement

Refer to illustration 18.5

Caution: *The mirror glass breaks easily; protection such as safety glasses and gloves should be worn to prevent injury.*

5   Using a plastic trim tool, insert the tool between the two tabs **(see illustration)** in the outer corner and twist until the glass is free of the motor. **Note:** *On 2007 and earlier models, insert the trim tool from the top of the mirror.*
6   Disconnect the electrical connectors, if equipped with heated mirrors.
7   Connect the wires to the mirror glass and snap the mirror glass onto the motor.

Inside mirror

8   Disconnect the sensor cover clips, remove the cover(s) and electrical connector.
9   To remove/install the mirror, remove/install the Torx screw or set screw at the base on the windshield.
10   If the mount plate itself has come off the windshield, adhesive kits are available at auto parts stores to re-secure it. Follow the instructions included with the kit.

19   Trunk lid - removal and installation

Refer to illustrations 19.1, 19.2 and 19.4
Note: *The trunk lid is heavy and awkward to*

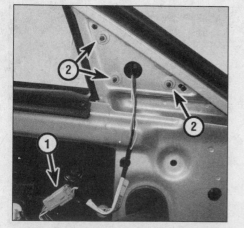

18.3 Mirror electrical connector (1) and mounting nuts (2)

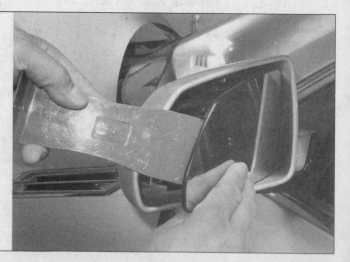

18.5 Insert a flat plastic trim tool between the two tabs

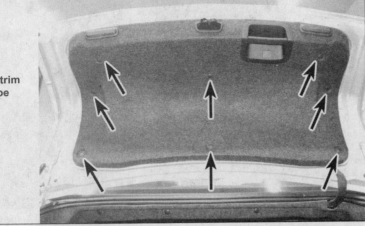

19.1 Trunk lid trim panel pin-type fasteners

19.2 Pull down handle fasteners

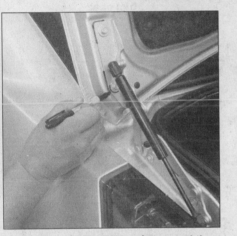

19.4 Draw alignment marks around the trunk hinges to ensure proper alignment, then remove the trunk lid hinge fasteners

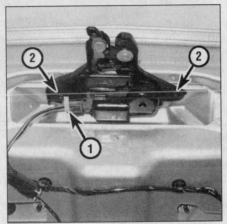

20.2 Trunk lid latch electrical connector (1) and mounting nuts (2)

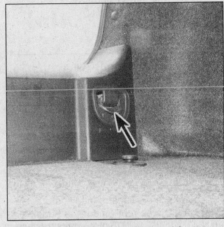

20.5 Remove the trunk sill panel fasteners from each corner

remove and install, so have a helper handy to assist you.

1   Remove the trunk lid trim panel fasteners (see illustration).

2   Remove the pull down handle fastener covers and fasteners (see illustration), then remove the panel.

3   Disconnect the electrical connectors from all wiring between the vehicle body and

the trunk lid. Disengage all wiring harness clips and set the harnesses aside.

4   Make marks around the trunk lid hinges to ensure proper alignment during installation (see illustration).

5   With an assistant helping you to support the trunk lid, remove the fasteners from the trunk lid hinges and remove the trunk lid.

6   Installation is the reverse of removal.

20 Trunk lid latch and striker - removal and installation

Trunk latch

Refer to illustration 20.2

1   Remove the trunk lid trim panel (see Section 19).

2   Disconnect the electrical connector from the trunk lid latch (see illustration).

3   Remove the latch mounting fasteners and remove the latch.

4   Installation is the reverse of removal.

Trunk striker

Refer to illustrations 20.5 and 20.6

5   Remove the trunk sill panel fasteners from each end and pry the panel out (see illustration).

6   Disconnect the emergency release cable from the trunk striker (see illustration).

7   Remove the striker mounting fasteners and remove the striker.

8   Installation is the reverse of removal.

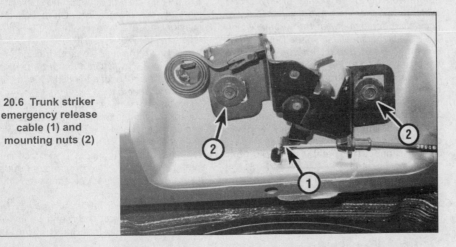

20.6 Trunk striker emergency release cable (1) and mounting nuts (2)

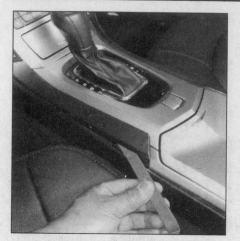

23.7 Pry out the outer trim panels from the center console

23.8 Carefully pry up the shift lever boot

23.9 Carefully pry off the shift lever trim ring

21   Liftgate trim panels (wagon) - removal and installation

Caution: *If the liftgate or liftgate actuator is removed, the liftgate must be recalibrated to open and close properly. This will have to be done by a dealer service department because the maximum and minimum openings and air temperature for the liftgate control module must be programmed.*

1   To replace the liftgate, the liftgate actuator mounted to the roof (under the headliner) must be disconnected. To disconnect the actuator, the headliner must be removed; we do not recommend attempting this repair. **Warning:** *Head impact energy-absorbing material is glued to the headliner and trims. If this is damaged during removal, it could cause personal injury (see Chapter 12).*

Interior trim panels

2   Open the liftgate.

Upper trim panel

3   Carefully pry the upper trim panel out, disengaging the retaining clips around the edge of the panel.
4   Remove the panel from the liftgate.
5   Installation is the reverse of removal.

Lower trim panel

6   Remove the upper trim panel (see Steps 3 and 4).
7   Using a small screwdriver, remove the retaining screw covers and screws from inside the pull down handle openings on both sides of the liftgate.
8   To detach the liftgate trim panel from its mounting clips, work your way around the edge of the trim panel, carefully prying loose the clips with a suitable door trim removal tool. Pull off the panel and disconnect any electrical connectors.
9   Installation is the reverse of removal.

Exterior trim panel

10   Remove the upper interior trim panel (see Steps 3 and 4).
11   Disconnect the electrical connectors to the radio antenna module and high mount brake light. Disconnect the rear wiper washer hose.
12   From inside the vehicle, remove the plastic access plugs and remove the exterior panel mounting nuts.
13   Use a small 12 point (8 mm) socket to push over the three center retainers and disengage them.
14   Detach the liftgate trim panel from the last two outer mounting clips, carefully prying loose the clips with a suitable door trim removal tool.
15   Installation is the reverse of removal.

22   Liftgate strut - removal and installation

Warning: *The models covered by this manual are equipped with Supplemental Restraint Systems (SRS), more commonly known as airbags. Always disable the airbag system before working in the vicinity of any airbag system component to avoid the possibility of accidental deployment of the airbag, which could cause personal injury (see Chapter 12).*
Warning: *Head impact energy-absorbing material is glued to the headliner and trims. If this is damaged during removal, it could cause personal injury (see Chapter 12).*

1   Open and support the liftgate.
2   Carefully remove the rear headliner trim and pull the rear of the headliner down enough to access the end of the strut.
3   Disconnect the metal locking clip from the ends of the strut.
4   Remove the strut from the ball studs.
5   Installation is the reverse of removal. Make sure the arrow on the strut is pointing towards the roof of the vehicle.

23   Center floor console - removal and installation

2007 and earlier models

1   Slide the front seats all the way rearward, pry out the console side trim panels and remove the bolts from the front of the console, one on each side, then slide the seats all the way forward.
2   Remove the four bolts in the rear of the console, two from each side.
3   Using a trim removal tool, carefully pry off the shift lever trim ring from the console and disconnect the wiring.
4   Lift up the console and disconnect all electrical connectors from the console.
5   Remove the center console.
6   Installation is the reverse of removal.

2008 and later models

Refer to illustrations 23.7, 23.8, 23.9, 23.10, 23.11, 23.12, 23.13 and 23.14

7   Slide the front seats all the way forward, then pry up the console outer trim panels **(see illustration)**.
8   Pry the shift boot out of the shift console trim ring **(see illustration)**. On manual transmission models, remove the shifter handle (see Chapter 7A).
9   Pry out the shift console trim ring **(see illustration)**. **Note:** *On manual transmission models, the shift boot and ring should be pried out as an assembly.*
10   On 2010 and later models, remove the console top panel fasteners **(see illustration)** and pry out the panel, starting from the rear of the panel working your way towards the front.
11   Remove the console storage compartment fasteners, lift the compartment out and disconnect the electrical connectors **(see illustration)**.
12   Slide the front seats all the way rearward, pull the carpet down and remove the bolt from each side **(see illustration)**, then

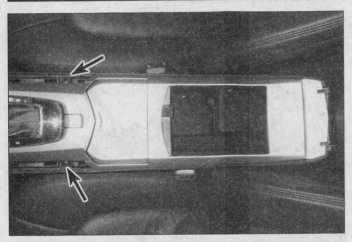

23.10 Remove the console top panel fasteners, then pry the panel out from the rear (2010 and later models)

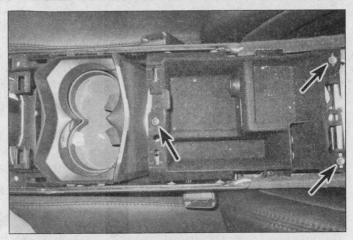

23.11 Remove the storage bin fasteners and storage bin from the console, then disconnect the electrical connector underneath

23.12 Pull down the carpet and remove the console front lower fasteners

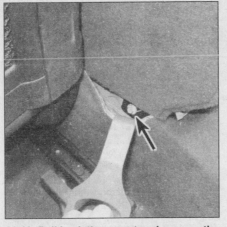

23.13 Pull back the carpet and remove the console rear fasteners

23.14 Center console forward upper mounting screws

slide the seats all the way forward.

13 Pull the carpet back and remove the bolts from the rear of the console, one from each side **(see illustration)**.

14 Remove the console mounting bolts at the top of the console **(see illustration)**.

15 Lift up the console and disconnect all electrical connectors from the console. Remove the center console.

16 Installation is the reverse of removal.

---

24 Dashboard trim panels - removal and installation

Warning: *Models covered by this manual are equipped with a Supplemental Restraint System (SRS), more commonly known as airbags. Always disable the airbag system before working in the vicinity of any airbag system component to avoid the possibility of accidental deployment of the airbag, which could cause personal injury (see Chapter 12).* **Note:** *Refer to Section 6 for fastener and trim removal.*

1 Removing various dashboard trim panels provides access to electrical/electronic components such as the instrument cluster, the audio unit, the heater and air conditioning control unit and various instrument panel-mounted switches. If you're going to remove the entire instrument panel, you'll need to remove all of the trim panels to access the instrument panel mounting bolts.

Left or right dashboard end trim panels

Refer to illustration 24.2

2 Carefully pry off the end trim panel **(see illustration)**.

3 Installation is the reverse of removal.

Instrument cluster trim panel

Refer to illustration 24.6

4 On 2007 and earlier models, the cluster trim panel is a thin narrow trim piece that runs along the lower edge of the instrument clus-

ter. Lower the column and pry the panel out.

5 On 2008 and later models, remove the defroster and speaker panel (see Steps 40 through 42).

24.2 Pry off the end trim panel

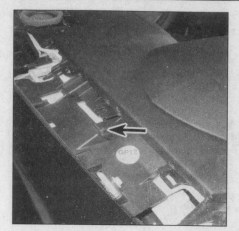

24.6 Instrument cluster mounting fastener location (2008 and later models)

24.8a Pry out the left appliqué . . .

24.8b . . . the center appliqué . . .

6   On 2008 and later models, remove the cluster trim panel mounting fastener **(see illustration)**, then pull the panel forward and out.

7   Installation is the reverse of removal.

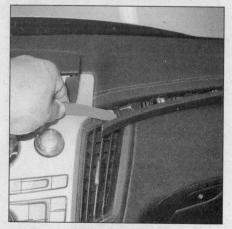

24.8c . . . and the right appliqué from the instrument panel

Left, center and right appliqués (2008 and later models)

Refer to illustrations 24.8a, 24.8b and 24.8c

8   Carefully pry off the left, center or right appliqué **(see illustrations)**.

9   Installation is the reverse of removal.

Center trim panel

2007 and earlier models

10   Remove the radio (see Chapter 12).

11   Remove the air conditioning control unit (see Chapter 3).

12   Remove the center trim panel fasteners.

13   Carefully pry off the center trim panel.

14   Installation is the reverse of removal.

2008 and later models

Refer to illustration 24.17, 24.19 and 24.20

15   Remove the center floor console top panel (see Section 23).

16   Remove the center and right trim appliqué (see Step 8).

17   Remove the upper trim cover **(see illustration)**.

18   Unclip the display panel and set it out of the way.

19   Remove the center trim panel fasteners **(see illustration)**.

20   Carefully pry the center trim panel forward **(see illustration)**, and disconnect all electrical connectors.

21   Remove the radio and air conditioning control module fasteners from the trim panel and separate the units as needed.

22   Installation is the reverse of removal.

Knee bolster trim panel and knee bolster

Refer to illustrations 24.23, 24.24 and 24.25

23   Remove the driver's side insulator panel fasteners and remove the insulator panel **(see illustration)**.

24   Carefully pry off the knee bolster trim panel **(see illustration)**.

25   Remove the fasteners securing the knee bolster **(see illustration)** and remove the bolster.

26   Installation is the reverse of removal.

24.17 Pry up the upper trim panel from the center console

24.19 Center trim panel fastener locations

24.20 Carefully pry the center trim panel forward

24.23 Driver's side insulator panel fastener locations

24.24 Carefully pry out the knee bolster panel

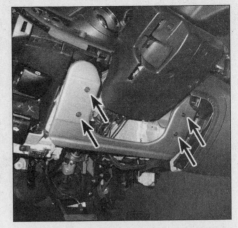

24.25 Remove the knee bolster support fasteners

Air register panels (2008 and later models)

Refer to illustrations 24.29a and 24.29b

27   Remove the left or right side end trim panel (see Step 2).

28   Remove the left or right trim appliqué (see Step 8).

29   Carefully pry out the register panel **(see illustrations)**. **Note:** *On some models, disconnect the LED light electrical connector.*

30   Disconnect the electrical connectors from the switches (driver's side).

31   Installation is the reverse of removal.

Glove box

2007 and earlier models

32   Open the glove box door, depress the tabs where the hinge arms meet the door and disconnect the arms.

33   Remove the door mounting screws and remove the door.

34   Remove the mounting fasteners around the opening of the glove box and slide the box out, disconnecting any electrical connectors.

35   Installation is the reverse of removal.

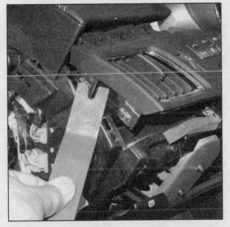

24.29a Carefully pry out the driver's side air register/switch panel

2008 and later models

Refer to illustrations 24.37 and 24.38

36   Remove the passenger's side insulator panel fasteners, then remove the insulator panel.

37   Remove the glove box mounting fasten-

24.29b Carefully pry out the passenger's side air register panel

ers below the box **(see illustration)**.

38   Open the glove box and remove the mounting fasteners **(see illustration)** then slide the box out, disconnecting any electrical connectors.

39   Installation is the reverse of removal.

24.37 Remove the mounting fasteners from below the glove box

24.38 Remove the mounting fasteners from inside the glove box

24.41 Pry up the defrost panel, working towards the opposite side, disengaging the retaining clips

24.42 Disconnect the electrical connector to the light sensor

25.9 Lower steering column cover retaining screw locations

Defroster/speaker trim panel

Refer to illustrations 24.41 and 24.42

40   Carefully pry out the A-pillar trim covers and disconnect the connector (see Section 26).
41   Start prying the defrost panel up, disconnecting the retaining clips from one end to the other **(see illustration)**.
42   Disconnect the electrical connector **(see illustration)** in the center of the panel and remove the panel.
43   Installation is the reverse of removal.

---

25   Steering column covers - removal and installation

Warning: *Models covered by this manual are equipped with a Supplemental Restraint System (SRS), more commonly known as airbags. Always disable the airbag system before working in the vicinity of any airbag system component to avoid the possibility of accidental deployment of the airbag, which could cause personal injury (see Chapter 12).*

1   Disconnect the cable from the negative terminal of the battery (see Chapter 5).

2007 and earlier models

2   Remove the steering wheel (see Chapter 10).
3   Unscrew the tilt lever from the column.
4   Remove the ignition lock cylinder (see Chapter 12).
5   Remove the column lower cover fasteners then slide the end of the cover down and in. Unhook the cover from the front and remove the cover.
6   Remove the upper cover fasteners and remove the cover.
7   Installation is the reverse of removal.

2008 and later models

Refer to illustrations 25.9, 25.10a, 25.10b and 25.11

8   Remove the knee bolster retaining screws and remove the knee bolster (see Section 24).
9   Remove the mounting fasteners from the lower steering column covers **(see illustration)**.

10   Press in on the sides of the lower covers to disengage the clips from the upper cover and separate the two covers **(see illustrations)**.
11   To remove the upper column cover, use a trim removal tool to separate the column cover flexible extension from the instrument cluster trim panel **(see illustration)** and remove the upper cover.
12   Installation is the reverse of removal.

---

26   Instrument panel - removal and installation

Refer to illustrations 26.2a, 26.2b, 26.3 and 26.9

Warning: *Models covered by this manual are equipped with a Supplemental Restraint System (SRS), more commonly known as airbags. Always disable the airbag system before working in the vicinity of any airbag system component to avoid the possibility of accidental deployment of the airbag, which*

25.10a Disengage the lower left cover from the upper cover locking tabs . . .

25.10b . . . then do the same for the right side lower cover, and remove the covers

25.11 Using a trim tool, disconnect the upper cover from the instrument panel

could cause personal injury (see Chapter 12).
Note: This is a difficult procedure for the home mechanic. There are many hidden fasteners, difficult angles to work in and many electrical connectors to tag and disconnect/connect. We recommend that this procedure be done only by an experienced do-it-yourselfer.
Note: During removal of the instrument panel, make careful notes of how each piece comes off, where it fits in relation to other pieces and what holds it in place. If you note how each part is installed before removing it, getting the instrument panel back together again will be much easier.

1   Remove the following parts:
   Steering wheel (see Chapter 10)
   All the dashboard trim panels and the glove box (see Section 24)
   Air conditioning and heater control assembly (see Chapter 3)
   Instrument cluster and radio (see Chapter 12)
   Defrost/speaker panel (see Section 24), if equipped.
   Front seats (though not absolutely necessary, removing both front seats allows more room to work and eliminates the possibility of the occurrence of damage to the seats during this procedure)
   Center floor console (see Section 23)
2   Carefully remove the left and right A-pillar (windshield pillar) trim panels **(see illustrations)**.
3   Grasp each front door opening weather strip/sill panel/kick panels and pull it off **(see illustration)**.
4   In the glove box area, disconnect all air conditioning system electrical connectors.
5   Disconnect all electrical connectors and wiring harness clips located on the floor between the two front seats.
6   Disconnect any other connectors, not already specifically mentioned, that connect wiring between the vehicle and the instrument panel.
7   Check to be sure all electrical wiring is out of the way, where it will not interfere with

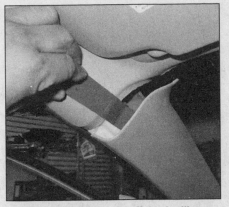

26.2a Carefully pry off the A-pillar trim panels

instrument panel removal.
8   Remove the steering column (see Chapter 10).
9   Remove the instrument panel dash trim fasteners around the panel **(see illustration)**.
10   Remove the two hood release handle screws and set the handle aside (see Section 8).
11   Remove the parking brake pedal fasteners and lower the assembly.
12   If equipped with a manual transmission, remove the clutch master cylinder (see Chapter 8).
13   Disconnect the in-vehicle temperature sensor aspirator hoses from the heater core and evaporator core housing, if equipped, as follows: Separate the aspirator hose retaining clips from the heater core/evaporator core housing, then pull the hose away from the heater core/evaporator core housing.
14   Remove the two bolts in the instrument cluster opening.
15   Remove the instrument panel center brace fasteners and brace.
16   Remove the bolts from the left and right lower corners of the instrument panel.
17   Remove the instrument panel end bolts.
Caution: To avoid damage to the instru-

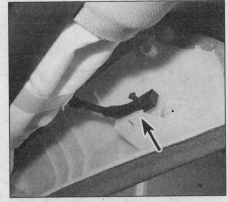

26.2b Disconnect the plastic retainer from the A-pillar trim panels

ment panel when removing these last three bolts, have an assistant support the instrument panel. You'll also need an assistant's help when installing the instrument panel and these three bolts.
18   With an assistant helping you, remove the instrument panel from the vehicle.
19   Installation is the reverse of removal.

27 Seats - removal and installation

Front seats

Refer to illustrations 27.3 and 27.6
Warning: All models covered by this manual are equipped with a Supplemental Restraint System (SRS), more commonly known as airbags. Always disable the airbag system before working in the vicinity of any airbag system component to avoid the possibility of accidental deployment of the airbag, which could cause personal injury (see Chapter 12).
Caution: The seats are heavy, so have an assistant handy to help you lift the seat from the vehicle.
Note: This procedure applies to the driver's and passenger's seats.

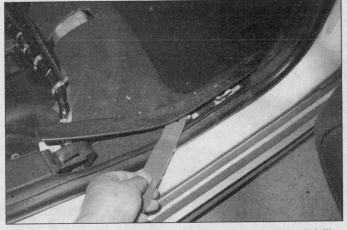

26.3 Remove each of the front door opening weather strip/sill panel/kick panels

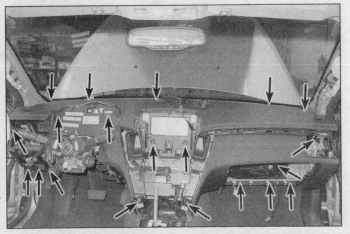

26.9 Instrument panel fastener locations (2010 model shown, other models similar)

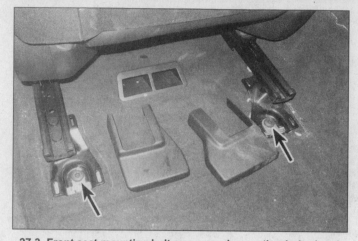

27.3 Front seat mounting bolt covers and mounting bolts (rear)

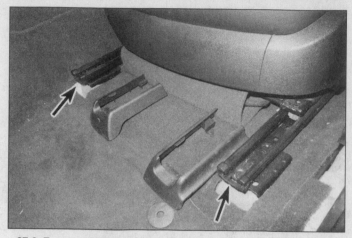

27.6 Front seat track mounting covers removed and track tabs locked into floor

1   Disconnect the battery (see Chapter 5).
2   On models equipped with the seatbelt anchor, remove the cover from the seatbelt anchor, then remove the anchor bolt and disconnect the seatbelt from the seat.
3   Remove the covers from the seat mounting bolts and remove the seat mounting bolts **(see illustration)**.
4   Tilt the seat forward and disconnect all electrical connectors underneath the seat.
5   Using a helper, carefully slide the seat back disengaging the locking tab at the front of the seat and lift the seat out of the vehicle. Warning: The seat is heavy, so trying to remove it by yourself could cause injury.
6   Installation is the reverse of removal. Make sure the tabs on the seat track lock into the floor **(see illustration)**.

Rear seat cushion

Refer to illustration 27.7

7   On wagon models, open the left rear door, insert your hand between the carpet and the lower edge of the rear seat cushion, then push your hand toward the other side of the

vehicle. The release lever for the rear seat cushion latches is located about 18 inches from the left rear door. On all models, push the rear seat cushion firmly to the rear to disengage the wire hoops on the underside of the rear part of the cushion from their retainer hooks **(see illustration)**.
8   Lift out the seat cushion. The cushion isn't that heavy, but get help if you need it, so that you don't hurt your back.
9   When installing the seat cushion, make SURE that the wire hoops at the lower rear edge of the cushion engage the rear retainer hooks. And make sure that the two latches fully engage the lower front edge of the seat cushion.

Rear seat backs

Coupe and Sedan

Refer to illustration 27.13

10   Remove the rear seat cushion (see Steps 7 through 9).
11   Open the trunk and remove the trunk liner pushpin fasteners and pull the liner from

the back side of the seat. Remove the four nuts securing the upper section of the rear seat back.
12   On 2007 and earlier models, remove the center seat belt and shoulder buckle mounting nuts the place the belt and buckle out of the way.
13   Remove the lower fasteners from the front side of the seat back at the bottom **(see illustration)**.
14   Remove the seat back from the vehicle
15   Installation is the reverse of removal.

Wagon

16   Remove the rear seat cushion (see Steps 7 and 8).
17   Pull the release handle and lower the seat backs to the down position.
18   Remove the mounting fastener at the bottom of the rear seat back bolster then unclip the top of the bolster to remove it.
19   Remove the mounting bolt at the lower corner of each seat.
20   Slide the seat backs off the rear center pivot pin and remove the seat back
21   Installation is the reverse of removal.

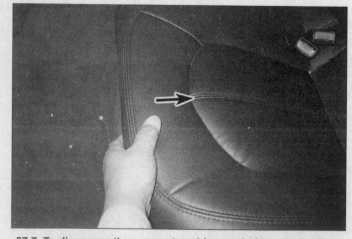

27.7 To disengage the rear seat cushion push down on the front of the seat and then push back and up

27.13 Seat back front side lower mounting nuts (Coupe and Sedan models)

28.12 To remove a C-pillar trim panel, pry off the trim cap, remove the pillar retaining screw, and then carefully pry off the panel with a trim removal tool

28 Package tray - removal and installation

Warning: *All models covered by this manual are equipped with a Supplemental Restraint System (SRS), more commonly known as airbags. Always disable the airbag system before working in the vicinity of any airbag system component to avoid the possibility of accidental deployment of the airbag, which could cause personal injury (see Chapter 12).*

1   Disconnect the battery (see Chapter 5).
2   Remove the rear seat cushion and seat backs (see Section 27).

2007 and earlier models

3   Remove the trim cap and screw from the left and right C-pillar trim panels.

28.13 Remove the plastic push pins from the front of the package tray panel

4   Disengage the shoulder belt trim cover by prying the front end of the trim up and pulling it out of the package tray.
5   It is not necessary to disconnect the center seatbelt to remove the package tray. Instead, pull the package tray up slightly, then disengage the seatbelt from the tray by threading the belt through the gap in the tray.
6   Lift up and in to disengage the retaining clips and remove the package tray. **Warning:** *Pay close attention to how the seatbelt is routed. It must be installed exactly the same way. Failure to do so could result in serious injury to someone secured by an incorrectly routed seatbelt in the event of an accident.*
7   Installation is the reverse of removal.

2008 and later models
Coupe

8   Remove the trim cap and screw from the left and right C-pillar trim panels.
9   Remove the pushpins that secure the front of the package tray.

10   Lift the panel up, then slide it forward and remove the package tray.
11   Installation is the reverse of removal.

Sedan

Refer to illustrations 28.12 and 28.13

12   Remove the trim cap and screw from the left and right C-pillar trim panels **(see illustration)**, then remove the trim panels.
13   Remove the pushpins that secure the front of the package tray **(see illustration)**.
14   Lift the panel up and slide it forward. If the panel is being replaced, remove the seat belt anchor and rout the seatbelt through the panel. Remove the package tray. **Warning:** *Pay close attention to how the seatbelts are routed. They must be installed exactly the same way. Failure to do so could result in serious injury to someone secured by an incorrectly routed seatbelt in the event of an accident.*
15   Installation is the reverse of removal.

Notes

Chapter 12
Chassis electrical system

Contents

1 General information

The electrical system is a 12-volt, negative ground type. Power for the lights and all electrical accessories is supplied by a lead/acid-type battery that is charged by the alternator.

This Chapter covers repair and service procedures for the various electrical components not associated with the engine. Information on the battery, alternator, ignition system and starter motor can be found in Chapter 5.

It should be noted that when portions of the electrical system are serviced, the negative cable should be disconnected from the battery to prevent electrical shorts and/or fires.

2 Electrical troubleshooting - general information

Refer to illustrations 2.5a, 2.5b, 2.6 and 2.9

A typical electrical circuit consists of an electrical component, any switches, relays, motors, fuses, fusible links or circuit breakers related to that component and the wiring and connectors that link the component to both the battery and the chassis. To help you pinpoint an electrical circuit problem, wiring diagrams are included at the end of this Chapter.

Before tackling any troublesome electrical circuit, first study the appropriate wiring diagrams to get a complete understanding of what makes up that individual circuit. Trouble spots, for instance, can often be narrowed down by noting if other components related to the circuit are operating properly. If several components or circuits fail at one time, chances are the problem is in a fuse or ground connection, because several circuits are often routed through the same fuse and ground connections.

Electrical problems usually stem from simple causes, such as loose or corroded connections, a blown fuse, a melted fusible link or a failed relay. Visually inspect the condition of all fuses, wires and connections in a problem circuit before troubleshooting the circuit.

If test equipment and instruments are going to be utilized, use the diagrams to plan ahead of time where you will make the necessary connections in order to accurately pinpoint the trouble spot.

The basic tools needed for electrical troubleshooting include a circuit tester or voltmeter (a 12-volt bulb with a set of test leads can also be used), a continuity tester, which includes a bulb, battery and set of test leads, and a jumper wire, preferably with a circuit breaker incorporated, which can be used to bypass electrical components **(see illustrations)**. Before attempting to locate a problem with test instruments, use the wiring diagram(s) to decide where to make the connections.

Voltage checks

Voltage checks should be performed if a circuit is not functioning properly. Connect one lead of a circuit tester to either the negative battery terminal or a known good ground. Connect the other lead to a connector in the circuit being tested, preferably nearest to the battery or fuse **(see illustration)**. If the bulb of the tester lights, voltage is present, which

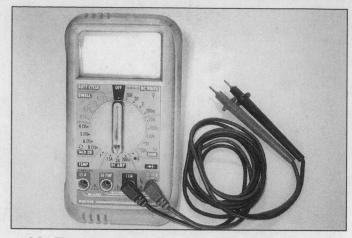

2.5a The most useful tool for electrical troubleshooting is a digital multimeter that can check volts, amps, and test continuity

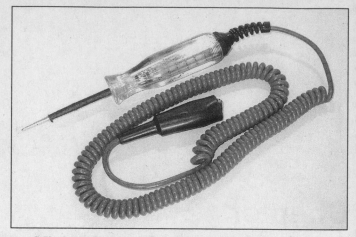

2.5b A test light is a very handy tool for checking voltage

means that the part of the circuit between the connector and the battery is problem free. Continue checking the rest of the circuit in the same fashion. When you reach a point at which no voltage is present, the problem lies between that point and the last test point with voltage. Most of the time the problem can be traced to a loose connection. **Note:** *Keep in mind that some circuits receive voltage only when the ignition key is in the Accessory or Run position.*

Finding a short

One method of finding shorts in a circuit is to remove the fuse and connect a test light or voltmeter in place of the fuse terminals. There should be no voltage present in the circuit. Move the wiring harness from side-to-side while watching the test light. If the bulb goes on, there is a short to ground somewhere in that area, probably where the insulation has rubbed through. The same test can be performed on each component in the circuit, even a switch.

Ground check

Perform a ground test to check whether a component is properly grounded. Disconnect the battery and connect one lead of a continuity tester or multimeter (set to the ohms scale), to a known good ground. Connect the other lead to the wire or ground connection being tested. If the resistance is low (less than 5 ohms), the ground is good. If the bulb on a self-powered test light does not go on, the ground is not good.

Continuity check

A continuity check is done to determine if there are any breaks in a circuit - if it is passing electricity properly. With the circuit off (no power in the circuit), a self-powered continuity tester or multimeter can be used to check the circuit. Connect the test leads to both ends of the circuit (or to the power end and a good ground), and if the test light comes on the circuit is passing current properly **(see illustration).** If the resistance is low (less than 5

ohms), there is continuity; if the reading is 10,000 ohms or higher, there is a break somewhere in the circuit. The same procedure can be used to test a switch, by connecting the continuity tester to the switch terminals. With the switch turned On, the test light should come on (or low resistance should be indicated on a meter).

Finding an open circuit

When diagnosing for possible open circuits, it is often difficult to locate them by sight because the connectors hide oxidation or terminal misalignment. Merely wiggling a connector on a sensor or in the wiring harness may correct the open circuit condition. Remember this when an open circuit is indicated when troubleshooting a circuit. Intermittent problems may also be caused by oxidized or loose connections.

Electrical troubleshooting is simple if you keep in mind that all electrical circuits are basically electricity running from the battery, through the wires, switches, relays, fuses

2.6 In use, a basic test light's lead is clipped to a known good ground, then the pointed probe can test connectors, wires or electrical sockets - if the bulb lights, the part being tested has battery voltage

2.9 With a multimeter set to the ohms scale, resistance can be checked across two terminals - when checking for continuity, a low reading indicates continuity, a high reading indicates lack of continuity

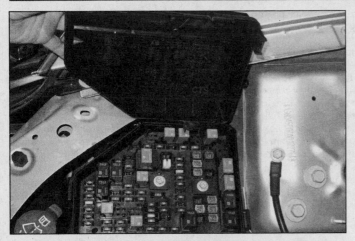

3.1a The engine compartment fuse and relay panel is located at the right side of the engine compartment

3.1b The interior compartment fuse box is located in the trunk or hatch next to the battery (2010 model shown)

and fusible links to each electrical component (light bulb, motor, etc.) and to ground, from which it is passed back to the battery. Any electrical problem is an interruption in the flow of electricity to and from the battery.

3 Fuses and fusible links - general information

Fuses

Refer to illustrations 3.1a, 3.1b and 3.3

The electrical circuits of the vehicle are protected by a combination of fuses, circuit breakers and fusible links. The main fuse/relay panel is in the engine compartment **(see illustration)**, while the interior fuse/relay panel (depending on the year and model) are located: under the instrument panel, under the left side rear seat, under the right side rear seat or inside the rear trunk or hatch next to the battery **(see illustration)**. Each of the fuses is designed to protect a specific circuit, and the various circuits are identified on the fuse panel itself.

Several sizes of fuses are employed in the fuse blocks. There are small, medium and large sizes of the same design, all with the same blade terminal design. The medium and large fuses can be removed with your fingers, but the small fuses require the use of pliers or the small plastic fuse-puller tool found in most fuse boxes.

If an electrical component fails, always check the fuse first. The best way to check the fuses is with a test light. Check for power at the exposed terminal tips of each fuse. If power is present at one side of the fuse but not the other, the fuse is blown. A blown fuse can also be identified by visually inspecting it **(see illustration)**.

Be sure to replace blown fuses with the correct type. Fuses (of the same physical size) of different ratings may be physically interchangeable, but only fuses of the proper rating should be used. Replacing a fuse with

one of a higher or lower value than specified is not recommended. Each electrical circuit needs a specific amount of protection. The amperage value of each fuse is molded into the top of the fuse body.

If the replacement fuse immediately fails, don't replace it again until the cause of the problem is isolated and corrected. In most cases, this will be a short circuit in the wiring caused by a broken or deteriorated wire.

Fusible links

Some circuits are protected by fusible links. The links are used in circuits which are not ordinarily fused, or which carry high current, such as the circuit between the alternator and the battery. Fusible links, which are usually several wire gauges smaller in size than the circuit that they protect, are designed to melt if the circuit is subjected to more current than it was designed to carry. If you have to replace a blown fusible link, make sure that you replace it with one of the same specification. If the replacement fusible link blows in the same circuit, make sure that you troubleshoot the circuit in which the fusible link melted BEFORE installing another fusible link.

4 Circuit breakers - general information

Circuit breakers protect certain circuits, such as the power windows or heated seats. Depending on the vehicle's accessories, there may be one or two circuit breakers, located in the fuse/relay box in the engine compartment.

Because the circuit breakers reset automatically, an electrical overload in a circuit breaker-protected system will cause the circuit to fail momentarily, then come back on. If the circuit does not come back on, check it immediately.

For a basic check, pull the circuit breaker up out of its socket on the fuse panel, but just

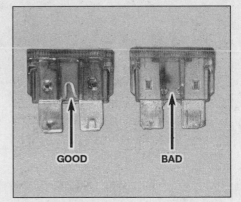

3.3 When a fuse blows, the element between the terminals melts

far enough to probe with a voltmeter. The breaker should still contact the sockets. With the voltmeter negative lead on a good chassis ground, touch each end prong of the circuit breaker with the positive meter probe. There should be battery voltage at each end. If there is battery voltage only at one end, the circuit breaker must be replaced.

Some circuit breakers must be reset manually.

5 Relays - general information

Several electrical accessories in the vehicle, such as the fuel injection system, horns, starter, and fog lamps use relays to transmit the electrical signal to the component. Relays use a low-current circuit (the control circuit) to open and close a high-current circuit (the power circuit). If the relay is defective, that component will not operate properly. Most relays are mounted in the engine compartment and interior fuse/relay boxes **(see illustrations 3.1a and 3.1b)**.

6   Electrical connectors - general information

Most electrical connections on these vehicles are made with multiwire plastic connectors. The mating halves of many connectors are secured with locking clips molded into the plastic connector shells. The mating halves of some large connectors, such as some of those under the instrument panel, are held together by a bolt through the center of the connector.

To separate a connector with locking clips, use a small screwdriver to pry the clips apart carefully, then separate the connector halves. Pull only on the shell, never pull on the wiring harness, as you may damage the individual wires and terminals inside the connectors. Look at the connector closely before trying to separate the halves. Often the locking clips are engaged in a way that is not immediately clear. Additionally, many connectors have more than one set of clips.

Each pair of connector terminals has a male half and a female half. When you look at the end view of a connector in a diagram, be sure to understand whether the view shows the harness side or the component side of the connector. Connector halves are mirror images of each other, and a terminal shown on the right side end-view of one half will be on the left side end-view of the other half.

It is often necessary to take circuit voltage measurements with a connector connected. Whenever possible, carefully insert a small straight pin (not your meter probe) into the rear of the connector shell to contact the terminal inside, then clip your meter lead to the pin. This kind of connection is called "backprobing." When inserting a test probe into a terminal, be careful not to distort the terminal opening. Doing so can lead to a poor connection and corrosion at that terminal later. Using the small straight pin instead of a meter probe results in less chance of deforming the terminal connector.

Electrical connectors

Most electrical connectors have a single release tab that you depress to release the connector

Some electrical connectors have a retaining tab which must be pried up to free the connector

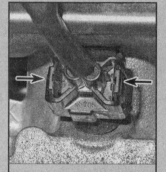

Some connectors have two release tabs that you must squeeze to release the connector

Some connectors use wire retainers that you squeeze to release the connector

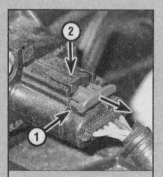

Critical connectors often employ a sliding lock (1) that you must pull out before you can depress the release tab (2)

Here's another sliding-lock style connector, with the lock (1) and the release tab (2) on the side of the connector

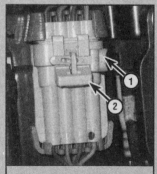

On some connectors the lock (1) must be pulled out to the side and removed before you can lift the release tab (2)

Some critical connectors, like the multi-pin connectors at the Powertrain Control Module employ pivoting locks that must be flipped open

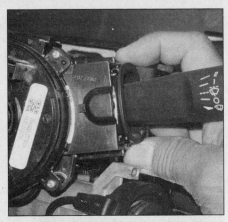

7.4 Depress the retaining tabs and remove the windshield wiper switch

7.7 Depress the retaining tabs and remove the headlight/turn signal switch

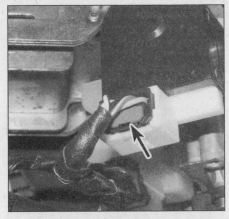

8.9 Disconnect the ignition switch electrical connector

7 Steering column switches - replacement

Warning: *The models covered by this manual are equipped with Supplemental Restraint Systems (SRS), more commonly known as airbags. Always disable the airbag system before working in the vicinity of any airbag system components to avoid the possibility of accidental deployment of the airbags, which could cause personal injury (see Section 28).*

1   Disconnect the cable from the negative terminal of the battery (see Chapter 5).

2   Remove the knee bolster trim panel, the knee bolster and the steering column covers (see Chapter 11).

Windshield wiper switch

Refer to illustration 7.4

3   On 2007 and earlier models, remove the retaining screws from the top and side of the windshield wiper switch, then remove the switch from the switch housing.

4   On 2008 and later models, depress the locking tabs on the top and bottom of the wiper switch and remove the switch from the switch housing **(see illustration)**.

5   Installation is the reverse of removal.

Headlight/turn signal switch

Refer to illustration 7.7

6   On 2007 and earlier models, remove the retaining screws from the top and side of the headlight switch, then remove the switch from the switch housing.

7   On 2008 and later models, depress the locking tabs on the top and bottom of the wiper switch and remove the switch from the switch housing **(see illustration)**.

8   Installation is the reverse of removal.

8 Ignition switch and key lock cylinder - replacement

Warning: *The models covered by this manual are equipped with Supplemental Restraint Systems (SRS), more commonly known as airbags. Always disable the airbag system before working in the vicinity of any airbag system components to avoid the possibility of accidental deployment of the airbags, which could cause personal injury (see Section 28).*

1   Disconnect the cable from the negative terminal of the battery (see Chapter 5).

2   Remove the knee bolster trim panel, the knee bolster and the upper and lower steering column covers (see Chapter 11). Lower the steering column to its lowest position.

Ignition switch

2007 and earlier models

3   Remove the wiring harness from the harness retainer.

4   Remove the two electrical connectors from the bottom of the multifunction switch housing.

5   Rotate the ignition key alarm connector down, then pull the connector outwards to release the connector fastener.

6   On 2004 and earlier models, remove the ignition switch screws. Remove the switch from the steering column and disconnect the wiring connector.

7   On 2005 through 2007 models, disconnect the electrical connector from the ignition switch. Carefully remove the two wires in the ignition switch clip (side of the switch), insert special tool J-42759 into the lock cylinder housing to release the igniting switch, and slide the switch out. **Note:** *On 2007 models only, first remove the ignition lock cylinder, then disconnect the theft deterrent module electrical connector and remove module from the end of the key lock housing.*

8   Installation is the reverse of removal. Lock the key alarm connector in place.

2008 and later models

Refer to illustrations 8.9, 8.10a and 8.10b

9   Remove the locking pin and disconnect the electrical connector from the ignition switch **(see illustration)**.

10   Remove the mounting fasteners **(see illustration)**, lift the rod out of the actuator arm **(see illustration)** and remove the ignition switch from the steering column.

11   When installing the switch, make sure that it snaps into place. Installation is otherwise the reverse of removal.

8.10a Remove the ignition switch mounting fasteners . . .

8.10b . . . then lift the rod out of the actuator arm

8.13 On 2008 and later models, insert a suitable tool through this hole and push the release button to release the ignition key lock cylinder

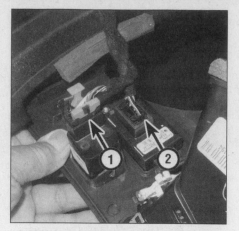

9.4 Disconnect the electrical connector for the dimmer switch (1), then the driver information center switch (2)

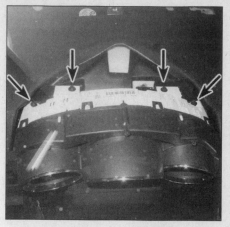

10.4 Instrument cluster mounting screws (2008 and later models)

Key lock cylinder

Refer to illustration 8.13

12   Turn the ignition key to the RUN position.

13   Using a suitable tool, depress the key lock cylinder release button. On 2007 and earlier models, the release button hole is on the bottom of the key lock cylinder housing; on 2008 and later models, it is located at the top **(see illustration)**. Remove the key lock cylinder.

14   To install the key lock cylinder, insert it into the lock cylinder housing and push it in until it clicks into place.

15   Verify that the ignition switch operates correctly in the OFF, ACC, RUN and START positions.

16   Installation is otherwise the reverse of removal.

Key lock cylinder illumination ring

Note: *Removal of the lock cylinder illumination ring is not necessary for lock cylinder replacement.*

17   Disconnect the electrical connector from the illumination ring.

18   Disengage the lock tabs and remove the illumination ring.

19   Installation is the reverse of removal. Make sure that the ring snaps into place.

9   Instrument panel switches - replacement

Warning: *The models covered by this manual are equipped with Supplemental Restraint Systems (SRS), more commonly known as airbags. Always disable the airbag system before working in the vicinity of any airbag system components to avoid the possibility of accidental deployment of the airbags, which could cause personal injury (see Section 28).*

Dimmer switch/Driver Information Center (DIC) switches

Refer to illustration 9.4

Note: *On 2007 and earlier models, the dimmer switch is mounted in the overhead console.*

1   Disconnect the cable from the negative terminal of the battery (see Chapter 5).

2   Remove the left end trim panel from the instrument panel and the left side trim strips (see Chapter 11).

3   Using a trim tool, pry out the driver's side switch panel (see Chapter 11).

4   Disconnect the electrical connectors **(see illustration)** from the switches on the backside of the trim panel.

5   To remove the dimmer switch, pry the switch panel out of the trim panel using a small screwdriver.

6   To remove the driver information center switch, remove the mounting fasteners and the switch.

7   Disconnect the electrical connector and remove the dimmer switch from the trim panel.

8   Pop a new instrument panel dimmer switch into the bezel and make sure that it snaps into place. Installation is otherwise the reverse of removal.

Hazard flasher switch

2007 and earlier models

9   Pry out the center air vent and disconnect the hazard switch electrical connector.

10   Release the tabs securing the switch to the vent panel.

11   Installation is the reverse of removal.

2008 and later models

Note: *The hazard flasher is an integral part of the radio control assembly and must be replaced as an assembly.*

12   Remove the center trim radio and heater/air control panel (see Chapter 11).

13   Remove the radio control assembly from the trim panel and have the unit tested.

14   Installation is the reverse of removal.

10   Instrument cluster - removal and installation

Refer to illustration 10.4

Warning: *The models covered by this manual are equipped with Supplemental Restraint Systems (SRS), more commonly known as airbags. Always disable the airbag system before working in the vicinity of any airbag system components to avoid the possibility of accidental deployment of the airbags, which could cause personal injury (see Section 28).*

1   Disconnect the cable from the negative battery terminal (see Chapter 5).

2   Release the tilt wheel lever and lower the steering wheel to its lowest position.

3   Remove the instrument cluster trim panel (see Chapter 11).

4   Remove the instrument cluster mounting screws **(see illustration)**. On 2007 and earlier models, the screws are on the face of the cluster; on 2008 and later models, they are on the top of the instrument cluster.

5   Carefully pull out the instrument cluster from the instrument panel and disconnect the electrical connectors.

6   Installation is the reverse of removal.

11   Radio and speakers - removal and installation

Warning: *The models covered by this manual are equipped with Supplemental Restraint Systems (SRS), more commonly known as airbags. Always disable the airbag system before working in the vicinity of any airbag system components to avoid the possibility of accidental deployment of the airbags, which could cause personal injury (see Section 28).*

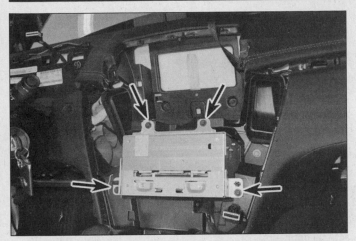

11.11 Radio mounting screws (2008 and later models)

11.14 Door speaker mounting screws

Radio

2007 and earlier models

1   Disconnect the cable from the negative battery terminal (see Chapter 5).
2   Remove the center trim panel vent panel and disconnect the hazard flasher switch (see Chapter 11).
3   Remove the ashtray from the center console (see Chapter 11).
4   Pry the air conditioning control panel out of the instrument panel and disconnect the wiring.
5   Remove the four radio-to-instrument panel fasteners.
6   Pull out the radio and disconnect the electrical connectors and antenna cable from the back of the radio.
7   Installation is the reverse of removal.

2008 and later models

Refer to illustration 11.11

Note: *The radio consists of the Front Radio Control Module. The FRCM (the controls) is what you see in the center trim panel; the radio is a separate component in the dash behind the FRCM. You can't replace the radio or FRCM at home. You can remove both units to access something else, or to remove the instrument panel, but if the radio or FRCM must be replaced, it will have to be done by a dealer service department because module configuration must be programmed into the new unit. Without the correct module configuration, the new radio will not work.*

8   Disconnect the cable from the negative battery terminal (see Chapter 5).
9   Remove the center radio and heater/air control panel (see Chapter 11).
10   If you're removing the FRCM (the radio controls), or the center trim panel, remove the screws and detach the FRCM from the center trim panel.
11   If you're removing the radio, remove the radio mounting screws **(see illustration)**, then pull out the radio unit and disconnect the antenna cable and all electrical connectors.
12   Installation is the reverse of removal.

11.22a Instrument panel center speaker fastener locations

11.22b Instrument panel corner/tweeter speaker fastener locations

Speakers

Door speakers

Refer to illustration 11.14

Note: *This procedure applies to front and rear door speakers.*

13   Remove the door trim panel (see Chapter 11).
14   Remove the speaker mounting screws **(see illustration)**.
15   Pull the speaker out of its enclosure and disconnect the speaker electrical connectors.
16   Installation is the reverse of removal.

Door tweeters

17   Remove the door trim panel and the sail panel (see Chapter 11).
18   Disconnect the tweeter electrical connector.
19   Pry the tweeter grille from the panel.
20   Installation is the reverse of removal.

Instrument panel speakers

Refer to illustration 11.22a and 11.22b

Note: *Depending on the year and model, there are various configurations of front speakers and tweeters. This procedure applies to any of them.*

21   Carefully pry out the defrost panel from instrument panel cover (see Chapter 11).
22   Remove the center speaker and the corner speaker fasteners **(see illustrations)**.
23   Lift the speaker out of the instrument panel and disconnect the electrical connector.
24   Installation is the reverse of removal.

Rear speakers

Note: *Depending on the year and model, there are various configurations of rear speakers and woofers located behind the back seat, underneath the package tray. This procedure applies to any of them.*

25   Remove the package tray (see Chapter 11).
26   Remove the speaker mounting fasteners, then lift up the speaker and disconnect the electrical connector.
27   Installation is the reverse of removal.

13.2 Remove the low-beam cover fasteners

13.3 Disconnect the electrical connector from the low-beam bulb (A), then rotate the bulb holder counterclockwise

13.6 Remove the high-beam cover fasteners

12   Antenna, module and cables - removal and installation

Antenna

1   The antenna is an integral component of the rear window. It cannot be serviced separately from the rear window.

Antenna module

2   Remove the C-pillar trim (see Chapter 11, Section 28), and pull down the rear of the headliner.
3   Disconnect the electrical connectors from the antenna module.
4   Remove the module mounting fastener and remove the module.
5   Installation is the reverse of removal.

Antenna cables

6   The antenna cable consists of two cables: front and rear. The rear cable is routed down the right C-pillar, between the body and the left and right ends of the back seat, then along the rocker, under the front and rear door sill panels and carpeting, ending at the

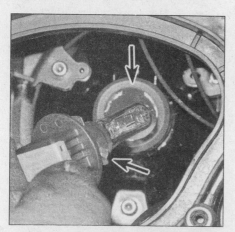

13.9 Align the lugs on the bulb holder with the cutouts in the headlight housing

right kick panel, where it connects to the front cable. The front cable is routed up behind the right kick panel, then turns left and goes across the glove box area and connects to the backside of the radio. The antenna cables are an integral part of the wiring harness under the carpeting. If one of these cables must be replaced, it's impractical to try to extricate it from the wiring harness. Instead, simply disconnect it at both ends and leave it in place, install a new cable and plug it in.

Rear antenna cable

7   To access the rear antenna cable, remove the following components (see Chapter 11):

    Back seat cushion
    Right C-pillar
    Front and rear door sills
    Front passenger seat
    Carpeting
    Right kick panel

8   Disconnect the antenna cable from the antenna module and from the front antenna cable, then install the new cable and plug it in.

Front antenna cable

9   To access the front antenna cable, remove the following components (see Chapter 11, unless otherwise noted):

    Right kick panel
    Glove box
    Radio (see Section 11)

10   Disconnect the front antenna cable from the radio and from the rear antenna cable, then install the new cable and plug it in.

13   Headlight bulb - replacement

Warning: *Halogen bulbs are gas-filled and under pressure and might shatter if the surface is scratched or the bulb is dropped. Wear eye protection and handle the bulbs carefully, grasping only the base whenever possible. Don't touch the surface of the bulb with your fingers because the oil from your skin could cause it to overheat and fail prematurely. If*

you do touch the bulb surface, clean it with rubbing alcohol.
Note: *To access the headlight bulb, turn signal, parking, side marker and cornering bulb, the headlight housing must be removed (see Section 14).*

Halogen headlight

1   To access headlight bulbs, remove the headlight housing (see Section 14).

Low-beam bulbs

Refer to illustrations 13.2 and 13.3

2   Remove the cover mounting fasteners from the back of the headlight housing **(see illustration)** and remove the cover.
3   Disconnect the electrical connector from the bulb **(see illustration)**.
4   Turn the bulb counterclockwise **(see illustration 13.3)** and remove it from the headlight housing.
5   When installing the bulb, align the lugs on the bulb's locking flange with their corresponding cutouts in the headlight housing, insert the bulb into the headlight housing and twist it clockwise to lock it into place. When installing the new bulb, make sure that you don't touch it with your fingers, because the oil from your hands will cause the bulb to overheat and fail prematurely. If you do touch the bulb, wipe it off with alcohol and a clean soft cloth. Installation is otherwise the reverse of removal.

High-beam bulbs

Refer to illustrations 13.6 and 13.9

6   Remove the protective cover fasteners and cover **(see illustration)**.
7   Disconnect the electrical connector from the bulb.
8   Turn the bulb counterclockwise and remove it from the headlight housing.
9   When installing the bulb, align the lugs on the bulb's locking flange with their corresponding cutouts in the headlight housing **(see illustration)**. Insert the bulb into the headlight housing and twist it clockwise to lock it into place. When installing the new

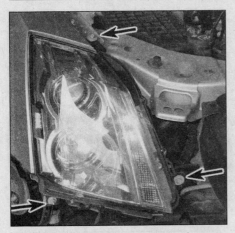

14.7 Headlight housing mounting fastener locations (2008 and later model shown)

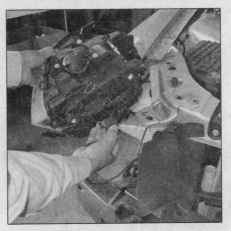

14.8 Disconnect the harness from the housing (2008 and later model shown)

7   Remove the headlight housing fasteners (see illustration).
8   Pull out the headlight housing and disconnect the electrical connector (see illustration).
9   Installation is the reverse of removal.

15   Headlights - adjustment

Refer to illustrations 15.1 and 15.2
Warning: *The headlights must be aimed correctly. If adjusted incorrectly, they could temporarily blind the driver of an oncoming vehicle and cause an accident or seriously reduce your ability to see the road. The headlights should be checked for proper aim every 12 months and any time a new headlight is installed or front-end bodywork is performed. The following procedure is only an interim step to provide temporary adjustment until the headlights can be adjusted by a properly equipped shop.*
1   The headlight adjustment screw (see illustration) controls up-and-down movement. Left-and-right movement is not adjustable.
2   There are several methods of adjusting the headlights. The simplest method requires a blank wall 25 feet in front of the vehicle and a level floor (see illustration).
3   Position masking tape on the wall in reference to the vehicle centerline and the centerlines of both headlights.
4   Measure the height of the headlight reference marks (in the centers of the headlight lenses) from the ground. Position a horizontal

bulb, make sure that you don't touch it with your fingers, because the oil from your hands will cause the bulb to overheat and fail prematurely. If you do touch the bulb, wipe it off with alcohol and a clean soft cloth. Installation is otherwise the reverse of removal.

Xenon (HID) headlights

Warning: *Some models use High Intensity Discharge (HID) bulbs instead of conventional halogen bulbs. According to the manufacturer, the high voltages produced by this system can be fatal in the event of shock. Also, the voltage can remain in circuit even after the headlight switch has been turned to OFF and the ignition key has been removed. Therefore, for your safety, we don't recommend that you try to replace one of these bulbs yourself Instead, have this service performed by a dealer service department or other qualified repair shop.*

14   Headlight housing - removal and installation

2007 and earlier models

1   Remove the front bumper cover (see

Chapter 11).
2   Remove the pin-type retainers and the headlight housing bolts.
3   Disconnect the headlight washer hose, if equipped.
4   Pull headlight housing straight out to release the housing from the ball stud and disconnect the electrical connectors.
5   Installation is the reverse of removal.

2008 and later models

Refer to illustration 14.7 and 14.8
6   Remove the front bumper cover (see Chapter 11).

15.1 Vertical adjustment screw location, insert through the body hole

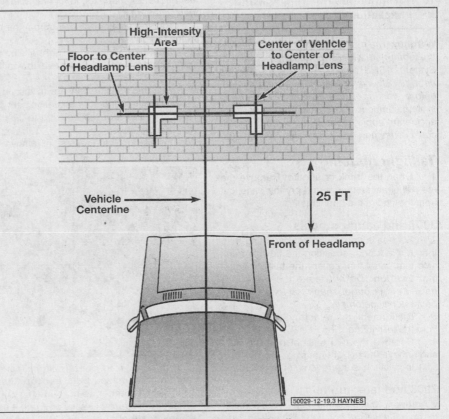

15.2 Headlight adjustment details

High-Intensity Area
Floor to Center of Headlamp Lens
Center of Vehicle to Center of Headlamp Lens
Vehicle Centerline
25 FT
Front of Headlamp
50029-12-19.3 HAYNES

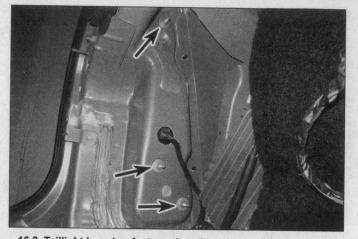

16.8 Taillight housing fastener locations (sedan model shown)

17.2 Headlight housing bulb cover mounting fastener locations (2008 and later model shown)

tape line on the wall at the same height as the headlight reference marks. **Note:** *It may be easier to position the tape on the wall with the vehicle parked only a few inches away.*

5   Adjustment should be made with the vehicle sitting level, the gas tank half-full and no unusually heavy load in the vehicle.

6   Turn on the low beams. Turn the adjusting screw to position the high intensity zone so it is two inches below the horizontal line.

7   Have the headlights adjusted by a dealer service department at the earliest opportunity.

16   Taillight housing - removal and installation

Warning: *The models covered by this manual are equipped with Supplemental Restraint Systems (SRS), more commonly known as airbags. Always disable the airbag system before working in the vicinity of any airbag system components to avoid the possibility of accidental deployment of the airbags, which could cause personal injury (see Section 28).*

Taillight housing

1   Open the trunk or liftgate. Remove the rear sill panel fasteners and pry the panel out from the end of the opening.

2007 and earlier models

2   Fold back the trunk floor carpeting mat, then pull out and reposition the flexible trunk side trim panel that covers the taillight housing. **Caution:** *Do not leave the trunk side panel bent or out of shape too long, or it will permanently deform it.*

3   Disconnect the electrical connectors from the taillight housing.

4   Remove the two taillight housing nuts and remove the taillight housing.

5   Installation is the reverse of removal.

2008 and later models

Caution: *To disconnect the electrical connector from the taillight housing LED unit on 2010*

and later models, use only a flat blade screwdriver (or equivalent) that is 3/8 inch (9.5 mm) wide. Insert the blade into the housing no more than 5/8 inch (15.8 mm) deep to depress the locking tab and disconnect the connector, or damage to the housing may occur.

Sedan and V-series

Refer to illustration 16.8

6   Fold back the trunk floor carpeting mat, then pull out and reposition the flexible trunk side trim panel that covers the taillight housing and the wheelhousing (see Chapter 11). **Caution:** *Do not leave the trunk side panel bent or out of shape too long, or it will permanently deform it.*

7   Pull the weather-stripping from the back of the taillight section.

8   Remove the three taillight housing nuts **(see illustration)** and remove the taillight housing.

9   Pull the housing forward to disconnect the electrical connectors and alignment pins. **Note:** *Lift and turn the housing to clear the rear bumper cover.*

10   Installation is the reverse of removal.

17.3 To remove a front turn signal/parking light or side marker bulb, squeeze these two tabs together, then rotate the bulb holder counterclockwise and pull it out of the headlight housing (2008 and later model shown)

Wagon

11   Remove the side trim panel screw covers, then remove the screws. Carefully pry out the panels, disengaging the retaining clips.

12   Remove the liftgate side trim panel screws and remove the panels.

13   Remove the three taillight housing nuts and remove the taillight housing.

14   Pull the taillight housing downwards and unhook the taillight hook from the trim end cap.

15   Remove the housing and disconnect the electrical connector (see **Caution** above). from the taillight housing.

16   Remove the three taillight housing nuts and remove the taillight housing.

17   Installation is the reverse of removal.

17   Bulb replacement

Exterior light bulbs

Front turn signal/parking and sidemarker light bulbs

Refer to illustrations 17.2 and 17.3

1   Remove the headlight housing (see Section 14).

2   On 2007 and earlier models, rotate the bulb cover and remove it from the headlight housing. On 2008 and later models, remove the bulb cover mounting fasteners and remove the cover **(see illustration)**.

3   On 2007 and earlier models, turn the bulb holder counterclockwise and remove it from the headlight housing. It's not necessary to disconnect the electrical connector to replace the bulb. On 2008 and later models, squeeze the tabs on both sides of the bulb holder, then rotate the holder counterclockwise **(see illustration)**.

4   To remove the bulb, pull it straight out of the holder.

5   Installation is the reverse of removal.

Bulb removal

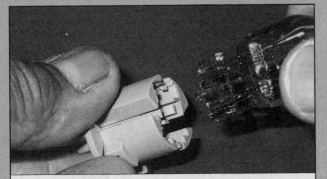

To remove many modern exterior bulbs from their holders, simply pull them out

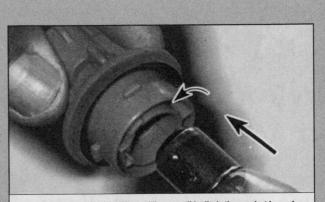

On bulbs with a cylindrical base ("bayonet" bulbs), the socket is spring-loaded; a pair of small posts on the side of the base hold the bulb in place against spring pressure. To remove this type of bulb, push it into the holder, rotate it 1/4-turn counterclockwise, then pull it out

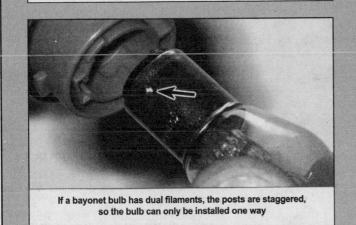

If a bayonet bulb has dual filaments, the posts are staggered, so the bulb can only be installed one way

To remove most overhead interior light bulbs, simply unclip them

Fog light bulbs

Warning: *Halogen bulbs are gas-filled and under pressure and might shatter if the surface is scratched or the bulb is dropped. Wear eye protection and handle the bulbs carefully, grasping only the base whenever possible. Don't touch the surface of the bulb with your fingers because the oil from your skin could cause it to overheat and fail prematurely. If you do touch the bulb surface, clean it with rubbing alcohol.*

6   Raise the front of the vehicle and support it securely on jackstands.

7   On 2007 and earlier models, remove the splash shield below the fog lamp. On 2008 and later models, remove the inner fender splash shield (see Chapter 11).

8   Disconnect the fog light bulb electrical connector.

9   Turn the fog light bulb counterclockwise and remove it from the fog light housing.

10   To install the new fog light bulb, insert it into the fog light housing and turn it clockwise to lock it into place.

11   Installation is otherwise the reverse of removal.

Center high-mounted brake light

Note: *The high-mounted brake light LEDs are an integral part of the housing, and not separately serviceable.*

2007 and earlier models

12   Open the trunk lid.

13   Remove the trunk lid trim panel (see Chapter 11).

14   Remove the trunk lid lighting and badge panel fasteners and separate the panel from the trunk lid.

15   Disconnect the electrical connectors.

16   Remove the brake light to badge panel fasteners and remove the brake light panel.

17   Installation is the reverse of removal.

2008 and later sedan and V-series models

Refer to illustration 17.20

18   Open the trunk lid.

19   Remove the trunk lid trim panel (see Chapter 11).

20   Remove the four mounting nuts **(see illustration)**, squeeze the two release tabs and push the lamp assembly out. Remove the

high-mounted brake light. No further disassembly is possible. The LEDs are an integral part of the housing, and not separately serviceable.

21   Installation is the reverse of removal.

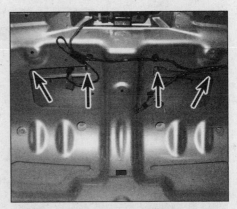

17.20   High mount brake light assembly fasteners (2008 and later Sedan model shown)

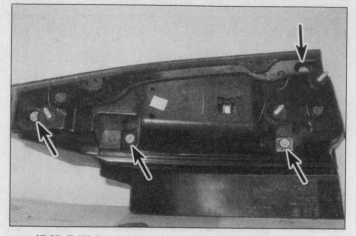

17.27 Taillight assembly fasteners (2008 and later Sedan model shown)

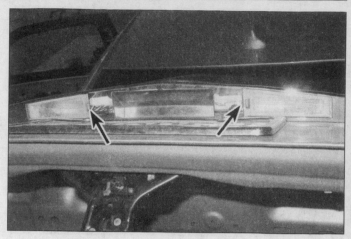

17.35 License plate lens release tab locations (2008 and later Sedan model shown)

Wagon models

22   Open the liftgate and remove the liftgate exterior panel fasteners from the inside of the liftgate (see Chapter 11).

23   Disconnect the electrical connectors.

24   Remove the eight mounting nuts and remove the high-mounted brake light assembly from the exterior trim panel. No further disassembly is possible. The LEDs are an integral part of the housing, and not separately serviceable.

25   Installation is the reverse of removal.

Taillight bulbs

Refer to illustration 17.27

26   Remove the taillight housing (see Section 16).

27   Remove the taillight assembly mounting screws **(see illustration)** and remove the assembly from the housing. No further disassembly is possible. The LEDs are an integral part of the assembly, and not separately serviceable.

28   Installation is the reverse of removal.

License plate light bulbs

2007 and earlier models

29   Remove the trunk lid lighting and badge panel fasteners and separate the panel from the trunk lid.

30   Unclip the license plate light lens and remove the lens and bulb.

31   Rotate the bulb socket counterclockwise and remove the socket and bulb.

32   Pull the bulb from the socket.

33   Installation is the reverse of removal.

2008 and later sedan and V-series models

Refer to illustration 17.35

34   Open the trunk lid.

35   Insert a small screwdriver into the slot in the lens, press the release tab, then remove the lens **(see illustration)**.

36   Disconnect the electrical connector, rotate the bulb socket counterclockwise and remove the socket and bulb.

37   Pull the bulb from the socket.

38   Installation is the reverse of removal.

Wagon models

39   Open the liftgate.

40   Depress the tabs on the left sides of the lenses and remove the lens.

41   Disconnect the electrical connector, rotate the bulb socket counterclockwise and remove the socket and bulb.

42   Pull the bulb from the socket.

43   Installation is the reverse of removal.

Interior light bulbs

Front or rear overhead light bulbs

Refer to illustrations 17.44 and 17.45

44   Carefully pry off the overhead lens **(see illustration)**.

45   Remove the lighting assembly-to-overhead panel fasteners and remove the lighting assembly **(see illustration)**.

46   Pull the bulb straight out of its sockets.

47   Installation is the reverse of removal.

Cargo light bulbs (wagon models)

48   Carefully pry out the cargo light from the side panel.

49   Disconnect the electrical connector and

17.44 To remove an overhead panel, carefully pry it off with a trim removal tool or screwdriver

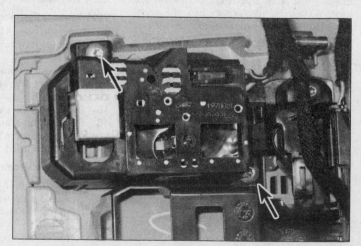

17.45 Remove the bulb holder mounting fasteners

18.1 Remove the wiper arm trim cap and the wiper arm nut

18.3 Wiper motor electrical connector (1) and assembly mounting bolts (2)

remove the bulb from the terminals.

50   Installation is the reverse of removal.

18   Wiper motor - replacement

Windshield wiper motor

Refer to illustrations 18.1, 18.3 and 18.5

1   Remove the wiper arm nuts and mark the relationship of the wiper arms to their shafts **(see illustration)**. Remove both wiper arms.

2   Remove the plastic cowl covers (see Chapter 11).

3   Disconnect the electrical connector from the wiper motor **(see illustration)**.

4   Remove the two wiper motor and link assembly mounting bolts and remove the wiper motor and link assembly.

5   Remove the nut that secures the crank arm to the motor shaft **(see illustration)**.

6   Mark the relationship of the crank arm to the motor shaft and remove the crank arm

from the shaft.

7   Remove the two motor mounting bolts **(see illustration 18.5)** and remove the motor from its mounting bracket.

8   Installation is the reverse of removal.

Liftgate wiper motor

9   Remove the wiper arm nut and mark the relationship of the wiper arms to their shaft.

10   Remove the liftgate rear trim panel (see Chapter 11).

11   Remove the three mounting fasteners and disconnect the electrical connector.

12   Pull the motor out of the rubber grommet and remove the motor.

13   Installation is the reverse of removal.

19   Horn - replacement

Refer to illustration 19.4

Note: *The horn is located at the lower right corner of the vehicle, in the void ahead of the right front wheel well.*

1   Raise the vehicle and support it securely on jackstands.

2   On 2007 and earlier models, remove the lower splash shield.

3   On 2008 and later models, remove the left front fender splash shield screws and pull down the splash shield (see Chapter 11).

4   Disconnect the horn electrical connector **(see illustration)**.

5   Remove the horn mounting bolt, then remove the horn.

6   Installation is the reverse of removal.

20   Daytime Running Lights (DRL) - general information

The Daytime Running Lights (DRL) system used on all models illuminates the low beam headlights at reduced intensity when the engine is running. The only exception is with the engine running and the shift lever in Park. Once the parking brake is released or the shift lever is moved, the lights will remain on as long as the ignition switch is on.

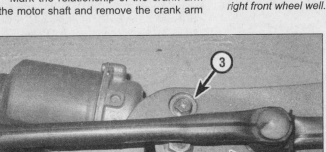

18.5 Wiper motor mounting details

1   Crankshaft arm nut
2   Crankshaft arm
3   Wiper motor mounting fasteners

19.4 Horn assembly details

1   Electrical connector
2   Horn mounting nuts
3   Horn bracket mounting bolts

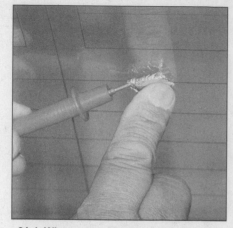

21.4 When measuring the voltage at the rear window defogger grid, wrap a piece of aluminum foil around the positive probe of the voltmeter and press the foil against the wire with your finger

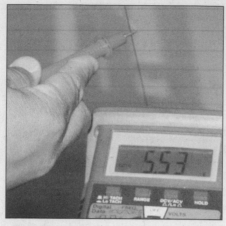

21.5 To determine if a heating element has broken, check the voltage at the center of each element; if the voltage is 5 or 6 volts, the element is unbroken, but if the voltage is 10 or 12 volts, the element is broken between the center and the ground side. If there is no voltage, the element is broken between the center and the positive side

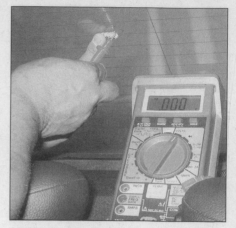

21.7 To find the break, place the voltmeter negative lead against the defogger ground terminal, place the voltmeter positive lead with the foil strip against the heating element at the positive terminal end and slide it toward the negative terminal end. The point at which the voltmeter reading changes abruptly is the point at which the element is broken

21   Rear window defogger - check and repair

1   The rear window defogger consists of a number of horizontal elements baked onto the glass surface.
2   Small breaks in the element can be repaired without removing the rear window.

Check

Refer to illustrations 21.4, 21.5 and 21.7

3   Turn the ignition switch and defogger system switches to the ON position. Using a voltmeter, place the positive probe against the defogger grid positive terminal and the negative probe against the ground terminal. If battery voltage is not indicated, check the fuse, defogger switch and related wiring. If voltage is indicated, but all or part of the defogger doesn't heat, proceed with the following tests.
4   When measuring voltage during the

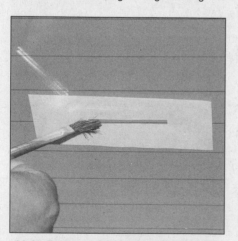

21.13 To use a defogger repair kit, apply masking tape to the inside of the window at the damaged area, then brush on the special conductive coating

next two tests, wrap a piece of aluminum foil around the tip of the voltmeter positive probe and press the foil against the heating element with your finger **(see illustration)**. Place the negative probe on the defogger grid ground terminal.
5   Check the voltage at the center of each heating element **(see illustration)**. If the voltage is 5 or 6-volts, the element is okay (there is no break). If the voltage is zero, the element is broken between the center of the element and the positive end. If the voltage is 10 to 12-volts, the element is broken between the center of the element and ground. Check each heating element.
6   Connect the negative lead to a good body ground. The reading should stay the same. If it doesn't, the ground connection is bad.
7   To find the break, place the voltmeter negative probe against the defogger ground terminal. Place the voltmeter positive probe with the foil strip against the heating element at the positive terminal end and slide it toward the negative terminal end. The point at which the voltmeter deflects from several volts to zero is the point at which the heating element is broken **(see illustration)**.

Repair

Refer to illustration 21.13

8   Repair the break in the element using a repair kit specifically recommended for this purpose, available at most auto parts stores. Included in this kit is plastic conductive epoxy.
9   Prior to repairing a break, turn off the system and allow it to cool off for a few minutes.
10   Lightly buff the element area with fine steel wool, then clean it thoroughly with rubbing alcohol.

11   Use masking tape to mask off the area being repaired.
12   Thoroughly mix the epoxy, following the instructions provided with the repair kit.
13   Apply the epoxy material to the slit in the masking tape, overlapping the undamaged area about 3/4-inch on either end **(see illustration)**.
14   Allow the repair to cure for 24 hours before removing the tape and using the system.

22   Cruise control system - description and check

1   The cruise control system maintains vehicle speed with the Body Control Module (BCM), Engine Control Module (ECM), throttle actuator control motor, Brake Pedal Position (BPP) sensor, Vehicle Speed Sensor (VSS) control switches and associated wiring. There is no mechanical connection, such as a vacuum servo or cable. Some features of the system require special testers and diagnostic procedures that are beyond the scope of the home mechanic. Listed below are some general procedures that may be used to locate common problems.
2   Check the fuses (see Section 3).
3   The BPP switch (or brake light switch) deactivates the cruise control system. Have an assistant press the brake pedal while you check the brake light operation.
4   If the brake lights do not operate properly, correct the problem and retest the cruise control.
5   Check the wiring between the PCM and throttle actuator motor for opens or shorts and repair as necessary.
6   The cruise control system uses information from the PCM, including the VSS, which is located in the transmission or transfer case.

Refer to Chapter 6 for more information on the VSS.

7   Test drive the vehicle to determine if the cruise control is now working. If it isn't, take it to a dealer service department or other qualified repair shop for further diagnosis.

23   Power window system - description and check

Note: *These models are equipped with a Body Control Module (BCM). Several systems are linked to this centralized control module, which allows simple and accurate troubleshooting, but only with a professional-grade scan tool. The BCM governs the door locks, the power windows, the ignition lock and security system, the interior lights, the Daytime Running Lights system, the horn, the windshield wipers, the heating/air conditioning system and the power mirrors. In the event of malfunction with this system, have the vehicle diagnosed by a dealership service department or other qualified automotive repair facility.*

1   The power window system operates electric motors, mounted in the doors, which lower and raise the windows. The system consists of the control switches, the motors, regulators, glass mechanisms, the Body Control Module (BCM) and associated wiring.

2   The power windows can be lowered and raised from the master control switch by the driver or by remote switches located at the individual windows. Each window has a separate motor that is reversible. The position of the control switch determines the polarity and therefore the direction of operation.

3   The circuit is protected by a fuse and a circuit breaker. Each motor is also equipped with an internal circuit breaker; this prevents one stuck window from disabling the whole system.

4   The power window system will only operate when the ignition switch is ON, and for a period of time after the ignition key has been turned Off (unless one of the doors is opened). In addition, many models have a window lockout switch at the master control switch which, when activated, disables the switches at the rear windows and, sometimes, the switch at the passenger's window also. Always check these items before troubleshooting a window problem.

5   These procedures are general in nature, so if you can't find the problem using them, take the vehicle to a dealer service department or other properly equipped repair facility.

6   If the power windows won't operate, always check the fuse and circuit breaker first.

7   If only the rear windows are inoperative, or if the windows only operate from the master control switch, check the rear window lockout switch for continuity in the unlocked position. Replace it if it doesn't have continuity.

8   Check the wiring between the switches and fuse panel for continuity. Repair the wiring, if necessary.

9   If only one window is inoperative from the master control switch, try the other con-

trol switch at the window. **Note:** *This doesn't apply to the driver's door window.*

10   If the same window works from one switch, but not the other, check the switch for continuity.

11   If the switch tests OK, check for a short or open in the circuit between the affected switch and the window motor.

12   If one window is inoperative from both switches, remove the switch panel from the affected door. Check for voltage at the switch and at the motor (refer to Chapter 11 for door panel removal) while the switch is operated.

13   If voltage is reaching the motor, disconnect the glass from the regulator (see Chapter 11). Move the window up and down by hand while checking for binding and damage. Also check for binding and damage to the regulator. If the regulator is not damaged and the window moves up and down smoothly, replace the motor. If there's binding or damage, lubricate, repair or replace parts, as necessary.

14   If voltage isn't reaching the motor, check the wiring in the circuit for continuity between the switches and the body control module, and between the body control module and the motors. You'll need to consult the wiring diagram at the end of this Chapter. If the circuit is equipped with a relay, check that the relay is grounded properly and receiving voltage.

15   Test the windows after you are done to confirm proper repairs.

24   Power door lock and keyless entry system - description and check

Note: *These models are equipped with a Body Control Module (BCM). Several systems are linked to this centralized control module, which allows simple and accurate troubleshooting, but only with a professional-grade scan tool. The BCM governs the door locks, the power windows, the ignition lock and security system, the interior lights, the Daytime Running Lights system, the horn, the windshield wipers, the heating/air conditioning system and the power mirrors. In the event of malfunction with this system, have the vehicle diagnosed by a dealership service department or other qualified automotive repair facility.*

1   The power door lock system operates the door lock actuators mounted in each door. The system consists of the switches, actuators, BCM and associated wiring. Diagnosis can usually be limited to simple checks of the wiring connections and actuators for minor faults that can be easily repaired.

2   Power door lock systems are operated by bi-directional solenoids located in the doors. The lock switches have two operating positions: Lock and Unlock. These switches send a signal to the BCM, which in turn sends a signal to the door lock solenoids.

3   If you are unable to locate the trouble using the following general steps, consult your dealer service department.

24.14 Using a coin, carefully pry the halves of the transmitter apart

4   Always check the circuit protection first. Some vehicles use a combination of circuit breakers and fuses. Refer to the wiring diagrams at the end of this Chapter.

5   Check for voltage at the switches. If no voltage is present, check the wiring between the fuse panel and the switches for shorts and opens.

6   If voltage is present, test the switch for continuity. Replace it if there's not continuity in both switch positions. To remove the switch, use a flat-bladed trim tool to pry out the door/window switch assembly (see Chapter 11).

7   If the switch has continuity, check the wiring between the switch and door lock solenoid.

8   If all but one lock solenoids operate, remove the trim panel from the affected door (see Chapter 11) and check for voltage at the solenoid while the lock switch is operated. One of the wires should have voltage in the Lock position; the other should have voltage in the Unlock position.

9   If the inoperative solenoid is receiving voltage, replace the solenoid.

10   If the inoperative solenoid isn't receiving voltage, check for an open or short in the wire between the lock solenoid and the relay.

11   On the models covered by this manual, power door lock system communication goes through the Body Control Module (BCM). If the above tests do not pinpoint a problem, take the vehicle to a dealer or qualified shop with the proper scan tool to retrieve trouble codes from the BCM.

Keyless entry system

12   The keyless entry system consists of a remote control transmitter that sends a coded infrared signal to a receiver, which then operates the door lock system.

13   Replace the battery when the transmitter doesn't operate the locks at a distance of ten feet. Normal range should be about 30 feet.

Key remote control battery replacement

Refer to illustrations 24.14 and 24.15

14   Use a plastic trim tool or coin to carefully separate the case halves **(see illustration)**.

24.15 Carefully pry out the old battery

15   Replace the battery **(see illustration)**.
16   Snap the case halves together.

Transmitter programming

17   Programming replacement transmitters requires the use of a specialized scan tool. Take the vehicle and the transmitter(s) to a dealer service department or other qualified repair shop equipped with the necessary tool to have the transmitter(s) programmed to the vehicle.

25   Electric side view mirrors - description

Note: *On these models, the outside mirrors are controlled by the Driver Door Switch Assembly (DDSA), which houses the mirror control switches, the Driver Door Module (DDM), and the front Passenger Door Module (PDM). The DDSA interprets the mirror control switch movements while the door modules supply the battery voltage and ground to their different mirror motors to move the mirrors.*

1   The electric rear view mirrors use two motors to move the glass; one for up and down adjustments and one for left-right adjustments.
2   The control switch has a selector portion which sends voltage to the left or right side mirror. With the ignition in the ACC position and the engine OFF, roll down the windows and operate the mirror control switch through all functions (left-right and up-down) for both the left and right side mirrors.
3   Listen carefully for the sound of the electric motors running in the mirrors.
4   If the motors can be heard but the mirror glass doesn't move, there's probably a problem with the drive mechanism inside the mirror. Power mirrors have no user-serviceable parts inside - a defective mirror must be replaced as a unit (see Chapter 11).
5   If the mirrors don't operate and no sound comes from the mirrors, check the fuses (see Section 3).
6   If the fuses are OK, remove the mir-

ror control switch. Have the switch continuity checked by a dealer service department or other qualified shop.
7   Check the ground connections.
8   If the mirror still doesn't work, remove the mirror and check the wires at the mirror for voltage.
9   If there's not voltage in each switch position, check the circuit between the mirror and control switch for opens and shorts.
10   If there's voltage, remove the mirror and test it off the vehicle with jumper wires. Replace the mirror if it fails this test.

26   Power seats - description

1   These models feature a six-way seat that goes forward and backward, up and down and tilts forward and backward. The seats are powered by three reversible motors, mounted in one housing, that are controlled by switches on the side of the seat. Each switch changes the direction of seat travel by reversing polarity to the drive motor.
2   Diagnosis is usually a simple matter, using the following procedures.
3   Look under the seat for any object which may be preventing the seat from moving.
4   If the seat won't work at all, check the circuit breaker (see Section 4).
5   With the engine off to reduce the noise level, operate the seat controls in all directions and listen for sound coming from the seat motors.
6   If the motors make noise or don't work, check for voltage at the motors while an assistant operates the switch. With the door open, try the seat switch again. If the dome light dims while trying to operate the seat, this indicates something may be jammed in the seat tracks.
7   If the motor is getting voltage but doesn't run, test it off the vehicle with jumper wires. If it still doesn't work, replace it.
8   If the motor isn't getting voltage, remove the switch and check for voltage. If there's no voltage to the switch, check the wiring between the fuse block and the switch. If there's battery voltage at the switch, check the other terminals for voltage while moving the switch around. If the switch is OK, check for a short or open in the wiring between the switch and motor.
9   Test the completed repairs.

27   Data Link Communication system - description

1   The vehicles covered by this manual have a complex electrical system, encompassing many power accessories, and a number of separate electronic modules.
2   The Powertrain Control Module (PCM) is mainly responsible for engine and transmission control, but also communicates with other modules around the vehicle through

a Data Link Communication system, which sends serial port data very quickly between the various modules. Many of the computer functions involved in the operation of body systems are routed through the Body Control Module (BCM) which communicates with the PCM.
3   Among the modules in the Data Link system besides the BCM and PCM are the Sensing Diagnostic Module (airbag system), the Electronic Brake Control Module and the instrument panel cluster. The BCM further communicates with various body subsystems.
4   All of the modules in the vehicle have associated trouble codes. When other troubleshooting procedures fail to pinpoint the problem, check the wiring diagrams at the end of this Chapter to see if the BCM or PCM are involved in the circuit. If so, take your vehicle to a dealer service department or other qualified repair shop with the proper diagnostic tools to extract the trouble codes.

28   Airbag system - general information

All models are equipped with a Supplemental Inflatable Restraint (SIR) system, more commonly known as the airbag system. The airbag system is designed to protect the driver and the front seat passenger from serious injury in the event of a head-on or frontal collision. It consists of the impact sensors, a driver's airbag module in the center of the steering wheel, a passenger's airbag module in the glove box area of the instrument panel and a sensing/diagnostic module mounted under the center console, side-curtain airbags and seat belt pre-tensioners.

Airbag modules

Driver's airbag

The airbag inflator module contains a housing incorporating the cushion (airbag) and inflator unit, mounted in the center of the steering wheel. The inflator assembly is mounted on the back of the housing over a hole through which gas is expelled, inflating the bag almost instantaneously when an electrical signal is sent from the system. A spiral cable (or clockspring) assembly on the steering column under the steering wheel carries this signal to the module. This clockspring can transmit an electrical signal regardless of steering wheel position.

Passenger's airbag

The airbag is mounted inside the right side of the instrument panel, in the area above the glove box. It's similar in design to the driver's airbag, except that it's larger than the steering wheel unit. The trim cover (on the side of the instrument panel that faces toward the passenger) is textured and colored to match the instrument panel and has a molded seam that splits open when the bag inflates.

28.8 The 10 amp AIRBAG fuse is located in the interior fuse box in the trunk or hatch on 2010 and later models - see the fuse cover for exact fuse location for your model

Side curtain airbags

In addition to the side-impact airbags, extra side-impact protection is also provided by side-curtain airbags. These are long airbags that, in the event of a side impact, come out of the headliner at each side of the car and come down between the side windows and the seats. They are designed to protect the heads of both front seat and rear seat passengers.

Sensing and diagnostic module

The sensing and diagnostic module supplies the current to the airbag system in the event of a collision, even if battery power is cut off. It checks this system every time the vehicle is started, causing the "AIR BAG" light to go on then off, if the system is operating properly. If there is a fault in the system, the light will go on and stay on, flash, or the dash will make a beeping sound. If this happens, the vehicle should be taken to your dealer immediately for service. This module is mounted under the center console. There is also a roll-over sensor located directly behind it on later models.

Seat belt pre-tensioners

These models are equipped with pyrotechnic (explosive) units in the front seat belt retracting mechanisms. During an impact that would trigger the airbag system, the airbag control unit also triggers the seat belt retractors. When the pyrotechnic charges go off, they accelerate the retractors to instantly take up any slack in the seat belt system to more fully prepare the driver and front seat passenger for impact.

The airbag system should be disabled any time work is done to or around the seats. **Warning:** *Never strike the pillars or floorpan with a hammer or use an impact-driver tool in these areas unless the system is disabled.*

Disarming the system and other precautions

Refer to illustration 28.8
Warning: *Failure to follow these precautions could result in accidental deployment of the airbag and personal injury.*

Whenever working in the vicinity of the steering wheel, steering column or any of the other SIR system components, the system must be disarmed.

To disarm the airbag system:

a) *Point the wheels straight ahead and turn the key to the Lock position.*
b) *Remove the 10A SIR/AIRBAG fuse(s)* **(see illustration)**. **Note:** *See Section 3 for fuse box locations.*
c) *Turn the ignition key to the On position and look at the AIR BAG light on the instrument panel for at least 30 seconds. If you removed the correct fuse, the light will remain lit continuously (not flash). If the light doesn't remain lit continuously, remove the proper fuse.*
d) *Turn the ignition key to the Off position.*
e) *Disconnect the cable from the negative battery terminal (see Chapter 5).*
f) *Wait at least two minutes for the back-up power supply to be depleted.*

To re-arm the airbag system:

a) *Turn the ignition key to the On position, then reinstall the SIR fuse.*
b) *Make sure there is nobody inside the vehicle and that there are no objects near any of the airbag modules, then reconnect the cable to the negative terminal of the battery.*
c) *Turn the ignition switch to the Off position, wait ten seconds, then turn it to the On position. The AIR BAG light on the instrument panel should come on continuously for about six seconds, then turn off.* **Note:** *The light might take up to 30 seconds to come on after the key is turned to the On position (during this time the Restraints Control Module is performing a self-check of the system). If the light fails to come on, or if it flashes, or if a chime sounds in patterns of five sets of five beeps, have the vehicle diagnosed by a dealer service department or other qualified repair shop.*

Whenever handling an airbag module:

Always keep the airbag opening (the trim side) pointed away from your body. Never place the airbag module on a bench or other surface with the airbag opening facing the surface. Always place the airbag module in a safe location with the airbag opening facing up.

Never measure the resistance of any SIR component. An ohmmeter has a built-in battery supply that could accidentally deploy the airbag.

Never use electrical welding equipment on a vehicle equipped with an airbag without first disconnecting the electrical connector for each airbag.

Never dispose of a live airbag module. Return it to a dealer service department or other qualified repair shop for safe deployment and disposal.

Component removal and installation

Driver's side airbag module and spiral cable

Refer to Chapter 10, *Steering wheel - removal and installation*, for the driver's side airbag module and clockspring removal and installation procedures.

Passenger's airbag module and other airbag modules

Even if you ever have to remove the instrument panel, it's not necessary to remove the passenger airbag module to do so; it can simply remain installed in the instrument panel. We don't recommend removing any of the other airbag modules either. These jobs are best left to a professional.

29 Wiring diagrams - general information

Since it isn't possible to include all wiring diagrams for every year and model covered by this manual, the following diagrams are those that are typical and most commonly needed.

Prior to troubleshooting any circuits, check the fuse and circuit breakers (if equipped) to make sure they're in good condition. Make sure the battery is properly charged and check the cable connections (see Chapter 1).

When checking a circuit, make sure that all connectors are clean, with no broken or loose terminals. When disconnecting a connector, do not pull on the wiring; pull only on the connector.

Notes

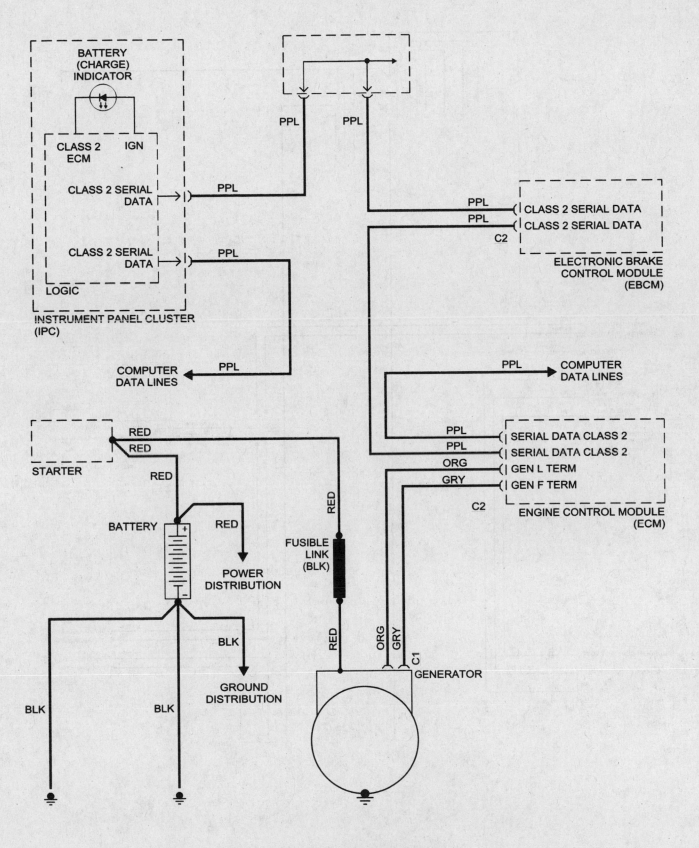

Charging system - 2007 and earlier CTS

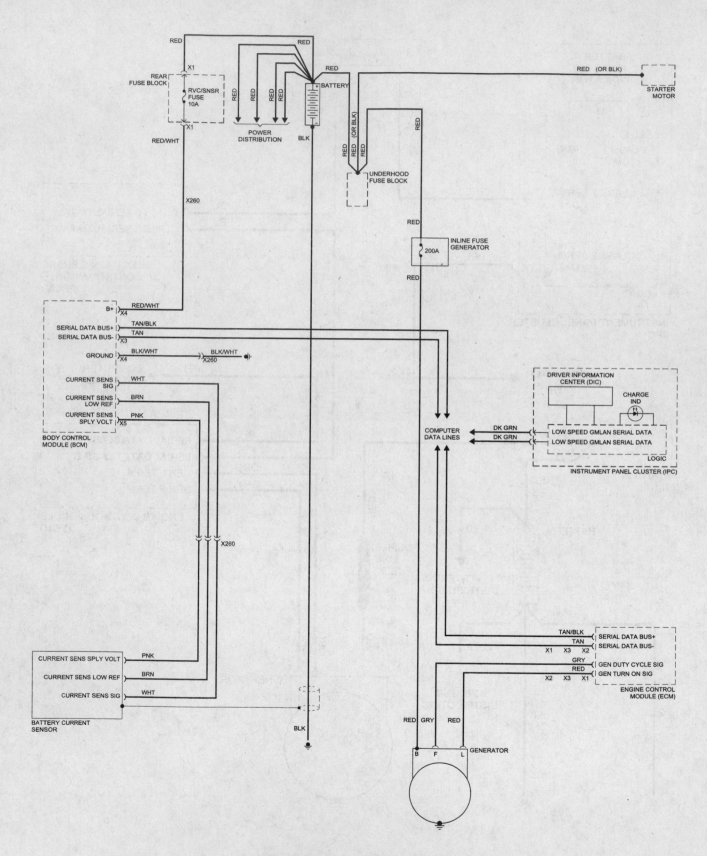

Charging system - 2008 and later CTS

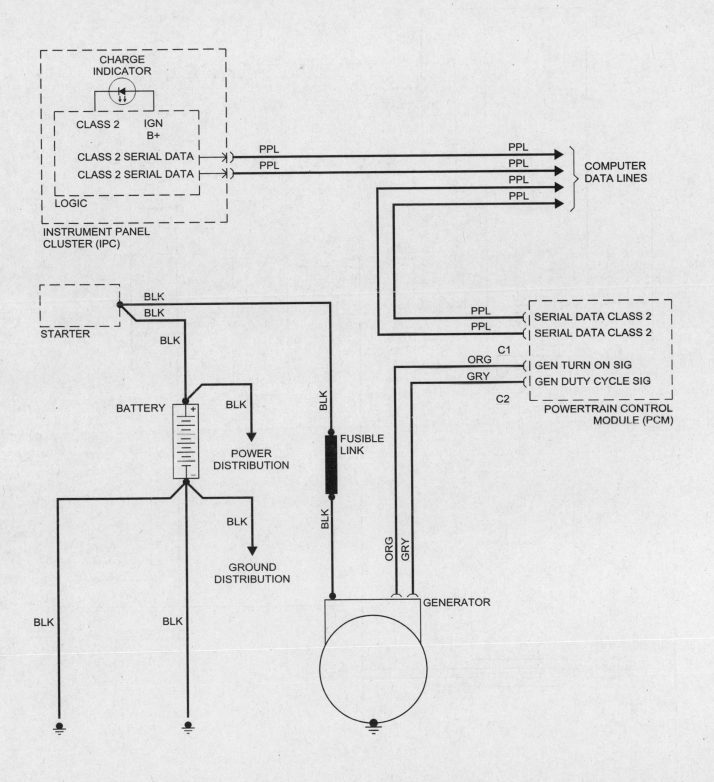

Charging system - CTS-V (typical)

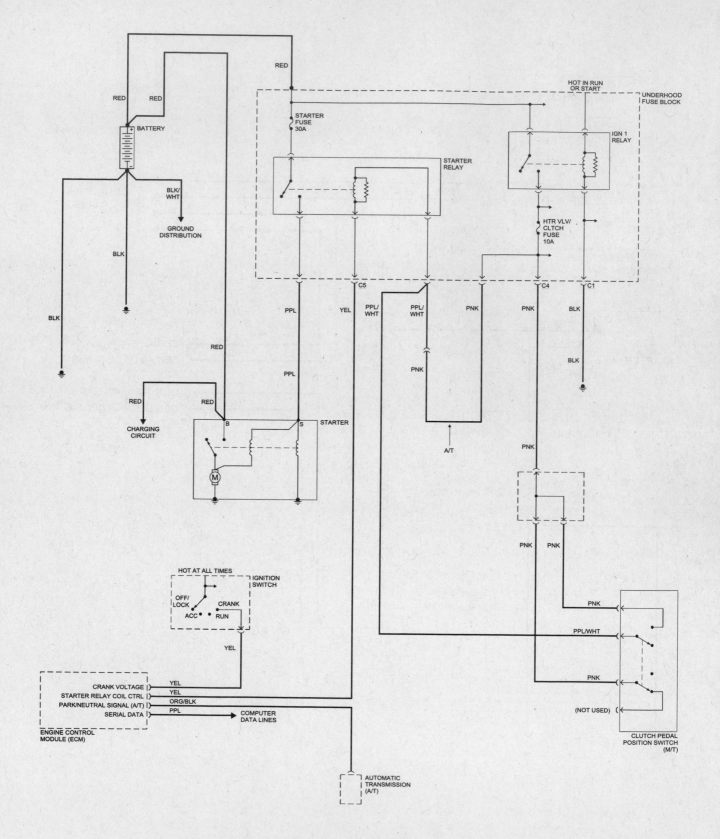

Starting system - 2007 and earlier CTS

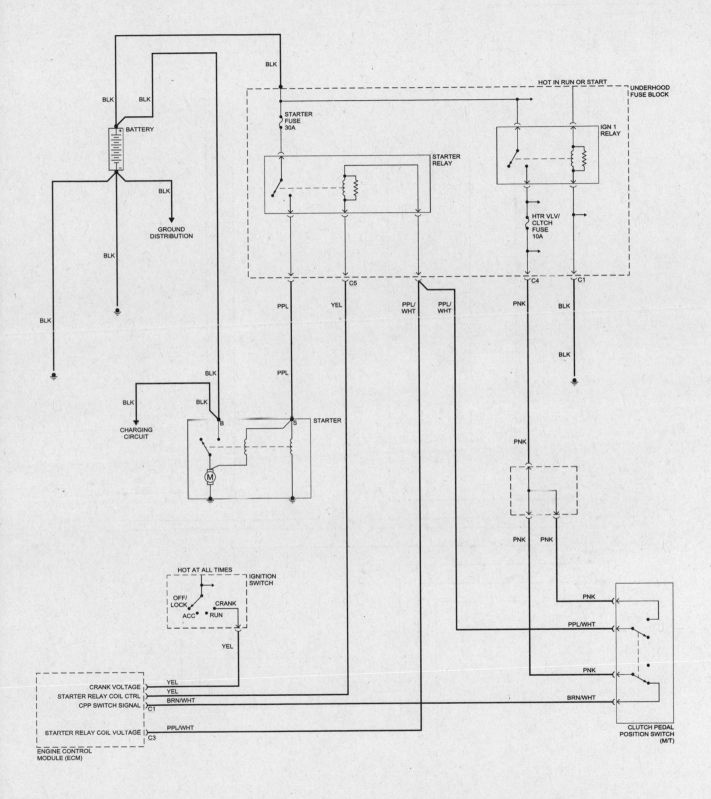

Starting system - 2007 and earlier CTS-V

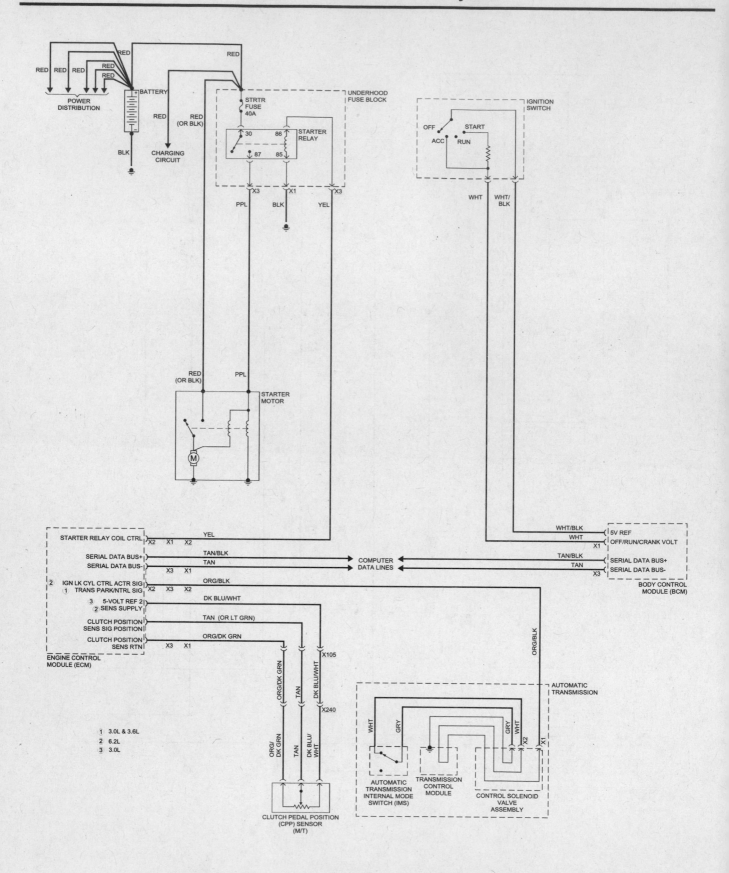

Starting system - 2008 and later CTS and CTS-V

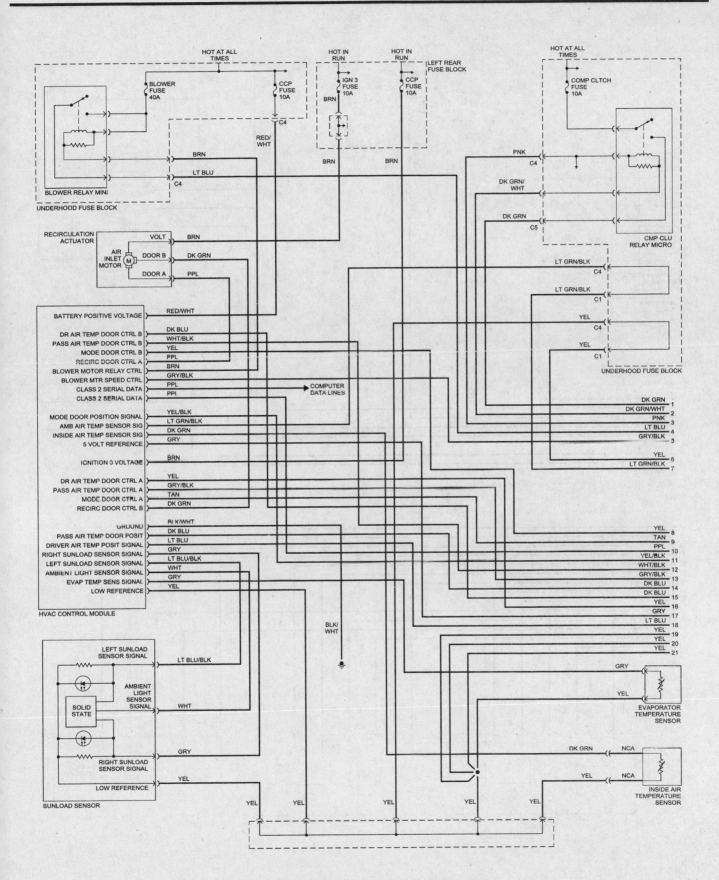

Air conditioning system - 2007 and earlier (1 of 3)

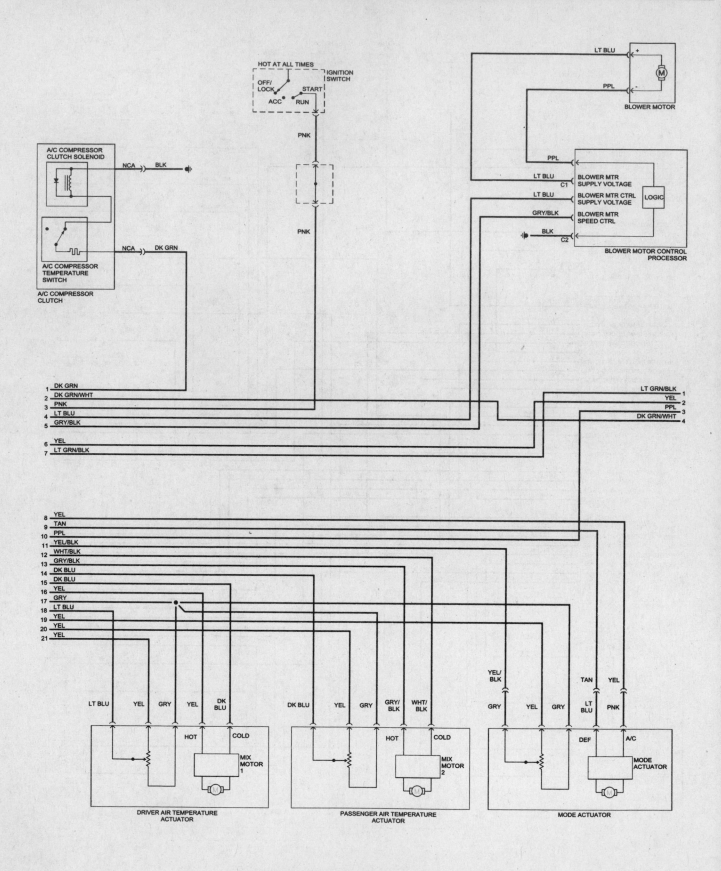

Air conditioning system - 2007 and earlier (2 of 3)

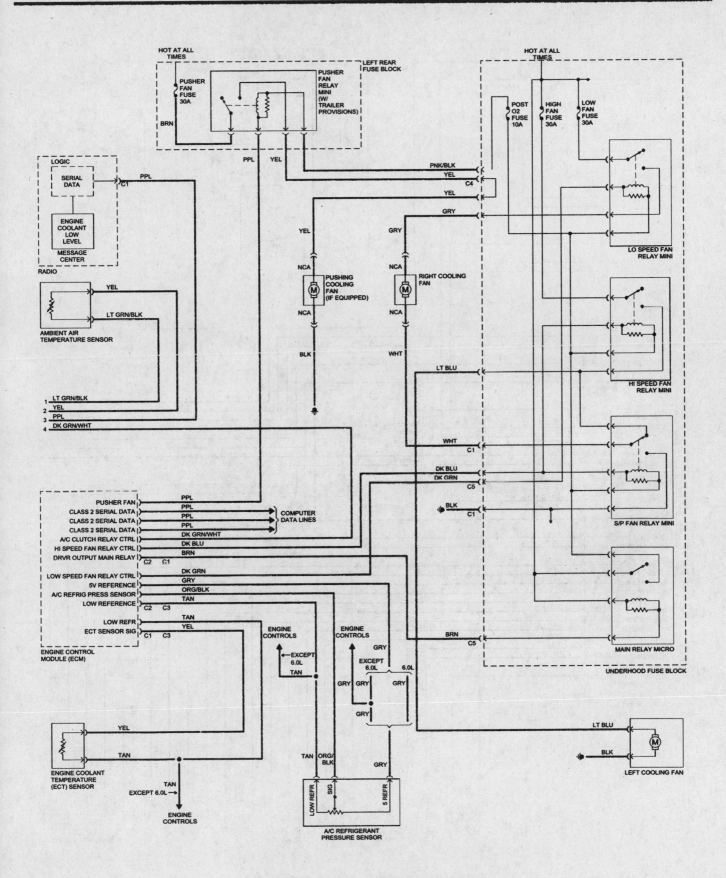

Air conditioning system - 2007 and earlier (3 of 3)

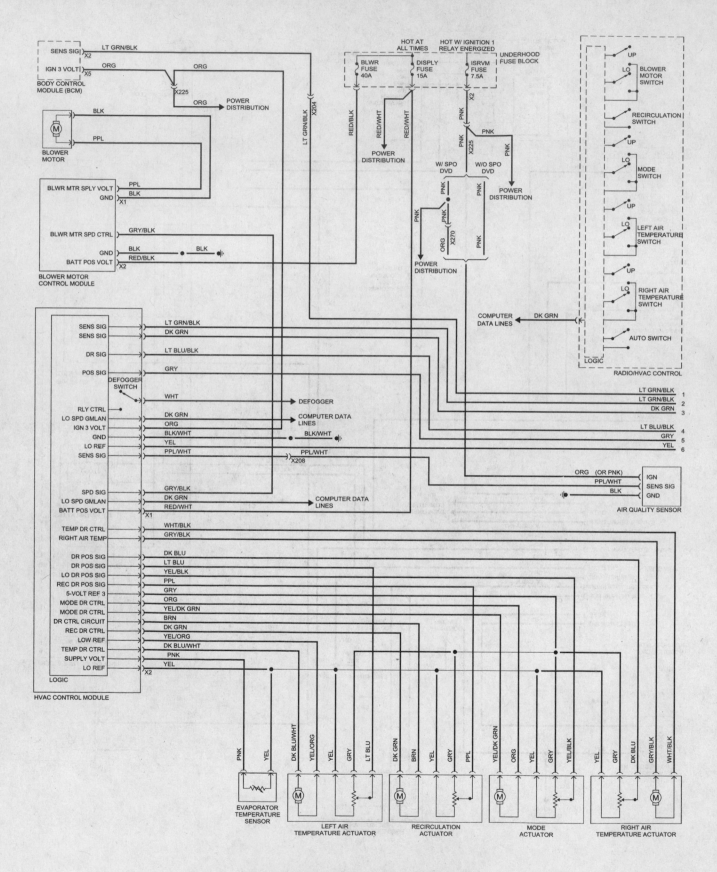

Air conditioning system - 2008 and later (1 of 2)

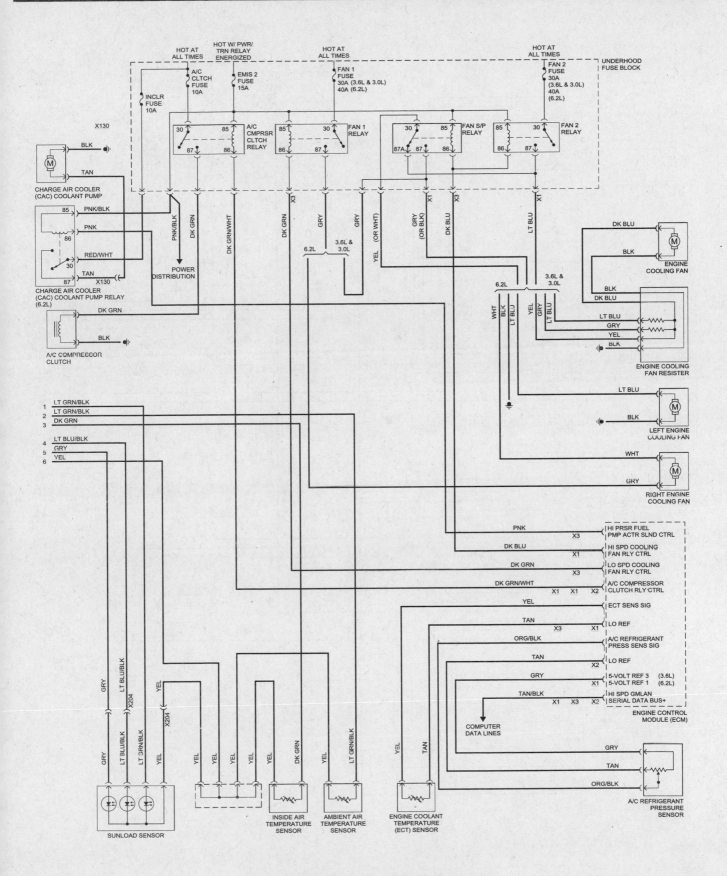

Air conditioning system - 2008 and later (2 of 2)

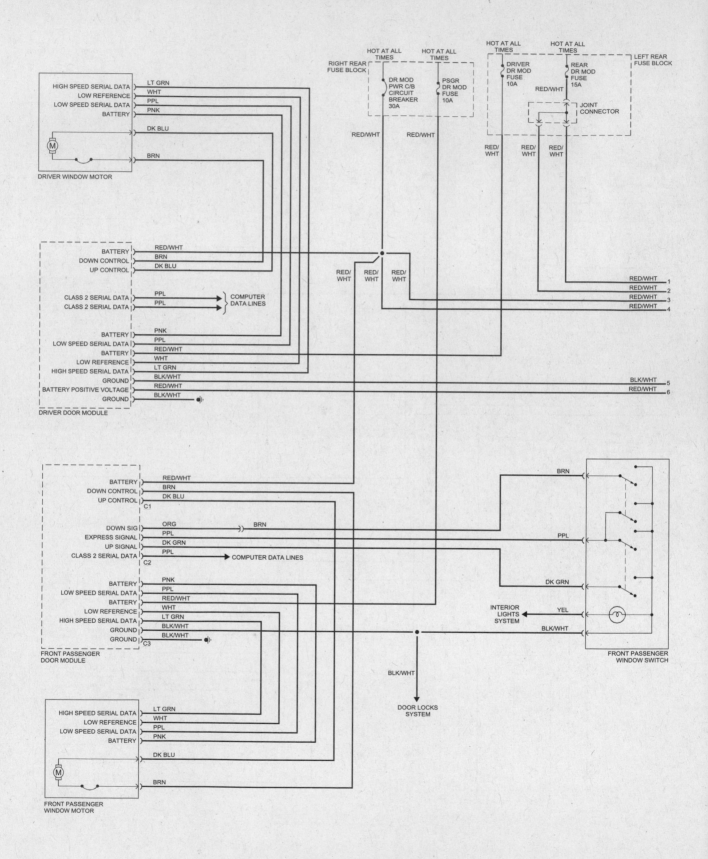

Power window system - 2007 and earlier (1 of 2)

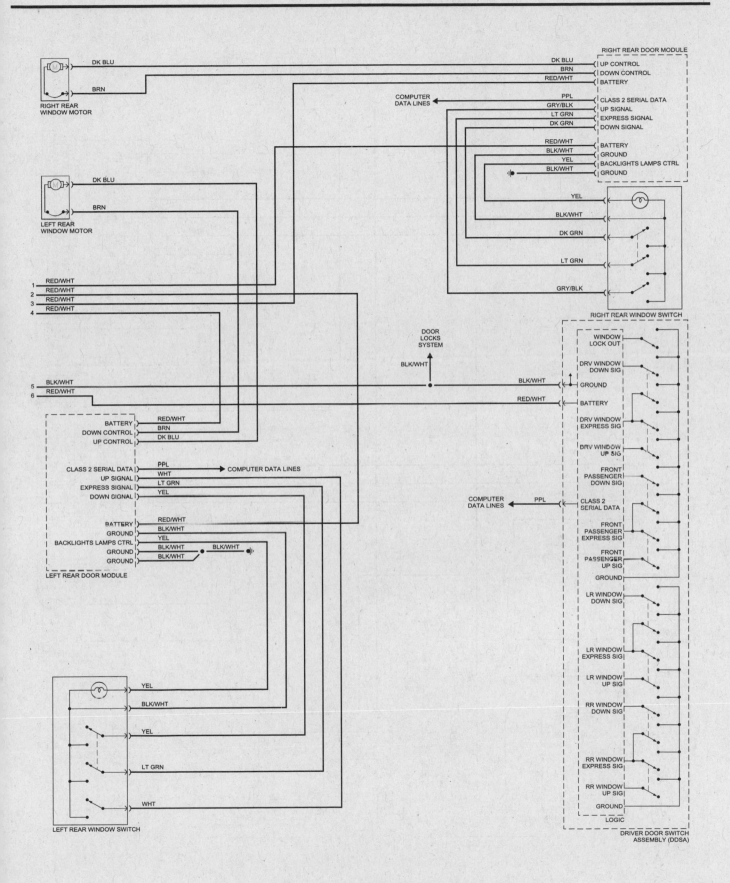

Power window system - 2007 and earlier (2 of 2)

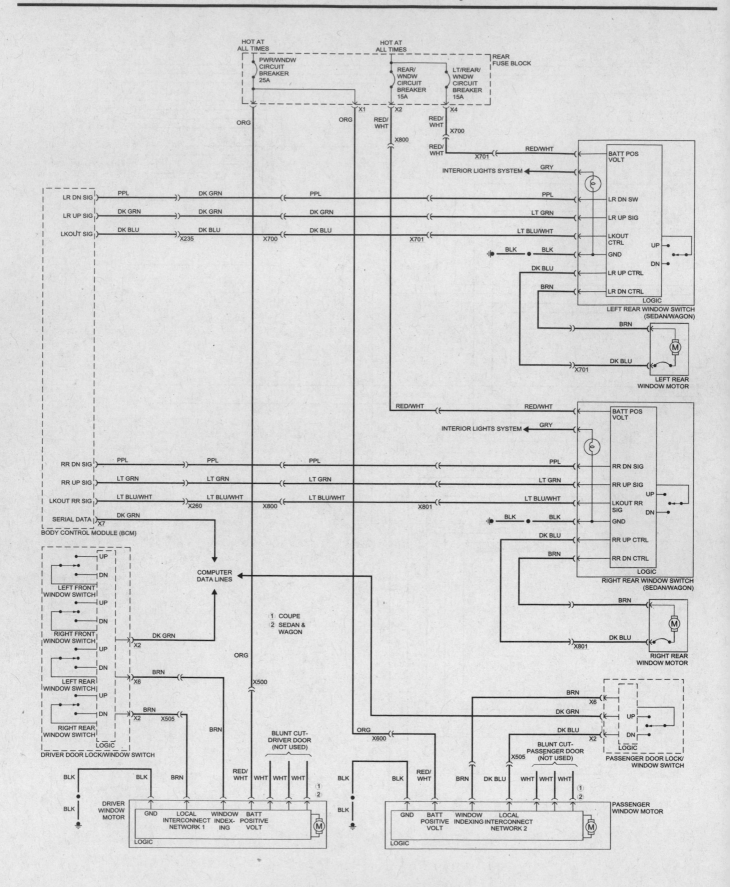

Power window system - 2008 and later

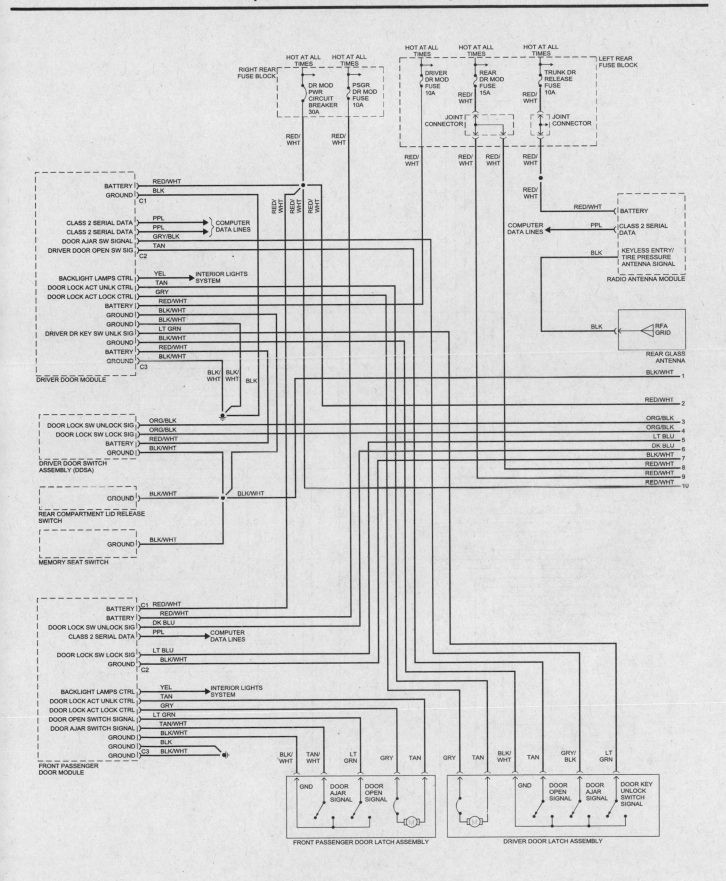

Power door locks - 2007 and earlier (1 of 2)

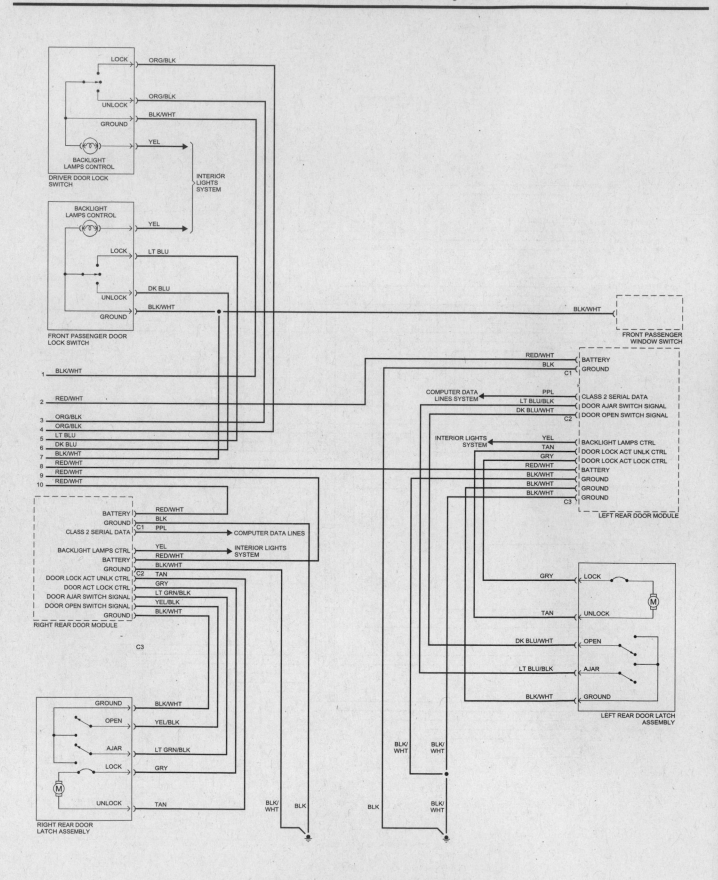

Power door locks - 2007 and earlier (2 of 2)

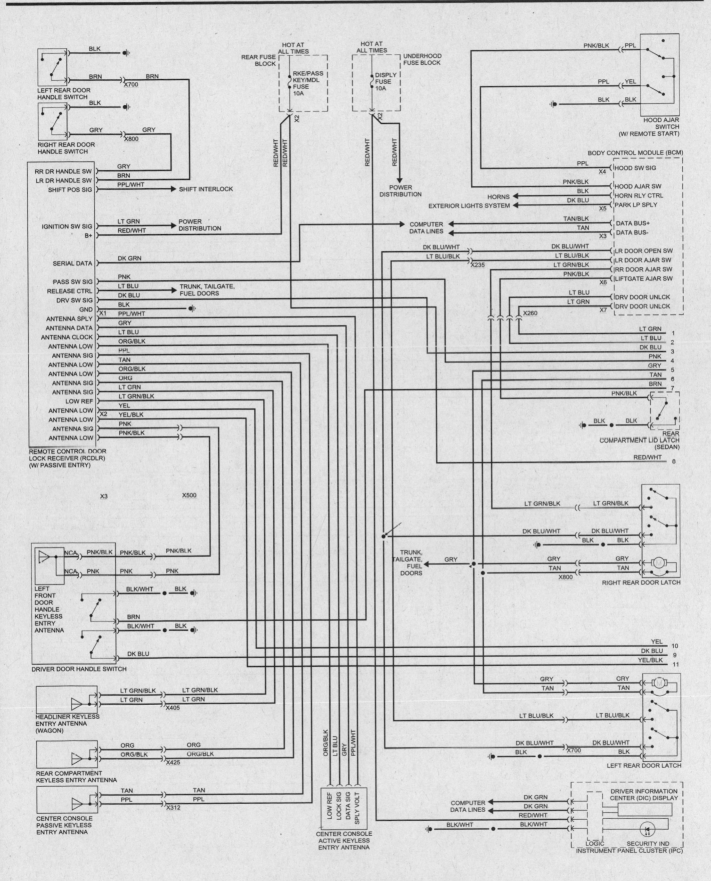

Power door locks - 2008 and later (1 of 2)

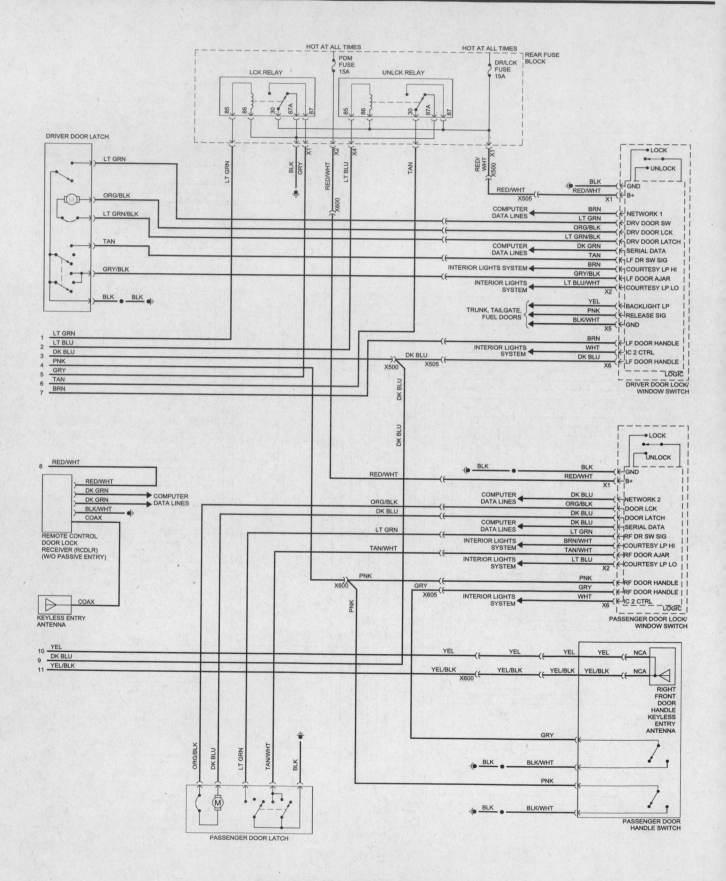

Power door locks - 2008 and later (2 of 2)

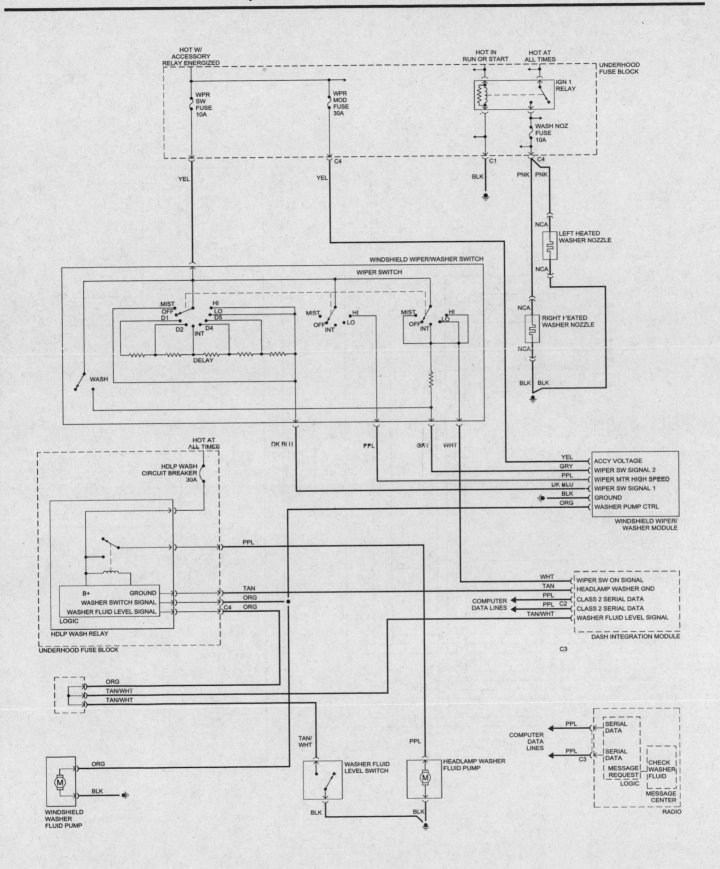

Windshield wiper/washer system - 2007 and earlier

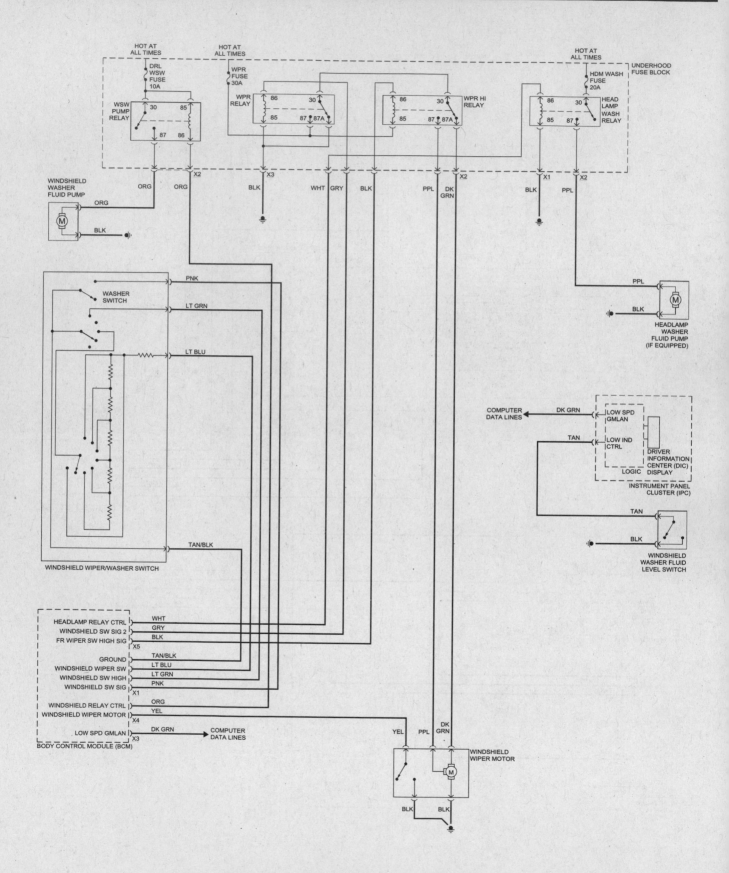

Windshield wiper/washer system - 2008 and later sedan

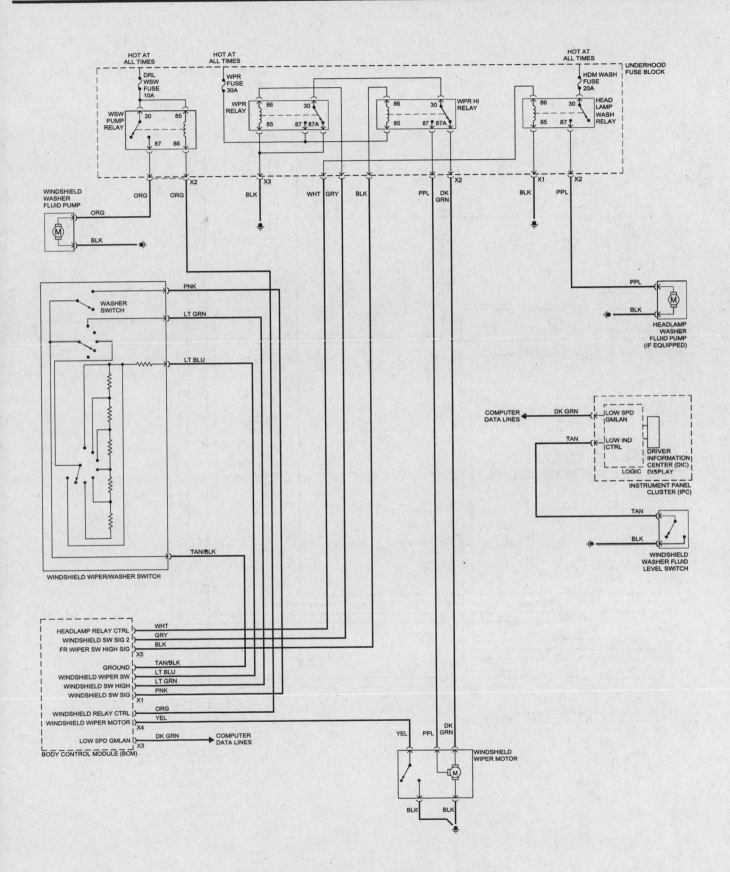

Windshield wiper/washer system - 2011 CTS coupe

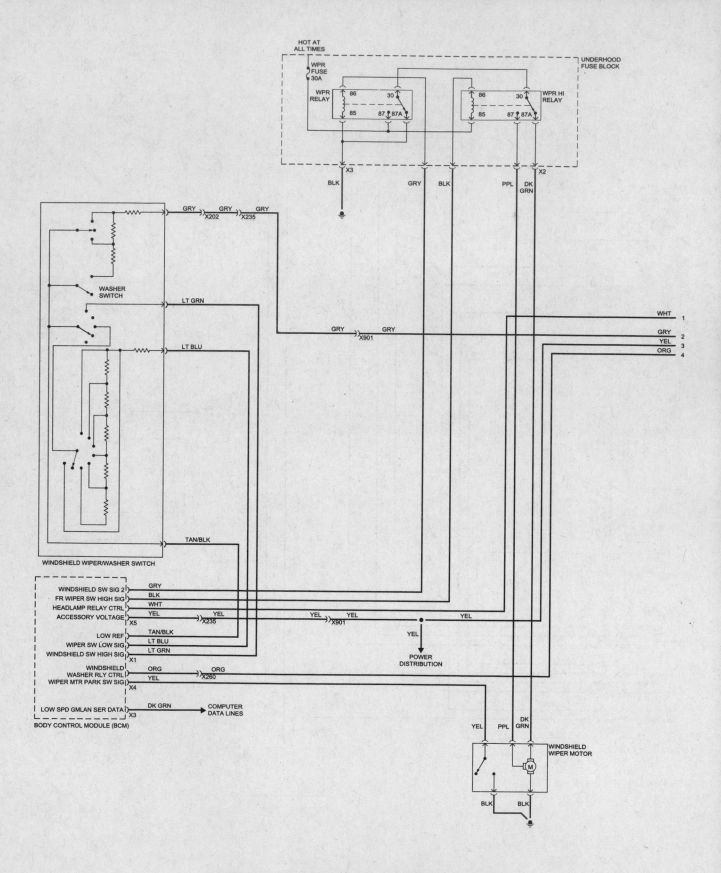

Windshield wiper/washer system - 2011 CTS wagon (1 of 2)

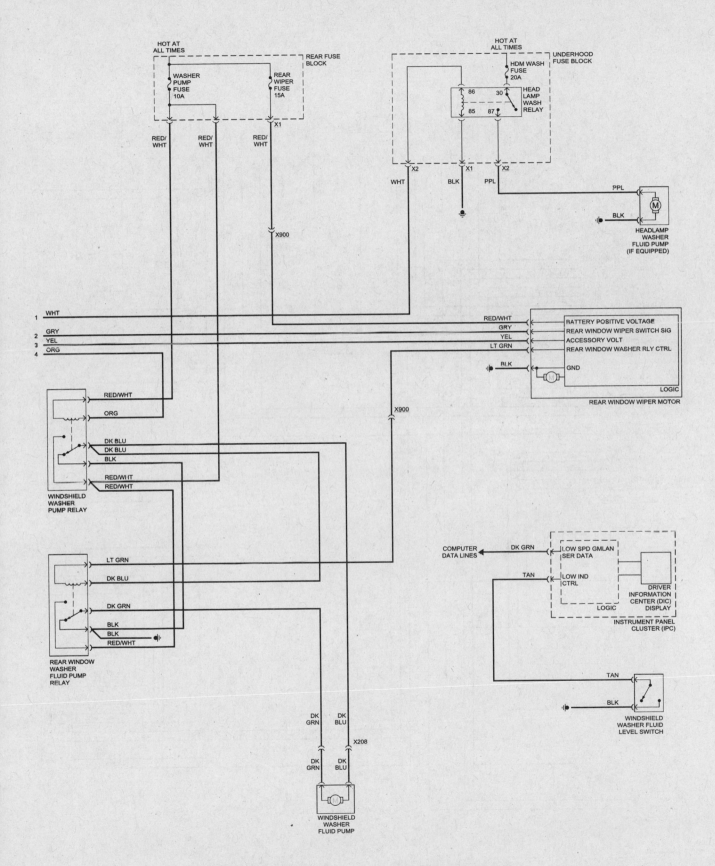

Windshield wiper/washer system - 2011 CTS wagon (2 of 2)

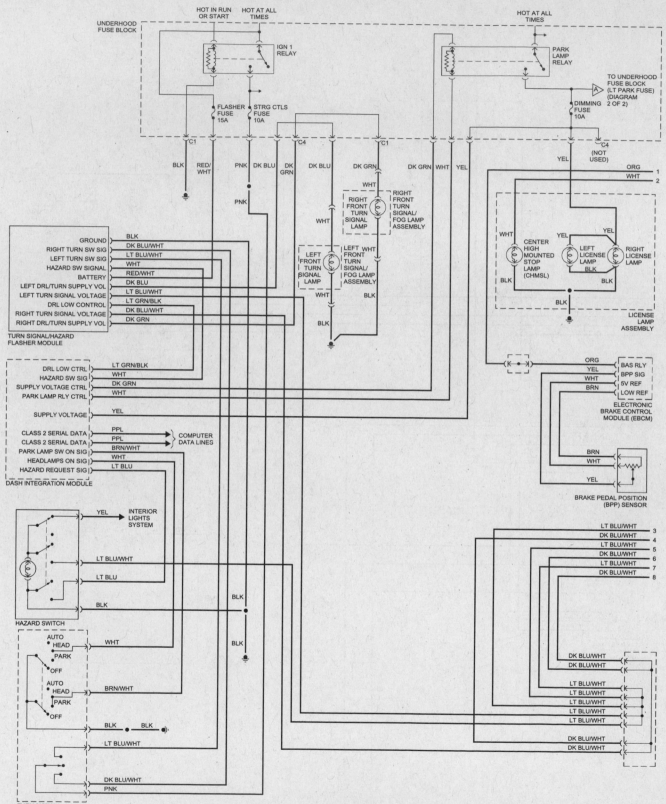

Exterior lighting system (except backup lights) - 2007 and earlier (1 of 2)

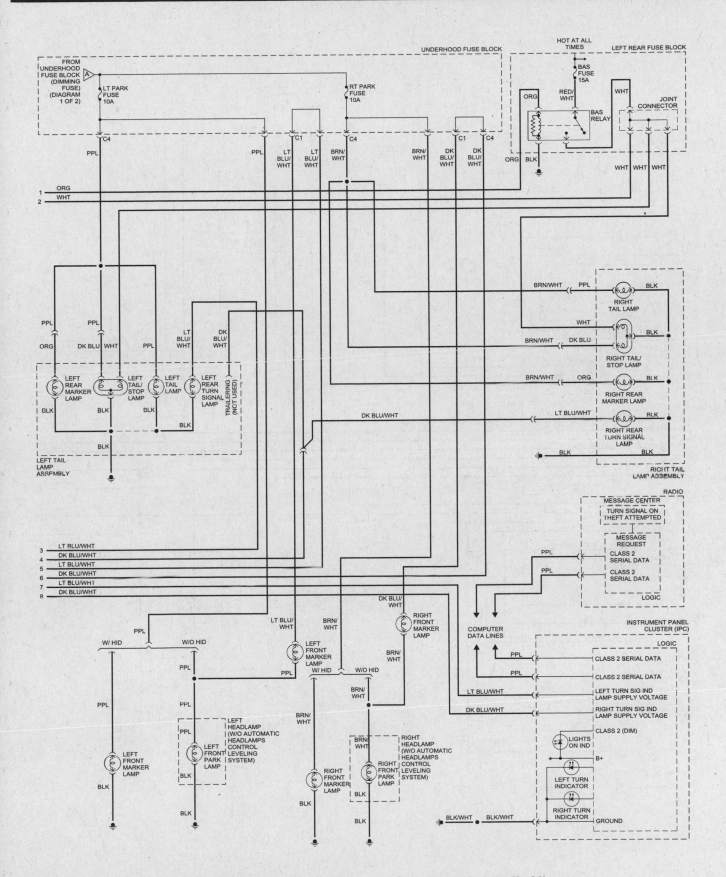

Exterior lighting system (except backup lights) - 2007 and earlier (2 of 2)

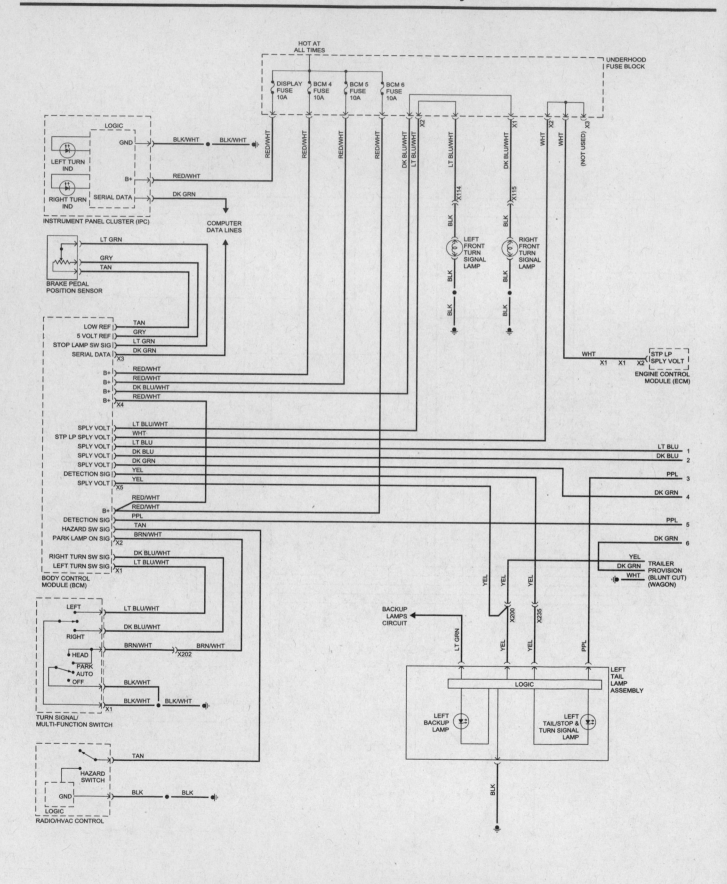

Exterior lighting system (except backup lights) - 2008 and later (1 of 2)

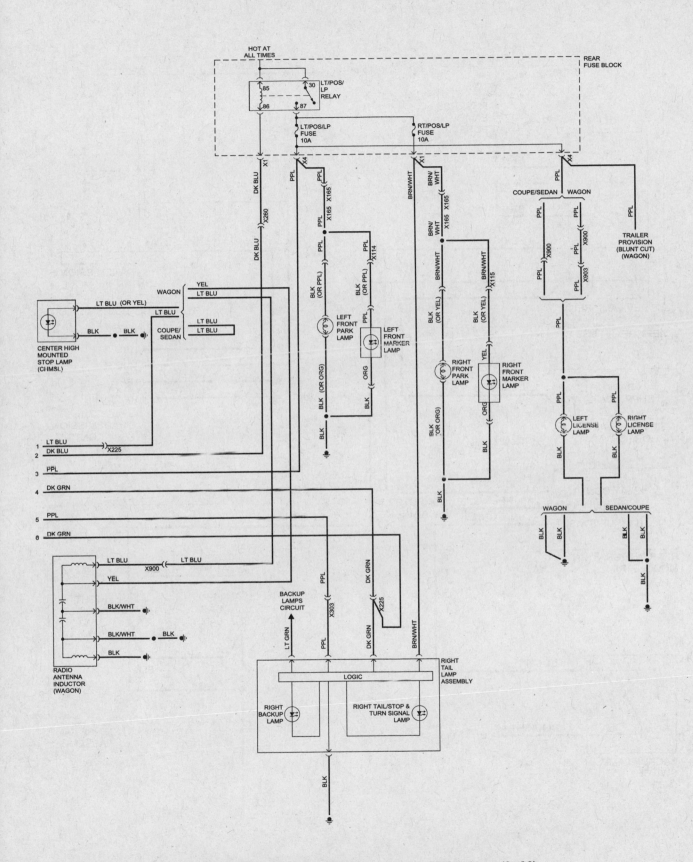

Exterior lighting system (except backup lights) - 2008 and later (2 of 2)

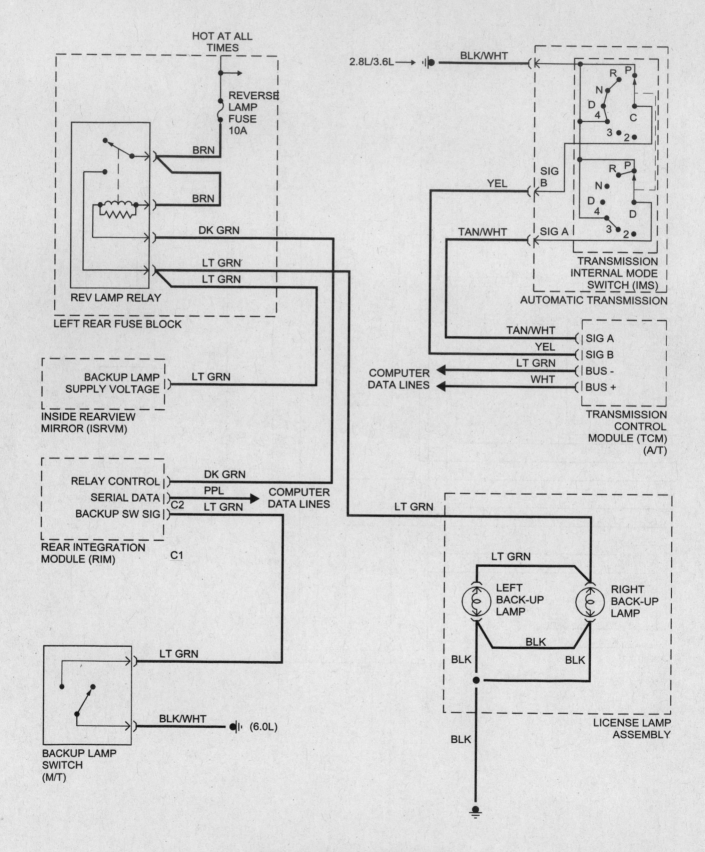

Backup light system - 2007 and earlier

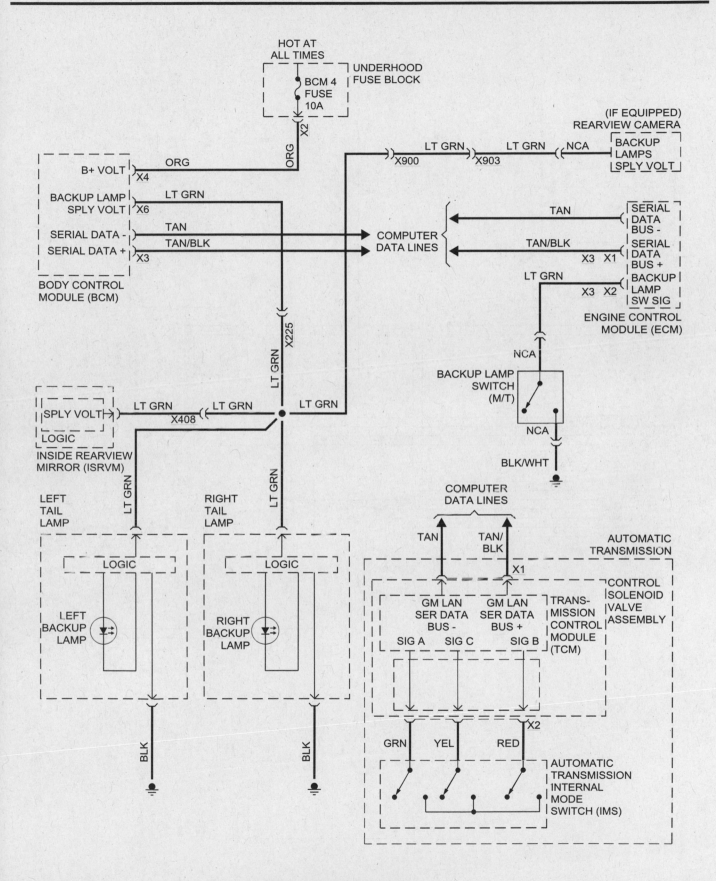

Backup light system - 2008 and later

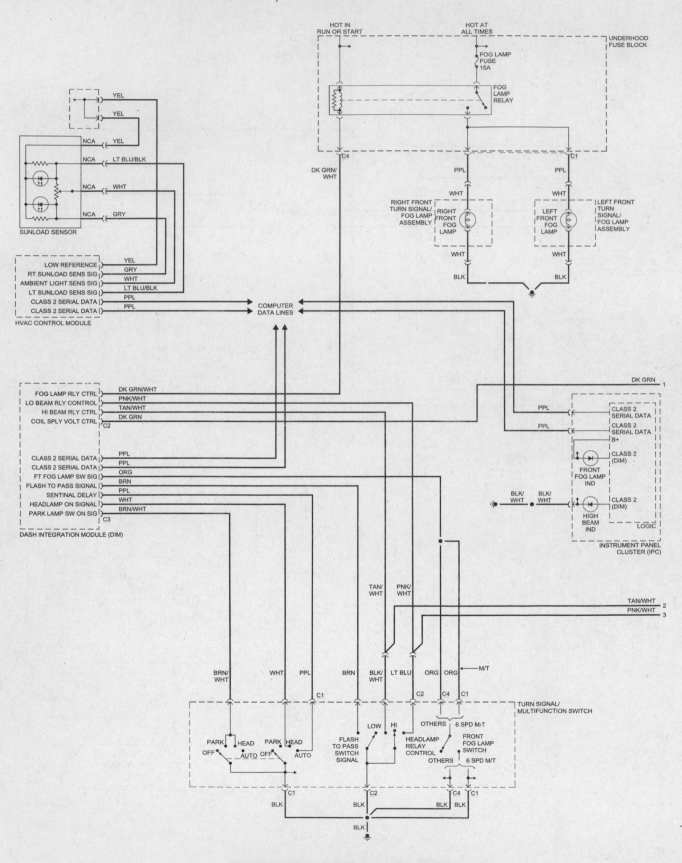

Headlight system - 2007 and earlier (1 of 2)

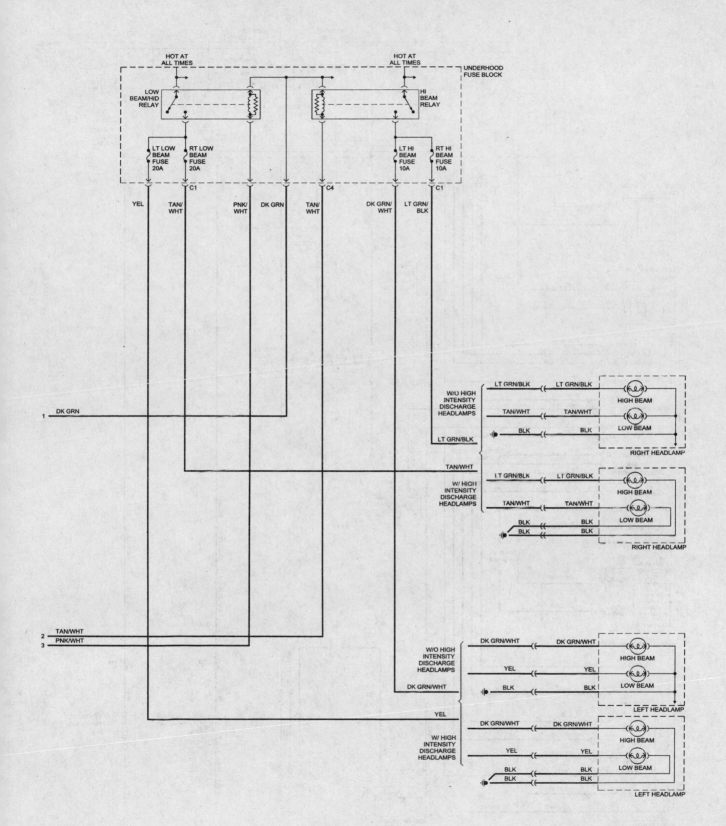

Headlight system - 2007 and earlier (2 of 2)

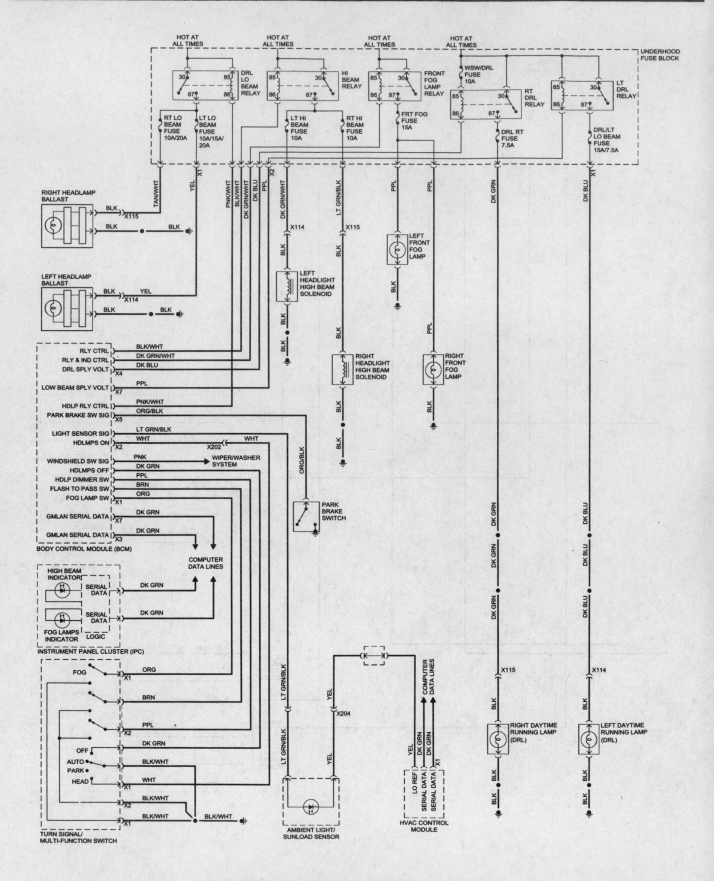

Headlight system (with Xenon headlights) - 2008 and later

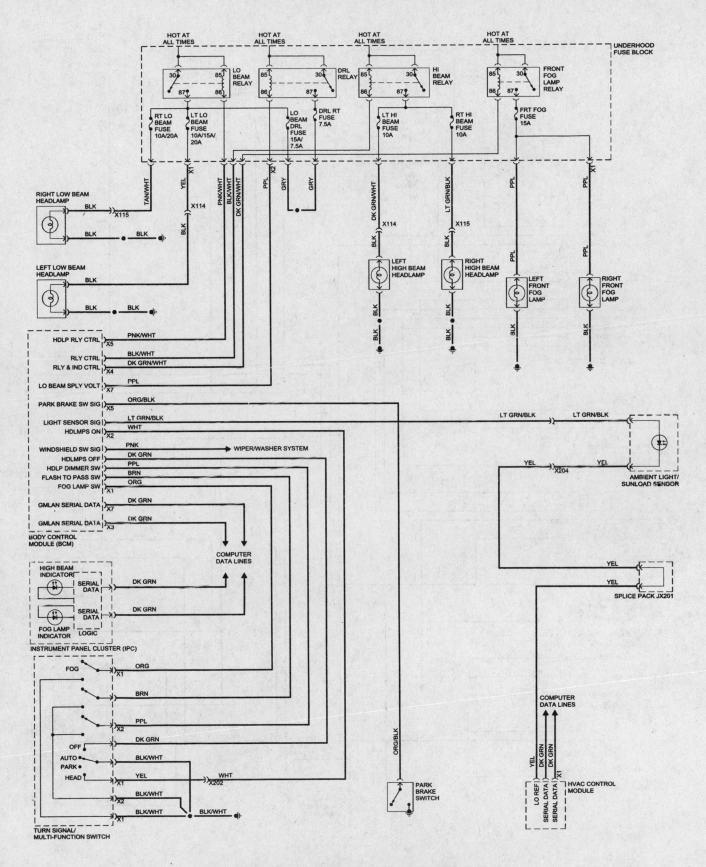

Headlight system (with halogen headlights) - 2008 and later

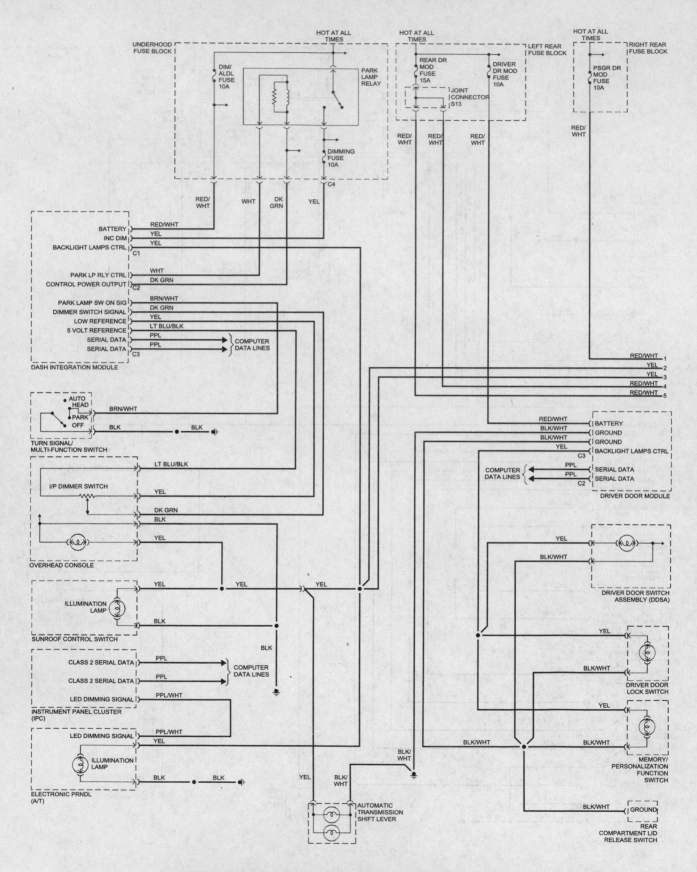

Instrument and switch illumination system - 2007 and earlier (1 of 2)

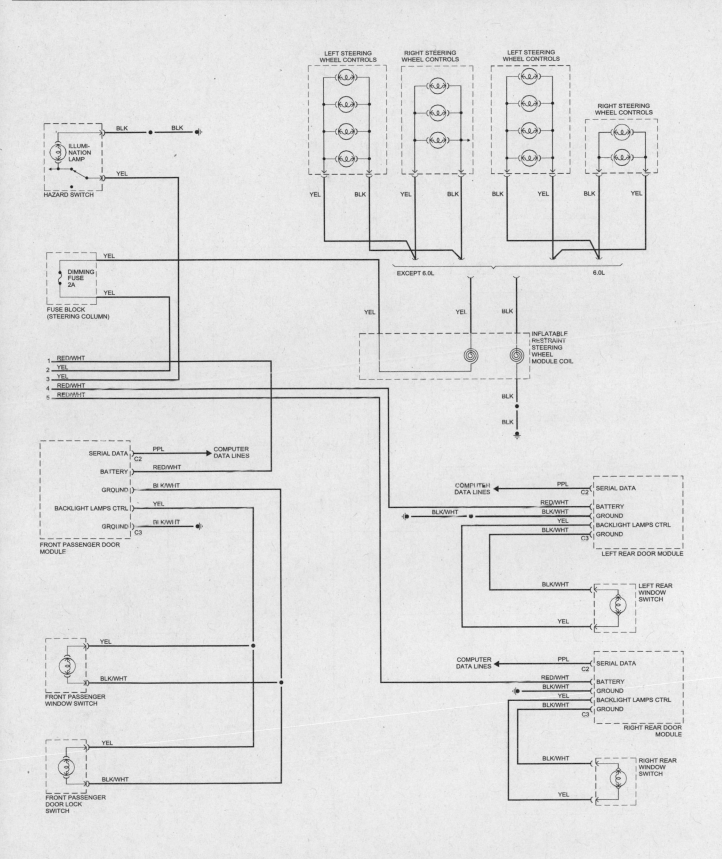

Instrument and switch illumination system - 2007 and earlier (2 of 2)

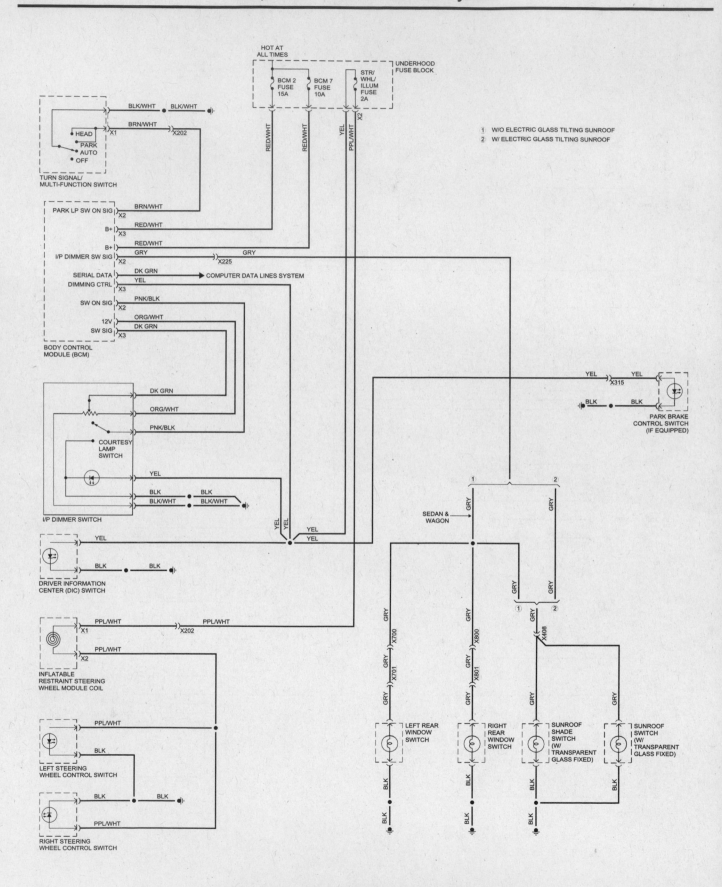

Instrument and switch illumination system - 2008 and later

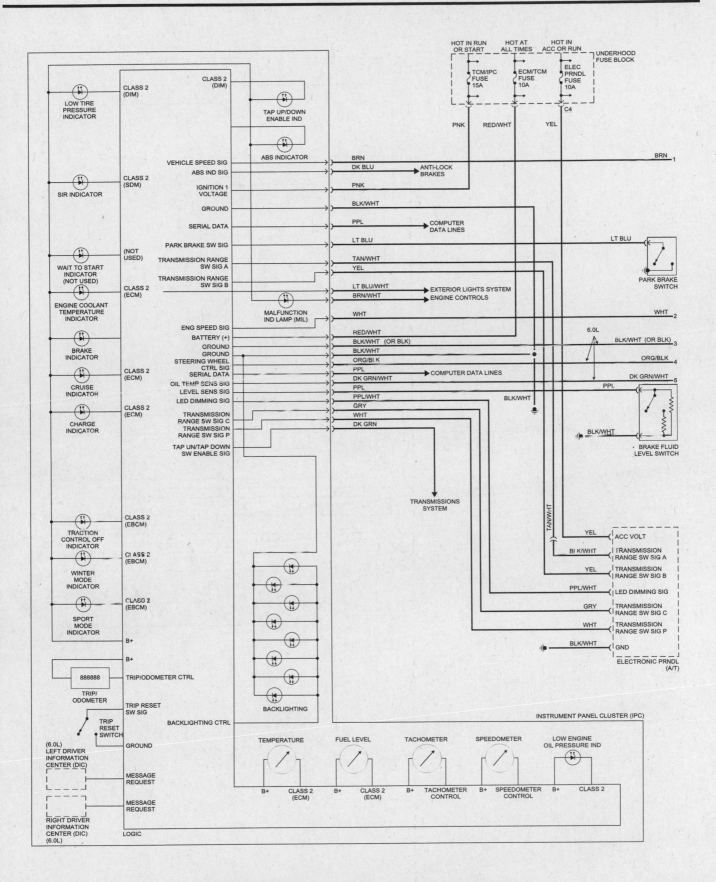

Warning lights and gauges system - 2007 and earlier (1 of 2)

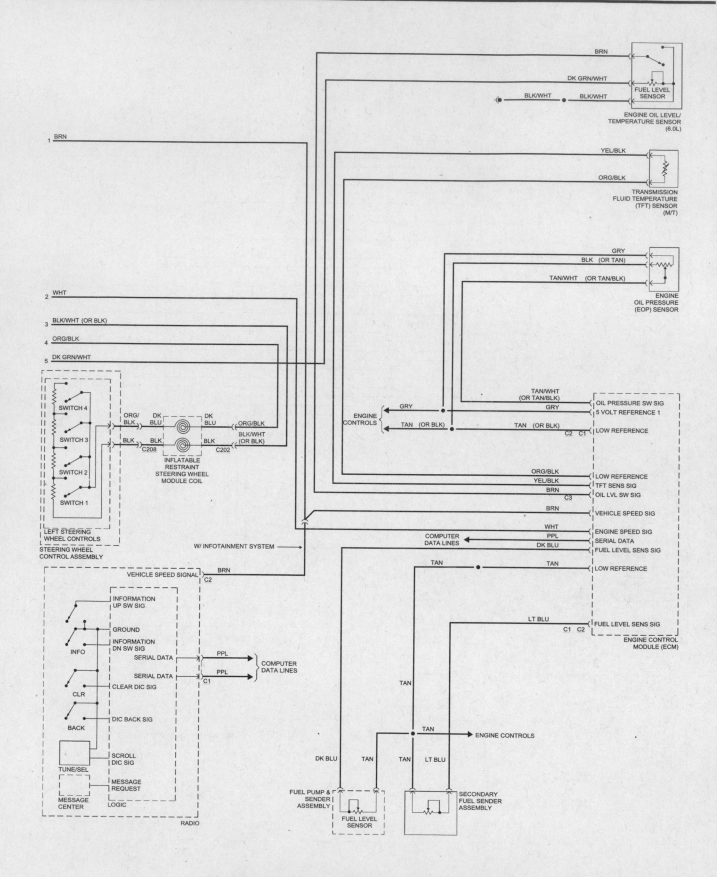

Warning lights and gauges system - 2007 and earlier (2 of 2)

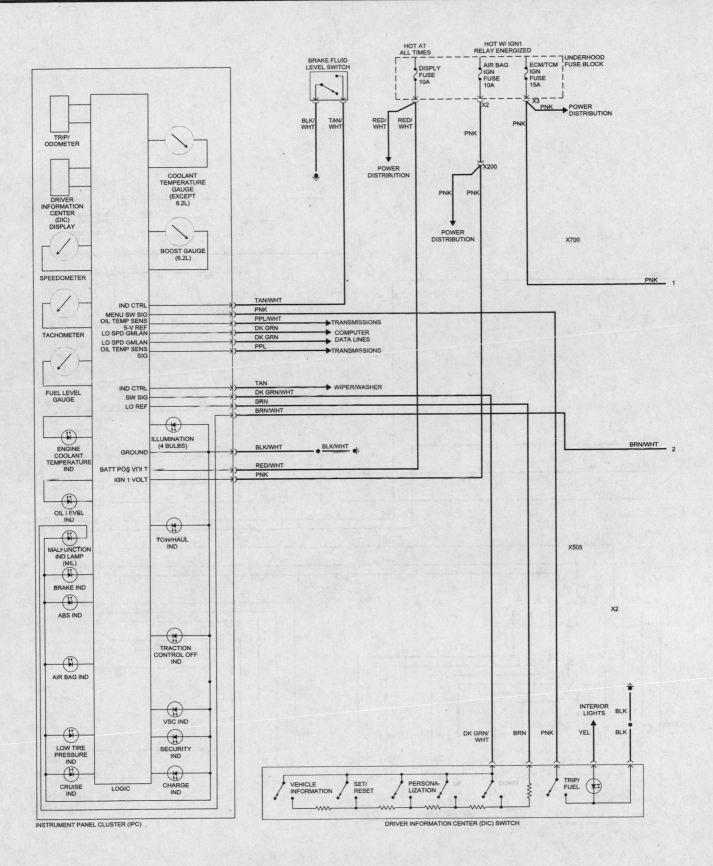

Warning lights and gauges system - 2008 and later (1 of 2)

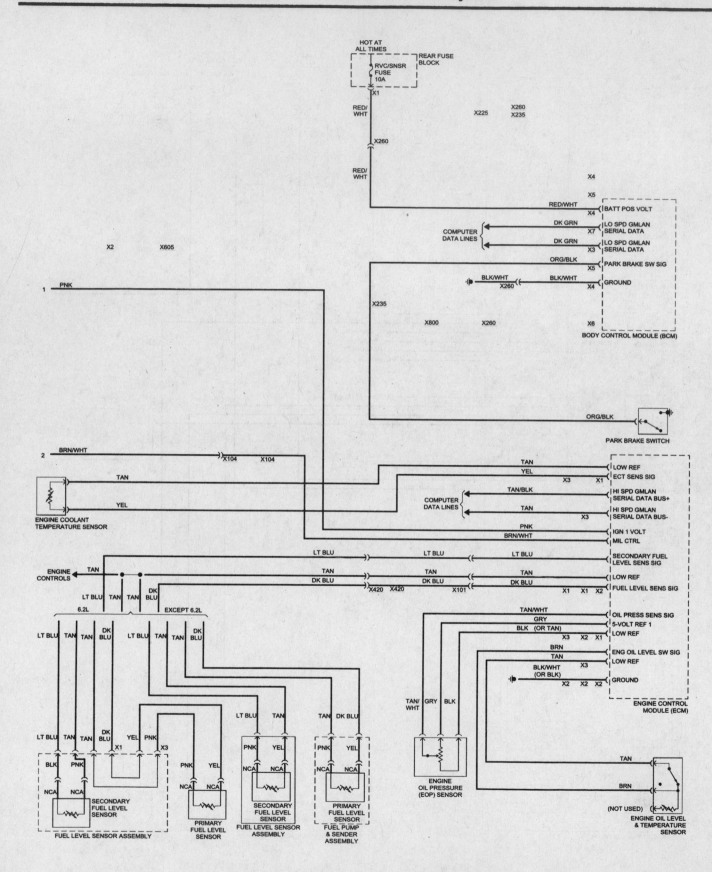

Warning lights and gauges system - 2008 and later (2 of 2)

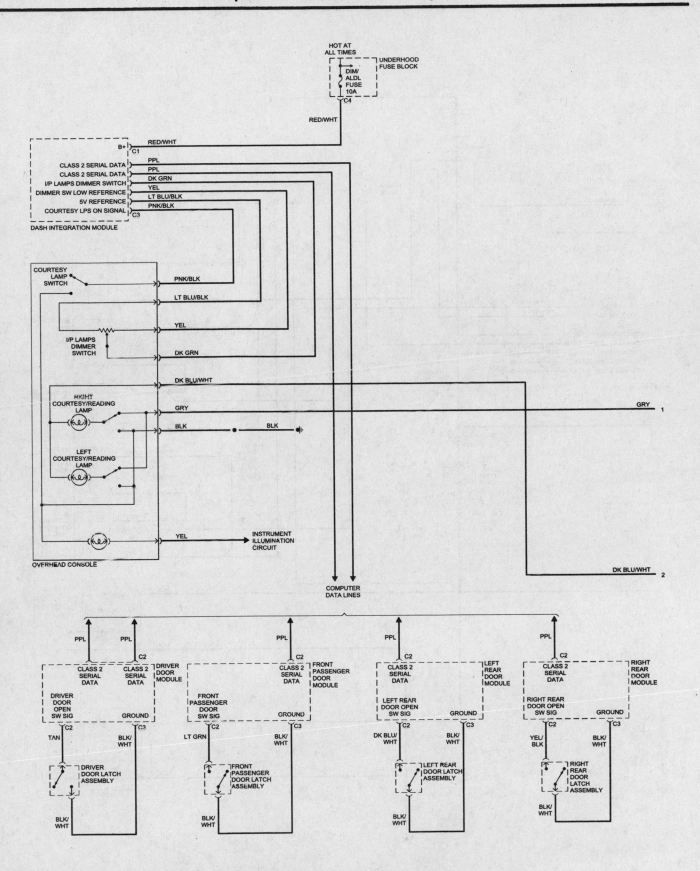

Courtesy light system - 2007 and earlier (1 of 2)

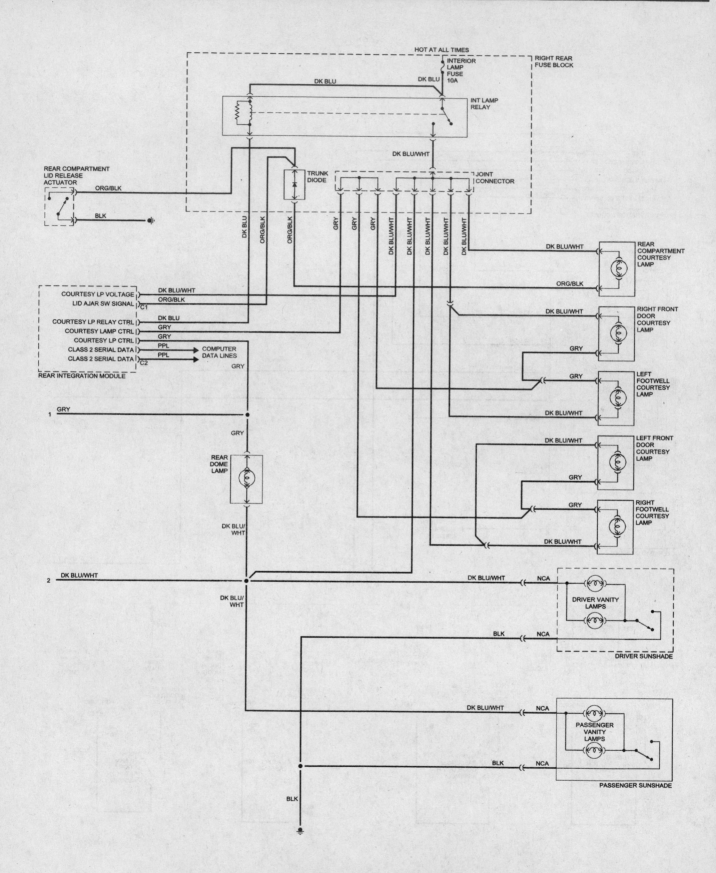

Courtesy light system - 2007 and earlier (2 of 2)

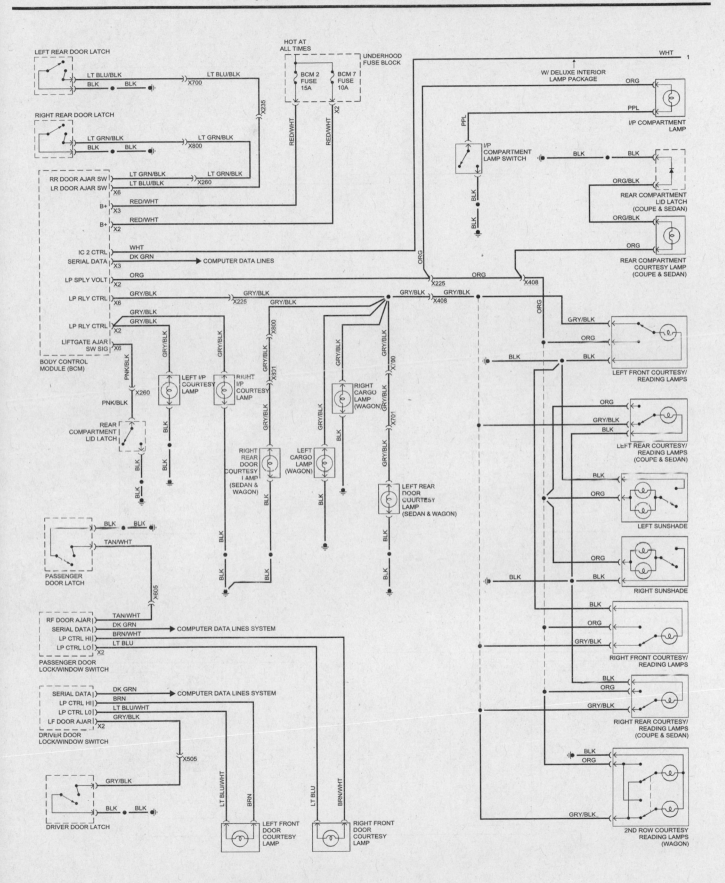

Courtesy light system - 2008 and later (1 of 2)

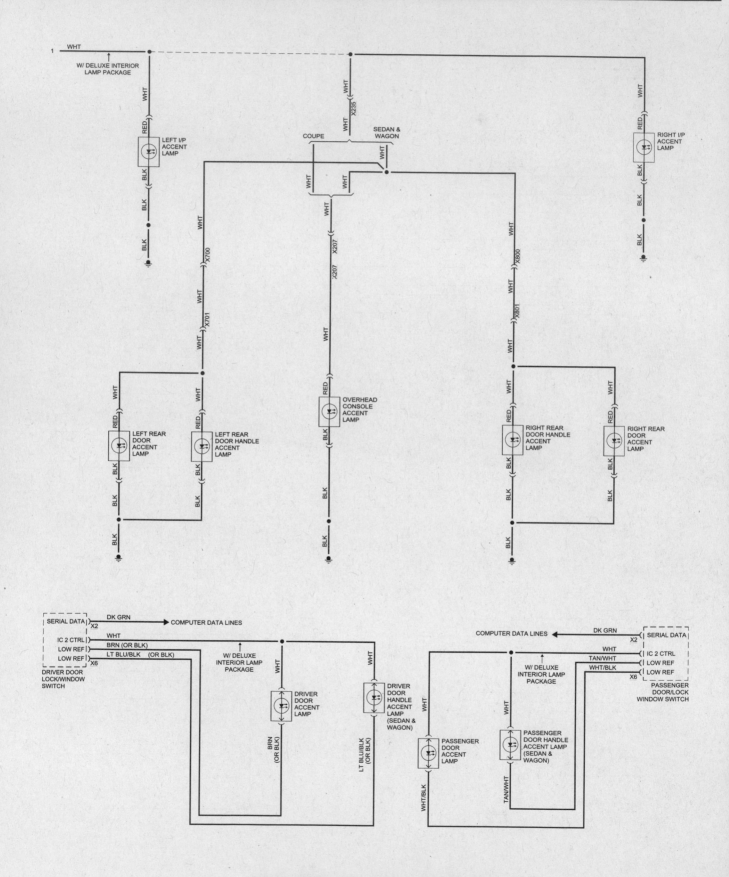

Courtesy light system - 2008 and later (2 of 2)

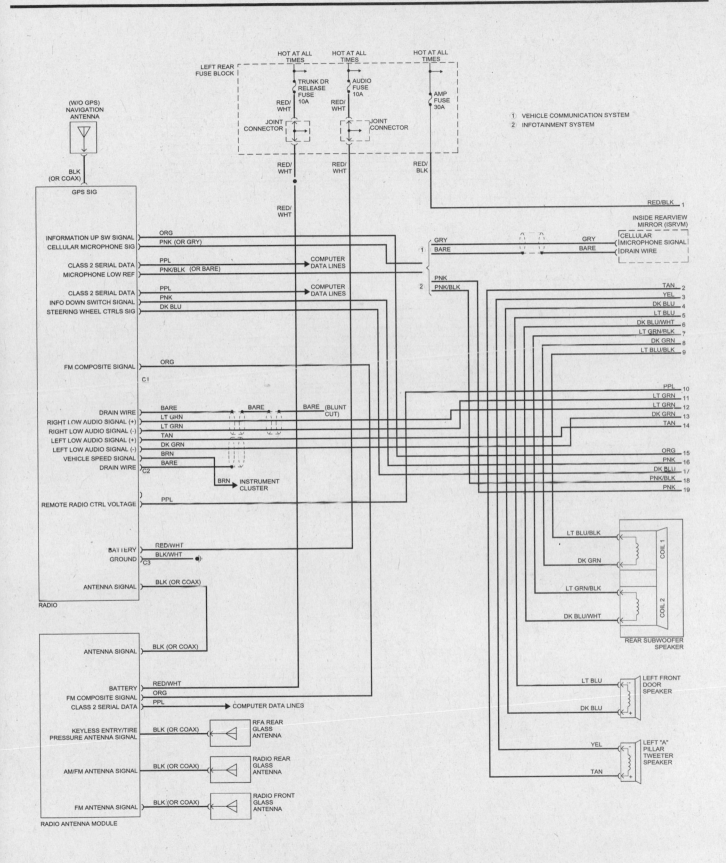

Base audio system - 2007 and earlier (1 of 2)

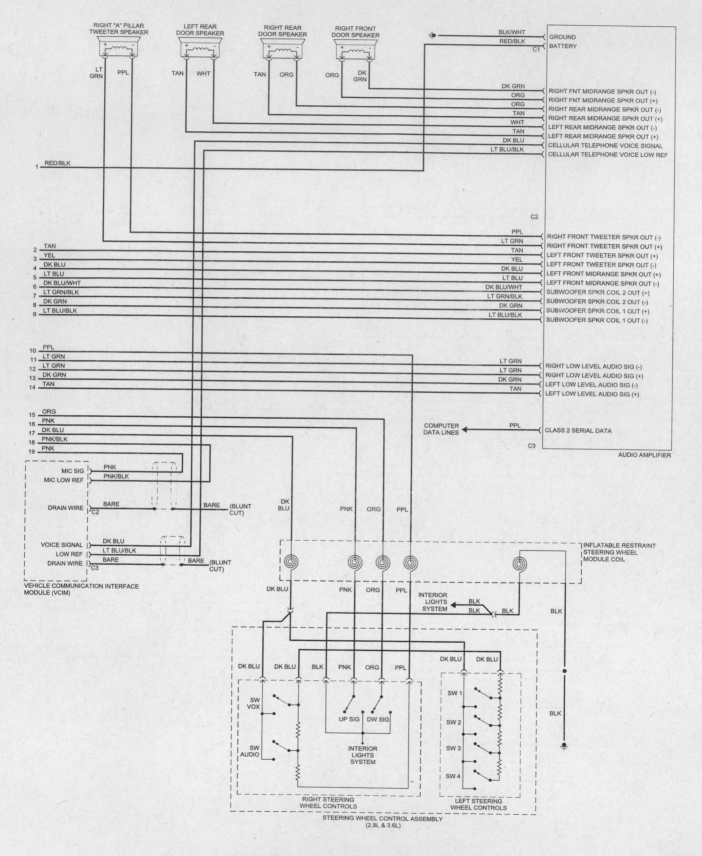

Base audio system - 2007 and earlier (2 of 2)

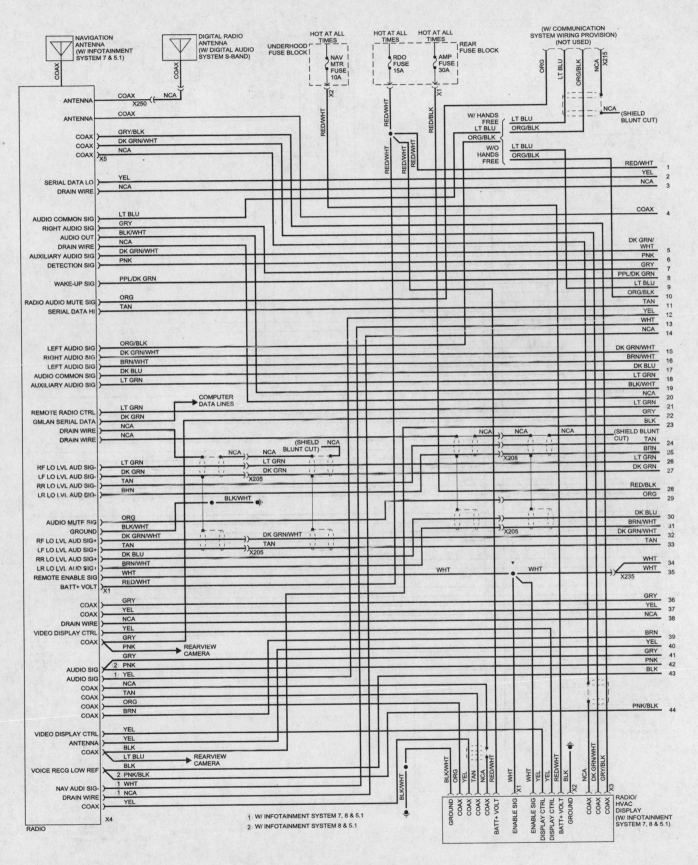

Base audio system - 2008 and later (1 of 4)

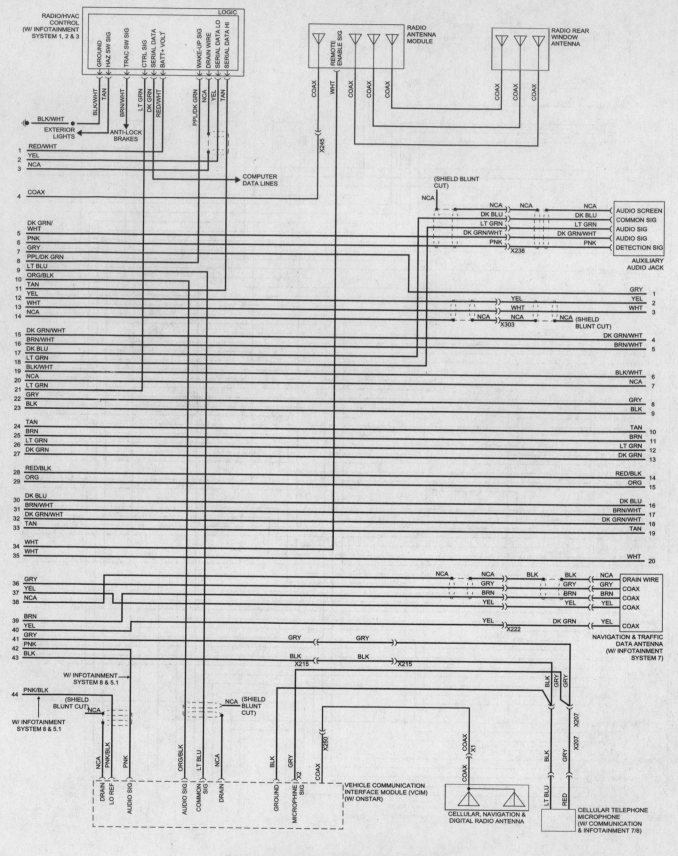

Base audio system - 2008 and later (2 of 4)

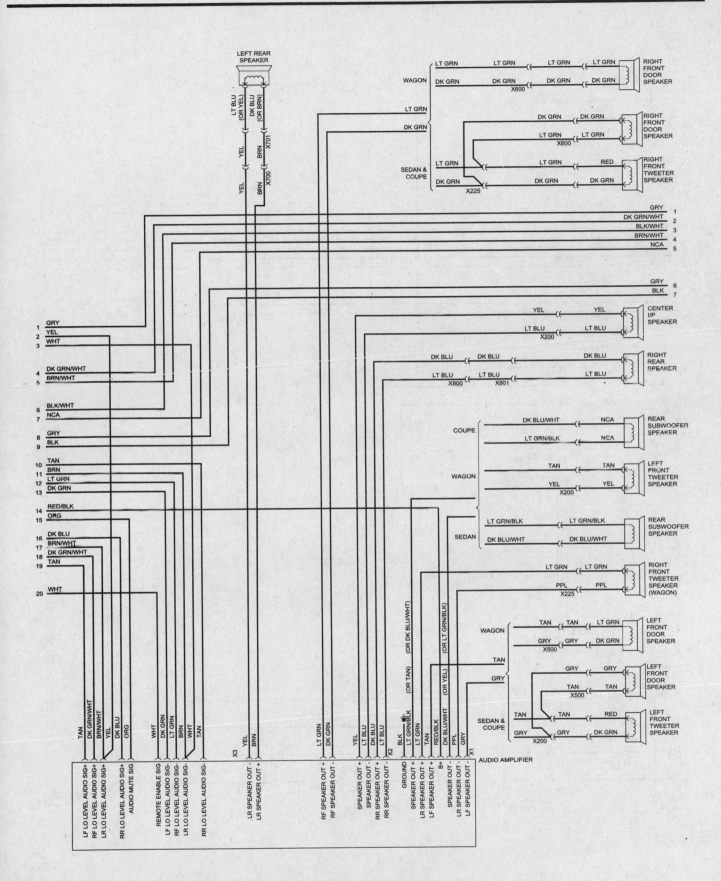

Base audio system - 2008 and later (3 of 4)

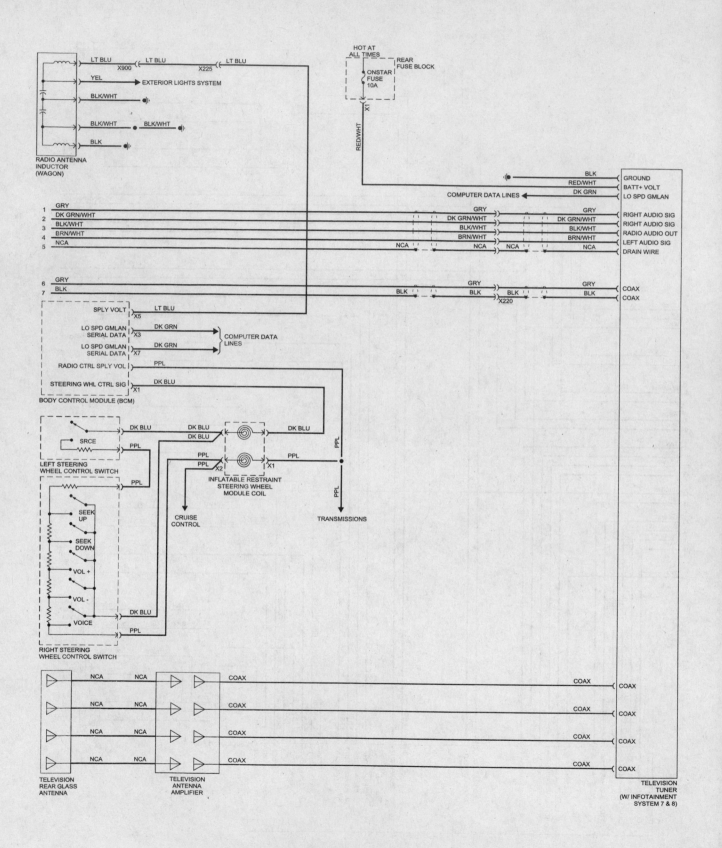

Base audio system - 2008 and later (4 of 4)

Index

Haynes Automotive Manuals

NOTE: If you do not see a listing for your vehicle, consult your local Haynes dealer for the latest product information.

ACURA

12020 **Integra** '86 thru '89 & **Legend** '86 thru '90
12021 **Integra** '90 thru '93 & **Legend** '91 thru '95
Integra '94 thru '00 - *see HONDA Civic (42025)*
MDX '01 thru '07 - *see HONDA Pilot (42037)*
12050 **Acura TL** all models '99 thru '08

AMC

Jeep CJ - *see JEEP (50020)*
14020 **Mid-size models** '70 thru '83
14025 **(Renault) Alliance & Encore** '83 thru '87

AUDI

15020 **4000** all models '80 thru '87
15025 **5000** all models '77 thru '83
15026 **5000** all models '84 thru '88
Audi A4 '96 thru '01 - *see VW Passat (96023)*
15030 **Audi A4** '02 thru '08

AUSTIN-HEALEY

Sprite - *see MG Midget (66015)*

BMW

18020 **3/5 Series** '82 thru '92
18021 **3-Series** incl. Z3 models '92 thru '98
18022 **3-Series** incl. Z4 models '99 thru '05
18023 **3-Series** '06 thru '10
18025 **320i all 4 cyl models** '75 thru '83
18050 **1500 thru 2002** except Turbo '59 thru '77

BUICK

19010 **Buick Century** '97 thru '05
Century (front-wheel drive) - *see GM (38005)*
19020 **Buick, Oldsmobile & Pontiac Full-size (Front-wheel drive)** '85 thru '05
Buick Electra, LeSabre and Park Avenue; **Oldsmobile** Delta 88 Royale, Ninety Eight and Regency; **Pontiac** Bonneville
19025 **Buick, Oldsmobile & Pontiac Full-size (Rear wheel drive)** '70 thru '90
Buick Estate, Electra, LeSabre, Limited, **Oldsmobile** Custom Cruiser, Delta 88, Ninety-eight, **Pontiac** Bonneville, Catalina, Grandville, Parisienne
19030 **Mid-size Regal & Century** all rear-drive models with V6, V8 and Turbo '74 thru '87
Regal - *see GENERAL MOTORS (38010)*
Riviera - *see GENERAL MOTORS (38030)*
Roadmaster - *see CHEVROLET (24046)*
Skyhawk - *see GENERAL MOTORS (38015)*
Skylark - *see GM (38020, 38025)*
Somerset - *see GENERAL MOTORS (38025)*

CADILLAC

21015 **CTS & CTS-V** '03 thru '12
21030 **Cadillac Rear Wheel Drive** '70 thru '93
Cimarron - *see GENERAL MOTORS (38015)*
DeVille - *see GM (38031 & 38032)*
Eldorado - *see GM (38030 & 38031)*
Fleetwood - *see GM (38031)*
Seville - *see GM (38030, 38031 & 38032)*

CHEVROLET

10305 **Chevrolet Engine Overhaul Manual**
24010 **Astro & GMC Safari Mini-vans** '85 thru '05
24015 **Camaro V8** all models '70 thru '81
24016 **Camaro** all models '82 thru '92
24017 **Camaro & Firebird** '93 thru '02
Cavalier - *see GENERAL MOTORS (38016)*
Celebrity - *see GENERAL MOTORS (38005)*
24020 **Chevelle, Malibu & El Camino** '69 thru '87
24024 **Chevette & Pontiac T1000** '76 thru '87
Citation - *see GENERAL MOTORS (38020)*
24027 **Colorado & GMC Canyon** '04 thru '10
24032 **Corsica/Beretta** all models '87 thru '96
24040 **Corvette** all V8 models '68 thru '82
24041 **Corvette** all models '84 thru '96
24045 **Full-size Sedans** Caprice, Impala, Biscayne, Bel Air & Wagons '69 thru '90
24046 **Impala SS & Caprice and Buick Roadmaster** '91 thru '96
Impala '00 thru '05 - *see LUMINA (24048)*
24047 **Impala & Monte Carlo** all models '06 thru '11
Lumina '90 thru '94 - *see GM (38010)*
24048 **Lumina & Monte Carlo** '95 thru '05
Lumina APV - *see GM (38035)*
24050 **Luv Pick-up** all 2WD & 4WD '72 thru '82
Malibu '97 thru '00 - *see GM (38026)*
24055 **Monte Carlo** all models '70 thru '88
Monte Carlo '95 thru '01 - *see LUMINA (24048)*
24059 **Nova** all V8 models '69 thru '79
24060 **Nova and Geo Prizm** '85 thru '92
24064 **Pick-ups** '67 thru '87 - Chevrolet & GMC
24065 **Pick-ups** '88 thru '98 - Chevrolet & GMC
24066 **Pick-ups** '99 thru '06 - Chevrolet & GMC
24067 **Chevrolet Silverado & GMC Sierra** '07 thru '12
24070 **S-10 & S-15 Pick-ups** '82 thru '93, **Blazer & Jimmy** '83 thru '94,
24071 **S-10 & Sonoma Pick-ups** '94 thru '04, including **Blazer, Jimmy & Hombre**
24072 **Chevrolet TrailBlazer, GMC Envoy & Oldsmobile Bravada** '02 thru '09
24075 **Sprint** '85 thru '88 & **Geo Metro** '89 thru '01
24080 **Vans - Chevrolet & GMC** '68 thru '96
24081 **Chevrolet Express & GMC Savana** Full-size Vans '96 thru '10

CHRYSLER

10310 **Chrysler Engine Overhaul Manual**
25015 **Chrysler Cirrus, Dodge Stratus, Plymouth Breeze** '95 thru '00
25020 **Full-size Front-Wheel Drive** '88 thru '93
K-Cars - *see DODGE Aries (30008)*
Laser - *see DODGE Daytona (30030)*
25025 **Chrysler LHS, Concorde, New Yorker, Dodge** Intrepid, **Eagle** Vision, '93 thru '97
25026 **Chrysler LHS, Concorde, 300M, Dodge** Intrepid, '98 thru '04
25027 **Chrysler 300, Dodge Charger & Magnum** '05 thru '09
25030 **Chrysler & Plymouth Mid-size** front wheel drive '82 thru '95
Rear-wheel Drive - *see Dodge (30050)*
25035 **PT Cruiser** all models '01 thru '10
25040 **Chrysler** Sebring '95 thru '06, **Dodge** Stratus '01 thru '06, **Dodge** Avenger '95 thru '00

DATSUN

28005 **200SX** all models '80 thru '83
28007 **B-210** all models '73 thru '78
28009 **210** all models '79 thru '82
28012 **240Z, 260Z & 280Z** Coupe '70 thru '78
28014 **280ZX** Coupe & 2+2 '79 thru '83
300ZX - *see NISSAN (72010)*
28018 **510 & PL521 Pick-up** '68 thru '73
28020 **510** all models '78 thru '81
28022 **620 Series Pick-up** all models '73 thru '79
720 Series Pick-up - *see NISSAN (72030)*
28025 **810/Maxima** all gasoline models '77 thru '84

DODGE

400 & 600 - *see CHRYSLER (25030)*
30008 **Aries & Plymouth Reliant** '81 thru '89
30010 **Caravan & Plymouth Voyager** '84 thru '95
30011 **Caravan & Plymouth Voyager** '96 thru '02
30012 **Challenger/Plymouth Saporro** '78 thru '83
30013 **Caravan, Chrysler Voyager, Town & Country** '03 thru '07
30016 **Colt & Plymouth Champ** '78 thru '87
30020 **Dakota Pick-ups** all models '87 thru '96
30021 **Durango** '98 & '99, **Dakota** '97 thru '99
30022 **Durango** '00 thru '03 **Dakota** '00 thru '04
30023 **Durango** '04 thru '09, **Dakota** '05 thru '11
30025 **Dart, Demon, Plymouth Barracuda, Duster & Valiant** 6 cyl models '67 thru '76
30030 **Daytona & Chrysler Laser** '84 thru '89
Intrepid - *see CHRYSLER (25025, 25026)*
30034 **Neon** all models '95 thru '99
30035 **Omni & Plymouth Horizon** '78 thru '90
30036 **Dodge and Plymouth Neon** '00 thru '05
30040 **Pick-ups** all full-size models '74 thru '93
30041 **Pick-ups** all full-size models '94 thru '01
30042 **Pick-ups** full-size models '02 thru '08
30045 **Ram 50/D50 Pick-ups & Raider and Plymouth Arrow Pick-ups** '79 thru '93
30050 **Dodge/Plymouth/Chrysler** RWD '71 thru '89
30055 **Shadow & Plymouth Sundance** '87 thru '94
30060 **Spirit & Plymouth Acclaim** '89 thru '95
30065 **Vans - Dodge & Plymouth** '71 thru '03

EAGLE

Talon - *see MITSUBISHI (68030, 68031)*
Vision - *see CHRYSLER (25025)*

FIAT

34010 **124 Sport Coupe & Spider** '68 thru '78
34025 **X1/9** all models '74 thru '80

FORD

10320 **Ford Engine Overhaul Manual**
10355 **Ford Automatic Transmission Overhaul**
11500 **Mustang '64-1/2 thru '70 Restoration Guide**
36004 **Aerostar Mini-vans** all models '86 thru '97
36006 **Contour & Mercury Mystique** '95 thru '00
36008 **Courier Pick-up** all models '72 thru '82
36012 **Crown Victoria & Mercury Grand Marquis** '88 thru '10
36016 **Escort/Mercury Lynx** all models '81 thru '90
36020 **Escort/Mercury Tracer** '91 thru '02
36022 **Escape & Mazda Tribute** '01 thru '11
36024 **Explorer & Mazda Navajo** '91 thru '01
36025 **Explorer/Mercury Mountaineer** '02 thru '10
36028 **Fairmont & Mercury Zephyr** '78 thru '83
36030 **Festiva & Aspire** '88 thru '97
36032 **Fiesta** all models '77 thru '80
36034 **Focus** all models '00 thru '11
36036 **Ford & Mercury Full-size** '75 thru '87
36044 **Ford & Mercury Mid-size** '75 thru '86
36045 **Fusion & Mercury Milan** '06 thru '10
36048 **Mustang V8** all models '64-1/2 thru '73
36049 **Mustang II** 4 cyl, V6 & V8 models '74 thru '78
36050 **Mustang & Mercury Capri** '79 thru '93
36051 **Mustang** all models '94 thru '04
36052 **Mustang** '05 thru '10
36054 **Pick-ups & Bronco** '73 thru '79
36058 **Pick-ups & Bronco** '80 thru '96
36059 **F-150 & Expedition** '97 thru '09, **F-250** '97 thru '99 & **Lincoln Navigator** '98 thru '09
36060 **Super Duty Pick-ups, Excursion** '99 thru '10
36061 **F-150** full-size '04 thru '10
36062 **Pinto & Mercury Bobcat** '75 thru '80
36066 **Probe** all models '89 thru '92
Probe '93 thru '97 - *see MAZDA 626 (61042)*
36070 **Ranger/Bronco II** gasoline models '83 thru '92
36071 **Ranger** '93 thru '10 & **Mazda Pick-ups** '94 thru '09
36074 **Taurus & Mercury Sable** '86 thru '95
36075 **Taurus & Mercury Sable** '96 thru '05
36078 **Tempo & Mercury Topaz** '84 thru '94
36082 **Thunderbird/Mercury Cougar** '83 thru '88
36086 **Thunderbird/Mercury Cougar** '89 thru '97
36090 **Vans** all V8 Econoline models '69 thru '91
36094 **Vans** full size '92 thru '10
36097 **Windstar Mini-van** '95 thru '07

GENERAL MOTORS

10360 **GM Automatic Transmission Overhaul**
38005 **Buick Century, Chevrolet Celebrity, Oldsmobile Cutlass Ciera & Pontiac 6000** all models '82 thru '96
38010 **Buick Regal, Chevrolet Lumina, Oldsmobile Cutlass Supreme & Pontiac Grand Prix** (FWD) '88 thru '07
38015 **Buick Skyhawk, Cadillac Cimarron, Chevrolet Cavalier, Oldsmobile Firenza & Pontiac J-2000 & Sunbird** '82 thru '94
38016 **Chevrolet Cavalier & Pontiac Sunfire** '95 thru '05
38017 **Chevrolet Cobalt & Pontiac G5** '05 thru '11
38020 **Buick Skylark, Chevrolet Citation, Olds Omega, Pontiac Phoenix** '80 thru '85
38025 **Buick Skylark & Somerset, Oldsmobile Achieva & Calais and Pontiac Grand Am** all models '85 thru '98
38026 **Chevrolet Malibu, Olds Alero & Cutlass, Pontiac Grand Am** '97 thru '03
38027 **Chevrolet Malibu** '04 thru '10
38030 **Cadillac Eldorado, Seville, Oldsmobile Toronado, Buick Riviera** '71 thru '85
38031 **Cadillac Eldorado & Seville, DeVille, Fleetwood & Olds Toronado, Buick Riviera** '86 thru '93
38032 **Cadillac DeVille** '94 thru '05 & **Seville** '92 thru '04
Cadillac DTS '06 thru '10
38035 **Chevrolet Lumina APV, Olds Silhouette & Pontiac Trans Sport** all models '90 thru '96
38036 **Chevrolet Venture, Olds Silhouette, Pontiac Trans Sport & Montana** '97 thru '05
General Motors Full-size Rear-wheel Drive - *see BUICK (19025)*
38040 **Chevrolet Equinox** '05 thru '09 **Pontiac Torrent** '06 thru '09
38070 **Chevrolet HHR** '06 thru '11

GEO

Metro - *see CHEVROLET Sprint (24075)*
Prizm - *'85 thru '92 see CHEVY (24060), '93 thru '02 see TOYOTA Corolla (92036)*
40030 **Storm** all models '90 thru '93
Tracker - *see SUZUKI Samurai (90010)*

GMC

Vans & Pick-ups - *see CHEVROLET*

HONDA

42010 **Accord CVCC** all models '76 thru '83
42011 **Accord** all models '84 thru '89
42012 **Accord** all models '90 thru '93
42013 **Accord** all models '94 thru '97
42014 **Accord** all models '98 thru '02
42015 **Accord** '03 thru '07
42020 **Civic 1200** all models '73 thru '79
42021 **Civic 1300 & 1500 CVCC** '80 thru '83
42022 **Civic 1500 CVCC** all models '75 thru '79

(Continued on other side)

Haynes North America, Inc., 861 Lawrence Drive, Newbury Park, CA 91320-1514 • (805) 498-6703 • http://www.haynes.com

Haynes Automotive Manuals (continued)

NOTE: If you do not see a listing for your vehicle, consult your local Haynes dealer for the latest product information.

42023 Civic all models '84 thru '91
42024 Civic & del Sol '92 thru '95
42025 Civic '96 thru '00, CR-V '97 thru '01, Acura Integra '94 thru '00
42026 Civic '01 thru '10, CR-V '02 thru '09
42035 Odyssey all models '99 thru '10
Passport - see ISUZU Rodeo (47017)
42037 Honda Pilot '03 thru '07, Acura MDX '01 thru '07
42040 Prelude CVCC all models '79 thru '89

HYUNDAI
43010 Elantra all models '96 thru '10
43015 Excel & Accent all models '86 thru '09
43050 Santa Fe all models '01 thru '06
43055 Sonata all models '99 thru '08

INFINITI
G35 '03 thru '08 - see NISSAN 350Z (72011)

ISUZU
Hombre - see CHEVROLET S-10 (24071)
47017 Rodeo, Amigo & Honda Passport '89 thru '02
47020 Trooper & Pick-up '81 thru '93

JAGUAR
49010 XJ6 all 6 cyl models '68 thru '86
49011 XJ6 all models '88 thru '94
49015 XJ12 & XJS all 12 cyl models '72 thru '85

JEEP
50010 Cherokee, Comanche & Wagoneer Limited all models '84 thru '01
50020 CJ all models '49 thru '86
50025 Grand Cherokee all models '93 thru '04
50026 Grand Cherokee '05 thru '09
50029 Grand Wagoneer & Pick-up '72 thru '91
Grand Wagoneer '84 thru '91, Cherokee & Wagoneer '72 thru '83, Pick-up '72 thru '88
50030 Wrangler all models '87 thru '11
50035 Liberty '02 thru '07

KIA
54050 Optima '01 thru '10
54070 Sephia '94 thru '01, Spectra '00 thru '09, Sportage '05 thru '10

LEXUS
ES 300/330 - see TOYOTA Camry (92007) (92008)
RX 330 - see TOYOTA Highlander (92095)

LINCOLN
Navigator - see FORD Pick-up (36059)
59010 Rear-Wheel Drive all models '70 thru '10

MAZDA
61010 GLC Hatchback (rear-wheel drive) '77 thru '83
61011 GLC (front-wheel drive) '81 thru '85
61012 Mazda3 '04 thru '11
61015 323 & Protogé '90 thru '03
61016 MX-5 Miata '90 thru '09
61020 MPV all models '89 thru '98
Navajo - see Ford Explorer (36024)
61030 Pick-ups '72 thru '93
Pick-ups '94 thru '00 - see Ford Ranger (36071)
61035 RX-7 all models '79 thru '85
61036 RX-7 all models '86 thru '91
61040 626 (rear-wheel drive) all models '79 thru '82
61041 626/MX-6 (front-wheel drive) '83 thru '92
61042 626, MX-6/Ford Probe '93 thru '02
61043 Mazda6 '03 thru '11

MERCEDES-BENZ
63012 123 Series Diesel '76 thru '85
63015 190 Series four-cyl gas models '84 thru '88
63020 230/250/280 6 cyl sohc models '68 thru '72
63025 280 123 Series gasoline models '77 thru '81
63030 350 & 450 all models '71 thru '80
63040 C-Class: C230/C240/C280/C320/C350 '01 thru '07

MERCURY
64200 Villager & Nissan Quest '93 thru '01
All other titles, see FORD Listing.

MG
66010 MGB Roadster & GT Coupe '62 thru '80
66015 MG Midget, Austin Healey Sprite '58 thru '80

MINI
67020 Mini '02 thru '11

MITSUBISHI
68020 Cordia, Tredia, Galant, Precis & Mirage '83 thru '93
68030 Eclipse, Eagle Talon & Ply. Laser '90 thru '94
68031 Eclipse '95 thru '05, Eagle Talon '95 thru '98
68035 Galant '94 thru '10
68040 Pick-up '83 thru '96 & Montero '83 thru '93

NISSAN
72010 300ZX all models including Turbo '84 thru '89
72011 350Z & Infiniti G35 all models '03 thru '08
72015 Altima all models '93 thru '06
72016 Altima '07 thru '10
72020 Maxima all models '85 thru '92
72021 Maxima all models '93 thru '04
72025 Murano '03 thru '10
72030 Pick-ups '80 thru '97 Pathfinder '87 thru '95
72031 Frontier Pick-up, Xterra, Pathfinder '96 thru '04
72032 Frontier & Xterra '05 thru '11
72040 Pulsar all models '83 thru '86
Quest - see MERCURY Villager (64200)
72050 Sentra all models '82 thru '94
72051 Sentra & 200SX all models '95 thru '06
72060 Stanza all models '82 thru '90
72070 Titan pick-ups '04 thru '10 Armada '05 thru '10

OLDSMOBILE
73015 Cutlass V6 & V8 gas models '74 thru '88
For other OLDSMOBILE titles, see BUICK, CHEVROLET or GENERAL MOTORS listing.

PLYMOUTH
For PLYMOUTH titles, see DODGE listing.

PONTIAC
79008 Fiero all models '84 thru '88
79018 Firebird V8 except Turbo '70 thru '81
79019 Firebird all models '82 thru '92
79025 G6 all models '05 thru '09
79040 Mid-size Rear-wheel Drive '70 thru '87
Vibe '03 thru '11 - see TOYOTA Matrix (92060)
For other PONTIAC titles, see BUICK, CHEVROLET or GENERAL MOTORS listing.

PORSCHE
80020 911 except Turbo & Carrera 4 '65 thru '89
80025 914 all 4 cyl models '69 thru '76
80030 924 all models including Turbo '76 thru '82
80035 944 all models including Turbo '83 thru '89

RENAULT
Alliance & Encore - see AMC (14020)

SAAB
84010 900 all models including Turbo '79 thru '88

SATURN
87010 Saturn all S-series models '91 thru '02
87011 Saturn Ion '03 thru '07
87020 Saturn all L-series models '00 thru '04
87040 Saturn VUE '02 thru '07

SUBARU
89002 1100, 1300, 1400 & 1600 '71 thru '79
89003 1600 & 1800 2WD & 4WD '80 thru '94
89100 Legacy all models '90 thru '99
89101 Legacy & Forester '00 thru '06

SUZUKI
90010 Samurai/Sidekick & Geo Tracker '86 thru '01

TOYOTA
92005 Camry all models '83 thru '91
92006 Camry all models '92 thru '96
92007 Camry, Avalon, Solara, Lexus ES 300 '97 thru '01
92008 Toyota Camry, Avalon and Solara and Lexus ES 300/330 all models '02 thru '06
92009 Camry '07 thru '11
92015 Celica Rear Wheel Drive '71 thru '85
92020 Celica Front Wheel Drive '86 thru '99
92025 Celica Supra all models '79 thru '92
92030 Corolla all models '75 thru '79
92032 Corolla all rear wheel models '80 thru '87
92035 Corolla all front wheel drive models '84 thru '92
92036 Corolla & Geo Prizm '93 thru '02
92037 Corolla models '03 thru '11
92040 Corolla Tercel all models '80 thru '82
92045 Corona all models '74 thru '82
92050 Cressida all models '78 thru '82
92055 Land Cruiser FJ40, 43, 45, 55 '68 thru '82
92056 Land Cruiser FJ60, 62, 80, FZJ80 '80 thru '96
92060 Matrix & Pontiac Vibe '03 thru '11
92065 MR2 all models '85 thru '87
92070 Pick-up all models '69 thru '78
92075 Pick-up all models '79 thru '95
92076 Tacoma, 4Runner, & T100 '93 thru '04
92077 Tacoma all models '05 thru '09
92078 Tundra '00 thru '06 & Sequoia '01 thru '07
92079 4Runner all models '03 thru '09
92080 Previa all models '91 thru '95
92081 Prius all models '01 thru '08
92082 RAV4 all models '96 thru '10
92085 Tercel all models '87 thru '94
92090 Sienna all models '98 thru '09
92095 Highlander & Lexus RX-330 '99 thru '07

TRIUMPH
94007 Spitfire all models '62 thru '81
94010 TR7 all models '75 thru '81

VW
96008 Beetle & Karmann Ghia '54 thru '79
96009 New Beetle '98 thru '11
96016 Rabbit, Jetta, Scirocco & Pick-up gas models '75 thru '92 & Convertible '80 thru '92
96017 Golf, GTI & Jetta '93 thru '98, Cabrio '95 thru '02
96018 Golf, GTI, Jetta '99 thru '05
96019 Jetta, Rabbit, GTI & Golf '05 thru '11
96020 Rabbit, Jetta & Pick-up diesel '77 thru '84
96023 Passat '98 thru '05, Audi A4 '96 thru '01
96030 Transporter 1600 all models '68 thru '79
96035 Transporter 1700, 1800 & 2000 '72 thru '79
96040 Type 3 1500 & 1600 models '63 thru '73
96045 Vanagon all air-cooled models '80 thru '83

VOLVO
97010 120, 130 Series & 1800 Sports '61 thru '73
97015 140 Series all models '66 thru '74
97020 240 Series all models '76 thru '93
97040 740 & 760 Series all models '82 thru '88
97050 850 Series all models '93 thru '97

TECHBOOK MANUALS
10205 Automotive Computer Codes
10206 OBD-II & Electronic Engine Management
10210 Automotive Emissions Control Manual
10215 Fuel Injection Manual '78 thru '85
10220 Fuel Injection Manual '86 thru '99
10225 Holley Carburetor Manual
10230 Rochester Carburetor Manual
10240 Weber/Zenith/Stromberg/SU Carburetors
10305 Chevrolet Engine Overhaul Manual
10310 Chrysler Engine Overhaul Manual
10320 Ford Engine Overhaul Manual
10330 GM and Ford Diesel Engine Repair Manual
10333 Engine Performance Manual
10340 Small Engine Repair Manual, 5 HP & Less
10341 Small Engine Repair Manual, 5.5 - 20 HP
10345 Suspension, Steering & Driveline Manual
10355 Ford Automatic Transmission Overhaul
10360 GM Automatic Transmission Overhaul
10405 Automotive Body Repair & Painting
10410 Automotive Brake Manual
10411 Automotive Anti-lock Brake (ABS) Systems
10415 Automotive Detaling Manual
10420 Automotive Electrical Manual
10425 Automotive Heating & Air Conditioning
10430 Automotive Reference Manual & Dictionary
10435 Automotive Tools Manual
10440 Used Car Buying Guide
10445 Welding Manual
10450 ATV Basics
10452 Scooters 50cc to 250cc

SPANISH MANUALS
98903 Reparación de Carrocería & Pintura
98904 Manual de Carburador Modelos Holley & Rochester
98905 Códigos Automotrices de la Computadora
98906 OBD-II & Sistemas de Control Electrónico del Motor
98910 Frenos Automotriz
98913 Electricidad Automotriz
98915 Inyección de Combustible '86 al '99
99040 Chevrolet & GMC Camionetas '67 al '87
99041 Chevrolet & GMC Camionetas '88 al '98
99042 Chevrolet & GMC Camionetas Cerradas '68 al '95
99043 Chevrolet/GMC Camionetas '94 al '04
99048 Chevrolet/GMC Camionetas '99 al '06
99055 Dodge Caravan & Plymouth Voyager '84 al '95
99075 Ford Camionetas y Bronco '80 al '94
99076 Ford F-150 '97 al '09
99077 Ford Camionetas Cerradas '69 al '91
99088 Ford Modelos de Tamaño Mediano '75 al '86
99089 Ford Camionetas Ranger '93 al '10
99091 Ford Taurus & Mercury Sable '86 al '95
99095 GM Modelos de Tamaño Grande '70 al '90
99100 GM Modelos de Tamaño Mediano '70 al '88
99106 Jeep Cherokee, Wagoneer & Comanche '84 al '00
99110 Nissan Camioneta '80 al '96, Pathfinder '87 al '95
99118 Nissan Sentra '82 al '94
99125 Toyota Camionetas y 4Runner '79 al '95

Over 100 Haynes motorcycle manuals also available

7-12